AMC Concord /Hornet Spirit /Gremlin Automotive Repair Manual

by David Hayden
and John H Haynes
Member of the Guild of Motoring Writers

Models covered
All models 1970 through 1983; 3-speed, 4-speed, 5-speed and automatic transmissions; 151 cu in four-cylinder, 199, 232 and 258 cu in six-cylinder, 304 and 360 cu in V8 engines.
Does not include Audi/VW 4-cylinder OHC engines

ISBN 0 85696 694 0

Printed in the USA

(2Z4 - 14020)
(694)

ABCDE
FGHIJ
KLMNO
PQRST 2

Haynes ®

APAA
AUTOMOTIVE PARTS & ACCESSORIES ASSOCIATION

Haynes Publishing Group
Sparkford Nr Yeovil
Somerset BA22 7JJ England

Haynes North America, Inc
861 Lawrence Drive
Newbury Park
California 91320 USA

Acknowledgements

We are grateful for the help and cooperation of American Motors Corporation, who supplied technical information, certain illustrations and vehicle photos, and the Champion Spark Plug Company, who supplied the illustrations showing the various spark plug conditions.

About this manual

Its purpose

The purpose of this manual is to help you get the best value from your vehicle. It can do so in several ways. It can help you decide what work must be done even if you choose to get it done by a dealer service department or a repair shop; it provides information and procedures for routine maintenance and servicing; and it offers diagnostic and repair procedures to follow when trouble occurs.

It is hoped that you will use the manual to tackle the work yourself. For many simpler jobs, doing it yourself may be quicker than arranging an appointment to get the vehicle into a shop and making the trips to leave it and pick it up. More importantly, a lot of money can be saved by avoiding the expense the shop must pass on to you to cover its labor and overhead costs. An added benefit is the sense of satisfaction and accomplishment that you feel after having done the job yourself.

Using the manual

The manual is divided into Chapters. Each Chapter is divided into numbered Sections, which are headed in bold type between horizontal lines. Each Section consists of consecutively numbered paragraphs.

The two types of illustrations used (figures and photographs), are referenced by a number preceding their captions. Figure reference numbers denote Chapter and numerical sequence in the Chapter; i.e. Fig. 12.4 means Chapter 12, figure number 4. Figure captions are followed by a Section number which ties the figure to a specific portion of the text. All photographs apply to the Chapter in which they appear, and the reference number pinpoints the pertinent Section and paragraph; i.e. 3.2 means Section 3, paragraph 2.

Procedures, once described in the text, are not normally repeated. When it is necessary to refer to another Chapter, the reference will be given as Chapter and Section number; i.e. Chapter 1/16. Cross references given without use of the word 'Chapter' apply to Sections and/or paragraphs in the same Chapter. For example, 'see Section 8' means in the same Chapter.

Reference to the left or right side of the vehicle is based on the assumption that one is sitting in the driver's seat facing forward.

Even though extreme care has been taken during the preparation of this manual, neither the publisher nor the author can accept responsibility for any errors in, or omissions from, the information given.

Introduction to the AMC Gremlin, Hornet, Spirit and Concord

This manual covers service and repair operations for the Gremlin, Hornet, Spirit and Concord models.

The engines available in each of these models include V8, four and six-cylinder engines with the exception of the Hornet, which was not available as a four-cylinder model.

Transmission options include a four-speed manual introduced in 1977 and a five-speed introduced in 1982 (four-speeds became standard equipment in 1979). A three-speed automatic transmission was also available.

The independent front suspension is equipped with coil springs and the solid rear axle is supported by leaf springs. Independently mounted shock absorbers are used front and rear.

Power assisted front disc brakes were optional through 1976 and became standard equipment in 1977. Rear drum brakes are standard equipment.

Contents

	Page	
Acknowledgements	2	
About this manual	2	
Introduction to the AMC Gremlin, Hornet, Spirit and Concord	2	
General dimensions	10	
Buying parts	10	
Vehicle identification numbers	11	
Maintenance techniques, tools and working facilities	12	
Automotive chemicals and lubricants	18	
Jacking and towing	19	
Safety first!	20	
Troubleshooting	21	
Chapter 1 Tune-up and routine maintenance	30	1
Chapter 2 Part A General engine overhaul procedures	56	2A
Chapter 2 Part B Four-cylinder engine (151 cu in)	69	2B
Chapter 2 Part C Six-cylinder engine	84	2C
Chapter 2 Part D V8 engine	103	2D
Chapter 3 Cooling, heating and air conditioning systems	115	3
Chapter 4 Fuel and exhaust systems	122	4
Chapter 5 Engine electrical systems	159	5
Chapter 6 Emissions control systems	172	6
Chapter 7 Part A Manual transmission	181	7A
Chapter 7 Part B Automatic transmission	208	7B
Chapter 8 Driveline	213	8
Chapter 9 Brakes	221	9
Chapter 10 Chassis electrical system	234	10
Chapter 11 Suspension and steering systems	261	11
Chapter 12 Body	277	12
Conversion factors	286	
Index	287	

1973 Hornet Hatchback

1979 Gremlin

1979 Concord four-door Sedan

1979 Concord Wagon

1979 Spirit Liftback

1980 Spirit Sedan

General dimensions

	Gremlin and Spirit sedan	Hornet and Concord sedan	Hornet and Concord wagon	Hornet and Spirit hatchback
Length				
1971 and 1972	161.2 in	179.2 in	–	–
1973	166.0 in	185.5 in	185.5 in	–
1974 through 1977	169.8 in	186.5 in	187.1 in	186.5 in
1978 through 1982	166.7 in	184.3 in	184.3 in	167.2 in
Width	70.6 in	71 in	71 in	70.6 to 71.1 in
Height	51.6 to 52.4 in	51.3 to 52.5 in	51.5 to 52.9 in	51.5 to 52.5 in

Buying spare parts

Replacement parts are available from many sources, which generally fall into one of two categories – authorized dealer parts departments and independent retail auto parts stores. Our advice concerning these parts is as follows:

Retail auto parts stores: Good auto parts stores will stock frequently needed components which wear out relatively fast, such as clutch components, exhaust systems, brake parts, tune-up parts, etc. These stores often supply new or reconditioned parts on an exchange basis, which can save a considerable amount of money. Discount auto parts stores are often very good places to buy materials and parts needed for general vehicle maintenance such as oil, grease, filters, spark plugs, belts, touch-up paint, bulbs, etc. They also usually sell tools and general accessories, have convenient hours, charge lower prices and can often be found not far from home.

Authorized dealer parts department: This is the best source for parts which are unique to the vehicle and not generally available elsewhere (such as major engine parts, transmission parts, trim pieces, etc.).

Warranty information: If the vehicle is still covered under warranty, be sure that any replacement parts purchased – regardless of the source – do not invalidate the warranty!

To be sure of obtaining the correct parts, have engine and chassis numbers available and, if possible, take the old parts along for positive identification.

Vehicle identification numbers

Regardless from which source parts are obtained, it is essential to provide correct information concerning the vehicle model and year of production, plus the engine serial number and the Vehicle Identification Number (VIN). The VIN can be found on the dashboard edge as you look into the windshield on the driver's side and on the right fender panel in the engine compartment. A data plate including the date of production can be found on the latch post of the driver's door. An emissions hose routing diagram and tune-up information (Emission Control Information label on later models) are located on the underside of the hood.

VIN Decoding Chart

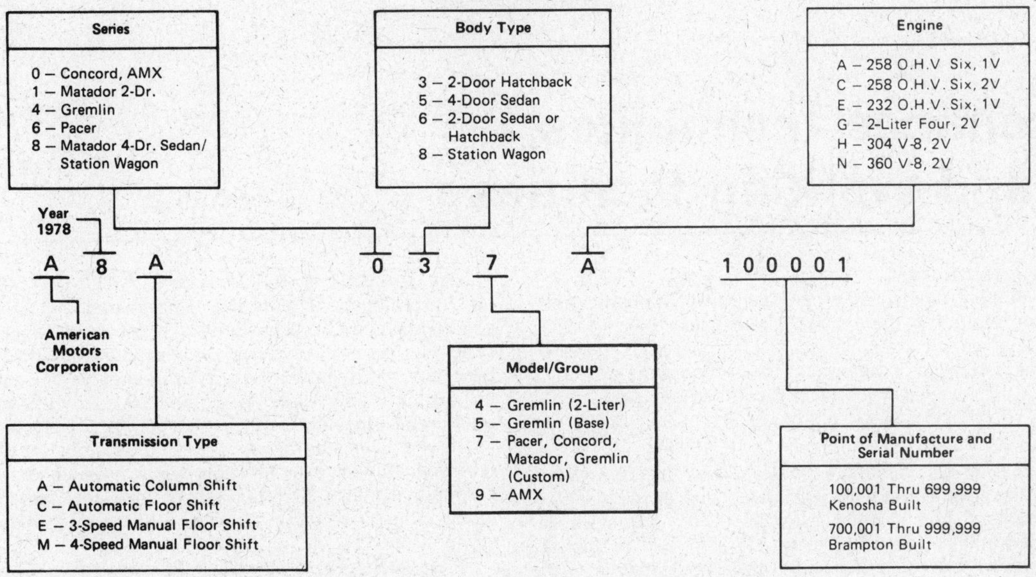

Typical Vehicle Identification Number (VIN) and decoding chart

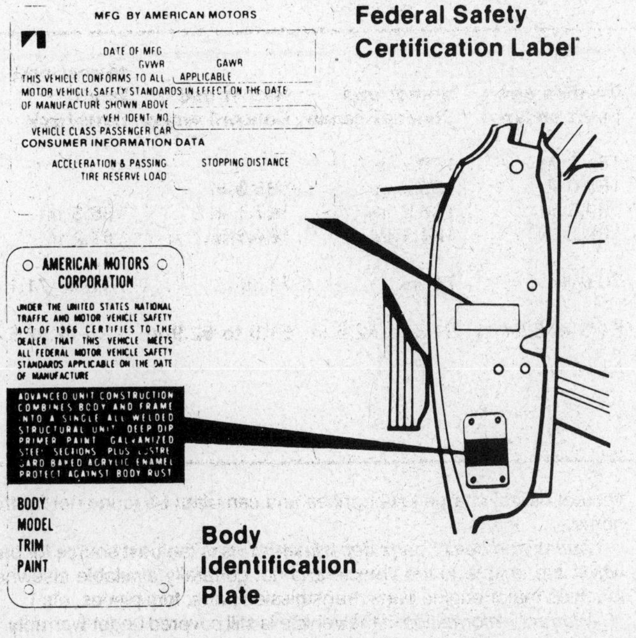

The location of the body identification plate

AMC
VEHICLE EMISSION CONTROL INFORMATION
ENGINE FAMILY
EVAPORATIVE FAMILY
EMISSION CONTROL SYSTEM
ENGINE
CID
THIS VEHICLE CONFORMS TO U S E P A AND CALIFORNIA REGULATIONS APPLICABLE TO 1978 MODEL YEAR NEW MOTOR VEHICLE INTENDED FOR SALE AT ALTITUDE 4000 FEET
PROPER MAINTENANCE AND ADJUSTMENT ARE NECESSARY FOR CONTINUED EFFECTIVENESS MAKE ADJUSTMENTS WITH ENGINE AT NORMAL OPERATING TEMPERATURE AIR CLEANER ON AIR CONDITIONING OFF SET IGNITION TIMING WITH DISTRIBUTOR VACUUM OFF AND PLUGGED SOLENOID DISCONNECTED
SPECIFICATIONS
TRANSMISSION
AUTO
MANUAL
IGNITION TIMING
2 BTDC R P M
CARB IDLE SPEED
100 R P M
HIGH IDLE SPEED
100 RPM(N)SEC STEP
IDLE MIXTURE
LEAN IDLE DROP
SPARK PLUG GAP
HOT VALVE LASH
INTAKE
EXHAUST
CAM DWELL
SEE OWNER OR SERVICE MANUAL FOR INSTRUCTIONS

Typical federal Vehicle Emission Control Information label

Maintenance techniques, tools and working facilities

Maintenance techniques

There are a number of techniques involved in maintenance and repair that will be referred to throughout this manual. Application of these techniques will enable the home mechanic to be more efficient, better organized and capable of performing the various tasks properly, which will ensure that the repair job is thorough and complete.

Fasteners

Fasteners, are nuts, bolts, studs and screws used to hold two or more parts together. There are a few things to keep in mind when working with fasteners. Almost all of them use a locking device of some type; either a lock washer, locknut, locking tab or thread adhesive. All threaded fasteners should be clean and straight, with undamaged threads and undamaged corners on the hex head where the wrench fits. Develop the habit of replacing damaged nuts and bolts with new ones. Special locknuts with nylon or fiber inserts can only be used once. If they are removed, they lose their locking ability and must be replaced with new ones.

Rusted nuts and bolts should be treated with a penetrating fluid to ease removal and prevent breakage. Some mechanics use turpentine in a spout-type oil can, which works quite well. After applying the rust penetrant, let it "work" for a few minutes before trying to loosen the nut or bolt. Badly rusted fasteners may have to be chiseled or sawed off or removed with a special nut breaker, available at tool stores.

If a bolt or stud breaks off in an assembly, it can be drilled and removed with a special tool commonly available for this purpose. Most automotive machine shops can perform this task, as well as other repair procedures (such as repair of threaded holes that have been stripped out).

Flat washers and lock washers, when removed from an assembly should always be replaced exactly as removed. Replace damaged washers with new ones. Always use a flat washer between a lock washer and any soft metal surface (such as aluminum), thin sheet metal or plastic.

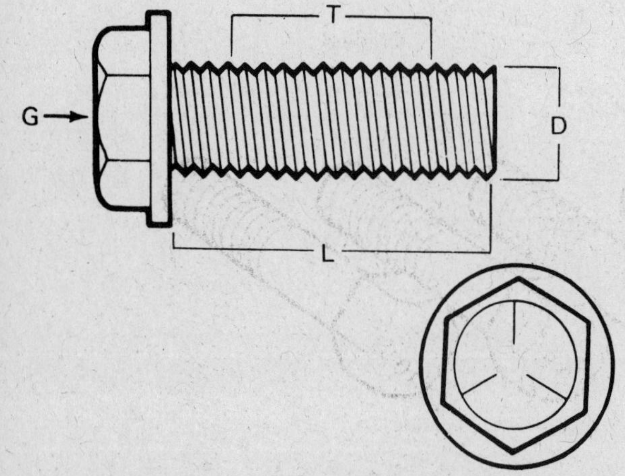

Standard (SAE) bolt dimensions/grade marks

G – Grade marks (bolt strength)
L – Length (in inches)
T – Thread pitch (number of threads per inch)
D – Nominal diameter (in inches)

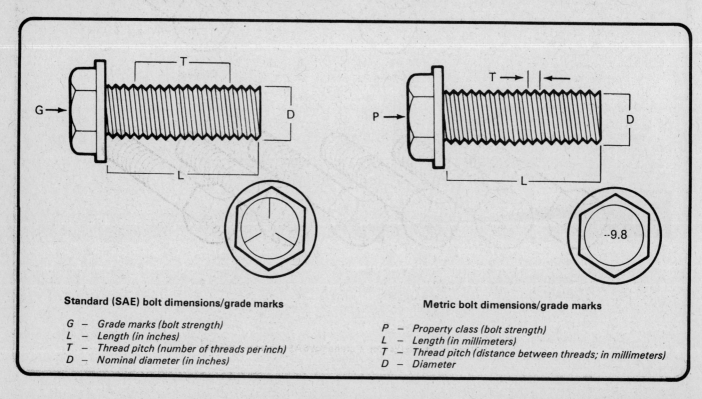

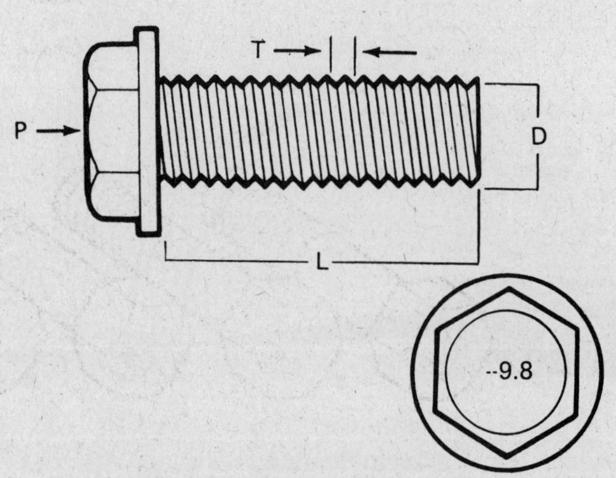

Metric bolt dimensions/grade marks

P – Property class (bolt strength)
L – Length (in millimeters)
T – Thread pitch (distance between threads; in millimeters)
D – Diameter

Fastener sizes

For a number of reasons, automobile manufacturers are making wider and wider use of metric fasteners. Therefore, it is important to be able to tell the difference between standard (sometimes called U.S., English or SAE) and metric hardware, since they cannot be interchanged.

All bolts, whether standard or metric, are sized according to diameter, thread pitch and length. For example, a standard $\frac{1}{2}$ – 13 x 1 bolt is $\frac{1}{2}$ inch in diameter, has 13 threads per inch and is 1 inch long. An M12 – 1.75 x 25 metric bolt is 12 mm in diameter, has a thread pitch of 1.75 mm (the distance between threads) and is 25 mm long. The 2 bolts are nearly identical, and easily confused, but they are not interchangeable.

In addition to the differences in diameter, thread pitch and length, metric and standard bolts can also be distinguished by examining the bolt heads. To begin with, the distance across the flats on a standard bolt head is measured in inches, while the same dimension on a metric bolt is measured in millimeters (the same is true for nuts). As a result, a standard wrench should not be used on a metric bolt and a metric wrench should not be used on a standard bolt. Also, standard bolts have slashes radiating out from the center of the head to denote the grade or strength of the bolt (which is an indication of the amount of torque that can be supplied to it). The greater the number of slashes, the greater the strength of the bolt (grades 0 through 5 are commonly used on automobiles). Metric bolts have a property class (grade) number, rather than a slash, molded into their heads to indicate bolt strength. In this case, the higher the number the stronger the bolt (property class numbers 8.8, 9.8 and 10.9 are commonly used on automobiles).

Strength markings can also be used to distinguish standard hex nuts from metric hex nuts. Standard nuts have dots stamped into one side, while metric nuts are marked with a number. The greater the number of dots, or the higher the number, the greater the strength of the nut.

Metric studs are also marked on their ends according to property class (grade). Larger studs are numbered (the same as metric bolts), while smaller studs carry a geometric code to denote grade.

It should be noted that many fasteners, especially Grades 0 through 2, have no distinguishing marks on them. When such is the case, the only way to determine whether it is standard or metric is to measure the thread pitch or compare it to a known fastener of the same size.

Since fasteners of the same size (both standard and metric) may have different strength ratings, be sure to reinstall any bolts, studs or nuts removed from your vehicle in their original locations. Also, when replacing a fastener with a new one, make sure that the new one has a strength rating equal to or greater than the original.

Tightening sequences and procedures

Most threaded fasteners should be tightened to a specific torque value (torque is basically a twisting force). Over-tightening the fastener can weaken it and lead to eventual breakage, while under-tightening can cause it to eventually come loose. Bolts, screws and studs, depending on the materials they are made of and their thread diameters, have specific torque values (many of which are noted in the Specifications at the beginning of each Chapter). Be sure to follow the torque recommendations closely. For fasteners not assigned a specific torque, a general torque value chart is presented here as a guide. As was previously mentioned, the sizes and grade of a fastener determine the amount of torque that can safely be applied to it. The figures listed here are approximate for Grade 2 and Grade 3 fasteners (higher grades can tolerate higher torque values).

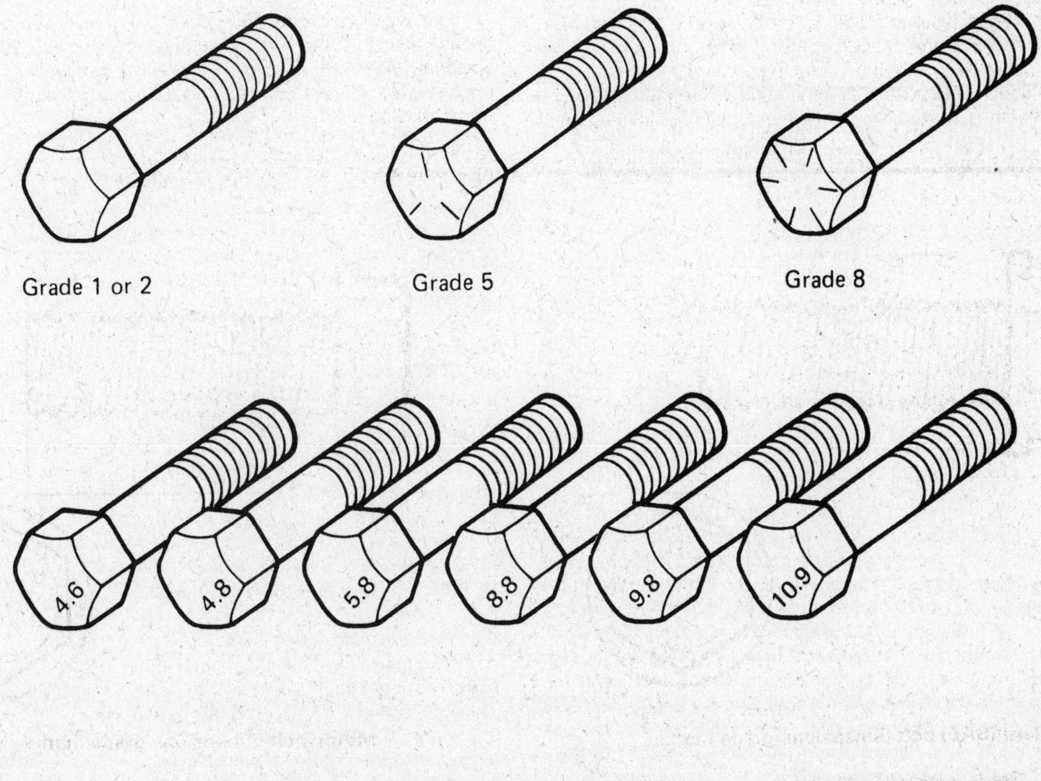

Bolt strength marks (top – standard/SAE; bottom – metric)

General torque values

	ft-lb	Nm
Metric thread sizes		
M-6	6 to 9	9 to 12
M-8	14 to 21	19 to 28
M-10	28 to 40	38 to 54
M-12	50 to 71	68 to 96
M-14	80 to 140	109 to 154
Pipe thread sizes		
$\frac{1}{8}$	5 to 8	7 to 10
$\frac{1}{4}$	12 to 18	17 to 24
$\frac{3}{8}$	22 to 33	30 to 44
$\frac{1}{2}$	25 to 35	34 to 47
U.S. thread sizes		
$\frac{1}{4}$ - 20	6 to 9	9 to 12
$\frac{5}{16}$ - 18	12 to 18	17 to 24
$\frac{5}{16}$ - 24	14 to 20	19 to 27
$\frac{3}{8}$ - 16	22 to 32	30 to 43
$\frac{3}{8}$ - 24	27 to 38	37 to 51
$\frac{7}{16}$ - 14	40 to 55	55 to 74
$\frac{7}{16}$ - 20	40 to 60	55 to 81
$\frac{1}{2}$ - 13	55 to 80	75 to 108

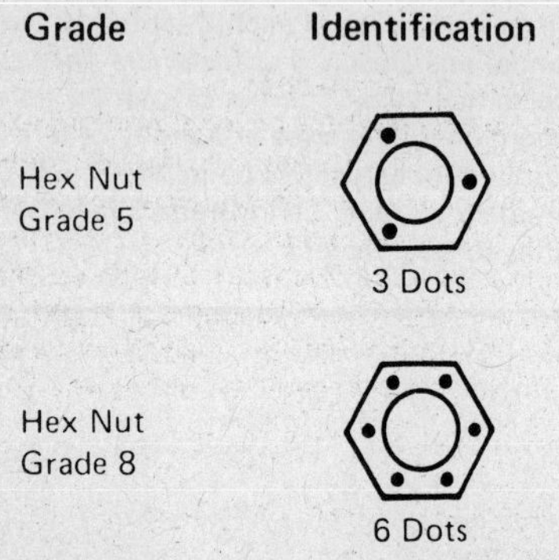

Standard hex nut strength marks

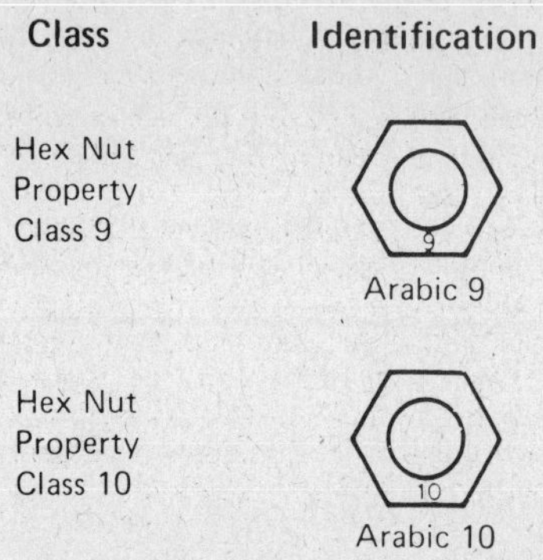

Metric hex nut strength marks

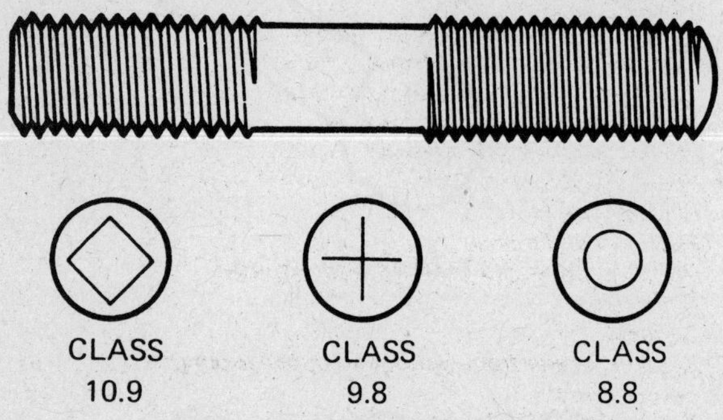

Metric stud strength marks

Fasteners laid out in a pattern (i.e. cylinder head bolts, oil pan bolts, differential cover bolts, etc.) must be loosened and tightened in a definite sequence to avoid warping the component. This sequence will normally be shown in the appropriate Chapter. If a specific pattern is not given, the following procedures can be used to prevent warping. Initially, the bolts or nuts should be assembled finger-tight only. Next, they should be tightened one full turn each, in a criss-cross or diagonal pattern. After each one has been tightened one full turn, return to the first one and tighten them all one half turn, following the same pattern. Finally, tighten each of them one-quarter turn at a time until they all have been tightened to the proper torque value. To loosen and remove them the procedure would be reversed.

Component disassembly

Component disassembly should be done with care and purpose to help ensure that the parts go back together properly. Always keep track of the sequence in which parts are removed. Make note of special characteristics or marks on parts that can be installed more than one way (such as a grooved thrust washer on a shaft). It is a good idea to lay the disassembled parts out on a clean surface in the order that they were removed. It may also be helpful to make simple sketches or take instant photos of components before removal.

When removing fasteners from an assembly, keep track of their locations. Sometimes threading a bolt back in a part or putting the washers and nut back on a stud can prevent mixups later. If nuts and bolts cannot be returned to their original locations, they should be kept in a compartmented box or a series of small boxes. A cupcake or muffin tin is ideal for this purpose, since each cavity can hold the bolts and nuts from a particular area (i.e. oil pan bolts, valve cover bolts, engine mount bolts, etc.). A pan of this type is especially helpful when working on assemblies with very small parts such as the carburetor, alternator, valve train or interior dash and trim pieces. The cavities can be marked with paint or tape to identify the contents.

Whenever wiring looms, harnesses or connectors are separated, it's a good idea to identify them with numbered pieces of masking tape so that they can be easily reconnected.

Gasket sealing surfaces

Throughout any vehicle, gaskets are used to seal the mating surfaces between two parts and keep lubricants, fluids, vacuum or pressure contained in an assembly.

Many times these gaskets are coated with a liquid or paste-type gasket sealing compound before assembly. Age, heat and pressure can sometimes cause the two parts to stick together so tightly that they are very difficult to separate. Often, the assembly can be loosened by striking it with a soft-faced hammer near the mating surfaces. A regular hammer can be used if a block of wood is placed between the hammer and the part. Do not hammer on cast parts or parts that could be easily damaged. With any particularly stubborn part, always recheck to see that every fastener has been removed.

Avoid using a screwdriver or bar to pry apart an assembly, as they can easily mar the gasket sealing surfaces of the parts (which must remain smooth). If prying is absolutely necessary, use an old broom handle, but keep in mind that extra clean-up will be necessary if the wood splinters.

After the parts are separated, the old gasket must be carefully scraped off and the gasket surfaces cleaned. Stubborn gasket material can be soaked with rust penetrant or treated with a special chemical to soften it so that it can be easily scraped off. A scraper can be fashioned from a piece of copper tubing by flattening and sharpening one end. Copper is recommended because it is usually softer than the surfaces to be scraped, which reduces the chance of gouging the part. Some gaskets can be removed with a wire brush, but regardless of the method used, the mating surfaces must be left clean and smooth. If, for some reason the gasket surface is gouged, then a gasket sealer thick enough to fill scratches will have to be used upon reassembly of the components. For most applications, a non-drying (or semi-drying) gasket sealer should be used.

Hose removal tips

Caution: *If the vehicle is equipped with air conditioning, do not disconnect any of the a/c hoses without first having the system depressurized by a dealer service department on air conditioning specialist.*

Hose removal precautions closely parallel gasket removal precautions. Avoid scratching or gouging the surface that the hose mates against or the connection may leak. This is especially true for radiator hoses. Because of various chemical reactions, the rubber in hoses can bond itself to the metal spigot that the hose fits over. To remove a hose, first loosen the hose clamps that secure it to the spigot. Then, with slip-joint pliers, grab the hose at the clamp and rotate it around the spigot. Work it back-and-forth until it is completely free, then pull it off. Silicone or other lubricants will ease removal if they can be applied between the hose and the spigot. Apply the same lubricant to the inside of the hose and the outside of the spigot to simplify installation.

As the last resort (and if the hose is to be replaced with a new one anyway), the rubber can be slit with a knife and the hose peeled from its spigot. If this must be done, be careful that the metal connection is not damaged.

If a hose clamp is broken or damaged, do not re-use it. Wire-type clamps usually weaken with age, so it is a good idea to replace them with screw-type clamps whenever a hose is removed.

Tools

A selection of good tools is a basic requirement for anyone who plans to maintain and repair his or her own vehicle. For the owner who has few tools, if any, the initial investment might seem high, but when compared to the spiraling costs of professional auto maintenance and repair, it is a wise one.

To help the owner decide which tools are needed to perform the tasks detailed in this manual, the following tool lists are offered: *Maintenance and minor repair, Repair and overhaul* and *Special.* The newcomer to practical mechanics should start off with the *Maintenance and minor repair* tool kit, which is adequate for the simpler jobs performed on a vehicle. Then, as his confidence and experience grow, he can tackle more difficult tasks, buying additional tools as they are needed. Eventually the basic kit will be expanded into the *Repair and overhaul* tool set. Over a period of time, the experienced do-it-yourselfer will assemble a tool set complete enough for most repair and overhaul procedures and will add tools from the *Special* category when he feels the expense is justified by the frequency of use.

Maintenance and minor repair tool kit

The tools in this list should be considered the minimum for performance of routine maintenance, servicing and minor repair work. We recommend the purchase of combination wrenches (box end and open end combined in one wrench); while more expensive than open-ended ones, they offer the advantages of both types of wrench.

Combination wrench set ($\frac{1}{4}$ in to 1 in or 6 mm to 19 mm)
Adjustable wrench – 8 in
Spark plug wrench (with rubber insert)
Spark plug gap adjusting tool
Feeler gauge set
Brake bleeder wrench
Standard screwdriver ($\frac{5}{16}$ in x 6 in)
Phillips screwdriver (No.2 x 6 in)
Combination pliers – 6 in
Hacksaw and assortment of blades
Tire pressure gauge
Grease gun
Oil can
Fine emery cloth
Wire brush
Battery post and cable cleaning tool
Oil filter wrench
Funnel (medium size)
Safety goggles
Jack stands (2)
Drain pan

Note: *If basic tune-ups are going to be a part of routine maintenance, it will be necessary to purchase a good quality stroboscopic timing light and a combination tachometer/dwell meter. Although they are included in the list of Special tools, they are mentioned here because they are absolutely necessary for tuning most vehicles properly.*

Repair and overhaul tool set

These tools are essential for anyone who plans to perform major repairs and are in addition to those in the *Maintenance and minor repair tool kit.* Included is a comprehensive set of sockets which, though expensive, are invaluable because of their versatility (especially when various extensions and drives are available). We recommend the $\frac{1}{2}$ in drive over the $\frac{3}{8}$ in drive. Although the larger drive is bulky and more expensive, it has the capability of accepting a very wide range of large sockets (ideally, the mechanic would have a $\frac{3}{8}$ in drive set and a $\frac{1}{2}$ in drive set).

Socket set(s)
Reversible ratchet
Extension – 10 in
Universal joint
Torque wrench (same size drive as sockets)
Ballpein hammer – 8 oz
Soft-faced hammer (plastic/rubber)
Standard screwdriver ($\frac{1}{4}$ in x 6 in)
Standard screwdriver (stubby – $\frac{5}{16}$ in)
Phillips screwdriver (No.3 x 8 in)
Phillips screwdriver (stubby – No.2)
Pliers – vise grip
Pliers – lineman's
Pliers – needle nose
Pliers – spring clip (internal and external)
Cold chisel – $\frac{1}{2}$ in
Scriber
Scraper (made from flattened copper tubing)
Center punch
Pin punches ($\frac{1}{16}$, $\frac{1}{8}$, $\frac{3}{16}$ in)
Steel rule/straightedge – 12 in
Allen wrench set ($\frac{1}{8}$ to $\frac{3}{8}$ in or 4 mm to 10 mm)
A selection of files
Wire brush (large)
Jack stands (second set)
Jack (scissor or hydraulic type)

Note: *Another tool which is often useful is an electric drill motor with a chuck capacity of $\frac{3}{8}$ in (and a set of good quality drill bits).*

Special tools

The tools in this list include those which are not used regularly, are expensive to buy, or which need to be used in accordance with their manufacturer's instructions. Unless these tools will be used frequently, it is not very economical to purchase many of them. A consideration would be to split the cost and use between yourself and a friend or friends. In addition, most of these tools can be obtained from a tool rental shop on a temporary basis.

This list contains only those tools and instruments widely available to the public, and not those special tools produced by vehicle

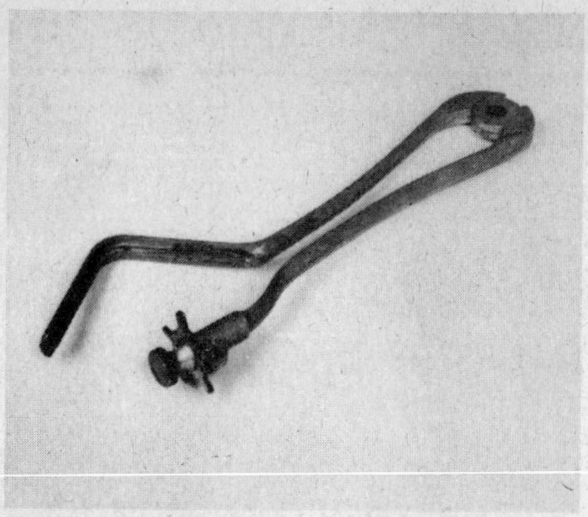

Piston ring groove cleaning tool

Piston ring compressor

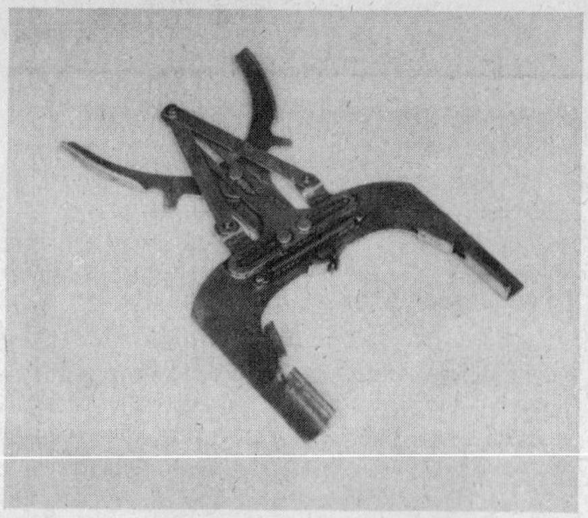

Piston ring removal/installation tool

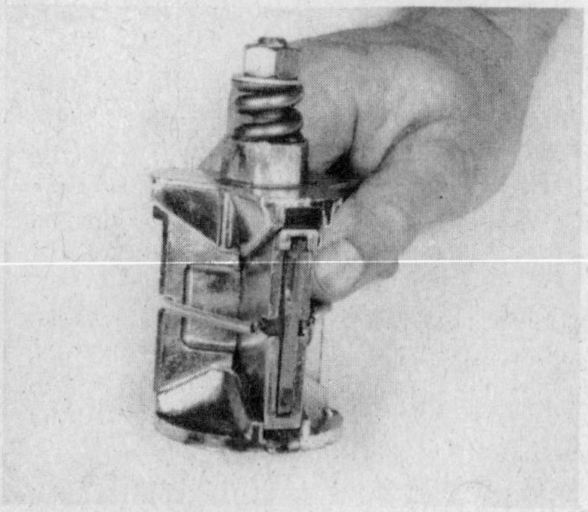

Cylinder ridge reamer

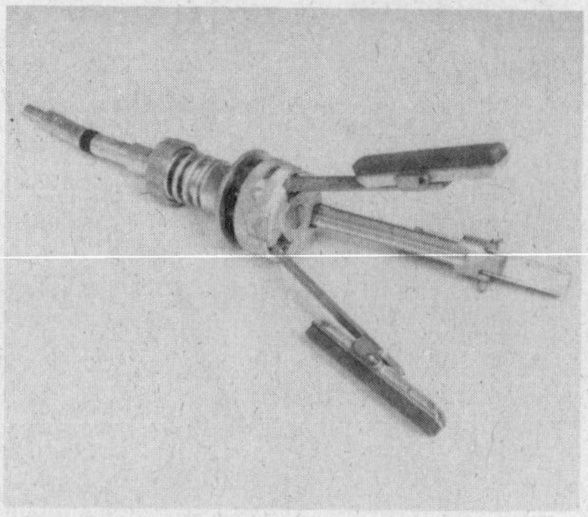

Cylinder surfacing hone

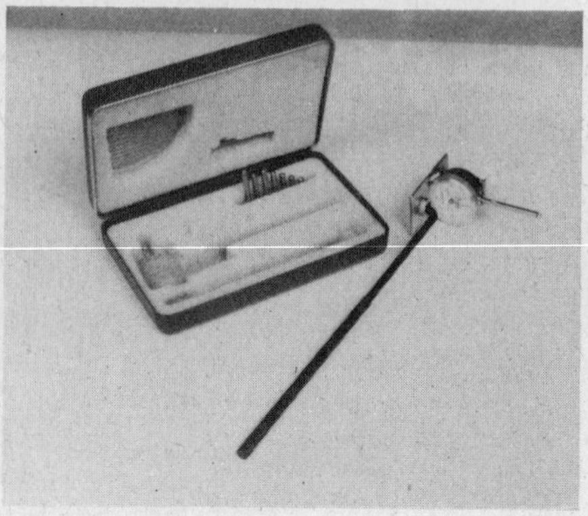

Cylinder bore gauge

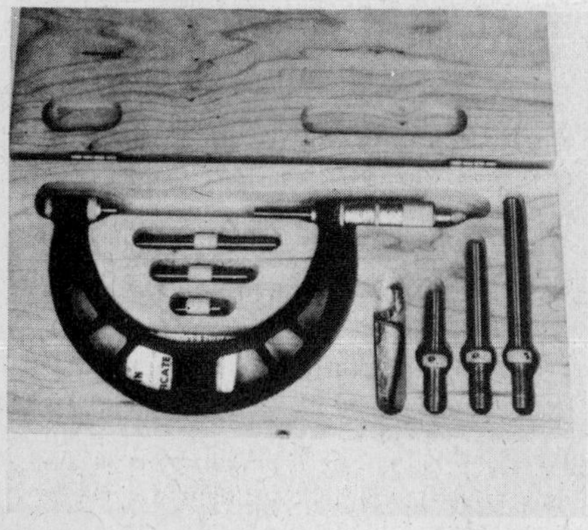

Micrometer set

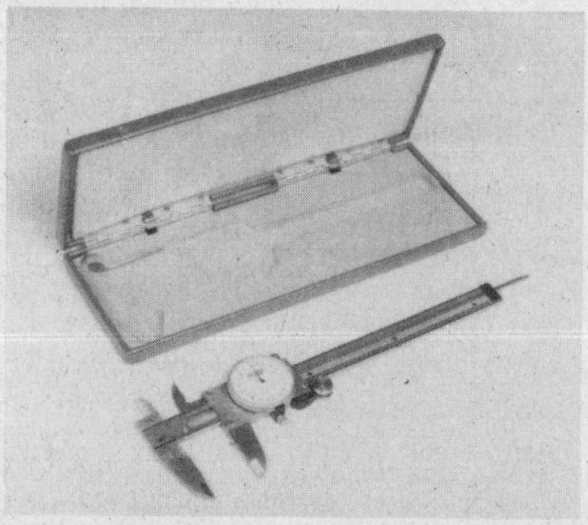

Dial caliper

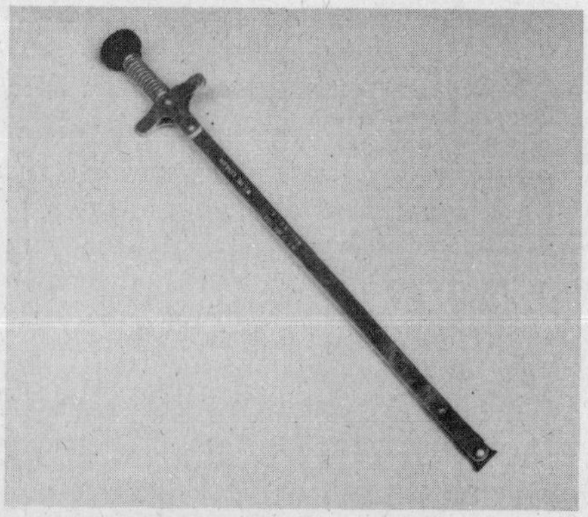

Hydraulic lifter removal tool

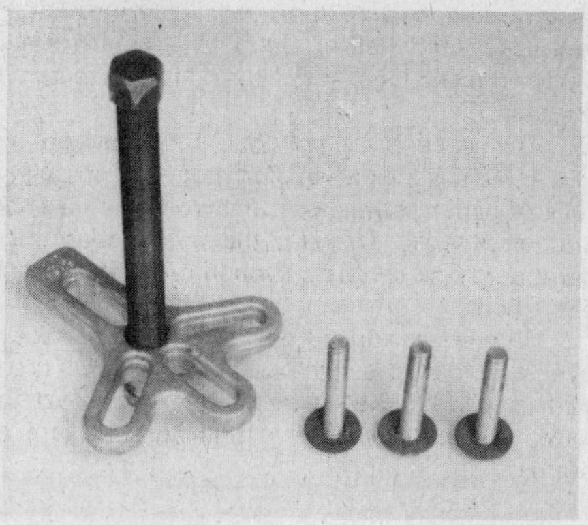

Universal-type puller

Dial indicator set

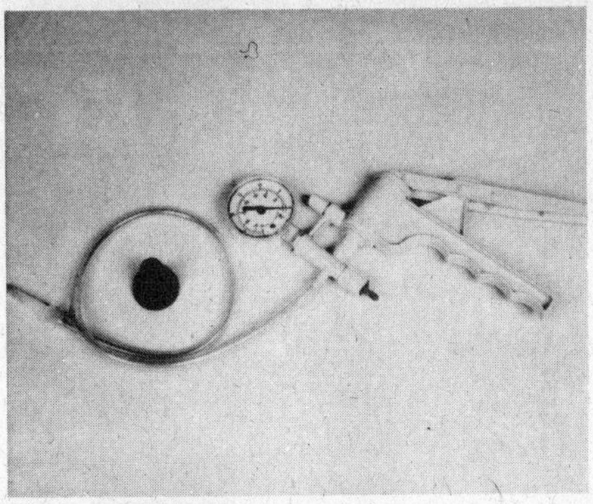

Hand operated vacuum pump

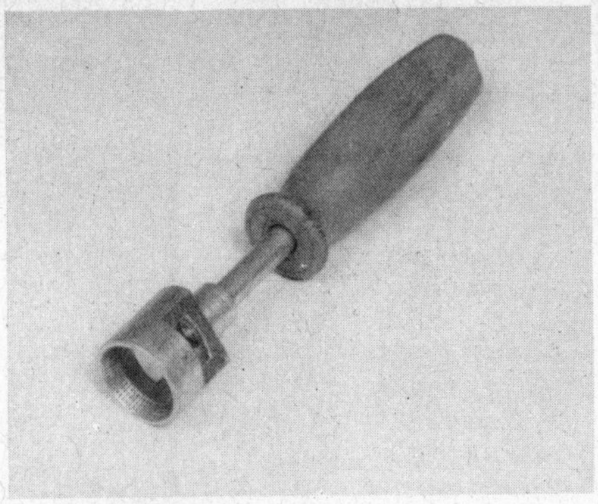

Brake shoe spring tool

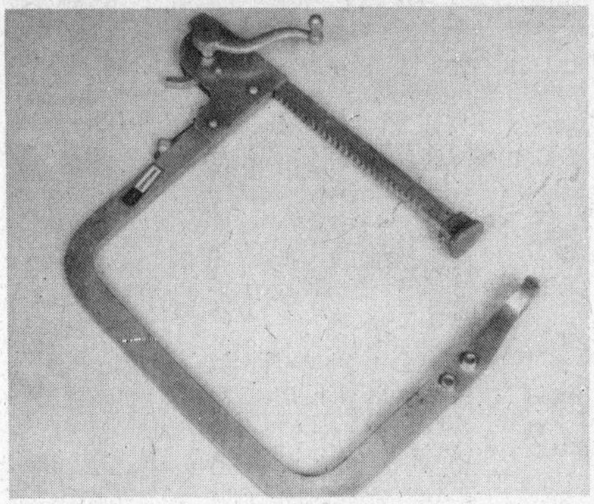

Valve spring compressor

manufacturers for distribution to dealer service departments. Occasionally, references to the manufacturer's special tools are included in the text of this manual. Generally, an alternate method of doing the job without the special tool is offered. However, sometimes there is no alternative to their use. Where this is the case, and the tool cannot be purchased or borrowed, the work should be turned over to the dealer, a repair shop or an automotive machine shop.

Valve spring compressor
Piston ring groove cleaning tool
Piston ring compressor
Piston ring installation tool
Cylinder compression gauge
Cylinder ridge reamer
Cylinder surfacing hone
Cylinder bore gauge
Micrometer(s) and/or dial calipers
Hydraulic lifter removal tool
Balljoint separator
Universal-type puller
Impact screwdriver
Dial indicator set
Stroboscopic timing light (inductive pickup)
Hand-operated vacuum/pressure pump
Tachometer/dwell meter
Universal electrical multimeter
Cable hoist
Brake spring removal and installation tools
Floor jack

Buying tools

For the do-it-yourselfer who is just starting to get involved in vehicle maintenance and repair, there are a couple of options available when purchasing tools. If maintenance and minor repair is the extent of the work to be done, the purchase of individual tools is satisfactory. If, on the other hand, extensive work is planned, it would be a good idea to purchase a modest tool set from one of the large retail chain stores. A set can usually be bought at substantial savings over the individual tool prices (and they often come with a tool box). As additional tools are needed, add-on sets, individual tools and a larger tool box can be purchased to expand the tool selection. Building a tool set gradually allows the cost of the tools to be spread over a longer period of time and gives the mechanic the freedom to choose only those tools that will actually be used.

Tool stores will often be the only source of some of the special tools that are needed, but regardless of where tools are bought, try to avoid cheap ones (especially when buying screwdrivers and sockets) because they won't last very long. The expense involved in replacing cheap tools will eventually be greater than the initial cost of quality tools.

Care and maintenance of tools

Good tools are expensive, so it makes sense to treat them with respect. Keep them in a clean and usable condition and store them properly when not in use. Always wipe off any dirt, grease or metal chips before putting them away. Never leave tools lying around in the work area. Upon completion of a job, always check closely under the hood for tools that may have been left there (so they don't get lost during a test drive).

Some tools, such as screwdrivers, pliers, wrenches and sockets, can be hung on a panel mounted on the garage or workshop wall, while others should be kept in a tool box or tray. Measuring instruments, gauges, meters, etc. must be carefully stored where they cannot be damaged by weather or impact from other tools.

When tools are used with care and stored properly, they will last a very long time. Even with the best of care, tools will wear out if used frequently. When a tool is damaged or worn out, replace it; subsequent jobs will be safer and more enjoyable if you do.

For those who desire to learn more about tools and their uses, a book entitled *How to Choose and Use Car Tools* is available from the publishers of this manual.

Working facilities

Not to be overlooked when discussing tools is the workshop. If anything more than routine maintenance is to be carried out, some sort of suitable work area is essential.

It is understood, and appreciated, that many home mechanics do not have a good workshop or garage available and end up removing an engine or doing major repairs outside. It is recommended, however, that the overhaul or repair be completed under the cover of a roof.

A clean, flat workbench or table of comfortable working height is an absolute necessity. The workbench should be equipped with a vise that has a jaw opening of at least 4 inches.

As mentioned previously, some clean, dry storage space is also required for tools, as well as the lubricants, fluids, cleaning solvents, etc. which soon become necessary.

Sometimes waste oil and fluids, drained from the engine or transmission during normal maintenance or repairs, present a disposal problem. To avoid pouring oil on the ground or into the sewage system, simply pour the used fluids into large containers, seal them with caps and deliver them to a local recycling center or disposal facility. Plastic jugs (such as old antifreeze containers) are ideal for this purpose.

Always keep a supply of old newspapers and clean rags available. Old towels are excellent for mopping up spills. Many mechanics use rolls of paper towels for most work because they are readily available and disposable. To keep the area under the vehicle clean, a large cardboard box can be cut open and flattened to protect the garage or shop floor.

Whenever working over a painted surface (such as when leaning over a fender to service something under the hood), always cover it with an old blanket or bedspread to protect the finish. Vinyl covered pads, made especially for this purpose, are available at auto parts stores.

Automotive chemicals and lubricants

A number of automotive chemicals and lubricants are available for use in vehicle maintenance and repair. They include a wide variety of products ranging from cleaning solvents and degreasers to lubricants and protective sprays for rubber, plastic and vinyl.

Contact point/spark plug cleaner is a solvent used to clean oily film and dirt from points, grime from electrical connectors and oil deposits from spark plugs. It is oil free and leaves no residue. It can also be used to remove gum and varnish from carburetor jets and other orifices.

Carburetor cleaner is similar to contact point/spark plug cleaner but it is a stronger solvent and may leave a slight oily residue. It is not recommended for cleaning electrical components or connections.

Brake system cleaner is used to remove grease or brake fluid from brake system components where clean surfaces are absolutely necessary and petroleum-based solvents cannot be used. It also leaves no residue.

Silicone-based lubricants are used to protect rubber parts such as hoses, weatherstripping and grommets and are used as lubricants for hinges and locks.

Multi-purpose grease is an all-purpose lubricant used whenever grease is more practical than a liquid lubricant such as oil. Some multi-purpose grease is white and specially formulated to be more resistant to water than ordinary grease.

Bearing grease/wheel bearing grease is a heavy grease used where increased loads and friction are encountered (i.e. wheel bearings, universal joints, etc.).

High temperature wheel bearing grease is designed to withstand the extreme temperatures encountered by wheel bearings in disc brake equipped vehicles. It usually contains molybdenum disulfide, which is a 'dry' type lubricant.

Gear oil (sometimes called gear lube) is a specially designed oil used in differentials, manual transmissions and transfer cases, as well as other areas where high friction, high temperature lubrication is required. It is available in a number of viscosities (weights) for various applications.

Motor oil, of course, is the lubricant specially formulated for use in the engine. It normally contains a wide variety of additives to prevent corrosion and reduce foaming and wear. Motor oil comes in various weights (viscosity ratings) of from 5 to 80. The recommended weight of the oil depends on the seasonal temperature and the demands on the engine. Light oil is used in cold climates and under light load conditions; heavy oil is used in hot climates and where high loads are encountered. Multi-viscosity oils are designed to have characteristics of both light and heavy oils and are available in a number of weights from 5W-20 to 20W-50.

Oil additives range from viscosity index improvers to slick chemical treatments that purportedly reduce friction. It should be noted that most oil manufacturers caution against using additives with their oils.

Gas additives perform several functions, depending on their chemical makeup. They usually contain solvents that help dissolve gum and varnish that build up on carburetor and intake parts. They also serve to break down carbon deposits that form on the inside surfaces of the combustion chambers. Some additives contain upper cylinder lubricants for valves and piston rings.

Brake fluid is a specially formulated hydraulic fluid that can withstand the heat and pressure encountered in brake systems. Care must be taken that this fluid does not come in contact with painted surfaces or plastics. An opened container should always be resealed to prevent contamination by water or dirt.

Undercoating is a petroleum-based, tar-like substance that is designed to protect metal surfaces on the underside of a vehicle from corrosion. It also acts as a sound deadening agent by insulating the bottom of the vehicle.

Weatherstrip cement is used to bond weatherstripping around doors, windows and trunk lids. It is sometimes used to attach trim pieces as well.

Degreasers are heavy-duty solvents used to remove grease and grime that accumulate on engine and chassis components. They can be sprayed or brushed on and, depending on the type, are rinsed with either water or solvent.

Solvents are used alone or in combination with degreasers to clean parts and assemblies during repair and overhaul. The home mechanic should use only solvents that are non-flammable and that do not produce irritating fumes.

Gasket sealing compounds may be used in conjunction with gaskets, to improve their sealing capabilities, or alone, to seal metal-to-metal joints. Many gaskets can withstand extreme heat, some are impervious to gasoline and lubricants, while others are capable of filling and sealing large cavities. Depending on the intended use, gasket sealers either dry hard or stay relatively soft and pliable. They are usually applied by hand, with a brush, or are sprayed on the gasket sealing surfaces.

Thread cement is an adhesive locking compound that prevents threaded fasteners from loosening because of vibration. It is available in a variety of types for different applications.

Moisture dispersants are usually sprays that can be used to dry out electrical components such as the distributor, fuse block and wiring connectors. Some types can also be used as a treatment for rubber and as a lubricant for hinges, cables and locks.

Waxes and polishes are used to help protect painted and plated surfaces from the weather. Different types of paint may require the use of different types of wax or polish. Some polishes utilize a chemical or abrasive cleaner to help remove the top layer of oxidized (dull) paint in older vehicles. In recent years, many non-wax polishes that contain a wide variety of chemicals such as polymers and silicones have been introduced. These non-wax polishes are usually easier to apply and last longer than conventional waxes and polishes.

Jacking and towing

Jacking

The jack supplied with the vehicle should be used for raising the vehicle during a tire change or when placing jackstands under the frame. **Under no circumstances should work be performed beneath the vehicle or the engine started while this jack is being used as the only means of support.**

All AMC vehicles come equipped with a ratchet-type jack designed to lift one corner of the vehicle from either the front or rear bumper. All types are used in basically the same fashion, the differences being in the design of the bumper hooking bracket.

The vehicle should be on level ground with the transmission in Park (automatic) or Reverse (manual transmission). The parking brake should be firmly set. Blocking the front and rear of the wheel on the same side as the one being changed will help prevent the vehicle from rolling.

With the lever on the jack in the Up position, locate the load rest bracket or hook (depending on the design) on the bumper. Before the load is taken up, remove the hubcap using the flat end of the lug wrench and loosen each of the lug nuts on the wheel to be changed. Using the lug wrench as a handle, raise the vehicle enough to remove the wheel.

Before installing the spare, remove any built-up corrosion or dirt from the drum or hub and the rear side of the spare.

Place the spare into position and install the lug nuts with the cone-shaped end of the nut toward the wheel, Making sure that the wheel is centered on the hub, change the lever to the Down position and carefully lower the vehicle. Once the wheel is resting completely on the ground, tighten all the lug nuts in a diagonal fashion until they are tight. The hub cap can be installed at this point by placing it into position and using the heel of your hand or a rubber mallet to seat it.

Towing

The vehicle can be towed with all four wheels on the ground provided speeds do not exceed 35 mph and the distance is not over 50 miles, otherwise transmission damage can result.

Towing equipment specifically designed for that purpose should be used and should be attached to the main structural members of the vehicle and not the bumper or brackets.

Safety is a major consideration when towing a vehicle and all applicable state and local laws must be obeyed. A safety chain system must be used for all towing.

While towing, the parking brake should be fully released and the transmission should be in Neutral. The steering must be unlocked (ignition switch in the Off position). Remember that power steering and power brakes will not work with the engine off.

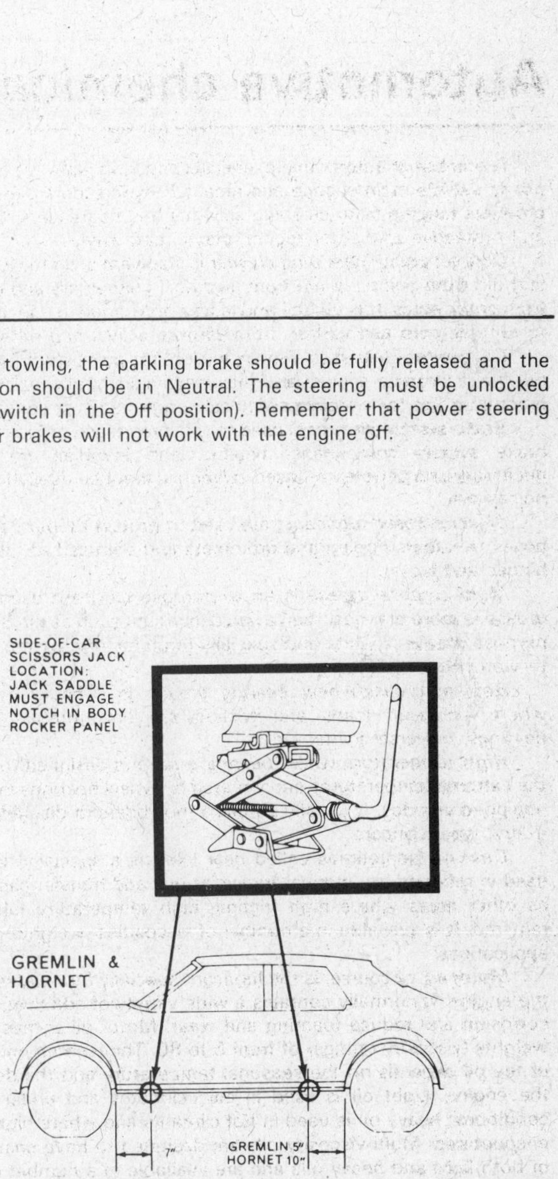

Jacking locations for the AMC vehicles covered in this manual

Safety first!

Regardless of how enthusiastic you may be about getting on with the job at hand, take the time to ensure that your safety is not jeopardized. A moment's lack of attention can result in an accident, as can failure to observe certain simple safety precautions. The possibility of an accident will always exist, and the following points should not be considered a comprehensive list of all dangers. Rather, they are intended to make you aware of the risks and to encourage a safety conscious approach to all work you carry out on your vehicle.

Essential DOs and DON'Ts

DON'T rely on a jack when working under the vehicle. Always use approved jackstands to support the weight of the vehicle and place them under the recommended lift or support points.
DON'T attempt to loosen extremely tight fasteners (i.e. wheel lug nuts) while the vehicle is on a jack — it may fall.
DON'T start the engine without first making sure that the transmission is in Neutral (or Park where applicable) and the parking brake is set.
DON'T remove the radiator cap from a hot cooling system — let it cool or cover it with a cloth and release the pressure gradually.
DON'T attempt to drain the engine oil until you are sure it has cooled to the point that it will not burn you.
DON'T touch any part of the engine or exhaust system until it has cooled sufficiently to avoid burns.
DON'T siphon toxic liquids such as gasoline, antifreeze and brake fluid by mouth, or allow them to remain on your skin.
DON'T inhale brake lining dust — it is potentially hazardous (see *Asbestos* below)
DON'T allow spilled oil or grease to remain on the floor — wipe it up before someone slips on it.
DON'T use loose fitting wrenches or other tools which may slip and cause injury.
DON'T push on wrenches when loosening or tightening nuts or bolts. Always try to pull the wrench toward you. If the situation calls for pushing the wrench away, push with an open hand to avoid scraped knuckles if the wrench should slip.
DON'T attempt to lift a heavy component alone — get someone to help you.
DON'T rush or take unsafe shortcuts to finish a job.
DON'T allow children or animals in or around the vehicle while you are working on it.
DO wear eye protection when using power tools such as a drill, sander, bench grinder, etc. and when working under a vehicle.
DO keep loose clothing and long hair well out of the way of moving parts.
DO make sure that any hoist used has a safe working load rating adequate for the job.
DO get someone to check on you periodically when working alone on a vehicle.
DO carry out work in a logical sequence and make sure that everything is correctly assembled and tightened.
DO keep chemicals and fluids tightly capped and out of the reach of children and pets.
DO remember that your vehicle's safety affects that of yourself and others. If in doubt on any point, get professional advice.

Asbestos

Certain friction, insulating, sealing, and other products — such as brake linings, brake bands, clutch linings, torque converters, gaskets, etc. — contain asbestos. *Extreme care must be taken to avoid inhalation of dust from such products since it is hazardous to health.* If in doubt, assume that they *do* contain asbestos.

Fire

Remember at all times that gasoline is highly flammable. Never smoke or have any kind of open flame around when working on a vehicle. But the risk does not end there. A spark caused by an electrical short circuit, by two metal surfaces contacting each other, or even by static electricity built up in your body under certain conditions, can ignite gasoline vapors, which in a confined space are highly explosive. Do not, under any circumstances, use gasoline for cleaning parts. Use an approved safety solvent.

Always disconnect the battery ground (–) cable *at the battery* before working on any part of the fuel system or electrical system. Never risk spilling fuel on a hot engine or exhaust component.

It is strongly recommended that a fire extinguisher suitable for use on fuel and electrical fires be kept handy in the garage or workshop at all times. Never try to extinguish a fuel or electrical fire with water.

Fumes

Certain fumes are highly toxic and can quickly cause unconsciousness and even death if inhaled to any extent. Gasoline vapor falls into this category, as do the vapors from some cleaning solvents. Any draining or pouring of such volatile fluids should be done in a well ventilated area.

When using cleaning fluids and solvents, read the instructions on the container carefully. Never use materials from unmarked containers.

Never run the engine in an enclosed space, such as a garage. Exhaust fumes contain carbon monoxide, which is extremely poisonous. If you need to run the engine, always do so in the open air, or at least have the rear of the vehicle outside the work area.

If you are fortunate enough to have the use of an inspection pit, never drain or pour gasoline and never run the engine while the vehicle is over the pit. The fumes, being heavier than air, will concentrate in the pit with possibly lethal results.

The battery

Never create a spark or allow a bare light bulb near the battery. The battery normally gives off a certain amount of hydrogen gas, which is highly explosive.

Always disconnect the battery ground (–) cable *at the battery* before working on the fuel or electrical systems.

If possible, loosen the filler caps or cover when charging the battery from an external source. Do not charge at an excessive rate or the battery may burst.

Take care when adding water and when carrying a battery. The electrolyte, even when diluted, is very corrosive and should not be allowed to contact clothing or skin.

Always wear eye protection when cleaning the battery to prevent the caustic deposits from entering your eyes.

Household current

When using an electric power tool, inspection light, etc., which operates on household current, always make sure that the tool is correctly connected to its plug and that, where necessary, it is properly grounded. Do not use such items in damp conditions and, again, do not create a spark or apply excessive heat in the vicinity of fuel or fuel vapor.

Secondary ignition system voltage

A severe electric shock can result from touching certain parts of the ignition system (such as the spark plug wires) when the engine is running or being cranked, particularly if components are damp or the insulation is defective. In the case of an electronic ignition system, the secondary system voltage is much higher and could prove fatal.

Troubleshooting

Contents

Symptom — **Applicable Section**

Engine and performance

Battery will not hold a charge ... 11
Engine backfires ... 18
Engine 'diesels' (continues to run) after switching off ... 21
Engine hard to start when cold ... 4
Engine hard to start when hot ... 5
Engine lacks power ... 17
Engine 'lopes' while idling or idles erratically ... 8
Engine misses at idle speed ... 9
Engine misses throughout driving speed range ... 14
Engine rotates but will not start ... 2
Engine stalls ... 16
Engine starts but stops immediately ... 7
Engine surges while holding accelerator steady ... 19
Engine will not rotate when attempting to start ... 1
Excessive fuel consumption ... 24
Excessively high idle speed ... 10
Excessive oil consumption ... 23
Fuel odor ... 25
Hesitation or stumble on acceleration ... 15
Ignition light fails to come on when key is turned ... 13
Ignition light fails to go out ... 12
Low oil pressure ... 22
Miscellaneous engine noises ... 26
Pinging or knocking engine sounds during hard acceleration or uphill ... 20
Starter motor noisy or excessively rough in engagement ... 6
Starter motor operates without rotating engine ... 3

Engine cooling system

Abnormal coolant loss ... 31
Corrosion ... 33
External coolant leakage ... 29
Internal coolant leakage ... 30
Overcooling ... 28
Overheating ... 27
Poor coolant circulation ... 32

Clutch

Clutch pedal stays on floor when disengaged ... 39
Clutch slips (engine speed increases with no increase in vehicle speed) ... 35
Fails to release (pedal depressed to the floor – shift lever does not move freely in and out of Reverse) ... 34
Grabbing (chattering) on take-up ... 36
Squeal or rumble with clutch fully disengaged (pedal depressed) ... 38
Squeal or rumble with clutch fully engaged (pedal released) ... 37

Manual transmission

Difficulty in engaging gears ... 45
Oil leakage ... 44
Noise occurs while shifting gears ... 46
Noisy in all gears ... 41
Noisy in Neutral with engine running ... 40
Noisy in one particular gear ... 42
Slips out of gear ... 43

Symptom — **Applicable Section**

Automatic transmission

Engine will start in gears other than P (Park) or N (Neutral) ... 50
Fluid leakage ... 47
General shift mechanism problems ... 48
Transmission slips, shifts rough, is noisy or has no drive in forward or reverse gears ... 51
Transmission will not downshift with the accelerator pedal pressed to the floor ... 49

Driveshaft

Knock or clunk when the transmission is under initial load (just after transmission is put into gear) ... 53
Leakage of fluid at front of driveshaft ... 52
Metallic grating sound consistent with vehicle speed ... 54
Scraping noise ... 56
Vibration ... 55
Whining or whistling noise ... 57

Rear axle and differential

Knocking sound when starting or gear shifting ... 59
Noise – same when in drive as when vehicle is coasting ... 58
Noise while turning ... 60
Oil leakage ... 62
Vibration ... 61

Brakes

Brake pedal feels spongy when depressed ... 66
Brake pedal pulsates during brake application ... 69
Brakes drag (indicated by sluggish engine performance or wheels being very hot after driving) ... 70
Excessive brake pedal travel ... 65
Excessive effort required to stop vehicle ... 65
Noise (high-pitched squeak) ... 64
Pedal travels to the floor with little resistance ... 68
Rear brakes lock up under heavy brake application (indicated by a skidding effect) ... 72
Rear brakes lock up under light brake application (indicated by a skidding effect) ... 71
Vehicle pulls to one side during braking ... 63

Suspension and steering

Vehicle pulls to one side ... 73
Excessively stiff steering ... 77
Excessive pitching and/or rolling around corners or during braking ... 75
Excessive play in steering ... 78
Excessive tire wear (not specific to one area) ... 84
Excessive tire wear on inside edge ... 86
Excesive tire wear on outside edge ... 85
Lack of power assistance (with power steering system) ... 79
Miscellaneous noises ... 83
Noisy power steering pump ... 82
Shimmy, shake or vibration ... 74
Steering effort not the same in both directions (power system) .. 81
Steering wheel fails to return to straight-ahead position ... 80
Tire tread worn in one place ... 87
Wandering or general instability ... 76

This section provides an easy-reference guide to the more common faults which may occur during the operation of your AMC vehicle. These faults and their probable causes are grouped under their respective systems i.e. Engine, Cooling system, etc., and also refer to the Chapter and/or Section which deals with the problem.

Remember that successful troubleshooting is not a mysterious 'black art' practiced only by professional mechanics; it's simply the result of a bit of knowledge combined with an intelligent, systematic approach to the problem. Always work by a process of elimination, starting with the simplest solution and working through to the most complex – and never overlook the obvious. Anyone can forget to fill the gas tank or leave the lights on overnight, so don't assume that you are above such oversights.

Finally, always get clear in your mind why a problem has occurred and take steps to ensure that it doesn't happen again. if the electrical system fails because of a poor connection, check all other connections in the system to make sure that they don't fail as well; if a particular fuse continues to blow, find out why – don't just go on replacing fuses. Remember, failure or incorrect functioning of a small component can often be indicative of potential failure or incorrect functioning of a more important component or system.

Engine and performance

1 Engine will not rotate when attempting to start

1 Battery terminal connections loose or corroded. Check the cable terminals at the battery; tighten or clean off corrosion as necessary.
2 Battery discharged or faulty. If the cable connectors are clean and tight on the battery posts, turn the key to the On position and switch on the headlights and/or windshield wipers. If these fail to function, the battery is discharged.
3 Automatic transmission not fully engaged in Park or Neutral (N).
4 Broken, loose or disconnected wiring in the starting circuit. Inspect all wiring and connectors at the battery, starter solenoid and ignition switch (on steering column).
5 Starter motor pinion jammed on flywheel ring gear. If manual transmission, place transmission in gear and rock the vehicle to manually turn the engine. Remove starter and inspect pinion (Chapter 5) and flywheel (Chapter 2) at earliest convenience.
6 Starter solenoid faulty (Chapter 5).
7 Starter motor faulty (Chapter 5).
8 Ignition switch faulty (Chapter 10).

2 Engine rotates but will not start

1 Fuel tank empty.
2 Battery discharged (engine rotates slowly). Check the operation of electrical components as described in previous Section.
3 Battery terminal connections loose or corroded. See previous Section.
4 Fuel not reaching carburetor. Check for clogged fuel filter or lines, or defective fuel pump. Also make sure the tank vent lines are not clogged (Chapter 4).
5 Choke not operating properly (Chapter 1).
6 Faulty distributor components. Check the cap and rotor (Chapters 1 and 5).
7 Low cylinder compression. Have the cylinder compression tested by your dealer or other reputable repair shop.
8 Valve clearances not properly adjusted (Chapter 1).
9 Water in fuel. Drain and fill with new fuel.
10 Defective ignition module (Chapter 5).
11 Dirty, clogged or misadjusted carburetor. Check particularly the float level adjustment (Chapter 4).
12 Excessive moisture on, or damage to ignition components (Chapter 5).
13 Worn, faulty or incorrectly adjusted spark plugs (Chapter 1).
14 Broken, loose or disconnected wiring in the starting circuit (see previous Section).
15 Distributor loose, thus changing ignition timing. Turn the distributor body as necessary to start the engine, then set ignition timing as soon as possible (Chapter 1).
16 Broken, loose or disconnected wires at the ignition coil, or faulty coil (Chapter 5).

3 Starter motor operates without rotating engine

1 Starter pinion sticking. Remove the starter (Chapter 5) and inspect.
2 Starter pinion or engine flywheel teeth worn or broken. Remove the starter and inspect (Chapter 5).

4 Engine hard to start when cold

1 Battery discharged or low. Check as described in Section 1.
2 Fuel not reaching the carburetor. Check the fuel filter, lines and fuel pump (Chapters 1 and 4).

5 Engine hard to start when hot

1 Air filter in need of replacement.
2 Fuel not reaching carburetor (see Section 4). Check particularly for a vapor lock situation, brought about by clogged fuel tank vent lines.

6 Starter motor noisy or excessively rough in engagement

1 Pinion or flywheel gear teeth worn or broken. Remove the starter and inspect (Chapter 5).
2 Starter motor retaining bolts loose or missing.

7 Engine starts but stops immediately

1 Loose or faulty electrical connections at distributor, coil or alternator.
2 Vacuum leak at the gasket surfaces of the intake manifold. Check that all mounting bolts are tightened to specifications and all vacuum hoses connected to the manifold are positioned properly and are in good condition.
3 Fuel not reaching carburetor (see Section 2).

8 Engine 'lopes' while idling or idles erratically

1 Vacuum leakage. Check mounting bolts at the intake manifold for tightness. Check that all vacuum hoses are connected and in good condition. Use a stethoscope or a length of fuel line hose held against your ear to listen for vacuum leaks while the engine is running. A hissing sound will be heard. A soapy water solution will also detect leaks. Check the intake manifold gasket surfaces.
2 Leaking EGR valve (Chapter 6) or plugged PCV valve (Chapter 6).
3 Air cleaner clogged and in need of replacement (Chapter 1).
4 Fuel pump not delivering sufficient fuel (Section 4).
5 Leaking head gasket. If this is suspected, have a cylinder compression check performed by your dealer or other reputable repair shop.
6 Timing chain or gears worn and need replacement (Chapter 2).
7 Camshaft lobes worn, necessitating the removal of the camshaft for inspection (Chapter 2).
8 Valve clearance out of adjustment (Chapter 1).
9 Ignition timing out of adjustment (Chapter 1).
10 Ignition system not operating properly (Chapter 5).
11 Forced air preheat system not operating properly (Chapter 6).
12 Choke not operating properly (Chapter 1).
13 Carburetor dirty, clogged or out of adjustment. Check particularly the float level adjustment (Chapter 4).
14 Idle speed out of adjustment (Chapter 1).

9 Engine misses at idle speed

1 Spark plugs faulty or not gapped properly (Chapter 1).
2 Faulty spark plug wires (Chapter 1).

3 Excessive moisture on or damage to distributor components (Chapter 5).
4 Shorts in ignition, coil or spark plug wires.
5 Sticking or faulty emissions systems (see Chapter 6).
6 Clogged fuel filter and/or foreign matter in fuel. Remove the fuel filter (Chapter 1) and inspect.
7 Vacuum leaks at intake manifold or at hose connections. Check as described in Section 8.
8 Incorrect idle speed (Chapter 1) or idle mixture (Chapter 4).
9 Incorrect ignition timing (Chapter 1).
10 Uneven or low cylinder compression. Have a cylinder compression check performed by your dealer or other reputable repair shop.
11 Choke not operating properly (Chapter 1).

10 Excessively high idle speed

1 Snagged throttle linkage (Chapter 4).
2 Choke opened excessively at idle (Chapter 4).
3 Idle speed incorrectly adjusted (Chapter 1).
4 Defective automatic choke system (Chapter 6).
5 Valve clearances incorrectly adjusted (Chapter 1).
6 Dash pot out of adjustment (Chapter 4).

11 Battery will not hold a charge

1 Alternator drivebelt defective or not adjusted properly (Chapter 1).
2 Battery terminals loose or corroded (Chapter 1).
3 Alternator not charging properly (Chapter 5).
4 Loose, broken or faulty wiring in the charging circuit (Chapter 5).
5 Short in vehicle circuitry causing a continual drain on battery (Chapter 10).
6 Battery defective internally.
7 Faulty regulator (Chapter 5).

12 Ignition light fails to go out

1 Fault in alternator or charging circuit (Chapter 5).
2 Alternator drivebelt defective or not properly adjusted (Chapter 1).

13 Ignition light fails to come on when key is turned

1 Ignition light bulb faulty (Chapter 10).
2 Alternator faulty (Chapter 5).
3 Fault in the printed circuit, dash wiring or bulb holder (Chapter 10).

14 Engine misses throughout driving speed range

1 Fuel filter clogged and/or impurities in the fuel system. Check fuel filter (Chapter 1) or clean system (Chapter 4).
2 Faulty or incorrectly gapped spark plugs (Chapter 1).
3 Incorrectly set ignition timing (Chapter 1).
4 Cracked distributor cap, disconnected distributor wires, or damage to the distributor components (Chapter 1).
5 Leaking spark plug wires (Chapter 1).
6 Emissions system components faulty (Chapter 6).
7 Low or uneven cylinder compression pressures. Have a cylinder compression check performed by your dealer or other reputable repair facility.
8 Weak or faulty ignition coil (Chapter 5).
9 Weak or faulty ignition system (Chapter 5).
10 Vacuum leaks at intake manifold or vacuum hoses (see Section 8).
11 Dirty or clogged carburetor (Chapter 4).
12 Leaky EGR valve (Chapter 6).
13 Carburetor out of adjustment (Chapter 4).

15 Hesitation or stumble on acceleration

1 Ignition timing incorrectly set (Chapter 1).
2 Ignition system not operating properly (Chapter 5).
3 Dirty or clogged carburetor (Chapter 4).
4 Low fuel pressure. Check for proper operation of the fuel pump and for blockage in the fuel filter and lines (Chapter 4).
5 Carburetor out of adjustment (Chapter 4).

16 Engine stalls

1 Idle speed incorrectly set (Chapter 1).
2 Fuel filter clogged and/or water and impurities in the fuel system (Chapter 1).
3 Choke not operating properly (Chapter 1).
4 Distributor components damp, or damage to distributor cap, rotor etc. (Chapter 5).
5 Emissions system components faulty (Chapter 6).
6 Faulty or incorrectly gapped spark plugs (Chapter 1). Also check spark plug wires (Chapter 1).
7 Vacuum leak at the carburetor, intake manifold or vacuum hoses. Check as described in Section 8.
8 Valve clearance incorrectly set (Chapter 1).

17 Engine lacks power

1 Incorrect ignition timing (Chapter 1).
2 Excessive play in distributor shaft. At the same time check for faulty distributor cap, wires, etc. (Chapter 5).
3 Faulty or incorrectly gapped spark plugs (Chapter 1).
4 Air cleaner needs replacing (Chapter 1).
5 Spark control system not operating properly (Chapter 6).
6 Faulty coil (Chapter 5).
7 Brakes binding (Chapters 1 and 9).
8 Automatic transmission fluid level incorrect, causing slippage (Chapter 1).
9 Manual transmission clutch slipping (Chapter 8).
10 Fuel filter clogged and/or impurities in the fuel system (Chapters 1 and 4).
11 EGR system not functioning properly (Chapter 6).
12 Use of sub-standard fuel. Fill tank with proper octane fuel.
13 Low or uneven cylinder compression pressures. Have a cylinder compression test performed by your dealer or other reputable repair shop, which will also detect leaking valves and/or a blown head gasket.
14 Air leak at carburetor or intake manifold (check as described in Section 8).
15 Dirty or clogged carburetor (Chapter 4).
16 Malfunctioning choke (Chapter 1 and Chapter 4).

18 Engine backfires

1 EGR system not functioning properly (Chapter 6).
2 Ignition timing incorrect (Chapter 1).
3 Forced air preheat system not operating properly (Chapter 6).
4 Anti-backfire valve not operating properly (Chapter 4).
5 Vacuum leak (refer to Section 8).
6 Valve clearances not correctly adjusted (Chapter 1).
7 Damaged valve springs or sticking valves (Chapter 2).
8 Intake air leak (see Section 15).
9 Carburetor float level out of adjustment (Chapter 4).
10 Automatic choke system not operating properly (Chapter 6).

19 Engine surges while holding accelerator steady

1 Intake air leak (see previous Section).
2 Fuel pump not working properly (Chapter 4).

20 Pinging or knocking engine sounds during hard acceleration or uphill

1 Incorrect grade of fuel. Fill tank with fuel of the proper octane rating.
2 Ignition timing incorrect (Chapter 1).

3 Carbon build-up in combustion chambers. Remove cylinder head and have chambers cleaned (Chapter 2).
4 Improper spark plugs (Chapter 1).

21 Engine diesels (continues to run) after switching off

1 Idle speed too fast (Chapter 1).
2 Ignition timing incorrectly adjusted (Chapter 1).
3 Incorrect heat range of spark plugs (Chapter 1).
4 Intake air leak (see Section 15).
5 Carbon build-up in combustion chambers. Remove the cylinder head and have chambers cleaned (Chapter 2).
6 Valves sticking (Chapter 2).
7 Automatic choke system not operating properly (Chapter 6).
8 Valve clearance incorrectly adjusted (Chapter 1).
9 EGR system not operating properly (Chapter 6).
10 Deceleration fuel cut system not operating properly (Chapter 6).
11 Check for causes of overheating (Section 27).

22 Low oil pressure

1 Improper grade of oil.
2 Oil pump regulator valve not operating properly (Chapter 2).
3 Oil pump worn or damaged (Chapter 2).
4 Engine overheating (refer to Section 27).
5 Clogged oil filter (Chapter 1).
6 Clogged oil strainer (Chapter 2).
7 Oil pressure gauge not working properly (Chapters 2 and 10).

23 Excessive oil consumption

1 Loose oil drain plug.
2 Loose or damaged oil pan gasket (Chapter 2).
3 Loose or damaged timing chain cover gasket (Chapter 2).
4 Front or rear crankshaft oil seal leaking (Chapter 2).
5 Loose or damaged valve cover gasket (Chapter 2).
6 Oil filter not tightened all the way (Chapter 1).
7 Loose or damaged oil pressure switch (Chapter 2).
8 Pistons and cylinders excessively worn (Chapter 2).
9 Piston rings not positioned correctly on pistons (Chapter 2).
10 Worn or damaged piston rings (Chapter 2).
11 Intake and/or exhaust valve oil seals in need of replacement (Chapter 2).
12 Worn valve stems. Valves in need of replacement (Chapter 2).

24 Excessive fuel consumption

1 Dirty or clogged air filter element (Chapter 1).
2 Incorrectly set ignition timing (Chapter 1).
3 Incorrectly set idle speed (Chapter 1).
4 Low tire pressure or incorrect tire size (Chapter 11).
5 Fuel leakage. Check all connections, lines and components in the fuel system (Chapter 4).
6 Choke not operating properly (Chapter 1).
7 Dirty or clogged carburetor (Chapter 4).

25 Fuel odor

1 Fuel leakage. Check all connections, lines and components of the fuel system (Chapter 4).
2 Fuel tank overfilled. Fill only to automatic shut-off.
3 Charcoal canister filter in Evaporative Emissions Control system in need of replacement (Chapter 1).
4 Vapor leaks from Evaporative Emissions Control system lines (Chapter 6).

26 Miscellaneous engine noises

1 *A strong dull noise that becomes more rapid as the engine accelerates* indicates worn or damaged crankshaft bearings or an unevenly worn crankshaft. To pinpoint the trouble spot, remove the spark plug wire from one plug at a time and crank the engine over. If the noise stops, the cylinder with the removed plug wire indicates the problem area. Replace the bearing and/or service or replace the crankshaft (Chapter 2).
2 *A similar (yet slightly higher pitched) noise* to the crankshaft knocking described in the previous paragraph, that becomes more rapid as the engine accelerates, indicates worn or damaged connecting rod bearings (Chapter 2). The procedure for locating the problem cylinder is the same as described in paragraph 1.
3 *An overlapping metallic noise that increases in intensity as the engine speed increases, yet diminishes as the engine warms up* indicates abnormal piston and cylinder wear (Chapter 2). To locate the problem cylinder, use the procedure described in paragraph 1.
4 *A rapid clicking noise that becomes faster as the engine accelerates* indicates a worn piston pin or piston pin hole. This sound will happen each time the piston hits the highest and lowest points of its stroke (Chapter 2). The procedure for locating the problem piston is described in paragraph 1.
5 *A metallic clicking noise coming from the water pump* indicates worn or damaged water pump bearings or pump. Replace the water pump with a new one (Chapter 3).
6 *A rapid tapping sound or clicking sound that becomes faster as the engine speed increases* indicates "valve tapping" or improperly adjusted valve clearances. This can be identified by holding one end of a plastic hose to your ear and placing the other end at different spots along the length of the rocker cover. The point where the sound is loudest indicates the problem valve. Adjust the valve clearance (Chapter 1).
7 *A steady metallic rattling or rapping sound coming from the area of the timing chain cover* indicates a worn, damaged or out-of-adjustment timing chain. Service or replace the chain and related components (Chapter 2).

Engine cooling system

27 Overheating

1 Insufficient coolant in system (Chapter 1).
2 Fan belt defective or not adjusted properly (Chapter 1).
3 Radiator core blocked or radiator grille dirty and restricted (Chapter 3).
4 Thermostat faulty (Chapter 3).
5 Fan not functioning properly (Chapter 3).
6 Radiator cap not maintaining proper pressure. Have cap pressure tested by gas station or repair shop.
7 Ignition timing incorrect (Chapter 1).
8 Defective water pump (Chapter 3).
9 Improper grade of engine oil.
10 Inaccurate temperature gauge (Chapter 10).

28 Overcooling

1 Thermostat faulty (Chapter 3).
2 Inaccurate temperature gauge (Chapter 10).

29 External coolant leakage

1 Deteriorated or damaged hoses. Loose clamps at hose connections (Chapter 3).
2 Water pump seals defective. If this is the case, water will drip from the 'weep' hole in the water pump body (Chapter 3).
3 Leakage from radiator core or header tank. This will require the radiator to be professionally repaired (see Chapter 3 for removal procedures).
4 Engine drain plugs or water jacket freeze plugs leaking (Chapter 1 or 2).
5 Leak from water temperature gauge connections (Chapter 2).
6 Leak from damaged gaskets or small cracks (Chapter 2).
7 Damaged head gasket. This can be verified by checking the condition of the engine oil as noted in Section 30.

30 Internal coolant leakage

Note: *Internal coolant leaks can usually be detected by examining the oil. Check the dipstick and inside of valve cover for water deposits and an oil consistency like that of a milkshake.*

1 Faulty cylinder head gasket. Have the system pressure-tested professionally or remove the cylinder heads (Chapter 2) and inspect.
2 Cracked cylinder bore or cylinder head. Dismantle engine and inspect (Chapter 2).
3 Loose cylinder head bolts (tighten as described in Chapter 2).

31 Abnormal coolant loss

1 Overfilling system (Chapter 1).
2 Coolant boiling away due to overheating (see causes in Section 15).
3 Internal or external leakage (see Sections 29 and 30).
4 Faulty radiator cap. Have the cap pressure tested.

32 Poor coolant circulation

1 Inoperative water pump. A quick test is to pinch the top radiator hose closed with your hand while the engine is idling, then let it loose. You should feel a surge of coolant if the pump is working properly (Chapter 3).
2 Restriction in cooling system. Drain, flush and refill the system (Chapter 1). If it appears necessary, remove the radiator (Chapter 3) and have it reverse-flushed or professionally cleaned.
3 Loose water pump drivebelt (Chapter 1).
4 Thermostat sticking (Chapter 3).
5 Insufficient coolant (Chapter 1).

33 Corrosion

1 Excessive impurities in the water. Soft, clean water is recommended. Distilled or rainwater is satisfactory.
2 Insufficient antifreeze solution.
3 Infrequent flushing and draining of system. Regular flushing of the cooling system should be carried out at the specified intervals as described in Chapter 1.

Clutch

Note: *All clutch service information is contained in Chapter 8 unless otherwise noted.*

34 Fails to release (pedal depressed to the floor) – shift lever does not move freely in and out of Reverse)

1 Clutch face wet with oil. Remove clutch disc and inspect.
2 Clutch disc warped, bent or excessively damaged.
3 Diaphragm spring fatigued. Remove clutch cover/pressure plate assembly and inspect.
4 Leakage of fluid from clutch hydraulic system. Inspect master cylinder, operating cylinder and connecting lines.
5 Air in clutch hydraulic system. Bleed the system.
6 Insufficient pedal stroke. Check and adjust as necessary.
7 Piston cup in operating cylinder deformed or damaged.
8 Lack of grease on pilot bushing.

35 Clutch slips (engine speed increases with no increase in vehicle speed)

1 Worn or oil soaked clutch disc facing.
2 Clutch disc not seated in. It may take 30 or 40 normal starts for a new disc to seat.
3 Diaphragm spring weak or damaged. Remove clutch cover/pressure plate assembly and inspect.
4 Flywheel warped (Chapter 2).
5 Debris in master cylinder preventing the piston from returning to its normal position.
6 Clutch hydraulic line damaged.

36 Grabbing (chattering) on take-up

1 Oil on clutch disc facings. Remove disc and inspect. Correct any leakage source.
2 Worn or loose engine or transmission mounts. These units may move slightly when clutch is released. Inspect mounts and bolts.
3 Worn splines on clutch gear. Remove clutch components and inspect.
4 Warped pressure plate or flywheel. Remove clutch components and inspect.
5 Diaphragm spring fatigued. Remove clutch cover/pressure plate assembly and inspect.
6 Clutch disc facing hardened or warped.
7 Clutch disc rivets loose.

37 Squeal or rumble with clutch fully engaged (pedal released)

1 Improper pedal adjustment. Adjust pedal free play (Chapter 1).
2 Release bearing binding on transmission bearing retainer. Remove clutch components and check bearing. Remove any burrs or nicks, clean and relubricate before installation.
3 Pilot bushing worn or damaged.
4 Clutch disc rivets loose.
5 Clutch disc cracked.
6 Fatigued clutch disc torsion springs. Replace clutch disc.

38 Squeal or rumble with clutch fully disengaged (pedal depressed)

1 Worn, faulty or broken release bearing.
2 Worn or broken pressure plate diaphragm finger.

39 Clutch pedal stays on floor when disengaged

1 Bind in linkage or release bearing. Inspect linkage or remove clutch components as necessary.
2 Linkage springs being over-extended. Adjust linkage for proper lash.

Manual transmission

Note: *All service information on the manual transmission is contained within Chapter 7, Part A, unless otherwise noted.*

40 Noisy in Neutral with engine running

1 Input shaft bearing worn.
2 Damaged main drive gear bearing.
3 Insufficient transmission oil (Chapter 1).
4 Transmission oil in poor condition. Drain and fill with proper grade oil. Check old oil for water or debris (Chapter 1).
5 Noise can be caused by variations in engine torque. Change the idle speed and see if noise disappears.

41 Noisy in all gears

1 Any of the above causes, and/or:
2 Worn or damaged output gear bearings or shaft.

42 Noisy in one particular gear

1 Worn, damaged or chipped gear teeth for that particular gear.
2 Worn or damaged synchronizer for that particular gear.

43 Slips out of gear

1 Transmission loose on clutch housing.
2 Stiff shift lever seal.

3 Shift linkage binding.
4 Broken or loose input gear bearing retainer.
5 Dirt between clutch lever and engine housing.
6 Worn linkage.
7 Damaged or worn check balls, fork rod ball grooves or check springs.
8 Worn mainshaft or countershaft bearings.
9 Loose engine mounts (Chapter 2).
10 Excessive gear end play.
11 Wear in synchronizer units.

44 Oil leakage

1 Excessive amount of lubricant in transmission (see Chapter 1 for correct checking procedures). Drain lubricant as required.
2 Rear oil seal or speedometer oil seal in need of replacement.
3 To pinpoint a leak, first remove all built-up dirt and grime from around the transmission. Degreasing agents and/or steam cleaning will achieve this. With the underside clean, drive the vehicle at low speeds so the air flow will not blow the leak far from its source. Raise the vehicle and determine where the leak is coming from.

45 Difficulty in engaging gears

1 Clutch not releasing fully.
2 Loose or damaged shift linkage. Make a thorough inspection, replacing parts as necessary.
3 Insufficient transmission oil (Chapter 1).
4 Transmission oil in poor condition. Drain and fill with proper grade of oil. Check oil for water or debris (Chapter 1).
5 Worn or damaged shift fork shaft.
6 Sticking or jamming gears.

46 Noise occurs while shifting gears

1 Check for proper operation of the clutch (Chapter 8).
2 Faulty synchromesh assemblies. Measure synchronizer ring-to-gear clearance. Also, check for wear or damage to synchronizer rings or any parts of the synchromesh assemblies.

Automatic transmission

Note: *Due to the complexity of the automatic transmission, it is difficult for the home mechanic to properly diagnose and service this component. For problems other than the following, the vehicle should be taken to a reputable mechanic.*

47 Fluid leakage

1 Automatic transmission fluid is a deep red color, and fluid leaks should not be confused with engine oil which can easily be blown by air flow to the transmission.
2 To pinpoint a leak, first remove all built-up dirt and grime from around the transmission. Degreasing agents and/or steam cleaning will achieve this. With the underside clean, drive the vehicle at low speeds so the air flow will not blow the leak from its source. Raise the vehicle and determine where the leak is coming from. Common areas of leakage are:

a) *Fluid pan:* tighten mounting bolts and/or replace pan gasket as necessary (Chapter 1)
b) *Rear extension:* tighten bolts and/or replace oil seal as necessary
c) *Filler pipe:* replace the rubber seal where pipe enters transmission case
d) *Transmission oil lines:* tighten connectors where lines enter transmission case and/or replace lines
e) *Vent pipe:* transmission over-filled and/or water in fluid (see checking procedures, Chapter 1)
f) *Speedometer connector:* replace the O-ring where speedometer cable enters transmission case

48 General shift mechanism problems

Chapter 7 part B deals with checking and adjusting the shift linkage on automatic transmissions. Common problems which may be attributed to misadjusted linkage are:

a) Engine starting in gears other than (P) Park or (N) Neutral
b) Indicator on quadrant pointing to a gear other than the one actually being used
c) Vehicle will not hold firm when in (P) Park position

49 Transmission will not downshift with the accelerator pedal pressed to the floor

Chapter 7 Part B deals with adjusting the throttle linkage to enable the transmission to downshift properly.

50 Engine will start in gears other than P (Park) or N (Neutral)

Chapter 7 Part B deals with adjusting the neutral start switch used with automatic transmissions.

51 Transmission slips, shifts rough, is noisy or has no drive in forward or reverse gears

1 There are many probable causes for the above problems, but the home mechanic should concern himself with only one possibility; fluid level.
2 Before taking the vehicle to a specialist, check the level of the fluid and condition of the fluid as described in Chapter 1. Correct fluid level as necessary or change the fluid and filter if needed. If the problem persists, have a professional diagnose the probable cause.

Driveshaft

Note: *All service information on the driveshaft is contained in Chapter 8 unless otherwise noted.*

52 Leakage of fluid at front of driveshaft

Defective transmission rear oil seal. See Chapter 7 for replacing procedures. While this is done, check the splined yoke for burrs or a rough condition which may be damaging the seal. If found, these can be dressed with crocus cloth or a fine dressing stone.

53 Knock or clunk when the transmission is under initial load (just after transmission is put into gear)

1 Loose or disconnected rear suspension components. Check all mounting bolts and bushings (Chapters 1 and 11).
2 Loose driveshaft bolts. Inspect all bolts and nuts and tighten to torque specifications.
3 Worn or damaged universal joint bearings. Replace bearings (Chapter 8).
4 Worn sleeve yoke and mainshaft spline.
5 Defective center bearing or insulator, if so equipped.

54 Metallic grating sound consistent with vehicle speed

Pronounced wear in the universal joint bearings. Replace U-joints as necessary.

55 Vibration

Note: *Before it can be assumed that the driveshaft is at fault, make sure the tires are perfectly balanced and perform the following test.*

1 Install a tachometer inside the vehicle to monitor engine speed as the vehicle is driven. Drive the vehicle and note the engine speed at which the vibration (roughness) is most pronounced. Now, shift the transmission to a different gear and bring the engine speed to the same point.
2 If the vibration occurs at the same engine speed (rpm) regardless of which gear the transmission is in, the driveshaft is NOT at fault since the driveshaft speed varies.
3 If the vibration decreases or is eliminated when the transmission is in a different gear at the same engine speed, refer to the following probable causes.
4 Bent or dented driveshaft. Inspect and replace as necessary.
5 Undercoating or built-up dirt, etc. on the driveshaft. Clean the shaft thoroughly and retest.
6 Worn universal joint bearings. Remove the U-joints or driveshaft as necessary.
7 Driveshaft and/or companion flange out of balance. Check for missing weights on the shaft. Remove driveshaft and reinstall 180° from original position. Retest. Have driveshaft professionally balanced if problem persists.
8 Loose installation of the driveshaft.

56 Scraping noise

Make sure that the dust cover on the sleeve yoke is not rubbing on the transmission rear extension.

57 Whining or whistling noise

Defective center bearing (if so equipped).

Rear axle and differential

Note: *All information on the rear axle and differential is contained in Chapter 8 unless otherwise noted.*

58 Noise – same when in drive as when vehicle is coasting

1 Road noise. No corrective procedures available.
2 Tire noise. Inspect tires and tire pressures (Chapter 1).
3 Front wheel bearings loose, worn or damaged (Chapter 1).
4 Insufficient differential oil (Chapter 1).
5 Defective differential.

59 Knocking sound during starting or gear shifting

Defective or incorrectly adjusted differential.

60 Noise while turning

Defective differential.

61 Vibration

See probable causes under *Driveshaft.* Proceed under the guidelines listed for the driveshaft. If the problem persists, check the rear wheel bearings by raising the rear of the vehicle and spinning the wheels by hand. Listen for evidence of rough (noisy) bearings. Remove and inspect (Chapter 8).

62 Oil leakage

1 Pinion oil seal damaged (Chapter 8).
2 Axle shaft oil seals damaged (Chapter 8).
3 Loose filler or drain plug on differential (Chapter 1).
4 Clogged or damaged breather on differential.

Brakes

Note: *Before assuming a brake problem exists, make sure that the tires are in good condition and inflated properly (Chapter 1); the front end alignment is correct (Chapter 11); and that the vehicle is not loaded with weight in an unequal manner. All service procedures for the brakes are described in Chapter 9, unless otherwise noted.*

63 Vehicle pulls to one side during braking

1 Defective, damaged or oil-contaminated disc pad on one side. Inspect as described in Chapter 1. Refer to Chapter 9 if replacement is required.
2 Excessive wear of brake pad material or disc on one side. Inspect and correct as necessary.
3 Loose or disconnected front suspension components. Inspect and tighten all bolts to specifications (Chapter 11).
4 Defective caliper assembly. Remove caliper and inspect for stuck piston or damage.
5 Scored or out-of-round rotor.
6 Loose caliper mounting.
7 Incorrect adjustment of wheel bearings.

64 Noise (high-pitched squeak)

1 Front brake pads worn out. This noise comes from the wear sensor rubbing against the disc. Replace pads with new ones immediately.
2 Glazed or contaminated parts.
3 Dirty or scored rotor.
4 Bent support plate.

65 Excessive brake pedal travel

1 Partial brake system failure. Inspect entire system (Chapter 1) and correct as required.
2 Insufficient fluid in master cylinder. Check (Chapter 1) and add fluid and bleed system if necessary.
3 Air in system. Bleed system.
4 Excessive lateral play of discs.
5 Brakes out of adjustment. Inspect the operation of the automatic adjusters,
6 Defective check valve. Replace valve and bleed system.

66 Brake pedal feels spongy when depressed

1 Air in hydraulic lines. Bleed the brake system.
2 Faulty flexible hoses. Inspect all system hoses and lines. Replace parts as necessary.
3 Master cylinder mountings insecure. Inspect master cylinder bolts (nuts) and torque-tighten to specifications.
4 Master cylinder faulty.
5 Incorrect shoe clearance adjustment.
6 Defective check valve. Replace valve and bleed system.
7 Clogged reservoir cap vent hole.
8 Deformed rubber brake lines.
9 Soft or swollen caliper seals.
10 Poor quality brake fluid. Bleed entire system and fill with new approved fluid.

67 Excessive effort required to stop vehicle

1 Power brake booster not operating properly.
2 Excessively worn linings or pads. Inspect and replace if necessary.
3 One or more caliper pistons seized or sticking. Inspect and rebuild as required.
4 Brake pads or linings contaminated with oil or grease. Inspect and replace as required.
5 New pads or linings installed and not yet seated. It will take a while for the new material to seat against the rotor or drum.
6 Worn or damaged master cylinder or caliper assemblies. Check particularly for frozen pistons.
7 See also causes listed under Section 66.

68 Pedal travels to the floor with little resistance

Little or no fluid in the master cylinder reservoir caused by; leaking caliper piston(s); loose, damaged or disconnected brake lines. Inspect entire system and correct as necessary.

69 Brake pedal pulsates during brake application

1 Wheel bearings not adjusted properly or in need of replacement (Chapter 1).
2 Caliper not sliding properly due to improper installation or obstructions. Remove and inspect.
3 Rotor not within specifications. Remove the rotor and check for excessive lateral run-out and parallelism. Have the rotor professionally machined or replace it with a new one. Also check that all rotors are the same thickness.
4 Out of round rear brake drums. Remove the drums and have them professionally machined or replace them with new ones.

70 Brakes drag (indicated by sluggish engine performance or wheels being very hot after driving)

1 Output rod adjustment too long at the brake pedal.
2 Obstructed master cylinder compensator. Disassemble master cylinder and clean.
3 Master cylinder piston seized in bore. Overhaul master cylinder.
4 Caliper assembly in need of overhaul.
5 Brake pads or shoes need replacing.
6 Piston cups in master cylinder or caliper assembly deformed. Overhaul master cylinder.
7 Rotor not within specs. (Section 69).
8 Parking brake assembly will not release.
9 Clogged brake lines.
10 Wheel bearings out of adjustment (Chapter 1).
11 Brake pedal height improperly adjusted.
12 Wheel cylinder needs overhaul.
13 Improper shoe-to-drum clearance. Adjust as necessary.

71 Rear brakes lock up under light brake application (indicated by a skidding effect)

1 Tire pressures too high.
2 Tires excessively worn (Chapter 1).

72 Rear brakes lock up under heavy brake application (indicated by a skidding effect)

1 Tire pressures too high.
2 Tires excessively worn (Chapter 1).
3 Front brake pads contaminated with oil, mud or water. Clean or replace the pads.
4 Front brake pads excessively worn.
5 Poor front braking effect caused by defective master cylinder or caliper assembly.

Suspension and steering

73 Vehicle pulls to one side

1 Tire pressures uneven (Chapter 1).
2 Defective tire (Chapter 1).
3 Excessive wear in suspension or steering components (Chapter 1)
4 Front end in need of alignment.
5 Front brakes dragging. Inspect braking system as described in Section 70.
6 Wheel bearings improperly adjusted (Chapter 1).
7 Wheel lug nuts not tight.
8 Worn upper or lower control arm or strut bar bushing.

74 Shimmy, shake or vibration

1 Tire or wheel out of balance or out of round. Have professionally balanced.
2 Loose, worn or out of adjustment wheel bearings (Chapter 1).
3 Shock absorbers and/or suspension components worn or damaged. Check for worn bushings in the upper and lower control arms.
4 Wheel lug nuts not tight.
5 Incorrect tire pressures.
6 Excessively worn or damaged tire.
7 Loosely mounted steering gear housing.
8 Steering gear improperly adjusted.
9 Loose, worn or damaged steering components.
10 Damaged idler arm.
11 Worn balljoint.

75 Excessive pitching and/or rolling around corners or during braking

1 Defective shock absorbers (replace as a set).
2 Broken or weak leaf springs and/or suspension components.
3 Worn or damaged stabilizer bar or bushings.
4 Worn or damaged upper or lower control arms or bushings.

76 Wandering or general instability

1 Improper tire pressures.
2 Worn or damaged upper and lower control arm or strut bar.
3 Incorrect front end alignment.
4 Worn or damaged steering linkage or upper or lower control arm.
5 Improperly adjusted steering gear.
6 Out of balance wheels.
7 Loose wheel lug nuts.
8 Worn rear shock absorbers.
9 Fatigued or damaged rear leaf springs.

77 Excessively stiff steering

1 Lack of lubricant in power steering fluid reservoir where appropriate (Chapter 1).
2 Incorrect tire pressures (Chapter 1).
3 Lack of lubrication at balljoints (Chapter 1).
4 Front end out of alignment.
5 Steering gear out of adjustment or lacking lubrication.
6 Improperly adjusted wheel bearings.
7 Worn or damaged steering gear.
8 Tire pressures too low.
9 Worn or damaged balljoints.
10 Worn or damaged steering linkage.
11 See also Section 76.

78 Excessive play in steering

1 Loose wheel bearings (Chapter 1).
2 Excessive wear in upper or lower control arm or strut bar.
3 Steering gear improperly adjusted.
4 Incorrect front end alignment.
5 Steering gear mounting bolts not tight.
6 Worn steering linkage.

79 Lack of power assistance (with power steering system)

1 Steering pump drivebelt faulty or improperly adjusted (Chapter 1).
2 Fluid level low (Chapter 1).
3 Hoses or pipes restricting the flow. Inspect and replace parts as necessary.
4 Air in power steering system. Bleed system.
5 Defective power steering pump.

80 Steering wheel fails to return to straight-ahead position

1 Incorrect front end alignment.
2 Tire pressures too low.
3 Steering gears improperly engaged.
4 Steering column out of alignment.
5 Worn or damaged balljoint.
6 Worn or damaged steering linkage.
7 Improperly lubricated idler arm.
8 Insufficient oil in steering gear.
9 Lack of fluid in power steering pump.

81 Steering effort not the same in both directions (power system)

1 Fluid leakage from steering gear.
2 Clogged fluid passage in steering gear.

82 Noisy power steering pump

1 Insufficient oil in pump.
2 Clogged hoses or oil filter in pump.
3 Loose pulley.
4 Improperly adjusted drivebelt (Chapter 1).
5 Defective pump.

83 Miscellaneous noises

1 Improper tire pressures.
2 Insufficiently lubricated balljoint or steering linkage.
3 Loose or worn steering gear, steering linkage or suspension components.
4 Defective shock absorber.
5 Defective wheel bearing.
6 Worn or damaged upper or lower control arm or strut bar.
7 Damaged leaf spring.
8 Loose wheel lug nuts.
9 Worn or damaged rear axle shaft spline.
10 Worn or damaged rear shock absorber mounting bushing.
11 Incorrect rear axle end play adjustment.
12 See also causes of noises at the rear axle and driveshaft.

84 Excessive tire wear (not specific to one area)

1 Incorrect tire pressures.
2 Tires out of balance. Have professionally balanced.
3 Wheels damaged. Inspect and replace as necessary.
4 Suspension or steering components excessively worn (Chapter 1).

85 Excessive tire wear on outside edge

1 Inflation pressures not correct.
2 Excessive speed on turns.
3 Front-end alignment incorrect (excessive toe-in). Have professionally aligned.
4 Suspension arm bent or twisted.

86 Excessive tire wear on inside edge

1 Inflation pressures incorrect.
2 Front-end alignment incorrect (toe-out). Have professionally aligned.
3 Loose or damaged steering components (Chapter 1).

87 Tire tread worn in one place

1 Tires out of balance. Balance tires professionally.
2 Damaged or buckled wheel. Inspect and replace if necessary.
3 Defective tire.

Chapter 1 Tune-up and routine maintenance

Contents

Air filter and PCV filter replacement	16
Automatic transmission fluid change	37
Battery check and maintenance	5
Brake check	25
Carburetor choke check	33
Carburetor fuel/air mixture adjustment	35
Carburetor mounting torque check	34
Chassis lubrication	9
Clutch pedal free play check and adjustment	23
Cooling system check	10
Cooling system servicing (draining, flushing and refilling)	29
Contact points and condenser – replacement and adjustment	32
Cylinder compression check	30
Differential lubricant change	36
Engine drivebelts – check and adjustment	13
Engine idle speed adjustment	20
Engine oil and filter change	8
Exhaust Gas Recirculation (EGR) valve check	15
Exhaust manifold heat valve check	17
Exhaust system check	11
Fluid level checks	4
Fuel filter replacement	21
Fuel system check	14
Fuel vapor control system canister – filter replacement	24
Ignition timing check and adjustment	31
Introduction to routine maintenance	1
Positive Crankcase Ventilation (PCV) valve replacement	22
Routine maintenance intervals	3
Spark plug replacement	27
Spark plug wires, distributor cap and rotor check and replacement	28
Suspension and steering check	12
Thermo controlled air cleaner check	18
Tire rotation	19
Tire and tire pressure checks	6
Tune-up sequence	2
Underhood hoses – check and replacement	7
Wheel bearing check and service	26

Specifications

Note: *Additional specifications can be found in appropriate Chapters.*

Recommended lubricants, fluids and capacities

Engine oil	
Type	API rating SE or SF
Viscosity	
-30°F to 20°F	SAE 5W-20 SAE 5W-30
0°F to 60°F	SAE 10W SAE 5W-30 SAE 10W-30 SAE 10W-40
20°F to 100°F	SAE 20W SAE 10W-30 SAE 10W-40 SAE 20W-40 SAE 20W-50
Capacity (with new filter)	
Six-cylinder and V8	5.0 US qt
Four-cylinder (1977 through 1979)	4.9 US qt
Four-cylinder (1980 through 1983)	3.0 US qt
Engine coolant type	Ethylene glycol
Brake and clutch fluid type	Dot 3 or SAE J-1703
Automatic transmission fluid type	Dexron II ATF
Manual transmission lubricant	
Type	API GL-5 gear oil
Viscosity	80W-90
Power steering fluid type	AMC power steering fluid or equivalent
Manual steering gearbox lubricant	Multi-purpose chassis lubricant
Differential lubricant	
Type	
Standard differential	API GL-5 gear oil
Twin-grip (limited slip) differential	API rated limited slip gear oil
Viscosity	SAE 80W-90
Suspension and steering balljoint grease	Lithium-base multi-purpose chassis lubricant
Wheel bearing grease	EP lithium base grease

Brakes

Disc brake pad wear limit	Replace when worn to within $\frac{1}{16}$ in of the backing plate
Drum brake shoe wear limit	Replace when worn to within $\frac{1}{16}$ in of the rivet heads

Ignition system

Spark plug type *(Champion)*	
1970 through 1977 all models	N12Y or RN12Y
1978 and 1979	
Six-cylinder	N13L or RN13L
V8	N12Y or RN12Y
Four-cylinder	N8L or RN8L
1980 through 1983	
Six-cylinder	FN14LY or RFN14LY
Four-cylinder	(AC) R44SX
Spark plug gap	0.033 to 0.038 in
Ignition timing *(manual transmission)*	
V8 engines	
1971	2.5° BTDC
1972 through 1979	5° BTDC
Six-cylinder engines	
1971, 1974 and 1975 258 cu in and 1972 through 1975 232 cu in (except Calif.)	5° BTDC
1971 through 1975 (all others)	3° BTDC
1976 through 1978 258 cu in	
HA carburetor (1978 only)	10° BTDC
All others	6° BTDC
1976 through 1979 232 cu in	
1977 HA carburetor and Calif. only	10° BTDC
All others	8° BTDC
1979 258 cu in only	4° BTDC
1980 and 1981 258 cu in	
HA carburetor (1981 only)	15° BTDC
All others	6° BTDC
1982 and 1983 258 cu in	
HA carburetor	19° BTDC
All others	15° BTDC
Four-cylinder engines	
1978 and 1979 (121 cu in)	
With code EH on emission label (1979 only)	16° BTDC
All others	12° BTDC
1980 through 1983 (151 cu in)	
1980 Calif. only	12° BTDC
1982 and 1983 Calif. only	8° BTDC
1982 and 1983 HA carburetor	15° BTDC
All others	10° BTDC
Ignition timing *(automatic transmission)*	
V8 engines	
1971 through 1975	5° BTDC
1976 and 1977	
Calif. only	5° BTDC
All others	10° BTDC
1978	
304 cu in (Calif. only)	5° BTDC
All others	10° BTDC
1979	8° BTDC
Six-cylinder engines	
1971 through 1973 232 cu in and 1971 258 cu in	5° BTDC
1972 through 1975 258 cu in and 1974 and 1975 232 cu in	3° BTDC
1976 232 cu in and 1976 and 1977 258 cu in	8° BTDC
1976 through 1978 (all others)	10° BTDC
1979	
232 cu in (with 2.37 rear axle)	12° BTDC
232 cu in (all others)	10° BTDC
258 cu in	8° BTDC
1980 258 cu in	10° BTDC
1981 258 cu in	
HA carburetor	15° BTDC
All others	6° BTDC
1982 and 1983 258 cu in	
HA carburetor	19° BTDC
All others	15° BTDC
Four-cylinder engines	
1978 and 1979 (121 cu in)	
Calif. only	8° BTDC
All others	12° BTDC
1980 and 1981 (151 cu in)	
Calif. only	10° BTDC
All others	12° BTDC

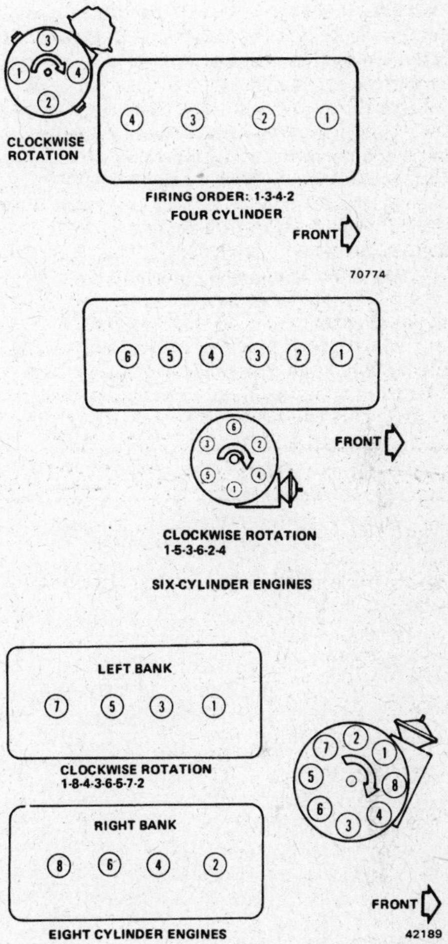

Cylinder location and distributor rotation

1982 and 1983 (151 cu in)	
Calif. only	8° BTDC
HA carburetor only	15° BTDC
All others	10° BTDC
Firing order	
Four-cylinder	1–3–4–2
Six-cylinder	1–5–3–6–2–4
V8	1–8–4–3–6–5–7–2
Distributor rotation	Clockwise
Point gap	0.016 in
Dwell angle	
Six-cylinder	31 to 34°
V8	29 to 31°

Radiator pressure cap rating

Radiator pressure cap rating	14 psi

Compression pressure

1970 through 1979 V8	
Standard	140 psi
Maximum difference between cylinders	20 psi
1970 through 1979 232 six-cylinder	
Standard	140 psi
Maximum difference between cylinders	20 psi
1970 through 1979 258 six-cylinder	
Standard	150 psi
Maximum difference between cylinders	20 psi
1980 through 1983 six-cylinder	
Standard	120 to 150 psi
Maximum difference between cylinders	30 psi
1978 and 1979 four-cylinder	116 to 160 psi
1980 through 1983 four-cylinder	140 psi

Idle speed

1971 through 1973	
Manual transmission	700 rpm
Automatic transmission	600 rpm
1974	
Six-cylinder (Calif. models with automatic transmission)	700 rpm
Six-cylinder (all others)	600 rpm
V8	700 rpm
1975 and 1976	
Six-cylinder	
Manual transmission	850 rpm
Automatic transmission	550 rpm
V8	
Manual transmission	750 rpm
Automatic transmission	700 rpm
1977 and 1978	
Four-cylinder	
Manual transmission	900 rpm
Automatic transmission	800 rpm
Six-cylinder (manual transmission)	
California	800 rpm
All others	600 rpm
Six-cylinder (automatic transmission)	
California	700 rpm
All others	550 rpm
1979	
Four-cylinder	
Manual transmission	800 rpm
Automatic transmission	700 rpm
232 cu in six-cylinder	
Manual transmission	600 rpm
Automatic transmission	550 rpm
258 cu in six-cylinder	
Manual transmission	700 rpm
Automatic transmission (Calif. only)	700 rpm
Automatic transmission (all others)	600 rpm
V8	
Manual transmission	800 rpm
Automatic transmission	600 rpm
1980 and 1981	
Four-cylinder (manual transmission)	
Air conditioning equipped models	900 rpm*
All others	500 rpm*

Four-cylinder (automatic transmission)	
Air conditioning equipped models	700 prm*
All others	500 rpm*
Six-cylinder	
Manual transmission	700 rpm
Automatic transmission	600 rpm
1982 and 1983	
Four-cylinder	
Manual transmission	500 rpm*
Automatic transmission	500 rpm*
Six-cylinder	
Manual transmission	600 rpm
Automatic transmission	500 rpm

**With air conditioning Off (if equipped) and solenoid disconnected*

Clutch

Clutch pedal height	$7\frac{1}{2} \pm \frac{1}{4}$ in (underside of pedal to floorpan)
Clutch pedal free play	
1970 through 1981	$\frac{7}{8}$ to $1\frac{1}{8}$ in (1 in preferred)
1982 and 1983	$\frac{3}{4}$ to $1\frac{1}{4}$ in ($1\frac{1}{8}$ in preferred)

Torque specifications

	Ft-lb *(except where noted)*
Spark plugs	
1970 through 1980	25 to 30
1981 through 1983	11
Automatic transmission oil pan bolts	150 **in-lb**
Manual transmission filler plug	20
Engine oil drain plug	25
Rear differential cover bolts	15 to 25
Front axle spindle nut	2 to 10 **in-lb**
1970 through 1974 caliper guide pin	35
1975 through 1981 caliper support key retaining screw	15
1982 caliper mounting pin	26
1970 through 1982 caliper anchor plate mounting bolt	80

1

1 Introduction to routine maintenance

This Chapter was designed to help the home mechanic maintain his (or her) vehicle for peak performance, economy, safety and long life.

On the following pages you will find a maintenance schedule along with Sections which deal specifically with each item on the schedule. Included are visual checks, adjustments and item replacements.

Servicing your vehicle using the time/mileage maintenance schedule and the sequenced Sections will give you a planned program of maintenance. Keep in mind that it is a comprehensive plan; maintaining only a few items at the specified intervals will not produce the same results.

You will find as you service your vehicle that many of the procedures can, and should, be grouped together, due to the nature of the job.

Examples of this are:

If the vehicle is raised for a chassis lubrication, it is an ideal time for the manual transmission oil, exhaust system, suspension, steering and fuel system checks.

If the tires and wheels are removed, as during a routine tire rotation, go ahead and check the brakes and wheel bearings at the same time.

If you must borrow or rent a torque wrench, it is a good idea to replace the spark plugs and/or repack (or replace) the wheel bearings all in the same day to save time and money.

The first step in this or any maintenance plan is to prepare yourself before the actual work begins. Read through the appropriate Sections for all work that is to be performed before you begin. Gather together all necessary parts and tools. If it appears that you could have a problem during a particular job, don't hesitate to ask advice from your local parts man or dealer service department.

2 Tune-up sequence

The term 'tune-up' is loosely applied to any general operation that puts the engine back into proper running condition. A tune-up is not a specific operation, but rather a combination of individual operations, such as replacing the spark plugs, adjusting the idle speed, setting the ignition timing, etc.

If, from the time the vehicle is new, the routine maintenance schedule (Section 3) is followed closely and frequent checks are made of fluid levels and high wear items, as suggested throughout this manual, the engine will be kept in relatively good running condition and the need for all inclusive tune-ups will be minimized.

More likely than not, however, there will be times when the engine is running poorly due to lack of regular maintenance. This is even more likely if a used vehicle which has not received regular and frequent maintenance checks is bought. In such cases an engine tune-up will be needed outside of the regular routine maintenance intervals.

The following series of operations are those most often needed to bring a generally poor running engine back into a proper state of tune.

Minor tune-up

Clean, inspect and test battery (Sec 5)
Check all engine-related fluids (Sec 4)
Check cylinder compression (Sec 30)
Check and adjust drivebelts (Sec 13)
Replace spark plugs (Sec 27)
Inspect distributor cap and rotor (Sec 28)
Check and/or replace breaker points and adjust dwell angle (Sec 32)
Inspect and/or replace spark plug and coil wires (Sec 28)
Change oil and filter (Sec 8)
Check and adjust idle speed (Sec 20)
Check and adjust timing (Sec 31)
Check and adjust fuel/air mixture (Sec 35)
Replace fuel filter (Sec 21)
Replace PCV valve (Sec 22)
Check cooling system (Sec 10)

Major tune-up

Perform all operations listed under *Minor tune-up*
Check ignition advance systems (Chapter 5)
Check EGR system (Chapter 6)
Test alternator and regulator (Chapter 5)
Test ignition system (Chapter 5)
Test charging system (Chapter 5)
Check fuel system (Chapter 4)

Fig. 1.1 Engine compartment components – typical

1 Transmission fluid dipstick (automatic transmission only)
2 Spark plug wires
3 Air cleaner housing
4 Brake master cylinder
5 Vacuum motor
6 TAC vacuum motor
7 Radiator coolant overflow reservoir
8 Windshield washer fluid reservoir
9 Power steering pump
10 Radiator cap
11 Fuel filter
12 Engine drivebelt
13 Oil filler cap
14 PCV valve
15 Upper radiator hose
16 Distributor cap
17 Air conditioning system compressor
18 Battery

Fig. 1.2 Typical view of the engine compartment underside

1 Alternator
2 Stabilizer bar
3 Relay rod
4 Pitman arm
5 Tie-rods
6 Balljoint grease fitting plugs
7 Lower control arms
8 Strut rods
9 Engine oil drain plug
10 Starter motor
11 Fuel line
12 Idler arm

3 Routine maintenance intervals

Note: *The following maintenance intervals are recommended by the manufacturer, not the publishers of this manual. It may be wise, in some cases, to perform the maintenance procedures at shorter intervals.*

Every 5000 miles or 4 months – whichever comes first

Change engine oil
Replace engine oil filter
Check all fluid levels

Every 7500 miles or 6 months – whichever comes first

Check and adjust drivebelts
Check tire pressures
Check exhaust system

Every 15 000 miles or 12 months – whichever comes first

Lubricate steering linkage and chassis components
Lubricate disc brake caliper abutment surfaces
Inspect and lubricate clutch linkage
Clean engine oil filler cap (filter type on older models only)
Check ignition wires
Check points and condenser (not all models)
Check ignition timing

Every 30 000 miles or 24 months – whichever comes first

Change rear axle differential oil
Lubricate front wheel bearings
Replace contact points and condenser (if not done previously)
Replace spark plugs
Adjust ignition timing
Check and lubricate exhaust manifold heat valve
Replace evaporative emission canister filter
Replace drivebelts
Replace PCV filter (some models are equipped with a reusable filter which can be cleaned)
Drain, flush and refill the cooling system
Inspect brake lines and hoses
Replace fuel filter
Replace air filter
Check distributor cap and rotor
Inspect disc brake pads
Inspect drum brake shoes and wheel cylinders

4 Fluid level checks

1 There are a number of components on a vehicle which rely on the use of fluids to perform their job. During the normal operation of the vehicle, the fluids are used up and must be replenished before damage occurs. See the *Recommended lubricants and fluids* Section at the front of this Chapter for the specific fluid to be used when additions are required. When checking fluid levels it is important to have the vehicle on a level surface.

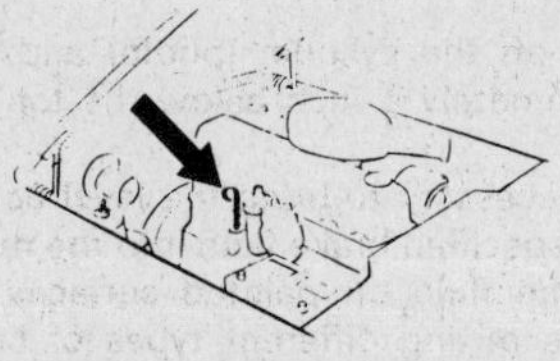

Fig. 1.3 Location of the engine oil dipstick (six-cylinder models) (Sec 4)

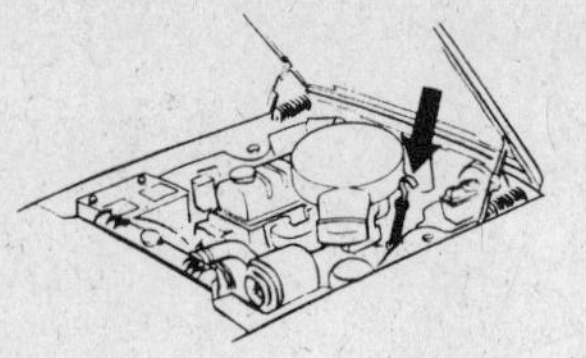

Fig. 1.4 Location of the engine oil dipstick (four-cylinder and V8 models) (Sec 4)

Engine oil

2 The engine oil level is checked with a dipstick which is located at the side of the engine block. The dipstick extends through a tube and into the oil pan at the bottom of the engine.
3 The oil level should be checked preferably before the vehicle has been driven, or about 15 minutes after the engine has been shut off. If the oil is checked immediately after driving the vehicle, some of the oil will remain in the upper engine components resulting in an inaccurate reading on the dipstick.
4 Pull the dipstick from the tube and wipe all the oil from the end with a clean rag. Insert the clean dipstick all the way back into the oil pan and pull it out again. Observe the oil at the end of the dipstick. At its highest point, the level should be between the Add and Full marks.
5 It takes approximately one (1) quart of oil to raise the level from the Add mark to the Full mark on the dipstick. Do not allow the level to drop below the Add mark as engine damage due to oil starvation may result. On the other hand, do not overfill the engine by adding oil above the Full mark as oil-fouled spark plugs, oil leaks or oil seal failures may occur.

4.6 Adding motor oil to the engine (six-cylinder shown)

6 Oil is added to the engine after removing a twist-off cap located on the rocker arm cover or through a raised tube near the front of the engine (photo). The cap should be marked *Engine oil* or something similar. An oil can spout or funnel will reduce spills as the oil is poured in.
7 Checking the oil level can also be an important preventative maintenance step. If you find the oil level dropping abnormally, it is an indication of oil leakage or internal engine wear, which should be corrected. If there are water droplets in the oil, or if it is milky looking, this also indicates component failure (the engine should be checked immediately). The condition of the oil should also be checked along with the level. With the dipstick removed from the engine, wipe your thumb and index finger up the dipstick, looking for small dirt and metal particles, which will cling to the dipstick. Their presence is an indication that the oil should be changed.

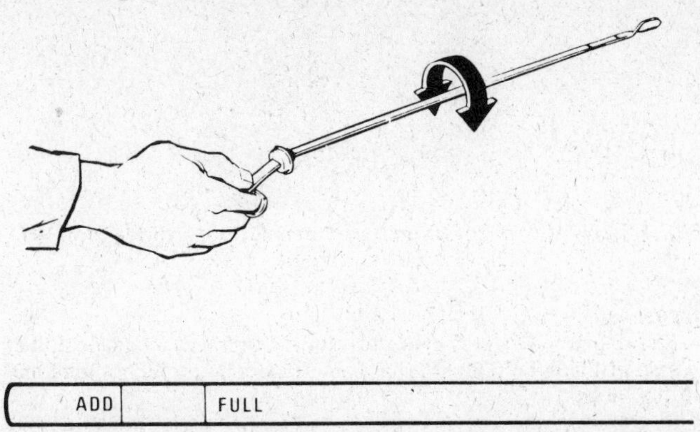

Fig. 1.5 Reading the engine oil dipstick – fluid level should be up to, but not above, the Full mark (Sec 4)

Engine coolant

8 Many vehicles are equipped with a pressurized coolant recovery system which makes coolant level checks very easy. A clear or white coolant reservoir attached to the inner fender panel is connected by a hose to the radiator neck. As the engine heats up during operation, coolant is forced from the radiator through the connecting tube and into the reservoir. As the engine cools, coolant is automatically drawn back into the radiator to maintain the correct level.

9 The coolant level should be checked when the engine is cold. Merely observe the level of fluid in the reservoir, which should be at or near the Full cold mark on the side of the reservoir. If the system is completely cooled, also check the level in the radiator by removing the cap. Some systems also have a Full hot mark to check the level when the engine is hot.

10 If your particular vehicle is not equipped with a coolant recovery system, the level should be checked by removing the radiator cap. **Warning**: *The cap should not, under any circumstances, be removed while the system is hot, as escaping steam could cause serious injury. Wait until the engine has completely cooled, then wrap a thick cloth around the cap and turn it to its first stop. If any steam escapes from the cap, allow the engine to cool further, then remove the cap and check the level in the radiator. It should be about 1-inch below the bottom of the filler neck.*

11 If only a small amount of coolant is required to bring the system up to the proper level, regular water can be used. However, to maintain the proper antifreeze/water mixture in the system, both should be mixed together to replenish a low level. High-quality antifreeze offering protection to -20°F should be mixed with water in the proportion specified on the container. Do not allow antifreeze to come in contact with your skin or painted surfaces of the vehicle. Flush contacted areas immediately wth plenty of water. **Caution**: *Antifreeze can be fatal to children and pets. They like it because it is sweet. Just a few drops can cause death. Wipe up garage floor and drip pan coolant spills immediately. Keep antifreeze containers covered. Repair leaks in your cooling system immediately.*

12 On systems with a recovery tank, coolant should be added to the reservoir after removing the reservoir cap. Coolant should be added directly to the radiator on systems without a coolant recovery tank.

13 As the coolant level is checked, note the condition of the coolant. It should be relatively clear. If it is brown or a rust color, the system should be drained, flushed and refilled (Sec 29).

14 If the cooling system requires repeated additions to maintain the proper level, have the radiator cap checked for proper sealing ability. Also, check for leaks in the system (cracked hoses, loose hose connections, leaking gaskets, etc.) (Sec 10).

Windshield washer fluid

15 The fluid for the windshield washer system is located in a plastic reservoir. The level inside the reservoir should be maintained at the Full mark.

16 An approved washer solvent should be added to the reservoir whenever replenishing is required. Do not use plain water alone in this system, especially in cold climates where the water could freeze.

Battery electrolyte

Note: *There are certain precautions to be taken when working on or near the battery: a) never expose a battery to open flames or sparks which could ignite the hydrogen gas given off by the battery; b) wear protective clothing and eye protection to reduce the possibility of the corrosive sulfuric acid solution inside the battery harming you (if the fluid is splashed or spilled, flush the contacted area immediately with plenty of water; c) remove all metal jewelry which could contact the positive terminal and another grounded metal source, causing a short circuit; d) always keep batteries and battery acid out of the reach of children.*

17 Vehicles equipped with maintenance-free batteries require no maintenance, as the battery case is sealed and has no removable caps for adding water.

4.18 Removing the battery caps to check the electrolyte level

18 If a maintenance-type battery is installed, the caps on the top of the battery should be removed periodically to check for a low electrolyte level (photo). This check will be more critical during the warm summer months.

19 Remove each of the caps and add *distilled* water to bring the level of each cell to the split ring in the filler opening.

20 At the same time the battery electrolyte level is checked, the overall condition of the battery and its related components should be inspected. If corrosion is present on the cable ends or battery terminals, remove the cables and clean away all corrosion using a baking soda/water solution or a wire brush cleaning tool designed for this purpose. See Section 5 for complete battery check and maintenance procedures.

Brake fluid

21 The brake master cylinder is located on the left side of the engine compartment firewall and has a cap which must be removed to check the fluid level.

22 Before removing the cap, use a rag to clean all dirt, grease, etc. from around the cap area. If any foreign matter enters the master cylinder with the cap removed, blockage of the brake system lines can occur. Also, make sure all painted surfaces around the master cylinder are covered, as brake fluid will ruin paint.

23 Release the clip(s) securing the cap to the top of the master cylinder. In most cases, a screwdriver can be used to pry the wire clip(s) free.

24 Carefully lift the cap off the cylinder (photo) and note the fluid level. It should be approximately $\frac{1}{4}$-inch below the top edge of each reservoir.

25 If additional fluid is necessary to bring the level up to the proper height, carefully pour the specified brake fluid into the master cylinder. Be careful not to spill the fluid on painted surfaces. Be sure the specified fluid is used, as mixing different types of brake fluid can cause damage to the system. See *Recommended lubricants and fluids* or your owner's manual.

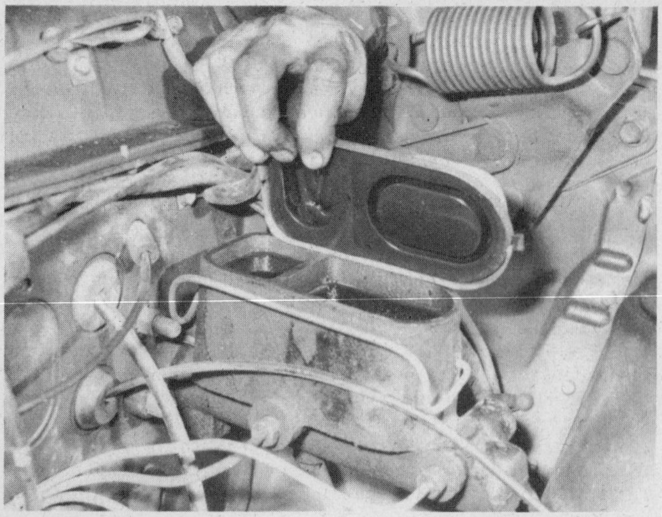

4.24 Removing the master cylinder cap to check the brake fluid level

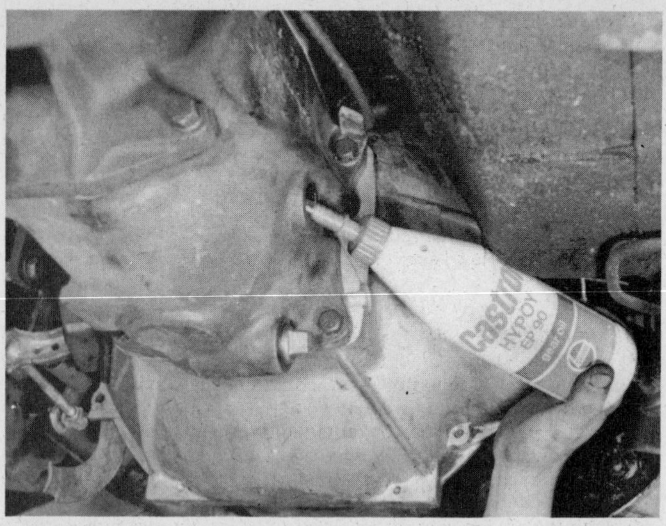

4.32 Adding lubricant to the transmission case (manual transmission)

26 At this time the fluid and master cylinder can be inspected for contamination. Normally, the hydraulic system will not require periodic draining and refilling, but if rust deposits, dirt particles or water droplets are seen in the fluid, the system should be drained and refilled with fresh fluid.
27 Reinstall the master cylinder cap and secure it with the clip(s). Make sure the cap is properly seated to prevent fluid loss.
28 The brake fluid level in the master cylinder will drop slightly as the brake shoes or pads at each wheel wear down during normal operation. If the master cylinder requires repeated replenishing to keep it at the proper level, this is an indication of leakage in the brake system which should be corrected immediately. Check all brake lines and connections, along with the wheel cylinders and booster (see Chapter 9 for more information).
29 If upon checking the master cylinder fluid level you discover one or both reservoirs empty or nearly empty, the system should be bled (Chapter 9). When the fluid level gets low, air can enter the system and should be removed by bleeding the brakes.

Manual transmission lubricant

30 Manual transmissions do not have a dipstick. The oil level is checked by removing a plug in the side of the transmission case. Locate the plug and use a rag to clean the plug and the area around it.
31 With the engine cold, remove the plug. If oil immediately starts leaking out, thread the plug back into the transmission because the level is all right. If there is no oil flow, completely remove the plug and place your little finger inside the hole. The fluid level should be just at the bottom of the plug hole.
32 If the transmission requires more oil, use a syringe to squeeze the appropriate lubricant into the plug hole to bring the oil up to the proper level (photo).
33 Thread the plug back into the transmission and tighten it securely. Drive the vehicle and check for leaks around the plug.

Automatic transmission fluid

34 The fluid inside the transmission must be at normal operating temperature to get an accurate reading on the dipstick. This is done by driving the vehicle for several miles, making frequent starts and stops to allow the transmission to shift through all gears.
35 Park the vehicle on a level surface, place the selector lever in Park and leave the engine running at an idle.
36 Remove the transmission dipstick (located on the right side, near the rear of the engine) and wipe all the fluid from the end of the dipstick with a clean rag.
37 Push the dipstick back into the transmission until the cap seats firmly on the dipstick tube. Now remove the dipstick again and observe the fluid on the end. The highest point of fluid should be between the

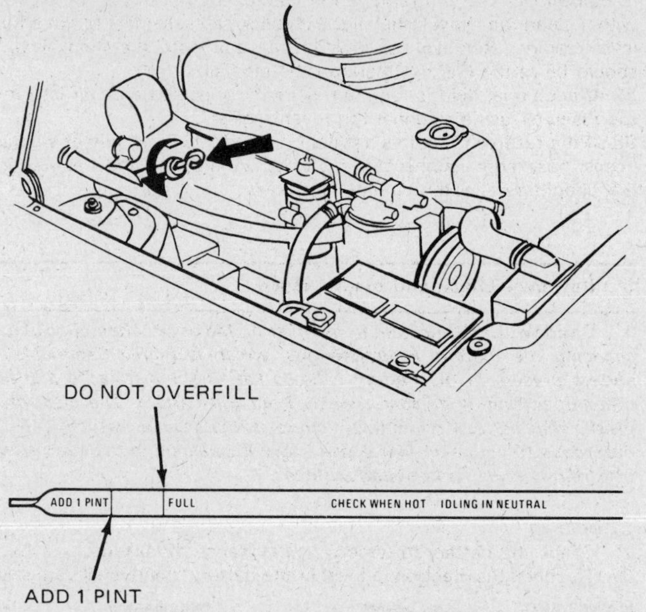

Fig. 1.6 The transmission oil dipstick and its location under the hood – fluid level should be between the Add and Full marks (Sec 4)

Full mark and $\frac{1}{4}$-inch below the Full mark.
38 If the fluid level is at or below the Add mark on the dipstick, add sufficient fluid to raise the level to the Full mark. One pint of fluid will raise the level from Add to Full. Fluid should be added directly into the dipstick guide tube, using a funnel to prevent spills.
39 It is important that the transmission is not overfilled. Under no circumstances should the fluid level be above the Full mark on the dipstick, as this could cause internal damage to the transmission. The best way to prevent overfilling is to add fluid a little at a time, driving the vehicle and checking the level between additions.
40 Use only transmission fluid specified by the manufacturer. This information can be found in the *Recommended lubricants and fluids* Section.
41 The condition of the fluid should also be checked along with the level. If the fluid at the end of the dipstick is a dark reddish-brown color, or if it has a 'burnt' smell, the transmission fluid should be changed. If you are in doubt above the condition of the fluid, purchase some new fluid and compare the two for color and smell.

Differential lubricant

42 Like the manual transmission, the differential has an inspection and fill plug which must be removed to check the level.

43 Remove the plug, which is located either in the removable cover plate or on the side of the differential carrier. Use your little finger to reach inside the housing to feel the level of the oil. It should be at the bottom of the plug hole.

44 If this is not the case, add the proper lubricant through the plug hole. A syringe or a small funnel can be used for this.

45 Make certain the correct lubricant is used.

46 Tighten the plug securely and check for leaks after the first few miles of driving.

Power steering fluid

47 Unlike manual steering, the power steering system relies on fluid which may, over a period of time, require replenishing.

48 The reservoir for the power steering pump will be located near the front of the engine, and can be mounted on either the left or right side.

49 The power steering fluid level should be checked only after the vehicle has been driven, with the fluid at operating temperature. The front wheels should be pointed straight ahead.

50 With the engine shut off, use a rag to clean the reservoir cap and the areas around the cap. This will help prevent foreign material from falling into the reservoir when the cap is removed.

51 Twist off the reservoir cap which has a built-in dipstick attached to it. Pull off the cap and remove the fluid at the bottom of the dipstick with a clean rag. Now reinstall the dipstick/cap assembly to get a fluid level reading. Remove the dipstick/cap and note the fluid level. It should be at the Full hot mark on the dipstick.

52 If additional fluid is required, pour the specified type directly into the reservoir using a funnel to prevent spills.

53 If the reservoir requires frequent fluid additions, all power steering hoses, hose connections, the power steering pump and the steering box should be checked carefully for leaks.

5 Battery – check and maintenance

1 **Caution:** *Certain precautions must be followed when checking or servicing the battery. Hydrogen gas, which is highly flammable, is always present in the battery cells so keep lighted tobacco and any other open flames or sparks away from the battery. The electrolyte inside the battery is actually dilute sulfuric acid, which can be hazardous to your skin and cause injury if splashed in the eyes. It will also ruin clothes and painted surfaces.*

Checking

2 Check the battery for cracks and evidence of leakage.

3 To check the electrolyte level in the battery, remove all vent caps. If the battery electrolyte level is low, add *distilled water* until the level is above the cell plates. There is an indicator in each cell to help you judge when enough water has been added. Do not overfill. **Note:** *Some models may be equipped with maintenance-free batteries, which have no provision (or need) for adding water. Also, some models may be equipped with translucent batteries so the electrolyte level can be observed without removing any vent caps. On these batteries the level should be between the upper and lower lines.*

4 Periodically check the specific gravity of the electrolyte with an hydrometer. This is especially important during cold weather. If the reading is below the specified range, the battery should be recharged. Maintenance-free batteries have a built-in hydrometer, which indicates the battery state-of-charge.

5 Check the tightness of the battery cable clamps to ensure good electrical connections. If corrosion is evident, remove the cables from the battery terminals (a puller may be required), clean them with a battery terminal brush, then reinstall them (photos). Corrosion can be kept to a minimum by applying a layer of petroleum jelly or grease to the terminal and cable clamps after they are assembled.

6 Inspect the entire length of each battery cable for corrosion, cracks and frayed conductors. Replace the cables with new ones if they are damaged.

7 Make sure that the rubber protector over the positive terminal is not torn or missing. It should completely cover the terminal.

8 Make sure that the battery is securely mounted, but do not overtighten the clamp bolts.

9 The battery case and caps should be kept clean and dry. If corrosion is evident, clean the battery as explained in Step 12.

10 If the vehicle is not being used for an extended period, disconnect the battery cables and have it charged approximately every six weeks.

Cleaning

11 Corrosion on the battery hold down components and inner fender panels can be removed by washing with a solution of water and baking soda. Once the area has been thoroughly cleaned, rinse it with clean water.

12 Corrosion on the battery case and terminals can also be removed with a solution of water and baking soda and a stiff brush. Be careful that none of the solution is splashed into your eyes or onto your skin (wear protective gloves). Do not allow any of the baking soda and water solution to get into the battery cells. Rinse the battery thoroughly once it is clean.

13 Metal parts of the vehicle which have been damaged by spilled battery acid should be painted with a zinc-based primer and paint. Do this only after the area has been thoroughly cleaned and dried.

Charging

14 As was mentioned before, if the battery's specific gravity is below the specified amount, the battery must be recharged.

15 If the battery is to remain in the vehicle during charging,

5.5A Battery terminal corrosion usually appears as a white fluffy powder

5.5B Removing the cable from the battery terminal post (always remove the ground cable first and hook it up last)

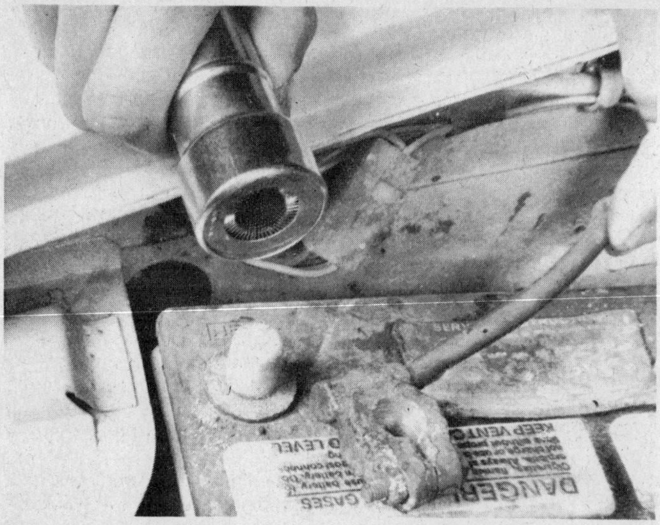

5.5C Cleaning the battery terminal post with a special tool

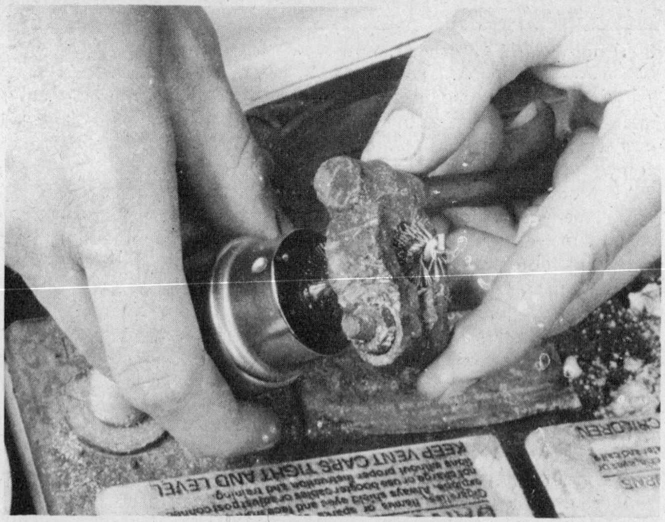

5.5D Cleaning the battery cable clamp

disconnect the cables from the battery to prevent damage to the electrical system.

16 When batteries are being charged, hydrogen gas (which is very explosive and flammable) is produced. *Do not smoke or allow an open flame near a charging or a recently charged battery. Also, do not plug in the battery charger until the connections have been made at the battery posts.*

17 The average time necessary to charge a battery at the normal rate is from 12 to 16 hours (sometimes longer). Always charge the battery slowly. A quick charge or boost charge is hard on a battery and will shorten its life. Use a battery charger that is rated at no more than 1/10 the amp/hour rating of the battery.

18 Remove all of the vent caps and cover the holes with a clean cloth to prevent the spattering of electrolyte. Hook the battery charger leads to the battery posts (positive to positive, negative to negative), then plug in the charger. Make sure it is set at 12 volts if it has a selector switch.

19 Watch the battery closely during charging to make sure that it does not overheat.

20 The battery can be considered fully charged when it is gassing freely and there is no increase in specific gravity during three successive readings taken at hourly intervals. Overheating of the battery during charging at normal charging rates, excessive gassing and continual low specific gravity readings are an indication that the battery should be replaced with a new one.

6 Tire and tire pressure checks

1 Periodically inspecting the tires may not only prevent you from being stranded with a flat tire, but can also give you clues as to possible problems with the steering and suspension systems before major damage occurs.

2 Proper tire inflation adds miles to the lifespan of the tires, allows the vehicle to achieve maximum miles per gallon figures and contributes to overall ride quality.

3 When inspecting the tires, first check the wear of the tread. Irregularities in the tread pattern (cupping, flat spots, more wear on one side than the other) are indications of front end alignment and/or balance problems. If any of these conditions are noted, take the vehicle to a reputable repair shop to correct the problem.

4 Also check the tread area for cuts and punctures. Many times a nail or tack will embed itself into the tire tread and yet the tire will hold its air pressure for a short time. In most cases, a repair shop or gas station can repair the punctured tire.

5 It is also important to check the sidewalls of the tires, both inside and outside. Check for deteriorated rubber, cuts, and punctures. Also inspect the inboard side of the tire for signs of brake fluid leakage, indicating that a thorough brake inspection is needed immediately.

6 Incorrect tire pressure cannot be determined merely by looking at the tire. This is especially true for radial tires. A tire pressure gauge must be used. If you do not already have a reliable gauge, it is a good idea to purchase one and keep it in the glove box. Built-in pressure gauges at gas stations are often unreliable.

7 Always check the tire inflation when the tires are cold. Cold, in this case, means the vehicle has not been driven more than one mile after sitting for three hours or more. It is normal for the pressure to increase 4 to 8 pounds or more when the tires are hot.

8 Unscrew the valve cap protruding from the wheel or hubcap and firmly press the gauge onto the valve stem. Observe the reading on the gauge and compare the figure to the recommended tire pressure listed on the tire placard. The tire placard is usually attached to the glove box door.

9 Check all tires and add air as necessary to bring them up to the recommended pressure levels. Do not forget the spare tire. Be sure to reinstall the valve caps (which will keep dirt and moisture out of the valve stem mechanism).

7 Underhood hoses – check and replacement

Caution: *Replacement of air conditioner hoses should be left to a dealer or air conditioning specialist who can depressurize the system and perform the work safely.*

1 The high temperatures present under the hood can cause deterioration of the numerous rubber and plastic hoses.

2 Periodic inspection should be made for cracks, loose clamps and leaks because some of the hoses are part of the emission control system and can affect the engine's performance.

3 Remove the air cleaner if necessary and trace the entire length of each hose. Squeeze each hose to check for cracks and look for swelling, discoloration and leaks.

4 If the vehicle has considerable mileage or if one or more of the hoses is suspect, it is a good idea to replace all of the hoses at one time.

5 Measure the length and inside diameter of each hose and obtain and cut the replacement to size. Since original equipment hose clamps are often good for only one or two uses, it is a good idea to replace them with screw-type clamps.

6 Replace each hose one at a time to eliminate the possibility of confusion. Hoses attached to the heater and radiator contain coolant so newspapers or rags should be kept handy to catch the spills when they are disconnected.

7 After installation, run the engine until it reaches operating temperature, shut it off and check for leaks. After the engine has cooled, retighten all of the screw-type clamps.

8 Engine oil and filter change

1 Frequent oil changes may be the best form of preventative maintenance available to the home mechanic. When engine oil is old, it gets diluted and contaminated, which ultimately leads to premature engine wear.
2 Although some sources recommend oil filter changes every other oil change, we feel that the minimal cost of an oil filter and the relative ease with which it is installed dictate that a new filter be used whenever the oil is changed.
3 The tools necessary for a normal oil and filter change are a wrench to fit the drain plug at the bottom of the oil pan, an oil filter wrench to remove the old filter, a container with a six quart capacity to drain the old oil into and a funnel or oil can spout to help pour fresh oil into the engine.
4 In addition you should have plenty of clean rags and newspapers handy to mop up any spills. Access to the underside of the vehicle is greatly improved if it can be lifted on a hoist, driven onto ramps or supported by jackstands. Do not work under a vehicle which is supported only by a bumper, hydraulic or scissors-type jack.
5 If this is your first oil change on the vehicle, it is a good idea to crawl underneath and familiarize yourself with the locations of the oil drain plug and the oil filter. Since the engine and exhaust components will be warm during the actual work, it is a good idea to figure out any potential problems before the engine and exhaust pipes are hot.
6 Allow the engine to warm up to normal operating temperature. If the new oil or any tools are needed, use the warm-up time to locate everything necessary for the job. The correct type of oil to buy for your application can be found in *Recommended lubricants and fluids* near the front of this Chapter.
7 With the engine oil warm (warm engine oil will drain better and more built-up sludge will be removed with the oil), raise the vehicle for access beneath it. Make sure the vehicle is firmly supported. If jackstands are used, they should be placed toward the front of the frame rails which run the length of the vehicle.
8 Move all necessary tools, rags and newspapers under the vehicle. Position the drain pan under the drain plug. Keep in mind that the oil will initially flow from the pan with some force, so position the pan accordingly.
9 Being careful not to touch any of the hot exhaust pipe components, use the wrench to remove the drain plug near the bottom of the oil pan. Depending on how hot the oil has become, you may want to wear gloves while unscrewing the plug the final few turns.
10 Allow the old oil to drain into the pan. It may be necessary to move the pan further under the engine as the oil flow reduces to a trickle.
11 After all the oil has drained, clean the drain plug thoroughly with a clean rag. Small metal particles may cling to the plug and immediately contaminate your new oil.
12 Clean the area around the drain plug opening and reinstall the plug. Tighten the plug securely.
13 Move the drain pan into position under the oil filter.
14 Now use the filter wrench to loosen the oil filter. Chain or metal band-type filter wrenches may distort the filter canister, but don't worry too much about this as the filter will be discarded anyway.
15 Sometimes the oil filter is on so tight it cannot be loosened, or it is positioned in an area which is inaccessible with a filter wrench. As a last resort, you can punch a metal bar or long screwdriver directly through the **bottom** of the canister and use it as a T-bar to turn the filter. If this must be done, be prepared for oil to spurt out of the canister as it is punctured.
16 Completely unscrew the old filter. Be careful, it is full of oil. Empty the old oil inside the filter into the drain pan.
17 Compare the old filter with the new one to make sure they are of the same type.
18 Use a clean rag to remove all oil, dirt and sludge from the area where the oil filter mounts to the engine. Check the old filter to make sure the rubber gasket is not stuck to the engine mounting surface. If the gasket is stuck to the engine (use a flashlight if necessary), remove it.
19 Open one of the cans of new oil and fill the new filter about half full with fresh oil. Also apply a light coat of fresh oil to the rubber gasket of the new oil filter.
20 Attach the new filter to the engine following the tightening directions printed on the filter canister or packing box. Most filter manufacturers recommend against using a filter wrench due to the possibility of overtightening and damage to the canister.
21 Remove all tools, rags, etc. from under the vehicle, being careful not to spill the oil in the drain pan. Lower the vehicle.
22 Move to the engine compartment and locate the oil filler cap on the engine. In most cases there will be a screw-off cap on the rocker arm cover or a cap at the end of a fill tube at the front of the engine. In any case, the cap will most likely be labeled *Engine Oil* or something similar.
23 If an oil can spout is used, push the spout into the top of the oil can and pour the fresh oil through the filler opening. A funnel placed in the opening may also be used.
24 Pour about three (3) quarts of fresh oil into the engine. Wait a few minutes to allow the oil to drain to the pan, then check the level on the oil dipstick (see Section 4 if necessary). If the oil level is at or above the Add mark, start the engine and allow the new oil to circulate.
25 Run the engine for only about a minute and then shut it off. Immediately look under the vehicle and check for leaks at the oil pan drain plug and around the oil filter. If either is leaking, tighten with a bit more force.
26 With the new oil circulated and the filter now completely full, recheck the level and add enough oil to bring the level to the Full mark on the dipstick.
27 During the first few trips after an oil change, make it a point to check frequently for leaks and correct oil level.
28 The old oil drained from the engine cannot be reused in its present state and should be disposed of. Oil reclamation centers, auto repair shops and gas stations will normally accept the oil, which can be refined and used again. After the oil has cooled, it can be drained into a suitable container (capped plastic jugs, topped bottles, milk cartons, etc.) for transportation to a disposal site.

9 Chassis lubrication

1 A grease gun and a cartridge filled with the proper grease (see *Recommended lubricants and fluids)* are the only equipment necessary to lubricate most chassis components.
2 Using the accompanying illustrations, locate the various grease fittings.
3 For easier access under the vehicle, raise it with a jack and place jackstands under the frame. *Make sure the vehicle is firmly supported by the stands.*
4 Before proceeding, force a little of the grease out of the nozzle to remove any dirt from the end of the gun. Wipe the nozzle clean with a rag.
5 Wipe the grease fitting clean and push the grease gun nozzle firmly over it. Squeeze the trigger on the grease gun to force grease into the component. The tie-rods and balljoints should be lubricated until the rubber reservoir is firm to the touch. Do not pump too much grease into the fittings, as it could rupture the reservoir. If the grease seeps out around the grease gun nozzle, the fitting is clogged or the nozzle is not fully seated on the fitting. Resecure the gun nozzle to the fitting and try again. If necessary, replace the fitting with a new one.
6 Wipe any excess grease from the components and the grease fitting.
7 While you are under the vehicle, clean and lubricate the brake cable.
8 Lower the vehicle to the ground for the remaining lubrication procedures.
9 Open the hood and smear a little chassis grease on the hood latch mechanism.
10 Lubricate all the hinges (door, hood and lift gate) with a few drops of light engine oil to keep them in proper working order.
11 Finally, the key lock cylinders can be lubricated with spray graphite or silicone, which is available at auto parts stores.

10 Cooling system check

1 Many major engine failures can be attributed to a faulty cooling system. If the vehicle is equipped with an automatic transmission the cooling system also plays an important role in prolonging its life.
2 The cooling system should be checked with the engine cold. Do this before the vehicle is driven for the day or after it has been shut off for at least three hours.
3 Remove the radiator cap and thoroughly clean the cap (inside and out) with clean water. Also clean the filler neck on the radiator. All

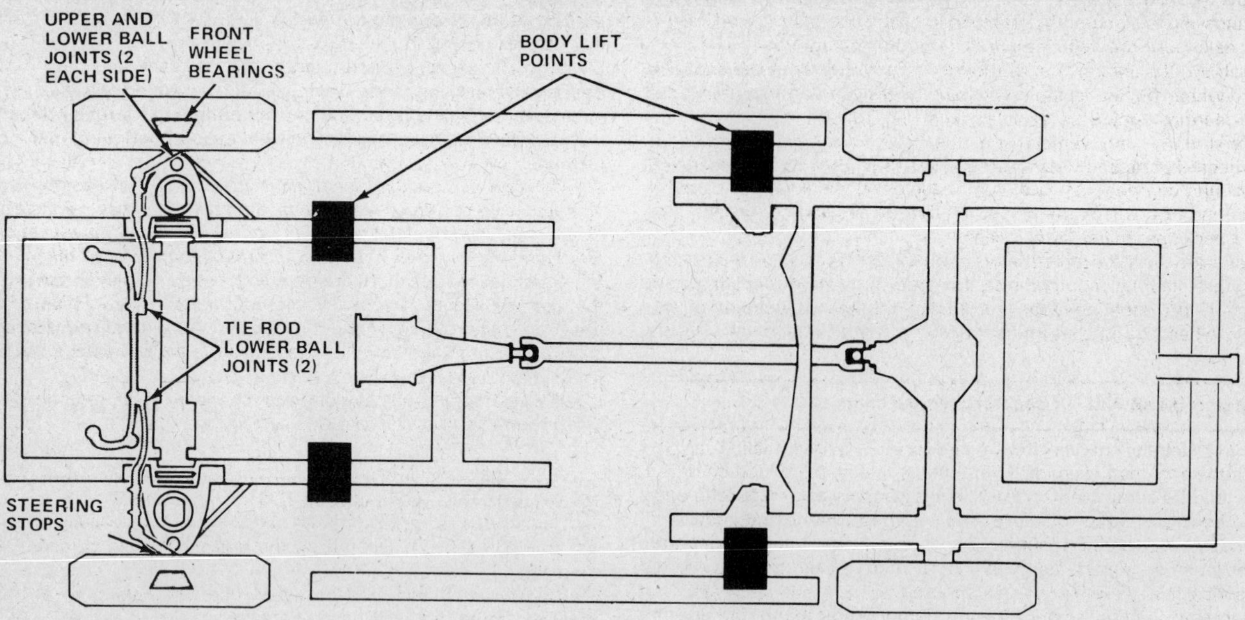

Fig. 1.7 Chassis lubrication points (typical) (Sec 9)

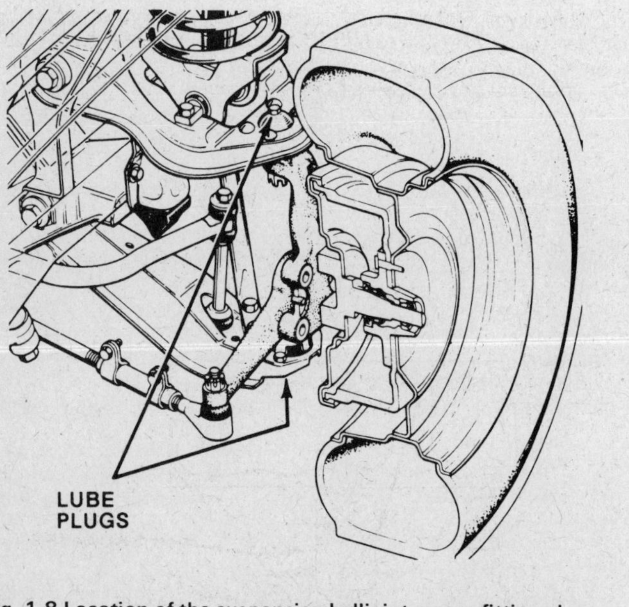

Fig. 1.8 Location of the suspension balljoint grease fitting plugs (Sec 9)

traces of corrosion should be removed.
4 Carefully check the upper and lower radiator hoses along with the smaller diameter heater hoses. Inspect each hose along its entire length, replacing any hose which is cracked, swollen or shows signs of deterioration. Cracks may become more apparent if the hose is squeezed.
5 Also make sure that all hose connections are tight. A leak in the cooling system will usually show up as white or rust colored deposits on the areas adjoining the leak.
6 Use compressed air or a soft brush to remove bugs, leaves, etc. from the front of the radiator or air-conditioning condenser. Be careful not to damage the delicate cooling fins, or cut yourself on them.
7 Finally, have the cap and system pressure tested. If you do not have a pressure tester, most gas stations and repair shops will do this for a minimal charge.

11 Exhaust system check

1 With the engine cold (at least three hours after the vehicle has been driven) check the complete exhaust system from its starting point at the engine to the end of the tailpipe. This should be done on a hoist where unrestricted access is available.
2 Check the pipes and connections for signs of leakage and/or corrosion indicating a potential failure. Make sure that all brackets and hangers are in good condition and tight.
3 At the same time, inspect the underside of the body for holes, corrosion, open seams, etc. which may allow exhaust gases to enter the passenger compartment. Seal all body openings with silicone or body putty.
4 Rattles and other noises can often be traced to the exhaust system, especially the mounts and hangers. Try to move the pipes, muffler and catalytic converter (if so equipped). If the components can come into contact with the body or driveline parts, secure the exhaust system with new mounts.
5 This is also an ideal time to check the running condition of the engine by inspecting inside the very end of the tailpipe. The exhaust deposits here are an indication of engine state-of-tune. If the pipe is black and sooty or coated with white deposits, the engine is in need of a tune-up (including a thorough carburetor inspection and adjustment).

12 Suspension and steering check

1 Whenever the front of the vehicle is raised for service, it is a good idea to visually check the suspension and steering components for wear.
2 Indications of a fault in these systems are excessive play in the steering wheel before the front wheels react, excessive sway around corners, body movement over rough roads or binding at some point as the steering wheel is turned.
3 Before the vehicle is raised for inspection, test the shock absorbers by pushing down to rock the vehicle at each corner. If you push the vehicle down and it does not come back to a level position within one or two bounces, the shocks are worn and must be replaced. As this is done, check for squeaks and strange noises from the suspension components. Information on shock absorber and suspension components can be found in Chapter 11.

4 Now raise the front end of the vehicle and support it firmly on jackstands placed under the frame rails. Because of the work to be done, make sure the vehicle cannot fall from the stands.
5 Grab the top and bottom of the front tire with your hands and rock the tire/wheel on the spindle. If there is noticeable movement, the wheel bearings should be serviced (see Sec 26).
6 Crawl under the vehicle and check for loose bolts, broken or disconnected parts and deteriorated rubber bushings on all suspension and steering components. Look for grease or fluid leaking from around the steering box. Check the power steering hoses and connections for leaks. Check the balljoints for wear.
7 Have an assistant turn the steering wheel from side-to-side and check the steering components for free movement, chafing and binding. If the steering does not react with the movement of the steering wheel, try to determine where the slack is located.

13 Engine drivebelts – check and adjustment

1 The drivebelts, or V-belts as they are sometimes called, at the front of the engine play an important role in the overall operation of the vehicle and its components. Due to their function and material make-up, the belts are prone to failure after a period of time and should be inspected and adjusted periodically to prevent major engine damage.
2 The number of belts used on a particular vehicle depends on the accessories installed. Drivebelts are used to turn the alternator, air injection smog pump, power steering pump, water pump, fan and air conditioning compressor. Depending on the pulley arrangement, a single belt may be used for more than one of these components.
3 With the engine off, open the hood and locate the various belts at the front of the engine. Using your fingers (and a flashlight if necessary) move along the belts checking for cracks and separation of the belt plies. Also check for fraying and glazing, which gives the belt a shiny appearance. Both sides of the belts should be inspected, which means you will have to twist the belt to check the underside.
4 The tension of each belt is checked by pushing on the belt at a distance halfway between the pulleys. Push firmly with your thumb and see how much the belt moves down (deflects). A rule of thumb, so to speak, is that if the distance (pulley center-to-pulley center) is between 7 and 11 inches the belt should deflect $\frac{1}{4}$-inch. If the belt is longer and travels between pulleys spaced 12 to 16 inches apart, the belt should deflect $\frac{1}{2}$-inch.
5 If it is necessary to adjust the belt tension, either to make the belt tighter or looser, it is done by moving the belt-driven accessory on the bracket.
6 For each component there will be an adjustment or strap bolt and a pivot bolt. Both bolts must be loosened slightly to enable you to move the component.
7 After the two bolts have been loosened, move the component away from the engine (to tighten the belt) or toward the engine (to loosen the belt). Hold the accessory in position and check the belt tension. If it is correct, tighten the two bolts until snug, then recheck the tension. If it is all right, tighten the two bolts completely.
8 It will often be necessary to use some sort of pry bar to move the accessory while the belt is adjusted. If this must be done to gain the proper leverage, be very careful not to damage the component being moved, or the part being pried against.

14 Fuel system check

1 **Caution:** *There are certain precautions to take when inspecting or servicing the fuel system components. Work in a well ventilated area and do not allow open flames (cigarettes, appliance pilot lights, etc.) to get near the work area. Mop up spills immediately and do not store fuel-soaked rags where they could ignite.*
2 The fuel system is under a small amount of pressure, so if any fuel lines are disconnected for servicing, be prepared to catch the fuel as it spurts out. Plug all disconnected fuel lines immediately after disconnection to prevent the tank from emptying itself.
3 The fuel system is most easily checked with the vehicle raised on a hoist where the components underneath the vehicle are readily visible and accessible.
4 If the smell of gasoline is noticed while driving, or after the vehicle has been in the sun, the system should be thoroughly inspected immediately.
5 Remove the gas filler cap and check for damage, corrosion and a proper sealing imprint on the gasket. Replace the cap with a new one if necessary.
6 With the vehicle raised, inspect the gas tank and filler neck for punctures, cracks and other damage. The connection between the filler neck and the tank is especially critical. Sometimes a rubber filler neck will leak due to loose clamps or deteriorated rubber; problems a home mechanic can usually rectify.
7 **Caution:** *Do not, under any circumstances, try to repair a fuel tank yourself (except rubber components) unless you have considerable experience. A welding torch or any open flame can easily cause the fuel vapors to explode if the proper precautions are not taken.*
8 Carefully check all rubber hoses and metal lines leading away from the fuel tank. Check for loose connections, deteriorated hoses, crimped lines and other damage. Follow the lines up to the front of the vehicle, carefully inspecting them all the way. Repair or replace damaged sections as necessary.
9 If a fuel odor is still evident after the inspection, refer to Section 24 on the evaporative emissions system.

15 Exhaust Gas Recirculation (EGR) valve check

1 The EGR valve is located on the intake manifold adjacent to the carburetor.
2 The valve should be checked while the engine is at normal operating temperature. Run the engine at idle speed and manually compress the EGR diaphragm (wear gloves to avoid burning your hand).
3 There should be a sudden drop in engine speed (about 200 rpm). If there is no change in engine speed but the engine idles properly, the EGR passage to the intake manifold is blocked.
4 If the engine is idling very poorly and compressing the diaphragm does not affect idle speed, the EGR valve is probably sticking open, causing full time exhaust gas recirculation.
5 To replace the EGR valve, refer to Chapter 6.

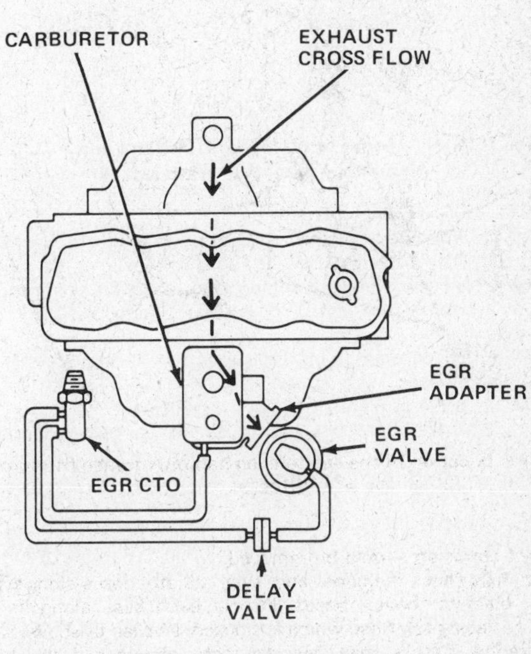

Fig. 1.9 EGR system – typical of four-cylinder models (Sec 15)

16 Air filter and PCV filter replacement

1 At the specified intervals, the air filter and PCV filter should be replaced with new ones. A thorough program of preventative maintenance would call for the two filters to be inspected periodically between changes.

1

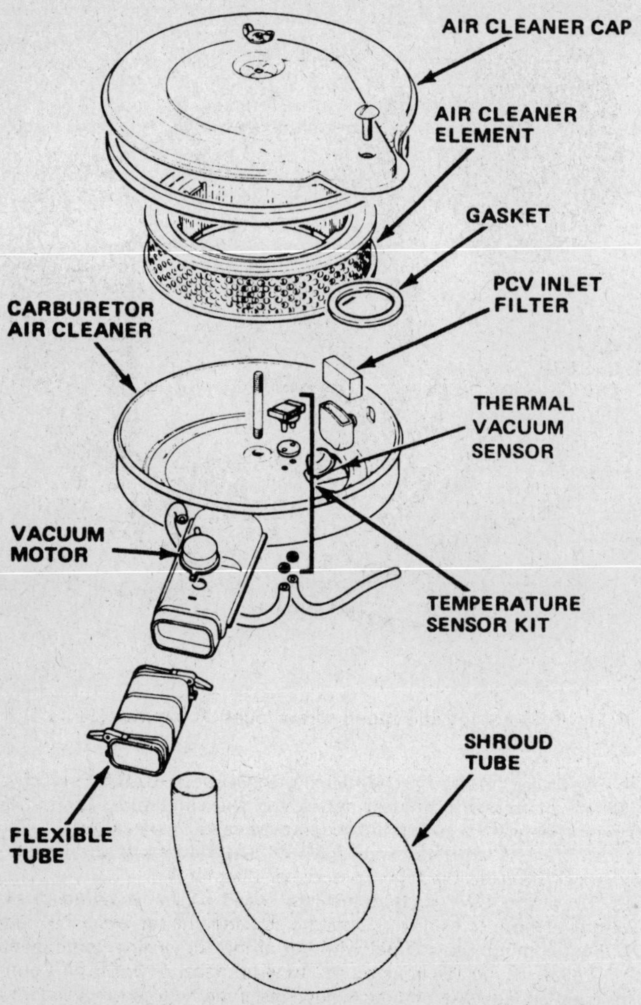

Fig. 1.10 Air cleaner assembly with air filter and PCV filter elements – exploded view (Sec 16)

2 The air filter is located inside the air cleaner housing on the top of the engine. The filter is generally replaced by removing the wing nut at the top of the air cleaner assembly and lifting off the top plate. If vacuum hoses are connected to the plate, note their positions and disconnect them.
3 While the top plate is off, be careful not to drop anything down into the carburetor.
4 Lift the air filter element out of the housing.
5 To check the filter, hold it up to sunlight, or place a flashlight or droplight on the inside of the filter. If you can see light coming through the paper element, the filter is still usable. Check all the way around the filter.
6 Wipe out the inside of the air cleaner housing with a rag.
7 Place the old filter (if in good condition) or the new filter (if specified interval has elapsed) back into the air cleaner housing. Make sure it seats properly in the bottom of the housing.
8 Connect any disconnected vacuum hoses to the top plate and reinstall it.
9 On later models, the PCV filter is located inside the air cleaner or the oil filler cap. Remove the top plate as described previously and locate the filter on the side of the housing or remove the filler cap.
10 Remove the filter element from the retainer or filler cap.
11 Wash the filter element thoroughly with kerosene or solvent and reinstall it. On some filler caps, the element is not removable and the assembly should be cleaned by blowing compressed air through the filler tube opening (the reverse of normal air flow) in the cap. If the element is badly clogged or contaminated, replace the entire cap assembly with a new one.
12 For more information on the filters and the systems they are part of, see Chapters 4 and 6.

17 Exhaust manifold heat valve check

1 The exhaust manifold heat valve (used until about 1980 on six-cylinder and V8 models to improve engine warm-up characteristics) is located at the junction of the exhaust pipe and manifold (right side on V8 models). It can be identified by an external weight and spring.
2 With the engine and exhaust pipe cold, try moving the weight by hand. It should move freely. Lubricate the valve with graphite at the time of inspection and at the specified intervals.
3 With the engine cold, start it and observe the heat valve. Upon starting, the weight should move to the closed position. As the engine warms to normal operating temperature, the weight should move the valve to the open position, allowing a free flow of exhaust gas through the tailpipe. Since it could take several minutes for the system to heat up, you could mark the position of the weight when cold, drive the vehicle and then recheck the position of the weight.

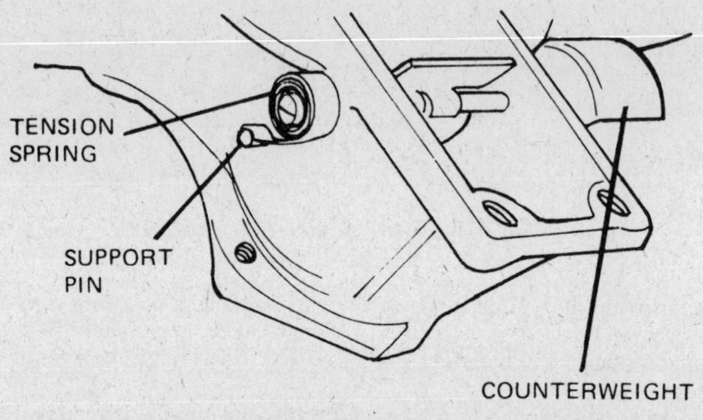

Fig. 1.11 Exhaust manifold heat valve in cold start position (typical) (Sec 17)

18 Thermo controlled air cleaner check

1 All models are equipped with a thermostatically controlled air cleaner, which directs air to the carburetor from different locations depending upon engine temperature.
2 This is a simple visual check. However, if access is tight, a small mirror may have to be used.
3 Open the hood and locate the air valve door in the air cleaner assembly. It will be located inside the long snorkel of the metal air cleaner housing. Make sure that the flexible air hose(s) are securely attached and undamaged.
4 If there is a flexible air duct attached to the end of the snorkel, leading to an area behind the grille, disconnect it at the snorkel. This will enable you to look through the end of the snorkel and see the air valve door inside.
5 The check should be done when the engine and outside air are cold. Start the engine and look through the snorkel at the air valve door, which should move to a closed position. With the door closed, air cannot enter through the end of the snorkel, but instead enters the air cleaner through the flexible duct attached to the exhaust manifold.
6 As the engine warms up to operating temperature, the door should open to allow air through the snorkel end. Depending on ambient temperature, this may take 10 to 15 minutes. To speed up this check you can reconnect the snorkel air duct, drive the vehicle and then check to see if the air valve door is open.
7 If the thermo controlled air cleaner is not operating properly, see Chapter 6 for more information.

19 Tire rotation

1 The tires should be rotated at the specified intervals and whenever

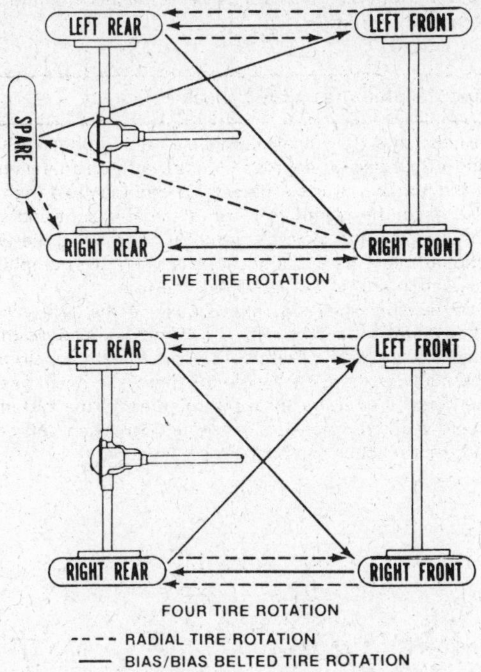

Fig. 1.12 Tire rotation diagram (Sec 19)

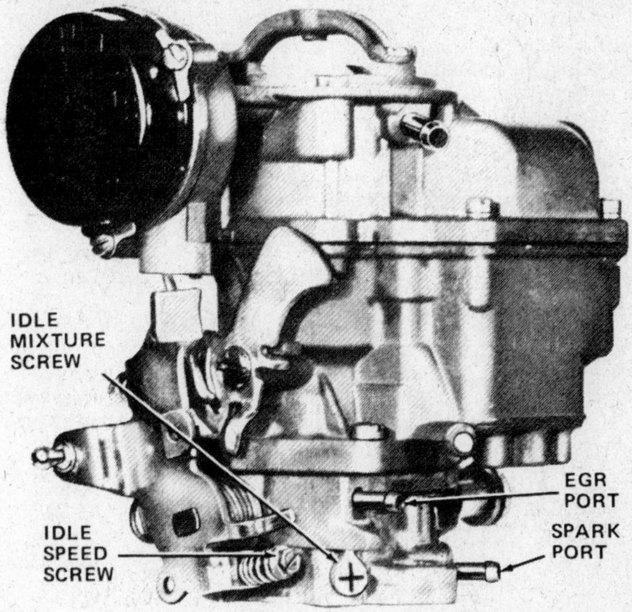

Fig. 1.13 Engine idle speed screw location (typical) (Sec 20)

uneven wear is noticed. Since the vehicle will be raised and the tires removed anyway, this is a good time to check the brakes (Sec 25) and/or repack the wheel bearings (Sec 26). Read over these Sections before beginning.

2 The location for each tire in the rotation sequence depends on the type of tire used on your vehicle. Tire type can be determined by reading the raised printing on the sidewall of the tire. The accompanying illustration shows the rotation sequence for each type of tire.

3 See the information in *Jacking and towing* at the front of this manual for the proper procedures to follow when raising the vehicle and changing a tire; however, if the brakes are to be checked, do not apply the parking brake as stated. Make sure the tires are blocked to prevent the vehicle from rolling.

4 Preferably, the entire vehicle should be raised at the same time. This can be done on a hoist or by jacking up each corner and then lowering the vehicle onto jackstands placed under the frame rails. Always use four jackstands and make sure the vehicle is firmly supported all around.

5 After rotation, check and adjust the tire pressures as necessary and be sure to check wheel lug nut tightness.

20 Engine idle speed adjustment

1 Engine idle speed is the speed at which the engine operates when no accelerator pedal pressure is applied. This speed is critical to the performance of the engine itself, as well as many engine sub-systems.

2 A hand-held tachometer must be used when adjusting idle speed to get an accurate reading. The exact hook-up for these meters varies with the manufacturer, so follow the particular directions included.

3 Since these models were equipped with many different carburetors in the time period covered by this manual, and each has its own peculiarities when setting idle speed, it would be impractical to cover all types in this Section. Chapter 4 contains information on each individual carburetor used. The carburetor used on your particular engine can be found in the Specifications Section of Chapter 4. However, all vehicles covered in this manual should have a tune-up decal or Emission Control Information label in the engine compartment, usually placed near the top of the radiator. The printed instructions for setting idle speed can be found on this decal or label and should be followed since they are for your particular engine.

4 Basically, for most applications, the idle speed is set by turning an adjustment screw located at the side of the carburetor. Turning the screw changes the position of the throttle valve in the carburetor. This screw may be on the linkage itself or may be part of the idle stop solenoid. Refer to the tune-up decal or Chapter 4.

5 Once you have located the idle speed screw, experiment with different length screwdrivers until the adjustments can easily be made, without coming into contact with hot or moving engine components.

6 Follow the instructions on the tune-up decal or Emission Control Information label, which may include disconnecting certain vacuum or electrical connections. To plug a vacuum hose after disconnecting it, insert a properly sized metal rod into the opening or thoroughly wrap the open end with tape to prevent any vacuum loss through the hose.

7 If the air cleaner is removed, the vacuum hose to the snorkel should be plugged.

8 Make sure the parking brake is firmly set and the wheels blocked to prevent the vehicle from rolling. This is especially true if the transmission is to be in Drive. An assistant inside the vehicle pushing on the brake pedal is the safest method.

9 For all applications, the engine must be completely warmed-up to operating temperature, which will automatically render the choke fast idle inoperative.

10 Turn the idle speed screw in or out, as required, until the idle speed listed in the Specifications is obtained.

21 Fuel filter replacement

Caution: *Gasoline is extremely flammable so extra safety precautions must be observed when working on any part of the fuel system. Do not smoke and do not allow bare light bulbs or open flames near the vehicle. Also, do not perform this maintenance procedure in a garage if a natural gas type water heater is located in the garage.*

1 These models were equipped with a variety of fuel filters. Some models are equipped with replaceable filters located in the fuel line, while others have screw-in type filters located at the carburetor fuel inlet.

2 This job should be done with the engine cold (after sitting for at least three hours). The necessary tools are pliers for the in-line filter or open end wrenches to fit the fuel line nuts of the screw-in type filter. Flare nut wrenches which wrap around the nut should be used if

available. In addition you will have to obtain a replacement filter (make sure it is correct for your specific vehicle and engine) and some clean rags.
3 Remove the air cleaner assembly. If vacuum hoses must be disconnected, make sure you note their positions and/or tag them to help during installation.
4 Place some rags under the filter to catch any spilled fuel.

In-line filter

5 Remove the retaining clips from the fuel lines and pull the filter free.
6 Install the new filter in the same position as the old one and push the fuel hoses into place, securing them with the clips. Later models have a breather fitting and hose which is part of the ECS system; it must be at the top.

Screw-in type filter

7 With the proper size wrench, hold the nut next to the carburetor body. Now loosen the nut fitting and the end of the metal fuel line. A flare-nut wrench on this fitting will prevent slipping and possible damage. However, an open-end wrench should do the job. Make sure the larger nut next to the carburetor is held firmly while the fuel line is disconnected.
8 With the fuel line disconnected, move it to the side slightly for better access to the inlet filter nut. *Do not crimp the fuel line.*
9 Now unscrew the fuel inlet filter nut which was previously held steady. As this fitting is drawn away from the carburetor body, be careful not to lose the thin washer-type gasket or the spring located behind the fuel filter. Also, pay close attention to how the filter was installed.
10 Compare the old filter with the new one to make sure they are of the same length and design.
11 Reinstall the spring in the carburetor body, after inspecting it for damage and defects.
12 Place the new filter into position behind the spring.
13 Install a new washer-type gasket on the fuel inlet filter nut (a new gasket is usually supplied with the new filter) and tighten the nut in the carburetor. Make sure it is not cross-threaded or over-tightened as fuel leaks could result.
14 On all models, reinstall the air cleaner assembly and return all hoses to their original positions. Start the engine and check for fuel leaks.

22 Positive Crankcase Ventilation (PCV) valve replacement

1 The PCV valve is located in the rocker arm cover on in-line engines and in the intake manifold on V8 engines. A hose connected to the valve runs to either the rocker arm cover, carburetor or intake manifold.
2 When purchasing a replacement PCV valve, make sure it is for your particular vehicle, model year and engine size.
3 Pull the valve (with hose attached) from the rubber grommet in the rocker arm cover or manifold.
4 Loosen the retaining clamp and pull the PCV valve from the end of the hose, noting its installed position and direction.
5 Compare the old valve with the new one to make sure they are the same.
6 Push the new valve into the end of the hose until it is fully seated and reinstall the clamp.
7 Inspect the rubber grommet for damage and replace it with a new one, if faulty.
8 Push the PCV valve and hose securely into position.
9 More information on the PCV system can be found in Chapter 6.

23 Clutch pedal free play check and adjustment

1 Proper clutch pedal free play is very important for proper clutch operation and to ensure normal clutch service life.
2 Clutch pedal free play is the distance the clutch pedal moves before the mechanical linkage or hydraulic pressure actually begins to disengage the clutch disc from the flywheel and pressure plate.
3 On 1970 and 1971 models with 232 and 258 cubic inch engines, the pedal height should be adjusted in the following manner before the pedal free play is checked. Insert a rod $\frac{5}{16}$-inch in diameter and $4\frac{1}{2}$ inches in length through the aligning holes in the clutch pedal support bracket. Now adjust the pedal stop until the pedal lever hole is in alignment with the other two and the rod can be slid freely through all three holes.
4 On all other models, adjust the pedal height by loosening the locknut on the pedal stop and turning the pedal stop in or out until the distance from the mid-point of the pedal rubber to the floor is equal to the pedal height in the Specifications.
5 When the pedal height is correct, tighten the locknut and adjust the pedal free play.
6 To check the free play, slowly depress the clutch pedal until the resistance offered by the clutch release mechanism is felt (the pedal will suddenly become much more difficult to move).
7 Measure the distance the clutch pedal has travelled and compare it to the Specifications. If adjustment is required, loosen the locknut on the bellcrank-to-throwout lever rod and turn the rod until the specified free play is obtained. Tighten the locknut when the adjustment is completed.

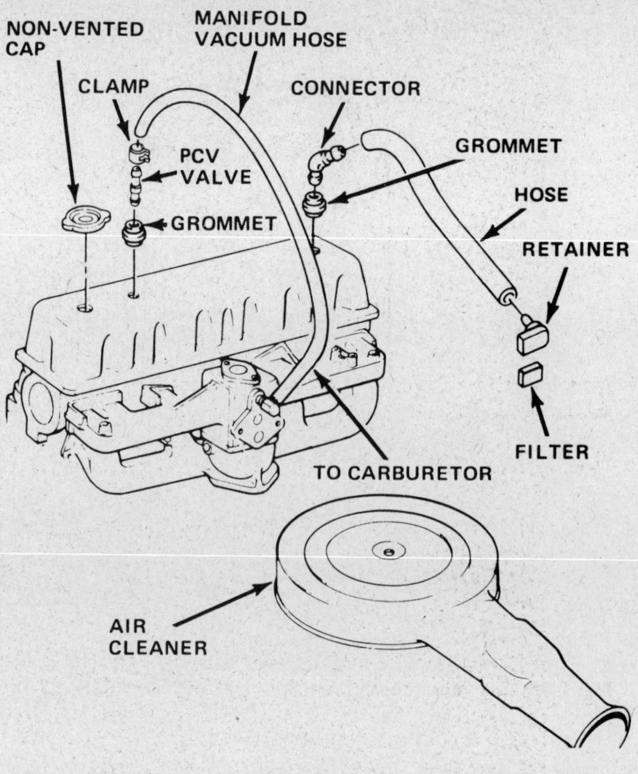

Fig. 1.14 PCV system components – exploded view (typical) (Sec 22)

24 Fuel vapor control system canister – filter replacement

1 The function of the fuel vapor control system is to draw fuel vapors from the tank and carburetor, store them in a charcoal canister, and then burn them during normal engine operation.
2 The filter at the bottom of the charcoal canister should be replaced at the specified intervals. If, however, a fuel odor is detected, the canister, filter and system hoses should immediately be inspected.
3 To replace the filter, locate the canister at the front of the engine compartment. It will have several hoses running out the top of it.
4 Remove the two bolts which secure the bottom of the canister to the body.
5 Turn the canister upside-down and pull out the old filter. If you cannot turn the canister enough, due to the short length of the hoses, the hoses must be marked with pieces of tape and then disconnected from the top.
6 Push the new filter into the bottom of the canister, making sure it is seated all the way around.
7 Place the canister back into position and tighten the two mounting bolts. Connect the various hoses if they were disconnected.

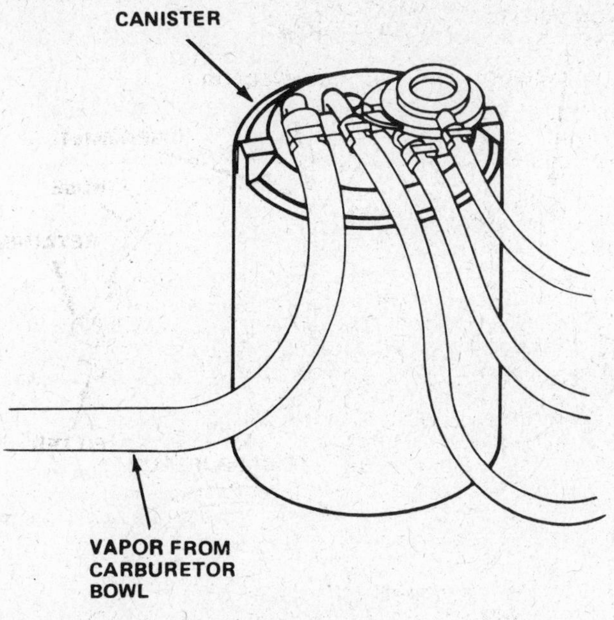

Fig. 1.15 Fuel vapor control system canister (typical) (Sec 24)

8 The fuel vapor control system is explained in more detail in Chapter 6.

25 Brake check

1 The brakes should be inspected every time the wheels are removed or whenever a problem is suspected. Indications of a potential brake system fault are: the vehicle pulls to one side when the brake pedal is depressed, noises coming from the brakes when they are applied, excessive brake pedal travel, pulsating pedal and leakage of fluid (which is usually seen on the inside of the tire or wheel).

Disc brakes

2 Disc brakes can be visually checked without the need to remove any parts except the wheels.
3 Raise the vehicle and place it securely on jackstands. Remove the front wheels (See *Jacking and towing* at the front of this manual, if necessary).
4 Now visible is the disc brake caliper, which contains the pads. There is an outer brake pad and an inner pad. Both should be inspected.
5 Most later model vehicles come equipped with a 'wear sensor' attached to the inner pad. This is a small, bent piece of metal which is visible from the inboard side of the brake caliper. When the pads wear to a danger limit, the metal sensor rubs against the disc and makes a screeching sound.
6 Inspect the pad thickness by looking at each end of the caliper and through the inspection hole in the caliper body (photo). If the wear sensor clip is very close to the rotor, or if the lining material is $\frac{1}{8}$-inch or less in thickness, the pads should be replaced. Keep in mind that the lining material is riveted or bonded to a metal backing shoe and the metal portion is not included in this measurement (if the lining material is worn to a point where it is thinner than the backing plate, new pads are required).
7 Since it will be difficult, if not impossible, to measure the exact thickness of the remaining lining material, if you are in doubt as to the pad quality, remove the pads for further inspection or replacement. See Chapter 9 for disc brake pad replacement.
8 Before installing the wheels, check for leakage around the brake hose connections and damage (cracking, splitting, etc.) to the brake hoses. Replace hoses or fittings as necessary, referring to Chapter 9.

25.6 Inspecting the disc brake pad lining thickness (arrow) through the caliper inspection hole

9 Also check the disc for scoring, gouging or burnt spots. If these conditions exist, the hub/disc assembly should be removed for servicing (Chapter 9).

1

Drum brakes

10 Raise the vehicle and support it securely on jackstands.
11 Remove the wheels, referring to *Jacking and towing* at the front of this manual if necessary.
12 *To remove the front brake drum(s),* pry off the dust cap, remove the cotter pin and nut lock, unscrew the spindle nut and pull the drum out about $\frac{1}{2}$-inch. Push the drum back in, remove the washer and outer wheel bearing, then pull the brake drum all the way off the spindle.
13 *The rear drum(s)* can be pulled off the hub after the wheel is removed (some models have drum retaining screws which must be removed first). **Note**: *If the brake drums are difficult to remove, the brake shoes can be retracted. Remove the access plug at the rear of the backing plate and disengage the automatic adjuster lever with a small screwdriver or section of welding rod. Turn the adjuster wheel until the drum can be removed.*
14 With the drum removed, carefully brush away any accumulations of dirt and dust. **Caution**: *Do not blow the dust out with compressed air. Make an effort not to inhale the dust, as it contains asbestos and is harmful to your health.*
15 Observe the thickness of the lining material on both the front and rear brake shoes. Measure the amount of remaining lining and compare it to the Specifications. If the linings look worn, but you are unable to determine their exact thickness, compare them with a new set at an auto parts store. The shoes should also be replaced if they are cracked, glazed (shiny surface), or contaminated with brake fluid.
16 Make sure that all the brake assembly springs are connected and in good condition.
17 Inspect the brake components for signs of fluid leakage. With your finger, carefully pry back the rubber cups on the wheel cylinder located at the top of the brake shoes. Any leakage is an indication that the wheel cylinders should be overhauled immediately (Chapter 9). Also check the hoses and connections for signs of leakage.
18 Wipe the inside of the drum with a clean rag and denatured alcohol or brake system cleaner. Again, be careful not to breathe the dangerous asbestos dust.
19 Check the inside of the drum for cracks, scoring, deep scratches and hard spots (which will appear as small discolorations). If these imperfections cannot be removed with fine emery cloth, the drum must be taken to a machine shop equipped to resurface the drums.
20 If, after the inspection process, all parts are in good condition, reinstall the brake drum and wheel and lower the vehicle to the ground. *On models with drum front brakes, refer to Section 26 for the hub/drum installation procedure.*

Parking brake

21 The easiest way to check the operation of the parking brake is to park the vehicle on a steep hill with the parking brake set and the transmission in Neutral. If the parking brake cannot prevent the vehicle from rolling, it is in need of adjustment (see Chapter 9).

26 Wheel bearing check and service

1 In most cases, the front wheel bearings will not need servicing until the brake pads or shoes are changed. However, the bearings should be checked whenever the front wheels are raised for any reason.

2 With the vehicle securely supported on jackstands, spin the wheel and check for noise, rolling resistance and free play. Now grab the top of the tire with one hand and the bottom of the tire with the other. Move the tire in and out on the spindle. If there is noticeable movement, the bearings should be checked, then repacked with grease or replaced if necessary.

3 To remove the bearings begin by removing the hub cap and wheel.

4 Remove the disc brake caliper (if so equipped) by referring to Chapter 9. On drum brake models, the brake drum is part of the hub.

5 Fabricate a wood block ($1\frac{1}{16}$-inch by $1\frac{1}{16}$-inch by 2 inches in length), which will be slid between the brake pads to keep them separated. Carefully slide the caliper off the disc and insert the wood block between the pads. Use wire to hang the caliper assembly out of the way. Be careful not to kink or damage the brake hose.

6 Using a screwdriver, pry the hub grease cap off the hub. This cap is located at the center of the hub (photo).

7 Use needle-nose pliers to straighten the bent ends of the cotter pin and then pull the cotter pin out of the locking nut (photo). Discard the cotter pin, as a new one should be used during reassembly.

8 Remove the nut retainer, spindle nut and washer from the end of the spindle (photo).

9 Pull the hub assembly out slightly, then push it back into its original position. This should force the outer bearing off the spindle enough so that it can be removed with your fingers. Remove the outer bearing, noting how it is installed on the end of the spindle (photo).

10 Now the hub assembly can be pulled off the spindle (photo).

11 On the rear side of the hub, use a screwdriver to pry out the inner bearing lip seal. As this is done, note the direction in which the seal is installed.

12 The inner bearing can now be removed from the hub, again noting how it is installed.

13 Use clean solvent to remove all traces of the old grease from the bearings, hub and spindle. A small brush may prove useful; however, make sure no bristles from the brush embed themselves inside the bearing rollers. Allow the parts to air dry.

26.6 Removing the front hub grease cap

26.7 Removing the front spindle cotter pin

26.8 Removing the nut retainer

26.9 Removing the outer bearing

26.10 Removing the front hub assembly

14 Carefully inspect the bearings for cracks, heat discoloration, bent rollers, etc. Check the bearing races inside the hub for cracks, scoring and uneven surfaces. If the bearing races are in need of replacement, this job is best left to a repair shop which can press the new races into position.
15 Use an approved high-temperature front wheel bearing grease to pack the bearings. Work the grease completely into the bearings, forcing the grease between the rollers, cone and cage.
16 Apply a thin coat of grease to the spindle at the outer bearing seat, inner bearing seat, shoulder and seal seat.
17 Put a small quantity of grease inboard of each bearing race inside the hub. Using your finger, form a dam at these points to provide extra grease availability and to keep thinned grease from flowing out of the bearing.
18 Place the grease-packed inner bearing into the rear of the hub and put a little more grease outboard of the bearing.
19 Place a new seal over the inner bearing and tap the seal with a flat plate and a hammer until it is flush with the hub.
20 Carefully place the hub assembly onto the spindle and push the grease-packed outer bearing into position.
21 Install the washer and spindle nut. Tighten the nut to 25 ft-lbs of torque while rotating the wheel to seat the bearings.
22 Remove any grease or burrs which could cause excessive bearing play later.
23 Put a little grease outboard of the outer bearing to provide extra lubrication.
24 Now make sure that the spindle nut is still tight (25 ft-lb).
25 Loosen the spindle nut $\frac{1}{3}$ of a turn.

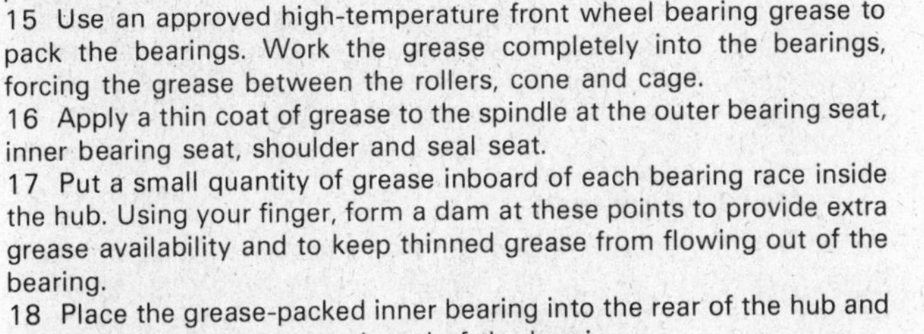

Fig. 1.16 Front hub components – exploded view (disc brake type) (typical) (Sec 26)

26 Using your hand (or a torque wrench calibrated in in-lb), tighten the spindle nut to 2 to 10 in-lb of torque. Install a new cotter pin through the hole in the spindle and spindle nut. If the slots do not line up, loosen the nut slightly until they do. From the hand-tight position the nut should not be loosened any more than one-half flat to install the cotter pin.
27 Bend the ends of the new cotter pin until they are flat against the nut. Cut off any extra length which could interfere with the dust cap.
28 Install the dust cap, tapping it into place with a rubber mallet.
29 If applicable, install the brake caliper by referring to Chapter 9.
30 Install the tire/wheel assembly and tighten the mounting nuts.
31 Grab the top and bottom of the tire and check the bearings in the same manner as described at the beginning of this Section.
32 Lower the vehicle to the ground and tighten the wheel nuts. Install the hub cap, using a rubber mallet to seat it.

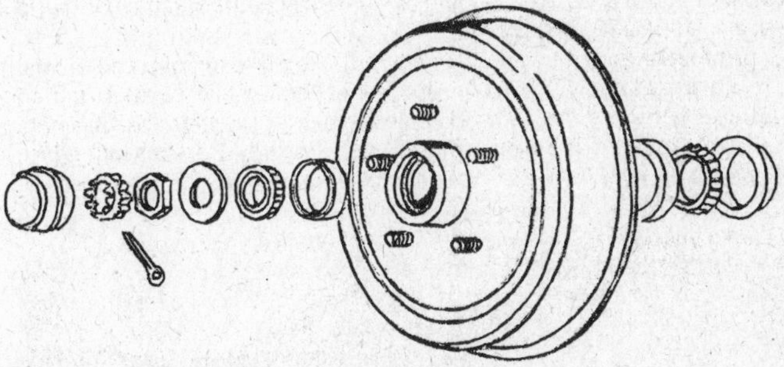

Fig. 1.17 Front hub components – exploded view (drum brake type) (typical) (Sec 26)

27 Spark plug replacement

1 The spark plugs are located on each side of the engine on a V8 and may or may not be easily accessible for removal. In-line engines generally have fewer spark plug accessibility problems. If the vehicle is equipped with air conditioning or power steering, some of the plugs may be difficult to remove (in which case special extension or swivel tools will be necessary). Make a survey under the hood to determine if special tools will be needed.
2 In most cases the tools necessary for a spark plug replacement job include a plug wrench or spark plug socket which fits onto a ratchet wrench (this special socket will be insulated inside to protect the porcelain insulator) and a feeler gauge to check and adjust the spark plug gap. If the vehicle is equipped with BID (electronic) ignition, a special spark plug wire removal tool is available for separating the wire boot from the spark plug.
3 The best procedure to follow when replacing the spark plugs is to purchase the new spark plugs beforehand, adjust them to the proper gap and then replace each plug one at a time. When buying the new spark plugs it is important to obtain the correct plugs for your specific engine. This information can be found in the Specifications Section but should be checked against the information found on the tune-up decal or Emission Control Information label located under the hood or in the factory owner's manual. If differences exist between these sources, purchase the spark plug type specified on the tune-up decal or emission label as it was printed for your specific engine.
4 With the new spark plugs on hand, allow the engine to cool thoroughly before attempting removal. During this time, each of the new spark plugs can be inspected for defects and the gap can be checked/adjusted.
5 The gap is checked by inserting the proper thickness gauge between the electrodes at the tip of the plug. The gap between these electrodes should be the same as that given in the Specifications or on the tune-up decal/emissions label. The wire should just touch each of the electrodes. If the gap is incorrect, use the notched adjuster on the feeler gauge body to bend the curved side electrode slightly until the proper gap is obtained. Also at this time check for cracks in the spark plug body, indicating the spark plug should not be used. If the side electrode is not exactly over the center one, use the notched adjuster to align them.

6 Cover the fenders of the vehicle to prevent damage to the exterior paint.
7 With the engine cool, remove the spark plug wire from one spark plug. Do this by grabbing the boot at the end of the wire, not the wire itself. Sometimes it is necessary to use a twisting motion while the boot and plug wire are pulled free. Use of a plug wire removal tool is recommended.
8 If compressed air is available, use it to blow any dirt or foreign material away from the spark plug area. A common bicycle pump will also work. The idea here is to eliminate the possibility of material falling into the engine cylinder as the spark plug is removed.
9 Now place the spark plug wrench or socket over the plug and remove it from the engine by turning in a counterclockwise direction.
10 Compare the spark plug with those shown in the accompanying color photos to get an indication of the overall running condition of the engine.
11 Carefully insert one of the new plugs into the spark plug hole and tighten it as much as possible by hand. The spark plug should screw easily into the engine. If it doesn't, change the angle of the spark plug slightly, as chances are the threads are not matched (cross-threaded).
12 Finally, tighten the spark plug with the wrench or socket. It is a good idea to use a torque wrench for this to ensure that the plug is seated correctly. The correct torque figure is given in the Specifications.
13 Before pushing the spark plug wire onto the end of the plug, inspect it following the procedures outlined in Section 28.
14 Attach the plug wire to the new spark plug, again using a twisting motion on the boot until it is firmly seated. Make sure the wire is routed away from the exhaust manifold.
15 Repeat the procedure for the remaining spark plugs, replacing them one at a time to prevent mixing up the plug wires.

28 Spark plug wires, distributor cap and rotor – check and replacement

1 The spark plug wires should be checked at the recommended intervals and whenever new spark plugs are installed in the engine.
2 The wires should be inspected one at a time to prevent mixing up the order, which is essential for proper engine operation.
3 Disconnect the plug wire from the spark plug. A removal tool can be used for this purpose or you can grab the rubber boot, twist slightly and pull the wire free. *Do not pull on the wire itself, only on the rubber boot.*
4 Inspect inside the boot for corrosion, which will look like a white crusty powder. Push the wire and boot back onto the end of the spark plug. It should be a tight fit on the plug end. If it is not, remove the wire and use a pliers to carefully crimp the metal connector inside the wire boot until it fits securely on the end of the spark plug.
5 Using a clean rag, wipe the entire length of the wire to remove any built-up dirt and grease. Once the wire is clean, check for burns, cracks and other damage. Do not bend the wire, since the conductor might break.
6 Disconnect the wire from the distributor. Again, pull only on the rubber boot. Check for corrosion and a tight fit in the same manner as the spark plug end. Replace the wire in the distributor.
7 Check the remaining spark plug wires, making sure they are securely fastened at the distributor and spark plug when the check is complete.
8 If new spark plug wires are required, purchase a set for your specific engine model. Wire sets are available pre-cut, with the rubber boots already installed. Remove and replace the wires one at a time to avoid mix-ups in the firing order.
9 Check the distributor cap and rotor for wear. Look for cracks, carbon tracks, and worn, burned or loose contacts. Replace the cap and rotor with new parts if defects are found. It is common practice to install a new cap and rotor whenever new spark plug wires are installed. When installing a new cap, remove the wires from the old cap one at a time and attach them to the new cap in the exact same location – do not simultaneously remove all the wires from the old cap or firing order mix-ups may occur.

29 Cooling system servicing (draining, flushing and refilling)

1 Periodically, the cooling system should be drained, flushed and refilled to replenish the antifreeze mixture and prevent the formation of rust and corrosion which can impair the performance of the cooling system and ultimately cause engine damage.
2 At the same time the cooling system is serviced, all hoses and the radiator cap should be inspected and replaced if faulty.
3 Since antifreeze is a poisonous solution, be careful not to spill any of the coolant mixture on the vehicle's paint or your own skin. If this happens, rinse immediately with plenty of clear water. Also, consult your local authorities about the dumping of antifreeze before draining the cooling system. In many areas reclamation centers have been set up to collect automobile oil and drained antifreeze/water mixtures rather than allowing these liquids to be added to the sewage system.
4 With the engine cold, remove the radiator cap.
5 Move a large container under the radiator to catch the coolant mixture as it is drained.
6 Drain the radiator. Most models are equipped with a drain plug at the bottom of the radiator, which can be opened using a wrench to hold the fitting while the petcock is turned to the open position. If the drain has excessive corrosion and cannot be turned easily, or if the radiator is not equipped with a drain, disconnect the lower radiator hose to drain the coolant. Be careful that none of the solution is splashed on your skin or in your eyes.
7 If accessible, remove the engine drain plug(s) from the lower edge(s) of the block, near the oil pan rail (Chapter 3).
8 On systems with a coolant reservoir, disconnect the overflow hose and remove the reservoir. Flush it out with clean water.
9 Place a water hose (a common garden hose is fine) in the radiator filler neck at the top of the radiator and flush the system until the water runs clear at all drain points.
10 In severe cases of contamination or clogging of the radiator, remove it (see Chapter 3) and reverse flush it. This involves simply inserting the hose in the bottom radiator outlet to allow the clear water to run against the normal flow, draining through the top. A radiator repair shop should be consulted if further cleaning or repair is necessary.
11 If the coolant is regularly drained and the system refilled with the correct antifreeze mixture there should be no need to employ chemical cleaners or descalers.
12 To refill the system, reconnect the radiator hose(s) and install the drain plugs securely in the engine. Special thread sealing tape (available at auto parts stores) should be used on the drain plugs installed in the engine block. Install the coolant reservoir and the overflow hose where applicable.
13 On vehicles without a coolant reservoir, refill the system through the radiator filler cap until the coolant level is about three inches below the filler neck.
14 On vehicles with a reservoir, fill the radiator up the base of the filler neck and then add more coolant to the reservoir.
15 Run the engine until normal operating temperature is reached, then with the engine idling, add coolant up to the correct level. Install the reservoir cap.
16 Always refill the system with a mixture of high quality antifreeze and water in the proportion called for on the antifreeze container or in your owner's manual. Chapter 3 also contains information on antifreeze mixtures.
17 Keep a close watch on the coolant level and the various cooling hoses during the first few miles of driving. Tighten the hose clamps and/or add more coolant mixture as necessary.

30 Cylinder compression check

1 A compression check will tell you what mechanical condition the engine is in. Specifically, it can tell you if the compression is down due to leakage caused by worn piston rings, defective valves and seats or a blown head gasket.
2 Begin by cleaning the area around the spark plugs before you remove them. This will keep dirt from falling into the cylinders while you are performing the compression test.
3 Remove the coil high-tension lead from the distributor and ground it on the engine block. Block the throttle and choke valves wide open.
4 With the compression gauge in the number one cylinder's spark plug hole, crank the engine over at least four compression strokes and observe the gauge. The compression should build up quickly in a healthy engine. Low compression on the first stroke, followed by gradually increasing pressure on successive strokes, indicates worn

Common spark plug conditions

NORMAL

Symptoms: Brown to grayish-tan color and slight electrode wear. Correct heat range for engine and operating conditions.
Recommendation: When new spark plugs are installed, replace with plugs of the same heat range.

WORN

Symptoms: Rounded electrodes with a small amount of deposits on the firing end. Normal color. Causes hard starting in damp or cold weather and poor fuel economy.
Recommendation: Plugs have been left in the engine too long. Replace with new plugs of the same heat range. Follow the recommended maintenance schedule.

CARBON DEPOSITS

Symptoms: Dry sooty deposits indicate a rich mixture or weak ignition. Causes misfiring, hard starting and hesitation.
Recommendation: Make sure the plug has the correct heat range. Check for a clogged air filter or problem in the fuel system or engine management system. Also check for ignition system problems.

ASH DEPOSITS

Symptoms: Light brown deposits encrusted on the side or center electrodes or both. Derived from oil and/or fuel additives. Excessive amounts may mask the spark, causing misfiring and hesitation during acceleration.
Recommendation: If excessive deposits accumulate over a short time or low mileage, install new valve guide seals to prevent seepage of oil into the combustion chambers. Also try changing gasoline brands.

OIL DEPOSITS

Symptoms: Oily coating caused by poor oil control. Oil is leaking past worn valve guides or piston rings into the combustion chamber. Causes hard starting, misfiring and hesitation.
Recommendation: Correct the mechanical condition with necessary repairs and install new plugs.

GAP BRIDGING

Symptoms: Combustion deposits lodge between the electrodes. Heavy deposits accumulate and bridge the electrode gap. The plug ceases to fire, resulting in a dead cylinder.
Recommendation: Locate the faulty plug and remove the deposits from between the electrodes.

TOO HOT

Symptoms: Blistered, white insulator, eroded electrode and absence of deposits. Results in shortened plug life.
Recommendation: Check for the correct plug heat range, over-advanced ignition timing, lean fuel mixture, intake manifold vacuum leaks, sticking valves and insufficient engine cooling.

PREIGNITION

Symptoms: Melted electrodes. Insulators are white, but may be dirty due to misfiring or flying debris in the combustion chamber. Can lead to engine damage.
Recommendation: Check for the correct plug heat range, over-advanced ignition timing, lean fuel mixture, insufficient engine cooling and lack of lubrication.

HIGH SPEED GLAZING

Symptoms: Insulator has yellowish, glazed appearance. Indicates that combustion chamber temperatures have risen suddenly during hard acceleration. Normal deposits melt to form a conductive coating. Causes misfiring at high speeds.
Recommendation: Install new plugs. Consider using a colder plug if driving habits warrant.

DETONATION

Symptoms: Insulators may be cracked or chipped. Improper gap setting techniques can also result in a fractured insulator tip. Can lead to piston damage.
Recommendation: Make sure the fuel anti-knock values meet engine requirements. Use care when setting the gaps on new plugs. Avoid lugging the engine.

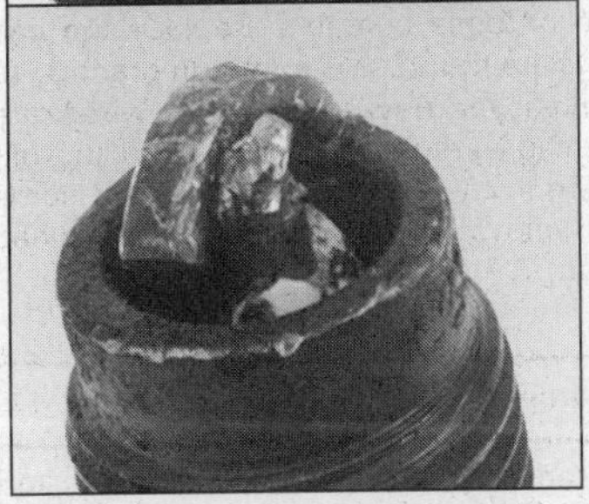

MECHANICAL DAMAGE

Symptoms: May be caused by a foreign object in the combustion chamber or the piston striking an incorrect reach (too long) plug. Causes a dead cylinder and could result in piston damage.
Recommendation: Repair the mechanical damage. Remove the foreign object from the engine and/or install the correct reach plug.

piston rings. A low compression reading on the first stroke, which does not build up during successive strokes, indicates leaking valves or a defective head gasket. Record the highest gauge reading obtained.
5 Repeat the procedure for the remaining cylinders and compare the results to the Specifications. Compression readings 10% above or below the specified amount can be considered normal.
6 Pour a couple of teaspoons of engine oil (a squirt can works great for this) into each cylinder, through the spark plug hole, and repeat the test.
7 If the compression increases after the oil is added, the piston rings are definitely worn. If the compression does not increase significantly, the leakage is occurring at the valves or head gasket. Leakage past the valves may be caused by burned valve seats/faces, warped, bent or cracked valves, valves that are out of adjustment, incorrect valve timing and broken valve springs.
8 If two adjacent cylinders have equally low compression, there is a strong possibility that the head gasket between them is blown. The appearance of coolant in the combustion chambers or the crankcase would verify this condition.
9 If the compression is higher than normal, the combustion chambers are probably coated with carbon deposits. If that is the case, the cylinder head(s) should be removed and decarbonized.
10 If compression is way down, or varies greatly between cylinders, it would be a good idea to have a leak-down test performed by a reputable automotive repair shop. This test will pinpoint exactly where the leakage is occurring and how severe it is.

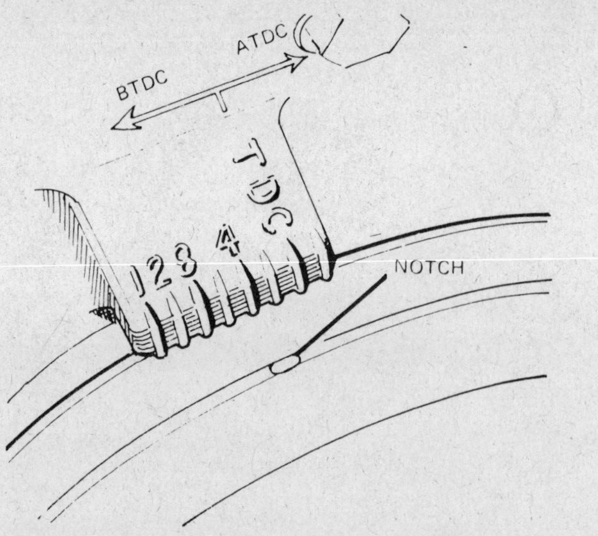

Fig. 1.18 Ignition timing marks – typical (Sec 31)

31 Ignition timing check and adjustment

1 All later model vehicles are equipped with a tune-up or Emission Control Information label inside the engine compartment. This label contains important ignition timing Specifications and procedures to be followed specific to that vehicle. If information on the label differs from the information given in this Section, the label should be followed.
2 At the specified intervals, whenever the contact points have been replaced, the distributor removed or a change made in the fuel type, the ignition timing must be checked and adjusted if necessary.
3 Before attempting to check the timing, make sure the contact point dwell angle is correct (if applicable) and the idle speed is as specified (Sec 20).
4 Disconnect the vacuum hose from the distributor and plug the now-open end of the hose with a rubber plug, rod or bolt of the proper size. Make sure the idle speed remains correct; adjust as necessary.
5 Connect a timing light in accordance with the manufacturer's instructions. Generally, the light will be connected to the battery terminals and to the number one (1) spark plug in some fashion. On V8 engines, the number one spark plug is the first one on the right as you are facing the engine from the front. On in-line engines it is the front spark plug.
6 Locate the numbered timing tag on the front cover of the engine. It is just behind the lower crankshaft pulley. Clean it off with solvent, if necessary, to read the printing and small grooves.
7 Locate the notched groove across the crankshaft pulley. It may be necessary to have an assistant temporarily turn the ignition off and on in short bursts without starting the engine to bring this groove into a position where it can easily be cleaned and marked. Stay clear of all moving engine components if the engine is turned over in this manner.
8 Use white soapstone, chalk or paint to mark the groove on the crankshaft pulley. Also put a mark on the timing tag in accordance with the number of degrees called for in the Specifications or on the label in the engine compartment. Each peak or notch on the timing tab represents 2°. The word *Before* or the letter A indicates advance and the letter O indicates Top Dead Center (TDC). As an example if your vehicle specifications call for 8° BTDC (Before Top Dead Center) you will make a mark on the timing tag 4 notches *before* the O. Some models have a T or TDC mark.
9 Make sure that the wiring for the timing light is clear of all moving engine components, then start the engine.
10 Point the flashing timing light at the timing marks, again being careful not to come in contact with moving parts. The marks you made should appear stationary. If the marks are in alignment, the timing is correct. If the marks are not aligned, turn off the engine.
11 Loosen the locknut at the base of the distributor. On some vehicles this task is made much easier with a special curved distributor wrench. Loosen the locknut only slightly, just enough to turn the distributor. (See Chapter 5 for further details, if necessary).
12 Now restart the engine and turn the distributor until the timing marks coincide.
13 Shut off the engine and tighten the distributor locknut, being careful not to move the distributor.
14 Start the engine and recheck the timing to make sure the marks are still in alignment.
15 Disconnect the timing light, unplug the distributor vacuum hose and connect the hose to the distributor.
16 Drive the vehicle and listen for 'pinging' noises. They will be most noticeable when the engine is hot and under a load (climbing a hill, accelerating from a stop). If you hear engine pinging, the ignition timing is too far advanced (Before Top Dead Center). Reconnect the timing light and turn the distributor to move the mark 1° or 2° in the retard direction. Road test the vehicle again to check for proper operation.
17 To keep pinging at a minimum, yet still allow you to operate the vehicle at the specified time setting, it is advisable to use gasoline of the same octane at all times. Switching fuel brands and octane levels can decrease performance and economy, and possibly damage the engine.

32 Contact points and condenser – replacement and adjustment

1 Although the contact points can be cleaned and dressed with a fine-cut file, it is recommended that the home mechanic replace them with new ones instead (photo).
2 The contact point set and condenser should be replaced as a set. Point alignment and spring tension are factory set and should not require further adjustment.
3 Whenever contact point replacement is required, it is a good idea to use magnetized tools to prevent screws or nuts from falling down into the distributor (which would require distributor disassembly to retrieve them).

Contact point removal and installation

4 Remove the distributor cap (Chapter 5).
5 Position the cap (with the spark plug wires still attached) out of the way. Use a length of wire or string to restrain it if necessary.
6 Remove the rotor, which is now visible at the top of the distributor shaft. On some models the rotor is held in position with screws (photo), while on others it is a push fit on the shaft and can be pulled off. Place the rotor in a safe place where it cannot be damaged.
7 Disconnect the primary and condenser wire leads at the contact point set. The wires may be attached with a small nut (which should be loosened, but not removed), a small screw or a quick-disconnect fitting (photos).
8 Remove the screw(s) which secure the contact point set to the

Fig. 1.19 Typical contact breaker point components (Sec 32)

1 Point mounting screw
2 Condenser lead wire
3 Primary lead wire
4 Condenser
5 Point cam
6 Point rubbing block
7 Adjustment slot

breaker plate (photo). *Do not completely remove the screw(s) if the breaker points have slots at these locations.* Separate the point set from the breaker plate.

9 The condenser can now be removed from the distributor. Loosen the mounting strap screw and slide the condenser out of the bracket, or completely remove the condenser and strap, depending on the particular mounting arrangement.

10 Before installing the new points and condenser, remove all old lubricant, dirt, etc. from the breaker plate and the point cam surface of the distributor shaft.

11 Lubricate the point cam with the special grease supplied with the new points or commercially available point cam lube *(do not use multi-purpose grease)*. Some models have a cam lubricator wick mounted on the breaker plate. The wick can be rotated to provide lubrication if it is still in good condition, but, if in doubt, replace the wick with a new one to provide adequate lubrication of the cam surface. It is removed by squeezing the base of the retainer together with long-nosed pliers and then lifting the unit out of the breaker plate. It is important that the cam lubricator wick be adjusted so the end of the wick just touches the cam lobes.

12 Place the new condenser in position and tighten the mounting screw.

13 Attach the new contact point set to the breaker plate and tighten the mounting screw(s) until just snug.

14 Connect the primary and condenser wire leads to the new point assembly. Make sure the condenser lead is positioned the same way it was before removal.

15 Although the gap between the contact points will be set when the dwell angle is adjusted, it is a good idea to adjust the initial gap to start the engine. With the points in position and the mounting screw(s) snug, but not completely tight, make sure that the point rubbing block is resting on one of the lobes of the cam (photo). To move the cam, turn the crankshaft by placing a wrench over the large bolt at the front of the crankshaft.

16 With the rubbing block on a cam lobe (points completely open), insert a blade-type feeler gauge between the contacts. The gap should be as specified. On some models the gap can be changed with a screwdriver. Insert the screwdriver into the adjustment slot and twist

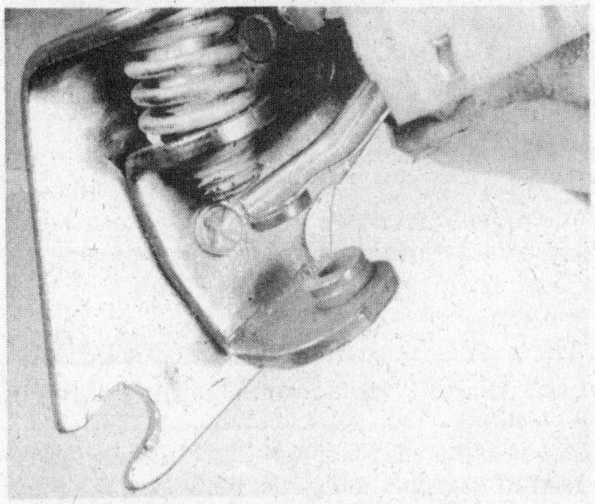

32.1 Although it is possible to clean contact points that are worn, they *should* be replaced instead

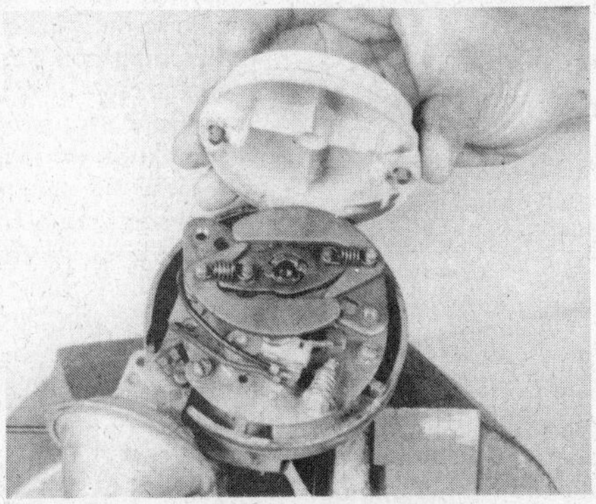

32.6 Some rotors are attached with screws

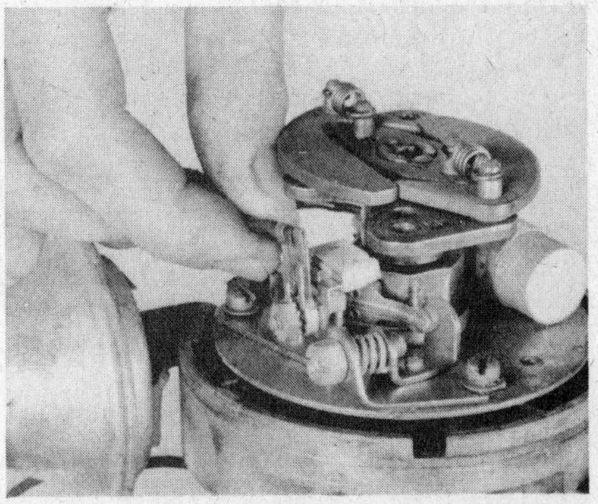

32.7A On some models, the wires are attached to the points by a nut or screw

32.7B On other models, the wires can be pulled off the points

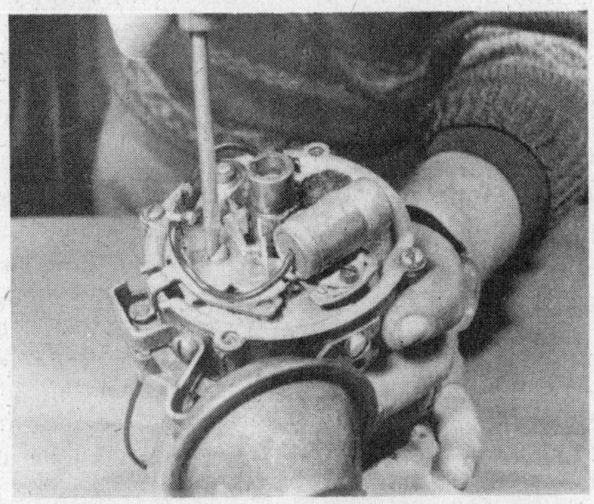

32.8 Removing the point mounting screw (on models with slotted mounting holes, the screw(s) should be loosened only)

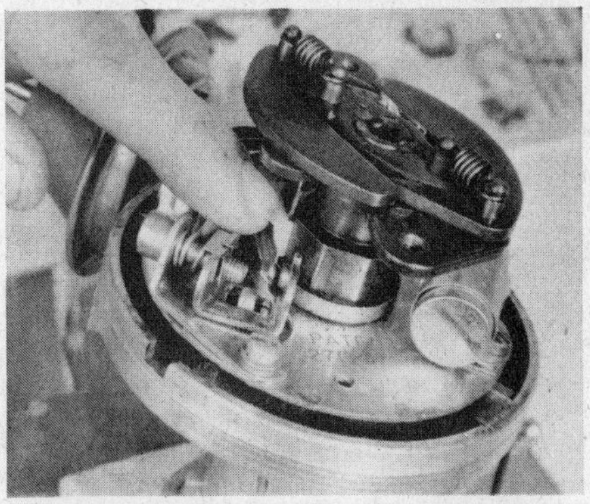

32.15 Before adjusting the point gap, the rubbing block must be resting on one of the cam lobes (which should open the points)

32.16A On some models, the point gap is adjusted by inserting a screwdriver into the slot and twisting it

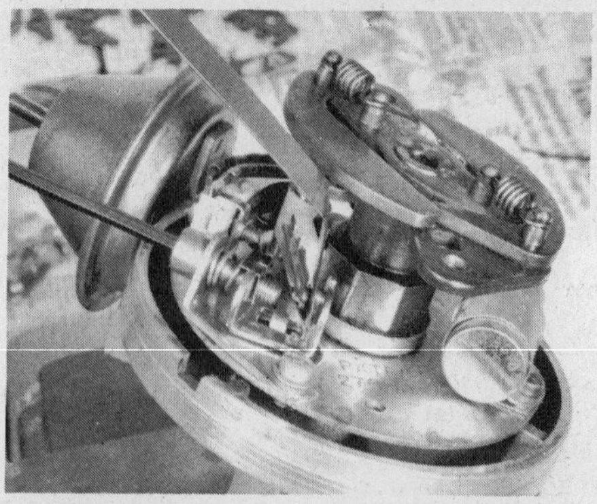

32.16B Some models have an adjusting screw which must be turned with an Allen wrench to change the point gap

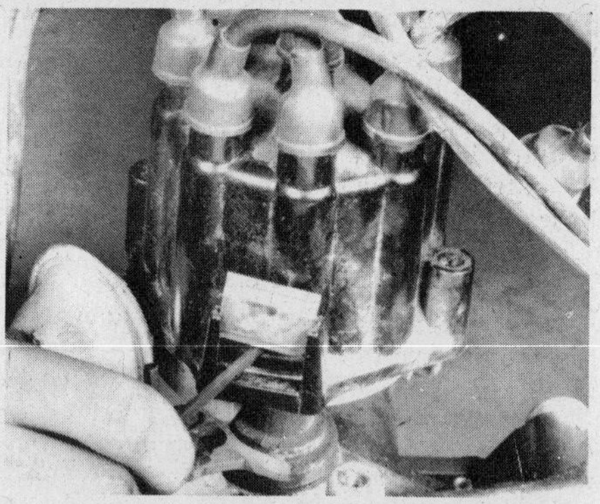

32.29 On some models, adjust the dwell by opening the window in the cap and turning the adjusting screw

it slightly to move the stationary point (photo). On other models, the gap is changed by turning the adjusting screw with an Allen wrench (photo). When the gap is correct, tighten the mounting screw(s) securely.

17 Before installing the rotor, inspect it for cracks and damage. Carefully check the condition of the metal contact at the top of the rotor. If in doubt as to its condition, replace it with a new one.

18 Install the rotor. It is keyed to fit on the shaft only one way.

19 Before installing the distributor cap, inspect it for cracks and damage. Closely examine the contacts on the inside of the cap for excessive corrosion. If in doubt as to the quality of the cap, replace it with a new one.

20 Install the distributor cap.

21 Start the engine and check the dwell angle and the ignition timing.

Dwell angle adjustment

22 Whenever new contact points are installed or the original points are cleaned, the dwell angle must be checked and adjusted.

23 Setting the dwell angle is actually quite easy; however, a dwell meter must be used for precise adjustment. Combination tach/dwell meters are common tune-up instruments which can be purchased at a reasonable cost.

24 Connect the dwell meter according to the manufacturer's instructions. Usually, one lead is attached to the primary wire at the distributor and the other lead is attached to a good ground on the engine. Make sure the engine selector switch on the meter is in the correct position.

25 Start the engine and allow it to idle until it has reached normal operating temperature. The engine must be warm to achieve an accurate reading.

26 Note the dwell meter reading. If it is within the specified range, shut off the engine and disconnect the meter. If it is not within the specified range, shut off the engine and remove the distributor cap and rotor. Some models have a distributor cap equipped with a metal 'window' which can be raised (and held up with tape, if necessary) for dwell adjustment, instead of having to remove the distributor cap.

27 *On non window-type distributors,* loosen the breaker point mounting screw slightly, then move the stationary point (Step 16) to change the point gap (dwell). Increasing the point gap will *decrease* the dwell reading, while decreasing the point gap will *increase* the dwell reading. Tighten the point mounting screw, install the rotor and distributor cap and recheck the dwell.

28 Repeat the procedure until the dwell reading is within the specified range (see Step 34).

29 *On window-type distributors,* insert a proper size Allen wrench through the window and into the adjusting screw socket (photo).

30 Start the engine and turn the adjusting screw as required to obtain the specified dwell reading on the meter. Remove your hand and recheck the reading.

31 Remove the Allen wrench and close the window. Shut off the engine and disconnect the dwell meter.

32 If you cannot obtain a dwell meter, you can get an approximate dwell setting on window-type distributors without one, using the following method.

33 With the engine at normal operating temperature, raise the window and insert the Allen wrench. Start the engine and turn the wrench clockwise until the engine starts to misfire. Then turn the screw *one-half turn counterclockwise.* Remove the Allen wrench and close the window. Have the dwell angle checked and/or adjusted with a meter as soon as possible.

34 **Note:** *On all models, try to obtain a dwell setting that is toward the lower end of the specified range. Then, as the points wear (which increases dwell), the dwell will remain within the specified range for a longer period of time.*

33 Carburetor choke check

1 The choke only operates when the engine is cold, so this check should be performed before the vehicle has been started for the day.

2 Open the hood and remove the top plate of the air cleaner assembly. It is usually held in place by a wing nut at the center. If any vacuum hoses must be disconnected, make sure you tag them to ensure reinstallation in their original positions. Place the top plate and wing nut aside, out of the way of moving engine components.

3 Look at the top of the carburetor at the center of the air cleaner housing. You will notice a flat plate at the carburetor opening.

4 Have an assistant press the accelerator pedal to the floor. The plate should close completely. Start the engine while you observe the plate at the carburetor. **Caution:** *Do not position your face directly over the carburetor, as the engine could backfire, causing serious burns.* When the engine starts, the choke plate should open slightly.

5 Allow the engine to continue running at an idle speed. As the engine warms up to operating temperature, the plate should slowly open, allowing more cold air to enter through the top of the carburetor.

6 After a few minutes, the choke plate should be fully open to the vertical position.

7 You will notice that the engine speed corresponds with the plate opening. With the plate completely closed, the engine should run at a fast idle speed. As the plate opens, the engine speed will decrease.

8 If a fault is detected during the above checks, refer to Chapter 4 for specific information related to adjusting and servicing the choke components.

34 Carburetor mounting torque check

1 The carburetor is attached to the top of the intake manifold by two or four nuts. These fasteners can sometimes work loose from vibration and temperature changes during normal engine operation and cause a vacuum leak.

2 To properly tighten the carburetor mounting nuts, a torque wrench is necessary. If you do not own one, they can usually be rented on a daily basis.

3 Remove the air cleaner assembly, tagging each hose to be disconnected with a piece of numbered tape to make reassembly easier.

4 Locate the mounting nuts at the base of the carburetor. Decide what special tools or adapters will be necessary, if any, to tighten the nuts with a properly sized socket and the torque wrench.

5 Tighten the nuts to a torque of about 12 ft-lbs. Do not overtighten the nuts, as the threads may strip.

6 If you suspect that a vacuum leak exists at the bottom of the carburetor, obtain a length of hose about the diameter of fuel hose. Start the engine and place one end of the hose next to your ear as you

probe around the base of the carburetor with the other end. You will hear a hissing sound if a leak exists.

7 If, after the nuts are properly tightened, a vacuum leak still exists, the carburetor must be removed and a new gasket installed. See Chapter 4 for more information.

8 After tightening the nuts, reinstall the air cleaner and return all hoses to their original positions.

35 Carburetor fuel/air mixture adjustment

Note: *On 1974 and later models, plastic limiter caps are installed over the idle mixture screws on the carburetor. On these models, fuel/air mixture adjustment should be performed only if the mixture screw(s) was removed and replaced during a carburetor overhaul.*

1 Connect a tachometer according to the manufacturer's instructions.

2 Start the engine and allow it to warm up to normal operating temperature. If the vehicle is equipped with an Air Guard system, stop the engine and disconnect the by-pass valve air inlet hose.

3 Adjust the engine idle speed to the specified rpm (refer to the Specifications). On 360 V8 models, adjust the idle speed by turning the throttle stop solenoid.

4 Set the parking brake firmly. On automatic transmission models, position the gear selector in Drive. Position the shift lever in Neutral on manual transmission models.

5 Turn the idle mixture screw clockwise until a loss of engine rpm is indicated.

6 Turn the idle mixture screw counterclockwise until the highest rpm reading is obtained. On carburetors incorporating two idle mixture screws, turn both screws equally, unless the engine demands otherwise.

7 Readjust the engine idle speed to the specified rpm.

8 Connect the by-pass valve air inlet hose (if so equipped).

36 Differential lubricant change

1 Some differentials can be drained by removing a drain plug, while on others it is necessary to remove the cover plate on the differential housing. Because of this, be sure to buy a new gasket at the same time the gear lubricant is purchased.

2 Move a drain pan (at least five pint capacity), rags, newspapers and wrenches under the vehicle.

3 On drain plug-equipped differentials, remove the fill plug, followed by the drain plug and allow the lubricant to drain into the pan. When it is completely drained, replace the drain plug and refill the differential with the specified lubricant to the base of the fill plug hole. Install the fill plug and tighten it securely.

4 On differentials without drain plugs, remove the bolts on the lower half of the differential cover plate. Use the upper bolts to keep the cover loosely attached to the differential. Allow the lubricant to drain into the drain pan, then completely remove the cover.

5 Using a lint-free rag, clean the inside of the cover and accessible areas of the differential housing. As this is done, check for chipped gears and metal particles in the lubricant, indicating the differential should be more thoroughly inspected and/or repaired (see Chapter 8 for more information).

6 Thoroughly clean the gasket mating surface on the cover and the differential housing. Use a gasket scraper or putty knife to remove all traces of the old gasket.

7 Apply a thin film of RTV-type gasket sealant to the cover flange and then press a new gasket into position on the cover. Make sure the bolt holes align properly.

8 Place the cover on the differential housing and install the bolts. Tighten the bolts a little at a time, working across the cover in a diagonal fashion until all bolts are tightened to 15 ft-lbs.

9 Remove the fill plug on the side of the differential housing or cover and fill the housing with the proper lubricant until the level is at the bottom of the plug hole.

10 Install the plug and tighten it securely.

37 Automatic transmission fluid change

1 At the specified time intervals, the transmission fluid should be changed and the filter replaced with a new one. Since there is no drain plug, the transmission oil pan must be removed from the bottom of the transmission to drain the fluid.

2 Before draining, purchase the specified transmission fluid (see *Recommended lubricants and fluids)* and a new filter. The necessary gaskets should be included with the filter; if not, purchase an oil pan gasket and an O-ring seal.

3 Other tools necessary for this job include:

Jackstands to support the vehicle in a raised position
A wrench to remove the oil pan bolts
A drain pan capable of holding at least six quarts
Newspapers and clean rags

4 The fluid should be drained immediately after the vehicle has been driven. This will remove any built-up sediment better than if the fluid were cold. Because of this, it may be wise to wear protective gloves (fluid temperature can exceed 350°F in a hot transmission).

5 After the vehicle has been driven to warm up the fluid, raise it and place it on jackstands for access underneath. Make sure the vehicle is firmly supported by the four stands (place them under the frame rails).

6 Move the necessary equipment under the vehicle, being careful not to touch any of the hot exhaust components.

7 Place the drain pan under the transmission oil pan and remove the oil pan bolts along the rear and sides of the pan. *Loosen, but do not remove, the bolts at the front of the pan.*

8 Carefully pry the oil pan down at the rear, allowing the hot fluid to drain into the pan. If necessary, use a screwdriver to break the gasket seat at the rear of the pan; however, do not damage the pan or transmission gasket surfaces in the process.

9 Support the pan and remove the remaining bolts at the front. Lower the pan and drain the remaining fluid into the container. As this is done, check the fluid for metal particles, which may be an indication of internal transmission failure.

10 Now visible on the bottom of the transmission is the filter/strainer held in place by screws.

11 Remove the screws, the filter and the O-ring seal from the pick-up pipe.

12 Thoroughly clean the transmission oil pan with solvent. Inspect it for metal particles and foreign matter. Dry it with compressed air (if available).

13 Clean the filter mounting surface on the valve body. This surface should be smooth and free of damage and nicks.

14 Place the new O-ring in position on the pick-up pipe and install the strainer and pipe assembly.

15 Place the new gasket in position and retain it with petroleum jelly.

16 Lift the pan up to the bottom of the transmission and install the mounting bolts. Tighten the bolts in a diagonal fashion, working around the pan, until the bolts are tightened to 150 in-lbs.

17 Lower the vehicle.

18 Open the hood and remove the transmission fluid dipstick from its guide tube.

19 Since fluid capacities vary between the various transmission types, it is best to add a little fluid at a time, continually checking the level with the dipstick. Allow the fluid time to drain into the pan. Add fluid until the level just registers on the end of the dipstick. In most cases, a good starting point will be five quarts added to the transmission through the filler tube (use a funnel to prevent spills).

20 With the selector lever in Park, apply the parking brake and start the engine without depressing the accelerator pedal (if possible). Allow the engine to run at a slow idle for a few minutes.

21 With the brake pedal depressed and the parking brake applied, shift the transmission through all positions and then place it in Park.

22 Check the fluid level on the dipstick, adding as necessary to bring the level up to the Add 1 pint mark. Do not allow the fluid level to go above this point, as the transmission may then be overfull, necessitating the removal of the oil pan to drain out the excess fluid.

23 Look under the vehicle for leaks around the oil pan mating surface.

24 Push the dipstick firmly back into its tube and drive the vehicle to reach normal operating temperature (15 miles of highway driving or its equivalent in the city). Park the vehicle on a level surface and check the fluid level on the dipstick with the engine idling and the transmission in Park. The level should now be at the Full mark on the dipstick. If not, add more fluid as necessary to bring the level up to this point. Again, do not overfill.

Chapter 2 Part A
General engine overhaul procedures

Contents

Crankshaft – inspection	16
Crankshaft – removal	12
Cylinder head – cleaning and inspection	8
Cylinder head – disassembly	7
Cylinder head – reassembly	10
Engine block – cleaning	13
Engine block – inspection	14
Engine disassembly – general information	6
Engine overhaul – general information	3
Engine rebuilding alternatives	4
Engine removal – methods and precautions	5
General information	1
Initial start-up and break-in after overhaul	20
Main and connecting rod bearings – inspection	17
Piston/connecting rod assembly – inspection	15
Piston/connecting rod assembly – installation and bearing oil clearance check	19
Piston/connecting rod assembly – removal	11
Piston rings – installation	18
Repair operations possible with the engine in the vehicle	2
Valves – servicing	9

1 General information

Included in this portion of Chapter 2 are general overhaul procedures common to all engines used in the vehicles covered by this manual. The material ranges from advice concerning how to prepare for and approach an engine overhaul to detailed, step-by-step procedures covering removal and installation of internal engine components and the inspection of parts.

Keep in mind that the information here should be used in conjunction with one of the other Parts of Chapter 2 (depending on the particular engine involved). To accomplish a typical engine overhaul, refer to the procedures in the appropriate Part of Chapter 2 to remove the engine from the vehicle and begin engine disassembly. Once the external components have been removed, proceed to Chapter 2, Part A, for the remainder of the engine teardown, certain cleaning and inspection procedures and the installation of internal parts. Return to the appropriate Part of Chapter 2 to complete engine reassembly and install it in the vehicle.

In order to avoid confusion and reduce the possibility of errors, all specifications and clearances for each particular engine are included in the appropriate Part of Chapter 2 – not Part A.

2 Repair operations possible with the engine in the vehicle

1 Many major repair operations can be accomplished without removing the engine from the vehicle.

2 It is a very good idea to clean the engine compartment and the exterior of the engine with some type of pressure washer before any work is begun. A clean engine will make the job easier and will prevent the possibility of getting dirt into internal areas of the engine.

3 Remove the hood (Chapter 12) and cover the fenders to provide as much working room as possible and to prevent damage to the painted surfaces.

4 If oil or coolant leaks develop, indicating a need for gasket or seal replacement, the repairs can generally be made with the engine in the vehicle. The oil pan gasket, the cylinder head gasket(s), intake and exhaust manifold gaskets, timing chain cover gaskets and the front and rear crankshaft oil seals are accessible with the engine in place. In the case of the rear crankshaft oil seal on the 151 cubic-inch four-cylinder engine, the transmission, the clutch components and the flywheel driveplate must be removed first.

5 Exterior engine components, such as the starter motor, the alternator, the distributor, the fuel pump and the carburetor, as well as the intake and exhaust manifolds, are quite easily removed for repair with the engine in place.

6 Since the cylinder head(s) can be removed without pulling the engine, valve component servicing can also be accomplished with the engine in the vehicle.

7 Replacement, repairs to or inspection of the timing gears or sprockets and chain and the oil pump are all possible with the engine in place.

8 In extreme cases caused by a lack of necessary equipment, repair or replacement of piston rings, pistons, connecting rods and rod bearings and reconditioning of the cylinder bores is possible with the engine in the vehicle. However, this practice is not recommended because of the cleaning and preparation work that must be done to the components involved.

9 Detailed removal, inspection, repair and installation procedures for the above mentioned components can be found in the appropriate Part of Chapter 2 or the other Chapters in this manual.

3 Engine overhaul – general information

It is not always easy to determine when, or if, an engine should be completely overhauled, as a number of factors must be considered.

High mileage is not necessarily an indication that an overhaul is needed while low mileage, on the other hand, does not preclude the need for an overhaul. Frequency of servicing is probably the single most important consideration. An engine that has regular (and frequent) oil and filter changes, as well as other required maintenance, will most likely give many thousands of miles of reliable service. Conversely, a neglected engine may require an overhaul very early in its life.

Excessive oil consumption is an indication that piston rings and/or valve guides are in need of attention (make sure that oil leaks are not responsible before deciding that the rings and guides are bad). Have a cylinder compression or leak-down test performed by an experienced tune-up mechanic to determine for certain the extent of the work required.

If the engine is making obvious 'knocking' or rumbling noises, the connecting rod and/or main bearings are probably at fault. Check the oil pressure with a gauge (installed in place of the oil pressure sending unit) and compare it to the Specifications. If it is extremely low, the bearings and/or oil pump are probably worn out.

Loss of power, rough running, excessive valve train noise and high fuel consumption rates may also point to the need for an overhaul (especially if they are all present at the same time). If a complete tune-up does not remedy the situation, major mechanical work is the only solution.

An engine overhaul generally involves restoring the internal parts to the specifications of a new engine. During an overhaul, the piston rings are replaced and the cylinder walls are reconditioned (rebored and/or honed). If a rebore is done, then new pistons are also required. The main and connecting rod bearings are replaced with new ones and, if necessary, the crankshaft may be reground to restore the journals. Generally, the valves are serviced as well, since they are usually in less-than-perfect condition at this point. While the engine is being overhauled, other components such as the carburetor, the distributor, the starter and the alternator can be rebuilt also. The end result should be a like-new engine that will give as many trouble-free miles as the original.

Before beginning the engine overhaul, read through the entire procedure to familiarize yourself with the scope and requirements of the job. Overhauling an engine is not that difficult, but it is time consuming. Plan on the vehicle being tied up for a minimum of two weeks, especially if parts must be taken to an automotive machine shop for repair or reconditioning. Check on availability of parts and make sure that any necessary special tools and equipment are obtained in advance. Most work can be done with typical shop hand tools, although a number of precision measuring tools are required for inspecting parts to determine if they must be replaced. Often a reputable automotive machine shop will handle the inspection of parts and offer advice concerning reconditioning and replacement. **Note:** *Always wait until the engine has been completely disassembled and all components, especially the engine block, have been inspected before deciding what service and repair operations must be performed by an automotive machine shop.* Since the block's condition will be the major factor to consider when determining whether to overhaul the original engine or buy a rebuilt one, never purchase parts or have machine work done on other components until the block has been thoroughly inspected. As a general rule, time is the primary cost of an overhaul, so it does not pay to install worn or sub-standard parts.

As a final note, to ensure maximum life and minimum trouble from a rebuilt engine, everything must be assembled with care in a spotlessly clean environment.

4 Engine rebuilding alternatives

1 The home mechanic is faced with a number of options when performing an engine overhaul. The decision to replace the engine block, piston/connecting rod assemblies and crankshaft depends on a number of factors, with the number one consideration being the condition of the block. Other considerations are cost, access to machine shop facilities, parts availability, time required to complete the project and experience.

2 Some of the rebuilding alternatives include:

Individual parts – *If the inspection procedures reveal that the engine block and most engine components are in reusable condition, purchasing individual parts may be the most economical alternative. The block, crankshaft and piston/connecting rod assemblies should all be inspected carefully. Even if the block shows little wear, the cylinder bores should receive a finish hone; a job for an automotive machine shop*

Master kit *(crankshaft kit) – This rebuild package usually consists of a reground crankshaft and a matched set of pistons and connecting rods. The pistons will already be installed on the connecting rods. Piston rings and the necessary bearings may or may not be included in the kit. These kits are commonly available for standard cylinder bores, as well as for engine blocks which have been bored to a regular oversize.*

Short block – *A short block consists of an engine block with a crankshaft and piston/connecting rod assemblies already installed. All new bearings are incorporated and all clearances will be correct. Depending on where the short block is purchased, a guarantee may be included. The existing camshaft, valve train components, cylinder head(s) and external parts can be bolted to the short block with little or no machine shop work necessary.*

Long block – *A long block consists of a short block plus oil pump, oil pan, cylinder head(s), valve cover(s), camshaft and valve train components, timing gears or sprockets and chain and timing gear/chain cover. All components are installed with new bearings, seals and gaskets incorporated throughout. The installation of manifolds and external parts is all that is necessary. Some form of guarantee is usually included with the purchase.*

3 Give careful thought to which alternative is best for you and discuss the situation with local automotive machine shops, auto parts dealers or dealership partsmen before ordering or purchasing replacement parts.

5 Engine removal – methods and precautions

If it has been decided that an engine must be removed for overhaul or major repair work, certain preliminary steps should be taken.

Locating a suitable work area is extremely important. A shop is, of course, the most desirable place to work. Adequate work space along with storage space for the vehicle is very important. If a shop or garage is not available, at the very least a flat, level, clean work surface made of concrete or asphalt is required.

Cleaning of the engine compartment and engine prior to removal will help keep tools clean and organized.

An engine hoist or A-frame will also be necessary. Make sure that the equipment is rated in excess of the combined weight of the engine and its accessories. Safety is of primary importance, considering the potential hazards involved in lifting the engine out of the vehicle.

If the engine is being removed by a novice, a helper should be available. Advice and aid from someone more experienced would also be helpful. There are many instances when one person cannot simultaneously perform all of the operations required when lifting the engine out of the vehicle.

Plan the operation ahead of time. Arrange for or obtain all of the tools and equipment you will need prior to beginning the job. Some of the equipment necessary to perform engine removal and installation safely and with relative ease are (in addition to an engine hoist) a heavy duty floor jack, complete sets of wrenches and sockets as described in the front of this manual, wooden blocks and plenty of rags and cleaning solvent for mopping up the inevitable spills. If the hoist is to be rented, make sure that you arrange for it in advance and perform beforehand all of the operations possible without it. This will save you money and time.

Plan for the vehicle to be out of use for a considerable amount of time. A machine shop will be required to perform some of the work which the home mechanic cannot accomplish due to a lack of special equipment. These shops often have a busy schedule so it would be wise to consult them prior to removing the engine in order to accurately estimate the amount of time required to rebuild or repair components that may need work.

Always use extreme caution when removing and installing the engine; serious injury can result from careless actions. Plan ahead. Take your time and a job of this nature, although major, can be accomplished successfully.

6 Engine disassembly – general information

It is much easier to dismantle and repair the engine if it is mounted on a portable-type engine stand. These stands can often be rented, for a reasonable fee, from an equipment rental yard. Before the engine is mounted on a stand, the flywheel/driveplate should be removed from the engine (refer to the appropriate Section).

If a stand is not available, it is possible to dismantle the engine with it blocked up on a sturdy workbench or on the floor. Be extra careful not to tip or drop the engine when working without a stand.

If you are obtaining a factory replacement or reconditioned engine, all external components must come off first – just as they will if you are doing a complete engine overhaul yourself. These include:

Alternator and brackets
Distributor and spark plug wires
Thermostat and cover
Oil filter
Carburetor
Intake and exhaust manifolds
Water pump
Engine mount brackets
Clutch and flywheel or driveplate

Note: *When removing the external components from the engine, pay close attention to details that may be helpful or important during installation. Look for the correct positioning of gaskets, seals, spacers,* *pins, washers, bolts and other small items.*

If you are obtaining what is termed a 'short block', which consists of the block, crankshaft, pistons and connecting rods all assembled, then the cylinder head(s), oil pan and oil pump will have to be removed also.

Remove all of the components according to the procedures described in the appropriate Chapters of this manual.

7 Cylinder head – disassembly

Note: *New and rebuilt cylinder heads are commonly available for most engines at dealerships and auto parts stores. Due to the fact that some specialized tools are necessary for the disassembly and inspection procedures, and replacement parts may not be readily available, it may be more practical and economical for the home mechanic to purchase a replacement head (or heads) rather than taking the time to disassemble, inspect and recondition the original head(s).*

1 Cylinder head disassembly involves removal and disassembly of the intake and exhaust valves and their related components. If so equipped, remove the rocker arm nuts/bolts, balls (or pivots) and rocker arms. Label the parts, or store then separately so they can be reinstalled in the same location.

2 Before the valves are removed, arrange to label and store them, along with their related components, so they can be kept separate and reinstalled in the same valve guides they are removed from. Also, measure the valve spring installed height (for each valve) and compare it to the Specifications. If it is greater than specified, the valve seats and valve faces need attention.

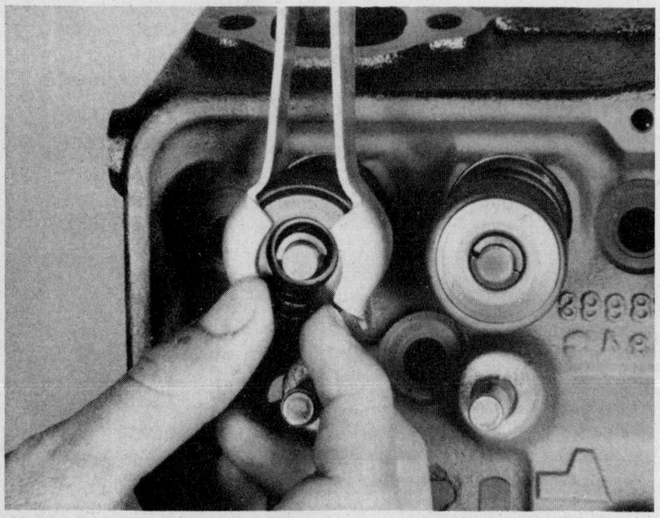

7.3 Use a valve spring compressor to compress the springs, then remove the keepers from the valve stem

3 Compress the valve spring on the first valve with a spring compressor and remove the keepers (photo). Carefully release the valve spring compressor and remove the retainer (or rotator), the shield (if so equipped), the springs, the seal (or oil deflector), the spring seat and the valve from the head. If the valve binds in the guide (won't pull through), push it back into the head and deburr the area around the keeper groove with a fine file or whetstone.

4 Repeat the procedure for the remaining valves. Remember to keep all the parts for each valve together so they can be resinstalled in the same locations.

5 Once the valves have been removed and safely stored, the head should be thoroughly cleaned and inspected. If a complete engine overhaul is being done, finish the engine disassembly procedures before beginning the cylinder head cleaning and inspection process.

8 Cylinder head – cleaning and inspection

1 Thorough cleaning of the cylinder head and related valve train

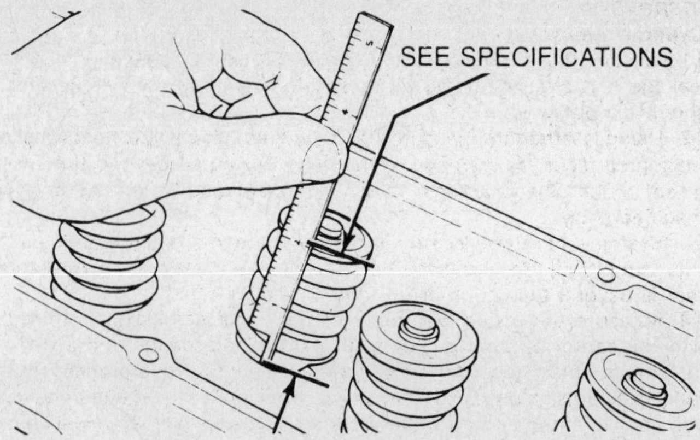

Fig. 2.1 Measuring the installed valve spring height with a steel rule (Sec 7)

components, followed by a detailed inspection, will enable you to decide how much valve service work must be done during the engine overhaul.

Cleaning

2 Scrape away all traces of old gasket material and sealing compound from the head gasket, intake manifold and exhaust manifold sealing surfaces.

3 Remove any scale built up around the coolant passages.

4 Run a stiff wire brush through the oil holes to remove any deposits that may have formed in them.

5 It is a good idea to run an appropriate size tap into each of the threaded holes to remove any corrosion or thread sealant that may be present. If compressed air is available, use it to clear the holes of debris produced by this operation.

6 Clean the exhaust and intake manifold stud threads in a similar manner with an appropriate size die. Clean the rocker arm pivot bolt or stud threads with a wire brush.

7 Next, clean the cylinder head with solvent and dry it thoroughly. Compressed air will speed the drying process and ensure that all holes and recessed areas are clean. **Note:** *Decarbonizing chemicals are available and may prove very useful when cleaning cylinder heads and valve train components. They are very caustic and should be used with caution. Be sure to follow the instructions on the container.*

8 Clean the rocker arms, pivots and pushrods with solvent and dry them thoroughly. Compressed air will speed the drying process and can be used to clean out the oil passages.

9 Clean all the valve springs, keepers, retainers, rotators, shields and spring seats with solvent and dry them thoroughly. Do the parts from one valve at a time so no mixing of parts between valves occurs.

10 Scrape off any heavy deposits that may have formed on the valves, then use a motorized wire brush to remove deposits from the valve heads and stems. Again, make sure the valves do not get mixed up.

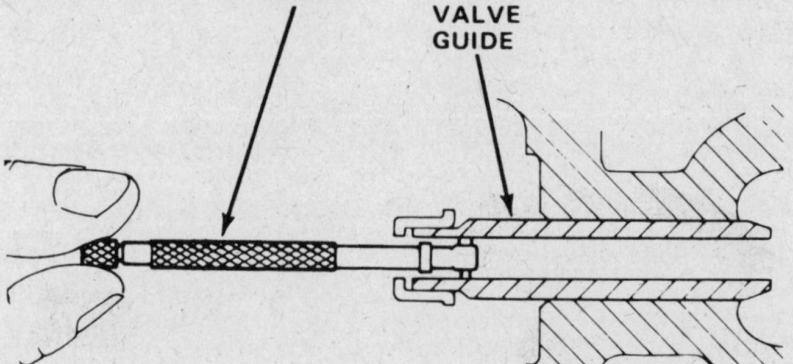

Fig. 2.2 Use a small hole gauge to determine the inside diameter of the valve guides (the gauge is then measured with a micrometer) (Sec 8)

Inspection

Cylinder head

11 Inspect the head very carefully for cracks, evidence of coolant leakage and other damage. If cracks are found, a new cylinder head should be obtained.

12 Using a straightedge and feeler gauges, check the head gasket mating surfaces for warpage. If the head is warped beyond the limits given in the Specifications, it can be resurfaced at an automotive machine shop.

13 Examine the valve seats in each of the combustion chambers. If they are pitted, cracked or burned, the head will require valve service that is beyond the scope of the home mechanic.

14 Measure the inside diameters of the valve guides (at both ends and the center of each guide) with a small hole gauge and a 0-to-1 inch micrometer. Record the measurements for future reference. These measurements, along with the valve stem diameter measurements, will enable you to compute the valve stem-to-guide clearances. These clearances, when compared to the Specifications, will be one factor that will determine the extent of valve service work required. The guides are measured at the ends and at the center to determine if they are worn in a bell-mouth pattern (more wear at the ends). If they are, guide reconditioning or replacement as necessary. As an alternative, use a dial indicator to measure the lateral movement of each valve stem with the valve in the guide and approximately $\frac{1}{16}$-inch off the seat (see the accompanying illustration).

Rocker arm components

15 Check the rocker arm faces (that contact the pushrod ends and valve stems) for pitting, wear and roughness. Check the pivot contact areas as well.

16 Inspect the pushrod ends for scuffing and excessive wear. Roll the pushrod on a flat surface, such as a piece of glass, to determine if it is bent.

17 Any damaged or excessively worn parts must be replaced with new ones.

Valves

18 Carefully inspect each valve face for cracks, pits and burned spots. Check the valve stem and neck for cracks. Rotate the valve and check for any obvious indication that it is bent. Check the end of the stem for pits and excessive wear. The presence of any of these conditions indicates the need for valve service by a properly equipped professional.

19 Measure the width of the valve margin (on each valve) and compare it to the Specifications. Any valve with a margin narrower than specified will have to be replaced with a new one.

20 Measure the valve stem diameter (photo). **Note**: *The exhaust valves used in the four-cylinder engine have tapered stems and are approximately 0.001 inch larger at the tip end than at the head end.* By subtracting the stem diameter from the corresponding valve guide diameter, the valve stem-to-guide clearance is obtained. Compare the results to the Specifications. If the stem-to-guide clearance is greater than specified, the guides will have to be reconditioned and new valves may have to be installed, depending on the condition of the old ones.

Valve components

21 Check each valve spring for wear (on the ends) and pits. Measure

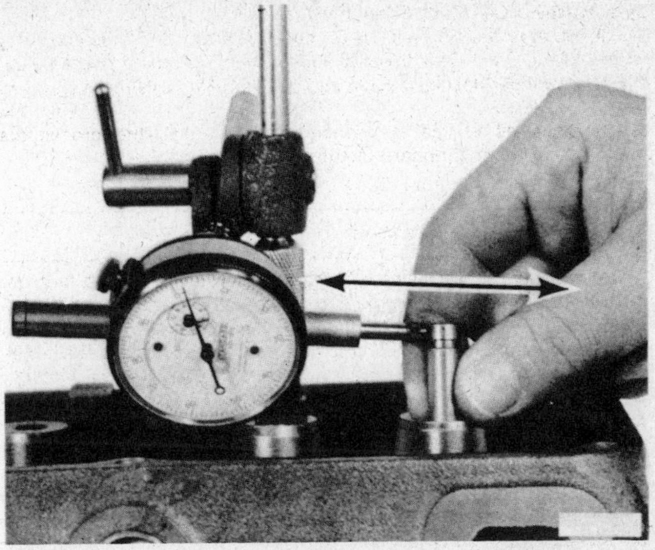

Fig. 2.3 A dial indicator can also be used to determine the valve stem-to-guide clearance (Sec 8)

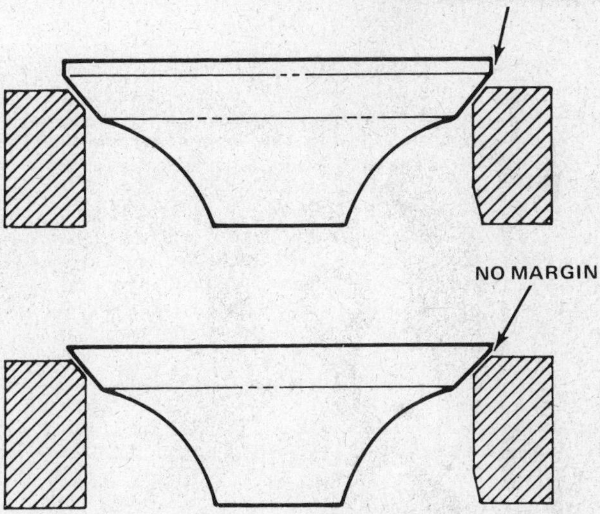

Fig. 2.4 The margin width on each valve must be as specified (if no margin exists, the valve must be replaced) (Sec 8)

2A

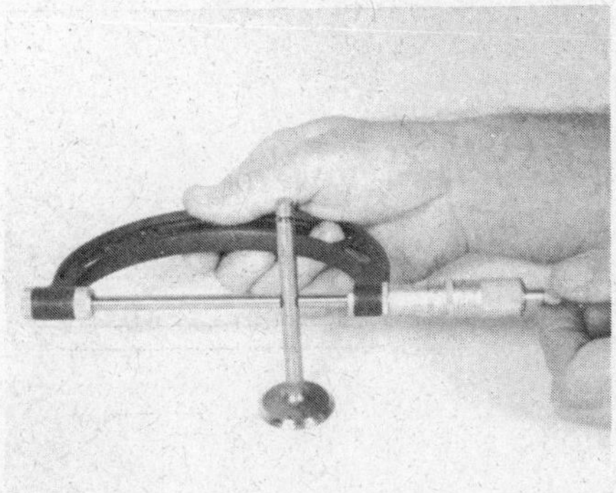

8.20 Measure the valve stem diameter at three points

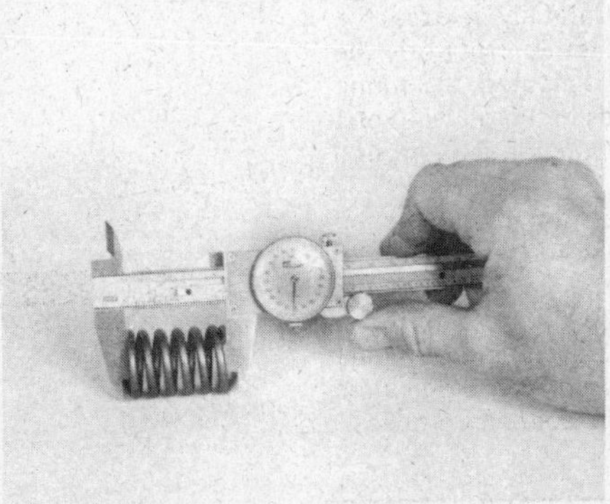

8.21A Measure the free length of each valve spring with a dial or Vernier caliper

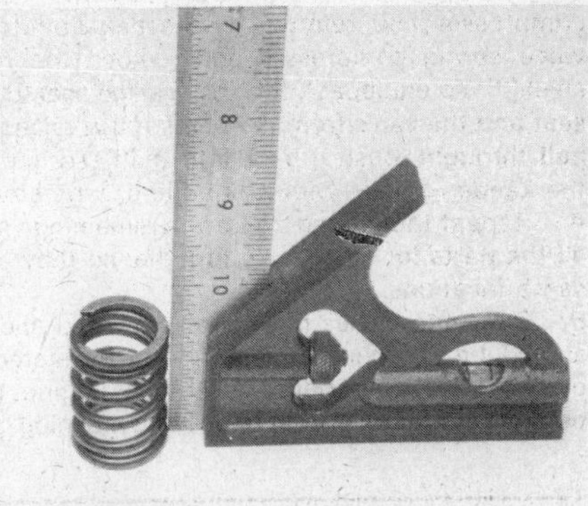

8.21B Check each valve spring for squareness

the free length (photo) and compare it to the Specifications. Any springs that are shorter than specified have sagged and should not be reused. Stand the spring on a flat surface and check it for squareness (photo).

22 Check the spring retainers (or rotators) and keepers for obvious wear and cracks. Any questionable parts should be replaced with new ones, as extensive damage will occur in the event of failure during engine operation.

23 If the inspection process indicates that the valve components are in generally poor condition and worn beyond the limits specified, which is usually the case in an engine that is being overhauled, reassemble the valves in the cylinder head and refer to Section 9 for valve servicing recommendations.

24 If the inspection turns up no excessively worn parts, and if the valve faces and seats are in good condition, the valve train components can be reinstalled in the cylinder head without major servicing. Refer to the appropriate Section for cylinder head reassembly procedures.

9 Valves – servicing

1 Because of the complex nature of the job and the special tools and equipment required, servicing of the valves, the valve seats and the valve guides (commonly known as a 'valve job') is best left to a professional.

2 The home mechanic can remove and disassemble the head, do the initial cleaning and inspection, then reassemble and deliver the head to a dealer service department or a reputable automotive machine shop for the actual valve servicing.

3 The dealer service department, or automotive machine shop, will remove the valves and springs, recondition or replace the valves and valve seats, recondition the valve guides, check and replace the valve springs, spring retainers or rotators and keepers (as necessary), replace the valve seals with new ones, reassemble the valve components and make sure the installed spring height is correct. The cylinder head gasket surface will also be resurfaced if it is warped.

4 After the valve job has been performed by a professional, the head will be in like-new condition. When the head is returned, be sure to clean it again, very thoroughly (before installation on the engine), to remove any metal particles and abrasive grit that may still be present from the valve service or head resurfacing operations. Use compressed air, if available, to blow out all the oil holes and passages.

10 Cylinder head – reassembly

1 Regardless of whether or not the head was sent to an automotive machine shop for valve servicing, make sure it is clean before beginning reassembly.

2 If the head was sent out for valve servicing, the valves and related components will already be in place.

3 Lay all the spring seats in position, then lubricate and install new seals (or deflectors) on each of the valve guides *(six-cylinder and V8 engines only). On four-cylinder engines* the seals are installed in the lower grooves in the valves after the springs are compressed (lubricate the seals before installation.

4 Next, install the valves (taking care not to damage the new seals), the springs, the shields (if so equipped) the retainers (or rotators) and the keepers. Coat the valve stems with clean multi-purpose grease (or engine assembly lube) before slipping them into the guides. When compressing the springs with the valve spring compressor, do not let the retainers contact the valve guide seals or deflectors (six-cylinder and V8 engines only). Make certain that the keepers are securely locked in their retaining grooves.

5 Double check the installed valve spring height. If it was correct before disassembly, it should still be within the specified limits.

6 On *four-cylinder engines* only, check the valve stem seals with a vacuum pump and adapter (photo). A properly installed seal should not leak.

7 Install the rocker arms and tighten the bolts/nuts to the specified torque. Be sure to lubricate the pivots with multi-purpose grease or engine assembly lube.

11 Piston/connecting rod assembly – removal

1 Prior to removing the piston/connecting rod assemblies, remove the cylinder head(s), and the oil pan by referring to the appropriate Sections.

2 Using a ridge reamer, completely remove the ridge at the top of each cylinder (follow the manufacturer's instructions provided with the ridge reaming tool) (photo). Failure to remove the ridge before attempting to remove the piston/connecting rod assemblies will result in piston breakage.

3 With the engine in the upside-down position, remove the oil pickup tube and oil pump from the bottom of the engine block.

4 Before the connecting rods are removed, check the end play as follows. Mount a dial indicator with its stem in-line with the crankshaft and touching the side of the number one cylinder connecting rod cap.

5 Push the connecting rod forward, as far as possible, and zero the dial indicator. Next, push the connecting rod all the way to the rear and check the reading on the dial indicator. The distance that it moves is the end play. If the end play exceeds the service limit, a new connecting rod will be required. Repeat the procedure for the remaining connecting rods.

6 An alternative method is to slip feeler gauges between the connecting rod and the crankshaft throw until the play is removed (photo). The end play is then equal to the thickness of the feeler gauge(s).

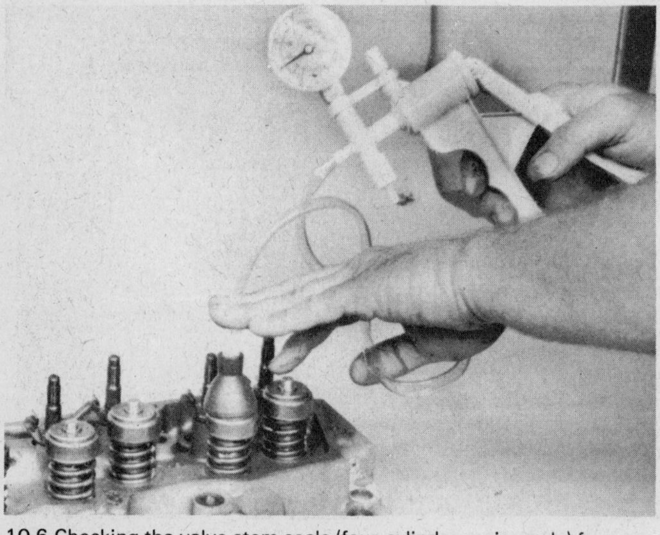

10.6 Checking the valve stem seals (four-cylinder engine only) for leakage

11.2 A special tool is required to remove the ridge from the top of each cylinder

11.6 Checking connecting rod end play with a feeler gauge

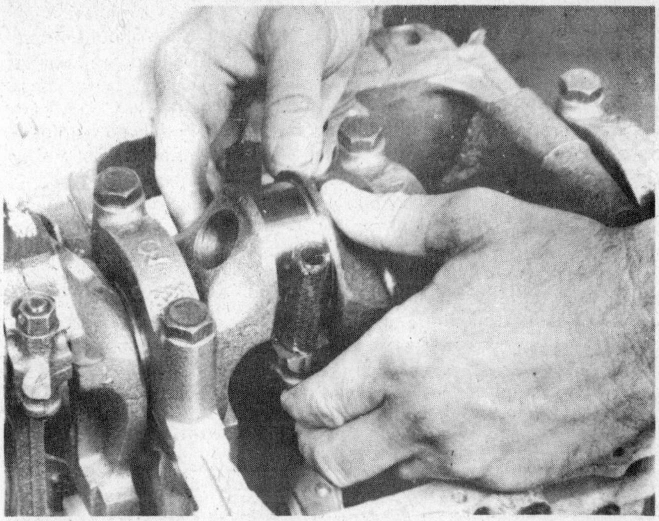

11.8 To prevent damage to the crankshaft journals and cylinder walls, slip sections of hose over the rod bolts before removing the pistons

7 Check the connecting rods and connecting rod caps for identification marks. If they are not plainly marked, identify each rod and cap using a small punch to make the appropriate number of indentations to indicate the cylinders they are associated with.

8 Loosen each of the connecting rod cap nuts approximately ½ turn each. Remove the number one connecting rod cap and bearing insert. Do not drop the bearing insert out of the cap. Slip a short length of plastic or rubber hose over each connecting rod cap bolt (to protect the crankshaft journal and cylinder wall when the piston is removed) (photo) and push the connecting rod/piston assembly out through the top of the engine. Use a wooden tool to push on the upper bearing insert in the connecting rod. If resistance is felt, double-check to make sure that all of the ridge was removed from the cylinder.

9 Repeat the procedure for the remaining cylinders. After removal, reassemble the connecting rod caps and bearing inserts in their respective connecting rods and install the cap nuts finger tight. Leaving the old bearing inserts in place until reassembly will help prevent the connecting rod bearing surfaces from being accidentally nicked or gouged.

12 Crankshaft – removal

1 Before beginning this procedure, the preliminary steps outlined in Chapters 2B, 2C or 2D (as appropriate) must be completed.

2 If not already done, remove the piston assemblies from the engine block, as described in Section 11. Be sure to mark each connecting rod and bearing cap so they will be properly mated during reassembly.

3 Before the crankshaft is removed, check the end play as follows. Mount a dial indicator with the stem in-line with the crankshaft and just touching one of the crank throws (see accompanying illustration).

4 Push the crankshaft all the way to the rear and zero the dial indicator. Next, pry the crankshaft to the front as far as possible and check the reading on the dial indicator. The distance that it moves is the end play. If it is greater than specified, check the crankshaft thrust surfaces for wear. If no wear is apparent, new main bearings should correct the end play.

5 If a dial indicator is not available, feeler gauges can be used. Gently pry or push the crankshaft all the way to the front of the engine. Slip the feeler gauges between the crankshaft and the front face of the thrust main bearing (photo) to determine the clearance (which is equivalent to crankshaft end play).

6 Loosen each of the main bearing cap bolts ¼ of a turn at a time, until they can be removed by hand. Check the main bearing caps to see if they are marked as to their locations. They are usually numbered consecutively (beginning with 1) from the front of the engine to the rear. If they are not, mark then with number stamping dies or a center punch (photo). Most main bearing caps have a cast-in arrow, which

12.5 Checking crankshaft end play with a feeler gauge (four-cylinder engine shown)

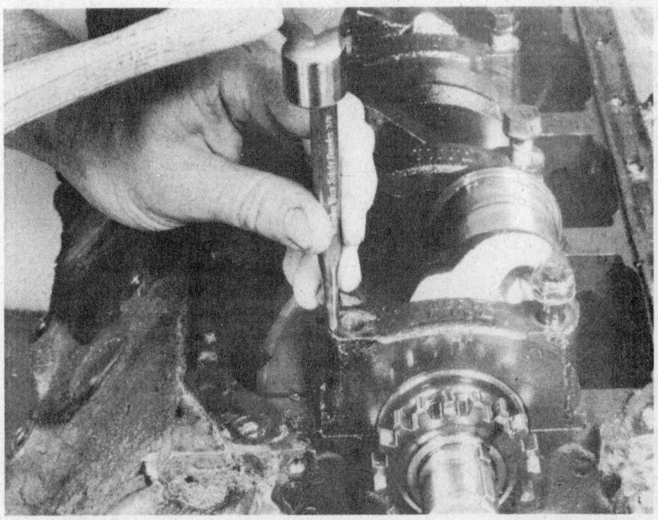

12.6 Mark the bearing caps with a center punch before removing them

points to the front of the engine.
7 Gently tap the caps with a soft-faced hammer, then separate them from the engine block. If necessary use the main bearing cap bolts as levers to remove the caps. Try not to drop the bearing if it comes out with the cap.
8 Carefully lift the crankshaft out of the engine. It is a good idea to have an assistant available, as the crankshaft is quite heavy. With the bearing inserts in place in the engine block and the main bearing caps, return the caps to their respective locations on the engine block and tighten the bolts finger tight.

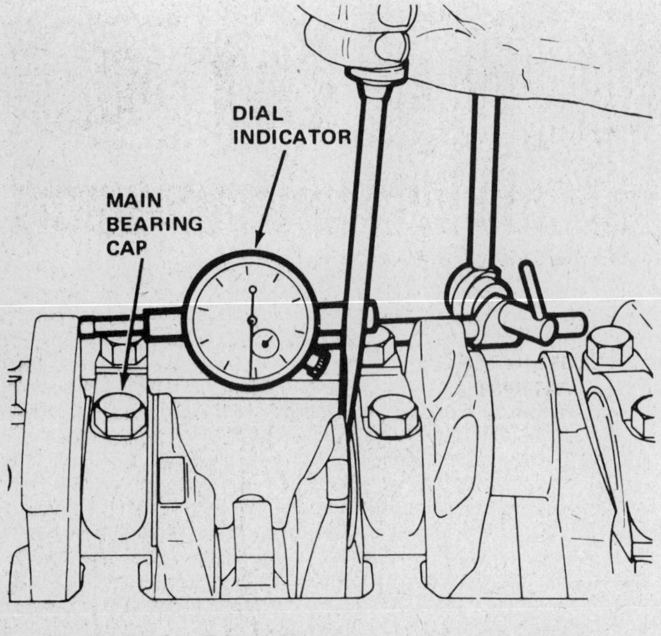

Fig. 2.5 Checking crankshaft end play with a dial indicator (Sec 12)

13 Engine block – cleaning

1 Remove the soft plugs from the engine block. To do this, knock the plugs into the block (using a hammer and punch), then grasp them with a large pliers and pull them back through the holes (photo).
2 Using a gasket scraper, remove all traces of gasket material from the engine block. Be very careful not to nick or gouge the gasket sealing surfaces.
3 Remove the main bearing caps and separate the bearing inserts from the caps and the engine block. Tag the bearings according to which cylinder they were removed from (and whether they were in the cap or the block) and set them aside.
4 Using a hex wrench of the appropriate size, remove the threaded oil gallery plugs from the front and back of the block.
5 If the engine is extremely dirty, it should be taken to an automotive machine shop to be steam cleaned or hot tanked. Any bearings left in the block (such as the camshaft bearings) will be damaged by the cleaning process, so plan on having new ones installed while the block is at the machine shop.
6 After the block is returned, clean all oil holes and oil galleries one more time (brushes for cleaning oil holes and galleries are available at most auto parts stores). Flush the passages with warm water (until the water runs clear), dry the block thoroughly and wipe all machined surfaces with a light, rust-preventative oil. If you have access to compressed air, use it to speed the drying process and to blow out all of the oil holes and galleries.
7 If the block is not extremely dirty or sludged up, you can do an adequate cleaning job with warm soapy water and a stiff brush. Take plenty of time and do a thorough job. Regardless of the cleaning method used, be very sure to thoroughly clean all oil holes and galleries, dry the block completely and coat all machined surfaces with light oil.
8 The threaded holes in the block must be clean to ensure accurate torque readings during reassembly. Run the proper size tap into each of the holes to remove any rust, corrosion, thread sealant or sludge and to restore any damaged threads. If possible, use compressed air to clear the holes of debris produced by this operation. Now is a good time to thoroughly clean the threads on the head bolts and the main bearing cap bolts as well.
9 Reinstall the main bearing caps and tighten the bolts finger tight.
10 After coating the sealing surfaces of the new soft plugs with a good quality gasket sealer, install them in the engine block. Make sure they are driven in straight and seated properly, or leakage could result. Special tools are available for this purpose, but equally good results can be obtained using a large socket (with an outside diameter slightly larger than the outside diameter of the soft plug) and a large hammer.
11 If the engine is not going to be reassembled right away, cover it with a large plastic trash bag to keep it clean.

14 Engine block – inspection

1 Thoroughly clean the engine block as described in Section 13 and double-check to make sure that the ridge at the top of each cylinder has been completely removed.
2 Visually check the block for cracks, rust and corrosion. Look for stripped threads in the threaded holes. It is also a good idea to have the block checked for hidden cracks by an automotive machine shop

13.1 Using a pliers to remove a soft plug from the block

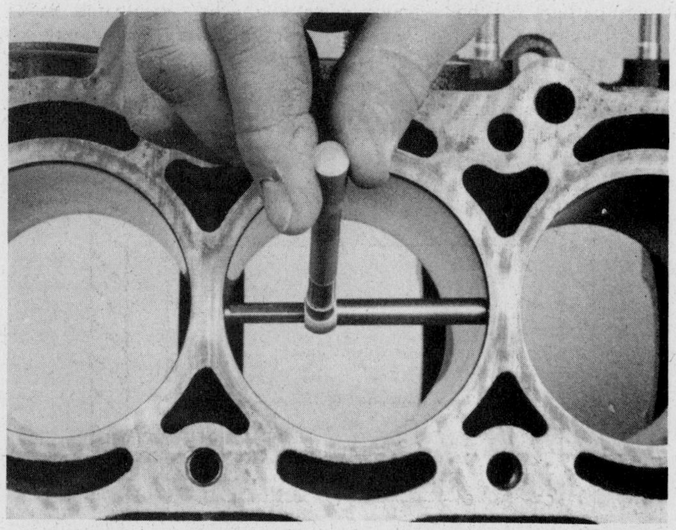

14.4A A telescoping gauge can be used to determine the cylinder bore diameter

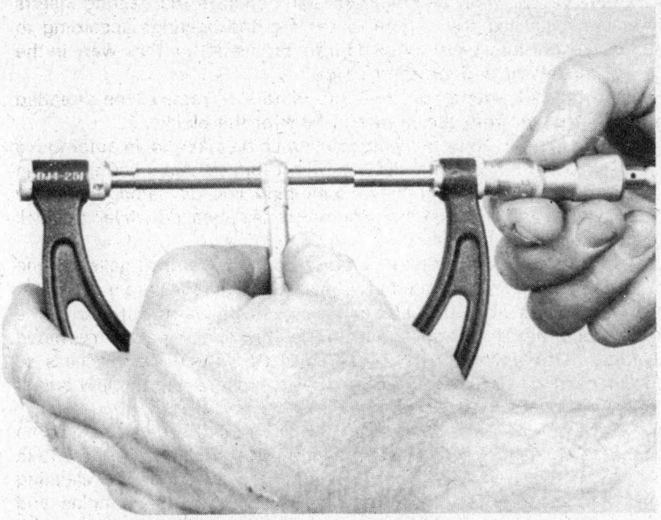
14.4B The gauge is then measured with a micrometer to determine the bore size in inches

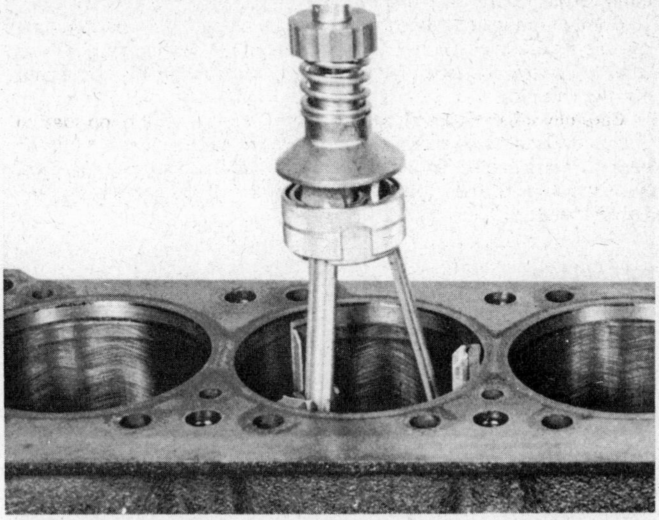
14.7 Honing a cylinder with a surfacing hone

that has the special equipment to do this type of work. If defects are found, have the block repaired, if possible, or replaced.

3 Check the cylinder bores for scuffing and scoring.

4 Using the appropriate precision measuring tools, measure each cylinder's diameter at the top (just under the ridge), center and bottom of the cylinder bore, parallel to the crankshaft axis (photos). Next, measure each cylinder's diameter at the same three locations across the crankshaft axis. Compare the results to the Specifications. If the cylinder walls are badly scuffed or scored, or if they are out-of-round or tapered beyond the limits given in the Specifications, have the engine block rebored and honed at an automotive machine shop. If a rebore is done, oversized pistons and rings will be required as well.

5 If the cylinders are in reasonably good condition and not worn to the outside of the limits, and if the piston-to-cylinder clearances can be maintained properly, then they do not have to be rebored; honing is all that is necessary.

6 Before honing the cylinders, install the main bearing caps (without the bearings) and tighten the bolts to the specified torque.

7 To perform the honing operation, you will need the proper size flexible hone (with fine stones), plenty of light oil or honing oil, some rags and an electric drill motor. Mount the hone in the drill motor, compress the stones and slip the hone into the first cylinder (photo). Lubricate the cylinder thoroughly, turn on the drill and move the hone up and down in the cylinder at a pace which will produce a fine cross-hatch pattern on the cylinder walls (with the cross-hatch lines intersecting at approximately a 60° angle). Be sure to use plenty of lubricant, and do not take off any more material than is absolutely necessary to produce the desired finish. Do not withdraw the hone from the cylinder while it is running. Instead, shut off the drill and continue moving the hone up and down in the cylinder until it comes to a complete stop, then compress the stones and withdraw the hone. Wipe the oil out of the cylinder and repeat the procedure on the remaining cylinders. Remember, do not remove too much material from the cylinder wall. If you do not have the tools or do not desire to perform the honing operation, most automotive machine shops will do it for a reasonable fee.

8 After the honing job is complete, chamfer the top edges of the cylinder bores with a small file so the rings will not catch when the pistons are installed.

9 Next, the entire engine block must be thoroughly washed again with warm soapy water to remove all traces of the abrasive grit produced during the honing operation. Be sure to run a brush through all oil holes and galleries and flush them with running water. After rinsing, dry the block and apply a coat of light rust preventative oil to all machined surfaces. Wrap the block in a plastic trash bag to keep it clean and set it aside until reassembly.

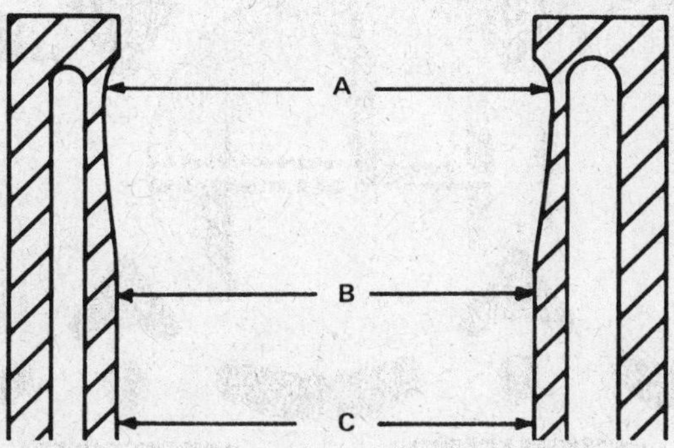

Fig. 2.6 Measure the diameter of each cylinder just under the wear ridge (A), at the center (B) and at the bottom (C) (Sec 14)

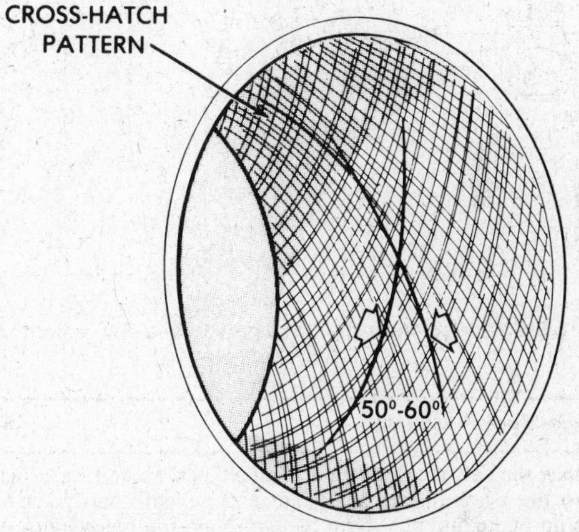

Fig. 2.7 The cylinder hone should leave a cross-hatch pattern with the lines intersecting at approximately a 60° angle (Sec 14)

15 Piston/connecting rod assembly – inspection

1 Before the inspection process can be carried out, the piston/connecting rod assemblies must be cleaned and the original rings removed from the pistons. **Note**: *Always use new piston rings when the engine is reassembled.*

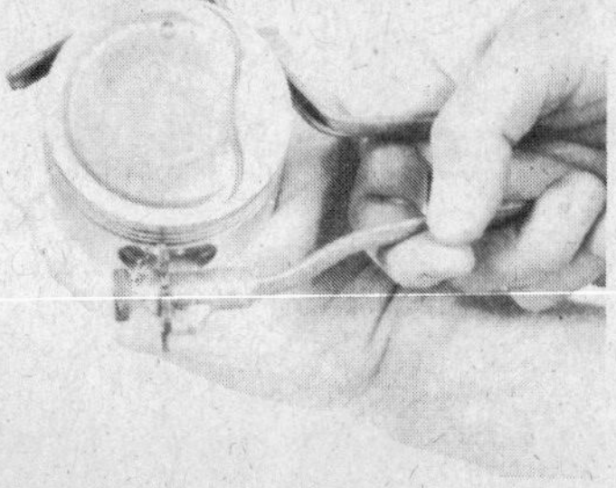

15.4 Cleaning the piston ring grooves with a piston ring groove cleaning tool

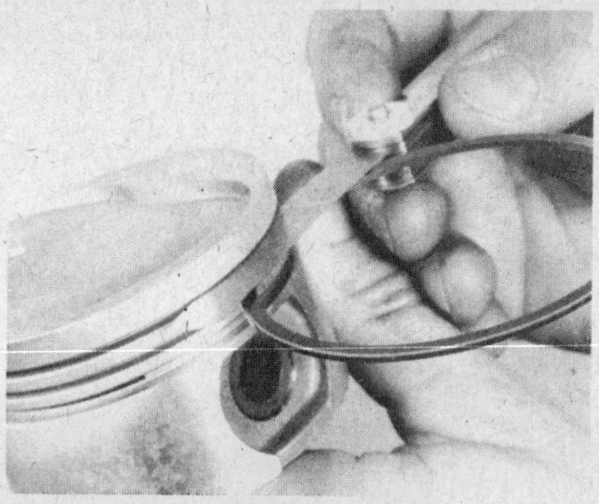

15.10 Checking the piston ring side clearance with a feeler gauge

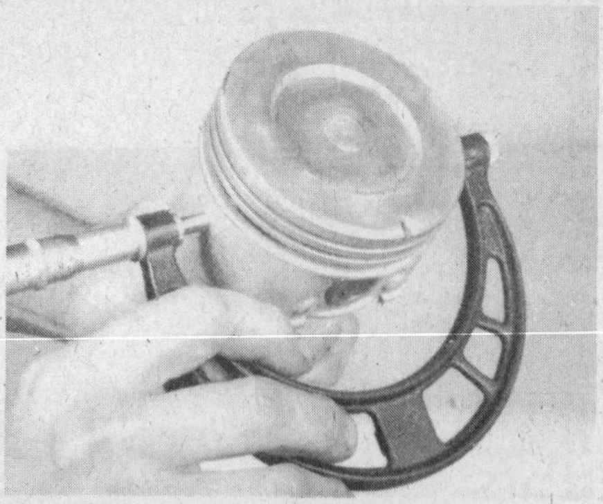

15.11 Measure the piston diameter directly in line with the piston pin hole

2 Using a piston ring installation tool, carefully remove the rings from the pistons. Do not nick or gouge the pistons in the process.
3 Scrape all traces of carbon from the top (or crown) of the piston. A hand-held wire brush or a piece of fine emery cloth can be used once the majority of the deposits have been scraped away. Do not, under any circumstances, use a wire brush mounted in a drill motor to remove deposits from the pistons. The piston material is soft and will be eroded away by the wire brush.
4 Use a piston ring groove cleaning tool to remove any carbon deposits from the ring grooves. If a tool is not available, a piece broken off the old ring will do the job. Be very careful to remove only the carbon deposits. Do not remove any metal and do not nick or scratch the sides of the ring grooves (photo).
5 Once the deposits have been removed, clean the piston/rod assemblies with solvent and dry them thoroughly. Make sure that the oil hole in the big end of the connecting rod and the oil return holes in the back sides of the ring grooves are clear.
6 If the pistons are not damaged or worn excessively, and if the engine block is not rebored, new pistons will not be necessary. Normal piston wear appears as even vertical wear on the piston thrust surfaces and slight looseness of the top ring in its groove. New piston rings, on the other hand, should always be used when an engine is rebuilt.
7 Carefully inspect each piston for cracks around the skirt, at the pin bosses and at the ring lands.
8 Look for scoring and scuffing (on the thrust faces of the skirt), holes (in the piston crown) and burned areas (at the edge of the crown). If the skirt is scored or scuffed, the engine may have been suffering from overheating and/or abnormal combustion, which caused excessively high operating temperatures. The cooling and lubrication systems should be checked thoroughly. A hole in the piston crown, an extreme to be sure, is an indication that abnormal combustion (preignition) was occurring. Burned areas at the edge of the piston crown are usually evidence of spark knock (detonation). If any of the above problems exist, the causes must be corrected or the damage will occur again.
9 Corrosion of the piston (evidenced by pitting) indicates that coolant is leaking into the combustion chamber and/or the crankcase. Again, the cause must be corrected or the problem may persist in the rebuilt engine.
10 Measure the piston ring side clearance by laying a new piston ring in each ring groove and slipping a feeler gauge in beside it (photo). Check the clearance at three or four locations around each groove. Be sure to use the correct ring for each groove; they are different. If the side clearance is greater than specified, new pistons and/or rings will have to be used.
11 Check the piston-to-bore clearance by measuring the bore (see Section 14) and the piston diameter (photo). Make sure that the pistons and bores are correctly matched. Measure the piston across the skirt, on the thrust faces (at a 90° angle to the piston pin), directly in line with the center of the pin hole. Subtract the piston diameter from the bore diameter to obtain the clearance. If it is greater than specified, the block will have to be rebored and new pistons and rings installed. Check the piston pin-to-rod clearance by twisting the piston and rod in opposite directions. Any noticeable play indicates that there is excessive wear, which must be corrected. The piston/connecting rod assemblies should be taken to an automotive machine shop to have new piston pins installed and the pistons and connecting rods rebored.
12 If the pistons must be removed from the connecting rods, such as when new pistons must be installed, or if the piston pins have too much play in them, they should be taken to an automotive machine shop. While they are there, it would be convenient to have the connecting rods checked for bend and twist, as automotive machine shops have special equipment for this purpose. Unless new pistons or connecting rods must be installed, do not disassemble the pistons.
13 Check the connecting rods for cracks and other damage. Temporarily remove the rod cap, lift out the old bearing inserts, wipe the rod and cap bearing surfaces clean and inspect them for nicks, gouges and scratches. After checking the rods, replace the old bearings, slip the caps into place and tighten the nuts finger tight.

16 Crankshaft – inspection

1 Clean the crankshaft with solvent (be sure to clean the oil holes with a stiff brush and flush them with solvent) and dry it thoroughly. Check the main and connecting rod bearing journals for uneven wear, scoring, pitting and cracks. Check the remainder of the crankshaft for cracks and damage.
2 Using an appropriate size micrometer, measure the diameter of the main and connecting rod journals (photo) and compare the results to the Specifications. By measuring the diameter at a number of points around the journal's circumference, you will be able to determine whether or not the journal is worn out-of-round. Take the measurement at each end of the journal, near the crank throw, to determine whether the journal is tapered.

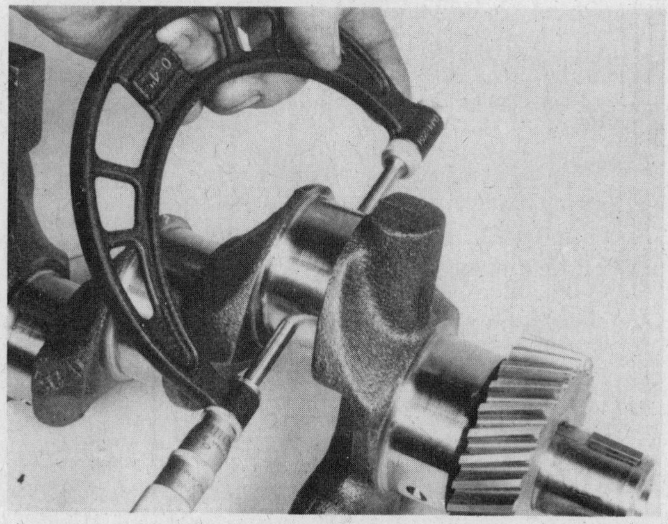

16.2 Measure the diameter of each crankshaft journal at several points to detect taper and out-of-round conditions

3 If the crankshaft journals are damaged, tapered, out-of-round or worn beyond the limits given in the Specifications, have the crankshaft reground by a reputable automotive machine shop. Be sure to use the correct undersize bearing inserts if the crankshaft is reconditioned.
4 Refer to Section 17 and examine the main and rod bearing inserts. If the bearing inserts and journals are all in good condition, do not decide to reuse the bearings until the oil clearances have been checked.

17 Main and connecting rod bearings – inspection

1 Even though the main and connecting rod bearings should be replaced with new ones during the engine overhaul, the old bearings should be retained for close examination, as they may reveal valuable information about the condition of the engine.
2 Bearing failure occurs mainly because of lack of lubrication, the presence of dirt or other foreign particles, overloading the engine and/or corrosion. Regardless of the cause of bearing failure, it must be corrected before the engine is reassembled to prevent it from happening again.
3 When examining the bearings, remove them from the engine block, the main bearing caps, the connecting rods and the rod caps and lay them out on a clean surface in the same general position as their location in the engine. This will enable you to match any noted bearing problems with the corresponding crankshaft journal.
4 Dirt and other foreign particles get into the engine in a variety of ways. It may be left in the engine during assembly, or it may pass through filters or breathers. It may get into the oil, and from there into the bearings. Metal chips from machining operations and normal engine wear are often present. Abrasives are sometimes left in engine components after reconditioning, especially when parts are not thoroughly cleaned using the proper cleaning methods. Whatever the source, these foreign objects often end up embedded in the soft bearing material and are easily recognized. Large particles will not embed in the bearing and will score or gouge the bearing and shaft. The best prevention for this cause of bearing failure is to clean all parts thoroughly and keep everything spotlessly clean during engine assembly. Frequent and regular engine oil and filter changes are also recommended.
5 Lack of lubrication (or lubrication breakdown) has a number of interrelated causes. Excessive heat (which thins the oil), overloading (which squeezes the oil from the bearing face) and oil leakage or throw-off (from excessive bearing clearances, worn oil pump or high engine speeds) all contribute to lubrication breakdown. Blocked oil passages, which usually are the result of misaligned oil holes in a bearing shell, will also oil-starve a bearing and destroy it. When lack of lubrication is the cause of bearing failure, the bearing material is wiped or extruded from the steel backing of the bearing. Temperatures may increase to the point where the steel backing turns blue from overheating.
6 Driving habits can have a definite effect on bearing life. Full-throttle low-speed operation (or 'lugging' the engine) puts very high loads on bearings, which tends to squeeze out the oil film. These loads cause the bearings to flex, which produces fine cracks in the bearing face (fatigue failure). Eventually the bearing material will loosen in pieces and tear away from the steel backing. Short-trip driving leads to corrosion of bearings, as insufficient engine heat is produced to drive off the condensed water and corrosive gases produced. These products collect in the engine oil, forming acid and sludge. As the oil is carried to the engine bearings, the acid attacks and corrodes the bearing material.
7 Incorrect bearing installation during engine assembly will lead to bearing failure as well. Tight-fitting bearings, which leave insufficient bearing oil clearance, result in oil starvation. Dirt or foreign particles trapped behind a bearing insert result in high spots on the bearing which lead to failure.

18 Piston rings – installation

1 Before installing the new piston rings, the ring end gaps must be checked. It is assumed that the piston ring side clearance has been checked and verified correct (Section 15).
2 Lay out the piston/connecting rod assemblies and the new ring sets so the ring sets will be matched with the same piston and cylinder during the end gap measurement and engine assembly.
3 Insert the top (number one) ring into the first cylinder and square it up with the cylinder walls by pushing it in with the top of the piston (photo). The ring should be near the bottom of the cylinder at the lower limit of ring travel. To measure the end gap, slip a feeler gauge between the ends of the ring (photo). Compare the measurement to the Specifications.
4 If the gap is larger or smaller than specified, double-check to make sure that you have the correct rings before proceeding.
5 If the gap is too small, it must be enlarged or the ring ends may come in contact with each other during engine operation, which can cause serious damage to the engine. The end gap can be increased by filing the ring ends very carefully with a fine file. Mount the *file* in a vise equipped with soft jaws, slip the ring over the file with the ends contacting the file face and slowly move the ring to remove material from the ends. *When performing this operation, file only from the outside in.*
6 Excess end gap is not critical unless it is greater than 0.040 in (1 mm). Again, double-check to make sure you have the correct rings for your engine.

2A

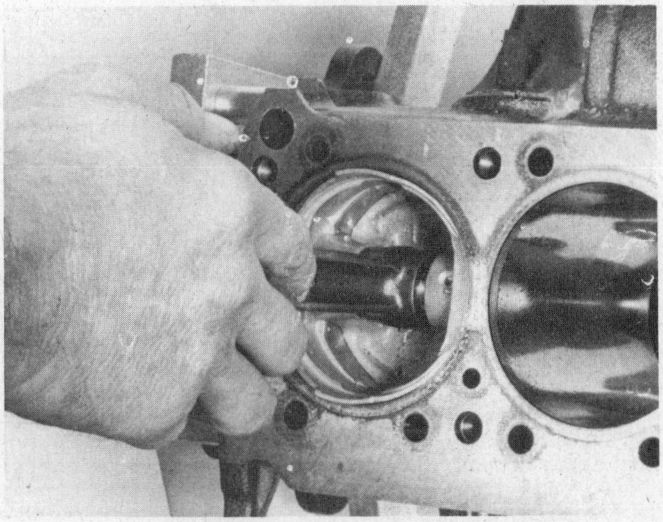

18.3A Use the piston to square up the ring in the cylinder prior to checking the ring end gap

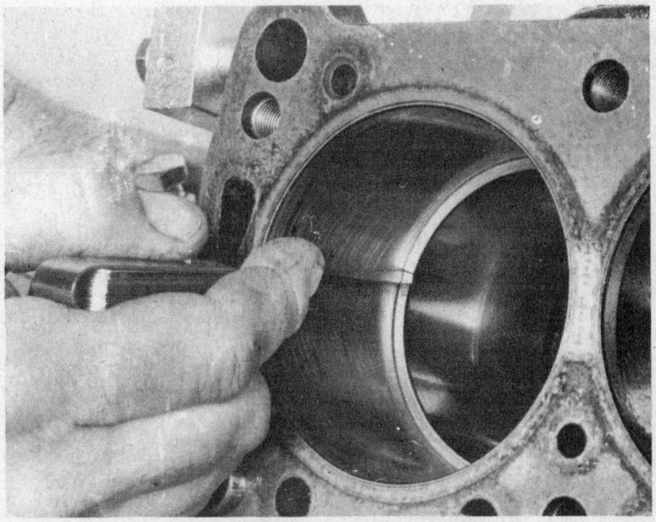

18.3B Measure the ring end gap with a feeler gauge

18.9A Installing the spacer/expander in the oil control ring groove

18.9B *Do not* use a piston ring tool when installing the oil ring side rails

7 Repeat the procedure for each ring that will be installed in the first cylinder and for each ring in the remaining cylinders. Remember to keep rings, pistons and cylinders matched up.
8 Once the ring end gaps have been checked/corrected, the rings can be installed on the pistons.
9 The oil control ring (lowest one on the piston) is installed first. It is composed of three separate components. Slip the spacer expander into the groove (photo) then install the upper side rail. *Do not use a piston ring installation tool on the oil ring side rails, as they may be damaged.* Instead, place one end of the side rail into the groove between the space expander and the ring land, hold it firmly in place and slide a finger around the piston while pushing the rail into the groove (photo). Next, install the lower side rail in the same manner.
10 After the three oil ring components have been installed, check to make sure that both the upper and lower side rails can be turned smoothly in the ring groove.
11 The number two (middle) ring is installed next. It is stamped with a mark so it can be readily distinguished from the top ring (the top ring is marked Top or T). *Do not mix the top and middle rings up, as they have different cross sections.*
12 Use a piston ring installation tool and *make sure that the identification mark is facing up,* then slip the ring into the middle groove on the piston (photo). Do not expand the ring any more than is necessary to slide it over the piston.
13 Finally, install the number one (top) ring in the same manner. Make sure the identifying mark is facing up.
14 Repeat the procedure for the remaining pistons and rings. Be careful not to confuse the number one and number two rings.

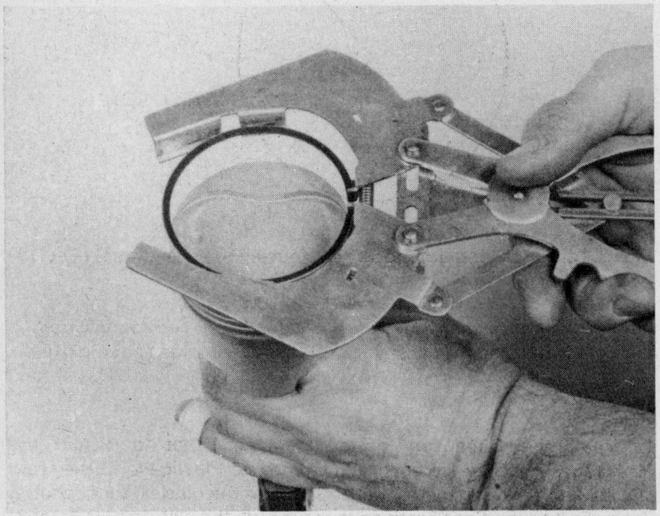

18.12 Installing the compression rings (note the special tool)

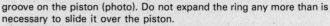

Fig. 2.8 Typical piston ring marks (always install the ring with the marks facing *up* (Sec 18)

19 Piston/connecting rod assembly – installation and bearing oil clearance check

1 Before installing the piston/connecting rod assemblies, the cylinder walls must be perfectly clean, the top edge of each cylinder must be chamfered, and the crankshaft must be in place.
2 Remove the connecting rod cap from the end of the number one connecting rod. Remove the old bearing inserts and wipe the bearing surfaces of the connecting rod and cap with a clean, lint-free cloth (they must be spotlessly clean).
3 Clean the back side of the new upper bearing half, then lay it in place in the connecting rod. Make sure that the tab on the bearing fits into the recess in the rod. Do not hammer the bearing insert into place and be very careful not to nick or gouge the bearing face. *Do not lubricate the bearing at this time.*
4 Clean the back side of the other bearing insert and install it in the rod cap. Again, make sure the tab on the bearing fits into the recess in the cap, and do not apply any lubricant. It is critically important that the mating surfaces of the bearing and connecting rod are perfectly clean and oil-free when they are assembled.
5 Position the piston ring gaps as shown in the accompanying illustrations, then slip a section of plastic or rubber hose over the connecting rod cap bolts.
6 Lubricate the piston and rings with clean engine oil and attach a piston ring compressor to the piston. Leave the skirt protruding about $\frac{1}{4}$-inch to guide the piston into the cylinder. The rings must be compressed as far as possible.
7 Rotate the crankshaft until the number one connecting rod journal is as far from the number one cylinder as possible (bottom dead center), and apply a uniform coat of engine oil to the cylinder walls.

8 With the notch or arrow on top of the piston (or the F on the skirt) facing to the front of the engine, gently place the piston/connecting rod assembly into the number one cylinder bore and rest the bottom edge of the ring compressor on the engine block. Tap the top edge of the ring compressor to make sure it is contacting the block around its entire circumference. **Note:** *On six-cylinder engines the oil holes in the connecting rods must face the camshaft. On four-cylinder engines the projections on the rods must face the front of the engine. On V8's, the numbers on the rods and caps must face out and the oil holes must face in.*

9 Clean the number one connecting rod journal on the crankshaft and the bearing faces in the rod.

10 Carefully tap on the top of the piston with the end of a wooden hammer handle (photo) while guiding the end of the connecting rod into place on the crankshaft journal. The piston rings may try to pop out of the ring compressor just before entering the cylinder bore, so keep some downward pressure on the ring compressor. Work slowly, and if any resistance is felt as the piston enters the cylinder, stop immediately. Find out what is hanging up and fix it before proceeding. *Do not, for any reason, force the piston into the cylinder, as you will break a ring and/or the piston.*

11 Once the piston/connecting rod assembly is installed, the connecting rod bearing oil clearance must be checked before the rod cap is permanently bolted in place.

12 Cut a piece of the appropriate type Plastigage slightly shorter than the width of the connecting rod bearing and lay it in place on the number one connecting rod journal, parallel with the journal axis (it must not cross the oil hole in the journal) (photo).

13 Clean the connecting rod cap bearing face, remove the protective hoses from the connecting rod bolts and gently install the rod cap in place. Make sure the mating mark on the cap is on the same side as the mark on the connecting rod. Install the nuts and tighten them to the specified torque, working up to it in three steps. *Do not rotate the crankshaft at any time during this operation.*

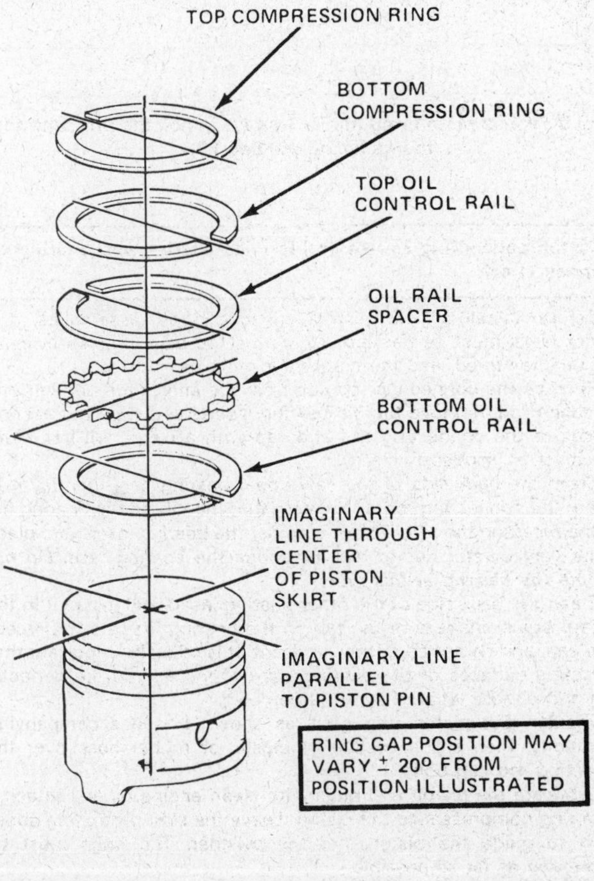

2.10 Piston ring gap positions (six-cylinder engines) (Sec 19)

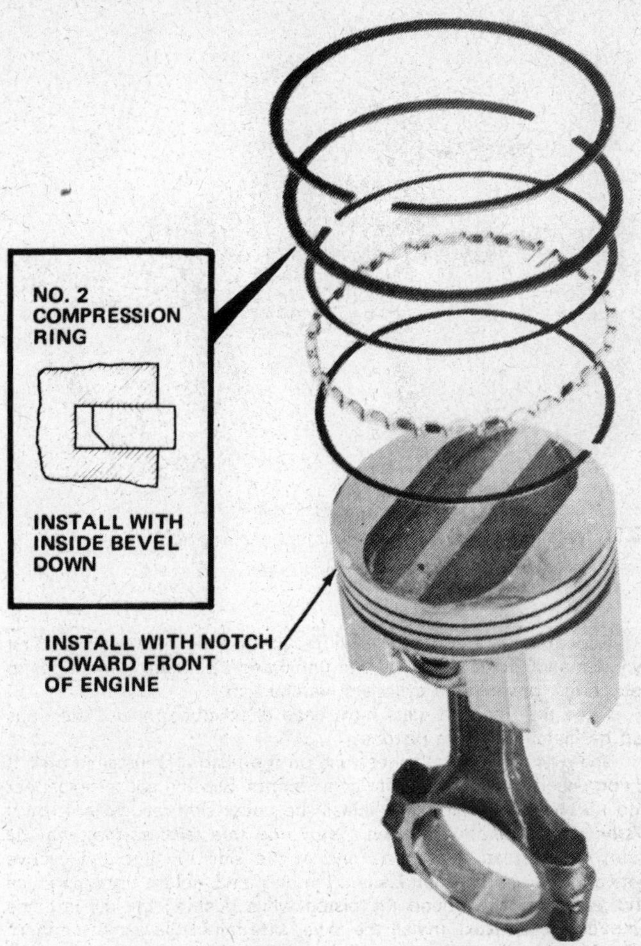

Fig. 2.9 Piston ring gap positions (V8 engines) (Sec 19)

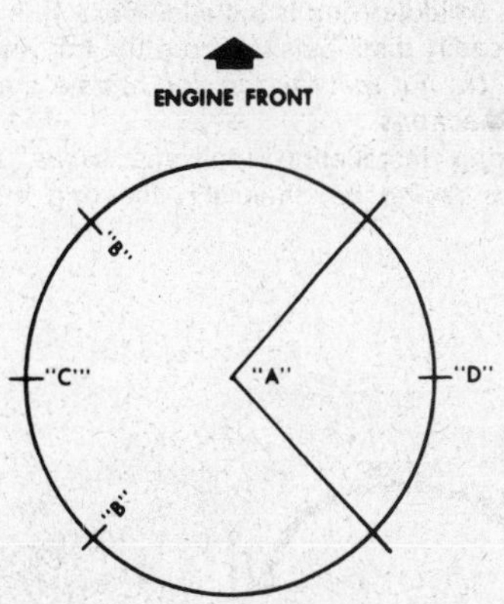

Fig. 2.11 Piston ring gap positions (four-cylinder engines) (Sec 19)

A	Oil ring spacer gap	C	2nd compression ring gap
B	Oil ring side rail gaps	D	Top compression ring gap

14 Remove the rod cap, being very careful not to disturb the Plastigage. Compare the width of the crushed Plastigage to the scale printed on the Plastigage container to obtain the oil clearance (photo). Compare it to the Specifications to make sure the clearance is correct. If the clearance is not correct, double-check to make sure that you have the correct size bearing inserts. Also, recheck the crankshaft connecting rod journal diameter and make sure that no dirt or oil was

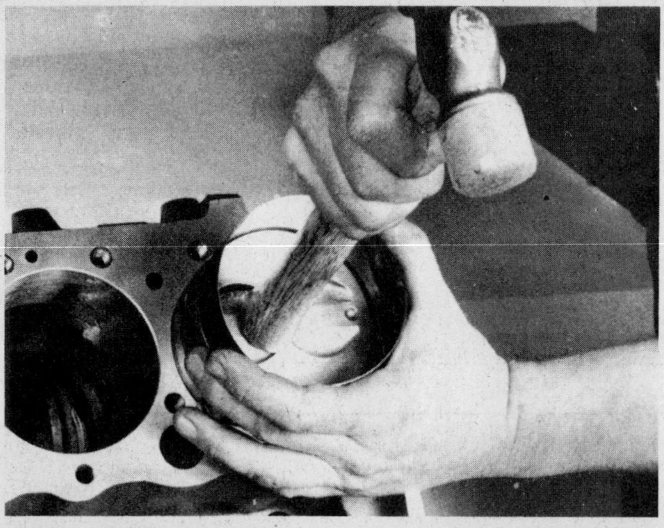

19.10 If resistance is encountered when tapping the piston/connecting rod assembly into the block, *stop immediately* and make sure the rings are fully compressed

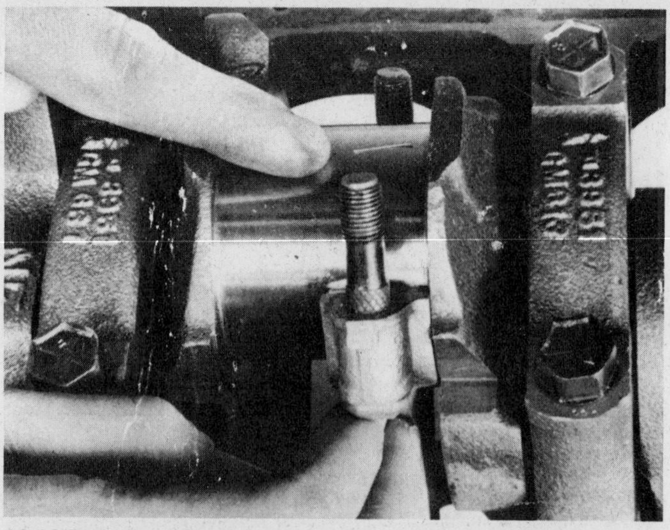

19.12 Position the Plastigage strip on the bearing journal, parallel to the journal axis

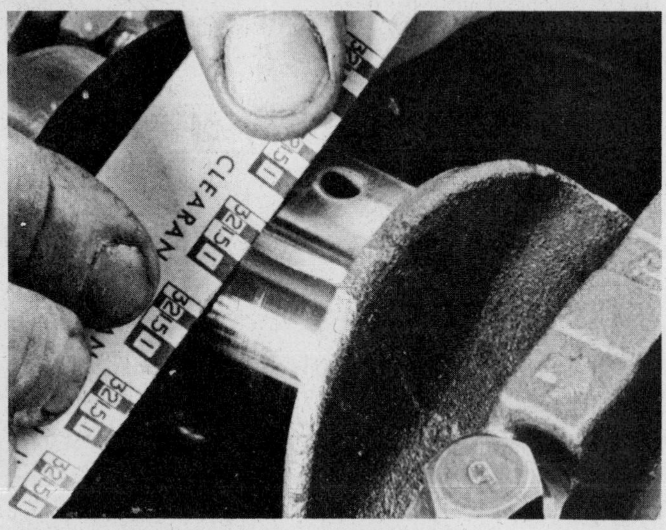

19.14 The crushed Plastigage is compared to the scale printed on the container to obtain the bearing oil clearance

between the bearing inserts and the connecting rod or cap when the clearance was measured.

15 Carefully scrape all traces of the Plastigage material off the rod journal and/or bearing face (be very careful not to scratch the bearing – use your fingernail or a piece of hardwood). Make sure the bearing faces are perfectly clean, then apply a uniform layer of clean high quality moly-based grease or engine assembly lube to both of them. You will have to push the piston into the cylinder to expose the face of the bearing insert in the connecting rod; be sure to slip the protective hoses over the rod bolts first.

16 Slide the connecting rod back into place on the journal, remove the protective hoses from the rod cap bolts, install the rod cap and tighten the nuts to the specified torque. Again, work up to the torque in three steps.

17 Repeat the entire procedure for the remaining piston/connecting rod assemblies. Keep the back sides of the bearing inserts and the inside of the connecting rod and cap perfectly clean when assembling them. Make sure you have the correct piston for the cylinder and that the notch (or arrow) on the piston faces to the front of the engine when the piston is installed. Remember, use plenty of oil to lubricate the piston before installing the ring compressor and be sure to match up the mating marks on the connecting rod and rod cap. Also, when installing the rod caps for the final time, be sure to lubricate the bearing faces adequately.

18 After all the piston/connecting rod assemblies have been properly installed, rotate the crankshaft a number of times by hand and check for any obvious binding.

19 As a final step, the connecting rod end play must be checked. Refer to Section 11 for the procedure to follow. Compare the measured end play to the Specifications to make sure it is correct.

20 Initial start-up and break-in after overhaul

1 Once the engine has been properly installed in the vehicle, double-check the engine oil and coolant levels.

2 With the spark plugs out of the engine and the coil high-tension lead grounded to the engine block, crank the engine over until oil pressure registers on the gauge (if so equipped) or until the oil light goes off.

3 Install the spark plugs, hook up the plug wires and the coil high-tension lead.

4 Make sure the carburetor choke plate is closed, then start the engine. It may take a few moments for gasoline to reach the carburetor, but the engine should start without a great deal of effort.

5 As soon as the engine starts, it should be set at a fast idle (to ensure proper oil circulation) and allowed to warm up to normal operating temperature. While the engine is warming up, make a thorough check for oil and coolant leaks.

6 Shut the engine off and recheck the engine oil and coolant levels. Also, check the ignition timing and the engine idle speed (refer to Chapter 1) and make any necessary adjustments.

7 Drive the vehicle to an area with minimum traffic, accelerate at full throttle from 30 to 50 mph, then allow the vehicle to slow to 30 mph with the throttle closed. Repeat the procedure 10 or 12 times. This will load the piston rings and cause them to seat properly against the cylinder walls. Check again for oil and coolant leaks.

8 Drive the vehicle gently for the first 500 miles (no sustained high speeds) and keep a constant check on the oil level. It is not unusual for an engine to use oil during the break-in period.

9 At approximately 500 to 600 miles, change the oil and filter, retorque the cylinder head bolts and recheck the valve clearances (if applicable).

10 For the next few hundred miles, drive the vehicle normally. Do not pamper it or abuse it.

11 After 2000 miles, change the oil and filter again and consider the engine fully broken in.

Chapter 2 Part B
Four-cylinder engine (151 cu in)

Contents

Camshaft and bearings – removal and installation 40
Crankshaft – inspection .... Chapter 2A
Crankshaft – installation and main bearing oil clearance check 42
Crankshaft – removal 41
Crankshaft pulley hub and front oil seal – removal and installation 33
Cylinder head – cleaning and inspection .... Chapter 2A
Cylinder head – disassembly .... Chapter 2A
Cylinder head – installation 32
Cylinder head – reassembly .... Chapter 2A
Cylinder head – removal 31
Engine – installation 45
Engine – removal 22
Engine/automatic transmission – rejoining 44
Engine/automatic transmission – separation 24
Engine block – cleaning .... Chapter 2A
Engine block – inspection .... Chapter 2A
Engine disassembly – general information .... Chapter 2A
Engine/manual transmission – rejoining 43
Engine/manual transmission – separation 23
Engine overhaul – general information .... Chapter 2A
Engine rebuilding alternatives .... Chapter 2A
Engine removal – methods and precautions .... Chapter 2A
Exhaust manifold – removal and installation 30
Flywheel and rear main oil seal – removal and installation 39
General information 21
Hydraulic lifters – removal, inspection and installation 28
Initial start-up and break-in after overhaul .... Chapter 2A
Intake manifold – removal and installation 29
Main and connecting rod bearings – inspection .... Chapter 2A
Oil pan – removal and installation 36
Oil pump – disassembly, inspection and reassembly 38
Oil pump – removal and installation 37
Oil pump driveshaft – removal and installation 35
Piston/connecting rod assembly – inspection .... Chapter 2A
Piston/connecting rod assembly – installation and bearing oil clearance check .... Chapter 2A
Piston/connecting rod assembly – removal .... Chapter 2A
Piston rings – installation .... Chapter 2A
Pushrod cover – removal and installation 27
Repair operations possible with the engine in the vehicle .... Chapter 2A
Rocker arm cover – removal and installation 25
Rocker arms, pushrods and valve springs – removal and installation (engine in vehicle) 26
Timing gear cover – removal and installation 34
Valves – servicing .... Chapter 2A

Specifications

General

Displacement	151 cu in
Bore and stroke	4.0 x 3.0 in
Compression ratio	8.24 : 1
Oil pressure	36 to 41 psi at 2000 rpm

Cylinder bores

Taper limit	
1980	0.0005 in max.
1981 through 1983	0.002 in max.
Out-of-round limit	
1980	0.0005 in max.
1981 through 1983	0.0015 in max.

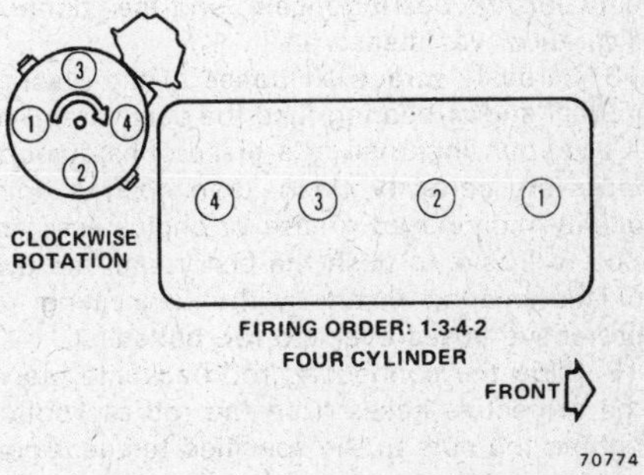

Cylinder location and distributor rotation

Pistons and rings

Piston diameter	3.9968 to 3.992 in
Piston-to-cylinder bore clearance	
Top	0.0025 to 0.0033 in
Bottom	0.0017 to 0.0041 in
Piston ring side clearance	0.003 in
Piston ring end gap	
Top ring	0.010 to 0.022 in
2nd ring	0.010 to 0.028 in
Oil ring side rails	0.015 to 0.055 in
Piston pin diameter	0.92705 to 0.92745 in
Piston pin-to-piston clearance	
Standard	0.0003 in
Service limit	0.0005 in
Piston pin-to-connecting rod clearance	Press fit

Crankshaft and connecting rods

Main journal	
Diameter	2.2988 in
Taper limit	0.0005 in max.
Out-of-round limit	0.0005 in max.
Main bearing oil clearance	
Standard	0.0005 in
Service limit	0.0022 in
Connecting rod journal	
Diameter	2.000 in
Taper limit	0.0005 in max.
Out-of-round limit	0.0005 in max.
Connecting rod bearing oil clearance	
Standard	0.0005 in
Service limit	0.0026 in
Connecting rod end play	0.017 in
Crankshaft end play	0.0035 to 0.0085 in

Camshaft

Bearing journal diameter	1.869 in
Bearing oil clearance	
Standard	0.0007 in
Service limit	0.0027 in
Lobe lift	0.230 in
End play	0.0015 to 0.0050 in

Cylinder head and valve train

Cylinder head warpage limit	0.008 in max.
Valve seat angle	46°
Valve seat width	
Intake	0.0353 to 0.0747 in
Exhaust	0.058 to 0.097 in
Valve face angle	45°
Valve margin minimum width	$\frac{1}{32}$ in
Valve stem-to-guide clearance	
Standard	
1982 and 1983 *exhaust* only	0.020 in
All others	0.010 in
Service limit	0.0027 in
Valve spring pressure (lbs @ specified length)	
Closed	78 to 86 @ 1.66 in
Open	172 to 180 @ 1.254 in
Valve lash adjustment	Zero
Lifter leakdown rate	12 to 90 sec with a 50-lb load
Lifter diameter	0.8120 to 0.8427 in
Lifter bore diameter	0.8435 to 0.8445 in
Lifter-to-bore clearance	0.0025 in
Pushrod length	8.927 in

Torque specifications

	Ft-lb	Nm
Adapter-to-intake manifold	10 to 16	14 to 20
Camshaft thrust plate-to-block screws	4.4 to 9	6 to 12
Carburetor-to-manifold nuts	10 to 16	14 to 20
Connecting rod nuts	30	40
Crankshaft pulley hub bolt	157 to 163	217 to 223
Cylinder head bolts	92	125
Distributor clamp bolt	6 to 12	9 to 15
Distributor clamp pivot bolt	9 to 15	14 to 21
Driveplate-to-crankshaft bolts	42 to 48	57 to 63
Driveplate-to-converter bolts	40	54
EGR valve-to-manifold	6.6 to 11	9 to 15
Exhaust manifold bolts	36 to 42	47 to 53
Exhaust pipe-to-manifold nuts	34 to 40	49 to 55
Fan and pulley-to-water pump	15 to 21	21 to 27
Flywheel-to-crankshaft bolts	65 to 71	90 to 96
Fuel pump-to-block	12 to 18	17 to 23
Intake manifold	34 to 40	47 to 53
Main bearing cap bolts	65	88
Oil filter adapter-to-block	32 to 38	44 to 50
Oil pan drain plug	23 to 28	31 to 37
Oil pan bolts	45 to 48	53 to 59
Oil pump cover bolts	6 to 12	14 to 20
Oil pump-to-block bolts	15 to 21	22 to 28
Oil pump-to-driveshaft plate	7 to 13	11 to 17
Oil screen support nut	25 to 31	35 to 41

Air injection bracket	34 to 40	47 to 54
Pressure plate-to-flywheel bolts	15 to 22	20 to 30
Crankshaft pulley bolt	22 to 28	31 to 37
Pushrod cover bolts	4.4 to 9	6 to 12
Rocker arm cover bolts	4 to 10	7 to 13
Rocker arm stud	57 to 63	73 to 79
Rocker arm-to-stud nuts	17 to 23	24 to 30
Starter bolts	14 to 20	21 to 27
Thermostat housing bolts	19 to 25	27 to 33
Timing cover	5	2 to 8
Timing cover-to-block	9	6 to 12
Water outlet housing	14 to 20	20 to 26
Water pump	14 to 20	20 to 26

21 General information

The 151 cubic-inch, four-cylinder engine features a crossflow cylinder head, hydraulic valve lifters and ball and socket-type rocker arms. The camshaft is mounted in the engine block and is gear driven by the crankshaft.

The oil pump is mounted in the crankcase and is driven by a shaft actuated by the crankshaft. The crankshaft is supported by five replaceable main bearings.

22 Engine – removal

1 The engine and transmission are removed and installed as a unit on these models.
2 Disconnect the negative battery cable from the battery.
3 Drain the coolant into a suitable container. The drain plug is located at the left rear corner of the engine block.
4 Disconnect the radiator hoses at the radiator.
5 Remove the hood, making sure to mark the location of the hinges to ensure installation in the same position.
6 Remove the air cleaner, cooling fan and shroud.
7 Disconnect the fluid cooler lines (automatic transmission) at the radiator and plug them.
8 Remove the radiator (Chapter 3).
9 Remove the power steering pump drivebelt and, on non-air conditioned models, disconnect the alternator wiring harness.
10 On air conditioner equipped models, unbolt the compressor and condenser, move them out of the way and remove the evaporator-to-drier line from the sill clips. **Caution**: *Do not disconnect any of the air conditioner hoses. If it is necessary to disconnect any of the hoses, have the system depressurized by a qualified technician.*
11 Disconnect the heater hose from the intake manifold and remove the throttle cable and clip from the bracket.
12 On air conditioned models, disconnect the alternator wiring harness and pull the wires through the tube.
13 Disconnect the power steering hoses at the steering gear and plug them.
14 Tag the vacuum hoses so they can be reinstalled in their original locations and disconnect them.
15 Disconnect the wide open throttle switch, choke heater, idle solenoid and coolant temperature sending unit wires.
16 Remove the dipstick and tube assembly.
17 Raise the vehicle and support it securely.
18 Remove the engine mount cushion nuts at the crossmember and disconnect the ground cable from the engine block.
19 Disconnect the rubber fuel hose from the steel fuel line on the right frame rail.
20 Disconnect the wires from the starter, distributor and oil pressure sending unit.
21 Loosen the crossmember, lower it slightly and disconnect the cooler lines, speedometer, transmission linkage, backup light switch and rear mount from the transmission. Remove the crossmember.
22 Remove the exhaust pipe-to-manifold retaining nuts and secure the pipe to the strut rod bushing with a piece of wire.
23 Mark the rear universal joint caps so they can be reinstalled in their original positions and remove the caps and the driveshaft.
24 Lower the vehicle and connect an engine hoist to the rear bracket (where it attaches to the cylinder head) and the air conditioner or alternator mounting bracket.
25 Carefully lift the engine/transmission unit from the vehicle. Initially, the assembly should be raised at a steep angle until it is clear of the engine compartment. Once clear of the vehicle, the engine/transmission unit can be leveled and lowered carefully to the floor or workbench. Brace the assembly securely with blocks of wood to ensure that it does not fall over.

23 Engine/manual transmission – separation

1 Remove the transmission-to-clutch housing retaining bolts and withdraw the transmission, taking care to support the clutch plate and pilot bearing so they do not fall.
2 Remove the throwout bearing and the pilot bushing lubricating wick. The lubricating wick should be soaked in clean engine oil prior to installation.
3 Unbolt and remove the clutch housing, taking care to support the rear of the engine so the flywheel starter ring gear is not damaged.

24 Engine/automatic transmission – separation

1 Remove the starter motor.
2 Remove the cover from the front of the converter housing.
3 Mark the relative position of the driveplate and converter for ease of installation in their original positions.
4 Remove the converter-to-driveplate attaching bolts, rotating the crankshaft pulley bolt with a wrench to provide access to each bolt.
5 Remove the transmission-to-engine attaching bolts and carefully withdraw the transmission and converter to the rear.
6 Remove the converter from the transmission input shaft.

25 Rocker arm cover – removal and installation

Note: *If the engine has been removed from the vehicle, disregard the following steps which do not apply.*
1 Remove the air cleaner.
2 Remove the PCV valve and hose.
3 If so equipped, remove the PULSAIR air hose from the air valve.
4 Remove the spark plug wires from the plugs and mounting clips, labeling each wire as to its proper position.
5 Remove the rocker cover bolts.
6 Remove the rocker arm cover. To break the gasket seal, it may be necessary to tap the cover with your hand or a rubber mallet. Do not pry on the cover.
7 Prior to installation, clean all dirt, oil and old gasket material from the sealing surfaces of the cover and cylinder head with a degreaser.
8 Place a continuous $\frac{3}{16}$-inch (5 mm) diameter bead of RTV-type sealant or equivalent around the sealing lip of the cover. Be sure to apply the sealant to the inside of the mounting bolt holes.
9 Place the rocker arm cover on the cylinder head while the sealant is still wet, install the mounting bolts and tighten them to the specified torque.
10 Complete the installation by reversing the removal procedure.

26 Rocker arms, pushrods and valve springs – removal and installation (engine in vehicle)

Note: *Valve mechanism components must be reinstalled in their original positions. Place all removed components in a compartmented box to aid in identification.*

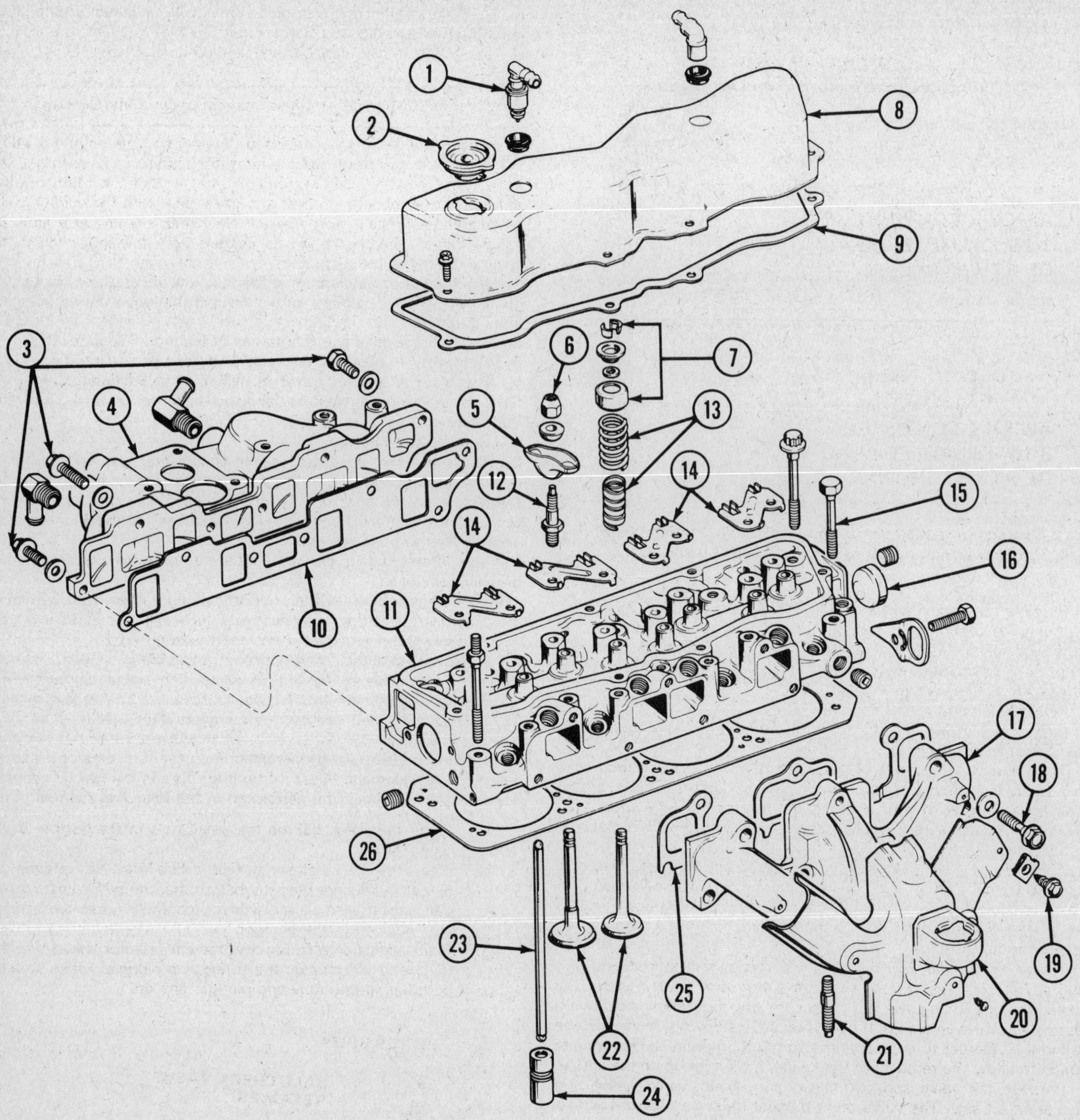

Fig. 2.12 Cylinder head components – exploded view

1 PCV valve
2 Oil filler cap
3 Intake manifold attaching bolts
4 Intake manifold
5 Rocker arm
6 Rocker arm pivot ball and nut
7 Valve spring retainer assembly
8 Rocker arm cover
9 Rocker arm cover gasket
10 Intake manifold gasket
11 Cylinder head
12 Rocker arm stud
13 Valve spring
14 Pushrod guide
15 Cylinder head bolts
16 Cylinder head core plug
17 Exhaust manifold
18 Exhaust manifold bolt
19 Dipstick tube attaching screw
20 Exhaust manifold heat shield
21 Exhaust manifold-to-exhaust pipe stud
22 Valves
23 Pushrod
24 Valve lifter
25 Exhaust manifold gasket
26 Cylinder head gasket

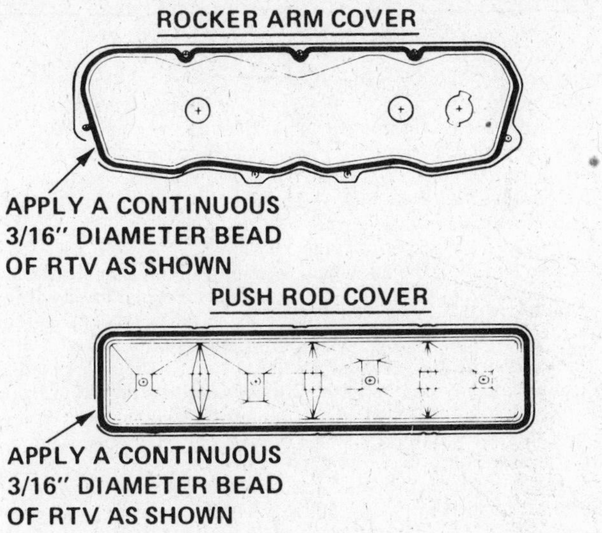

Fig. 2.13 Recommended sealant application for installation of the rocker arm and pushrod covers (Secs 25 and 26)

1 Remove the rocker arm cover as described in Section 25.
2 If only the pushrod is to be replaced, loosen the rocker nut enough so the rocker arm can be rotated away from the pushrod. If the rocker arm or valve spring is to be replaced, remove the rocker arm nut and ball and lift off the rocker arm.
3 Pull the pushrod out of the hole.
4 If the valve spring is to be removed, remove the spark plug from the cylinder being serviced.
5 There are two methods of keeping the valve in place while the valve spring is removed. If you have access to compressed air, attach an air hose adapter to your air hose and insert it into the spark plug hole. When air pressure is applied, the valves will be held in place by the pressure.
6 If you do not have access to compressed air, bring the piston to top dead center (TDC). Feed a long piece of $\frac{1}{4}$-inch nylon cord in through the spark plug hole until it fills the combustion chamber. Be sure to leave the end of the cord hanging out of the spark plug hole so it can be removed easily.
7 Thread the rocker arm nut onto the rocker arm stud. Position a valve spring compressor tool over the spring and hook it under the rocker arm nut. Using the nut to secure the tool, apply downward pressure to the valve spring. If care is taken, a screwdriver can also be used in this manner to compress the spring. Compress the spring just enough to allow the removal of the keepers, then let up on the spring.
8 Remove the valve spring retainer, cup shield, valve spring and valve stem oil seal. The valve stem oil seal must be replaced with a new one whenever the keepers have been disturbed.
9 Inspection procedures for the various valve components are detailed in Chapter 2A.
10 Installation is the reverse of the removal procedure. Prior to installing the rocker arms, coat the bearing surfaces of the arms and rocker arm balls with engine assembly lube or moly-based grease. The valve mechanisms require no special lash adjustment.

27 Pushrod cover – removal and installation

1 Remove the intake manifold as described in Section 29.
2 Remove the pushrod cover bolts and lift off the cover. If the gasket seal is difficult to break, tap lightly on the cover with a rubber mallet. Do not pry on the cover.
3 Using a degreaser, thoroughly clean the sealing surfaces on the cover and engine block to remove all oil and old gasket material.
4 Prior to installation of the cover, place a continuous $\frac{3}{16}$-inch (5 mm) bead of RTV-type sealant or equivalent to the sealing lip of the pushrod cover.
5 With the sealant still wet, place the cover in position on the block, install the cover bolts and tighten them to the specified torque.
6 Install the intake manifold and related components.

28 Hydraulic lifters – removal, inspection and installation

1 A noisy valve lifter is easiest to detect when the engine is idling. Place a length of hose or tubing near the position of each intake and exhaust valve while listening at the other end of the tube. Another method is to remove the rocker arm cover and, with the engine idling, place a finger on each of the valve spring retainers one at a time. If a valve lifter is defective it will be evident from the shock felt at the retainer as the valve seats.
2 Provided that adjustment is correct, the most likely cause of a noisy valve lifter is a piece of dirt trapped between the plunger and lifter body.
3 Remove the rocker arm cover as described in Section 25.
4 Remove the intake manifold as described in Section 29.
5 Remove the pushrod cover as described in Section 27.
6 Loosen the rocker arm nut and rotate the rocker arm away from the pushrod.
7 Remove the pushrod.
8 To remove the lifters, a special hydraulic lifter removal tool can be used, or a sharp scribe can be positioned at the top of the lifter and used to force the lifter up. Do not use pliers or other tools on the outside of the lifter body, as they will damage the machined surface and render the lifter useless.
9 The lifters should be kept separate for reinstallation in their original positions.
10 To dismantle a valve lifter, hold the plunger down with a pushrod and then extract the pushrod seat retainer using a small screwdriver.
11 Remove the pushrod seat and the metering valve.
12 Remove the plunger, ball check valve and plunger spring. Remove the ball check valve and spring by prying with a small screwdriver.
13 Examine all components for wear. Check the ball for flat spots. If any defects are noted, replace the complete lifter assembly. **2B**
14 Examine each lifter for scoring, wear and erosion of the camshaft lobe mating surface. Any imperfections on the lifter body surface are cause for replacement. Wear in the lifter bore in the block is rare.
15 Reassembly should be performed in the following manner:

- a) Place the check ball on the small hole in the bottom of the plunger.
- b) Insert the check ball spring on the seat in the ball retainer and place the retainer over the ball so that the spring rests on the ball. Using a small screwdriver, carefully press the retainer into position in the plunger.
- c) Place the plunger spring over the ball retainer, invert the lifter body and slide it over the spring and plunger. Make sure the oil holes in the body and plunger line up.

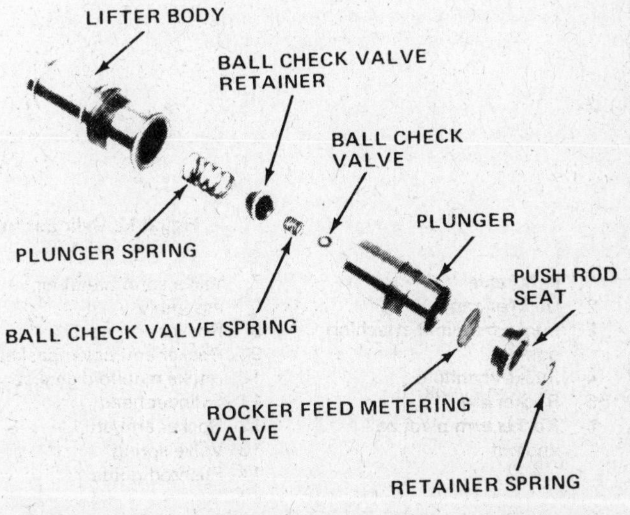

Fig. 2.14 Exploded view of the hydraulic valve lifter (Sec 28)

d) Fill the assembly with SAE 10W oil. Place the metering valve and pushrod seat into position, press down on the seat and install the pushrod seat retainer.

16 When installing the lifters, make sure they are replaced in their original bores and coat them with engine assembly lube or moly-based grease.
17 Complete the installation by reversing the steps in the removal procedure.

29 Intake manifold – removal and installation

1 Remove the air cleaner, being sure to label the lines and hoses as to their proper location.
2 Remove the PCV hose.
3 Disconnect the negative battery cable.
4 Drain the cooling system as described in Chapter 1.
5 Remove the carburetor as described in Chapter 4.
6 Remove the carburetor base gasket.
7 Disconnect the vacuum lines from the carburetor spacer.
8 Remove the EGR valve.
9 Remove the carburetor spacer.
10 Remove the carburetor spacer gasket.
11 Remove the throttle linkage and set it to one side for clearance.
12 Remove the heater hose from the intake manifold.
13 Remove the upper alternator bracket.
14 If equipped, remove the PULSAIR air valve bracket.
15 Remove the bolts that secure the intake manifold to the cylinder head and lift off the intake manifold.

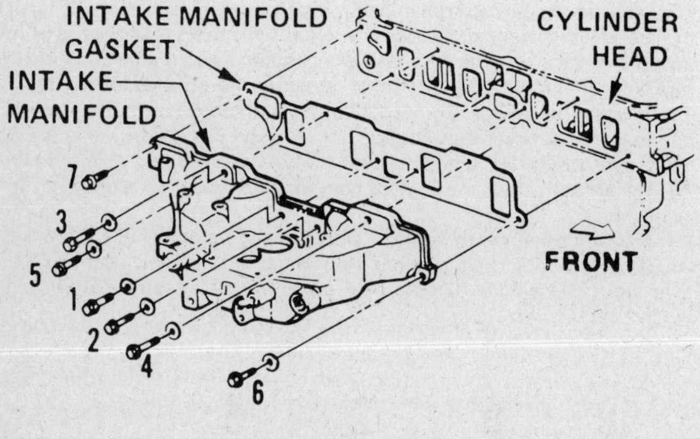

Fig. 2.15 Recommended tightening sequence for the intake manifold mounting bolts (Sec 19)

16 Remove the manifold gasket.
17 If the intake manifold is to be replaced with another, transfer any remaining components still attached to the old manifold to the new one.
18 Before installing the manifold, clean the cylinder head and manifold gasket surfaces. All extra gasket material and sealing compound must be removed prior to installation.
19 Apply a thin bead of RTV-type sealant to the intake manifold and cylinder head mating surfaces. Be certain that the sealant will not spread into the air or coolant passages when the manifold is installed.
20 Place a new intake manifold gasket on the manifold, place the manifold in position against the cylinder head and install the mounting bolts finger tight.
21 Tighten the manifold mounting bolts to the specified torque in the sequence shown in the accompanying illustration. Work up to the torque in three or four steps.
22 Install the remaining components in the reverse order of removal.
23 Fill the radiator with coolant, start the engine and check for leaks. Check the carburetor idle speed and adjust if necessary, as described in Chapter 1.

30 Exhaust manifold – removal and installation

1 If the vehicle is equipped with air conditioning, carefully examine the routing of the hoses and the mounting of the compressor. You may be able to remove the exhaust manifold without disconnecting the air conditioning system. If you are in doubt, take the vehicle to a dealer or other qualified automotive repair shop to have the system depressurized. **Caution:** *Do not under any circumstances disconnect any air conditioning lines while the system is under pressure.*
2 Remove the air cleaner.
3 Remove the carburetor pre-heat tube.
4 Remove the engine oil dipstick tube.
5 Remove the exhaust sensor located on the exhaust manifold.
6 Remove the air conditioning compressor mounting bracket.
7 Label the four spark plug wires as to their positions. Disconnect them and secure them to the side for clearance.
8 Disconnect the exhaust pipe from the exhaust manifold. The exhaust pipe can be hung from a piece of wire attached to the frame.
9 Remove the exhaust manifold end bolts first, then remove the center bolts and the exhaust manifold.
10 Remove the exhaust manifold gasket.
11 Before installing the exhaust manifold, clean the mating surfaces on the cylinder head and manifold. All old gasket material should be removed.
12 Place a new exhaust manifold gasket into position on the cylinder head, then place the manifold into position and install the mounting bolts finger tight.

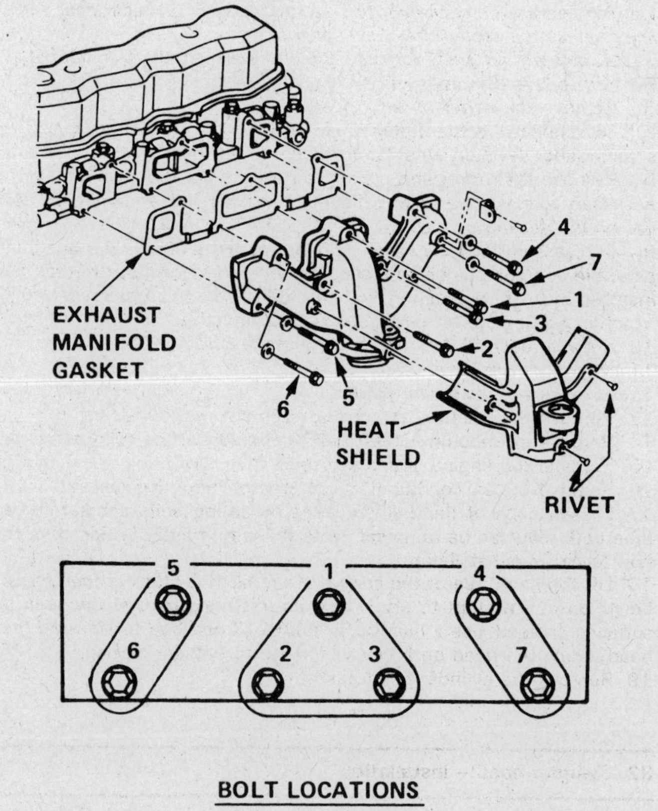

Fig. 2.16 Exhaust manifold installation and bolt tightening sequence (Sec 30)

13 Tighten the manifold mounting bolts to the specified torque in the sequence shown in the accompanying illustration. Work up to the final torque in three or four steps.
14 Install the remaining components in the reverse order of removal, using new gaskets wherever one has been removed.
15 Start the engine and check for exhaust leaks between the manifold and cylinder head and between the manifold and exhaust pipe.

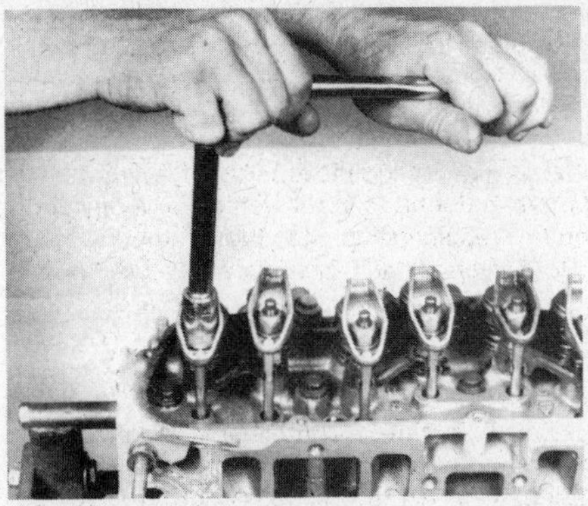

31.10 Removing the rocker arms from the pivots

31.12 Removing the pushrods

32.5 The cylinder head mounting bolts should be coated with sealant (arrows) prior to installation

31 Cylinder head – removal

Note: *If the engine has been removed from the vehicle, disregard the following steps which do not apply.*

1 Remove the intake manifold as described in Section 29.
2 Remove the exhaust manifold as described in Section 30.
3 Remove the bolts that secure the alternator bracket to the cylinder head.
4 Disconnect the air conditioning compressor and swing it out of the way for clearance. *Be sure not to disconnect any of the air conditioning lines unless the system has been depressurized.*
5 Disconnect all electrical and vacuum lines from the cylinder head. Be sure to label the lines as to their locations.
6 Remove the upper radiator hose.
7 Disconnect the spark plug wires and remove the spark plugs. Be sure to label the plug wires as to their correct locations.
8 Remove the rocker arm cover. To break the gasket seal it may be necessary to strike the cover with your hand or a rubber mallet. Do not pry on the sealing surfaces.
9 In disassembling the valve train components, it is important that all of the components be kept separate, once removed, so they can be installed in their original positions. A cardboard box or rack numbered according to engine cylinders can be used for this.
10 Remove each of the rocker arm nuts or bolts (photo).
11 Lift the rocker arms off.
12 Remove the pushrods (photo).
13 Remove the thermostat housing from the cylinder head.
14 Remove all vacuum valves and switches from the cylinder head.
15 Remove the engine lifting brackets.
16 Remove the air conditioning compressor mounting bracket.
17 Loosen each of the cylinder head mounting bolts one turn at a time until they can be removed. Note the length and position of each bolt to aid in reinstallation.
18 Lift the head free of the engine. If the head is stuck to the engine block, do not attempt to pry it free, as this may damage the sealing surfaces. Instead, use a hammer and a block of wood to dislodge the head. Place the head on a block of wood to prevent damage.
19 Remove the cylinder head gasket.

32 Cylinder head – installation

1 If not already done, thoroughly clean the gasket surfaces on both the cylinder head and the engine block. Do not scratch or otherwise damage the sealing areas.
2 To get the proper torque readings, the threads of the head bolts must be clean. This also holds true for the threaded holes in the engine block. Run a tap through these holes to ensure that they are clean.
3 Place the gasket in place over the engine block dowel pins.
4 Carefully lower the cylinder head onto the engine, over the dowel pins and the gaskets. Be careful not to move the gasket while doing this.
5 Coat both the threads of the cylinder head attaching bolts and the point at which the head and stem meet with a sealing compound and install each finger tight. Do not tighten any of the bolts at this time (photo).
6 Tighten each of the bolts, a little at a time, in the sequence shown in the accompanying illustration. Continue tightening in this sequence until the proper torque reading is obtained. As a final check, work around the head in a logical front-to-rear sequence to make sure none of the bolts have been overlooked.
7 Install the exhaust manifold as described in Section 30.
8 Install each of the valve lifters (if removed) into its proper bore. Engine assembly lube or clean oil should be used as a coating on each lifter.
9 Place a small amount of engine assembly lube on each end of the pushrods and install each in its original position. Make sure the pushrods are seated properly in the lifter cavities.
10 Place each of the rocker arms and corresponding rocker balls onto its original stud or bolt. The rocker balls and valve stem end of the rocker arms should receive a small amount of engine assembly lube.
11 Tighten the rocker arm nuts/bolts to the specified torque.
12 Install the rocker arm cover.
13 Install the intake manifold as described in Section 29.
14 Install the remaining engine components in the reverse order of removal.
15 Fill the radiator with coolant, start the engine and check for leaks. Adjust the ignition timing as required. Be sure to recheck the coolant level once the engine has warmed up to operating temperature and cooled back down again.

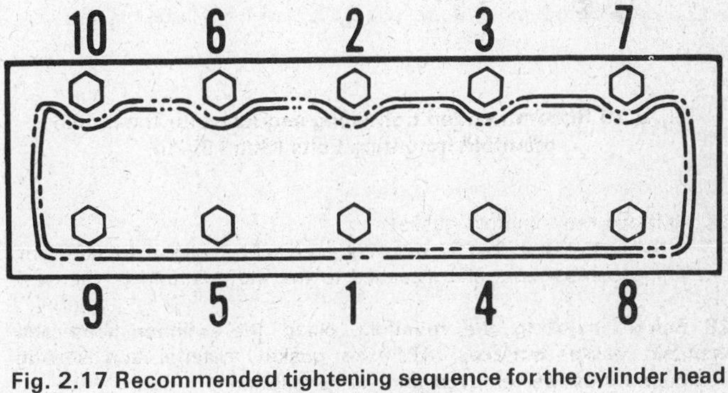

Fig. 2.17 Recommended tightening sequence for the cylinder head bolts (Sec 32)

33 Crankshaft pulley hub and front oil seal – removal and installation

Note: *If the engine has been removed from the vehicle, disregard the following steps which do not apply.*

1 Remove the engine drivebelts. Refer to the appropriate Chapters for each accessory.
2 Remove the radiator to provide working clearance.
3 With the parking brake applied and the shifter in Park (automatic)

2B

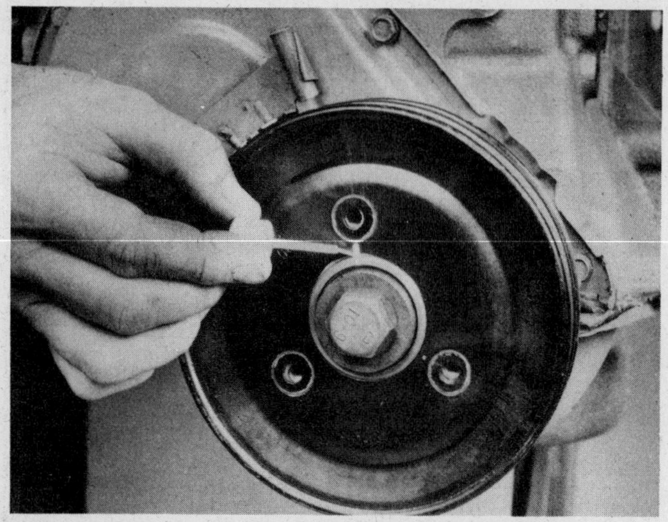

33.4 Marking the position of the crankshaft pulley in relation to the hub

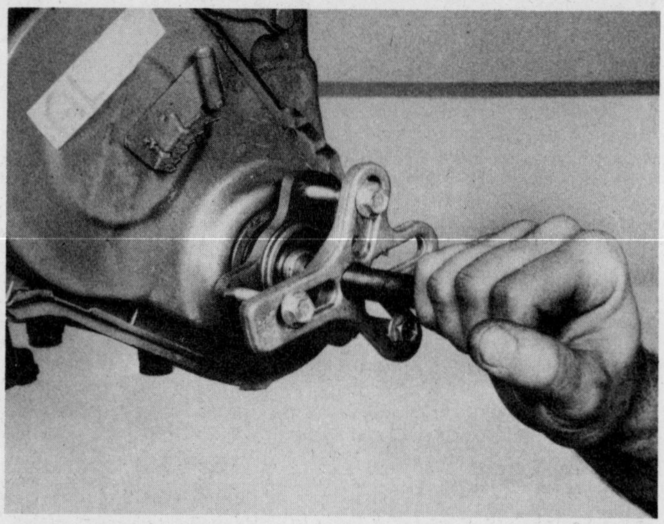

33.5 Using a hub puller to remove the hub from the crankshaft

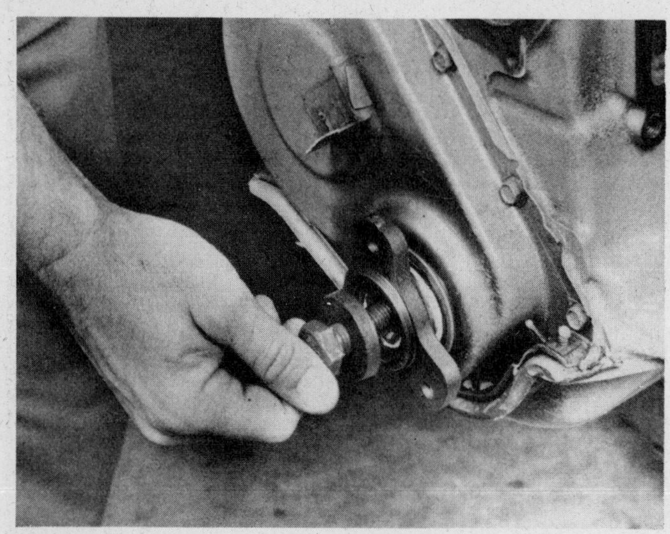

33.9 Drawing the hub onto the crankshaft with the hub bolt

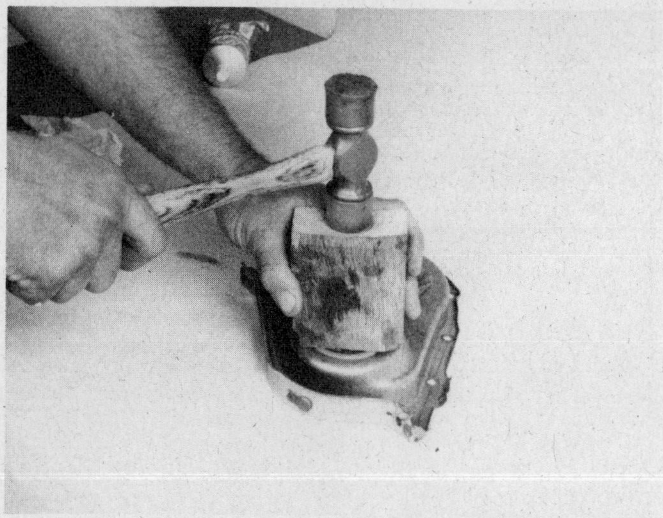

34.12 Using a block of wood to install the front oil seal in the timing gear cover.

or in gear (manual) to prevent the engine from turning over, remove the crank pulley bolt. As there is considerable torque on this bolt, a breaker bar will probably be necessary.

4 Mark the positon of the pulley in relation to the hub (photo). Remove the bolts that secure the crank pulley to the hub and lift off the pulley.

5 Using a hub puller, remove the hub from the crankshaft (photo).

6 Carefully pry out the oil seal from the front cover with a large screwdriver. Be sure not to distort the cover.

7 Install the new seal with the helical lip toward the rear of the engine. Drive the seal into place using a special front oil seal installing tool or an appropriate-size socket.

8 Apply a light coat of oil to the inside lip of the seal.

9 Position the pulley hub on the crankshaft and, using a slight twisting motion, slide it through the seal until it bottoms against the crankshaft gear. The crank pulley hub bolt can also be used to press the hub into position (photo).

10 Install the crank pulley onto the hub, aligning the marks made during removal.

11 Install the crank pulley hub bolt and tighten it to the specified torque.

12 Complete the installation by reversing the removal steps. Tighten the drivebelts to their proper tension.

34 Timing gear cover – removal and installation

Note: *If the engine has been removed from the vehicle, disregard the following steps which do not apply.*

1 Remove the crank pulley hub as described in Section 33.

2 Remove the lower alternator bracket.

3 Remove the nuts that secure the front engine mount to the cradle.

4 Remove the fan shroud and (if equipped) the air conditioner compressor bracket.

5 Loosen the drivebelts.

6 Remove the bolts that secure the timing gear cover to the engine block and oil pan.

7 Pull the cover forward slightly and, using a sharp knife or other suitable cutting tool, cut the front oil pan seal flush with the cylinder block at both sides of the cover.

8 Remove the timing gear cover.

9 Remove the timing gear cover gasket.

10 Using a degreaser, clean all dirt and old gasket material from the sealing surfaces of the timing gear cover, engine block and oil pan.

11 Replace the front oil seal by carefully prying it out of the timing gear cover with a large screwdriver. Be sure not to distort the cover.

12 Install the new seal with the helical lip toward the inside of the cover. Drive the seal into place using a special front oil seal installing

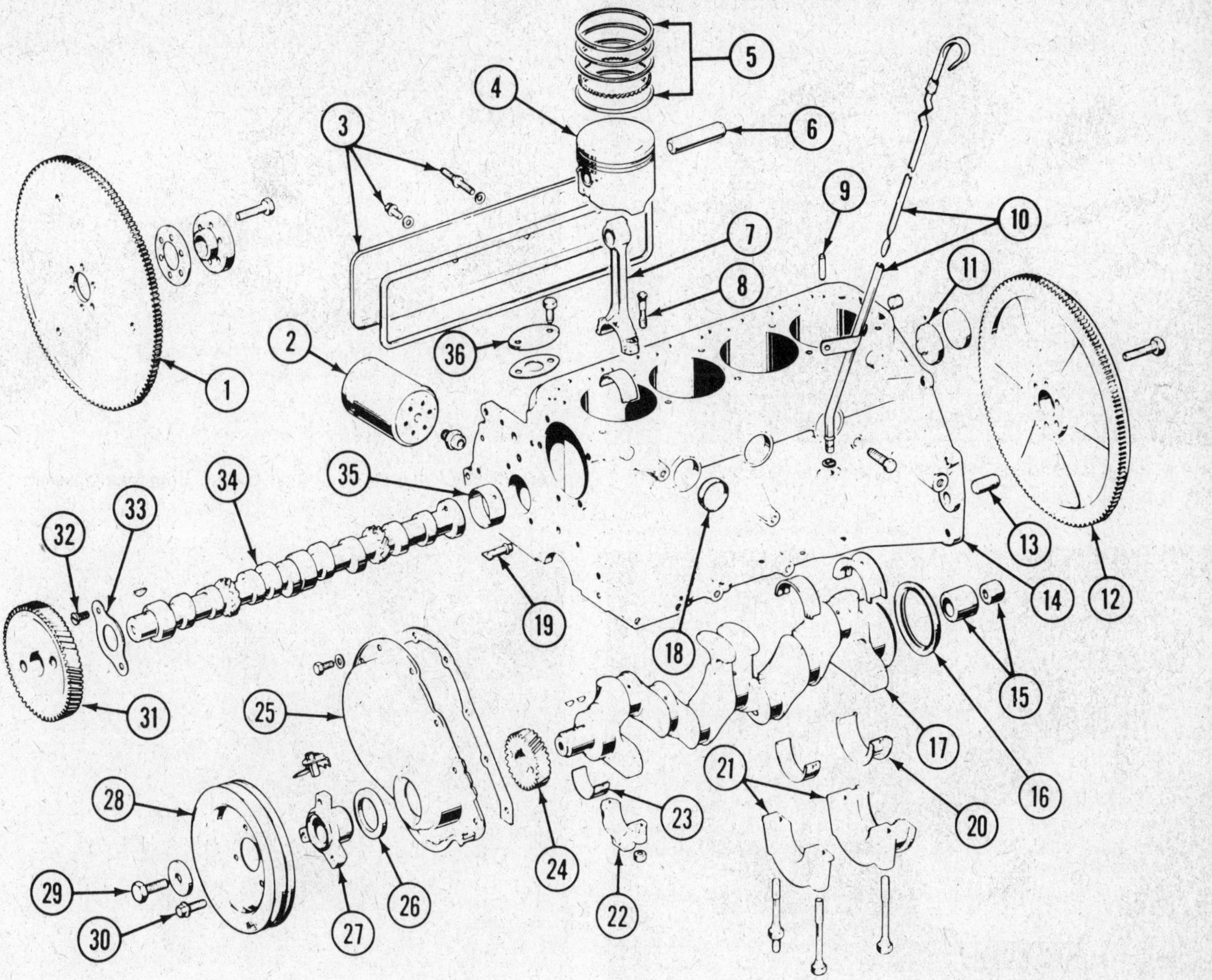

Fig. 2.18 Engine lower end components – exploded view

1 *Driveplate and ring gear (automatic transmission)*
2 *Oil filter*
3 *Pushrod cover and bolts*
4 *Piston*
5 *Piston rings*
6 *Piston pin*
7 *Connecting rod*
8 *Connecting rod bolt*
9 *Dowel pin*
10 *Dipstick and tube*
11 *Camshaft button*
12 *Flywheel and ring gear (manual transmission)*
13 *Dowel pin*
14 *Cylinder block*
15 *Pilot and/or converter bushing*
16 *Rear main oil seal*
17 *Crankshaft*
18 *Block core soft (freeze) plug*
19 *Timing gear oiler*
20 *Main bearings*
21 *Main bearing caps*
22 *Connecting rod bearing cap*
23 *Connecting rod bearing*
24 *Crankshaft gear*
25 *Timing gear cover*
26 *Timing gear cover oil seal*
27 *Crankshaft pulley hub*
28 *Crankshaft pulley*
29 *Crankshaft pulley hub bolt*
30 *Crankshaft pulley bolt*
31 *Camshaft timing gear*
32 *Camshaft thrust plate screw*
33 *Camshaft thrust plate*
34 *Camshaft*
35 *Camshaft bearing*
36 *Oil pump driveshaft retainer plate, gasket and bolt*

tool or an appropriate-size socket. A flat block of wood will also work (photo).

13 Prior to installing the cover, install a new front oil pan gasket. Cut the ends off of the gasket as shown in the accompanying figure and install it on the cover by pressing the rubber tips into the holes provided.

14 Apply a thin coat of RTV-type gasket sealant to the timing gear cover gasket and place it in position on the cover.

15 Apply a bead of RTV-type sealant to the joint between the oil pan and engine block.

16 Using the crank pulley hub as a centering tool, insert the hub into the front cover seal and place the cover in position on the block with the hub on the crankshaft.

17 Install the oil pan-to-cover bolts and partially tighten them.

18 Install the bolts that secure the cover to the block and tighten all of the mounting bolts to the specified torque.

19 Remove the hub from the front cover seal.

20 Complete the installation by reversing the removal procedure.

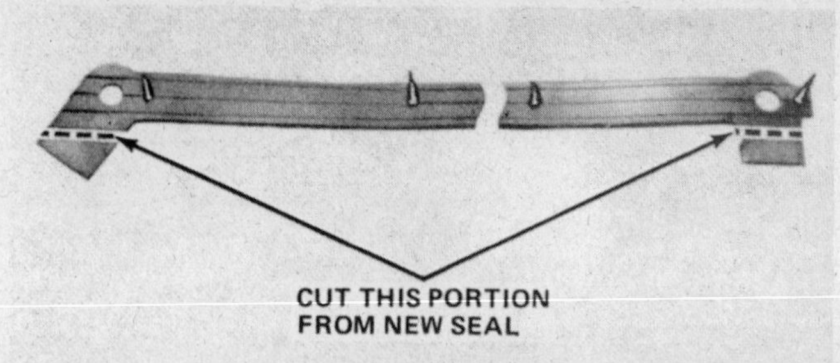

Fig. 2.19 The front oil pan gasket must be cut as shown to form a proper seal with the side gaskets (Sec 36)

35 Oil pump driveshaft – removal and installation

Note: *If the engine has been removed from the vehicle, disregard the following steps which do not apply.*

1 Remove the air cleaner.

2 Remove the carburetor bowl vent line at the rocker arm cover.

3 Remove the upper alternator bracket.

4 Remove the alternator.

5 Remove the oil pump driveshaft retainer plate bolts.

6 Remove the bushing.

7 Remove the shaft and gear assembly.

8 Thoroughly clean the sealing surfaces on the cylinder block and retainer plate.

9 Inspect the gear teeth to see if they are chipped or broken. Replace the gear if necessary.

10 Install the oil pump driveshaft into the block and turn it until it engages with the camshaft drive gear in the oil pump body.

11 Apply a $\frac{1}{16}$-inch (1.5 mm) diameter bead of RTV-type sealant to the retainer plate so that it completely seals around the oil pump driveshaft hole in the block (photo). Install the retainer plate mounting bolts and tighten them securely.

12 Complete the installation by reversing the removal procedure.

36 Oil pan – removal and installation

1 Due to clearance problems with the chassis crossmember, the oil pan can only be removed with the engine out of the vehicle.

2 Remove the oil pan retaining bolts and lift off the oil pan. It may be necessary to use a rubber mallet to break the seal.

3 Prior to installing the oil pan, clean any dirt or old gasket material from the sealing surfaces of the oil pan and engine block.

4 The oil pan gasket consists of four separate gasket pieces. Each

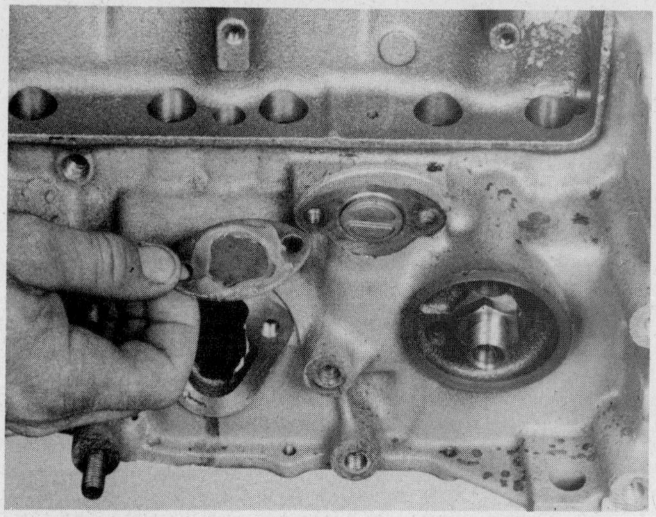

35.11 Apply sealant to the retainer plate prior to installation

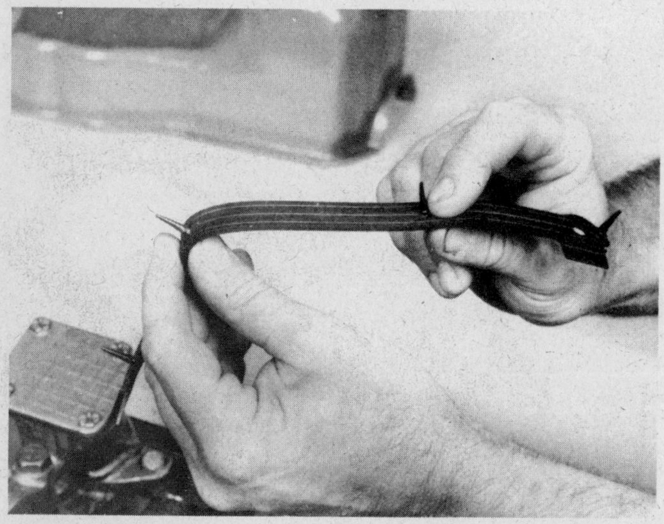

36.4 During installation the rubber tips on the front oil pan gasket should be pressed into the holes in the timing gear cover

36.5 Lower the oil pan carefully into position and do not disturb the gaskets

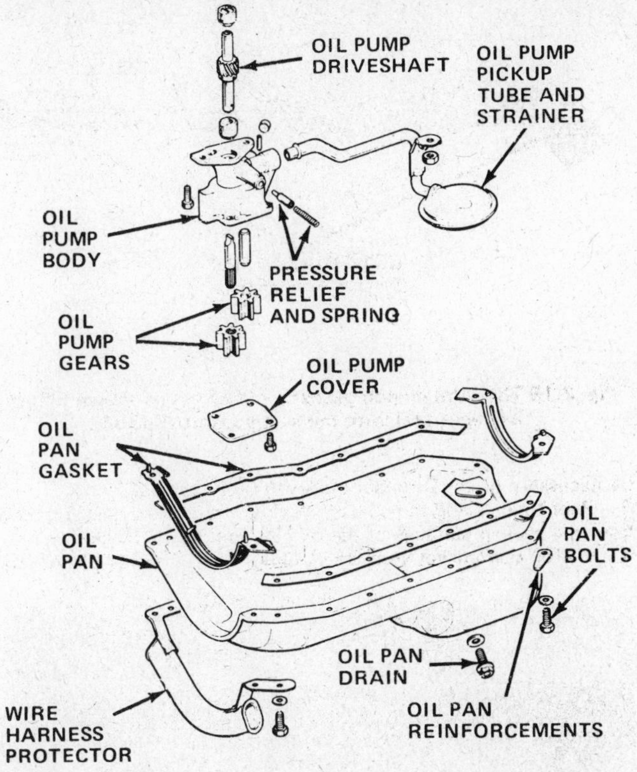

Fig. 2.20 Oil pump and pan components – exploded view

must be carefully installed in its proper place to form a good junction with the other pieces it joins with.

a) Install the rear oil pan gasket in the rear main bearing cap and apply a small quantity of RTV-type sealant in depressions where the pan gasket engages in the block.
b) Install the front oil pan gasket on the timing gear cover, pressing the tips into the holes provided in the cover (photo).
c) Install the side gaskets on the oil pan, using grease to hold them in place.
d) Trim the ends off of the front gasket as indicated in the accompanying illustration to form a good joint with the side gaskets.
e) Apply a bead of RTV-type sealant at the split lines between the front gasket and the side gaskets. The pan can now be installed.

5 Place the oil pan into position against the block (photo) and insert the rear and side mounting bolts. Tighten these bolts snugly before installing the front bolts into the timing cover. Tighten all of the bolts to the specified torque.

37 Oil pump – removal and installation

1 Remove the oil pan as described in Section 36.
2 Remove the two oil pump flange mounting bolts and the nut from the main bearing cap bolt.
3 Lift off the oil pump and screen as an assembly.
4 If the oil pump is to be overhauled, refer to Section 38.
5 To install the pump, align the shaft so it mates with the oil pump driveshaft tang.
6 Place the oil pump housing flange in position and install the mounting bolt(s). No gasket is needed between the pump flange and the block.
7 Install the oil pump screen bracket over the main bearing cap bolt and install the nut.
8 Tighten the pump mounting bolt(s) and screen support nut to the specified torque.
9 Install the oil pan.

38 Oil pump – disassembly, inspection and reassembly

1 In most cases it will be more practical and economical to replace a faulty oil pump with a new or rebuilt unit. If it is decided to overhaul the oil pump, check on availability of internal parts before beginning.
2 Remove the pump cover retaining screws and the pump cover. Index mark the gear teeth to permit reassembly in the same position.
3 Remove the idler gear, drive gear and shaft from the body (photo).
4 Remove the pressure regulator valve retaining pin (photo), the regulator valve and the related parts (photo).
5 The screen assembly is factory-fitted to the pump body and cannot be separated.
6 Wash all the parts in solvent and dry them thoroughly. Inspect the body for cracks, wear and damage. Inspect the gears (photo).
7 Check the drive gear shaft for looseness in the pump body and the inside of the pump cover for wear that would permit oil leakage past the ends of the gears (photo). If either the gears or body are worn or damaged, the entire oil pump assembly must be replaced.
8 Inspect the pickup screen and pipe assembly for damage to the screen, pipe and relief grommet.

2B

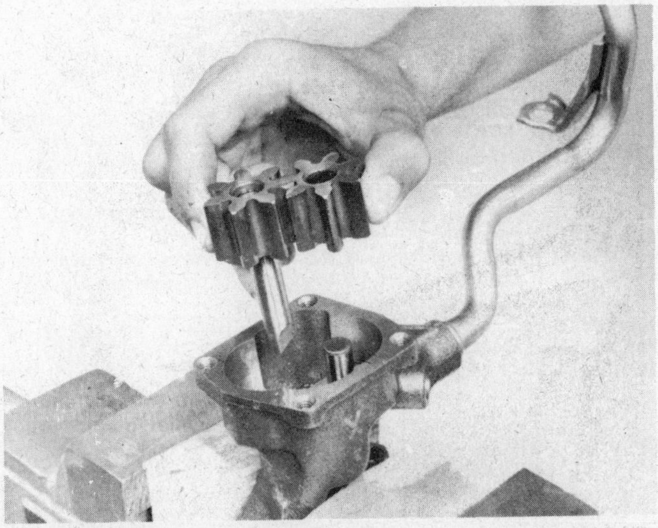

38.3 Removing the drive gear and shaft and the idler gear from the oil pump body

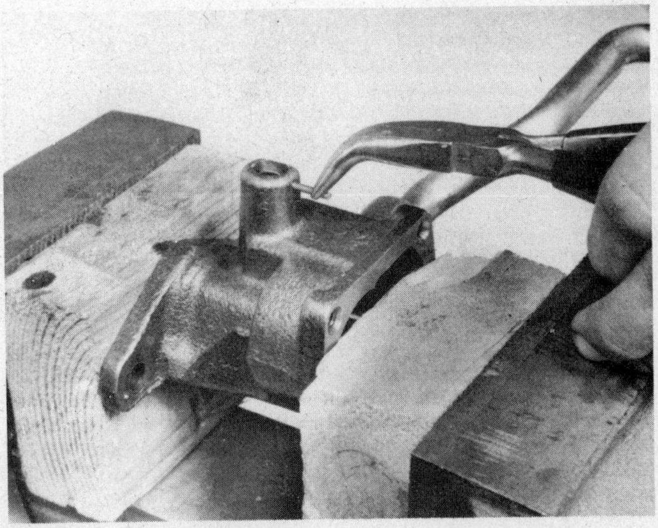

38.4A Removing the pressure regulator valve retaining pin with needle-nose pliers

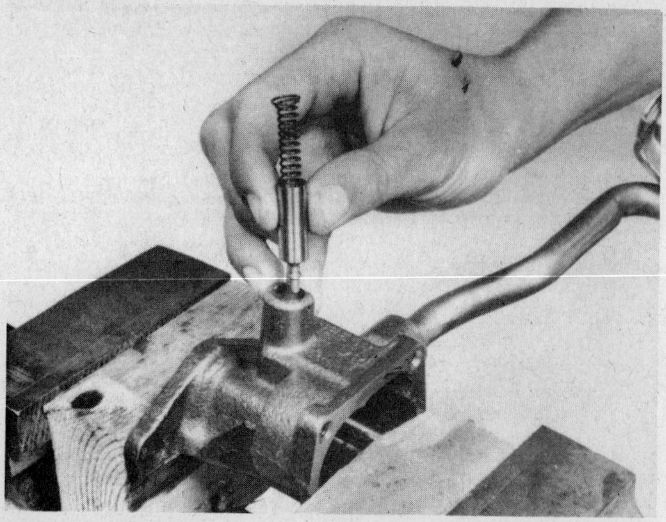
38.4B Withdrawing the pressure regulator valve assembly

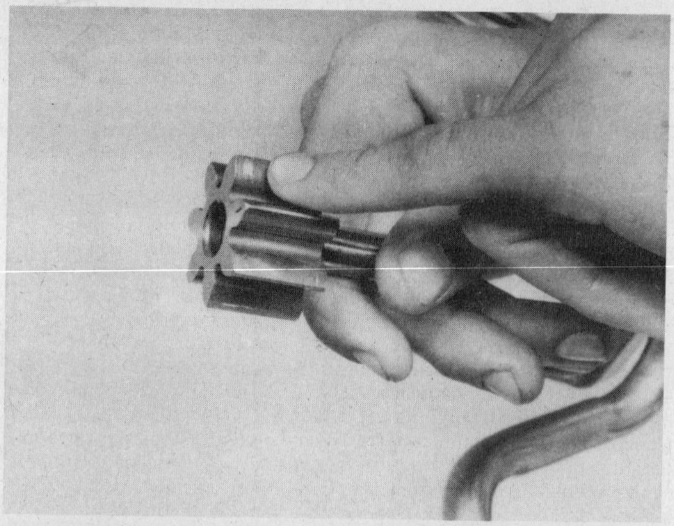
38.6 If the gears show signs of wear or damage they should be replaced with new ones

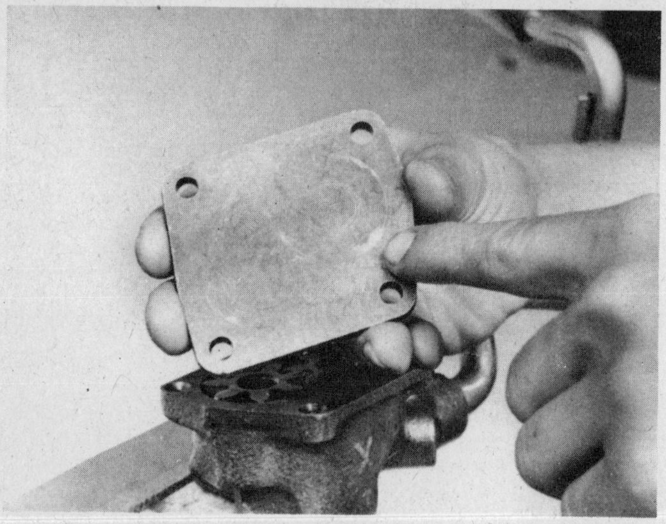
38.7 Inspect the pump cover for wear

39.3 A long screwdriver can be used to prevent the flywheel from turning during bolt removal

9 Install the pressure regulator valve and related parts.
10 Install the drive gear and shaft in the pump body, followed by the idler gear with the smooth side toward the pump cover opening. Lubricate the parts with engine oil.
11 Install the cover and tighten the screws to the specified torque.
12 Turn the driveshaft to ensure that the pump operates freely.

39 Flywheel and rear main oil seal – removal and installation

1 To gain access to the flywheel, either the engine or the transmission must be removed from the vehicle. If other engine work is needed, remove the engine as described in Section 22. If no other work necessitating the removal of the engine needs to be done it would be easier to remove the transmission as described in Chapter 7.
2 If equipped with a manual transmission remove the clutch from the flywheel as described in Chapter 8.
3 The flywheel can be unbolted from the rear flange of the crankshaft. To prevent the flywheel from turning, a long screwdriver or similar tool can be run through the flywheel and positioned against the engine block (photo).
4 Once the bolts are removed, the flywheel can be lifted off.
5 Remove the flywheel spacer if so equipped.
6 If the rear main bearing seal must be replaced, pry it out of its bore.
7 Examine the flywheel ring gear for any broken or chipped teeth. If this condition exists, the flywheel must be replaced with a new one.
8 On manual transmission flywheels, inspect the clutch friction face for scoring. Light scoring may be corrected using emery cloth, but where there is deep scoring the flywheel must be replaced with a new one or clutch damage will soon occur.
9 On automatic transmission flywheels, examine the converter securing bolt holes for distortion. This condition, too, necessitates the replacement of the flywheel.
10 Before installing the flywheel, clean the mating surfaces of the flywheel and the crankshaft.
11 If the oil seal was removed, apply a light coat of engine oil to the inside lip of the new seal and install it in its bore.
12 To install the flywheel, position it in place against the crankshaft using a new spacer, if equipped, and insert the mounting bolts, securing them only finger tight. It is a good idea to use a thread sealing agent such as Loc-tite, or equivalent, on the bolt threads.
13 Again, while preventing the flywheel from turning, tighten the bolts a little at a time until they are all at the specified torque.
14 Complete the remainder of the installation procedure by reversing the removal steps.

40 Camshaft and bearings – removal and installation

1 Remove the engine as described in Section 22 and mount it on a suitable stand.
2 Remove the rocker arm cover.
3 Loosen the rocker arm nuts/bolts and pivot the rocker arms clear of the pushrods.
4 Remove the pushrods.
5 Remove the pushrod cover.
6 Remove the valve lifters as described in Section 28.
7 Remove the distributor.
8 Remove the fuel pump.
9 Remove the oil pump driveshaft and gear assembly.
10 Remove the front pulley hub as described in Section 33.
11 Remove the timing gear cover as described in Section 34.
12 Remove the two camshaft thrust plate screws by working through the holes in the camshaft gear.
13 While supporting the camshaft with your fingers inserted through the fuel pump hole to prevent damaging the camshaft bearings, carefully and slowly pull the camshaft straight out from the block (photo).
14 If the gear must be removed from the camshaft, it must be pressed off. If you do not have access to a press, take it to your dealer or an automotive machine shop. The thrust plate must be positioned so that the woodruff key in the shaft does not damage it when the shaft is pressed out.
15 Examine the bearing surfaces and the surfaces of the cam lobes. The oil pan may have to be removed to thoroughly inspect the bearings. Surface scratches, if they are very shallow, can be removed by rubbing with a fine emery cloth or oilstone. Any deep scoring will necessitate a new camshaft.
16 Mount the camshaft on V-blocks and use a dial gauge to measure lobe lift. Reject a camshaft which does not meet the specified limits.
17 Using a micrometer, measure the journal diameters (photo). Again, reject a camshaft which does not meet the specified limits.
18 If the camshaft bearings are worn, they must be replaced using the following procedure:

a) Remove the oil pan if it is still in place.
b) Remove the flywheel.
c) Driving from the inside out, remove the expansion plug from the rear cam bearing.
d) Using a camshaft bearing remover set, available from a dealer or auto parts store, drive out the front bearing toward the rear.
e) Drive out the rear bearing toward the front.
f) Using an extension on the bearing remover, drive out the center bearing toward the rear.

40.13 Support the camshaft inside the block (arrow) during removal (withdraw the camshaft straight out, taking care not to gouge the bearing surfaces with the cam lobes)

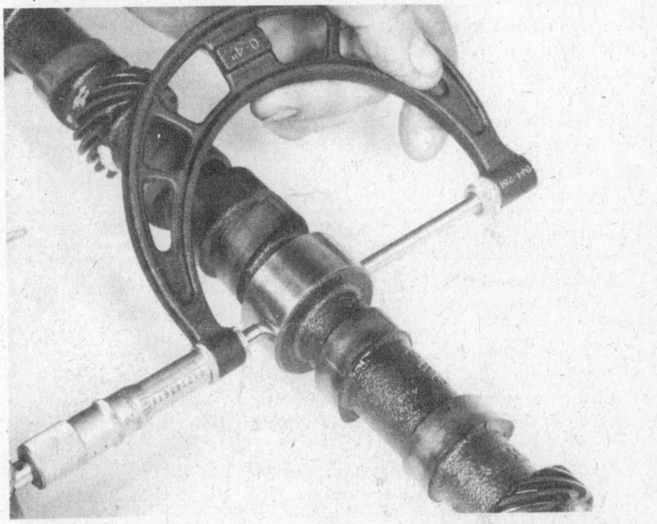

40.17 Measuring the cam bearing journal diameter with a micrometer

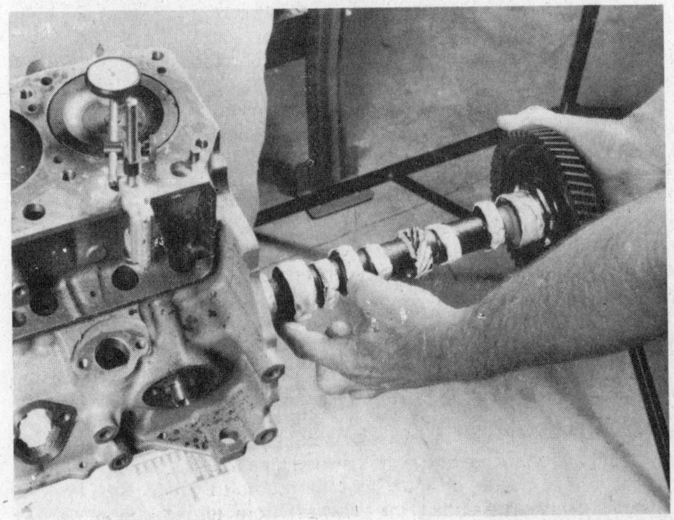

40.21 Lubricate the camshaft lobes and journals prior to installation of the shaft in the block (the dial indicator is used here to verify that the piston is at Top Dead Center)

40.22 The camshaft and crankshaft gears must be positioned with timing marks (arrows) aligned

g) Install the new bearings by reversing the removal procedure. Be sure all of the oil holes are aligned. **Note:** *The front bearing must be driven approximately $\frac{1}{8}$-inch from the front of the cylinder block in order to uncover the oil hole to the timing gear oil nozzle.*
h) After installing the new bearings, install a new camshaft rear expansion plug flush with the rear surface of the block.
i) Reinstall the flywheel and oil pan.

19 If the camshaft gear has been removed from the camshaft, it must be pressed on prior to installation of the camshaft.

a) Support the camshaft in an arbor press by using press plate adapters behind the front journal.
b) Place the gear spacer ring and the thrust plate over the end of the shaft.
c) Install the woodruff key in the shaft keyway.
d) Install the camshaft gear and press it onto the shaft until it bottoms against the gear spacer ring.
e) Use a feeler gauge to check the end clearance of the thrust plate. It should be 0.0015 to 0.0050 inch. If the clearance is less than 0.0015 inch the spacer ring should be replaced. If the clearance is more than 0.0050 inch the thrust plate should be replaced.

20 Prior to installing the camshaft, verify that the number 1 piston is at TDC. Coat each of the lobes and journals liberally with a moly-based grease or engine assembly lube.
21 Slide the camshaft into the engine block, again taking care not to damage the bearings (photo).
22 Position the camshaft and crankshaft gears so that the valve timing marks line up (photo). With the shafts in this position, the engine is in the number four (4) cylinder firing position.
23 Install the camshaft thrust plate mounting screws and tighten them to the specified torque.

41 Crankshaft – removal

1 Remove the engine from the vehicle as described in Section 22.
2 Remove the crankshaft pulley and hub assembly as described in Section 33.
3 Remove the oil pan.
4 Remove the oil pump assembly.
5 Remove the timing gear cover.
6 Remove the pistons and connecting rods from the crankshaft as described in Chapter 2A.
7 Remove the flywheel as described in Section 39.
8 Refer to Chapter 2A for the remainder of the crankshaft removal procedure.

42 Crankshaft – installation and main bearing oil clearance check

Note: *If a new or reground crankshaft is being installed, or if the original crankshaft has been reground, make sure the correct bearings are used.*
1 Crankshaft installation is generally one of the first steps in engine reassembly; it is assumed at this point that the engine block and crankshaft have been cleaned and inspected and repaired or reconditioned.
2 Position the engine with the bottom facing up.
3 Remove the main bearing cap bolts and lift out the caps. Lay them out in the proper order to help ensure correct installation.
4 If they are still in place, remove the old bearing inserts from the block and the main bearing caps. Wipe the main bearing surfaces of the block and caps with a clean, lint-free cloth (they must be kept spotlessly clean).
5 Clean the back side of the new main bearing inserts and lay one bearing half in each main bearing saddle (in the block) (photo) and the other bearing half from each bearing set in the corresponding main bearing cap. Make sure the tab on the bearing insert fits into the recess in the block or cap. Also, the oil holes in the block and cap must line up with the oil holes in the bearing insert. *Do not hammer the bearing into place and do not nick or gouge the bearing faces. No lubrication should be used at this time.*
6 The thrust bearings must be installed in the number five (rear) cap and saddle.
7 Clean the faces of the bearings in the block and the crankshaft main bearing journals with a clean, lint-free cloth. Check or clean the oil holes in the crankshaft, as any dirt here can only go one way – straight through the new bearings.
8 Once you are certain that the crankshaft is clean, carefully lay it in position (an assistant would be very helpful here) in the main bearings with the counterweights lying sideways.
9 Before the crankshaft can be permanently installed, the main bearing oil clearance must be checked.
10 Trim five pieces of the appropriate type of Plastigage (so they are slightly shorter than the width of the main bearings) and place one piece on each crankshaft main bearing journal, parallel with the journal axis (photo). Do not lay them across any oil holes.
11 Clean the faces of the bearings in the caps and install the caps in their respective positions (do not mix them up) with the arrows pointing toward the front of the engine. Do not disturb the Plastigage.
12 Starting with the center main and working out toward the ends, tighten the main bearing cap bolts, in three steps, to the specified torque. *Do not rotate the crankshaft at any time during this operation.*
13 Remove the bolts and carefully lift off the main bearing caps. Keep them in order. Do not disturb the Plastigage or rotate the crankshaft. If any of the main bearing caps are difficult to remove, tap gently from side-to-side with a soft-faced hammer to loosen them.
14 Compare the width of the crushed Plastigage on each journal to the scale printed on the Plastigage container to obtain the main bearing oil clearance (photo). Check the Specifications to make sure it is correct.
15 If the clearance is not correct, double-check to make sure that you have the right size bearing inserts. Also, recheck the crankshaft main bearing journal diameters and make sure that no dirt or oil was between the bearing inserts and the main bearing caps or the block when the clearance was measured.
16 Using a piece of hardwood or your fingernail, carefully scrape all traces of Plastigage material off the main bearing journals and/or the bearing faces. Do not nick or scratch the bearing faces.
17 Carefully lift the crankshaft out of the engine. Clean the bearing faces in the block, then apply a thin layer of clean, high-quality moly-based grease or engine assembly lube to each of the bearing faces. Be

42.5 Installing the main bearings in the block

42.10 Place the Plastigage strip (arrow) on the journal, parallel to the journal axis

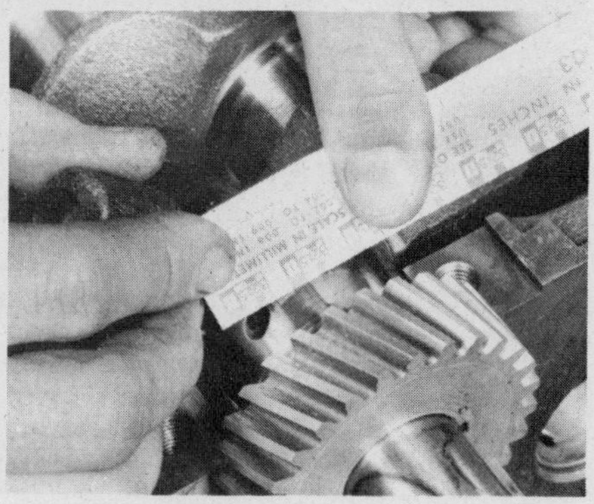
42.14 The oil clearance is obtained by comparing the crushed Plastigage to the scale printed on the container

sure to coat the thrust bearing faces as well. Make sure the crankshaft journals are clean, then carefully lay it back in place in the block. Clean the faces of the bearings in the caps, then apply a thin layer of clean, high-quality moly-based grease or engine assembly lube to each of the bearing faces and install the caps in their respective positions with the arrows pointing toward the front of the engine. Install the bolts and tighten the bolts in caps one through four to the specified torque, starting with the center main and working out towards the ends. Work up to the final torque in three steps. Tighten the bolts in the number five (rear) cap to 10 ft-lb, then use a lead or brass hammer to tap the crankshaft to the rear, then the front, to center the thrust bearing. Tighten the rear cap bolts to the specified torque.

18 Rotate the crankshaft a number of times by hand and check for any obvious binding.

19 Next, check the crankshaft end play. This can be done with a feeler gauge or a dial indicator set (refer to Section 12 in Chapter 2A).

20 Lubricate the seal lip with multi-purpose grease or engine assembly lube, then center the seal over the rear end of the crankshaft with the seal lip facing the *front* of the engine. Using a soft-faced hammer, carefully drive the seal into the groove in the main bearing cap and block until it is seated. Make sure it is driven in squarely.

21 Install the woodruff key in the front of the crankshaft, then slip the timing gear into place.

22 Refer to the appropriate Sections and install the piston/connecting rod assemblies, the camshaft, the oil pump, the oil pan, the flywheel, the timing gear cover and the pulley hub.

43 Engine/manual transmission – rejoining

1 Install the clutch housing and tighten the bolts to the specified torque.

2 Lubricate the pilot bushing with clean engine oil and install it.

3 Install the throwout bearing and attach the transmission, making sure it is properly aligned. Install the retaining bolts and tighten them to the specified torque.

44 Engine/automatic transmission – rejoining

1 Install the converter on the transmission input shaft.

2 Place the transmission in position on the engine, install the attaching bolts and tighten them to the specified torque.

3 Align the marks made on the converter and driveplate during removal. Apply thread-locking compound to the threads of the retaining bolts, install and tighten them to the specified torque.

4 Install the converter housing cover.

5 Install the starter motor.

45 Engine – installation

1 Connect the transmission to the engine and install a lifting device.

2 Lower the engine/transmission assembly into the engine compartment.

3 Raise the vehicle and support it securely.

4 Connect the transmission fluid cooler lines (automatic transmission), speedometer cable, shift linkage and Neutral start switch (if so equipped).

5 Install the rear transmission mount, raise the transmission and install the rear crossmember.

6 Connect the exhaust pipe to the manifold, install the bolts and tighten them to the specified torque.

7 Install the engine mount cushion nuts and tighten them to the specified torque.

8 Install the engine ground cable, raising the engine slightly to start the bolt.

9 Install the driveshaft.

10 Connect the starter motor cable and wire, distributor wires, oil pressure sending unit wire and fuel hose.

11 Lower the vehicle.

12 Insert the alternator wire harness and coolant temperature sending unit wire through the harness protector tube and connect them.

13 Install the air conditioning compressor and condenser with the large bracket on the condenser facing down. Have the system recharged by an air conditioning technician.

14 Connect the sill clips which retain the evaporator to the hose.

15 Install the radiator and connect the lower hose.

16 Install the fan, shroud and upper radiator hose.

17 Install the dipstick tube assembly, power steering pump and drivebelts. Adjust the drivebelt tension and refill the power steering pump reservoir.

18 Connect the vacuum hoses, choke, idle speed solenoid wire, MC solenoid (if so equipped) and heater hoses.

19 Connect the throttle cable to the carburetor and install the retainer.

20 Fill the radiator with the specified coolant.

21 Fill the engine to the correct level with the specified oil.

22 Connect the negative battery cable.

23 Install the hood.

24 Refer to Chapter 2A for the initial start-up and break-in procedures.

Chapter 2 Part C Six-cylinder engine

Contents

Camshaft – removal ... 58
Camshaft and bearings – inspection and replacement ... 66
Camshaft and timing chain/sprockets – installation ... 74
Crankshaft – inspection ... Chapter 2A
Crankshaft – installation and main bearing oil clearance check ... 71
Crankshaft – removal ... Chapter 2A
Cylinder head – cleaning and inspection ... Chapter 2A
Cylinder head – disassembly ... Chapter 2A
Cylinder head – reassembly ... Chapter 2A
Cylinder head – removal ... 55
Cylinder head and rocker gear – installation ... 76
Engine (1977 through 1983 models) – installation ... 79
Engine (1977 through 1983 models) – removal ... 50
Engine/automatic transmission (1970 through 1976 models) – separation ... 52
Engine block – cleaning ... Chapter 2A
Engine block – inspection ... Chapter 2A
Engine disassembly – general information ... Chapter 2A
Engine/manual transmission (1970 through 1976 models) – separation ... 51
Engine mount flexible cushions – replacement ... 48
Engine overhaul – general information ... Chapter 2A
Engine rebuilding alternatives ... Chapter 2A
Engine removal – methods and precautions ... Chapter 2A
Engine/transmission (1970 through 1976 models) – installation ... 78
Engine/transmission (1970 through 1976 models) – removal ... 49
External components – installation ... 77
External components – removal ... 53
Flywheel and starter ring gear – inspection and servicing ... 68
Flywheel/driveplate – installation ... 72
Flywheel/driveplate – removal ... 62
General information ... 46
Initial start-up and break-in after overhaul ... Chapter 2A
Lubrication system – general information ... 61
Main and connecting rod bearings – inspection ... Chapter 2A
Main and connecting rod bearings – selection ... 70
Oil pan – removal ... 59
Oil pump – disassembly, inspection and reassembly ... 67
Oil pump – removal ... 60
Oil pump and oil pan – installation ... 73
Oil seals – replacement ... 69
Oversize and undersize component designation ... 47
Piston/connecting rod assembly – inspection ... Chapter 2A
Piston/connecting rod assembly – installation and bearing oil clearance check ... Chapter 2A
Piston/connecting rod assembly – removal ... Chapter 2A
Piston rings – installation ... Chapter 2A
Repair operations possible with the engine in the vehicle ... Chapter 2A
Rocker gear – inspection and overhaul ... 63
Rocker gear – removal ... 54
Timing chain and sprockets – inspection ... 65
Timing cover, chain and sprockets – removal ... 57
Valve lifters – description and removal ... 56
Valve lifters – inspection and overhaul ... 64
Valve lifters – installation ... 75
Valves – servicing ... Chapter 2A

Specifications

General

Displacement	199, 232 or 258 cu in
Bore and stroke	
199 cu in engine	3.750 x 3.00 in
232 cu in engine	3.750 x 3.50 in
258 cu in engine	3.750 x 3.895 in
Oil pressure	
600 rpm	13 psi
Above 1600 rpm	37 to 75 psi

Engine block

Cylinder bore	
Diameter	3.7501 to 3.7533 in
Taper limit	
1971 through 1978	0.005 in
1979 through 1983	0.001 in
Out-of-round limit	
1971 through 1978	0.003 in
1979 through 1983	0.001 in
Deck warpage limit	0.006 in max.

Pistons and rings

Piston-to-cylinder bore clearance	
Standard	0.0009 to 0.0017 in
Preferred	0.0012 to 0.0013 in
Piston ring side clearance	
1971 and 1972	
Compression	0.0015 to 0.0035 in
Oil control	0.000 to 0.005 in
1973 through 1980	
Compression (standard)	0.0015 to 0.003 in
Compression (preferred)	0.0015 in
Oil control (standard)	0.001 to 0.008 in
Oil control (preferred)	0.003 in
1981 through 1983	
Compression (standard)	0.0017 to 0.0032 in
Compression (preferred)	0.0017 in
Oil control (standard)	0.001 to 0.008 in
Oil control (preferred)	0.003 in
Piston ring end gap	
Compression (all)	0.010 to 0.20 in
Oil control	
1971 and 1972 only	0.015 to 0.055 in
All others	0.010 to 0.025 in
Piston pin diameter	0.9304 to 0.9309 in
Piston pin-to-piston clearance	
Standard	0.0003 to 0.0005 in
Preferred	0.0005 in

Crankshaft

Main journal	
Diameter	
1971 through 1981	2.4986 to 2.5001 in
1982 and 1983	2.4996 to 2.5001 in
Taper limit	0.0005 in
Out-of-round limit	0.0005 in
Main bearing oil clearance	
1971 through 1973	0.001 to 0.002 in
1974 through 1980	
Standard	0.001 to 0.003 in
Preferred	0.0025 in
1981 through 1983	
Standard	0.001 to 0.0025 in
Preferred	0.002 in
Connecting rod journal	
Diameter	2.0934 to 2.0955 in
Taper limit	0.0005 in
Out-of-round limit	0.0005 in
Connecting rod bearing oil clearance	
1971 through 1973	0.001 to 0.002 in
1974 and 1975	
Standard	0.001 to 0.003 in
Preferred	0.0025 in
1976 through 1980	
Standard	0.001 to 0.0025 in
Preferred	0.0055 to 0.002 in
1981 through 1983	
Standard	0.001 to 0.003 in
Preferred	0.0015 to 0.002 in
Connecting rod end play	
1971 and 1972	0.008 to 0.010 in
1973 through 1980	0.005 to 0.014 in
1981 through 1983	0.010 to 0.019 in
Crankshaft end play	0.0015 to 0.0065 in

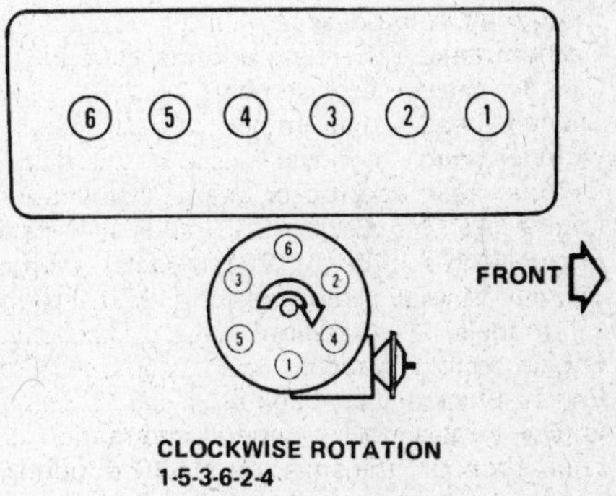

SIX-CYLINDER ENGINES

Cylinder location and distributor rotation

Camshaft

Bearing journal diameter	
Number 1	2.029 to 2.030 in
Number 2	2.019 to 2.020 in
Number 3	2.009 to 2.010 in
Number 4	1.999 to 2.000 in
Bearing oil clearance	0.001 to 0.003 in

Lobe lift	
1971 through 1974	0.254 in
1975 and 1976	0.232 in
1977 through 1979	
232/258 with 1 bbl. carb	0.232 in
258 with 2 bbl. carb	0.248 in
1980	0.248 in
1981 through 1983	0.253 in
End play	Zero (engine operating)

Cylinder head and valve train

Head warpage limit	0.006 in max
Intake valve seat angle	30°
Exhaust valve seat angle	44.5°
Intake valve seat width	
1971	0.050 to 0.075 in
1972 through 1983	0.040 to 0.060 in
Exhaust valve seat width	0.040 to 0.060 in
Valve seat runout limit	0.0025 in
Valve guide inside diameter	0.3735 to 0.3745 in
Intake valve face angle	29°
Exhaust valve face angle	44°
Valve margin width	$\frac{1}{32}$ in min
Valve stem diameter	0.3715 to 0.3725 in
Valve stem-to-guide clearance	0.001 to 0.003 in
Valve spring free length	
1971 through 1973	Not available
1974 through 1976	
With rotators	2.00 in (approx)
Without rotators	2.234 in (approx)
1977	
258 2 bbl. only	1.987 in (approx)
All others	2.234 in (approx)
1978 through 1983	1.99 in (approx)
Lifter/tappet type	Hydraulic
Valve lash adjustment	Zero
Lifter bore diameter	
1971 through 1973	Not available
1974 through 1980	0.905 to 0.906 in
1981 through 1983	0.9055 to 0.9065 in
Lifter diameter	
1971 through 1973	Not available
1974 through 1980	0.904 to 0.9045 in
Lifter-to-bore clearance	
1971 through 1973	Not available
1974 through 1980	0.001 to 0.002 in
1981 through 1983	0.001 to 0.0025 in
Pushrod diameter	
1971 through 1973 and 1975	Not available
1974	0.294 to 0.303 in
1976 through 1980	0.312 to 0.313 in
1981 through 1983	0.312 to 0.315 in
Pushrod length	
1971 through 1973 and 1975	Not available
1974	9.656 to 9.666 in
1976	9.595 to 9.615 in
1977 through 1983	9.640 to 9.660 in

Oil pump

Gear-to-body clearance	
1971 through 1980	0.0005 to 0.0025 in
1981 through 1983	0.002 to 0.004 in
Gear end clearance	
1971	0 to 0.004 in
1972 through 1976 and 1981 through 1983	0.002 to 0.006 in
1977 through 1980	0.002 to 0.008 in

Oversize and undersize component code letter definition

Code letter

B	All cylinder bores	0.010 in oversize
M	All crankshaft main bearing journals	0.010 in undersize
P	All connecting rod bearing journals	0.010 in undersize
C	All camshaft bearing bores	0.010 in oversize

Torque specifications

	Ft-lb
Camshaft sprocket bolts	45 to 55
Carburetor mounting nuts	12 to 15
Connecting rod cap nuts	
1971 through 1976	26 to 30
1977 through 1983	33
Cylinder head bolts	
1971 and 1972	80 to 85
1973 through 1980	105
1981 through 1983	85
Crankshaft pulley-to-damper bolt	20 to 25
Exhaust manifold bolts	20 to 25
Fan and hub assembly bolts	15 to 25
Driveplate-to-torque converter bolts	
1971	30 to 35
1972 through 1983	20 to 25
Flywheel/driveplate-to-crankshaft bolts	100 to 110
Intake manifold bolts	20 to 25
Main bearing cap bolts	75 to 85
Oil pump cover bolts	
1971	8 to 12
1972	6 to 7.5
1973 through 1983	6
Oil pump mounting bolts	
Short	8 to 12
Long	15 to 18
Oil pan bolts	
$\frac{1}{4}$ x 20	5 to 9
$\frac{5}{16}$ x 18	10 to 13
Bridged rocker pivot bolt	
1973, 1975 and 1976	21
1977 through 1983	19
Rocker arm shaft bolts	
1971	20 to 23
1972	19 to 22
1974	21
Vibration damper bolt	
1971 through 1976	50 to 60
1977 through 1983	80
Water pump bolts	10 to 15

46 General information

The six-cylinder in-line engine is made of cast iron, with a removable cylinder head, intake and exhaust manifolds.

The valves are mounted in the cylinder head and are actuated by a camshaft located in the block via pushrods, rocker arms and hydraulic lifters. Depending on the year of production, the rocker arms are mounted in either of two ways. Some models use a bridged rocker arm pivot, which is attached to the cylinder head by cap screws. On other models the rocker arms operate on a common shaft.

The crankshaft is supported in the block by seven main bearings. The plain bearing inserts for the crankshaft and connecting rods are removable.

The distributor is driven by a gear on the camshaft, which in turn drives the positive displacement oil pump.

Along with the cylinder head and manifolds, the water pump, timing chain cover and bellhousing can be unbolted from the block.

47 Oversize and undersize component designation

1 Some engines may be built with oversize or undersize cylinder bores, crankshaft main bearing journals, connecting rod journals or camshaft bearing bores.

2 A code designating the presence of oversize or undersize components is stamped on the cylinder block oil filter boss located between the distributor and the ignition coil.

3 Refer to the Specifications and compare the letter code with the information in the chart to determine which components are oversize or undersize.

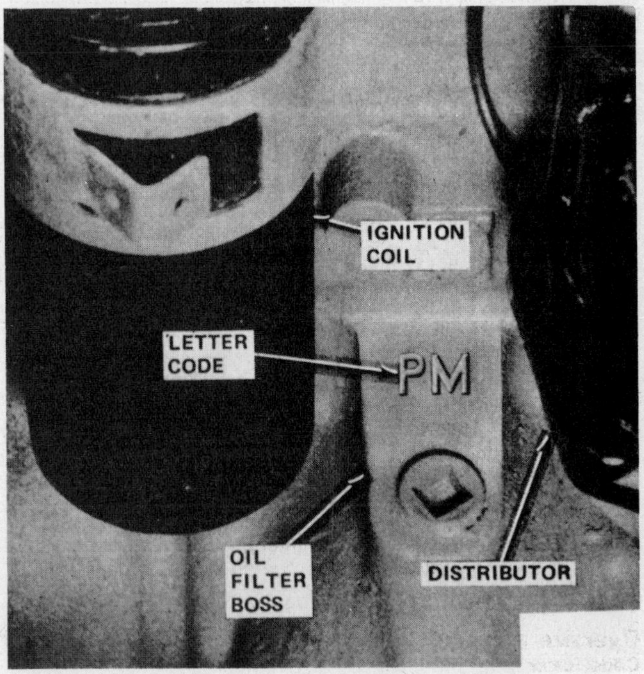

Fig. 2.21 Oversize/undersize component code location (Sec 47)

2C

48 Engine mount flexible cushions – replacement

1 Inspect the engine mount flexible cushions periodically to determine if they have become hard, split or separated from the metal backing.
2 If it is necessary to replace the cushions, it can be accomplished by supporting the weight of the engine or transmission in the area of the cushion.

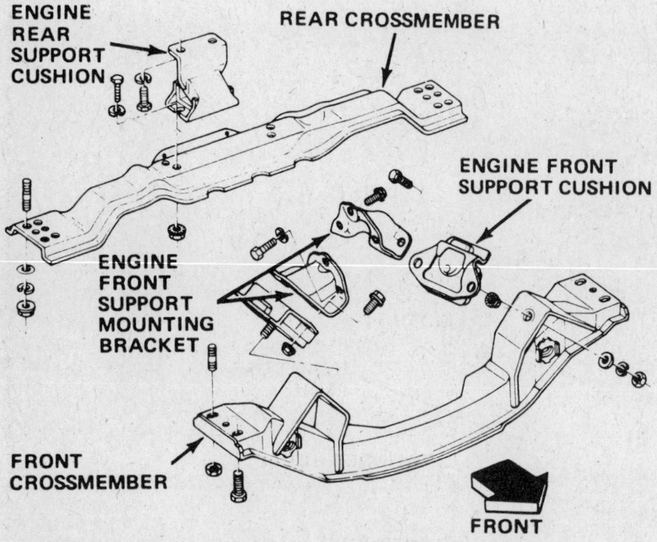

Fig. 2.22 Typical engine mount and flexible cushion component layout (Sec 48)

49 Engine/transmission (1970 through 1976 models) – removal

1 On 1970 through 1976 models the engine and transmission must be removed as a unit.
2 Mark the position of the hinge plates on the underside of the hood, then unbolt the hinges and remove the hood with the help of an assistant.
3 Disconnect the cable from the negative battery terminal. On some models it will be necessary to remove the battery.
4 Drain the cooling system and the engine oil.
5 Remove the radiator and upper baffle (if equipped).
6 Drain the transmission lubricant.
7 Remove the air cleaner.
8 Remove the fan and the drivebelt pulley. On later models insert a $\frac{1}{2}$-inch long $\frac{5}{16}$ bolt through the fan pulley to keep the pulley and water pump aligned.
9 *On vehicles equipped with power steering,* move the power steering pump to one side of the engine compartment.
10 *On vehicles equipped with an air conditioning system,* have the system discharged and remove the compressor and the condenser. **Caution:** *Never disconnect any part of the air conditioning system until the system has been discharged by a qualified technician, such action can be extremely dangerous.*
11 Disconnect all controls from the carburetor.
12 Disconnect all electrical leads from the engine.
13 Disconnect the heater hoses and the fuel hoses.
14 Disconnect the clutch operating rod and return spring.
15 Disconnect the shift lever or speed selector linkage from the transmission (see Chapter 7).
16 Disconnect the speedometer drive cable from the transmission (photo).
17 Disconnect the exhaust pipe(s) from the exhaust manifold.

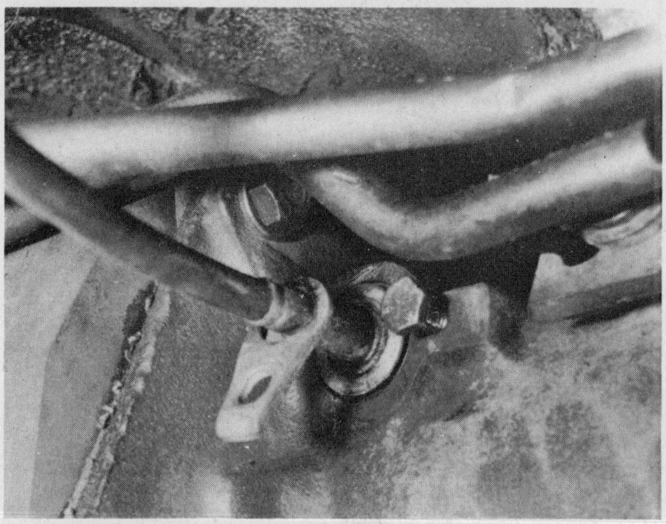

49.16 Disconnecting the speedometer cable from the transmission

49.29 Transmission rear mount crossmember (early models shown)

49.30 The engine/transmission must be lifted from the engine compartment at a steep angle

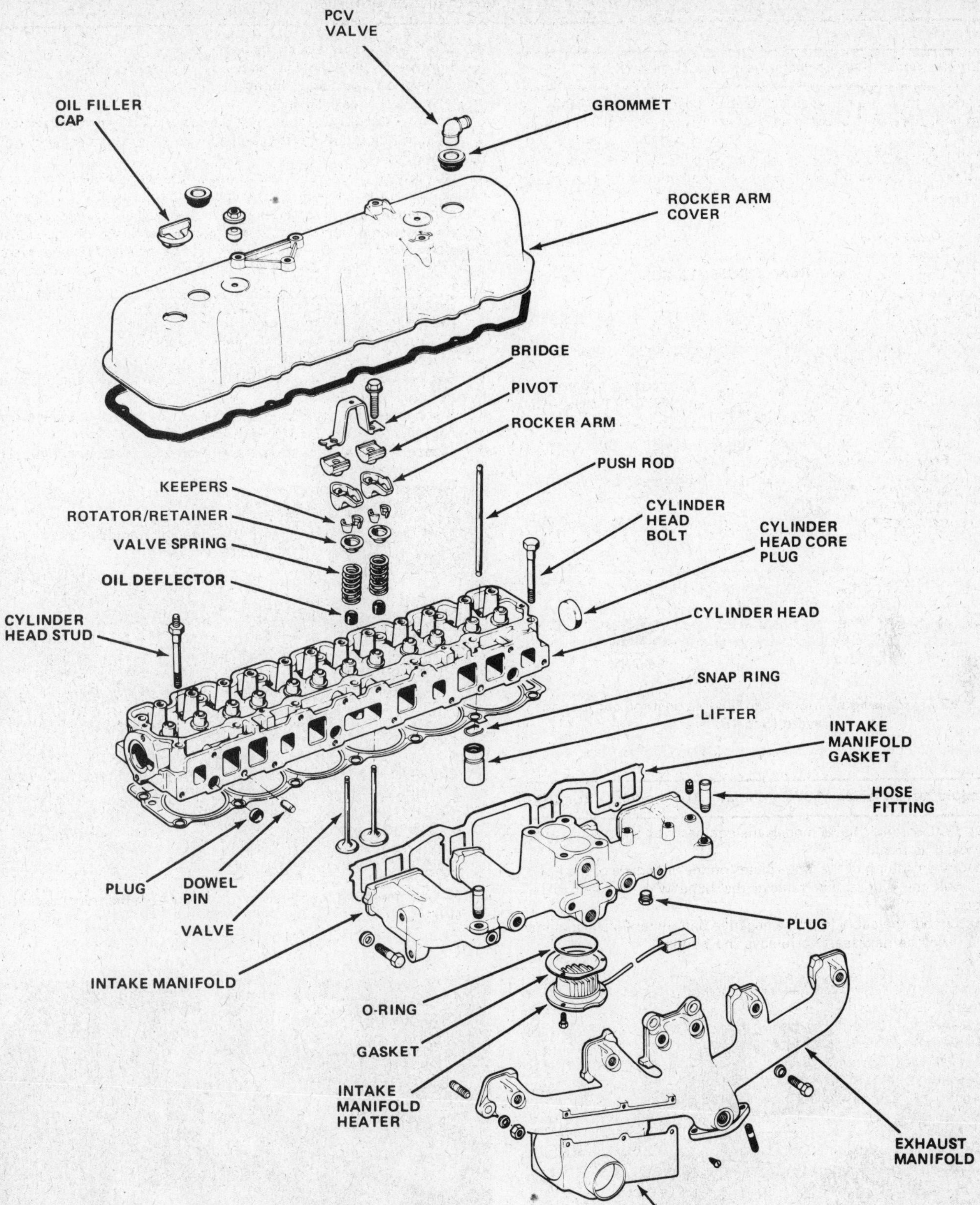

Fig. 2.23 Cylinder head components (typical) – exploded view

18 *On vehicles equipped with an automatic transmission,* disconnect the fluid cooler lines. Plug the open ends to prevent the entry of dirt.

On late model vehicles

19 Disconnect the leads from the neutral safety switch (manual transmission).
20 Disconnect the leads from the transmission controlled spark switch (TCS), used with manual transmissions.
21 Disconnect the TCS solenoid vacuum valve hose from the intake manifold.
22 Disconnect the line which supplies fluid pressure from the automatic transmission to the TCS switch (automatic transmission).
23 Disconnect the throttle stop solenoid.
24 Disconnect the vacuum line (for the fuel vapor storage canister) from the air cleaner.
25 Disconnect the brake booster vacuum line from the intake manifold.
26 Disconnect the vacuum line (for the heater damper doors) from the manifold.

On all models

27 Disconnect and remove the driveshaft (Chapter 8).
28 Using a suitable lifting device, support the weight of the engine and disconnect the engine front mount.
29 Remove the transmission rear mount crossmember from the transmission and the frame (photo).
30 Withdraw the engine/transmission (forward and up at a steeply inclined angle) from the engine compartment (photo).

50 Engine (1977 through 1983 models) – removal

1 Perform Steps 2 through 5 and 7 through 17 of Section 49. On 1977 through 1983 models, the engine can be removed without disturbing the transmission.
2 Remove the starter motor.
3 *On automatic transmission equipped models,* remove the torque converter cover. Remove the converter-to-driveplate bolts, rotating the crankshaft pulley bolt with a wrench to expose each bolt in turn. Mark the relationship of the converter to the driveplate so they can be reinstalled in the same position.
4 *On manual transmission equipped models,* remove the clutch housing cover and the bellcrank inner support screws. Disconnect the springs and remove the bellcrank, followed by the outer bellcrank-to-strut rod bracket retainer. Unplug the backup light wire harness at the dash panel for access to the clutch housing screw.
5 Remove the screws retaining the engine mount cushions to the brackets.
6 Unbolt the exhaust pipe at the manifold.
7 Remove the upper clutch or converter housing bolts and loosen the lower bolts.
8 Raise the front of the vehicle and support it securely.
9 Remove the air-conditioning idler pulley and bracket (if so equipped).
10 Connect a suitable lifting device to the engine.
11 Raise the engine weight off the front supports.
12 Place a jack or suitable support under the clutch or converter housing and remove the lower retaining bolts.
13 Move the engine slowly forward to disengage it from the transmission and then carefully lift it from the engine compartment.

51 Engine/manual transmission (1970 through 1976 models) – separation

1 Unbolt and remove the starter motor.
2 Unscrew and remove the bolts which secure the clutch housing to the engine block.
3 Pull the transmission straight back so it does not hang by the input shaft.

52 Engine/automatic transmission (1970 through 1976 models) – separation

1 Disconnect the transmission filler tube at its upper bracket.
2 Unscrew and remove the inspection cover from the lower part of the front of the torque converter bellhousing.
3 Turn the engine (with a wrench on the crankshaft pulley bolt) until the torque converter drain plug is at its lowest point. Unscrew the drain plug and drain the fluid from the torque converter.
4 Remove the fluid filler tube and starter motor.
5 Mark the position of the driveplate in relation to the torque converter and then remove the bolts with secure the driveplate to the torque converter.
6 Remove the bolts which secure the torque converter bellhousing to the engine block and separate the engine and the transmission.

53 External components – removal

1 With the engine removed from the vehicle and separated from the transmission, the external components should be removed before disassembly of the engine begins.
2 From the right-hand side of the engine, remove the following components:

The fuel pump
The engine mounting bracket
The oil filter cartridge (a chain wrench or oil filter removal tool will be required)
The ignition coil
The distributor and spark plug wires

3 From the left-hand side of the engine, remove the following components:

The alternator and mounts
The engine mounting bracket
The EGR valve, back pressure sensor and coolant temperature switch (emission control models)
The solenoid vacuum valve and connections (emission control models)
The intake manifold and carburetor (after disconnecting the PCV valve to cylinder head cover hose)
The exhaust manifold and air cleaner hot air intake

4 Unscrew and remove the vibration damper bolt.
5 Draw off the damper from the front of the crankshaft using a suitable puller if necessary.
6 *On vehicles with a manual transmission,* unbolt and remove the clutch assembly from the flywheel, as described in Chapter 7.
7 From the front face of the engine remove the following components:

The water pump
The thermostat housing cover and the thermostat

54.3 Separating the bridge-type rocker arm assembly from the cylinder head

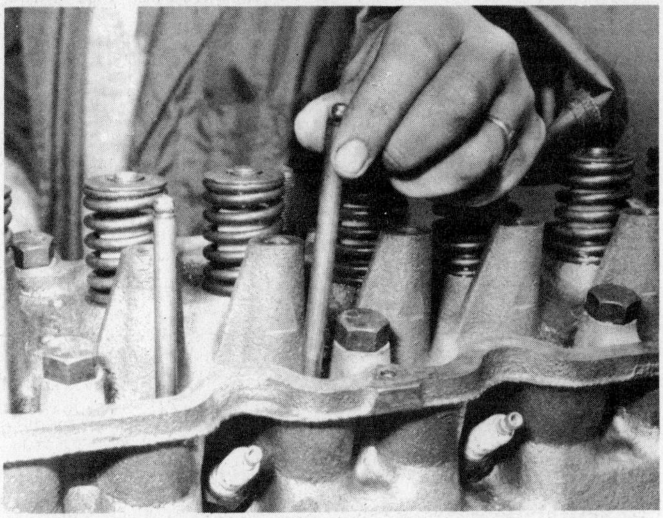

54.5 Remove the pushrods and mark them so they can be returned to their original locations

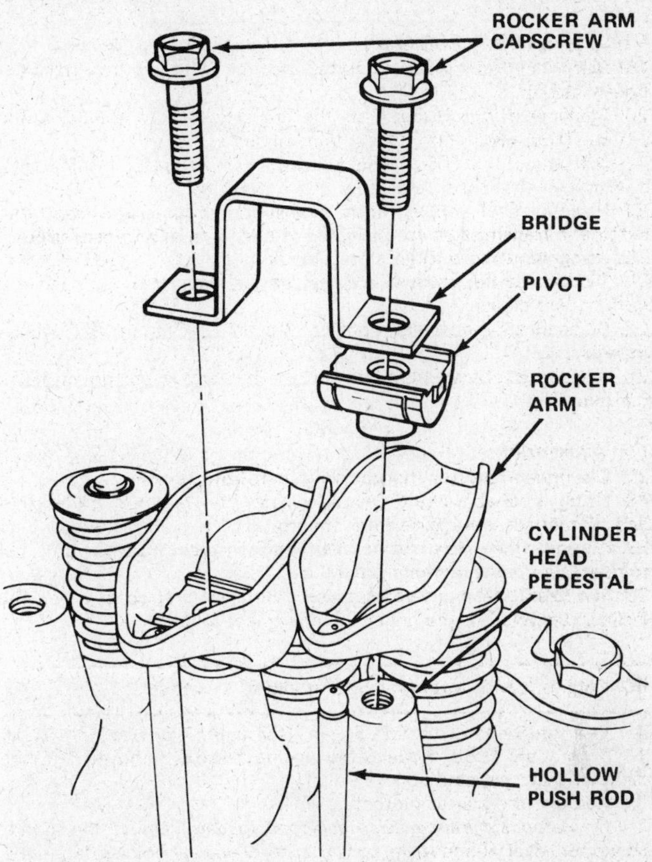

Fig. 2.24 Bridged rocker arm pivot components – exploded view (Sec 54)

54 Rocker gear – removal

1 Remove the rocker arm cover bolts and then lift off the cover and gasket.

2 *On all models except 1971, 1972 and 1974,* the rocker arms pivot on a bridge assembly and the pushrods are hollow to serve as oil galleries supplying oil to the rocker assemblies.

3 Remove the rocker arm bridge assemblies by unscrewing the two cap bolts. Keep all components in their original order (photo).

4 *On 1971, 1972 and 1974 models,* unscrew and remove the rocker shaft mounting bolts and lift the shaft, complete with the rocker arms, from the cylinder head.

5 Remove the pushrods and keep them in their original order (photo).

2C

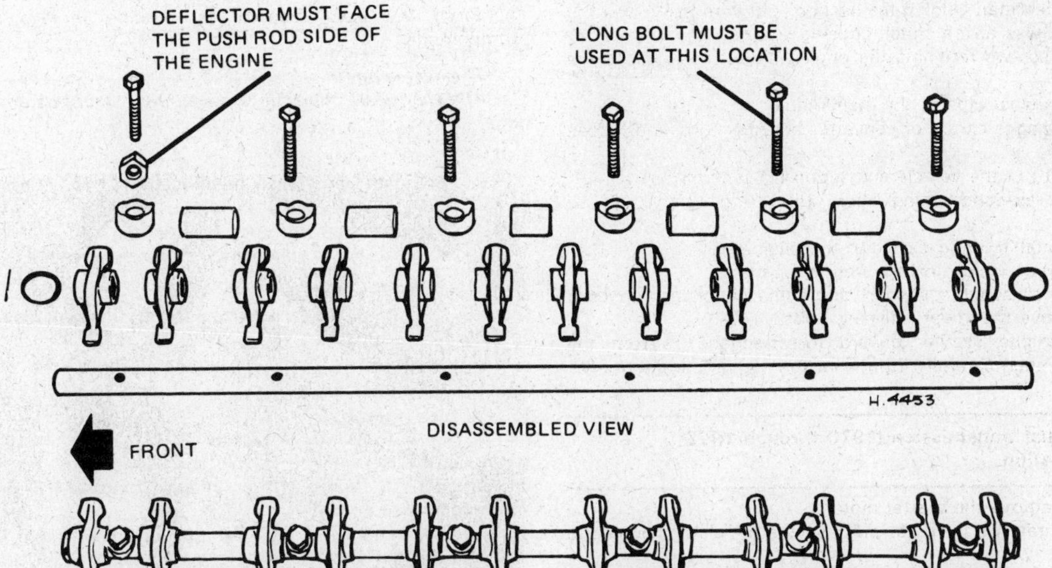

Fig. 2.25 Rocker shaft-type valve gear components – exploded view (Sec 54)

55 Cylinder head – removal

1 If the cylinder head is being removed with the engine still in the vehicle, remember to:

a) Drain the cooling system and disconnect the hoses
b) Remove the intake and exhaust manifolds
c) Remove the ignition coil and disconnect the spark plug wires

2 Remove the rocker arm cover and rocker gear.
3 Disconnect the wire from the coolant temperature sending unit.
4 Unscrew each of the cylinder head bolts, $\frac{1}{4}$- turn at a time and in a diagonal sequence, working from the center out.
5 Lift off the cylinder head and remove the gasket.

56 Valve lifters – description and removal

1 The lifters are hydraulic and consist of a body, plunger, spring, check valve, metering disc, cap and lock ring.
2 By means of charging and leak down cycles and the contact of the lifters with the lobes of the camshaft, zero lash in the valve train is maintained.
3 The lifters can be withdrawn (photo) after removing the cylinder head and pushrods as described elsewhere in this Chapter.
4 **Note:** *Removal of the lifters will most likely require a special valve lifter removal tool (available at tool and auto parts stores).*

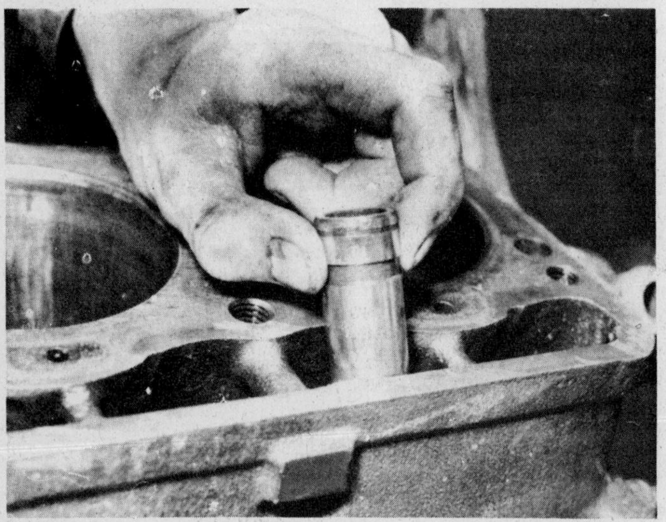
56.3 Removing a valve lifter

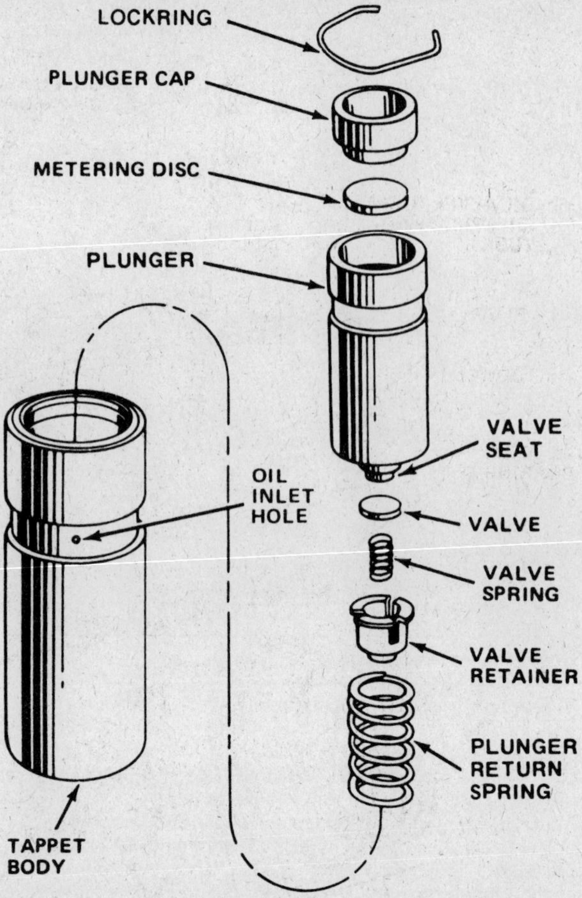

Fig. 2.26 Hydraulic valve lifter – exploded view (Sec 56)

57 Timing cover, chain and sprockets – removal

1 If these components are being removed with the engine in the vehicle, remember to:

a) Drain the cooling system
b) Remove the radiator
c) Remove the fan and pulley
d) Remove the vibration damper and pulley

2 Unscrew and remove the cover mounting bolts and the bolts which retain the front of the oil pan to the timing cover.
3 Lift the timing cover just enough to disengage the oil pan-to-cover sealing strip. Failure to observe this operation will cause damage to the oil pan gasket, which will then have to be replaced after removal of the oil pan.
4 Withdraw the timing cover and gasket and the oil slinger.
5 Unscrew and remove the camshaft retaining bolt and washer.
6 Withdraw the camshaft sprocket, crankshaft sprocket and timing chain as an assembly.

58 Camshaft – removal

1 If the camshaft is being removed with the engine in the vehicle, remember to:

a) Drain the radiator and air-conditioner condenser
b) Remove the cylinder head, pushrods and lifters
c) Remove the timing chain and sprockets
d) Remove the distributor and fuel pump
e) Remove the radiator grille and front bumper

2 Withdraw the camshaft from the front of the engine, taking great care not to damage the camshaft bearings with the lobes or eccentrics as they pass through.

59 Oil pan – removal

1 Raise the front of the vehicle and support it securely.
2 Support the engine with a suitable lifting device and disconnect the front engine mounts.
3 Disconnect the steering idler arm and loosen the sway bar link nuts to the end of their threads. Remove the sway bar clamp bolts and lower the sway bar.
4 Unbolt the front frame crossmember, pull it down and wedge it into position with wood blocks.
5 Remove the right-hand engine mount bracket from the engine.
6 Loosen the lower control arm strut rod bolts.
7 Drain the engine oil into a suitable container.
8 Remove the starter motor, if necessary, for clearance.
9 Remove the oil pan bolts and lower the pan from the engine.

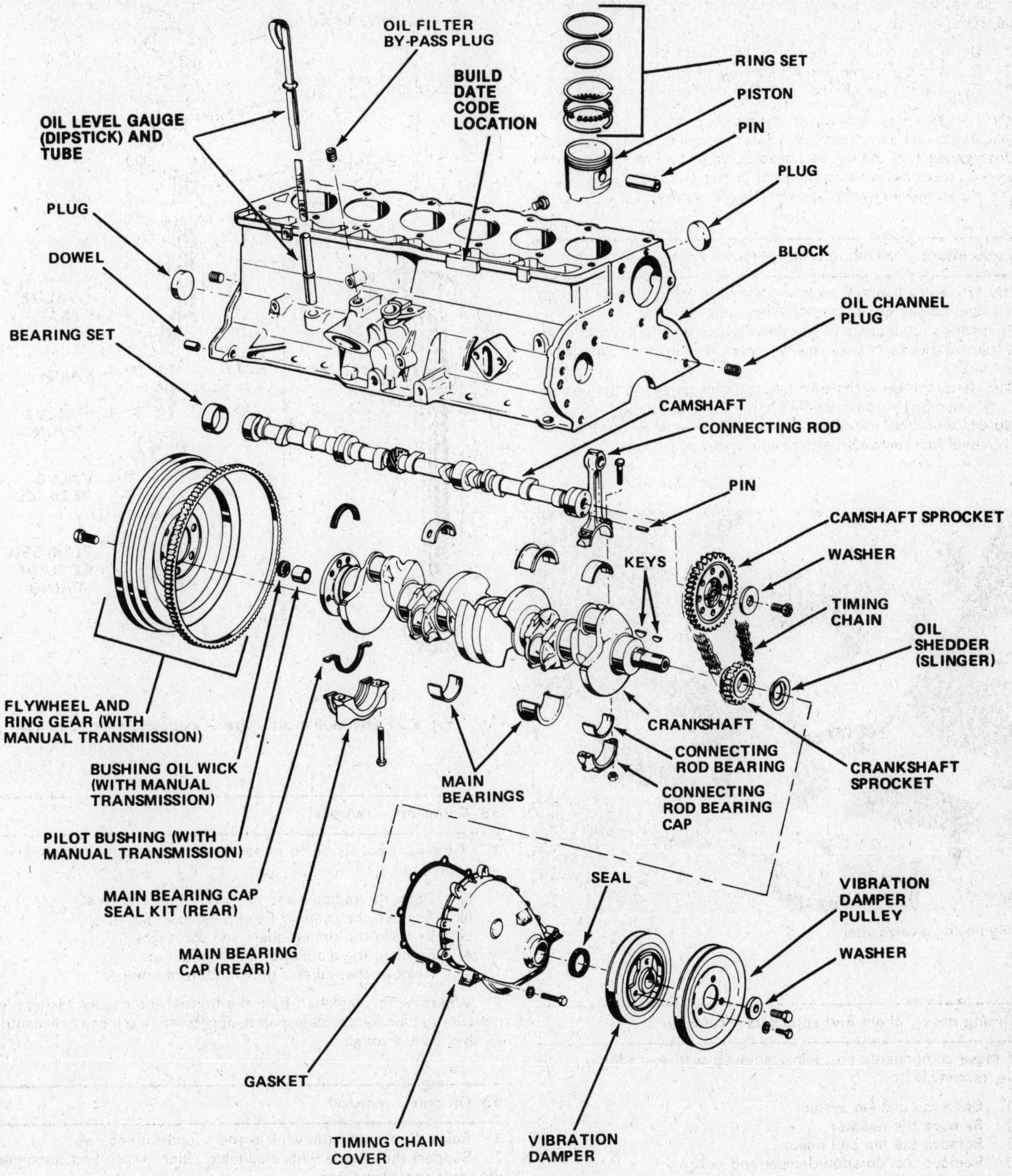

Fig. 2.27 Engine block components – exploded view

60 Oil pump – removal

1 With the oil pan removed, the oil pump can be unbolted from the engine block.
2 Do not attempt to dismantle or alter the position of the oil pick-up tube. If the pressure relief valve has to be dismantled, then the pick-up tube will have to be moved and this will necessitate replacing the tube assembly.

61 Lubrication system – general information

The oil pump is a gear type, driven by an extension of the distributor driveshaft, which in turn is driven by a gear on the camshaft.

The pressurized oil passes through the full-flow oil filter and then through galleries and passages to all moving components. Oil holes in the connecting rod bearing caps provide splash type lubrication of the camshaft lobes, distributor drive gear, cylinder walls and piston rings.

The hydraulic valve lifters receive oil directly from the main oil gallery.

An oil pressure switch is mounted on the right-hand side of the block.

62 Flywheel/driveplate – removal

1 Unscrew and remove the bolts which secure the flywheel (or driveplate) to the crankshaft rear flange.
2 If difficulty is experienced when loosening the bolts due to the rotation of the crankshaft, wedge a block of wood between the crankshaft web and the inside of the engine block. Alternatively, wedge the starter ring gear by inserting a cold chisel at the starter motor opening.
3 Lift the flywheel (or driveplate) from the crankshaft flange.
4 Unbolt and remove the engine endplate. Now is a good time to check the engine block rear core plug for security and evidence of leakage.

63 Rocker gear – inspection and overhaul

1 *On bridged rocker arm models,* this is simply a matter of examining the rocker arms and bridged pivot assemblies for wear and replacing parts as appropriate.
2 *On all other models,* examine the rocker arm faces for wear. If it is slight, it may be removed by gently rubbing on an oilstone. If the wear is deep or if the shaft is grooved or scored, dismantle the complete rocker assembly and replace parts as necessary.
3 Disassembly can be carried out after driving out the roll pin from one end of the shaft and removing the spring washer.
4 Reassemble as shown in the accompanying illustration. Make sure that the rocker shaft oil holes face toward the cylinder head.
5 Take the time to examine the pushrods for wear and distortion and replace any which require it.

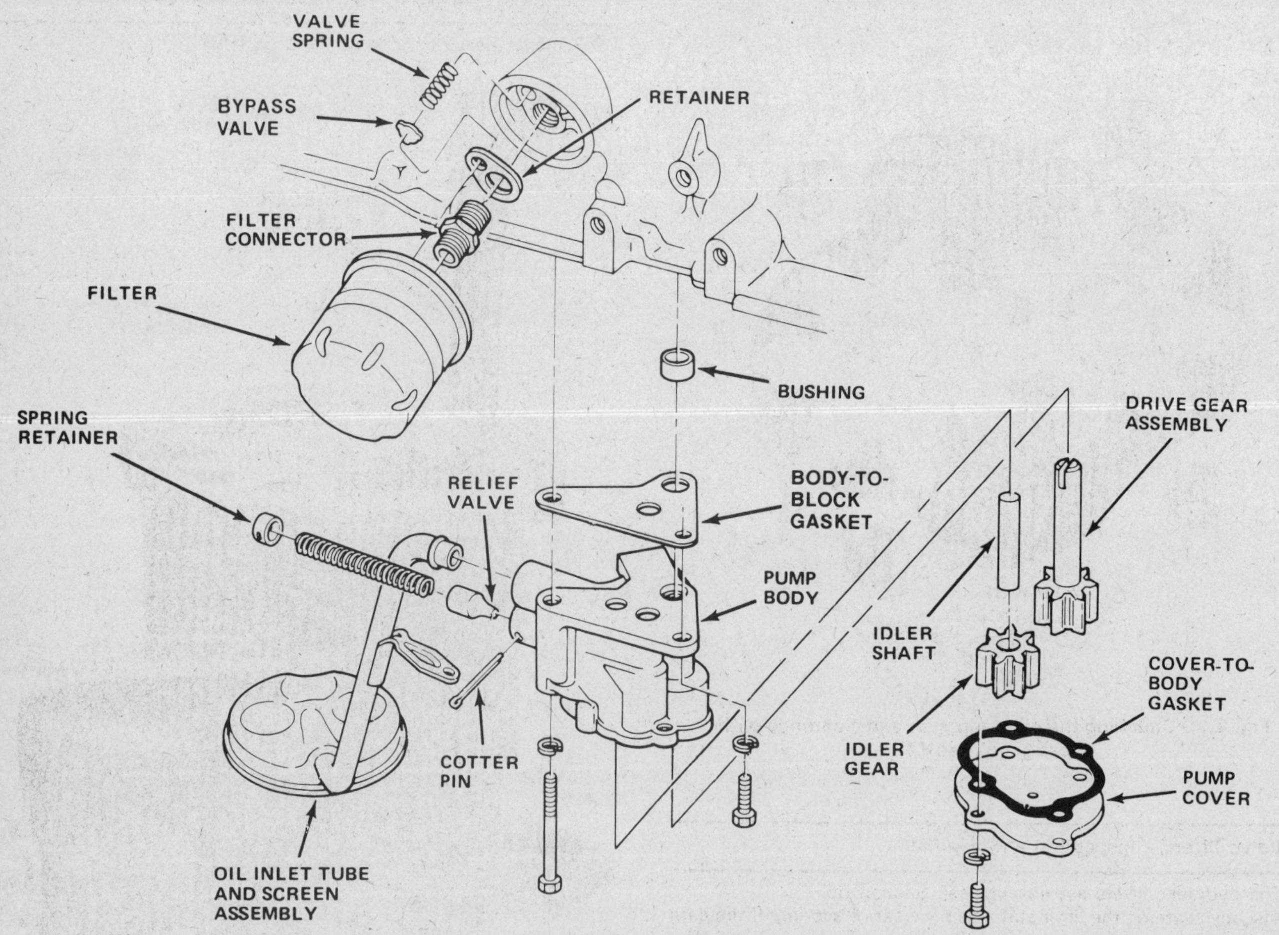

Fig. 2.28 Oil pump and filter components – exploded view (Sec 67)

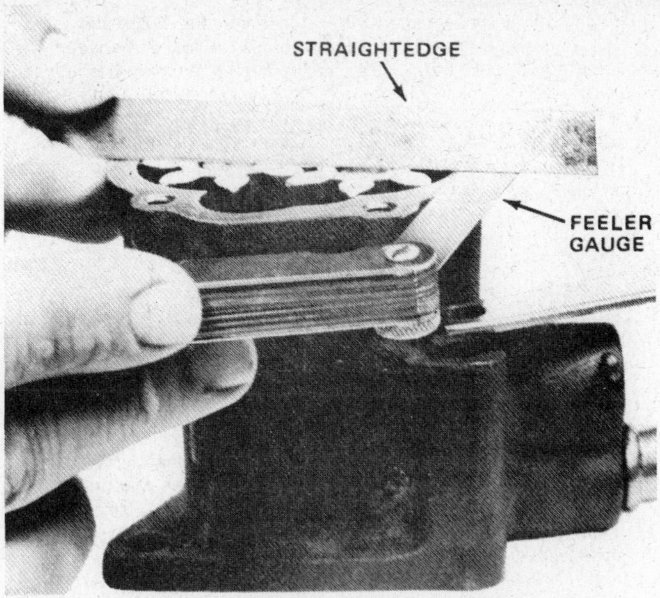

Fig. 2.29 Checking the oil pump gear end clearance with a straightedge and feeler gauge (Sec 67)

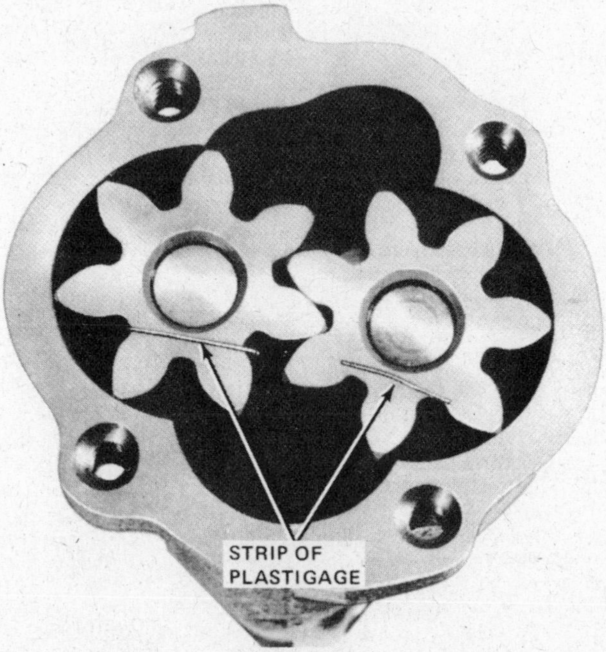

Fig. 2.30 Checking the oil pump gear end clearance with Plastigage (Sec 67)

64 Valve lifters – inspection and overhaul

1 The hydraulic lifters are described in Section 56.

2 Visually examine the lifter surfaces for wear or scoring. If the cam lobe contact face has worn concave, the lifter must be replaced. The camshaft will require changing as well. Never use a worn camshaft with new lifters or vice versa.

3 Checking the leak-down time for each lifter is a job for your AMC dealer who has the necessary testing device. Any that take more than the specified time (20 to 110 seconds) must be replaced.

65 Timing chain and sprockets – inspection

1 Examine the teeth of the camshaft and crankshaft sprockets. if they are worn or chipped, replace the sprocket.

2 Wear in the chain can only be satisfactorily checked by comparing it with a new one but, when installed on the sprockets, if it can be deflected more than *a total of* $\frac{1}{2}$-inch, then it should be replaced or the timing will be upset.

66 Camshaft and bearings – inspection and replacement

1 Examine the bearing surfaces and the surfaces of the cam lobes. Surface scratches, if shallow, can be removed by rubbing with fine emery cloth or an oilstone. Any deep scoring will necessitate a new camshaft.

2 The camshafts used in engines without EGR systems differ from those installed in engines with EGR systems and they are not interchangeable.

3 The camshaft runs in four plain insert type bearings which have larger bores at the front to permit easier withdrawal of the camshaft.

4 Replacement of the bearings is definitely a job for an automotive machine shop, as special equipment is required.

5 Camshaft end play is automatically maintained at zero while the engine is running by the action of the helical cut distributor/oil pump drive gear, which holds the camshaft sprocket thrust face against the cylinder block.

67 Oil pump – disassembly, inspection and reassembly

1 Remove the oil pump cover and gasket.

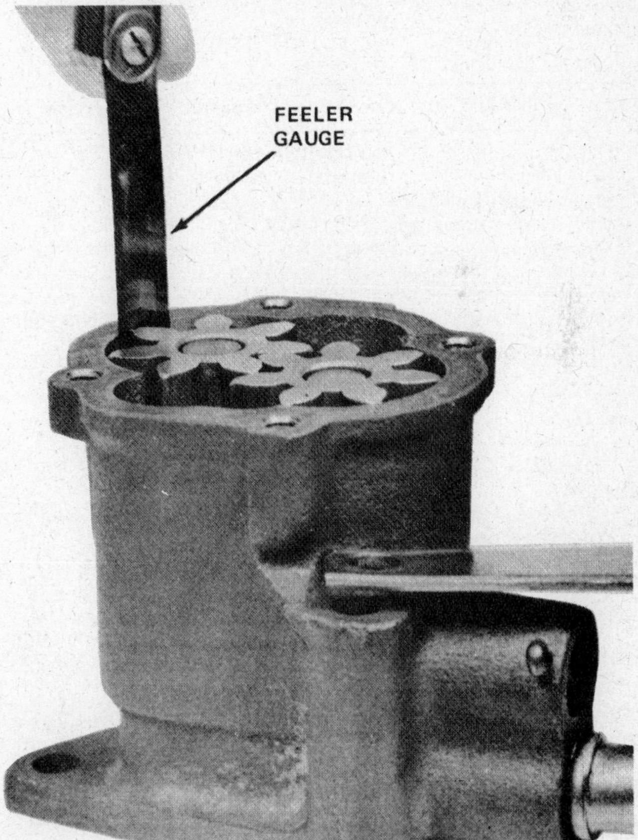

Fig. 2.31 Checking the oil pump gear-to-body clearance with a feeler gauge (Sec 67)

2C

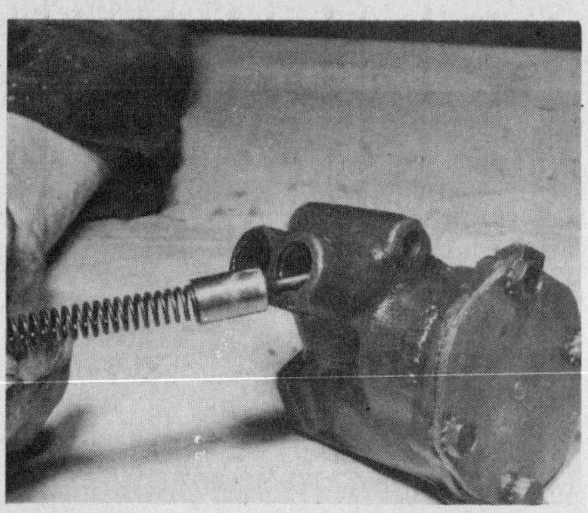

67.7A Insert the relief valve and spring

67.7B Insert the spring retainer

67.7C Push in on the retainer and install a new cotter pin

2 Place a straightedge across the gears and pump body and use a feeler gauge blade to measure the gear end clearance.
3 Alternatively, place a strip of Plastigage across the full width of each gear, install the cover and tighten the retaining screws evenly and securely. Remove the cover and measure the Plastigage with the scale on the envelope.
4 Compare the gear end clearance to the Specifications.
5 Check the gear-to-pump body inner wall clearance and compare this measurement to the Specifications.
6 If any of the measurements are out of the specified range, replace the oil pump assembly with a new one.
7 To remove the oil pressure relief valve, extract the cotter pin and withdraw the valve and spring. Installation is the reverse of removal and a new pickup tube must be installed (photos).
8 Pack the interior of the pump with petroleum jelly to provide a self-priming action and use a new gasket when reassembling the pump.

68 Flywheel and starter ring gear – inspection and servicing

1 Examine the clutch contact surface of the flywheel *(manual transmission models)* for scoring, burn marks, deep ridges and cracks. If any of these conditions exist, or if the surface is highly polished, have the flywheel resurfaced and balanced at an automotive machine shop.
2 Check the starter ring gear for worn and chipped teeth. If damage is evident, the ring gear must be replaced with a new one *(manual transmission models). On automatic transmission models,* the drive-plate must be replaced with a new one if the ring gear is damaged or worn.

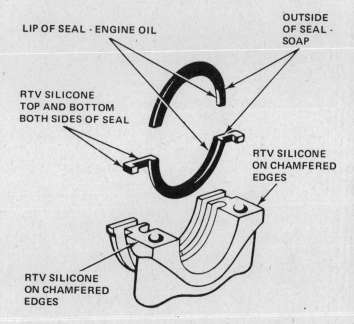

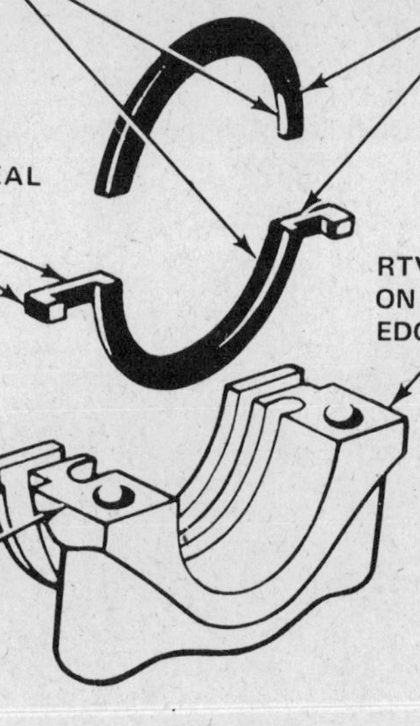

Fig. 2.32 Rear main oil seal installation details (Sec 69)

69 Oil seals – replacement

1 The timing cover seal and the crankshaft rear oil seal should be replaced as part of the engine overhaul procedure
2 Use a suitable diameter piece of tubing or a socket and a hammer to carefully drive the old seal out of the timing cover.
3 Apply a light coat of RTV-type sealant to the outer diameter of the new seal. Place the seal in position with the lip facing *in* and carefully drive it in until it bottoms in the recess.
4 Drive out the old rear main seal with a brass drift and a hammer until it protrudes sufficiently from the engine block to be gripped with pliers and removed. Remove the lower seal from the main bearing cap.
5 Clean the main bearing cap and engine block to remove any traces of gasket sealer.
6 Coat the lip of the seal with engine oil or grease and the upper contact surface with liquid soap. Insert the seal into the groove in the engine block with the lip facing *forward.*
7 Coat both sides of the lower seal ends with RTV-type sealant, taking care not to apply it to the seal surface. Coat the lip of the seal with engine oil or grease and the curved outer surface with liquid soap.
8 Install the lower seal into the main bearing cap with the lip facing *forward* and seat it securely.
9 When installing the main bearing cap, apply a coat of RTV-type sealant to the chamfered contact surfaces.

70 Main and connecting rod bearings – selection

1 The crankshaft and bearing inspection procedures are included in Chapter 2A. The condition and measured size of the crankshaft journals will determine the bearings to be installed when the engine is reassembled.
2 If a new or reground crankshaft is installed, the size of each journal should be indicated by a color coded mark on the adjacent cheek or counterweight, toward the rear (flanged) end of the crankshaft. The bearing inserts are also color coded (on the edge of the insert). The accompanying charts (one for main bearings, one for rod bearings) should be consulted to determine the correct bearings to use. **Caution**: *Always check the bearing oil clearance with Plastigage during final installation of the crankshaft and/or piston/connecting rod assemblies.*
3 If necessary to achieve the desired oil clearance, different size upper and lower bearing inserts may be used on the same journal but the size difference must never exceed 0.001 inch. **Caution**: *The odd size inserts must all be either in the caps or block (main bearings). In the case of connecting rod bearings the odd size inserts must all be either in the caps or rods.*
4 If the original crankshaft is reground, the automotive machine shop that reconditions the journals should supply bearings that will produce the desired oil clearance.

Crankshaft Connecting Rod Journal Color and Diameter in Inches (Journal Size)	Bearing Color Code	
	Upper Insert Size	Lower Insert Size
Yellow –2.0955 to 2.0948 (Standard)	Yellow – Standard	Yellow – Standard
Orange –2.0948 to 2.0941 (0.0007 Undersize)	Yellow – Standard	Black – .001-inch Undersize
Black –2.0941 to 2.0934 (0.0014 Undersize)	Black – .001-Inch Undersize	Black – .001-inch Undersize
Red –2.0855 to 2.0848 (0.010 Undersize)	Red – .010-Inch Undersize	Red – .010-inch Undersize

Fig. 2.33 Connecting rod bearing selection chart (Sec 70)

Crankshaft Main Bearing Journal Color Code and Diameter in Inches (Journal Size)	Bearing Color Code	
	Upper Insert Size	Lower Insert Size
Yellow –2.5001 to 2.4996 (Standard)	Yellow – Standard	Yellow – Standard
Orange –2.4996 to 2.4991 (0.0005 Undersize)	Yellow – Standard	Black – .001-inch Undersize
Black –2.4991 to 2.4986 (0.001 Undersize)	Black – .001-inch Undersize	Black – .001-inch Undersize
Green –2.4986 to 2.4981 (0.0015 Undersize)	Black – .001-inch Undersize	Green – .002-inch Undersize
Red –2.4901 to 2.4896 (0.010 Undersize)	Red – .010-inch Undersize	Red – .010-inch Undersize

Fig. 2.34 Main bearing selection chart (1970 through 1980 only) (Sec 70)

Crankshaft Main Bearing Journal 5 2-6 Color Code and Diameter in Inches (Journal Size)	Bearing Insert Color Code	
	Upper Insert Size	Lower Insert Size
Yellow – 2.5001 to 2.4996 (Standard) (63.5025 to 63.4898 mm)	Yellow – Standard	Yellow – Standard
Orange – 2.4996 to 2.4991 (0.0005 Undersize) (63.4898 to 63.4771 mm)	Yellow – Standard	Black – 0.001-inch Undersize (0.025mm)
Black – 2.4991 to 2.4986 (0.001 Undersize) (63.4771 to 63.4644 mm)	Black – 0.001-inch Undersize (0.025 mm)	Black – 0.001-inch Undersize (0.025mm)
Green – 2.4986 to 2.4981 (0.0015 Undersize) (63.4644 to 63.4517 mm)	Black – 0.001-inch Undersize (0.025 mm)	Green – 0.002-inch Undersize (0.051mm)
Red – 2.4901 to 2.4986 (0.010 Undersize) (63.2485 to 63.2358 mm)	Red – 0.010-inch Undersize (0.054 mm)	Red – 0.010-inch Undersize (0.254mm)

Fig. 2.35 Main bearing selection chart (1981 – journals 1-6; 1982 and 1983 – journals 2-6) (Sec 70)

Crankshaft Main Bearing Journal 7 Color Code and Diameter in Inches (Journal Size)	Bearing Insert Color Code	
	Upper Insert Size	Lower Insert Size
Yellow – 2.4995 to 2.4990 (Standard) (63.4873 to 63.4746 mm)	Yellow – Standard	Yellow – Standard
Orange – 2.4990 to 2.4985 (0.0005 Undersize) (63.4746 to 63.4619 mm)	Yellow – Standard	Black – 0.001-inch Undersize (0.025mm)
Black – 2.4985 to 2.4980 (0.001 Undersize) (63.4619 to 63.4492 mm)	Black – 0.001-inch Undersize (0.025mm)	Black – 0.001-inch Undersize (0.025mm)
Green – 2.4980 to 2.4975 (0.0015 Undersize) (63.4492 to 63.4365 mm)	Black – 0.001-inch Undersize (0.025mm)	Green – 0.002-inch Undersize (0.051mm)
Red – 2.4895 to 2.4890 (0.010 Undersize) (63.2333 to 63.2206 mm)	Red – 0.010-inch Undersize (0.254mm)	Red – 0.010-inch Undersize (0.254mm)

Fig. 2.36 Main bearing selection chart (1981 through 1983 – journal 7) (Sec 70)

Crankshaft No. 1 Main Bearing Journal Color Code and Diameter In Inches (mm)	Cylinder Block No. 1 Main Bearing Bore Color Code and Size In Inches (mm)	Bearing Insert Color Code	
		Upper Insert Size	Lower Insert Size
Yellow – 2.5001 to 2.4996 (Standard) (63.5025 to 63.4898mm)	Yellow – 2.6910 to 2.6915 (68.3514 to 68.3641 mm)	Yellow – Standard	Yellow – Standard
	Black – 2.6915 to 2.6920 (68.3641 to 68.3768 mm)	Yellow – Standard	Black – 0.001-inch Undersize (0.025mm)
Orange – 2.4996 to 2.4991 (0.0005 Undersize) (63.4898 to 63.4771mm)	Yellow – 2.6910 to 2.6915 (68.3514 to 68.3641 mm)	Yellow – Standard	Black – 0.001-inch Undersize (0.001mm)
	Black – 2.6915 to 2.6920 (68.3641 to 68.3768 mm)	Black – 0.001-inch Undersize (0.025mm)	Black – 0.001-inch Undersize (0.025mm)
Black – 2.4991 to 2.4986 (0.001 Undersize) (63.4771 to 63.4644mm)	Yellow – 2.6910 to 2.6915 (68.3514 to 68.3641 mm)	Black – 0.001-inch Undersize (0.025mm)	Black – 0.001-inch Undersize (0.025mm)
	Black – 2.6915 to 2.6920 (68.3641 to 68.3768 mm)	Black – 0.001-inch Undersize (0.025mm)	Green – 0.002-inch Undersize (0.051mm)
Green – 2.4986 to 2.4981 (0.0015 Undersize) (63.4644 to 63.4517mm)	Yellow – 2.6910 to 2.6915 (68.3514 to 68.3641 mm)	Black – 0.001-inch Undersize (0.025mm)	Green – 0.002-inch Undersize (0.051mm)
Red – 2.4901 to 2.4986 (0.010 Undersize) (63.2485 to 63.2358mm)	Yellow – 2.6910 to 2.6915 (68.3514 to 68.3641 mm)	Red – 0.010-inch Undersize (0.254mm)	Red – 0.010-inch Undersize (0.254mm)

Fig. 2.37 Main bearing selection chart (1982 and 1983 – journal 1) (Sec 70)

71 Crankshaft – installation and main bearing oil clearance check

1 Crankshaft installation is generally one of the first steps in engine reassembly; it is assumed at this point that the engine block and crankshaft have been cleaned and inspected and repaired or reconditioned. The rear main oil seal sections should also be in place in the rear bearing cap and block (Section 69).

2 Position the engine with the bottom facing up.

3 Remove the main bearing cap bolts and lift out the caps. Lay them out in the proper order to help ensure that they are installed correctly.

4 If they are still in place, remove the old bearing inserts from the block and the main bearing caps. Wipe the main bearing surfaces of the block and caps with a clean, lint-free cloth (they must be kept spotlessly clean).

5 Clean the back sides of the new main bearing inserts and lay one bearing half in each main bearing saddle (in the block) and the other bearing half from each bearing set in the corresponding main bearing cap. Make sure the tab on the bearing insert fits into the recess in the block or cap (photo). Also, the oil holes in the block and cap must line up with the oil holes in the bearing insert. *Do not hammer the bearing into place and do not nick or gouge the bearing faces. No lubrication should be used at this time.*

6 The flanged thrust bearing must be installed in the number three cap and saddle (photo).

7 Clean the faces of the bearings in the block and the crankshaft main bearing journals with a clean, lint-free cloth. Check or clean the oil holes in the crankshaft, as any dirt here can only go one way – straight through the new bearings.

8 Once you are certain that the crankshaft is clean, carefully lay it in position (an assistant would be very helpful here) in the main bearings with the counterweights lying sideways.

9 Before the crankshaft can be permanently installed, the main bearing oil clearance must be checked.

10 Trim seven pieces of the appropriate type of Plastigage (so they are slightly shorter than the width of the main bearings) and place one piece on each crankshaft main bearing journal, parallel with the journal axis. Do not lay them across any oil holes.

11 Clean the faces of the bearings in the caps and install the caps in their respective positions (do not mix them up) with the arrows pointing toward the front of the engine. Do not disturb the Plastigage.

12 Starting with the center main and working out toward the ends, tighten the main bearing cap bolts, in three steps, to the specified torque (photo). *Do not rotate the crankshaft at any time during this operation.*

13 Remove the bolts and carefully lift off the main bearing caps. Keep them in order. Do not disturb the Plastigage or rotate the crankshaft. If any of the main bearing caps are difficult to remove, tap gently from side-to-side with a soft-faced hammer to loosen them.

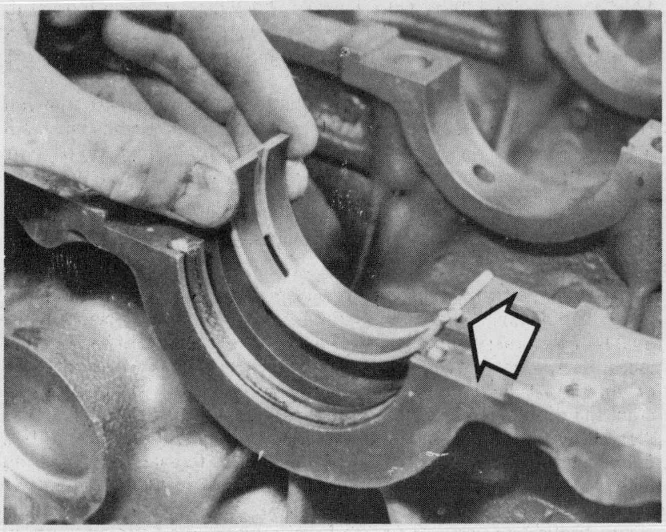

71.5 Make sure the tab (arrow) on the bearing insert fits into the recess in the block

71.6 The thrust bearing must be installed in the number three cap and saddle

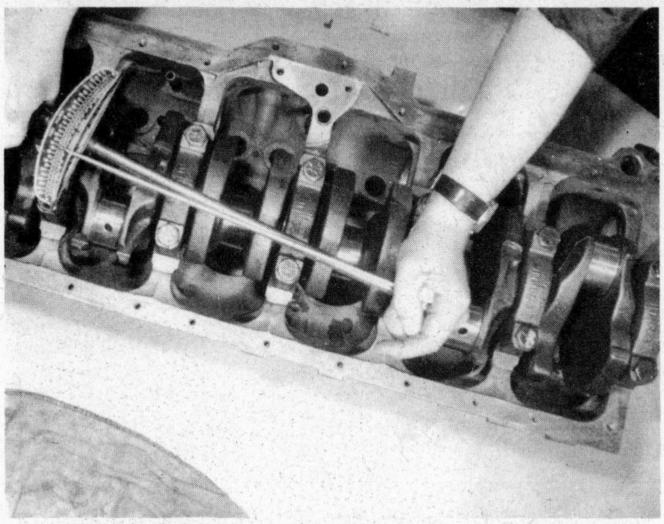

71.12 Tightening the main bearing cap bolts

73.1 Be sure to use a new gasket when installing the oil pump

14 Compare the width of the crushed Plastigage on each journal to the scale printed on the Plastigage container to obtain the main bearing oil clearance. Check the Specifications to make sure it is correct.
15 If the clearance is not correct, double-check to make sure that you have the right size bearing inserts. Also, recheck the crankshaft main bearing journal diameters and make sure that no dirt or oil was between the bearing inserts and the main bearing caps or the block when the clearance was measured.
16 Carefully scrape all traces of the Plastigage material off the main bearing journals and/or the bearing faces. Do not nick or scratch the bearing faces.
17 Carefully lift the crankshaft out of the engine. Clean the bearing faces in the block, then apply a thin, uniform layer of clean, high-quality moly grease (or engine assembly lube) to each of the bearing faces. Be sure to coat the thrust flange faces as well as the journal face of the thrust bearing in the number three main. Make sure the crankshaft journals are clean, then carefully lay it back in place in the block. Clean the faces of the bearings in the caps, then apply a thin, uniform layer of clean, high-quality moly grease to each of the bearing faces and install the caps in their respective positions with the arrows pointing toward the front of the engine. Refer to Section 69 and apply sealer to the rear cap as explained there. Install the bolts and tighten them to the specified torque, starting with the center main and working out toward the ends. Work up to the final torque in three steps.
18 Rotate the crankshaft a number of times by hand and check for any obvious binding.
19 The final step is to check the crankshaft end play. This can be done with a feeler gauge or a dial indicator set. Refer to Chapter 2A, Section 12, for the procedure to follow.

72 Flywheel/driveplate – installation

1 Install the engine rear plate over the locating dowels.
2 Attach the flywheel (or driveplate) to the crankshaft rear flange and tighten the bolts to the specified torque. Apply a wrench to the vibration damper bolt to prevent the crankshaft from rotating as the flywheel bolts are tightened.

73 Oil pump and oil pan – installation

1 Locate a new oil pump gasket on the lower flange of the block (photo).
2 Install the oil pump/pick-up tube assembly and tighten the long and short securing bolts (photo).
3 Position a new oil pan gasket on the block and then bolt on the oil pan, tightening the bolts to the specified torque. Follow a criss-cross

73.2 Installing the oil pump

pattern to avoid warping the pan. Make sure that the drain plug is tight.

74 Camshaft and timing chain/sprockets – installation

1 Lubricate the camshaft bearing journals and lobes with engine assembly lube or moly grease and carefully insert the camshaft from the front of the engine.
2 With the engine positioned with the cylinder head surface up, set the crankshaft so that the keyway is vertical and at the top.
3 Engage the camshaft and crankshaft sprockets within the timing chain and install them as an assembly so that a line drawn through the sprocket timing marks will also pass through the centers of the sprockets. Obviously the camshaft will have to be rotated and a certain amount of repositioning of the camshaft sprocket within the loop of the chain will be required to achieve this.
4 Secure the camshaft sprocket and then check the timing. To do this, set the camshaft sprocket timing mark to the 1 o'clock position. There should be 15 chain pins between the sprocket timing marks (as shown in the accompanying illustration).
5 Attach the oil slinger to the front of the crankshaft sprocket (photo).
6 Install a new oil seal in the timing chain cover (Section 69), then

2C

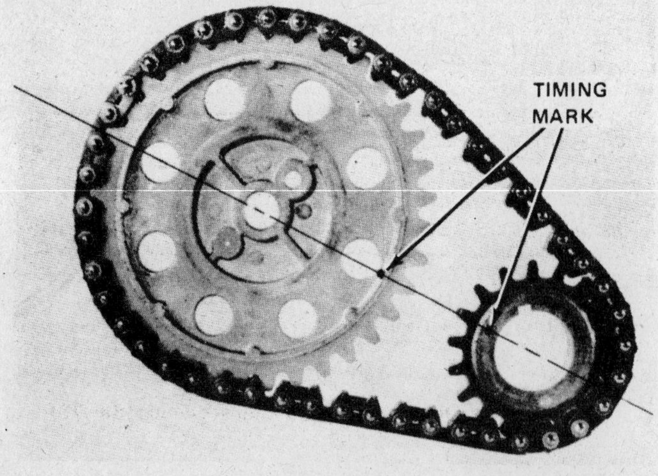

Fig. 2.38 Correct relationship of crankshaft and camshaft sprockets (Sec 74)

attach the cover to the engine with a new gasket. Tighten the bolts finger tight at this time (photo).

7 Apply grease to the oil seal contact surfaces of the vibration damper and push it into position. If necessary, tap the timing cover from side-to-side, or up-and-down, to center it and enable the damper to be withdrawn and installed correctly.

8 Now tighten the timing chain cover bolts securely.

9 Install the damper and tighten the mounting bolt to the specified torque. Use a block of wood inserted between the crankshaft and the engine block to prevent crankshaft rotation.

10 Locate a new gasket on the front face of the cylinder block (use RTV-type sealant on the gasket).

11 Install the water pump.

75 Valve lifters – installation

Note: *The camshaft must be in place before the lifters are installed.*

1 Apply engine assembly lube or moly grease to the lifters, then install them (in their original bores).

2 If new lifters are being installed, a new camshaft must also be installed. If a new camshaft was installed, then use new lifters as well. *Never install used lifters unless the original camshaft is used and the lifters can be installed in their original locations.*

76 Cylinder head and rocker gear – installation

Note: *The valve lifters must be in place before the head is installed.*

1 If not already done, thoroughly clean the gasket surfaces on both the cylinder head and the engine block. Do not scratch or otherwise damage the sealing areas.

2 To get the proper torque readings, the threads of the head bolts must be clean. This also holds true for the threaded holes in the engine block. Run a tap through these holes to ensure that they are clean.

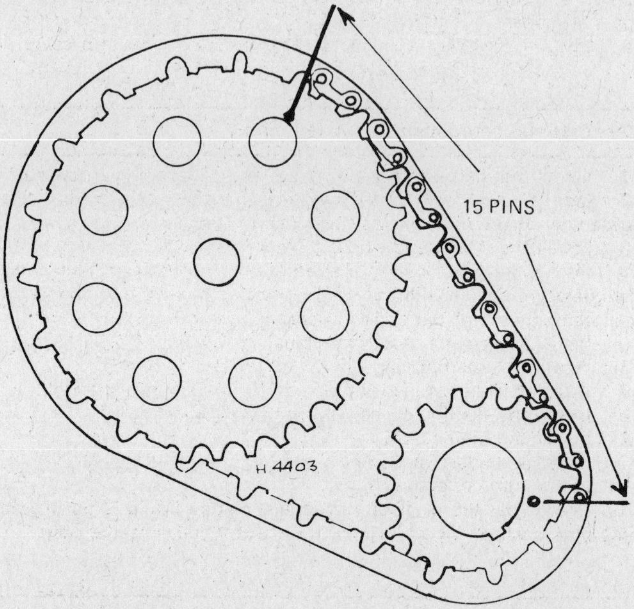

Fig. 2.39 With the camshaft sprocket timing mark at the 1 o'clock position, the timing marks must be 15 pins apart (Sec 74)

74.5 Remember to install the oil slinger (arrow) before attaching the timing chain cover to the block

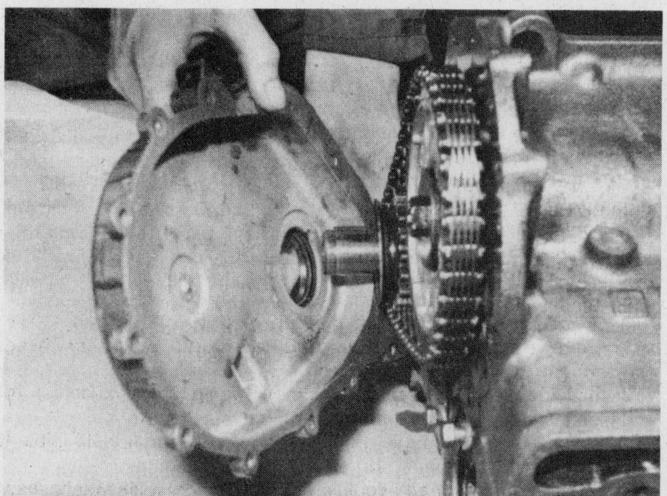

74.6 Be careful not to damage the seal when installing the timing chain cover

3 Apply a thin, even coat of AMC Perfect Seal gasket sealer (or equivalent) to *both* sides of the new head gasket. **Caution**: *Do not apply the gasket sealer to the cylinder head or block and do not allow any to enter the cylinder bores.* Place the gasket in position over the engine block dowel pins. Make sure the side marked TOP is facing up.
4 Carefully lower the cylinder head onto the engine, over the dowel pins and the gasket. Be careful not to move the gasket, while doing this.
5 Install the head bolts and tighten them finger tight.
6 Tighten each of the bolts, a little at a time, in the sequence shown in the accompanying illustration. Continue tightening in this sequence until the proper torque reading is obtained. As a final check, work around the head in a logical front-to-rear sequence to make sure none of the bolts have been overlooked.
7 Lubricate the pushrod ends with engine assembly lube or moly grease and install them. Make sure they are seated in the lifter cavities.
8 Lubricate the rocker arm contact surfaces, then install the rocker arms or shaft assembly and tighten the bolts to the specified torque. Be sure to lubricate the rocker arm pivots with engine assembly lube or moly grease.
9 Lay a new gasket in place, then install the rocker arm cover.

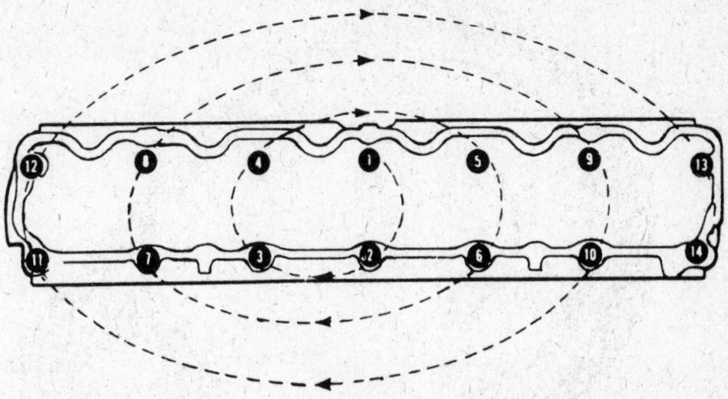

Fig. 2.40 Cylinder head bolt tightening sequence (Sec 76)

77 External components – installation

1 Install the thermostat (pin hole up) and cover using a new gasket.
2 *On vehicles with a manual transmission,* attach the clutch assembly to the flywheel, as described in Chapter 8.
3 Install the intake and exhaust manifolds.
4 Install the EGR valve, the back pressure sensor, the coolant temperature switch and the solenoid vacuum valve and connections (all components of the emission control system).
5 Install the engine mount brackets.
6 Install the alternator.
7 Attach the air cleaner hot air duct to the exhaust manifold.
8 Install the distributor, as described in Chapter 4.
9 Install the ignition coil.
10 Install the spark plugs and wires.
11 Install the fuel pump.
12 Check that the oil filter cartridge threaded fitting is tight, grease the filter sealing ring and screw it on with hand pressure only.

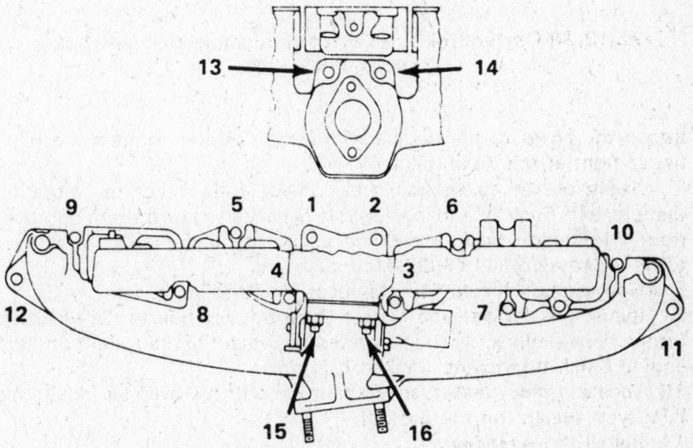

Fig. 2.41 Intake/exhaust manifold bolt tightening sequence (Sec 77)

78 Engine/transmission (1970 through 1976 models) – installation

1 Lower the engine/transmission assembly slowly and carefully into the engine compartment. Initially the assembly should be at a steep angle and then, once lowered into position, it can be leveled so the driveshaft slip joint can be engaged in the transmission.
2 Install the rear support cushion and tighten the retaining nuts securely.
3 Raise the rear crossmember into position with a jack and lower the engine until it contacts the front support cushions. Install the front cushions with the retaining nuts finger tight.
4 Install the rear crossmember-to-chassis retaining nuts and bolts and tighten them securely.
5 Lower the engine weight onto the front support cushions and tighten the retaining nuts.
6 Connect the exhaust pipe and brackets.
7 Connect the speedometer cable.
8 Connect all fuel and vacuum hoses.
9 Connect the throttle linkage.
10 Connect all electrical wires disconnected during removal.
11 Connect the transmission linkage. Refer to Chapter 7 for linkage adjustment procedures.
12 Install the power steering pump (if equipped) and adjust the drivebelt.
13 Connect the automatic transmission TCS switch fluid pipe (if equipped).
14 Install the radiator and cooling fan. Connect all lines and hoses to the radiator.
15 Install the air-conditioning compressor, condenser and receiver assembly. *Have the system purged of air and recharged by a qualified technician.*
16 Install the battery and air cleaner assembly. *Connect the positive cable to the battery first, then the negative cable.*
17 Fill the cooling system, crankcase and transmission to the specified level with the specified fluids.
18 Align the hood with the marks made during removal and install the retaining bolts.

79 Engine (1977 through 1983 models) – installation

1 Lower the engine slowly and carefully into the engine compartment.
2 *On manual transmission-equipped models,* insert the transmission shaft into the clutch splines and align the clutch housing with the engine. Install the lower clutch housing attaching bolts and tighten them securely.
3 *On automatic transmission-equipped vehicles,* align the transmission converter housing with the engine and install the lower attaching bolts finger tight. Install the next higher bolts and then tighten all four to the specified torque.
4 Remove the support from the clutch or converter housing.
5 Lower the engine onto the mount cushions, making sure the bolt holes are aligned. Install the bolts and tighten them securely.
6 With the front of the vehicle raised and supported securely, install the seal and connect the exhaust pipe to the manifold. Install the retaining nuts and tighten them securely.

2C

7 *On manual transmission-equipped vehicles,* install the flywheel housing cover and insert the clutch release bellcrank through the bushing in the throwout lever rod bracket. Install the retainer. Attach the bellcrank-to-throwout lever rod to the throwout lever and connect the springs. Attach the inner support bracket to the flywheel housing and connect the clutch pedal to the bellcrank rod. Plug in the backup light switch wiring harness at the dash panel.

8 *On automatic transmission-equipped vehicles,* make sure the marks on the converter and driveplate made during removal are aligned and install the converter drive bolts. Turn the crankshaft pulley bolt to provide access to each bolt in turn and tighten them to the specified torque. Install the housing spacer and the exhaust pipe support.

9 Install and tighten the remaining clutch or converter housing attaching bolts.

10 Install the starter motor and connect the electrical cable and lead.

11 Lower the vehicle and remove the engine lifting device.

12 Fill the engine to the correct level with the recommended oil.

Chapter 2 Part D V8 engine

Contents

Camshaft – installation 100
Camshaft – removal 94
Crankshaft – inspection .... Chapter 2A
Crankshaft – installation and main bearing oil clearance check 106
Crankshaft – removal 105
Cylinder head – cleaning and inspection .... Chapter 2A
Cylinder head – disassembly .... Chapter 2A
Cylinder head – installation 102
Cylinder head – reassembly .... Chapter 2A
Cylinder head – removal 90
Engine – disassembly and reassembly sequence 87
Engine/automatic transmission – connection 108
Engine/automatic transmission – separation 85
Engine block – cleaning .... Chapter 2A
Engine block – inspection .... Chapter 2A
Engine disassembly – general information .... Chapter 2A
Engine/manual transmission – connection 109
Engine/manual transmission – separation 86
Engine mounts – replacement 82
Engine (1977 through 1983 models) – installation 111
Engine (1977 through 1983 models) – removal 84
Engine overhaul – general information .... Chapter 2A
Engine rebuilding alternatives .... Chapter 2A
Engine removal – methods and precautions .... Chapter 2A
Engine/transmission (1970 through 1976 models) – installation 110
Engine/transmission (1970 through 1976 models) – removal 83
General information 80
Initial start-up and break-in after overhaul .... Chapter 2A
Intake manifold – installation 103
Intake manifold – removal 89
Main and connecting rod bearings – inspection .... Chapter 2A
Main and connecting rod bearings – selection 107
Oil pan – installation 104
Oil pan – removal 88
Oil pump – disassembly, inspection and reassembly 96
Oil pump – installation 98
Oil pump – removal 95
Oil seal replacement 97
Oversize and undersize component designation 81
Piston/connecting rod assembly – inspection .... Chapter 2A
Piston/connecting rod assembly – installation and bearing oil clearance check .... Chapter 2A
Piston/connecting rod assembly – removal .... Chapter 2A
Piston rings – installation .... Chapter 2A
Repair operations possible with the engine in the vehicle .... Chapter 2A
Timing chain and sprockets – installation 99
Timing chain and sprockets – removal 93
Timing chain cover – installation 101
Timing chain cover – removal 91
Timing chain wear – checking 92
Valves – servicing .... Chapter 2A

2D

Specifications

General

Displacement	304 or 360 cu in
Cylinder numbering (viewed from radiator, front-to-rear)	
Left bank	1-3-5-7
Right bank	2-4-6-8
Firing order	1-8-4-3-6-5-7-2
Compression pressure	140 psi
Maximum variation between cylinders	20 psi
Oil pressure	
600 rpm	13 psi
1600 rpm and above	37 psi minimum, 75 psi max.

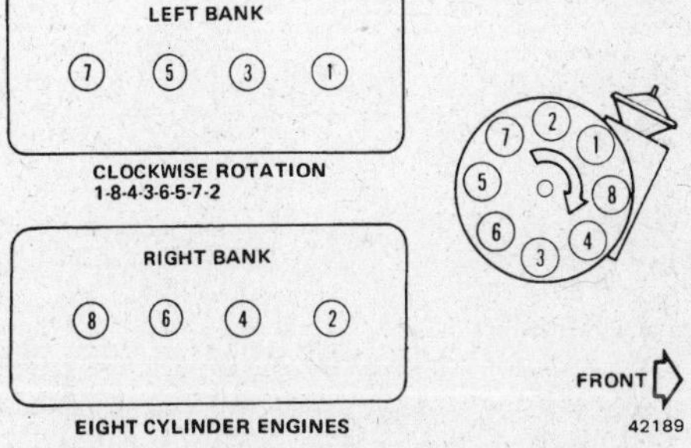

Cylinder location and distributor rotation

Cylinder bore

Taper limit	0.005 in
Out-of-round limit	0.003 in
Deck warpage limit	0.008 in

Pistons and rings

Piston-to-cylinder bore clearance	
304 cu in engine	
Standard	0.0010 to 0.0018 in
Preferred	0.0014 in
360 cu in engine	
Standard	0.0012 to 0.0020 in
Preferred	0.0016 in
Piston ring side clearance (304 cu in engine)	
Top ring	
Standard	0.0015 to 0.0035 in
Preferred	0.0015 in
2nd ring	
Standard	0.0015 to 0.003 in
Preferred	0.0015 in
Oil ring	0.0011 to 0.008 in
Piston ring side clearance (360 cu in engine)	
Top ring	
Standard	0.0015 to 0.003 in
Preferred	0.0015 in
2nd ring	
Standard	0.0015 to 0.0035 in
Preferred	0.0015 in
Oil ring	0.000 to 0.007 in
Piston ring end gap	
Top and 2nd ring	
Standard	0.010 to 0.020 in
Preferred	0.010 to 0.012 in
Oil ring	
304 cu in engine	0.010 to 0.025 in
360 cu in engine	0.015 to 0.045 in
Piston pin-to-rod clearance	Press fit
Piston pin-to-bore clearance	
Standard	0.0003 to 0.0005 in
Preferred	0.0005 in

Crankshaft and flywheel

Main journal diameter	
1, 2, 3 and 4	2.7474 to 2.7489 in
Rear main (5)	2.7464 to 2.7479 in
Main bearing oil clearance	
1, 2, 3 and 4	
Standard	0.001 to 0.003 in
Preferred	0.0017 to 0.0020 in
Rear main (5)	
Standard	0.002 to 0.004 in
Preferred	0.0025 to 0.003 in
Connecting rod journal	
Diameter	2.0934 to 2.0955 in
Taper limit	0.0005 in
Out-of-round limit	0.0005 in
Connecting rod bearing oil clearance	
Standard	0.001 to 0.003 in
Preferred	0.0015 to 0.002 in
Connecting rod end play	0.006 to 0.0018 in
Crankshaft end play	0.003 to 0.008 in

Camshaft

Bearing journal diameter	
1	2.1195 to 2.1205 in
2	2.0895 to 2.0905 in
3	2.0595 to 2.0605 in
4	2.0295 to 2.0305 in
5	1.9995 to 2.0005 in
Bearing oil clearance	
Standard	0.001 to 0.003 in
Preferred	0.0017 to 0.0020 in
Lobe lift	
1971 through 1978	0.266 in
1979	0.233 in
End play	Zero
Timing chain total allowable deflection	$\frac{7}{8}$ in

Cylinder heads and valve train

Head warpage limit	0.008 in max.
Valve seat angle	
Intake	30°
Exhaust	44.5°
Valve seat width	0.040 to 0.060 in
Valve seat runout limit	0.0025 in max.
Valve face angle	
Intake	29°
Exhaust	44°
Valve stem diameter	0.3715 to 0.3725 in
Valve guide diameter	0.3735 to 0.3745 in
Valve stem-to-guide clearance	0.001 to 0.003 in
Valve margin width	$\frac{1}{32}$ in minimum
Valve lifter type	Hydraulic
Lifter diameter	0.9040 to 0.9045 in
Lifter bore diameter	0.9055 to 0.9065 in
Lifter-to-bore clearance	0.001 to 0.0025 in

Oil pump

Gear end clearance	0.002 to 0.006 in
Gear-to-body clearance	0.0005 to 0.0025 in
Oil pressure relief valve opening pressure	75 psi

Oversize and undersize component code letter definition

Code letter		
B	Cylinder bore	0.010 in oversize
M	Main bearings	0.010 in undersize
F	Connecting rod bearings	0.010 in undersize
PM	Main and connecting rod bearings	0.010 in undersize
C	Camshaft bearing bores	0.010 in oversize

Torque specifications

	Ft-lbs	Nm
Camshaft gear screw	30	41
Carburetor adapter	12 to 15	16 to 20
Carburetor mounting nuts	12 to 15	16 to 20
Connecting rod nuts		
1971 through 1975	28	38
1976 through 1979	33	45
Crankshaft pulley-to-damper bolt	17 to 28	24 to 38
Cylinder head bolts	110	149
Driveplate-to-torque converter bolts	22	30
Exhaust manifold bolts		
$\frac{3}{8}$ in	25	34
$\frac{5}{16}$ in	15	20
Exhaust pipe-to-manifold	15 to 25	20 to 34
Fan and hub assembly	12 to 25	16 to 34
Flywheel or driveplate-to-crankshaft bolts	105	142
Intake manifold	43	58
Main bearing cap bolts	100	136
Oil pan bolts		
$\frac{1}{4}$ in	5 to 9	7 to 12
$\frac{5}{16}$ in	9 to 13	12 to 18
Oil pump cover	4.5	6.0
Oil relief valve cap	28	38
Rocker arm bolt	16 to 26	22 to 35
Spark plugs	22 to 33	30 to 45
Starter motor bolts	13 to 25	18 to 34
Thermostat housing bolts	10 to 18	14 to 24
Timing chain cover-to-block bolts	18 to 33	24 to 45
Vibration damper bolt*		
1971 through 1975	55	76
1976 and 1978	80	108
1977 and 1979	90	122
Water pump bolts	4 to 5	5 to 6

***Note**: *The vibration damper bolt on 1978 and 1979 models should be lubricated before installation.*

80 General information

The 90 degree V8 engine is made of cast-iron and features overhead valves. The camshaft is located in the V of the cylinder block and actuates the valves through hydraulic lifters, pushrods and rocker arms. The rocker arms are fastened to the cylinder head in pairs by bridged pivots on 304 cu in engines and on studs mounted in the head on 360 cu in engines.

The positive displacement, gear-type oil pump is incorporated into the timing case cover and is driven by the distributor shaft.

The crankshaft is supported by five two-piece insert-type main bearings.

81 Oversize and undersize component designation

1 Some engines may have oversize or undersize cylinder bores, crankshaft main bearing journals, connecting rod journals and/or camshaft bearing bores.
2 A code designating the presence of oversize or undersize components is stamped on the tag located on the right bank rocker arm cover. The oversize/undersize code is located adjacent to the engine build date code on the tag.
3 Refer to the Specifications Section and compare the letter code with the information in the chart to determine which components are oversize or undersize.

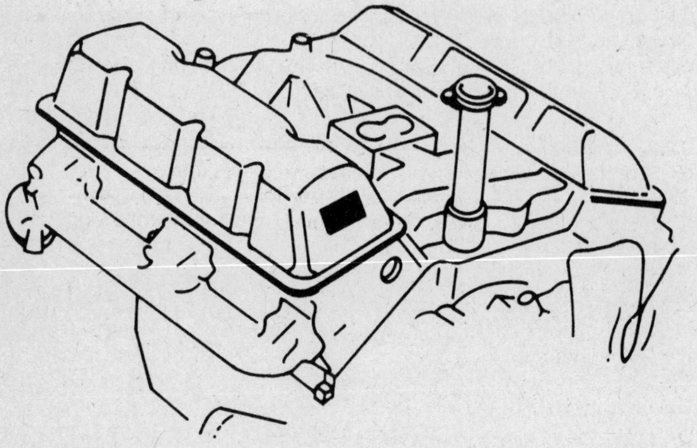

Fig. 2.42 The engine build date and oversize/undersize codes are located on the right side rocker arm cover (Sec 81)

82 Engine mounts – replacement

1 Rubber engine mounts support the engine at three points. These mounts should be inspected periodically to make sure they haven't become hard, split or separated from the metal backing.
2 The mount cushions can be replaced after supporting the engine/transmission weight with a jack, hoist or holding fixture.

83 Engine/transmission (1970 through 1976 models) – removal

Note: *The engine and transmission should be removed as a unit on these models.*
1 Remove the hood and (if equipped) the fender braces.
2 Remove the air cleaner assembly and the battery (disconnect the negative cable first, then the positive cable).
3 Drain the cooling system, crankcase and transmission.
4 Remove the radiator upper air baffle (if equipped), followed by the radiator and hoses.
5 Remove the engine cooling fan.
6 Remove the drivebelt, unbolt the power steering pump and support it out of the way.
7 If equipped with air conditioning, have the system discharged by a dealer or properly trained technician. **Caution:** *Do not attempt to disconnect the air conditioning system until it has been safely discharged as disconnecting could cause serious injury.*
8 Disconnect the condenser and evaporator lines and the receiver outlet. Remove the condenser and receiver assemblies.
9 Disconnect the wires from the starter motor, ignition coil, distributor, coolant temperature sending unit, alternator, oil pressure sending unit, solenoid vacuum and control switches and throttle stop solenoid.
10 Disconnect the lines and hoses from the fuel pump and fuel filter.
11 Disconnect the vacuum hoses for the power brake reservoir and heater damper doors at the intake manifold.
12 Disconnect the throttle linkage at the engine.

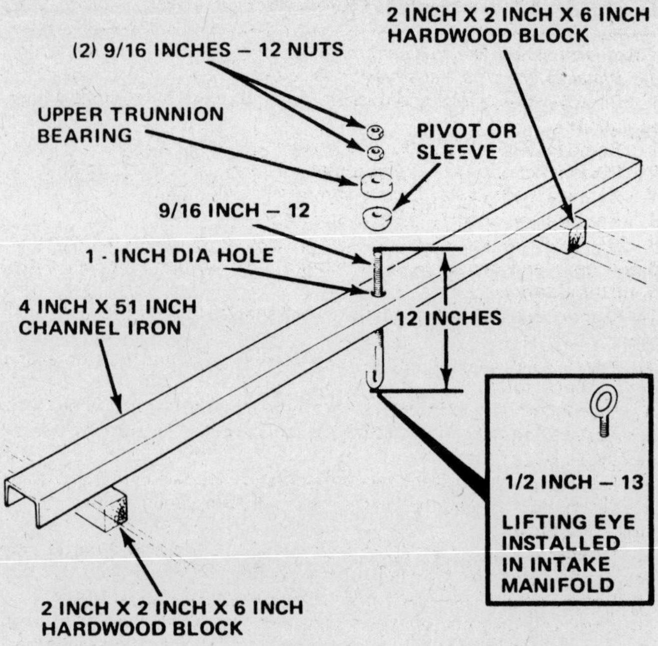

Fig. 2.43 An engine lifting/supporting fixture can be fabricated and used when replacing engine mount cushions (Sec 82)

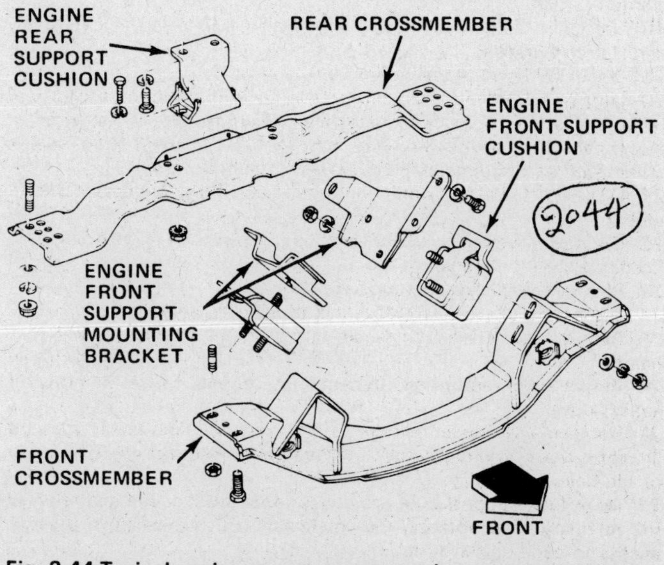

Fig. 2.44 Typical engine mount component layout – exploded view (Sec 82)

13 Disconnect the transmission linkage (Chapter 7).
14 Unbolt the exhaust pipes from the manifolds.
15 Disconnect the speedometer cable from the transmission.
16 Attach a suitable lifting device and raise the engine/transmission unit sufficiently to support its weight.
17 Remove the engine ground strap and unbolt the front engine mount support cushions.
18 Unbolt the rear engine mount support cushion and remove the rear crossmember.
19 Raise the engine/transmission unit slowly and carefully. Move the assembly forward sufficiently to disengage the transmission from the driveshaft slip joint and have an assistant support the driveshaft so it does not fall. Lift the engine/transmission unit from the engine compartment at a steep angle, taking care not to contact the fenders, firewall or radiator brace. Lower the assembly to the floor or workbench and brace it in an upright position with blocks of wood.

84 Engine (1977 through 1983 models) – removal

Note: *On these models the engine is removed after separating it from the transmission (the transmission is left in place in the vehicle).*

1 Remove the hood and disconnect the underhood light (if so equipped).
2 Remove the radiator cap and drain the cooling system.
3 Disconnect and plug the automatic transmission fluid cooler lines.
4 Remove the radiator hoses, shroud and radiator.
5 Remove the cooling fan and spacer.
6 Remove the air cleaner assembly and disconnect the canister purge hose and sensor hose. Disconnect the negative battery cable from the battery.
7 Disconnect the thermostatic air cleaner vacuum hose and heat tube.
8 Insert a $\frac{1}{2}$-in by $\frac{5}{16}$-in bolt through the fan pulley and into the water pump flange to maintain alignment.
9 Disconnect the alternator wires, the Neutral start switch wire harness and the throttle control switch harness. Fasten the wiring harnesses out of the way.
10 Disconnect the heater hose at the heater core and intake manifold.
11 Disconnect the heater and air conditioning vacuum hose at the intake manifold.
12 Disconnect the throttle cable, disengage it from the bracket and position it out of the way behind the power brake booster.
13 Remove the check valve from the power brake booster.
14 Disconnect the coolant temperature sending unit wire and throttle stop solenoid wire from the connector located adjacent to the ignition coil.
15 Disconnect the TCS solenoid control switch tube.
16 Disconnect the distributor and primary ignition leads from the coil.
17 Remove the return hose from the fuel filter after cutting off the clamp.
18 Unless it is located inside the wheel well, remove the vapor canister and bracket.
19 Disconnect and plug the flexible fuel line.
20 On air conditioner equipped models, have the system discharged by your dealer or a qualified technician. **Caution:** *Do not attempt to disconnect the air conditioning system until it has been safely discharged as disconnecting could lead to serious injury.*
21 Disconnect the air conditioner hoses and the compressor clutch wire.
22 On power steering equipped models, disconnect and plug the hoses. Drain the reservoir.
23 Raise the vehicle and support it securely.
24 Disconnect the starter cable and remove the starter motor.
25 Remove the flange nut, seals and heat valve from the exhaust flange.
26 Remove the automatic transmission torque converter housing spacer cover.
27 Remove the lower throttle valve bellcrank and inner manual linkage support and disconnect the throttle valve rod at the lower end of the bellcrank.
28 Mark the relationship of the converter and driveplate and remove the retaining bolts, rotating the crankshaft with a wrench to provide access to each bolt in turn.
29 Unbolt the exhaust system from the transmission extension housing. Lower the exhaust system.
30 Unbolt the front engine mounts from the engine block.
31 Remove the four upper torque converter housing bolts and loosen the lower bolts.
32 Lower the vehicle.
33 Remove the throttle cable housing bracket and connect a suitable lifting device to the engine.
34 Lift the engine slightly off the front supports and place a jack under the converter housing.
35 Remove the remaining converter housing-to-engine retaining bolts.
36 Lift the engine from the engine compartment.

85 Engine/automatic transmission – separation

1 Remove the converter inspection cover.
2 Remove the starter motor.
3 Remove the transmission filler tube.
4 Mark the relationship of the converter and driveplate.
5 Remove the converter-to-driveplate attaching bolts, using a wrench on the crankshaft pulley bolt to turn the driveplate and provide access to the bolts.
6 Remove the bolts attaching the converter support bracket and the transmission to the engine.
7 Withdraw the transmission from the engine, taking care to support the converter so it does not fall.

86 Engine/manual transmission – separation

1 Remove the starter motor.
2 Remove the clutch housing-to-engine block retaining bolts.
3 Withdraw the transmission/clutch housing assembly in a straight line so the weight does not hang on the input shaft while it is still engaged in the clutch.
4 Remove the lubricating wick from the pilot bearing and soak it in engine oil until the time of installation.

87 Engine – disassembly and reassembly sequence

1 To completely disassemble the engine, remove the following items in the order given:

Oil pan
Intake manifold
Cylinder head/valve train components
Timing chain cover
Timing chain and sprockets
Camshaft
Piston/connecting rod assemblies
Crankshaft
Oil pump

2 Engine reassembly is basically the reverse of disassembly. Install the following components in the order given:

Oil pump
Crankshaft
Piston/connecting rod assemblies
Timing chain and sprockets
Camshaft
Timing chain cover
Cylinder head/valve train components
Intake manifold
Oil pan

2D

88 Oil pan – removal

1 Remove the bolts attaching the oil pan to the engine block.
2 Tap on the pan with a soft-faced hammer, to break the gasket seal, and lift the oil pan off the engine.
3 Remove the oil pan neoprene seals.
4 Using a gasket scraper, remove all traces of gasket from the oil pan and engine block gasket surfaces.
5 Clean the oil pan with solvent and dry it thoroughly. Check the gasket sealing surfaces for distortion.

89 Intake manifold – removal

1 Remove the carburetor and linkage (Chapter 4).
2 Remove the retaining bolts and lift the manifold from the engine.
3 Remove the metal gasket and the end seals.

90 Cylinder head – removal

1 Remove the rocker arm covers. The covers are installed with a formed-in-place RTV-type gasket and it may be necessary to tap them sharply with a soft-faced hammer to break the seal.
2 Remove the intake manifold.
3 Remove the rocker arm assembly bolts/nuts.

4 Remove the rocker arm assemblies and pushrods, keeping them in order so they can be reinstalled in their original locations.

5 Loosen the cylinder head bolts $\frac{1}{4}$-turn at a time, working from the inside out. Remove the bolts, then lift off the cylinder head and gasket. It may be necessary to tap the head sharply with a soft-faced hammer around its circumference to break the gasket seal.

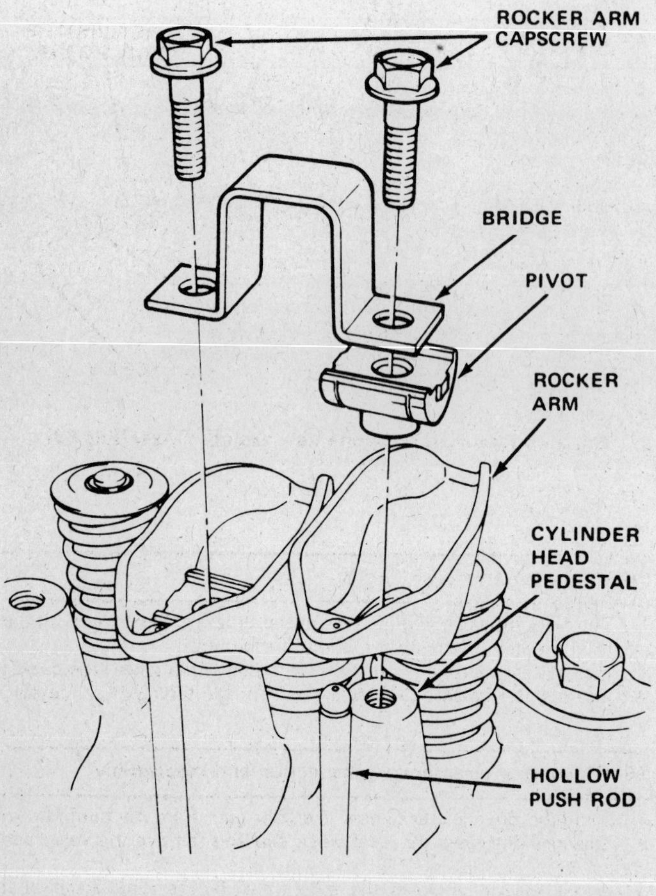

Fig. 2.45 Rocker arm assembly components – exploded view (304 cu in engine) (Sec 90)

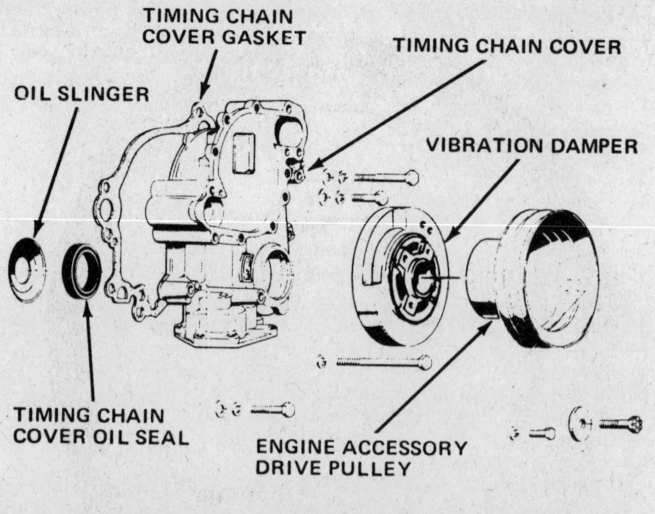

Fig. 2.46 Timing chain cover components – exploded view (Sec 91)

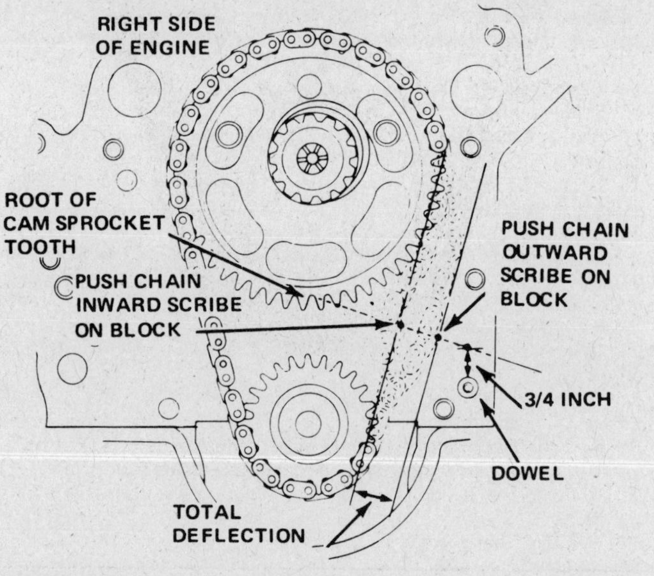

Fig. 2.47 Checking timing chain wear (deflection) (Sec 92)

91 Timing chain cover – removal

1 Remove the vibration damper bolt.

2 Using a suitable puller, remove the vibration damper.

3 Remove the timing cover mounting bolts. Since these bolts are of varying lengths, mark the location of each one at the time of removal so they can be reinstalled in the same location.

4 Remove the cover by pulling it straight out, off the locating dowels.

5 Pry the oil seal out and clean the bore. Clean the gasket surfaces of the timing cover and engine block.

92 Timing chain wear – checking

1 Remove the timing chain cover.

2 Rotate either the crankshaft or camshaft sprocket until there is no slack in the right side of the chain.

3 To determine a reference point for deflection measurement, move $\frac{3}{4}$ of an inch up from the dowel on the right side of the engine and make a mark at this location. Place a straightedge across the timing chain from a point at the lowest root of the camshaft sprocket to the marked position. Grasp the chain at this point to use as a reference, move the chain in toward the centerline of the engine and mark the point of maximum deflection. Move the chain out to the point of maximum deflection and make another mark.

4 Measure the distance between the two marks to determine the total deflection (as shown in the accompanying illustration).

5 If the deflection is beyond the maximum allowed in the Specifications, replace the chain with a new one. If the chain is replaced, new sprockets probably should be used as well.

93 Timing chain and sprockets – removal

1 Remove the vibration damper and pulley.

2 Remove the timing chain cover.

3 Remove the camshaft retaining screw and washer, distributor drive gear and fuel pump eccentric.

4 Rotate the crankshaft until the zero timing mark on the sprocket is aligned with and closest to the zero timing mark on the camshaft sprocket as shown in the accompanying illustration.

5 Remove the crankshaft and camshaft sprockets and the timing chain as an assembly.

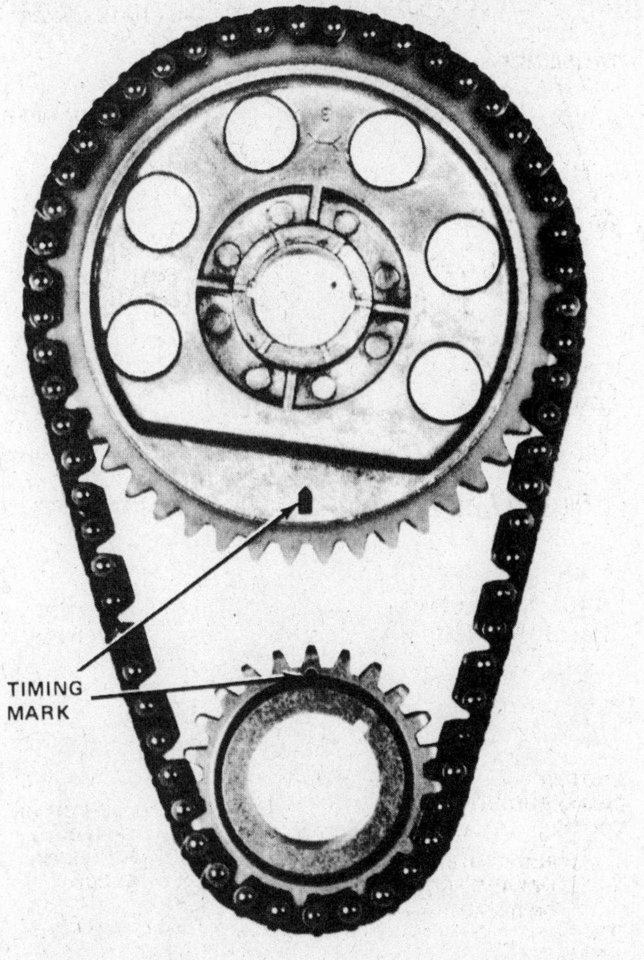

Fig. 2.48 The marks on the sprockets must be aligned before removing the chain and sprocket (Sec 93)

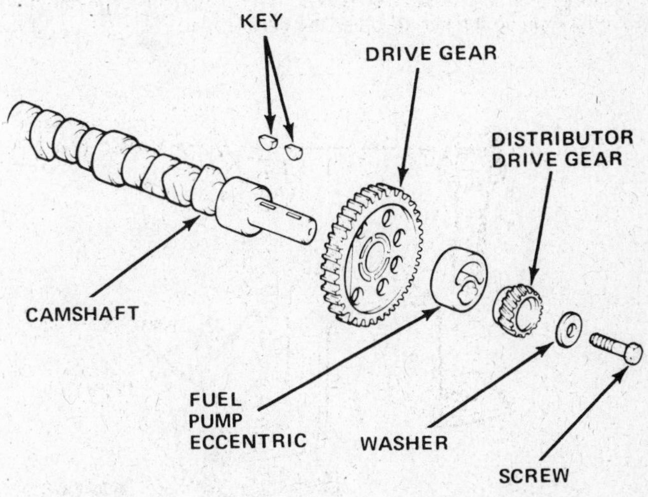

Fig. 2.49 Camshaft components – exploded view (Sec 94)

94 Camshaft – removal

1 Remove the pushrods and valve lifters.
2 Remove the distributor.
3 Remove the vibration damper and timing chain cover.
4 Install the vibration damper screw and two washers and use a wrench to rotate the crankshaft until the timing mark is aligned with the centerline of the camshaft sprocket.
5 Remove the retaining screws from the camshaft and crankshaft.
6 Remove the fuel pump eccentric and distributor drive gear from the camshaft.
7 Remove the crankshaft and camshaft sprockets and timing chain as an assembly.
8 Remove the camshaft from the engine block, taking care not to damage the lobes or bearing surfaces.
9 Inspect the distributor drivegear and fuel pump eccentric for wear and damage. Inspect the camshaft bearing journals for excessive wear and evidence of seizure. if the journals are damaged, the bearings in the block are probably damaged as well. Both the camshaft and bearings will have to be replaced with new ones. Check the cam lobes for pitting, grooves, scoring or flaking. Inspect the valve lifter faces (that ride on the cam lobes) for concave wear. **Note:** *Never install used lifters on a new camshaft. If the original camshaft and lifters are installed, make sure the lifters are returned to the bores they were removed from. If they get mixed up, new lifters must be used.*

95 Oil pump – removal

1 The oil pump is an integral part of the timing chain cover with the cavity in the cover forming the body of the pump.
2 Remove the retaining bolts and lift the oil pump cover, the gasket and the oil filter as an assembly away from the timing chain cover.

2D

96 Oil pump – disassembly, inspection and reassembly

1 Slide the drivegear assembly and idler gear from the pump body.
2 Unscrew the pressure relief valve cap and remove the valve and spring.
3 Check the operation of the relief valve by inserting the poppet valve and making sure it slides back and forth freely. If it does not, replace the pump cover and the valve with new components.
4 The distance between the end of the pump gear and the cover is the gear end clearance. This can be checked in either of two ways.

a) Place a strip of Plastigage across the full width of each gear, install the pump cover and tighten the bolts to the specified torque. Remove the cover and measure the Plastigage with the scale on the container to determine if the clearance is within the Specifications.
b) Place a straightedge across the gears and the pump body and select a feeler gauge which will fit freely but snugly between the straightedge and the body. Make sure the gears are pushed as far up into the body as possible.

5 If the clearance is excessive, check the gears for excessive wear. If the gear is obviously not badly worn and a thinner cover gasket will not bring the clearance within the specified limit, replace the gears and idler shaft.
6 To check the gear-to-body clearance, insert a feeler gauge between the gear tooth end and the pump body inner wall opposite the point of gear mesh as shown in the accompanying illustration. Select a gauge which fits snugly, yet can be inserted freely. Rotate the gears and measure the clearance of each tooth in turn.
7 If the gear-to-body clearance is greater than specified, replace the gears and idler shaft.
8 Slide the gear and idler shaft assembly into the pump body and insert the pressure relief valve and spring; secure it with the cap.
9 **Note:** *The oil pump must be packed with petroleum jelly (not grease) prior to installation to ensure self-priming action.*

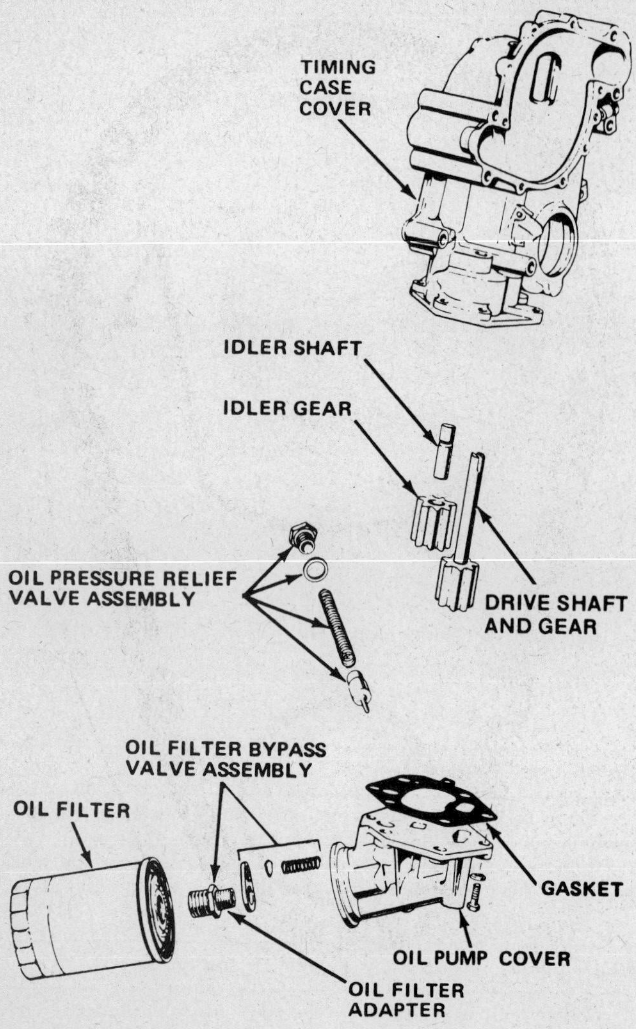

Fig. 2.50 Oil pump components – exploded view (Sec 96)

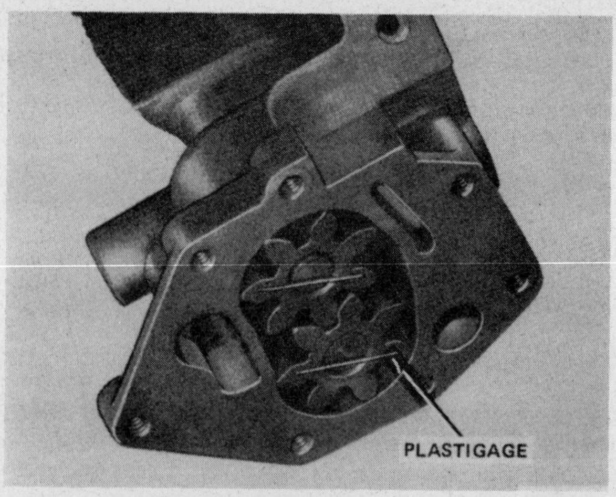

Fig. 2.51 Checking oil pump gear end clearance with Plastigage (Sec 96)

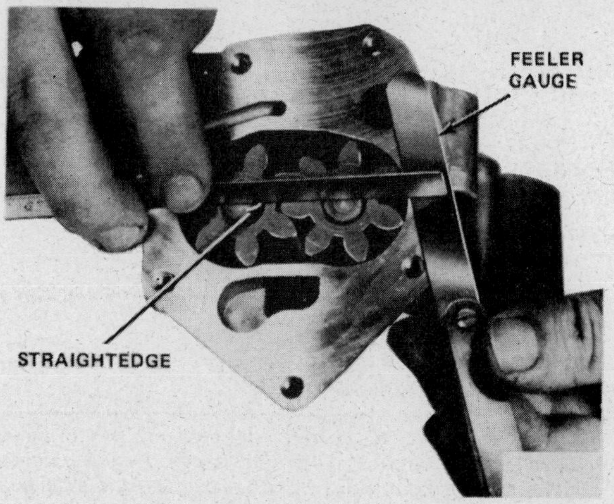

Fig. 2.52 Checking oil pump gear end clearance with a feeler gauge and straightedge (Sec 96)

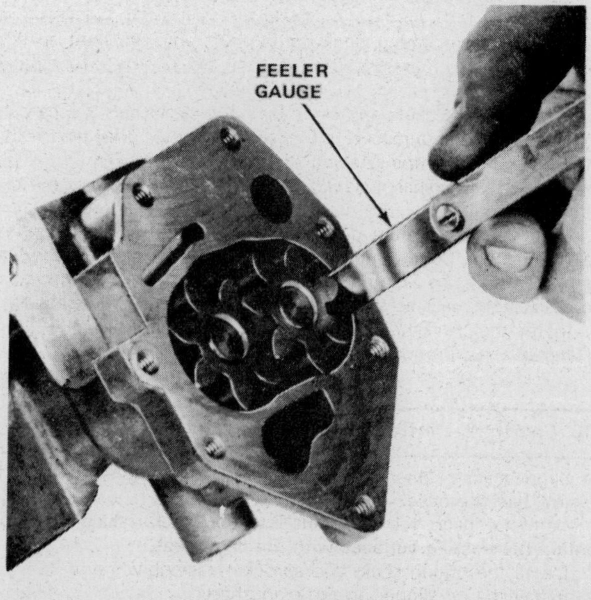

Fig. 2.53 Checking oil pump gear-to-body clearance (Sec 96)

97 Oil seal replacement

Front timing chain cover seal

1 The seal should be replaced with a new one whenever the timing chain cover is removed.

2 Remove the old seal and clean the cavity.

3 Apply a gasket sealant such as Permatex No. 2 or equivalent to the outer circumference of the seal.

4 Install the seal evenly in the timing case, using a suitable size socket or a block of wood and a hammer to seat it completely in the cavity.

5 Prior to installing the crankshaft vibration damper, apply a light coat of engine oil or grease to the seal-to-damper contact surface.

Rear main bearing oil seal

6 Remove the rear main bearing cap and discard the old lower seal.

7 Clean all traces of sealer from the main bearing cap.

8 Gently drive out the upper seal, using a hammer and brass drift, until it protrudes sufficiently to be grasped with pliers and pulled out.

9 If the crankshaft is in place, wipe the contact surface area clean and apply a light coat of engine oil.

10 Coat the lip of the seal with engine oil or grease and the upper contact surface with liquid soap. Insert the seal into the groove in the engine block with the lip facing forward.

11 Coat both sides of the lower seal ends with RTV-type sealant, taking care not to apply it to the seal surface. Coat the lip of the seal

with engine oil or grease and the curved outer surface with liquid soap as shown in the accompanying illustration.
12 Install the lower seal in the main bearing cap with the lip facing forward and seat it securely.
13 When installing the main bearing cap, apply a coat of RTV-type sealant to the chamfered contact surfaces.

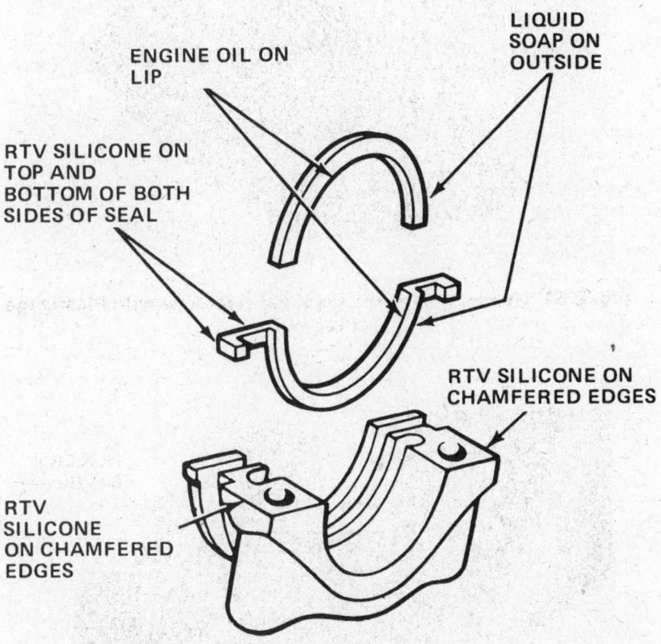

Fig. 2.54 Rear main bearing oil seal installation details (Sec 97)

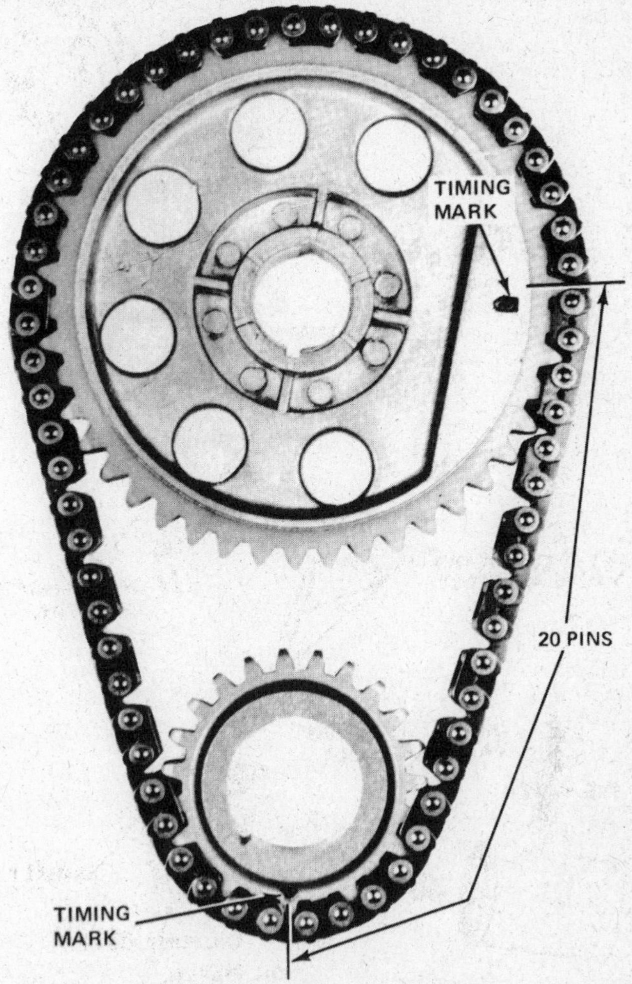

Fig. 2.55 For proper valve timing, there must be 20 pins between the sprocket timing marks (Sec 99)

98 Oil pump – installation

1 Pack the interior of the pump with petroleum jelly to provide a self-priming action. **Caution**: *Do not use grease for this purpose.*
2 Using a new gasket, place the pump and filter assembly in position and install the retaining bolts. Tighten them to the specified torque.

99 Timing chain and sprockets – installation

1 Assemble the timing chain, crankshaft and camshaft sprockets with the timing marks aligned as shown in the accompanying illustration.
2 Install the sprockets and chain onto the crankshaft and camshaft.
3 Install the fuel pump eccentric and distributor drivegear with the eccentric REAR stamping facing the camshaft sprocket.
4 Install the camshaft washer and screw. Tighten the screw to the specified torque.
5 Rotate the crankshaft until the camshaft timing mark is at the 3 o'clock position. Counting from the pin directly adjacent to the timing mark, there must be 20 pins between the camshaft sprocket mark and the crankshaft mark as shown in the accompanying illustration.
6 Install the crankshaft oil seal and timing chain cover.
7 Install the vibration damper and pulley.

100 Camshaft – installation

1 Lubricate the camshaft very thoroughly with engine assembly lube or moly-based grease.
2 Carefully insert the camshaft into the block, taking care not to contact the bearing surfaces with the cam lobes.
3 Install the timing chain and sprocket assembly.
4 Install the oil slinger on the crankshaft.
5 Install the fuel pump eccentric and drivegear on the camshaft, tightening the retaining screw to the specified torque.
6 Install the timing chain case using a new gasket and oil seal.
7 Install the vibration damper and pulley, tightening the retaining bolts to the specified torque.
8 Coat the hydraulic lifters with engine assembly lube or moly-based grease. Install each lifter into the bore from which it was originally removed.
9 Lubricate the ends of each pushrod with engine assembly lube or moly-based grease and install them in their original locations.
10 Install the rocker arm assemblies.
11 Install the rocker arm covers.
12 Install the fuel pump.
13 Rotate the crankshaft until the number 1 position is at top dead center (TDC) on the compression stroke. This can be determined by placing your finger over the number 1 cylinder spark plug hole and turning the crankshaft pulley bolt with a wrench in a clockwise direction until pressure is felt. The timing mark on the vibration damper should be aligned with the TDC index mark on the timing degree scale.
14 Insert the distributor so the rotor is aligned with the number 1 terminal of the cap when fully in place (Chapter 5). Install the distributor cap.

101 Timing chain cover – installation

1 Remove the lower locating dowel, taking care not to damage it.
2 Cut both sides of the oil pan gasket off flush with the engine block.
3 Apply RTV-type gasket sealant to both sides of the new timing

cover gasket and attach the gasket to the cover.
4 Attach the new front oil pan seal to the bottom of the timing chain cover.
5 If a new oil pan gasket is used, use the old gaskets as a guide and trim them to correspond to the amount cut off in Step 2. Line up the tongues of the new gasket pieces with the oil-pan seal and cement them into place on the cover with RTV-type gasket sealant. Apply gasket sealant to the cut off edges of the original pan gasket, place the timing cover in position and install the bolts. Tighten the bolts slowly and evenly until the cover aligns with the upper dowel. Insert the lower dowel and carefully drive it into position. Install the lower bolts and then tighten all of the cover bolts to the specified torque.
6 If RTV-type sealant is used, apply a $\frac{1}{8}$-inch bead to the timing cover flanges. Place the cover in position and install the bolts in their marked positions. Insert the lower locating dowel into the block and drive it into position. Install the remaining bolts and tighten them to the specified torque. Apply a bead of RTV-type sealant to the pan-to-cover joint and press it into place with your finger. Apply a thread-locking compound to the oil pan bolts and install them.
7 Install the vibration damper and tighten the bolt to the specified torque.

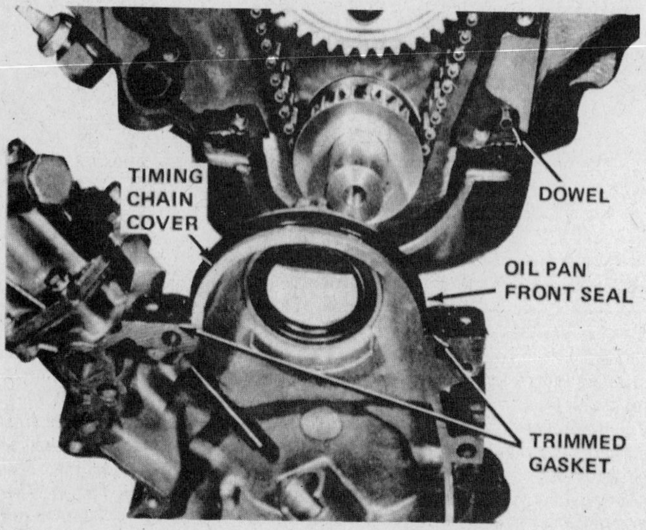

Fig. 2.56 Timing chain cover and oil pan seal installation details (Sec 101)

102 Cylinder head – installation

1 Apply an even coat of non-hardening gasket sealant to both sides of the new cylinder head gasket.
2 Place the gasket in position on the engine block with the stamped TOP designation facing up.
3 Prior to installing the head bolts, clean the threads with a wire brush so the bolts will not bind when installed.
4 Place the cylinder head in position on the engine block.
5 Install the bolts finger tight, making sure they thread smoothly into the block with no binding.
6 Tighten the bolts evenly to the specified torque in the sequence shown in the accompanying illustration.
7 Install the intake manifold.
8 Install the pushrods and rocker arm assemblies in their original positions. Make sure the pushrod ends are lubricated with a dab of engine assembly lube or moly-based grease and that the bottom end of each rod is centered in the valve lifter plunger cap. Tighten the rocker arm bolts/nuts one turn at a time, alternately, to avoid bending or breaking the bridge (if so equipped).
9 Apply a $\frac{1}{8}$-inch bead of RTV-type sealant to the gasket surface of the rocker arm cover.
10 Place the cover in position on the cylinder head, install the bolts and tighten them evenly and securely.

103 Intake manifold – installation

1 If a new intake manifold is to be installed, transfer the EGR valve and back pressure sensor, thermostat housing, coolant temperature sensor and CTO valve from the old unit.
2 Coat both sides of the manifold gasket with RTV-type sealant.
3 Place the gasket in position on the alignment locators at the rear of the cylinder heads. Hold the rear of the gasket in place and align it with the front locators.
4 Install the end seals and apply a coat of Permatex No. 2 sealant.
5 Lower the manifold into position and install the retaining bolts finger tight.
6 After making sure the bolts are properly started, with no binding, tighten them to the specified torque in a crisscross pattern.

104 Oil pan – installation

1 Install the front oil seal in the timing chain cover. Coat the ends of the seal with RTV-type sealant.
2 Coat the rear oil pan seal curved surface and the end seal cap. Make sure the seal is completely seated.
3 Cement the oil pan side gasket to the engine block sealing surfaces with gasket sealant. Apply a generous coat of RTV-type sealant to the gasket ends.
4 Install the oil pan and bolts and tighten the bolts to the specified torque in a crisscross pattern.

105 Crankshaft – removal

1 Before removing the crankshaft, you must remove the flywheel/driveplate, the rear oil seal housing, the cylinder heads, the oil pan, the timing chain cover and the timing chain and sprockets.
2 With the engine upside-down, remove the oil pick-up tube and screen assembly.
3 Remove the piston assemblies from the engine block as described in Chapter 2A.
4 Refer to Chapter 2A for the remaining crankshaft removal steps.

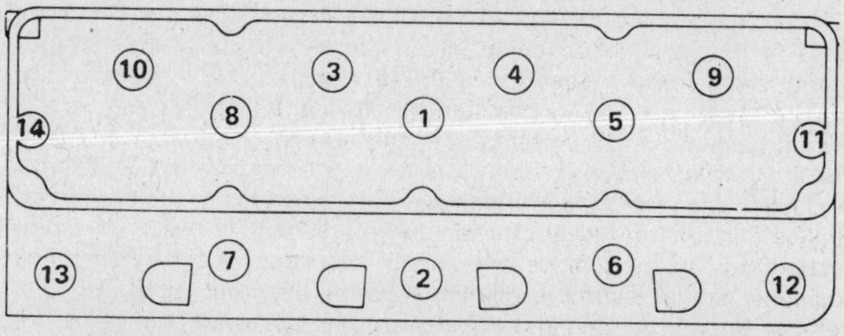

Fig. 2.57 Cylinder head bolt tightening sequence (Sec 102)

106 Crankshaft – installation and main bearing oil clearance check

1 Crankshaft installation is generally one of the first steps in engine reassembly; it is assumed at this point that the engine block and crankshaft have been cleaned and inspected and repaired or reconditioned. The new rear main oil seal sections should be installed before proceeding (Section 97).
2 Position the engine with the bottom facing up.
3 Remove the main bearing cap bolts and lift out the caps. Lay them out in the proper order to help ensure that they are installed correctly.
4 If they are still in place, remove the old bearing inserts from the block and the main bearing caps. Wipe the main bearing surfaces of the block and caps with a clean, lint-free cloth (they must be kept spotlessly clean).
5 Clean the back sides of the new main bearing inserts and lay one bearing half in each main bearing saddle (in the block) and the other

bearing half from each bearing set in the corresponding main bearing cap. Make sure the tab on the bearing insert fits into the recess in the block or cap. Also, the oil holes in the block and cap must line up with the oil holes in the bearing insert. *Do not hammer the bearing into place and do not nick or gouge the bearing faces. No lubrication should be used at this time.*

6 The flanged thrust bearing must be installed in the number three (3) (center) cap and saddle.

7 Clean the faces of the bearings in the block and the crankshaft main bearing journals with a clean, lint-free cloth. Check or clean the oil holes in the crankshaft, as any dirt here can only go one way – straight through the new bearings.

8 Once you are certain that the crankshaft is clean, carefully lay it in position (an assistant would be very helpful here) in the main bearings with the counterweights lying sideways.

9 Before the crankshaft can be permanently installed, the main bearing oil clearance must be checked.

10 Trim five pieces of the appropriate type of Plastigage (so they are slightly shorter than the width of the main bearings) and place one piece on each crankshaft main bearing journal, parallel with the journal axis. Do not lay them across any oil holes.

11 Clean the faces of the bearings in the caps and install the caps in their respective positions (do not mix them up) with the arrows pointing toward the front of the engine. Do not disturb the Plastigage.

12 Starting with the center main and working out toward the ends, tighten the main bearing cap bolts, in three steps, to the specified torque. *Do not rotate the crankshaft at any time during this operation.*

13 Remove the bolts and carefully lift off the main bearing caps. Keep them in order. Do not disturb the Plastigage or rotate the crankshaft. If any of the main bearing caps are difficult to remove, tap gently from side-to-side with a soft-faced hammer to loosen them.

14 Compare the width of the crushed Plastigage on each journal to the scale printed on the Plastigage container (photo) to obtain the main bearing oil clearance. Check the Specifications to make sure it is correct.

15 If the clearance is not correct, double-check to make sure that you have the right size bearing inserts. Also, make sure that no dirt or oil was between the bearing inserts and the main bearing caps or the block when the clearance was measured.

16 Carefully scrape all traces of the Plastigage material off the main bearing journals and/or the bearing faces. Do not nick or scratch the bearing faces.

17 Carefully lift the crankshaft out of the engine. Clean the bearing faces in the block, then apply a thin, uniform layer of clean, high-quality moly-based grease (or engine assembly lube) to each of the bearing faces. Be sure to coat the thrust flange faces as well as the journal face of the thrust bearing in the number three (center) main. Make sure the crankshaft journals are clean, then carefully lay it back in place in the block. Clean the faces of the bearings in the caps, then apply a thin, uniform layer of clean, high-quality moly-based grease to each of the bearing faces and install the caps in their respective positions with the arrows pointing toward the front of the engine. Refer to Section 97 and apply sealant to the rear main bearing cap as indicated there. Install the bolts and tighten them to the specified torque, starting with the center main and working out toward the ends. Work up to the final torque in three steps.

18 Rotate the crankshaft a number of times by hand and check for any obvious binding.

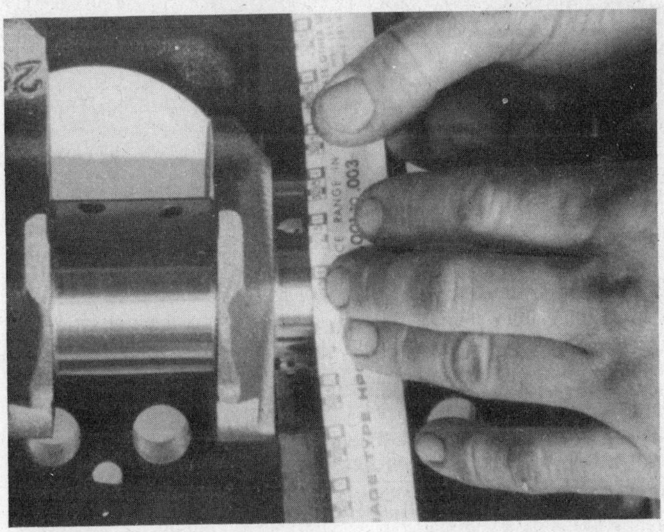

106.14 Comparing the width of the crushed Plastigage to the scale on the container

19 The final step is to check the crankshaft end play. This can be done with a feeler gauge or a dial indicator set. Refer to Chapter 2A, Section 12, for the procedure to follow.

107 Main and connecting rod bearings – selection

1 The crankshaft and bearing inspection procedures are included in Chapter 2A. The condition and measured size of the crankshaft journals will determine the bearings to be installed when the engine is reassembled.

2 If a new or reground crankshaft is installed, the size of each journal should be indicated by a color coded mark on the adjacent cheek or counterweight, toward the rear (flanged) end of the crankshaft. The bearing inserts are also color coded (on the edge of the insert). The accompanying charts (one for main bearings, one for rod bearings) should be consulted to determine the correct bearings to use. **Caution**: *Always check the bearing oil clearance with Plastigage during final installation of the crankshaft and/or piston/connecting rod assemblies.*

3 If necessary to achieve the desired oil clearance, different size upper and lower bearing inserts may be used on the same journal but the size difference must never exceed 0.001 inch. **Caution**: *The odd size inserts must all be either in the caps or block (main bearings). In the case of connecting rod bearings the odd size inserts must all be either in the caps or rods.*

4 If the original crankshaft is reground, the automotive machine shop that reconditions the journals should supply bearings that will produce the desired oil clearance.

Crankshaft Connecting Rod Journal Color Code and Diameter	Bearing Color Code	
	Upper Insert Size	Lower Insert Size
304 – 360 CID Engines		
Yellow –2.0955 to 2.0948 (Standard)	Yellow – Standard	Yellow – Standard
Orange –2.0948 to 2.0941 (0.0007 Undersize)	Yellow – Standard	Black – .001-inch Undersize
Black –2.0941 to 2.0934 (0.0014 Undersize)	Black – .001-inch Undersize	Black – .001-inch Undersize
Red –2.0855 to 2.0848 (0.010 Undersize)	Red – .010-inch Undersize	Red – .010-inch Undersize

Fig. 2.58 Connecting rod bearing selection chart (Sec 107)

Crankshaft Main Bearing Journal Color Code and Diameter in Inches (Journal Size)	Bearing Color Code	
	Upper Insert Size	Lower Insert Size
Yellow –2.7489 to 2.7484 (Standard)	Yellow – Standard	Yellow – Standard
Orange –2.7484 to 2.7479 (0.0005 Undersize)	Yellow – Standard	Black – .001-inch Undersize
Black –2.7479 to 2.7474 (0.001 Undersize)	Black – .001-inch Undersize	Black – .001-inch Undersize
Green –2.7474 to 2.7469 (0.0015 Undersize)	Black – .001-inch Undersize	Green – .002-inch Undersize
Red –2.7389 to 2.7384 (0.010 Undersize)	Red – .010-inch Undersize	Red – .010-inch Undersize

Fig. 2.59 Main bearing selection chart (Sec 107)

108 Engine/automatic transmission – connection

1 Prior to connection, make sure the converter is properly engaged with the transmission input shaft. Rotate the converter so the mark made at the time of removal is lined up with the one on the driveplate.
2 Engage the transmission pilot holes with the dowels on the engine and install the two lower retaining bolts. Tighten the bolts to draw the transmission against the engine.
3 Install the remaining bolts and tighten them securely.
4 Align the converter and driveplate marks, install the attaching bolts and tighten them to the specified torque.
5 Install the starter motor, converter inspection cover and transmission filler tube.

109 Engine/manual transmission – connection

1 Install the clutch housing/transmission unit and tighten the bolts securely.
2 Lubricate the pilot bushing with clean engine oil and install it.
3 Install the throwout bearing and insert the transmission, making sure the input shaft splines are properly aligned. Install the retaining bolts and tighten them securely.

110 Engine/transmission (1970 through 1976 models) – installation

1 Lower the engine/transmission unit carefully into the engine compartment at a steep angle initially to clear the fenders and radiator brace. Once in the engine compartment, the engine/transmission unit can be leveled and the transmission shaft engaged with the driveshaft slip joint.
2 Install the rear engine support cushion on the crossmember and tighten the hardware securely.
3 Raise the rear crossmember into position with a jack and lower the engine until it rests lightly on the front mount support cushions. Install the cushion retaining nuts finger tight.
4 Install the rear crossmember retaining nuts and washer and tighten the nuts securely.
5 Lower the engine onto the front support cushions and tighten the nuts.
6 Connect the speedometer cable to the transmission.
7 Attach the exhaust pipes to the manifolds.
8 Connect all wires, linkages, hoses and lines which were disconnected prior to engine removal.
9 Install the power steering pump and drivebelt.
10 Install the cooling fan.
11 Install the air conditioning components.
12 Install the radiator and hoses.
13 Connect the transmission fluid cooler lines to the radiator *(on automatic transmission equipped models).*
14 Install the radiator upper air baffle.
15 Install the battery and air cleaner assembly. Always hook up the negative cable *last* when installing the battery.
16 Install the hood assembly and fender braces (if equipped).
17 Fill the cooling system, crankcase and transmission with the specified fluids.
18 Have the air conditioning system purged of air and recharged by a qualified technician.

111 Engine (1977 through 1983 models) – installation

1 Lower the engine slowly and carefully into the engine compartment and align the engine with the converter bolt holes. Install the retaining bolts and tighten them securely. Remove the jack supporting the converter housing.
2 Lower the front of the engine and install the front engine mount supports and ground strap. Remove the lifting device.
3 Raise the front of the vehicle and support it securely.
4 Reach through the starter motor hole and pull the converter forward into the crankshaft pilot bushing. Align the converter with the marks on the driveplate during removal and install the retaining bolts. Install the converter cover.
5 Install the throttle valve bellcrank and manual linkage support. Connect the rod to the bellcrank.
6 Align the exhaust system and tighten the bolts.
7 Install the upper converter housing and tighten the bolts.
8 Attach the heat valve to the right exhaust manifold, followed by the front exhaust pipes, seals and nuts.
9 Lower the vehicle.
10 Connect the power steering hoses and fill the reservoir.
11 Connect the hoses and compressor clutch wire to the air conditioning system components.
12 Connect the power brake vacuum check valve.
13 Install the throttle cable housing bracket and the throttle return spring.
14 Install the throttle cable housing in the bracket and connect the cable.
15 Connect the heater and air conditioner vacuum hoses to the intake manifold.
16 Connect the flexible fuel line and clamp.
17 Install the vapor canister, bracket and hoses.
18 Attach the heater inlet hose and clamp to the intake manifold.
19 Connect the TCS solenoid control switch, wiring harness and control switch, if equipped.
20 Install the heater hose.
21 Install the ignition wire harness, distributor, throttle stop solenoid lead, coolant temperature sending unit and ignition coil leads.
22 Connect the alternator and oil pressure sending unit leads.
23 Connect the fuel return line and clamp to the fuel filter.
24 Remove the alignment screw from the fan pulley and water pump and install the spacer on the fan.
25 Install the radiator, shroud and hoses and connect the automatic transmission fluid cooler lines. Fill the cooling system with the specified coolant.
26 Install the battery (hook up the positive cable first, then the negative cable). Install the TAC heat tube, the air cleaner assembly, the TAC vacuum line, the canister purge hose and the sensor hose.
27 Install the hood.

Chapter 3 Cooling, heating and air conditioning systems

Contents

Air conditioning compressor – removal and installation 15
Air conditioning condenser – removal and installation 13
Air conditioning evaporator – removal and installation 14
Air conditioning receiver/drier – removal and installation 16
Air conditioning system check 12
Air conditioning system servicing – general information 11
Antifreeze – general note 2
Coolant level check ..... See Chapter 1
Coolant reserve system – testing 4
Cooling system – servicing, draining, flushing and refilling ..... See Chapter 1
Engine drivebelts – check and adjustment ..... See Chapter 1
General information 1
Heater assembly – removal and installation 9
Heater control panel – removal and installation 10
Heater controls – adjustment 8
Radiator – removal and installation 6
Radiator – servicing 5
Thermostat – removal and installation 3
Underhood hoses – check and replacement ..... See Chapter 1
Water pump – removal and installation 7

3

Specifications

Radiator

Pressure cap rating	14 psi

Thermostat

Type	Wax pellet
Starts to open at	195°F (90°C)

Torque specifications

Thermostat housing cover bolts	
1980 through 1983 4-cylinder	20 ft-lb (27 Nm)
All other models	14 ft-lb (19 Nm)

1 General information

The cooling system consists of a radiator, water pump, flow and return hoses and a vehicle interior heater. Coolant circulates through the engine block and head through cast-in passages, cooling the cylinder bores, combustion surfaces and valve seats. The system is pressurized to raise the boiling point of the water/antifreeze solution. A radiator cap with a spring-loaded relief valve is used to pressurize the system.

The belt-driven water pump uses an impeller to push the water through the passages around the block. When the coolant has reached a certain predetermined temperature, the thermostat opens and allows the coolant to move from the cylinder head into the top radiator hose and the radiator.

As the coolant travels down the radiator tubes it is cooled by the in-rush of air (when the vehicle is moving). A fan mounted on the water pump pulley assists this cooling action.

The coolant also circulates through the heater core, providing heat for the interior heating system.

Air conditioning is available as an option. All components of the system are mounted in the engine compartment.

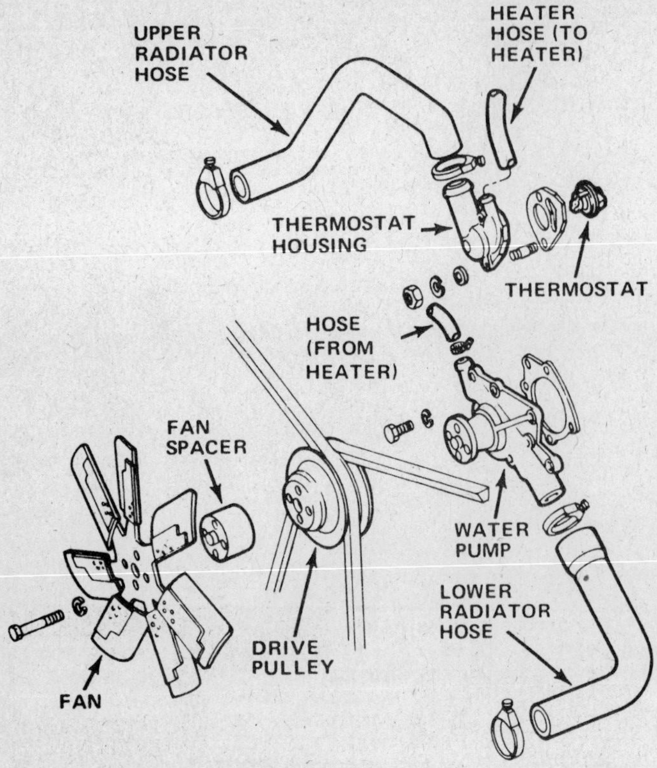

Fig. 3.1 Cooling system components – exploded view (typical of most models) (Sec 1)

2 Antifreeze – general note

Caution: *Children and pets may be attracted to coolant by its sweet odor and taste but a few licks of antifreeze solution can be lethal. Keep all containers closed and wipe up any spills under your vehicle as soon as you notice them. When handling antifreeze, be careful not to spill it on the vehicle paint, since it may cause damage if not removed immediately.*

1 It is recommended that the cooling system be filled with a water/ethylene glycol based antifreeze solution which will give protection down to at least -20°F at all times. This provides protection against corrosion and increases the coolant boiling point.

2 The cooling system should be drained, flushed and refilled every other year. The use of antifreeze solutions for periods longer than two years is likely to cause damage and encourage the formation of rust and scale due to the corrosion inhibitors gradually losing their efficiency.

3 Before adding antifreeze to the system, check all hose connections and the tightness of the cylinder head bolts.

4 The exact mixture of antifreeze-to-water which you should use depends upon the relative weather conditions. The mixture should contain at least 50 percent antifreeze, offering protection to -20°F. Under no circumstances should the mixture contain more than 70 percent antifreeze.

3 Thermostat – removal and installation

1 The thermostat is basically a restriction valve which is actuated by a heat sensitive element. It is designed to open and close at predetermined temperatures. If the thermostat is not functioning properly, it will affect the operating temperature of the engine. A thermostat stuck in the open position will cause the engine to warm up very slowly. If it is stuck closed, the engine will overheat easily. The thermostat is only one possible cause of such symptoms, but it can be replaced easily and inexpensively.

2 With the engine cool, drain about a gallon of coolant out of the radiator into a suitable container.

Fig. 3.2 Thermostat with housing removed (typical) (Sec 3)

3 Disconnect the top radiator hose from the thermostat housing cover on the front of the engine. Be careful, as antifreeze will irritate skin and strip paint away. On some models it may be necessary to remove some of the intake manifold hoses. Note where they are attached before removing them.

4 Unbolt and remove the thermostat housing cover. Note how the thermostat is installed before removing it.

5 Scrape all traces of the old gasket from the thermostat housing and cover. Do not nick or gouge the gasket surfaces.

6 Install the new thermostat. Check to be sure that it is seated in the machined recess and that the air bleed hole is facing *up.*

7 Apply a thin layer of RTV-type gasket sealer to both sides of a new gasket and place it on the housing.

8 Install the housing cover and tighten the bolts to the specified torque.

9 Refill the cooling system, start the engine, let it reach normal operating temperature, then check carefully for leaks.

4 Coolant reserve system – testing

1 Make sure the coolant level in the reserve system reservoir is at the Full mark.

2 With the radiator cap in place, open the radiator drain petcock (place a suitable container under the radiator to catch the coolant).

3 Coolant should be drawn from the reserve system reservoir into the radiator. Close the radiator drain petcock before the reserve system reservoir is completely drained.

4 If coolant is not drawn from the reservoir, check for leaks in the hose from the reservoir to the radiator filler neck, the radiator cap, and the radiator top tank.

5 It may be necessary to have the cap and system pressure checked to locate any leaks.

6 Be sure to remove the radiator pressure cap and replenish the coolant in the radiator and the reserve system reservoir.

5 Radiator – servicing

1 The radiator should be kept free of obstruction such as leaves, paper, insects, etc. which could affect the cooling efficiency.

2 Periodically, inspect the radiator for bent cooling fins, signs of coolant leakage and cracks around the upper and lower tanks. Carefully straighten any bent fins, using the blade of a screwdriver.

6.2 Disconnecting the upper radiator hose

6.5 Lifting out the radiator

3 Check the filler neck sealing surface for dents which could affect the radiator cap effectiveness.
4 If leaks are evident, remove it from the vehicle and have it repaired at a radiator shop.

6 Radiator – removal and installation

1 Remove the radiator cap. Drain the coolant from the radiator and engine block into a suitable container. On V8 models, there is usually one drain plug on each side of the engine block. Six-cylinder models usually have two on the left side of the block and four-cylinder models should have one drain plug at the left rear side of the engine block.
2 Remove the upper and lower radiator hoses (photo).
3 Remove the fan shroud, if so equipped.
4 If your vehicle is equipped with an automatic transmission, disconnect the transmission fluid cooler lines from the radiator. Plug the lines to prevent dirt from entering them.
5 Remove the radiator attaching bolts and lift out the radiator (photo). Do not gouge the cooling fins with the fan blade. Also, antifreeze can irritate the skin and strip paint away, so be careful not to spill any when lifting out the radiator.
6 The radiator can now be inspected for leaks and damage. If there are any leaks, the radiator should be taken to a radiator repair shop.
7 Bugs and dirt can be cleaned from the radiator using compressed air or a soft brush. Do not bend the cooling fins.
8 Installation is the reverse of the removal procedure. Add coolant and recheck the level after the engine has been running for a minute or two. Replace the cap and check for leaks after the engine has warmed up.

7 Water pump – removal and installation

1 If the water pump is not functioning properly, it must be replaced as a unit.
2 Disconnect the negative battery cable.
3 Drain the cooling system.
4 Disconnect the coolant hoses from the water pump.
5 Remove the necessary drivebelts.
6 Remove or loosen the alternator as needed to gain adequate clearance for water pump removal.
7 Disconnect the fan shroud. On some models, the fan shroud will have to be removed along with the fan and hub assembly. If possible, remove the fan shroud at this time. Turning the fan shroud ½-turn will sometimes aid in removal.
8 Remove the fan and hub assembly.
9 Remove or loosen the air pump, power steering pump and air conditioning compressor (if so equipped) as needed to gain adequate clearance.

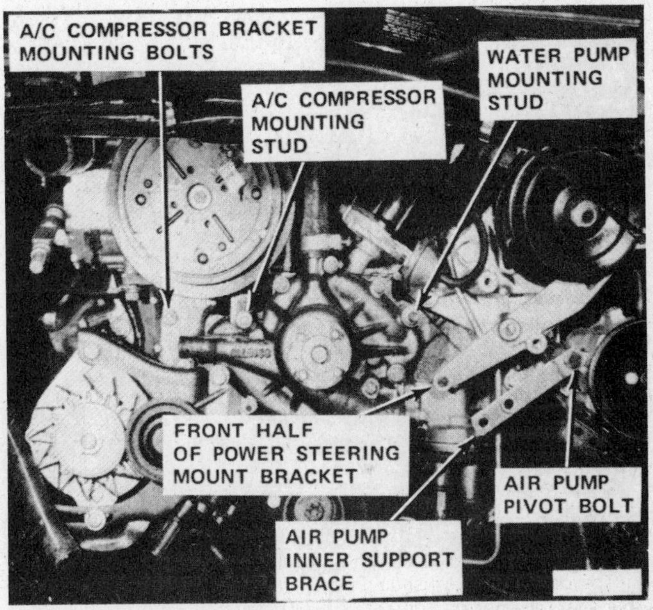

Fig. 3.3 Water pump and air conditioning compressor (typical of most V8 engines) (Sec 7)

10 Remove the water pump bolts, then separate the pump from the engine. You may have to tap it lightly with a soft-faced hammer to break the gasket seal.
11 Scrape all traces of the old gasket and gasket sealer off of the engine. Do not nick or gouge the gasket sealing surfaces.
12 Coat both sides of a new gasket with RTV-type gasket sealer, then install the new pump. Be sure the gasket lines up properly to ensure proper sealing.
13 The rest of the installation procedure is the reverse of removal. Adjust the drivebelts to their proper tension (Chapter 1).

8 Heater controls – adjustment

1970 through 1976 heater and defroster door cables

1 Either cable can be adjusted using the following procedure.
2 Remove the cable housing retaining clips at the damper doors.
3 With the heater air flow lever set at the Off position, hold the damper doors tightly closed and reinstall the clips.
4 Check the operation of the damper door to ensure positive closing.

3

1977 through 1983 heater and defroster door cable

5 Move the air flow lever to the Off position and move the heater-defroster door crank arm to the lowest position (full heat).
6 Slide the self-adjusting clip (accessible at the door crank on the heater housing) approximately ½-inch along the control cable wire. This would move the crank arm toward the cable clamp.
7 Move the heater air flow lever to the Defrost position, allowing the cable wire to slip through the self-adjusting clip for proper adjustment.

1970 through 1976 blend-air damper door cable

8 Early blend-air door cables use a turnbuckle for adjustment. The turnbuckle is located under the instrument panel and is accessible midway between the control and the housing.
9 Place the temperature control lever in the far left position.
10 Rotate the turnbuckle to obtain complete closing of the blend-air damper door.
11 Check damper door operation.

1977 through 1983 blend-air damper door cable

12 Hold the temperature control lever in the far right (Warm) position and move the blend-air door crank arm to the extreme right end of its travel (full heat position).
13 Slide the self-adjusting clip approximately ½-inch along the control cable wire, moving the crank arm toward the control panel.
14 Move the temperature control lever from Warm to Off, allowing the cable wire to slip through the self-adjusting clip for proper adjustment.

9 Heater assembly – removal and installation

1 Disconnect the negative battery cable.
2 Drain about two quarts of coolant from the radiator.
3 Disconnect the heater hose from the heater core tubes in the engine compartment. Plug the tubes to prevent spillage of the coolant during removal of the housing.
4 Disconnect the blower motor wire and remove the blower motor and fan assembly.
5 Remove the housing attaching nuts in the engine compartment.
6 Remove the package tray from the dashboard, if so equipped.
7 Disconnect the wire connector at the blower motor resistor.
8 Disconnect the heater, defroster and blend-air door cables at the heater housing.
9 Remove the door sill plate, if so equipped.
10 Remove the right cowl trim panel.
11 Remove the right windshield pillar moulding, the instrument panel

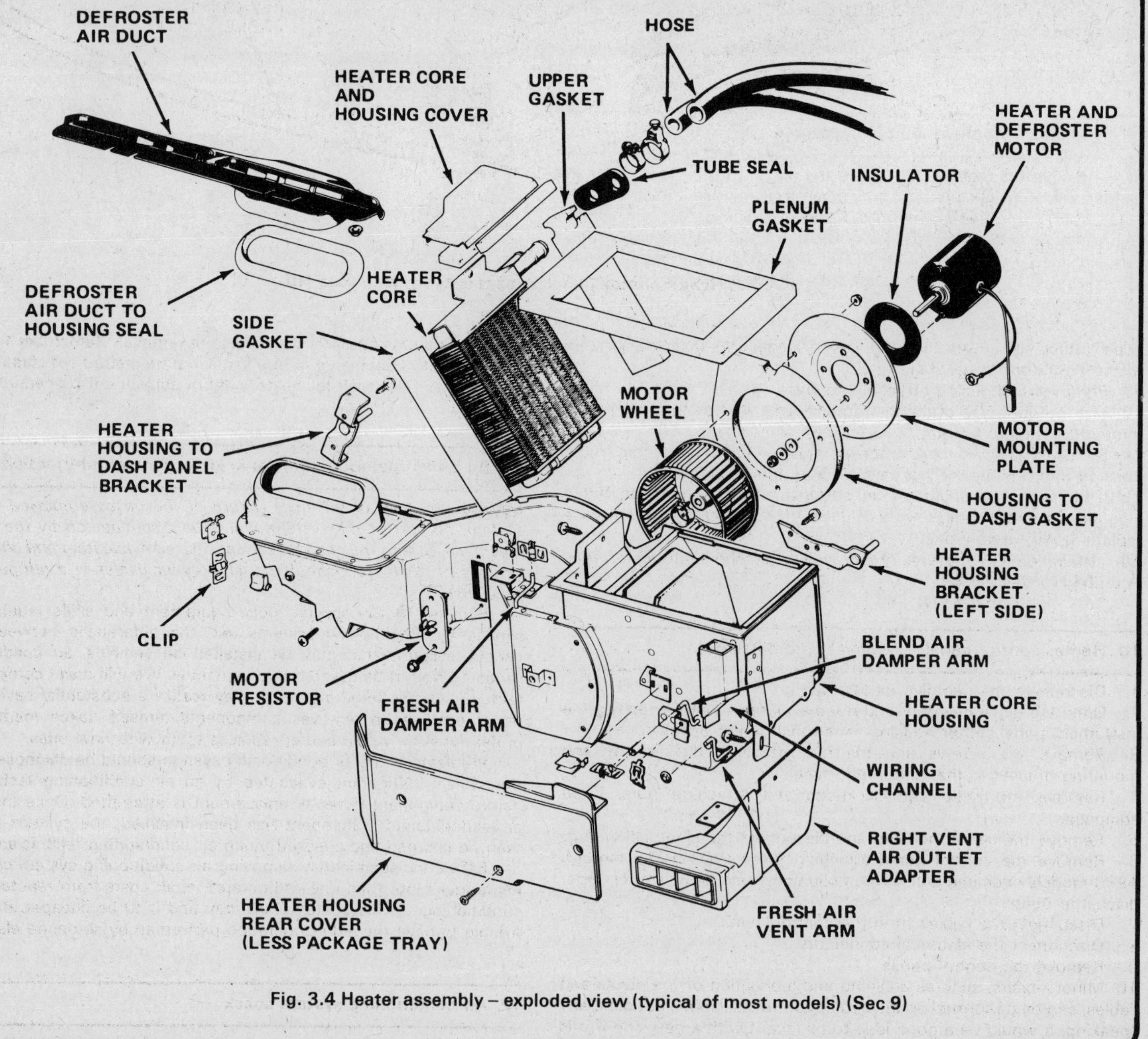

Fig. 3.4 Heater assembly – exploded view (typical of most models) (Sec 9)

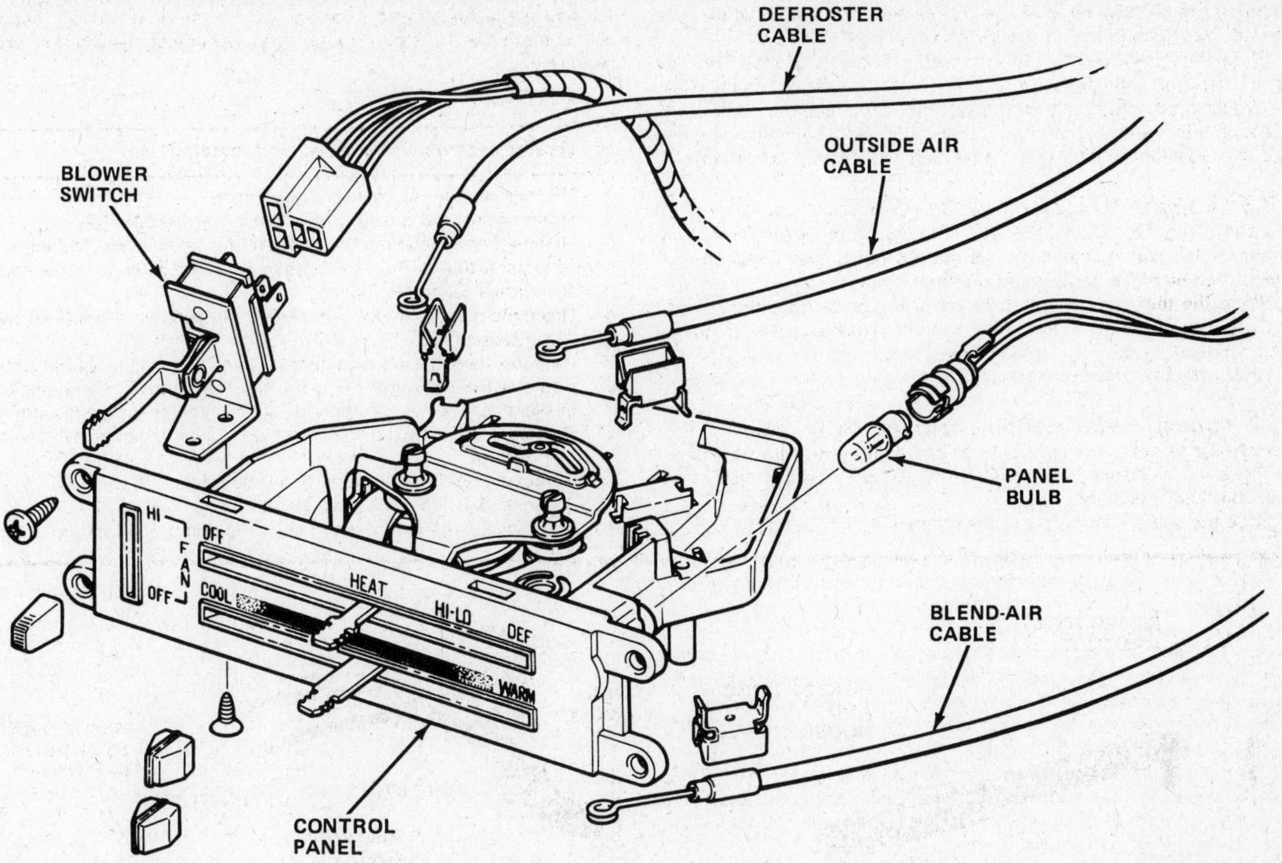

Fig. 3.5 Heater control panel components (typical) (Sec 10)

upper attaching screws and the screw attaching the instrument panel to the right door hinge post.

12 Remove the housing attaching screws.

13 Pull the right side of the instrument panel slightly to the rear and remove the heater housing.

14 Remove the cover and the screws attaching the heater core to the housing and remove the heater core from the housing.

15 If the core is leaking, it should be replaced with a new one. If it is clogged, reverse flushing with cold water might clear it, otherwise replace it with a new one.

16 Installation is the reverse of removal. Adjust the heater controls as described in Section 8.

10 Heater control panel – removal and installation

1 Disconnect the negative battery cable.

2 Open the glove box door and remove all the screws attaching the instrument panel center housing to the instrument panel.

3 Remove the screws and the nut attaching the ashtray and mounting bracket to the instrument panel.

4 Remove the radio control knobs and attaching nuts, if so equipped.

5 Remove the center housing and disconnect the electrical wiring.

6 Remove the control panel attaching screws. On 1975 through 1983 models equipped with air conditioning, remove the center upper discharge duct.

7 Disconnect the cables from the control levers.

8 Disconnect the electrical connectors.

9 Remove the control panel.

10 Minor repairs, such as cleaning and lubrication of the pivots and cables, can be performed on the heater control assembly, but generally speaking, it would be a good idea to replace it with a new one if it is not operating properly.

11 Installation is basically the reverse of removal. Remember to plug in the electrical connector before installing the instrument cluster rim.

12 Refer to Section 8 for heater control adjustment procedures.

3

11 Air conditioning system servicing – general information

Caution: *In view of the toxic nature of the gases employed in the system, no part of the system should be disconnected by the home mechanic. Due to the need for the specialized evacuating and charging equipment, such work should be left to your dealer or a refrigeration specialist.*

Because of the special tools, equipment and skills required to service air conditioning systems and the differences between the various systems that may be installed on vehicles, air conditioner servicing cannot be covered in this manual. We will cover component removal, as the home mechanic may realize a substantial savings in repair costs if he removes components himself, takes them to a professional for repair and/or replaces them with new ones.

Problems in the air conditioning system should be diagnosed and the system refrigerant evacuated by an air conditioning technician before component removal/replacement is attempted. Once the new or reconditioned component has been installed, the system should then be charged and checked by an air conditioning technician.

Before indiscriminately removing air conditioning system components, get more than one estimate of repair costs from reputable air conditioning service centers. You may find it to be cheaper and less trouble to have the entire operation performed by someone else.

12 Air conditioning system check

1 The following maintenance steps should be performed on a

regular basis to ensure that the air conditioner continues to operate at peak efficiency.

a) Check the tension of the drivebelt and adjust it if necessary. Refer to Chapter 1.
b) Visually inspect the condition of the hoses, checking for cracks, hardening and other deterioration. **Note**: *Do not replace hoses without first having the system discharged.*
c) Check that the fins of the condenser are not covered with foreign material, such as leaves or bugs. A soft brush and compressed air can be used to remove them.

2 The compressor should be run for about 10 minutes at least once every month. This is especially important to remember during the winter months because long-term non-use can cause hardening of the internal seals.
3 If the system should lose its cooling action, some causes can be diagnosed by the home mechanic. Look for symptoms of trouble such as those in the following list. In all cases, it's a good idea to have the system serviced by a professional.

a) If bubbles appear in the sight glass (located at the top of the receiver/drier), it is an indication of either a small refrigerant leak or air in the refrigerant. If air is in the refrigerant, the receiver/drier is suspect and should be replaced.
b) If the view glass takes on a mist-like appearance or shows many bubbles, it indicates a large refrigerant leak. In such a case, do not operate the compressor at all until the fault has been corrected.
c) If no bubbles appear, have an assistant switch the fan control on and off, to cycle the magnetic clutch. If bubbles then appear, the system is fully charged with refrigerant.
d) If no bubbles appear during the switching action just described, then the system lacks refrigerant and must be recharged by your dealer as soon as possible.
e) Sweating or frosting of the expansion valve inlet indicates that the expansion valve is clogged or defective. It should be cleaned or replaced as necessary.
f) Sweating or frosting of the suction line (which runs between the suction throttle valve and the compressor) indicates that the expansion valve is stuck open or defective. It should be corrected or replaced as necessary.
g) Frosting on the evaporator indicates a defective suction throttle valve, requiring replacement of the valve.
h) Frosting of the high pressure liquid line (which runs between the condenser, receiver/drier and expansion valve) indicates that either the drier or the high pressure line is restricted. The line will have to be cleared or the receiver/drier replaced.
i) The combination of bubbles in the sight glass, a very hot suction line and, possibly, overheating of the engine is an indication that either the condenser is not operating properly or the refrigerant is overcharged. Check the tension of the drivebelt and adjust if necessary (Chapter 1). Check for foreign matter covering the fins of the condenser and clean if necessary. Also check for proper operation of the cooling system. If no fault can be found in these checks, the condenser may have to be replaced.

13 Air conditioning condenser – removal and installation

1 Before removing the condenser, the system must be evacuated by an air conditioning technician. **Caution**: *Do not attempt to do this yourself; the refrigerant used in the system can cause serious injuries and respiratory irritation.*
2 On 1979 and later 4-cylinder models, remove the charcoal canister and mounting bracket, if necessary, to gain adequate clearance for condenser removal. Remove the ambient air inlet duct from the radiator on later 4-cylinder models.
3 Remove the attaching screws from the fan shroud and the radiator.
4 Remove the fan shroud and the radiator.
5 Disconnect the compressor discharge-to-condenser line.
6 Disconnect the receiver/drier-to-evaporator line. Plug all open connections to prevent dirt and moisture from entering the components.
7 Remove the mounting bolts and lift out the condenser and the receiver/drier assembly.
8 Installation is the reverse of removal. On 1980 through 1983 4-cylinder models, one ounce of air conditioning system lubricant must be added to the system after replacing this component.

14 Air conditioning evaporator – removal and installation

1 Before removing the evaporator, the system must be evacuated by an air conditioning technician. **Caution**: *Do not attempt to do this yourself; the refrigerant used in the system can cause serious injuries and respiratory irritation.*
2 Disconnect the negative battery cable. If your vehicle is equipped with a package tray, follow Steps 3 through 6. If there is no package tray, proceed to Step 7.
3 Disconnect the wiring harness from the courtesy lights.
4 Remove the screws attaching the package tray to the cowl trim panels.
5 Remove the hood release cable attaching screws, if so equipped.
6 Remove the screws attaching the package tray to the instrument panel and evaporator housing. Remove the package tray.
7 Remove the air duct assembly.
8 Remove the instrument panel center housing, as described in Section 10.
9 Remove the radio, if so equipped (refer to Chapter 10).
10 Remove the necessary air outlets to gain clearance for evaporator housing removal. Remove the air duct.
11 Remove the insulation and disconnect the inlet and discharge hoses.
12 Disconnect the control cables and remove the temperature sensing capillary tube at the evaporator housing.
13 Remove the evaporator housing-to-dash panel screws in the passenger compartment and the housing-to-dash nuts in the engine compartment.
14 Remove the evaporator housing.
15 To remove the evaporator core, remove the evaporator housing cover and the evaporator core attaching screws.
16 Installation is the reverse of removal. On 1980 through 1983 4-cylinder models, one ounce of air conditioning system lubricant must be added to the system after replacing this component.

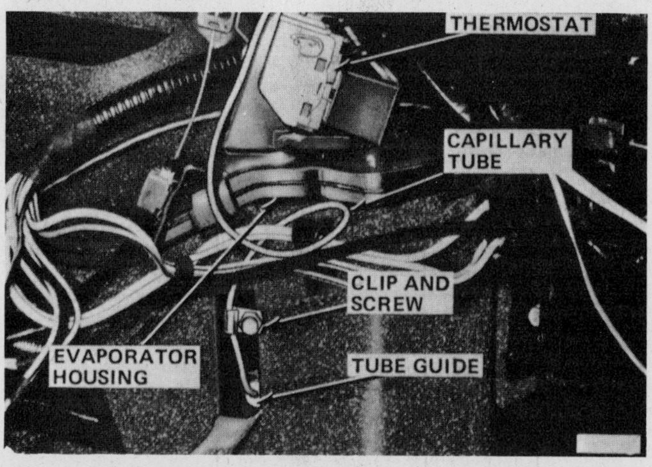

Fig. 3.6 Temperature control thermostat and temperature sensing capillary tube (typical of most models) (Sec 14)

15 Air conditioning compressor – removal and installation

1 Before removing the compressor, the system must be evacuated

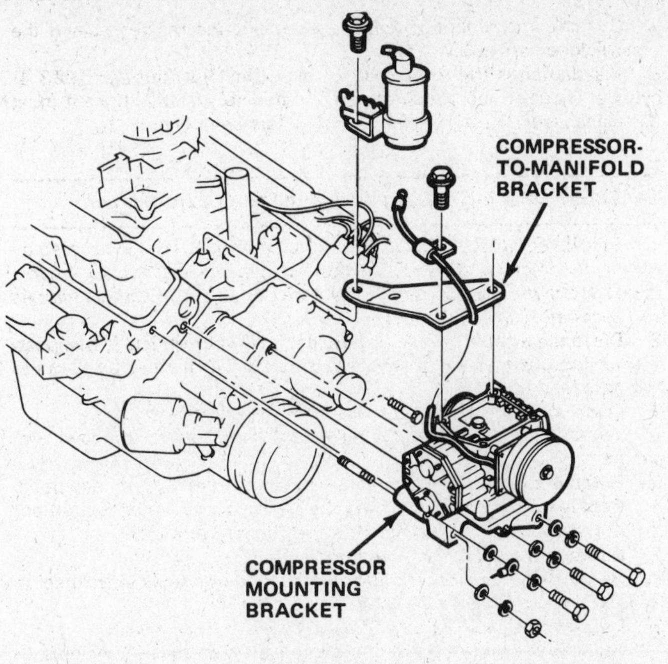

Fig. 3.7 Air conditioning compressor with mounting hardware (typical V8) (Sec 15)

by an air conditioning technician. **Caution**: *Do not attempt to do this yourself; the refrigerant used in the system can cause serious injuries and respiratory irritation.*

2 Remove both service valves and lines.

3 Loosen and remove the compressor drivebelt.

4 Disconnect the clutch wire.

5 On some models it may be necessary to loosen or remove the alternator to gain adequate clearance for compressor removal.

6 Remove any idler pulleys which would hinder compressor removal.

7 Remove the compressor mounting bolts and lift out the compressor.

8 Installation is the reverse of removal.

16 Air conditioning receiver/drier – removal and installation

1 Before removing the receiver/drier, the system must be evacuated by an air conditioning technician. **Caution**: *Do not attempt to do this yourself; the refrigerant used in the system can cause serious injuries and respiratory irritation.*

2 The condenser must be removed to gain access to the receiver attaching screws. Remove the condenser as described in Section 13.

3 Disconnect the receiver inlet and outlet lines.

4 Remove the receiver/drier from the condenser bracket. Plug all open connections to prevent dirt and moisture from entering.

5 Installation is the reverse of removal. On 1980 through 1983 4-cylinder models, one ounce of air conditioning system lubricant must be added to the system after replacing this component.

3

Chapter 4 Fuel and exhaust systems

Contents

Air filter replacement ... See Chapter 1
Autolite/Motorcraft 2100 and 2150 carburetors – overhaul and adjustment ... 12
Autolite/Motorcraft 4300 carburetor – overhaul and adjustment . 11
Carburetor – servicing ... 8
Carburetor application ... 7
Carburetor choke check ... See Chapter 1
Carburetor – removal and installation ... 9
Carter BBD carburetor – overhaul and adjustment ... 13
Carter YF carburetor – overhaul and adjustment ... 10
Engine idle speed adjustment ... See Chapter 1
Exhaust manifold heat valve check ... See Chapter 1
Exhaust system – component replacement ... 18
Exhaust system check ... See Chapter 1
Fuel filter replacement ... See Chapter 1
Fuel lines and hoses – check and replacement ... 6
Fuel pump – check ... 4
Fuel pump – general information ... 3
Fuel pump – removal and installation ... 5
Fuel system check ... See Chapter 1
Fuel tank – cleaning and repair ... 17
Fuel tank – removal and installation ... 16
General information ... 1
Holley-Weber 5210 carburetor – overhaul and adjustment ... 14
Rochester 2SE and E2SE carburetors – overhaul and adjustment ... 15
Throttle linkage – check and adjustment ... 2

Specifications

Note: *Refer to Chapter 1 for fast idle speed specifications*

Autolite/Motorcraft 2100 and 2150 carburetors

Dry float level	
1971 through 1973	$\frac{3}{8}$ in
1974 and 1975	0.400 in
1976 (manual transmission)	$\frac{35}{64}$ in
1976 (automatic transmission)	$\frac{13}{32}$ in
1977	$\frac{5}{16}$ in
1978	0.555 in
1979	0.313 in
Wet float level	
1971 through 1973	$\frac{3}{4}$ in
1974 through 1979	0.78 in
Initial choke plate clearance	
1971	$\frac{3}{16}$ in
1972 through 1976 (manual transmission)	0.130 in
1972 through 1976 (automatic transmission)	0.140 in
1977 and 1978	0.136 in
1979	0.125 in
Automatic choke setting	
1970 through 1973 (manual transmission)	1 notch rich
1970 through 1973 (automatic transmission)	2 notches rich
1974 and 1975	1 notch rich
1976	1 to 2 notches rich
1977 and 1978 (Calif.)	Index mark
1977 and 1978 (All others)	1 notch rich
1979	1 notch rich

Fast idle cam setting	
1971	0.170 in
1972 through 1975	0.130 in
1976 (manual transmission)	0.120 in
1976 (automatic transmission)	0.130 in
1977 and 1978	0.126 in
1978 (automatic transmission – Calif.)	0.120 in
1979	0.113 in
Dashpot	
1970 and 1971	$\frac{1}{8}$ in
1972 through 1974 (manual transmission)	0.110 in
1972 through 1974 (automatic transmission)	0.140 in
1975	0.095 in
1976	0.075 in
Choke unloader	
1972	0.200 in
1973 through 1978	0.250 in
1979	0.300 in
Bowl vent clearance	0.120 in

Autolite/Motorcraft 4300 carburetor

Float level	0.820 in
Initial choke plate clearance	
1972 and 1973	0.190 in
1974	0.170 in
Fast idle cam setting	
1972	0.190 in
1973 and 1974	0.160 in
Automatic choke setting	
1972	1 notch rich
1973 and 1974	2 notches rich
Dashpot	0.140 in
Choke unloader	
1972	0.300 in
1973	0.275 in
1974	0.325 in

Carter BBD carburetor

Float level	0.250 in
Vacuum piston gap	
1977 and 1978	0.040 in
1979 through 1983	0.035 in
Initial choke plate clearance	
1977 and 1978 (manual transmission)	0.128 in
1977 and 1978 (automatic transmission)	0.150 in
1979 (carburetor numbers 8185 and 8187)	0.140 in
1979 (carburetor numbers 8186 and 8221)	0.150 in
1980 (manual transmission)	0.150 in
1980 (automatic transmission)	0.140 in
1981	0.128 in
1982 and 1983	0.140 in
Automatic choke setting	
1977 through 1983 (except carburetor numbers 8216, 8246 and 8309)	1 notch rich
1980 (carburetor numbers 8216 and 8246)	2 notches rich
1982 (carburetor number 8309)	2 notches rich
Choke unloader	0.280 in
Accelerator pump setting	
1977 and 1978 (manual transmission)	0.520 in
1977 and 1978 (automatic transmission)	0.490 in
1979 (carburetor numbers 8185 and 8187)	0.470 in
1979 (carburetor number 8186)	0.520 in
1979 (carburetor number 8221)	0.530 in
1980 through 1983	0.520 in

Carter YF carburetor

Float level	
1970 and 1971	$\frac{3}{16}$ in
1972 and 1973	$\frac{29}{64}$ in
1974 through 1978	0.476 in
Float drop	
1970 through 1973	1.25 in
1974 through 1978	1.38 in
Initial choke plate clearance	
1970 through 1972	0.230 in
1973 through 1978	0.215 in

Fast idle cam setting	
1970 through 1973	Index mark (choke closed)
1974 through 1978	0.195 in
Dashpot	
1970 and 1971 (manual transmission)	$\frac{1}{16}$ in
1970 and 1971 (automatic transmission)	$\frac{1}{8}$ in
1972 and 1973	$\frac{3}{32}$ in
1974	0.095 in
1975 and 1976	0.075 in
Automatic choke setting	
1970 and 1971	$\frac{1}{2}$ notch rich
1972	Index mark
1973 through 1975	1 notch rich
1976 (carburetor numbers 7083, 7085 and 7112)	1 notch rich
1976 (carburetor numbers 7084 and 7086)	2 notches rich
1977 (carburetor numbers 7151, 7152, 7189 and 7195)	1 notch rich
1977 (carburetor numbers 7153 and 7223)	Index mark
1977 (carburetor number 7111)	2 notches rich
1978 (carburetor numbers 7201 and 7235)	Index mark
1978 (carburetor numbers 7228, 7229 and 7267)	1 notch rich

Holley-Weber 5210 carburetor

Float level	0.420 in
Initial choke valve clearance	
1978 (carburetor number 8163)	0.191 in
1978 (carburetor number 8164)	0.202 in
1978 (carburetor number 8165)	0.180 in
1979 (carburetor numbers 7846 and 8548)	0.191 in
1979 (carburetor number 8675)	0.177 in
1979 (carburetor number 8549)	0.266 in
Fast idle cam setting	
Carburetor numbers 7846, 8163 and 8549	0.193 in
Carburetor numbers 8164 and 8548	0.204 in
Carburetor numbers 8165 and 8675	0.177 in
Choke unloader	0.300 in
Automatic choke setting	
All models except those equipped for high altitude or hilly terrain	1 notch rich
Models equipped for high altitude or hilly terrain	Index mark

Rochester 2SE and E2SE carburetors

Float level	
1980 and 1981	0.208 in
1982	0.125 in
1983	0.138 in
Pump stem height	
1980	0.50 in
1981 through 1983	0.128 in
Fast idle cam setting	
1980	18°
1981	25°
1982 and 1983	18°
Air valve link	2°
Primary vacuum break	
1980	20°
1981 through 1983	19°
Choke unloader	
1980 and 1981	32°
1982 and 1983	34°
Secondary lockout	
1980	0.085 in
1981 (automatic transmission)	0.085 in
1981 (manual transmission)	0.050 to 0.080 in
1982 and 1983	0.050 to 0.080 in
Choke coil lever plug gauge	
1980	0.080 in
1981 through 1983 (manual transmission)	0.050 to 0.080 in
1981 through 1983 (automatic transmission	0.085 in

Torque specifications

	Ft-lb	Nm
Carburetor-to-intake manifold nuts	12 to 15	18 to 20
Fuel pump mounting bolt	16	21

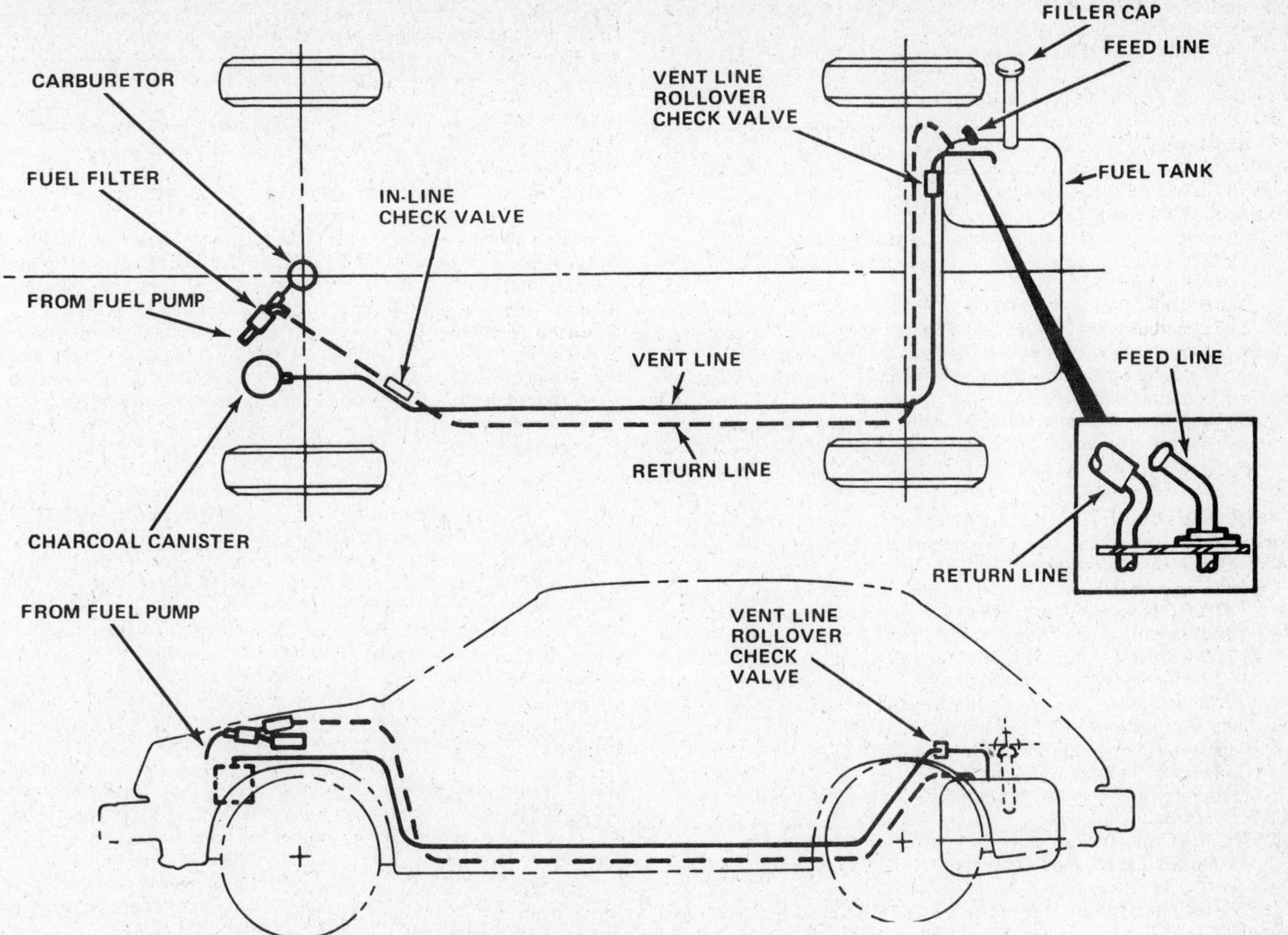

Fig. 4.1 Typical fuel system components

1 General information

The fuel system consists of the fuel tank, a fuel pump, which draws fuel to the carburetor, and associated hoses, lines and filters.

The exhaust system is composed of pipes, heat shields and mufflers for carrying exhaust gases from the engine to the rear of the vehicle. Later models incorporate catalytic converters into the system to reduce exhaust emissions. Catalytic converter-equipped vehicles must use unleaded fuel only.

2 Throttle linkage – check and adjustment

1 Periodically check the full length of the throttle linkage for wear, looseness and damage.
2 With the engine off, observe the linkage as an assistant pushes the throttle pedal down completely and releases it. Watch the action of the linkage to determine if there are any worn joints or bent links. Make sure the return springs are securely seated and not stretched. Replace any worn or damaged components with new ones.
3 Adjust the linkage if the throttle does not open completely.
4 Lubricate the linkage joints with a few drops of engine oil or spray lubricant such as graphite or silicone.

3 Fuel pump – general information

All models are equipped with mechanical fuel pumps which are actuated by an eccentric on the camshaft.

Some early model AMC vehicles are equipped with a double action fuel and vacuum booster pump. This pump, in addition to

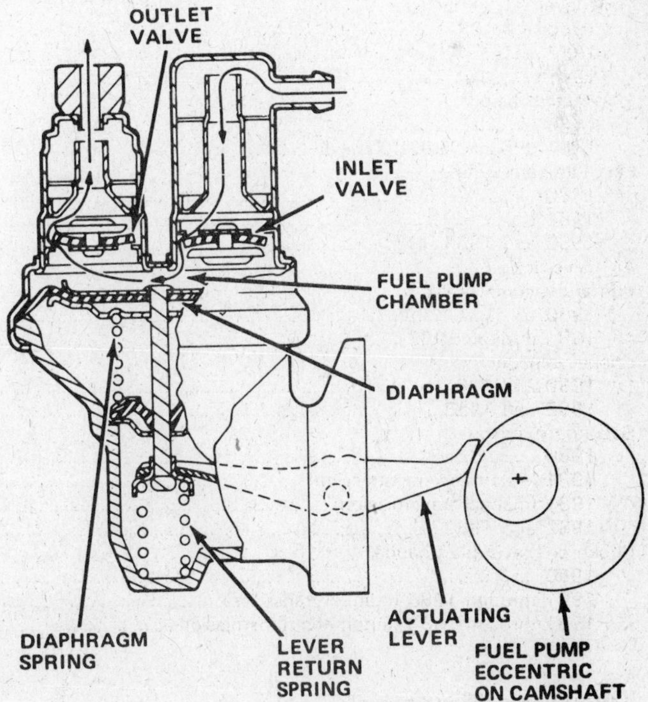

Fig. 4.2 Typical later model fuel pump (Sec 3)

4

supplying fuel pressure, powers the vacuum-operated windshield wipers.

Both types of pumps are sealed and must be replaced as a unit if a problem develops.

4 Fuel pump – check

Caution: *Gasoline is extremely flammable and extra precautions must be taken when working on any part of the fuel system. Do not smoke or allow open flames or bare light bulbs near the work area. Also, do not work in a garage if a natural gas type appliance with a pilot light is present.*

1 Inspect the fuel pump for signs of leakage. If the pump itself is leaking, replace it with a new one (Section 5). If the inlet or outlet connections are leaking, tighten or replace them as necessary.

2 To check the fuel pump operation, disconnect the outlet hose and route it into a suitable container.

3 Disconnect and ground the ignition coil wire and turn the engine over with the starter while observing the fuel pump outlet hose. The pump should produce definite spurts of fuel. If it does not, or if very little fuel is seen, replace the pump with a new one.

5 Fuel pump – removal and installation

Caution: *Gasoline is extremely flammable and extra precautions must be taken when working on any part of the fuel system. Do not smoke or allow open flames or bare light bulbs near the work area. Also do not work in a garage if a natural gas type appliance with a pilot light is present.*

1 Place clean rags or wadded-up newspapers under the fuel pump to catch any gasoline which may be spilled during removal.

2 To remove the pump, remove the fuel inlet and outlet (as well as all other) connections. Use two wrenches to prevent damage to the pump and flare-type fittings.

3 Remove the mounting bolts, pump and gasket (photo).

4 Remove all traces of gasket material from the pump and engine mating surfaces.

5 Coat both sides of a new gasket with RTV-type gasket sealant and place the gasket in position on the pump.

6 Place the pump in position, making sure the actuating lever seats securely against the camshaft eccentric. Install the mounting bolts.

7 Connect the fuel lines and other hoses or lines to the fuel pump.

8 Start the engine and check carefully for leaks.

5.3 Fuel pump removal

6 Fuel lines and hoses – check and replacement

Caution: *Gasoline is extremely flammable and extra precautions must be taken when working on any part of the fuel system. Do not smoke or allow open flames or bare light bulbs near the work area. Also, do not work in a garage if a natural gas type appliance with a pilot light is present.*

1 All fuel lines, hoses and connections should be inspected periodically for damage, leaks and deterioration.

2 Check all rubber hoses for cracks, splits and signs of hardening. Partially kink or squeeze the hoses to see if cracks appear. Grasp each hose at the points of connection to make sure they aren't brittle or hardened and move them back-and-forth to check for cracks.

3 Look for areas where oil or grease have accumulated, wipe the hose clean and inspect for damage. Petroleum products break down the rubber and make it soft.

4 Measure the length of each hose to be replaced and cut off a short (no more than $\frac{1}{2}$ inch) piece from the end. With the length measurement information and sample pieces, go to an automotive parts store to obtain replacement hose. The sample piece will make the selection of the proper inside diameter hose easier. It is a good idea to obtain replacement screw-type hose clamps to replace any original equipment clamps which are bent or damaged.

5 Inspect the metal fuel lines to make sure they aren't bent, dented, cracked or leaking. Check the flare nut connections for tightness, using two wrenches to avoid damage to the line and component. Be careful not to overtighten them. Replacement fuel line and fittings are also available at automotive parts stores. A tube-flaring tool will be necessary for installing the fittings. Use only seamless steel tubing for the fuel lines, as copper or aluminum tubing does not have enough durability to withstand normal operating conditions.

6 If only one section of a metal fuel line is damaged, it can be cut out and replaced with a piece of rubber tubing. The rubber tubing should be cut four inches longer than the section it is replacing so there will be about two inches of overlap between the rubber and metal tubing at either end of the section. Screw-type hose clamps should be used to secure both ends of the repaired section.

7 If a section of metal line longer than six inches is being removed, use a combination of metal tubing and rubber hose so the rubber hose lengths will not be longer than ten inches.

8 **Caution:** *Never use rubber hose within four (4) inches of any part of the exhaust system.*

7 Carburetor application

1 The models covered in this manual were equipped with a variety of carburetors over their long production life.

2 The Carter YF carburetor was used on six-cylinder engines from 1970 through 1978.

3 Later models of the six-cylinder engine were equipped with the Carter BBD carburetor, first used in 1977 along with the YF.

4 The Autolite/Motorcraft 4300 was first used in 1972 as standard equipment on Hornet models equipped with a 360 cubic inch engine. This carburetor, along with the 360 cubic inch engine, was dropped from the Hornet models in 1975.

5 The Autolite/Motorcraft 2100/2150 carburetors were used from 1970 through 1979 on smaller V8 engines. The 2150 differs from the 2100 in that it incorporates an altitude compensation device.

6 The Holley-Weber 5210 carburetor was used on all four-cylinder AMC models manufactured in 1978 and 1979.

7 In 1980, the Rochester 2SE/E2SE carburetors replaced the 5210, becoming standard equipment for four-cylinder models through 1983. The electronic E2SE is used on all vehicles manufactured for sale in California.

8 Carburetor – servicing

1 A thorough road test and check of carburetor adjustments should be done before any major carburetor service. Specifications for some adjustments are listed on the vehicle Emission Control Information label found in the engine compartment.

2 Some performance complaints directed at the carburetor are actually a result of loose, misadjusted or malfunctioning engine or electrical components. Others develop when vacuum hoses leak, are disconnected or are incorrectly routed. The proper approach to

analyzing carburetor problems should include a routine check of the following areas:
3 Inspect all vacuum hoses and actuators for leaks and proper installation (see Chapter 6, *Emission control systems).*
4 Tighten the intake manifold nuts and carburetor mounting nuts evenly and securely.
5 Perform a cylinder compression test (Chapter 1).
6 Clean or replace the spark plugs as necessary (Chapter 1).
7 Check the condition of the spark plug wires (Chapter 1).
8 Inspect the ignition primary wires and check the vacuum advance operation. Replace any defective parts.
9 Check the ignition timing with the vacuum advance line disconnected and plugged.
10 Set the carburetor idle mixture as described in the appropriate Section.
11 Check the fuel pump operation as described in Section 4.
12 Inspect the heat control valve in the air cleaner for proper operation (Chapter 1).
13 Remove the carburetor air filter element and blow out any dirt with compressed air. If the filter is extremely dirty, replace it with a new one.
14 Inspect the crankcase ventilation system (see Chapter 6).
15 Carburetor problems usually show up as flooding, hard starting, stalling, severe backfiring, poor acceleration and lack of response to idle mixture screw adjustments. A carburetor that is leaking fuel and/or covered with wet-looking deposits definitely needs attention.
16 Diagnosing carburetor problems may require that the engine be started and run with the air cleaner removed. While running the engine without the air cleaner, it is possible that it could backfire. A backfiring situation is likely to occur if the carburetor is malfunctioning, but removal of the air cleaner alone can lean the air/fuel mixture enough to produce an engine backfire.
17 Once it is determined that the carburetor is indeed at fault, it should be disassembled, cleaned and reassembled using new parts where necessary. Before dismantling the carburetor, make sure you have a carburetor rebuild kit, which will include all necessary gaskets and internal parts, carburetor cleaning solvent and some means of blowing out all the internal passages of the carburetor. To do the job properly, you will also need a clean place to work and plenty of time and patience.
18 It should be noted that it is often easier and more convenient to replace the carburetor with a rebuilt unit instead of overhauling the original carburetor. If a rebuilt carburetor is purchased, be sure to deal with a reputable auto parts store.
19 **Caution**: *Gasoline is extremely flammable and extra precautions must be taken when working on any part of the fuel system. Do not smoke or allow open flames or bare light bulbs near the work area. Also, do not work in a garage if a natural gas type appliance with a pilot light is present.*

9 Carburetor – removal and installation

Caution: *Gasoline is extremely flammable and extra precautions must be taken when working on any part of the fuel system. Do not smoke or allow open flames or bare light bulbs near the work area. Also, do not smoke in a garage if a natural gas type appliance with a pilot light is present.*

Removal

1 Remove the air cleaner assembly.
2 Mark or tag all hoses and lines connected to the carburetor to simplify reinstallation.
3 Disconnect the throttle linkage, vacuum hoses, choke linkage and other hoses and wires from the carburetor.
4 Remove the retaining nuts and lift the carburetor from the manifold.
5 Carefully clean the gasket surfaces of the carburetor, spacer or gasket and intake manifold. Inspect them for nicks or damage which could affect carburetor-to-manifold sealing. Replace the gasket or spacer with a new one if it is bent, damaged or distorted.

Installation

6 Place the carburetor and spacer or gasket in position and install the retaining nuts. Tighten the nuts evenly and securely in a crisscross pattern.
7 Connect the throttle linkage, vacuum hoses, fuel lines and other hoses and wires to the carburetor.
8 Install the air cleaner assembly.

10 Carter YF carburetor – overhaul and adjustment

1 Remove the carburetor as described in Section 9.

Overhaul

2 On models equipped with a choke pulldown motor, remove the retaining screws, disconnect the choke pulldown link and remove the motor assembly, disengaging the link from the choke shaft lever.
3 Remove the choke retaining screws, housing retainers, spring housing assembly, gasket, baffle plate and fast idle link.
4 Remove the screws securing the air horn assembly to the carburetor and remove the air horn, gasket and solenoid bracket assembly.
5 With the air horn assembly upside down, remove the float pin, float and lever assembly. Turn the air horn assembly over and catch the needle pin, spring and needle and remove the needle seat and gasket.
6 Remove the air cleaner bracket. File the staked ends off the screws retaining the choke plate and remove the screws and plate. Remove the choke link lever and screw.
7 Turn the main body casting upside down and catch the accelerating pump check ball and weight and (if equipped) hot idle compensator.
8 Remove the mechanical bowl vent operating lever assembly from the throttle shaft.
9 Loosen the throttle shaft screw and remove the arm and pump connector link.
10 Remove the fast idle cam and shoulder screw.
11 Remove the accelerating pump diaphragm housing screws and lift the pump diaphragm assembly out as a unit.
12 Disengage the metering rod spring from the rod and remove the rod from the arm assembly. Sketch the location of any washers which may be used in shimming the springs so they can be reinstalled in the same location. Compress the upper pump spring and remove the spring retainer, spring and pump diaphragm assembly from the housing.
13 Use the proper size jet tool or screwdriver to remove the main metering rod jet and low speed jet.
14 On models with a temperature-compensated accelerator pump, remove the bleed valve plug from the main body, using a punch. Loosen the bleed valve screw and remove the valve.
15 Remove the retaining screws and separate the throttle body from the main body of the carburetor.
16 File the staked throttle plate retaining screws and remove the screws and plate. Slide the throttle shaft and lever assembly from the carburetor. Be sure to note the location of the ends of the spring on the throttle shaft for proper reinstallation. Also be sure to note the position of the idle limiter cap tab to ensure proper assembly. After removing the cap, count the number of turns required to lightly seat the needle and make a note of this for reference during reassembly.
17 The carburetor is now completely disassembled and should be cleaned and inspected for wear. After the carburetor components have been soaked in the proper solvent to remove dirt, gum and carbon deposits, they should be rinsed in kerosene and dried, preferably with compressed air. Do not use a wire brush to clean the carburetor and clean all passages with compressed air rather than wire or drill bits, which could enlarge them. Inspect the throttle and choke shafts for grooves, wear and excessive looseness. Check the throttle and choke plates for nicks and smoothness of operation. Inspect the carburetor body and components for cracks. Check the floats for leaks by submerging them in water which has been heated to just below the boiling point. Leaks will be indicated by the appearance of bubbles. Check the float arm needle contact surface for grooves. If the grooves are light, polish the needle contact surface with crocus cloth or steel wool. Replace the floats if the shafts are badly worn. Inspect the gasket mating surfaces for burrs and nicks. Replace any distorted springs or screws or bolts which have stripped threads.
18 To begin reassembly, install the throttle shaft and lever assembly in the throttle body flange. Make sure the bushings and springs are in the positions noted during disassembly. Position the throttle plate on the throttle shaft with the notch aligned with the slotted idle port. Install the throttle plate, using new screws. Tighten the screws so they are snug and then move the throttle plate around to make sure that it

4

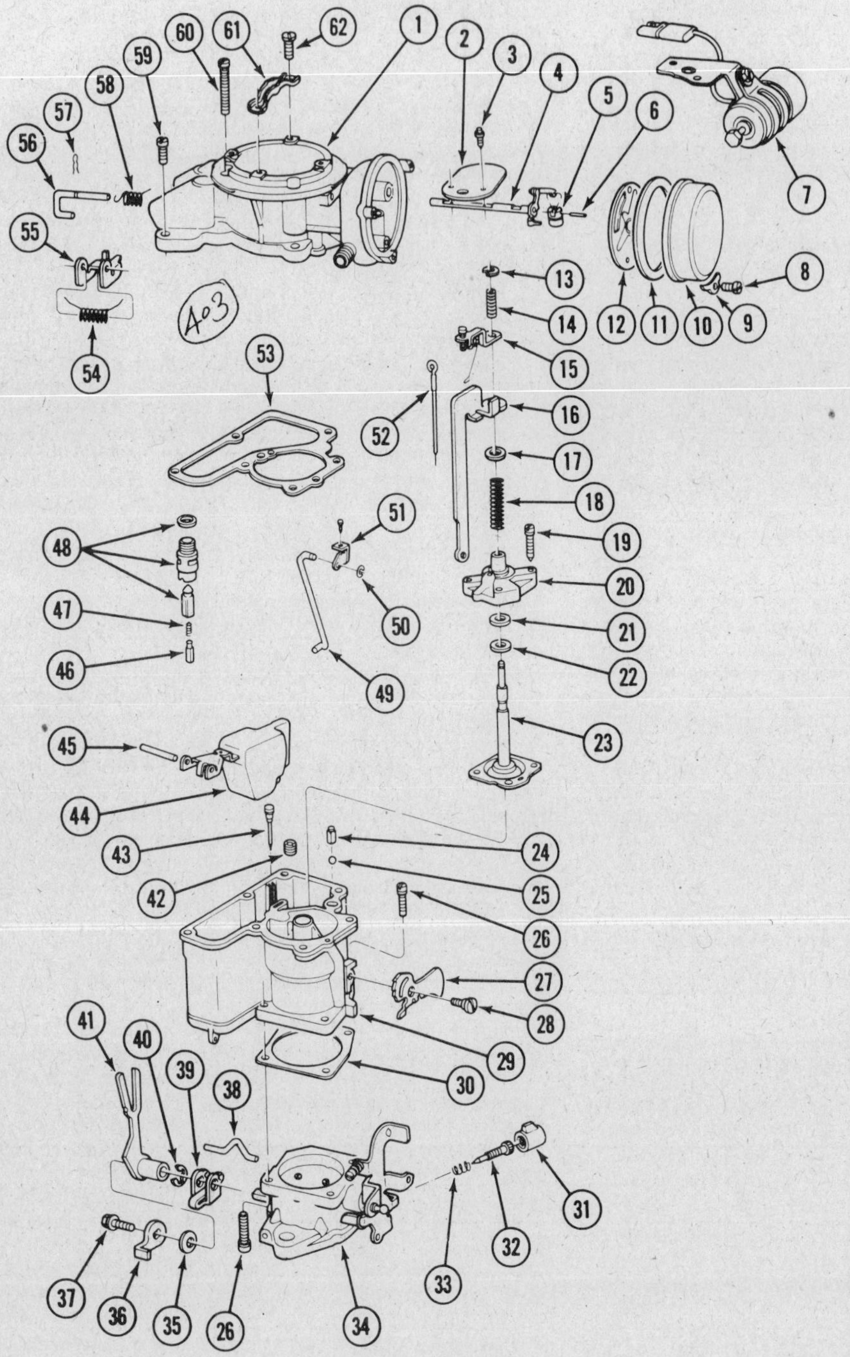

Fig. 4.3 Carter YF carburetor – exploded view (Sec 10)

1 Air horn
2 Choke
3 Screw
4 Shaft
5 Piston
6 Pin
7 Solenoid and bracket
8 Coil housing screw
9 Coil housing retainer
10 Choke cover
11 Coil housing gasket
12 Coil housing baffle plate
13 Upper pump spring retainer
14 Upper pump spring
15 Metering rod arm
16 Diaphragm lifter link
17 Washer
18 Diaphragm spring
19 Diaphragm housing screw
20 Diaphragm housing
21 Washer
22 Spacer
23 Diaphragm
24 Discharge ball weight
25 Discharge ball
26 Body flange screw
27 Fast idle cam
28 Fast idle cam screw
29 Main body
30 Body gasket
31 Idle screw limiter cap
32 Idle mixture screw
33 Spring
34 Throttle body
35 Wave washer
36 Arm
37 Screw
38 Pump connector link
39 Throttle shaft arm
40 Retainer
41 Lever
42 Metering rod jet
43 Low speed jet
44 Float
45 Float pin
46 Needle pin
47 Needle spring
48 Needle, needle seat, gasket
49 Choke connector rod
50 Choke connector rod retainer
51 Lever
52 Metering rod
53 Air horn gasket
54 Spring
55 Lifter
56 Bellcrank
57 Retainer
58 Spring
59 Air horn screw (short)
60 Air horn screw (long)
61 Stud support
62 Screw

doesn't bind in the bore. Make sure that the idle speed screw is backed off when checking the throttle plate fit. Reposition the plate as necessary, tighten the screws and stake or peen them in place. Install the idle speed screw and turn it out the same number of turns recorded during removal.
19 Attach the main body to the throttle body flange and tighten the screws evenly and securely.
20 Install the low speed jet and main metering rod jet.
21 Install the pump diaphragm in the pump diaphragm housing. Place the pump diaphragm spring on the diaphragm shaft and housing assembly. Install the spring shim washers, spring retainer, pump lifter link, metering rod arm and spring assembly and upper arm spring on the diaphragm shaft. Depress the spring and install the upper pump and spring retainer.
22 Assemble the metering rod on the metering rod arm and position the looped end of the metering rod arm spring. Align the diaphragm pump with the housing, making sure the holes are lined up. Install the housing attachment screws to maintain alignment.
23 Install the assembly in the carburetor main body, engage the pump lifter link with the body and insert the metering rod in the main metering rod jet. Install the pump housing screws so that they are snug, but not tight. Push down on the diaphragm shaft and then tighten the screws. Adjust the metering rod as described in Steps 40 through 42.
24 Place the pump bleed valve and washer in position and install the retaining screw. Install a new welch plug, using a $\frac{1}{4}$ inch flat drift punch to seat it.
25 Install the fast idle cam and shoulder screw, throttle shaft arm and pump connector link and tighten the lock screw.
26 Install the E-clip, spacer, wave washer and bowl vent actuating lever and tighten the retaining screw. Install the hot idle compensator valve and accelerator pump check ball and weight.
27 Insert the choke shaft assembly through the choke housing. Slip the pulldown link lever into the air horn and tighten the retaining screw.
28 Place the choke plate in position on the choke shaft and install the retaining screws snugly, but not tight. Check the choke plate for binding and tighten the screws and peen or stake them in place.
29 Install the needle seat and gasket in the air horn. Turn the air horn over and install the needle, pin spring, needle pin, float and lever assembly and float pin. Adjust the float level as described below.
30 Align the bowl vent flapper valve with the vent rod, making sure that the spring is properly installed on the vent rod shaft. Install the spring retainer.
31 Place a new air horn gasket in position and install the air horn, making sure that the mechanical fuel bowl vent engages the forked actuating lever. Install the solenoid bracket.
32 Install the choke coil housing (with the identification marks facing out), the gasket and baffle plate. The thermostatic spring must engage the choke lever tang and not be stopped by the baffle plate retaining tab (if equipped). Set the choke housing to the index mark specified on the Emission Control Information label and tighten the screws.
33 Install the air cleaner bracket and fast idle link.
34 Engage the choke pulldown link with the choke fast idle lever and the pulldown diaphragm rod. Place the diaphragm bracket on the air horn and install the attaching screws. Connect the pulldown vacuum hose to the diaphragm housing.
35 Adjust the carburetor to the specifications listed on the Emission Control Information label.

Float level adjustment

36 Invert the air horn and measure the clearance from the top of the float to the bottom of the air horn with a suitable gauge. The air horn should be held at eye level during this procedure and the float lever should be resting on the needle pin.
37 Bend the float arm as necessary to bring the float level within specifications. Do not bend the tab at the end of the float arm as this prevents the float from striking the bottom of the fuel bowl when the bowl is empty.

Float drop adjustment

38 With the carburetor air horn held upright and the float hanging free, measure the distance from the air horn gasket surface to the top of the end of the float. Compare this float drop measurement to the Specifications.
39 To adjust, bend the tab at the end of the float arm.

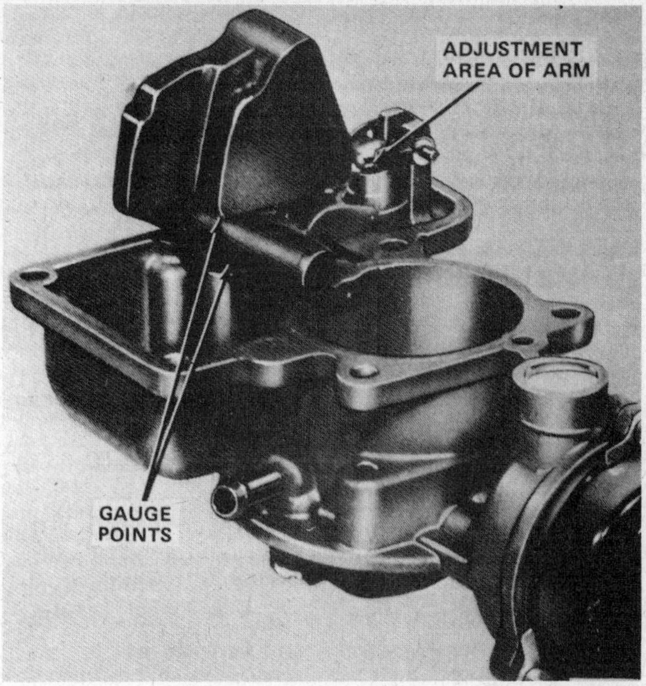

Fig. 4.4 Carter YF carburetor float level adjustment (Sec 10)

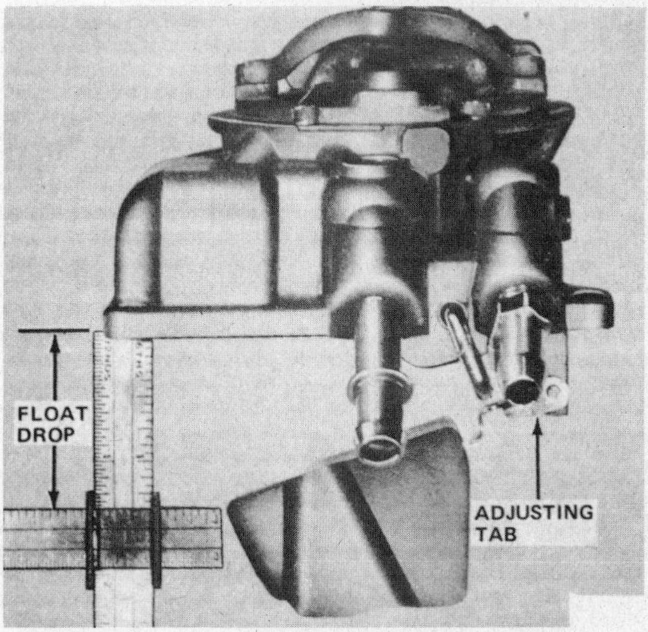

Fig. 4.5 Carter YF carburetor float drop measurement and adjustment (Sec 10)

Metering rod adjustment

40 With the air horn removed, back out the idle speed adjusting screw until the throttle plate is closed tightly in the bore.
41 Push down on the end of the pump diaphragm until it bottoms.
42 To adjust the metering rod, hold the diaphragm down and turn the adjustment screw until the metering rod just bottoms in the body casting as shown in the accompanying illustration. Turn the adjustment screw clockwise one additional turn for final adjustment.

4

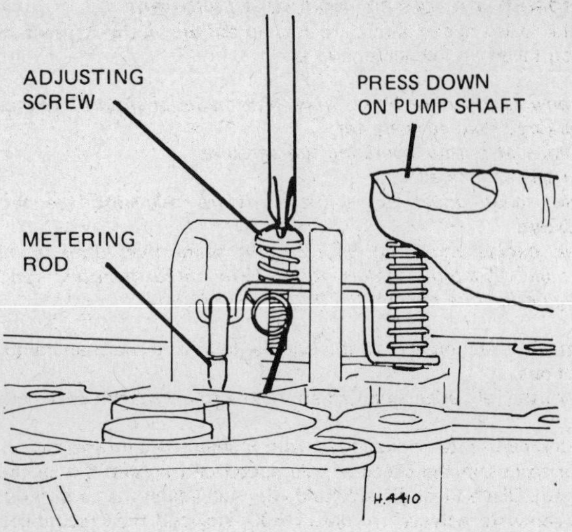

Fig. 4.6 Metering rod adjustment (YF carburetor) (Sec 10)

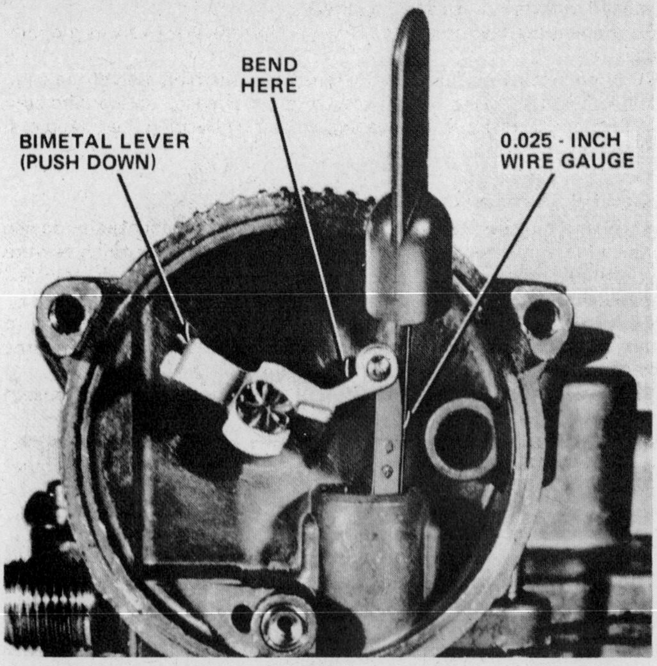

Fig. 4.7 Initial choke plate adjustment (YF carburettor) (Sec 10)

Initial choke plate-to-air horn clearance adjustment

43 Bend a 0.026-inch diameter wire at a 90° angle approximately $\frac{1}{8}$-inch from the end to fabricate a wire gauge as shown in the accompanying illustration.

44 Open the throttle partially and close the choke plate to position the choke piston at the top of its bore.

45 Hold the choke plate closed, release the throttle and insert the wire gauge into the piston slot and against the outboard (choke shaft right side) of the piston bore. Push down on the piston with the gauge until the bent end enters the piston bore slot. Keep the gauge in place and push on the choke piston lever to move the piston up and lock the gauge in position.

46 Measure the choke plate lower edge-to-air horn wall clearance with a suitable gauge or drill bit shank.

47 Use a pair of needle-nosed pliers to carefully bend the choke piston lever and adjust the clearance. Decrease the clearance by bending the lever toward the piston and increase it by bending the lever away from the piston.

48 Install the choke baffle plate, gasket cover and retaining screws. On 1973 through 1977 models, adjust the cover to the specified setting and tighten the retaining screws. On 1978 models, turn the cover toward the rich side (counterclockwise) and tighten one retaining screw. The final adjustment is made after the fast idle cam linkage is adjusted.

Fast idle cam linkage adjustment

49 Place the fast idle screw on the second step of the fast idle cam and against the shoulder of the high step.

50 Check the clearance between the lower edge of the choke plate and the air horn wall using a suitable gauge or drill bit shank. Compare this measurement to the Specifications.

51 To adjust, bend the choke plate connecting rod until the proper choke plate-to-air horn wall clearance is achieved.

Choke unloader adjustment

52 Hold the throttle completely open while pushing the choke plate toward the closed position. Measure the clearance between the choke plate lower edge and the air horn wall with a suitable drill bit shank. Compare this measurement to the Specifications.

53 To adjust, bend the unloader tang which contacts the fast idle cam.

54 After adjustment, operate the throttle to make sure the linkage does not bind.

55 There should be a 0.0701 inch clearance between the unloader tang and carburetor body with the throttle completely open after adjustment.

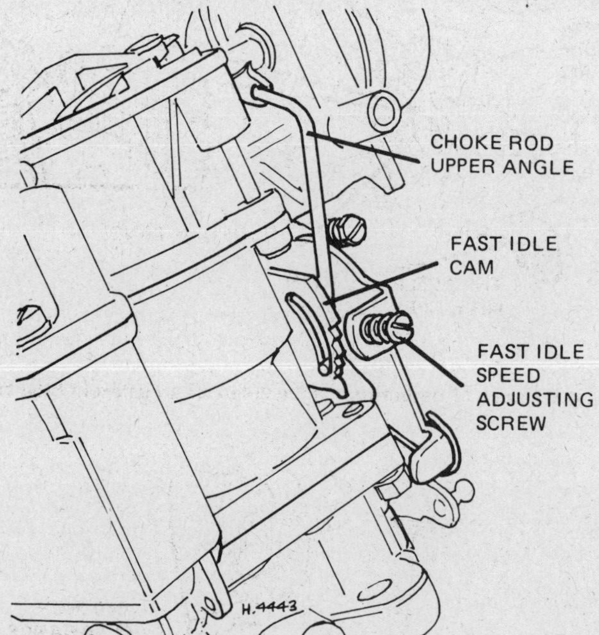

Fig. 4.8 Fast idle cam linkage adjustment (YF carburetor) (Sec 10)

Bowl vent adjustment

56 Disconnect the emissions canister hose from the carburetor and attach a new piece of clean hose to the bowl vent.

57 Place the throttle on the high step of the fast idle cam and blow into the hose. There should be considerable resistance felt, indicating the vent is closed.

58 Move the fast idle cam until the throttle screw drops to the third step of the cam. Blow into the hose to verify that the bowl vent has

opened and that pressure is relieved.
59 Repeat the test procedure to verify that the bowl vent is properly adjusted.
60 If no pressure is felt with the throttle on the high step of the cam, the vent is not closing. If the pressure is not released on the third step of the cam, the vent is not opening. Adjust by bending the forked end of the lever.

Altitude compensator adjustment

61 Some models are equipped wth an altitude compensation device which features a compensation circuit that prevents a too-rich mixture at altitudes above 4000 feet. The altitude compensator is adjusted manually.
62 When operating the vehicle above 4000 feet, use a screwdriver to turn the compensator plug counterclockwise approximately $2\frac{1}{2}$ turns to the outer (high altitude) seat position.
63 Below 4000 feet, adjust the plug clockwise to the inner seat position.
64 The plug has two positions; all the way in (low altitude) or all the way out (above 4000 feet). Do not adjust the plug to any other position.

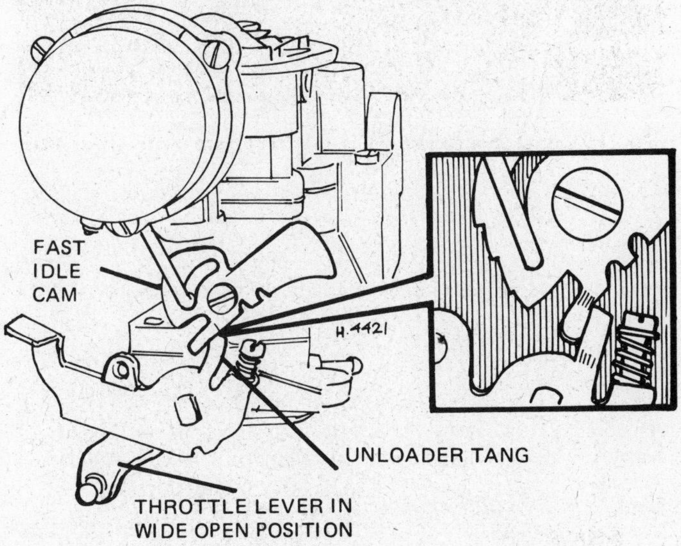

Fig. 4.9 Carter YF carburetor choke unloader adjustment (Sec 10)

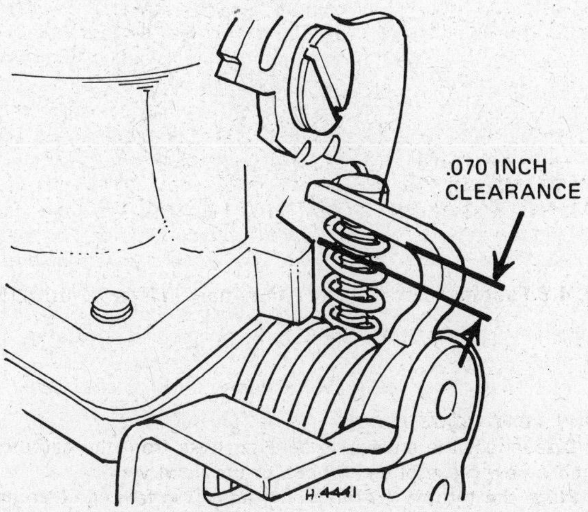

Fig. 4.10 Checking choke unloader-to-body clearance (Sec 10)

Idle speed and fuel/air mixture adjustment

65 Prior to idle speed or mixture adjustment the following precautions must be taken and conditions exist:

Transmission must be in Drive (automatic) or Neutral (manual)
Parking brake securely set
Engine at normal operating temperature
Air cleaner installed
Idle speed must be adjusted before adjusting the fuel/air mixture
The engine must not be idled for more than three minutes. If the adjustment takes more than three minutes, run the engine for one minute at 2000 rpm in Neutral)

66 Attach a tachometer to the engine, following the manufacturer's instructions.
67 Turn the idle speed adjustment screw to obtain the specified idle speed.
68 If the carburetor is equipped with a solenoid, turn the nut on the plunger to obtain the specified idle speed and tighten the locknut (if equipped). Disconnect the solenoid wire and adjust the carburetor idle speed screw to achieve an idle of 500 rpm and then reconnect the wire.
69 On non-catalytic converter-equipped vehicles, the manufacturer recommends that mixture adjustments be made using special infra-red analyzer equipment. Consequently these models should be taken to your dealer or a properly equipped shop for mixture adjustment. On catalytic-equipped models the idle drop procedure, described below, is used.
70 Adjust the idle mixture screw to the full rich stop (counterclockwise), note the position of the screw head slots and remove the plastic limiter caps. This can be accomplished by threading a No. 10 sheet metal screw into the center of the cap.
71 Connect a tachometer and perform the idle speed adjustment procedure described above.
72 Beginning at the full rich position (Step 70), turn the mixture screw clockwise in the lean direction until there is an rpm drop. Turn the screw in a counterclockwise direction until the highest rpm previously attained is obtained. This is the lean best idle.
73 Turn the idle mixture screw until the specified idle drop is reached.
74 If the final reading varies more than 30 rpm up or down from the idle speed specification, repeat the idle speed adjustment.
75 Install a new idle mixture screw limiter cap with the ear of the cap against the full rich stop, taking care not to alter the mixture setting.

Dashpot assembly adjustment

76 Set the throttle at the curb idle position, depress the dashpot stem completely and measure the stem-to-throttle lever clearance. Compare this measurement to the Specifications.
77 To adjust, loosen the locknut and turn the dashpot until the specified clearance is obtained.

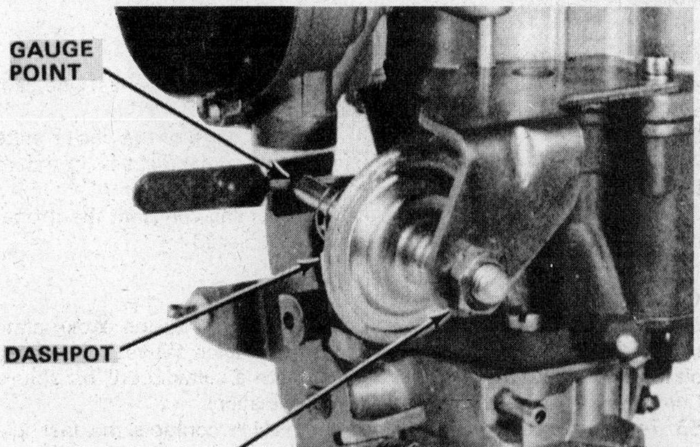

Fig. 4.11 Dashpot adjustment (YF carburetor) (Sec 10)

Fast idle adjustment

78 The fast idle adjustment is made with the engine at normal operating temperature, the EGR valve and TCS solenoid disconnected and the fast idle screw contacting the second step and against the shoulder of the high step of the fast idle cam. Turn the fast idle adjustment screw to obtain the specified rpm setting.

11 Autolite/Motorcraft 4300 carburetor – overhaul and adjustment

Overhaul

1 Remove the choke control rod retainer from the automatic choke lever and separate the rod from the lever.
2 Remove the accelerator pump spring and washer, then separate the pump rod from the lever.
3 Remove the air cleaner anchor stud and the air horn securing screws. Lift off the air horn.
4 Pull out the float pivot pin and lift out the float assembly.
5 Remove the main and auxiliary (supplemental) fuel inlet valve seats and gaskets.
6 Remove the secondary air valve lever pivot pin and the rod from the dampener piston assembly and air valve plate, then remove the air valve dampener piston rod and spring.
7 If it is necessary to remove the secondary air valve plates or shaft, remove the attaching screws, lift out the plates and then slide the shaft out of the air horn.
8 File off the staking on the choke plate securing screws, remove the screws, lift out the choke plate, then slide the shaft out of the air horn.
9 Turn the main body upside down and collect the accelerating pump discharge needle.
10 Using a socket wrench, unscrew the power valve from the fuel bowl.
11 Remove the main metering jets from the fuel bowl.
12 Using needle-nose pliers, remove the accelerating pump inlet check ball retainer, then turn the body over and collect the check ball.
13 Remove the throttle body-to-main body attaching screws and separate the two castings.
Note: *Do not remove the idle mixture limiter caps or the mixture screws.*
14 Remove the choke housing cover screws, cover, gasket and thermostatic spring.
15 Undo the choke piston lever retaining screw and remove the piston assembly.
16 Remove the secondary throttle lever-to-primary throttle connecting link retainers then lift away the link.
17 File off the staking on the throttle plate attaching screws, remove the screws and remove the plates.
18 Unscrew the nut from the secondary throttle shaft, then remove the lockout lever and slide the shaft and return spring out of the throttle body.
19 Remove the securing screw on the primary throttle shaft and remove the fast idle lever and adjusting screw. Slide the primary throttle shaft and lever assembly out of the throttle body.
20 Remove the retainer and slide the lever and springs off the primary throttle shaft.
21 Disassembly is now complete and all parts should be thoroughly cleaned with solvent. Remove any sediment from the fuel bowl and passages, taking care not to scratch any of the passages. Remove all traces of gaskets with a scraper.
22 Reassembly is basically the reverse of disassembly but note the following:

a) Check that all holes in new gaskets are properly punched and that they are free of foreign material.
b) After attaching the throttle plates to the main body, hold the assembly up to the light. Little or no light should be seen between the throttle plates and the bores. Tighten and stake the throttle plates at this time.

Dry float level measurement and adjustment

23 Turn the air horn assembly upside down and remove the gasket.
24 Using a T-scale, measure the distance from the float to the smooth surface on the air horn casting (between the main discharge nozzles).
25 Check the alignment and clearance of the float pontoons to the gauge. Both pontoons should just touch the gauge. If necessary, align the pontoons by twisting them slightly.

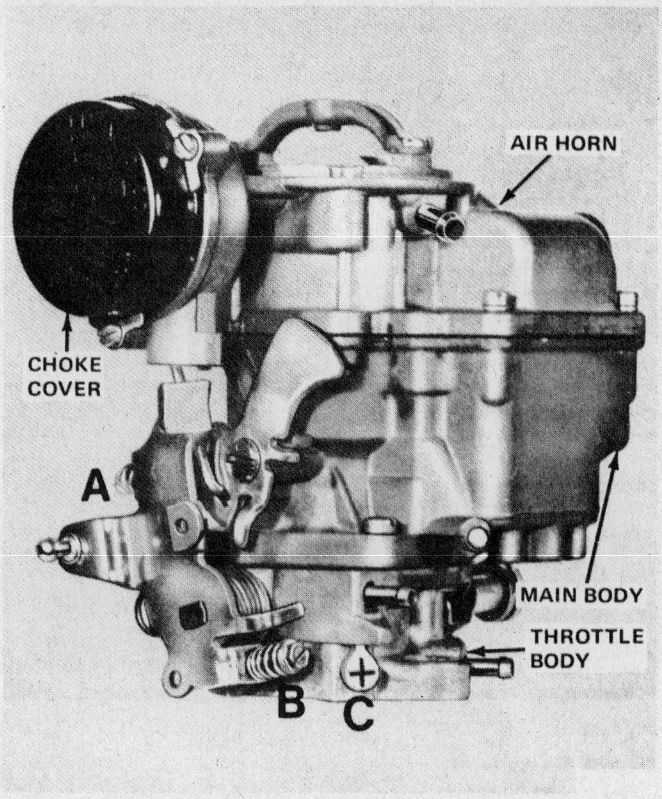

Fig. 4.12 Carter YF carburetor adjustment screw locations (Sec 10)

A Fast idle | *B Idle* | *C Fuel/air mixture*

26 Compare the measurement to the Specifications. Adjust, if necessary, by bending the tab on the end of the float assembly.

Initial choke plate clearance measurement and adjustment

27 Remove the air cleaner and the choke thermostatic spring housing.
28 Bend a wire of 0.036 inch diameter at a 90° angle approximately $\frac{1}{8}$ inch from one end. Block the throttle about half open so that the fast idle cam does not contact the fast idle adjustment screw, then insert the bent end of the wire gauge between the lower edge of the piston slot and the upper edge of the right-hand slot in the choke housing.
29 Pull the choke piston lever counterclockwise until the gauge is snug in the piston slot. Check the choke plate clearance (pulldown) between the lower edge of the choke plate and the wall of the air horn.
30 To adjust, if necessary, loosen the hex-head screw (left-hand thread) on the choke plate shaft and pry the link away from the tapered shaft.
31 Insert a drill, 0.010 inch less than the specified clearance, between the lower edge of the choke plate and the wall of the air horn. Hold the plate against the drill and with the choke piston snug against the 0.036 inch wire gauge, tighten the hex head screw in the choke plate shaft. The drill is used to allow for tolerances in the linkage. Use a drill with a diameter equal to the specified clearance for final checking.
32 Install the choke thermostatic spring housing and the air cleaner.

Automatic choke adjustment

33 Loosen the choke cover screws and rotate the cover in the desired direction. The rich setting is to the right (clockwise) and the lean to the left (counterclockwise).

Fast idle cam adjustment

34 Rotate the choke cover $\frac{1}{4}$ of a turn counterclockwise (towards the

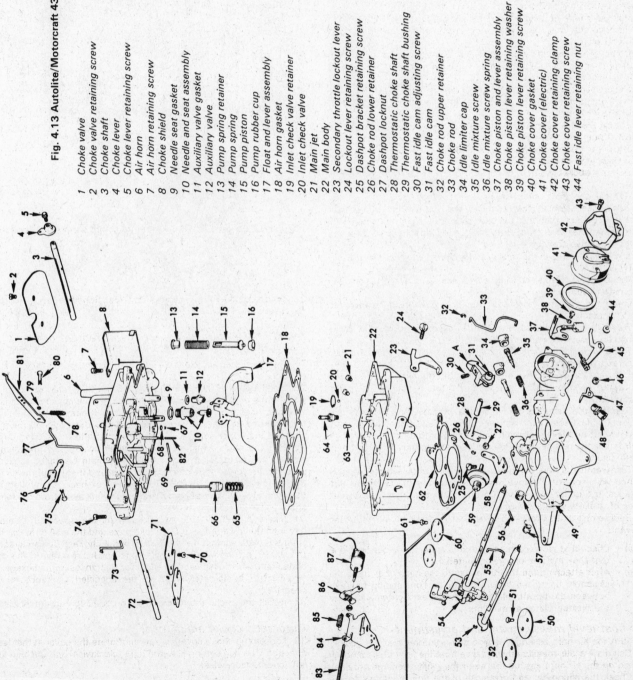

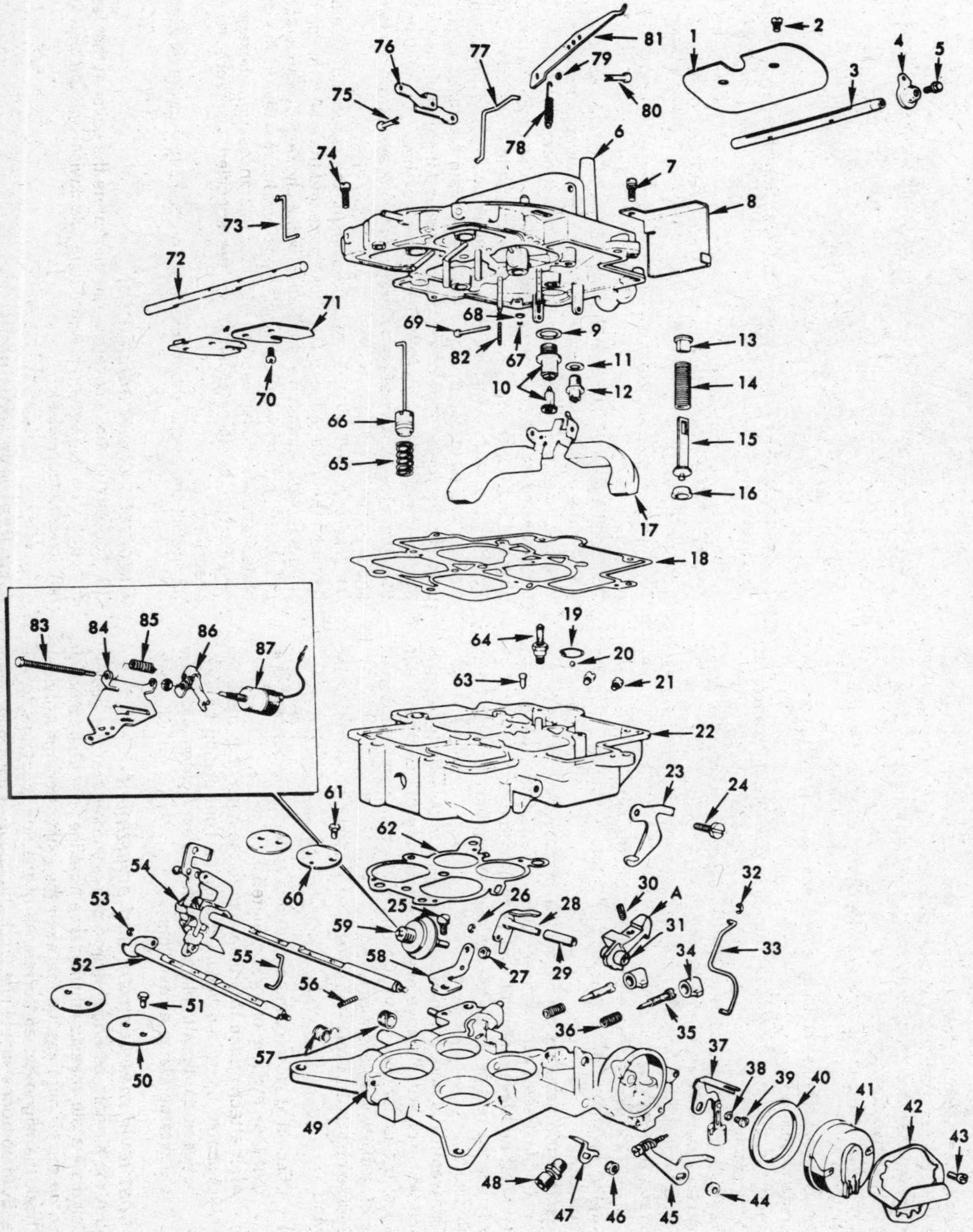

Fig. 4.13 Autolite/Motorcraft 4300 carburetor – exploded view (Sec 11)

1 *Choke valve*
2 *Choke valve retaining screw*
3 *Choke shaft*
4 *Choke lever*
5 *Choke lever retaining screw*
6 *Air horn*
7 *Air horn retaining screw*
8 *Choke shield*
9 *Needle seat gasket*
10 *Needle and seat assembly*
11 *Auxiliary valve gasket*
12 *Auxiliary valve*
13 *Pump spring retainer*
14 *Pump spring*
15 *Pump piston*
16 *Pump rubber cup*
17 *Float and lever assembly*
18 *Air horn gasket*
19 *Inlet check valve retainer*
20 *Inlet check valve*
21 *Main jet*
22 *Main body*
23 *Secondary throttle lockout lever*
24 *Lockout lever retaining screw*
25 *Dashpot bracket retaining screw*
26 *Choke rod lower retainer*
27 *Dashpot locknut*
28 *Thermostatic choke shaft*
29 *Thermostatic choke shaft bushing*
30 *Fast idle cam adjusting screw*
31 *Fast idle cam*
32 *Choke rod upper retainer*
33 *Choke rod*
34 *Idle limiter cap*
35 *Idle mixture screw*
36 *Idle mixture screw spring*
37 *Choke piston and lever assembly*
38 *Choke piston lever retaining washer*
39 *Choke piston lever retaining screw*
40 *Choke cover gasket*
41 *Choke cover (electric)*
42 *Choke cover retaining clamp*
43 *Choke cover retaining screw*
44 *Fast idle lever retaining nut*
45 *Fast idle lever*
46 *Secondary stop lever retaining nut*
47 *Secondary throttle stop lever*
48 *Choke heat inlet fitting*
49 *Throttle body*
50 *Secondary throttle valve*
51 *Throttle valve retaining screw*
52 *Secondary throttle shaft*
53 *Secondary link retainer*
54 *Primary throttle shaft assembly*
55 *Secondary throttle link*
56 *Curb idle adjusting screw*
57 *Throttle return spring*
58 *Dashpot bracket*
59 *Dashpot*
60 *Primary throttle valve*
61 *Throttle valve retaining screw*
62 *Throttle body gasket*
63 *Pump discharge needle*
64 *Power valve*
65 *Dampener spring*
66 *Dampener piston*
67 *Pump air bleed retainer*
68 *Pump air bleed (Viton Disc)*
69 *Float pin*
70 *Air valve retaining screw*
71 *Air valve*
72 *Air valve shaft*
73 *Air valve link*
74 *Air horn retaining screw*
75 *Pivot pin*
76 *Air valve lever*
77 *Pump rod*
78 *Pump return spring*
79 *Pump rod washer*
80 *Pivot pin*
81 *Pump lever*
82 *Atomizing screen*
83 *Adjusting screw*
84 *Mounting bracket*
85 *Adjusting screw spring*
86 *Carriage*
87 *Electric solenoid*

4

rich position). Tighten the cover screws.
35 Depress the throttle and allow the choke valve to close completely.
36 Push down on the fast idle cam lever until the fast idle adjusting screw is in contact with the index (second) step and against the shoulder of the high step.
37 Measure the choke plate lower edge-to-air horn wall clearance and check it against the Specifications.
38 Turn the fast idle cam lever screw to adjust the linkage.
39 Adjust the automatic choke and tighten the retaining screws.

Choke unloader adjustment

40 Hold the throttle completely open with pressure applied on the choke plate toward the closed position.
41 Measure the choke plate lower edge-to-air horn wall clearance and compare it to the Specifications.
42 Adjust the clearance by bending the choke unloader tang.
43 Check the unloader tang to make sure it does not bind or stick on any part of the carburetor casting or linkage.

Accelerator pump stroke adjustment

44 For most driving conditions, the pump will operate satisfactorily with the pivot pin in the center position of the three pivot holes.
45 If extreme weather conditions cause faltering acceleration, the pump rod pivot pin can be moved forward or backward to ensure smooth acceleration.

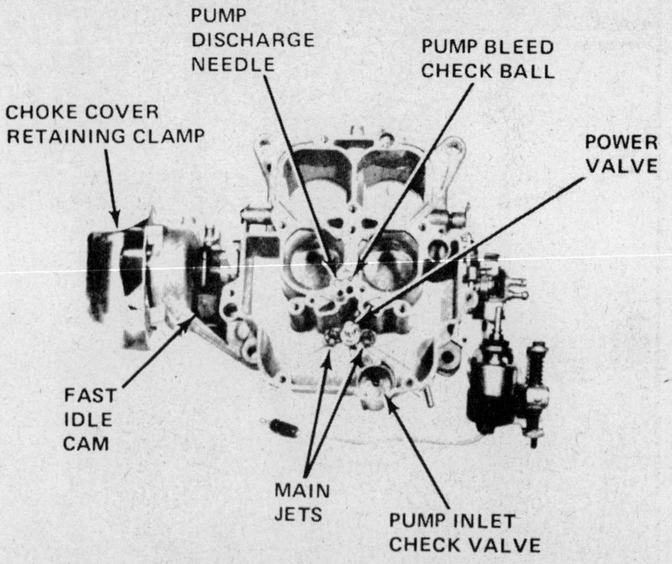

Fig. 4.14 Interior view of the fuel bowl (4300 carburetor) (Sec 11)

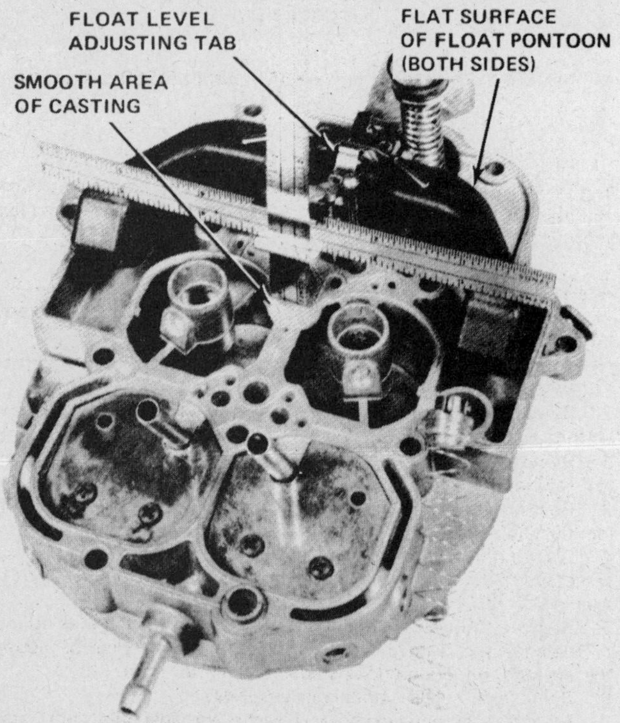

Fig. 4.15 Adjusting the float level (4300 carburetor) (Secs 11 & 12)

Fig. 4.16 Choke unloader adjustment on a 4300 carburetor (Sec 11)

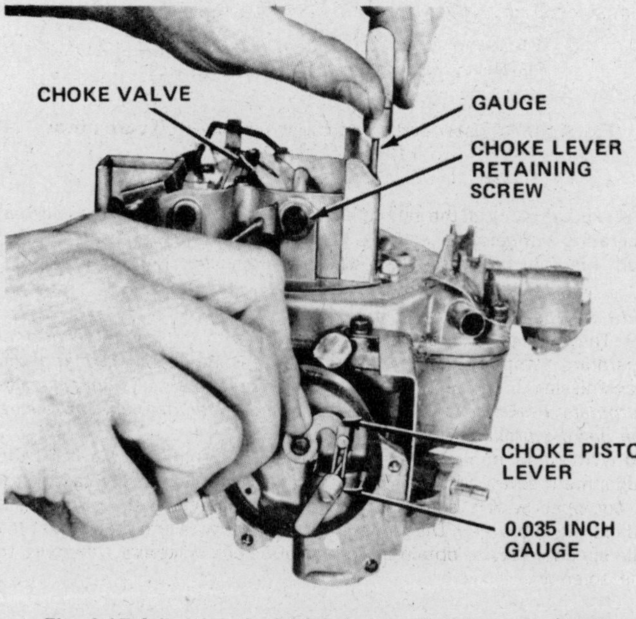

Fig. 4.17 Adjusting the initial choke valve clearance (4300 carburetor) (Sec 11)

Dashpot adjustment

46 With the throttle in the idle position, depress the dashpot stem and measure the stem-to-throttle lever clearance. Compare the measurement to the Specifications.
47 To adjust the clearance, loosen the locknut and turn the dashpot.

Fast idle speed adjustment

48 Connect a tachometer to the engine and set the fast idle speed with the fast idle adjusting screw against the index mark (located on

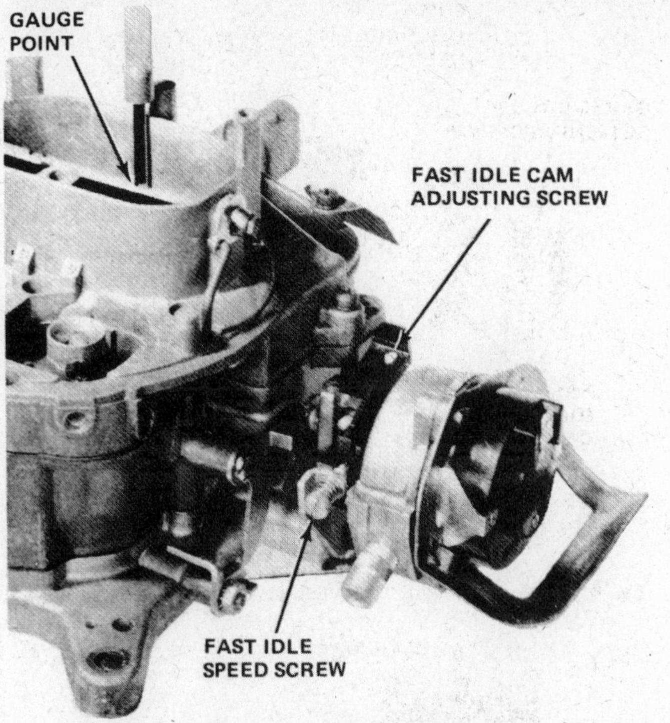

Fig. 4.18 Fast idle cam adjustment (Sec 11)

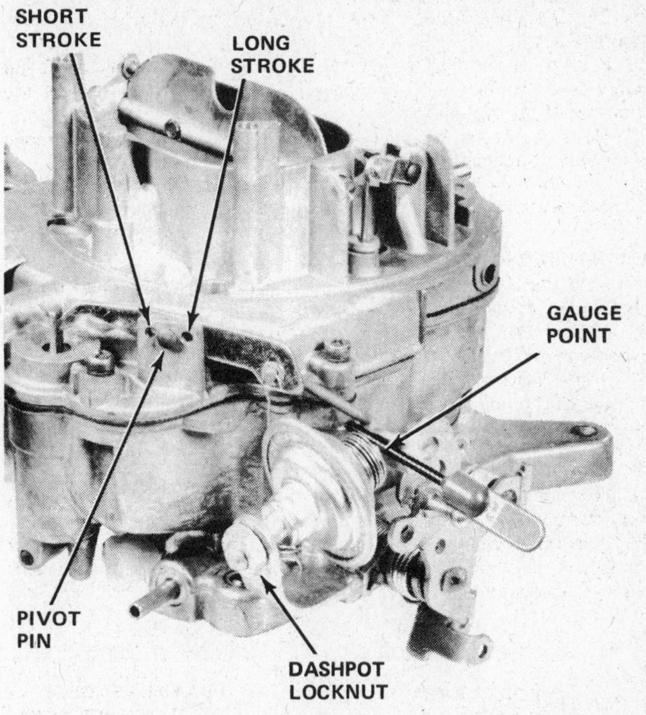

Fig. 4.19 Accelerator pump and dashpot (4200 carburetor) (Sec 11)

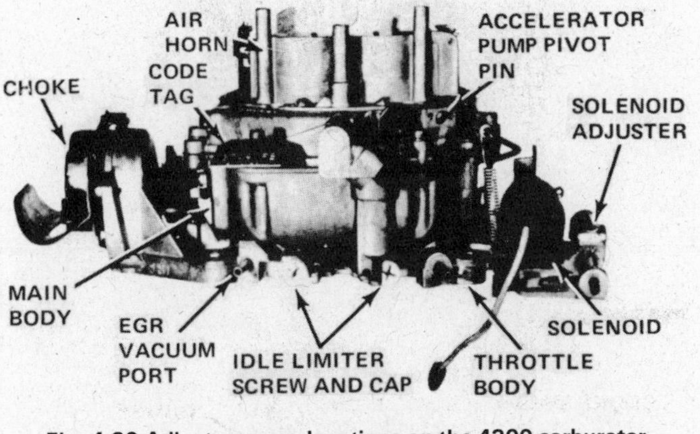

Fig. 4.20 Adjuster screw locations on the 4300 carburetor (Secs 11 & 12)

the second step) of the fast idle cam. The engine must be at normal operating temperature and the EGR and TCS solenoid disconnected. Turn the adjustment screw to obtain the specified setting.

Idle speed adjustment

49 The idle speed and must be adjusted with the engine at normal operating temperature, the air cleaner assembly installed and the transmission in Drive (automatic) or Neutral (manual). *Because the automatic transmission must be in Drive during adjustment, make sure the parking brake is firmly set.*

50 With a tachometer connected and the engine at idle, turn the adjustment screw to obtain the specified idle speed. If the carburetor is equipped with a solenoid, turn the hex screw on the solenoid to adjust the idle speed. Disconnect the solenoid wire and then adjust the idle speed screw to obtain an idle of 500 rpm. Reconnect the wire to the solenoid.

Mixture adjustment

51 The manufacturer recommends that mixture adjustment on these models be accomplished with special infra-red equipment. Consequently, the vehicle should be taken to a dealer or properly equipped shop for this adjustment.

12 Autolite/Motorcraft 2100 and 2150 carburetors – overhaul and adjustment

4

Overhaul

1 Before disassembly, clean the exterior of the carburetor with solvent and wipe it off using a lint-free rag.

2 Remove the air cleaner anchor screw and automatic choke control rod retainer.

3 Remove the air horn attaching screws, lockwashers, carburetor identification tag, air horn and gasket.

4 Loosen the screw securing the choke control rod to the choke shaft lever. Remove the choke control rod and slide out the plastic dust seal.

5 Remove the choke plate screws after filing off the staking marks on the ends and remove the choke plate by sliding it out of the top of the air horn. Slide the choke shaft from the air horn.

6 Remove the choke modulator assembly.

7 From the automatic choke, remove the fast idle cam retainer thermostatic choke spring housing, clamp and retainer.

8 Remove the choke housing assembly, gasket and fast idle cam and rod from the fast idle cam lever.

9 On the main body, use a screwdriver to pry the float shaft retainer from the fuel inlet seat. Remove the float, float shaft and fuel inlet needle assembly.

10 Remove the retainer and float shaft from the float lever and remove the fuel filler bowl.

11 Remove the fuel inlet needle, seat filter screen and main jets.

12 Remove the booster venturi, metering rod assembly and gasket. Turn the main body upside down and let the accelerator pump discharge weight and ball fall into your hand.

13 Disassemble the lift rod from the booster by removing the lift rod spring retaining clip and spring and separating the lift rod assembly from the booster. Do not remove the metering rod hanger from the lift rod.

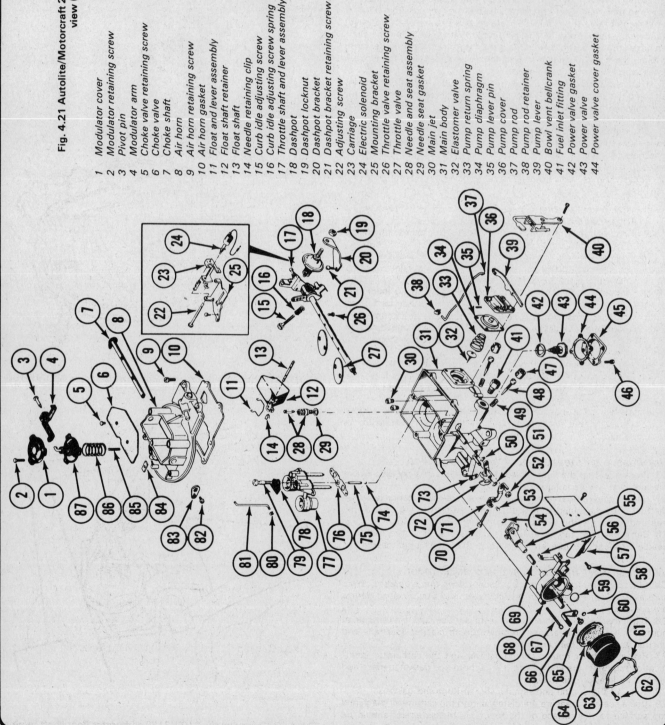

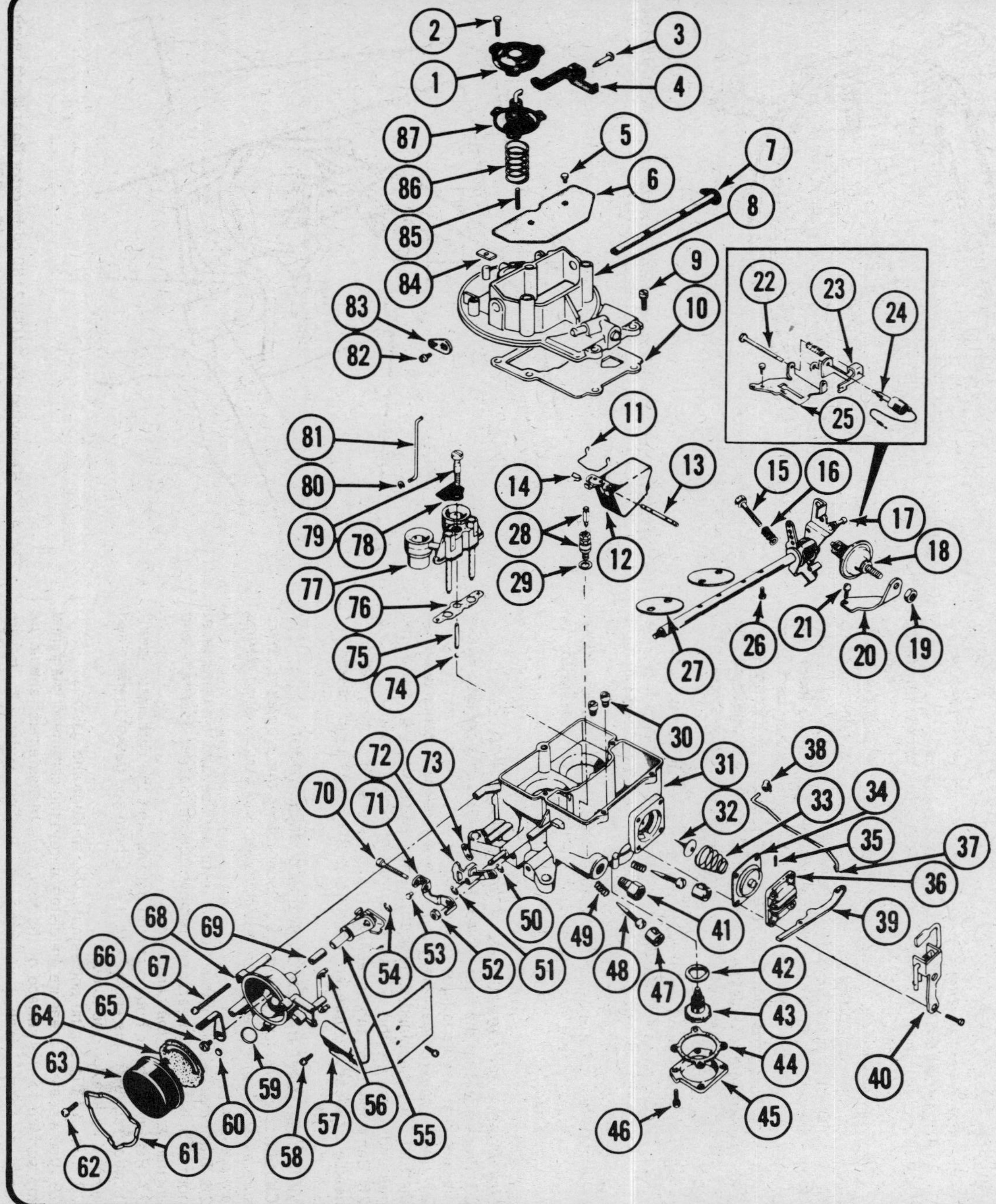

Fig. 4.21 Autolite/Motorcraft 2100/2150 carburetor – exploded view (Sec 12)

1 Modulator cover
2 Modulator retaining screw
3 Pivot pin
4 Modulator arm
5 Choke valve retaining screw
6 Choke valve
7 Choke shaft
8 Air horn
9 Air horn retaining screw
10 Air horn gasket
11 Float and lever assembly
12 Float shaft retainer
13 Float shaft
14 Needle retaining clip
15 Curb idle adjusting screw
16 Curb idle adjusting screw spring
17 Throttle shaft and lever assembly
18 Dashpot
19 Dashpot locknut
20 Dashpot bracket
21 Dashpot bracket retaining screw
22 Adjusting screw
23 Carriage
24 Electric solenoid
25 Mounting bracket
26 Throttle valve retaining screw
27 Throttle valve
28 Needle and seat assembly
29 Needle seat gasket
30 Main jet
31 Main body
32 Elastomer valve
33 Pump return spring
34 Pump diaphragm
35 Pump lever pin
36 Pump cover
37 Pump rod
38 Pump rod retainer
39 Pump lever
40 Bowl vent bellcrank
41 Fuel inlet fitting
42 Power valve gasket
43 Power valve
44 Power valve cover gasket
45 Power valve cover
46 Power valve cover retaining screw
47 Idle limiter cap
48 Idle mixture screw
49 Idle mixture screw spring
50 Retainer
51 Retainer
52 Fast idle lever retaining nut
53 Fast idle lever pin
54 Retainer
55 Lever and shaft
56 Fast idle cam rod
57 Choke shield
58 Choke shield retaining screw
59 Piston passage plug
60 Heat passage plug
61 Choke cover retaining clamp
62 Choke cover retaining screw
63 Choke cover
64 Choke cover gasket
65 Thermostat lever retaining screw
66 Thermostat lever
67 Choke housing retaining screw
68 Choke housing
69 Choke shaft bushing
70 Fast idle speed adjusting screw
71 Fast idle lever
72 Fast idle cam
73 Choke housing gasket
74 Pump discharge check ball
75 Pump discharge weight
76 Booster venturi gasket
77 Booster venturi assembly
78 Air distribution plate
79 Pump discharge screw
80 Retainer
81 Choke rod
82 Choke lever retaining screw
83 Choke plate lever
84 Choke rod seal
85 Stop screw
86 Modulator return spring
87 Modulator diaphragm assembly

14 Remove the roll pin from the accelerator pump cover, using a suitable punch. Retain the roll pin and remove the accelerator pump link and rod assembly, pump cover, diaphragm assembly and spring.
15 To remove the nylon valve from the accelerator pump assembly, grasp it firmly and pull it out. Examine the valve, and if the tip is broken off, be sure to remove it from the fuel bowl. Discard the valve.
16 Turn the main body upside down and remove the enrichment valve cover and gasket. Using an eight-point socket, remove the enrichment valve and gasket.
17 Remove the idle fuel mixture adjusting screws and springs. Remove the idle screw limiter caps.
18 Remove the fast idle adjusting lever assembly and then remove the idle screw and spring from the lever.
19 Before removing the throttle plates, lightly scribe along the throttle shaft and mark each plate for reinstallation in the proper bore. File off the staked portion of the throttle plate screws before removing them. Remove any burrs from the shaft after plate removal so that the shaft can be withdrawn without damage to the throttle shaft bores. Be ready to catch the mechanical high-speed cam located between the throttle plates when the shaft is removed.
20 If an altitude compensator is installed, remove the four screws attaching the assembly to the main body and remove the compensator assembly. Remove the three screws holding the aneroid valve and separate the aneroid, gasket and valve.
21 Disassembly is now complete and all parts should be thoroughly cleaned in solvent. Remove any sediment from the fuel bowl and passages, taking care not to scratch any of the passages. Remove all traces of gaskets with a scraper.
22 Reassembly is basically a reverse of disassembly, but note the following:

a) Check that all holes in new gaskets are properly punched and that they are free of foreign material.
b) When installing a new nylon valve in the accelerator pump assembly, lubricate the tip before inserting it into the accelerator pump cavity hole. Reach into the fuel bowl with needle-nose pliers and pull the valve tip into the fuel bowl. Cut off the tip ahead of the retainer shoulder.
c) Install the idle mixture adjusting screws by turning them with your fingers until they just contact the seat, then back them off two turns. Do not install the limiter caps at this time. The enrichment valve cover and gasket must be installed next as the limiter stops on the cover provide a positive stop for the limiter caps.
d) After installing the throttle plates in the main body, hold the assembly up to the light. Little or no light should be seen between the throttle plates and bores. Tighten and stake the throttle plate screws at this time.
e) When checking the float setting, make sure that the nylon valve in the accelerator pump does not interfere with the float.

Dry float level measurement and adjustment

23 Press down on the float tab to raise the float to a position where the fuel inlet needle is lightly seated.
24 Use a scale or float level gauge to measure the distance between the fuel bowl machined surface to the flat surface of the float at the free end. Compare this measurement to the Specifications.
25 Bend the float tab to adjust, taking care to hold the fuel inlet needle off its seat to prevent damage to the Viton-tipped needle.

Wet float level measurement and adjustment

Caution: *Because fuel vapors are present during this procedure, make sure all smoking materials are extinguished and that no open flames are present.*
26 With the vehicle parked on a level surface and the engine at normal operating temperature, remove the air cleaner assembly and anchor screw from the carburetor.
27 Remove the air horn retaining screws and the carburetor identification tag. Start the engine with the air horn and gasket in place and allow it to idle for one minute.
28 Turn off the engine and remove the air horn and gasket.
29 Use a scale to measure the distance from the carburetor machined top surface to the surface of the fuel. This measurement should be made at least $\frac{1}{4}$-inch away from any vertical surface to ensure accuracy, because the surface of the fuel is actually slightly higher at

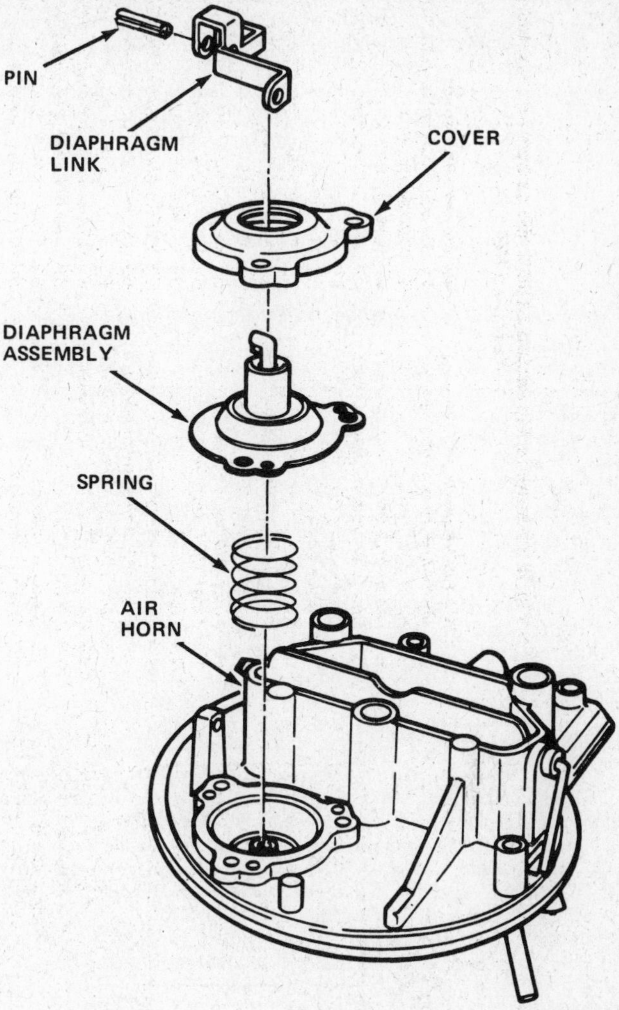

Fig. 4.22 Choke modulator assembly components (2100/2150 carburetor) (Sec 12)

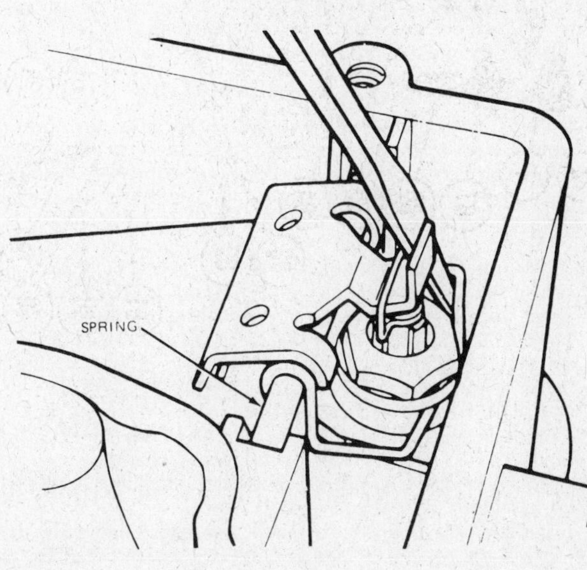

Fig. 4.23 Removing the 2100/2150 carburetor float shaft retainer with a screwdriver (Sec 12)

4

the edges. Compare the measurement to the Specifications.
30 To adjust the fuel level, bend the float tab up where it contacts the fuel inlet valve to raise the fuel level and down to lower it.
31 After adjustment, replace the air horn and gasket and run the engine for one minute before repeating the check and adjustment procedure.
32 Install the air horn (using a new gasket) and air cleaner assembly.

Automatic choke adjustment

33 Loosen the choke cover screws and rotate the cover in the desired direction. The rich setting is to the right (clockwise) and the lean to the left (counterclockwise).

Initial choke plate clearance measurement and adjustment

34 On standard models, rotate the choke cover $\frac{1}{4}$-turn counterclockwise, toward the rich setting side. On altitude compensator-equipped models, open the throttle and rotate the choke cover until the choke plate is closed. On all models, tighten one choke cover retaining screw.
35 On standard models, disconnect the choke heat inlet tube and align the fast idle speed adjusting screw with the index (second) step of the fast idle cam. On altitude compensator models, close the throttle with the fast idle speed screw on the top step of the cam and apply vacuum to the choke diaphragm to hold it against the set screw.
36 On standard models, start the engine (without moving the accelerator linkage) and turn the fast idle adjusting screw counterclockwise three full turns.
37 On all models, measure the clearance between the choke plate lower edge and the air horn wall with a suitable gauge or drill bit shank. Compare this measurement to the Specifications. After setting the choke to the specified position, tighten the choke cover screws.
38 To adjust the early model carburetor, grasp the modulator arm firmly with a pair of pliers at point A and twist the arm at point B with a second pair of pliers (see the accompanying illustration).
39 On later models the clearance is adjusted by turning the set screw located at the bottom of the modulator. On altitude compensator-equipped models, turn the adjustment screw on the back of the diaphragm to attain the specified clearance.
40 Shut off the engine and connect the choke heat tube. Reset the choke cover only after adjusting the fast idle cam linkage.

Fast idle cam adjustment

41 Push down on the fast idle cam lever until the fast idle adjusting screw is in contact with the index (second) step and against the shoulder of the high step.
42 Measure the choke plate lower edge-to-air horn wall clearance and check it against the Specifications.
43 Turn the fast idle cam lever screw to adjust the linkage.
44 Adjust the automatic choke and tighten the retaining screws.

Choke unloader adjustment

45 Hold the throttle completely open with pressure applied on the choke plate toward the closed position.
46 Measure the choke plate lower edge-to-air horn wall clearance and compare it to the Specifications.
47 Adjust the clearance by bending the choke unloader tang.
48 After adjustment, open the throttle until the unloader tang is directly below the fast idle cam pivot, check the clearance against the Specifications. Adjust as necessary and have an assistant push the throttle pedal down. Make sure the throttle linkage opens completely and, if it does not, adjust the throttle cable bracket or remove any excess padding from under the floor mat.

Accelerator pump stroke adjustment

49 The accelerator pump overtravel lever has four adjustment holes and the pump lever has two. During normal operation, the pump rod should be in the third hole of the overtravel lever and the inboard hole of the pump lever.
50 In extremely hot weather, the pump rod can be moved to the second hole of the overtravel lever and, in very cold weather, to the fourth hole to provide smoother acceleration.
51 Remove the operating rod from the retaining clip to move the rod to a different position on the overtravel lever. Move the clip to the desired position, insert the rod and snap the clip over the rod.

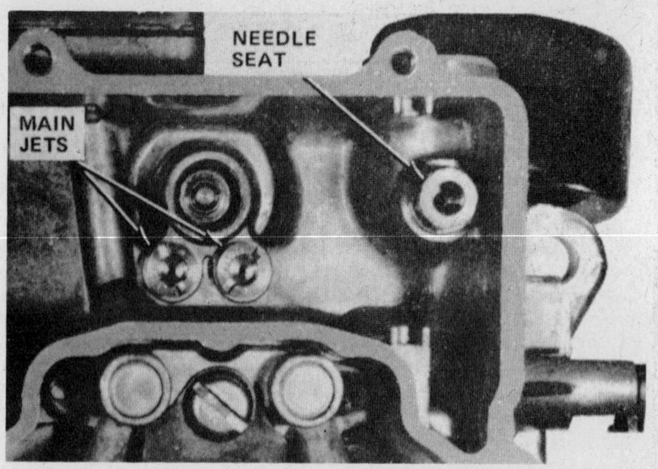

Fig. 4.24 2100/2150 carburetor fuel bowl component layout (Sec 12)

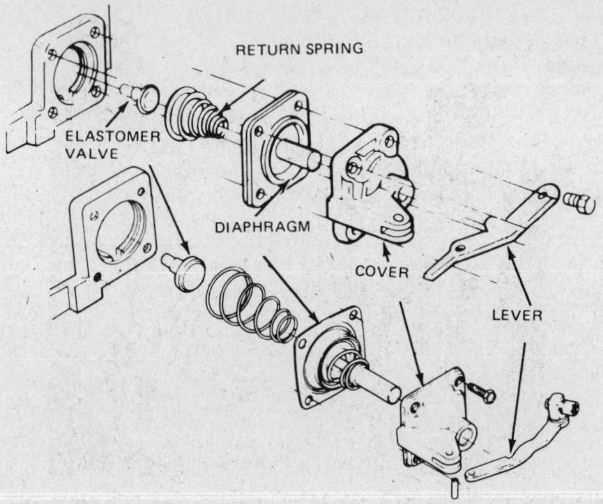

Fig. 4.25 Accelerator pump assembly components (2100/2150 carburetor) (Sec 12)

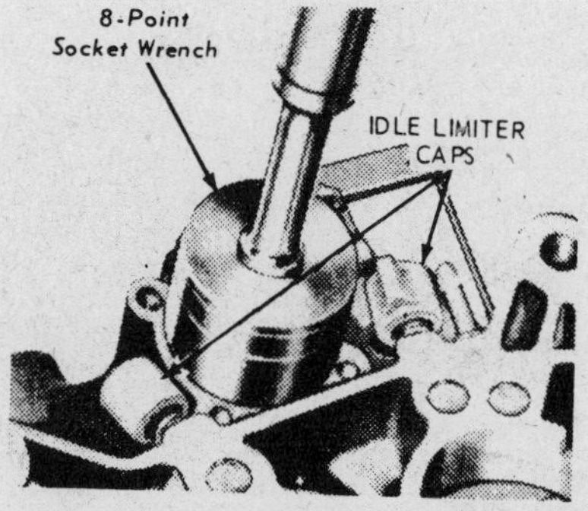

Fig. 4.26 A suitable size socket wrench is used to remove or install the enrichment valve assembly (2100/2150 carburetor) (Sec 12)

Dashpot adjustment

52 With the throttle in the idle position, depress the dashpot stem and measure the stem-to-throttle lever clearance. Compare this measurement to the Specifications.
53 To adjust the clearance, loosen the locknut and turn the dashpot.

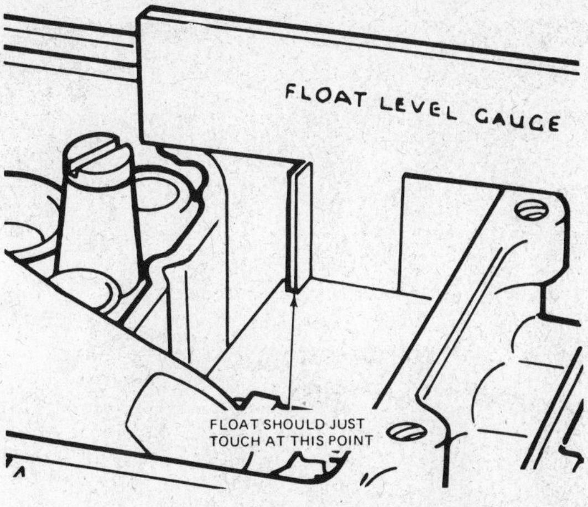

Fig. 4.27 Measuring the dry float level (2100/2150 carburetor) (Sec 12)

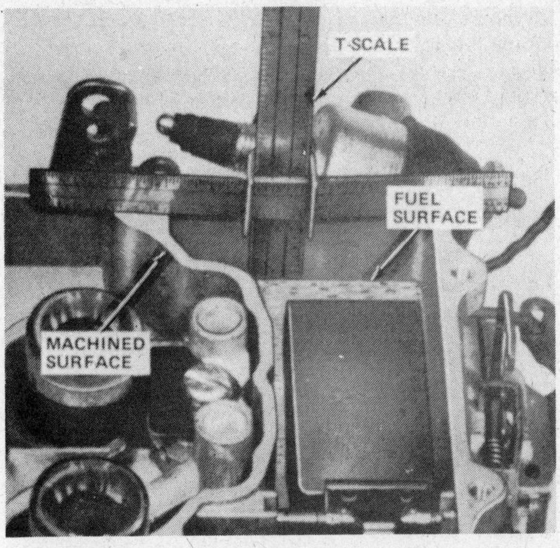

Fig. 4.28 Using a T-scale to measure the 2100/2150 carburetor wet float level (Sec 12)

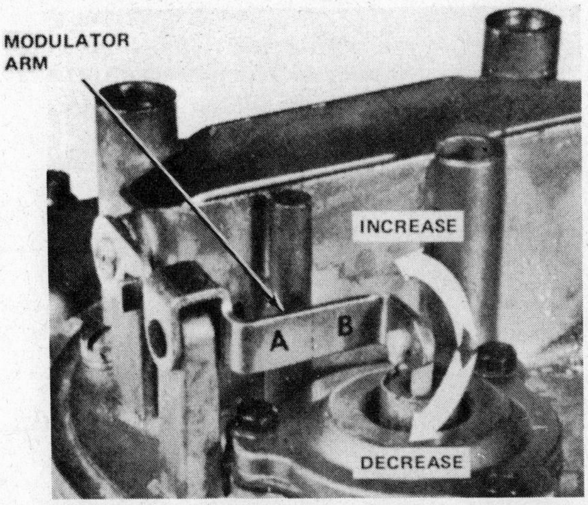

Fig. 4.29 *Early model* 2100/2150 initial choke plate clearance adjustment (Sec 12)

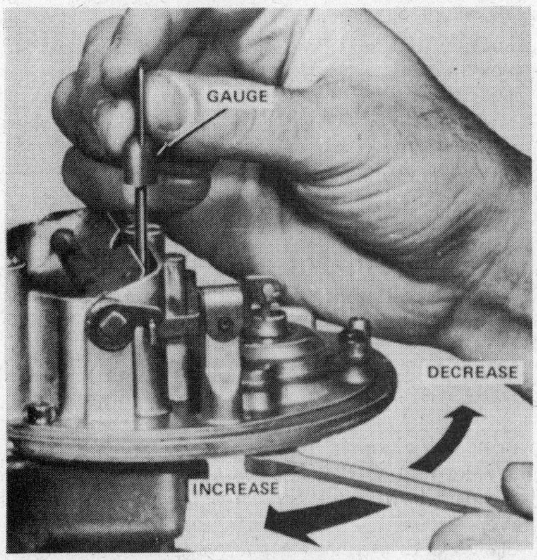

Fig. 4.30 *Later model* 2100/2150 carburetor initial choke plate clearance adjustment (Sec 12)

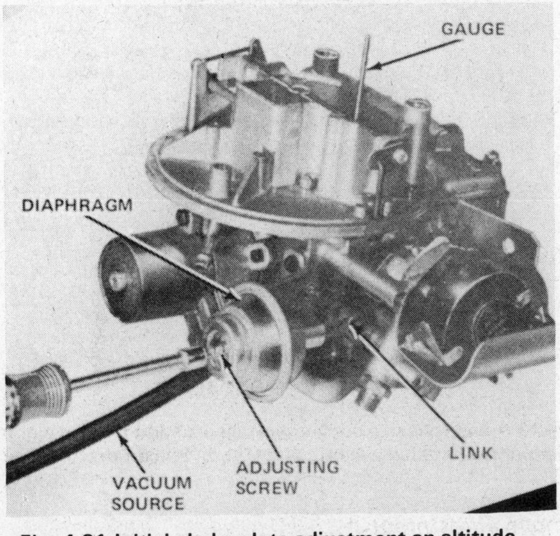

Fig. 4.31 Initial choke plate adjustment on altitude compensator – equipped 2150 carburetor (Sec 12)

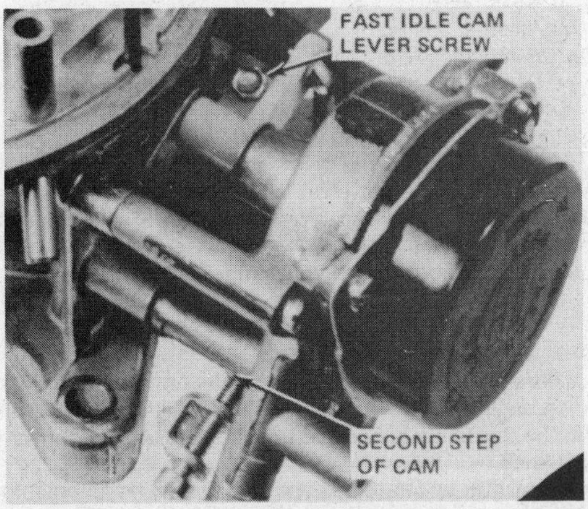

Fig. 4.32 Fast idle cam linkage adjustment (2100/2150 carburetor) (Sec 12)

4

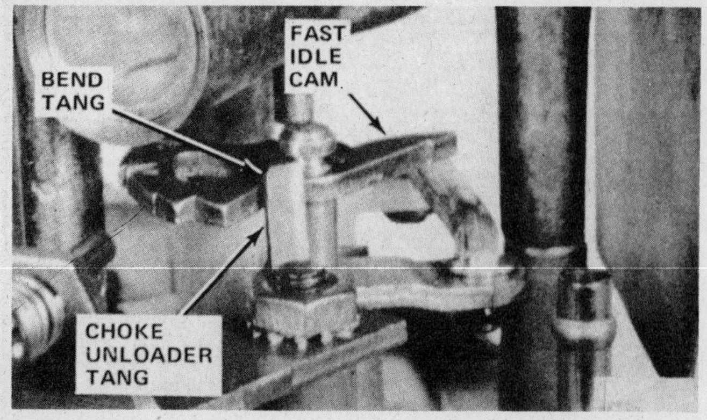

Fig. 4.33 2100/2150 carburetor choke unloader adjustment (Sec 12)

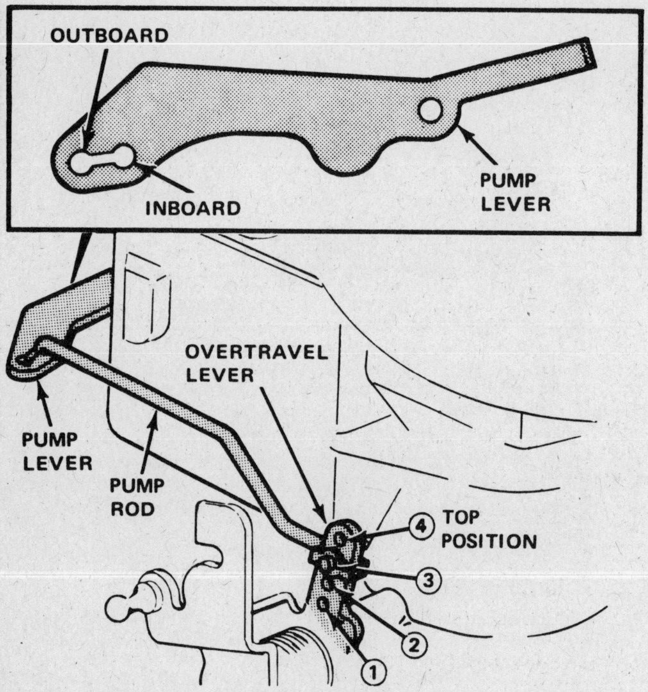

Fig. 4.35 Accelerator pump stroke adjustment (2100/2150 carburetor) (Sec 12)

Fast idle speed adjustment

54 Connect a tachometer to the engine and set the fast idle speed with the fast idle adjusting screw against the index mark (located on the second step) of the fast idle cam. The engine must be at normal operating temperature and the EGR and TCS solenoid disconnected. Turn the adjustment screw to obtain the specified setting.

Idle speed adjustment

55 The idle speed must be adjusted with the engine at normal operating temperature, the air cleaner assembly installed and the transmission in Drive (automatic) or Neutral (manual). *Because the automatic transmission must be in Drive during adjustment, make sure the parking brake is firmly set.*

56 With a tachometer connected and the engine at idle, turn the adjustment screw to obtain the specified idle speed. If the carburetor is equipped with a solenoid, turn the hex screw on the solenoid to adjust the idle speed. Disconnect the solenoid wire and then adjust the idle speed screw to obtain an idle of 500 rpm. Reconnect the wire to the solenoid.

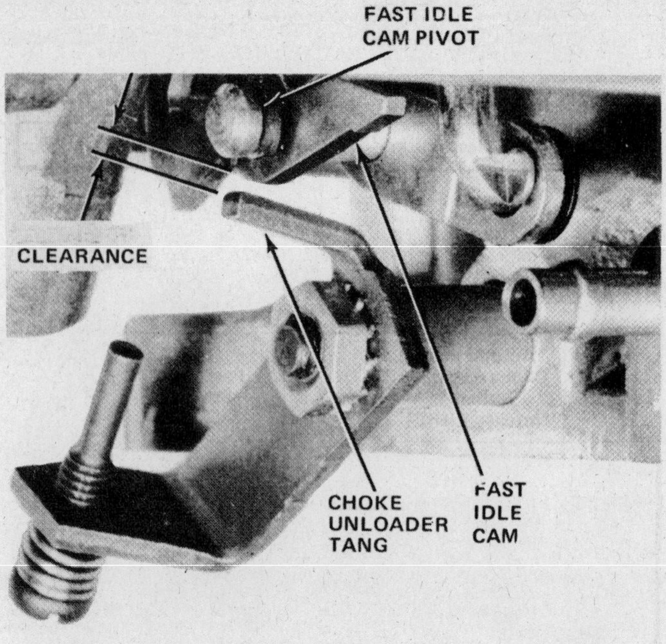

Fig. 4.34 Choke unloader fast idle cam clearance (2100/2150 carburetor) (Sec 12)

Mixture adjustment

57 The manufacturer recommends that mixture adjustment on these models be accomplished with special infra-red equipment. Consequently, the vehicle should be taken to a dealer or properly equipped shop for this adjustment.

13 Carter BBD carburetor – overhaul and adjustment

Overhaul

1 With the carburetor removed from the vehicle, clean away all external dirt.

2 Where applicable, remove the throttle position solenoid.

3 Where applicable, remove the vacuum throttle positioner.

4 Where applicable, remove the idle enrichment vacuum diaphragm, the vacuum nipple and diaphragm return spring (three screws).

5 Remove the retaining clip and take off the accelerator pump arm link.

6 Where applicable, remove the step-up piston cover plate and gasket.

7 Remove the screws and locks, then slide the accelerator pump arm lever out of the air horn. Lift out the vacuum piston and step-up rods.

8 Remove the main body-to-choke vacuum hose.

9 Remove the choke diaphragm, linkage and bracket.

10 Remove the fast idle cam and linkage.

11 Remove the screws and take off the air horn.

12 Invert the air horn, compress the accelerator pump drive spring and remove the S-link so the pump can be removed.

13 Remove the fuel needle valve, seat and gasket.

14 Remove the retainer and baffle, then lift out the floats and fulcrum pin.

15 Remove the main metering jets.

16 Remove the venturi cluster and gaskets, but don't remove the orifice tubes or main vent tubes.

17 Invert the carburetor and drop out the pump discharge and intake check balls.

18 Note the positions of the limiter caps, then remove them and count the exact number of turns required to just bottom the idle mixture screws. Remove the screws and springs.

19 Remove the screws and separate the throttle body from the main body.

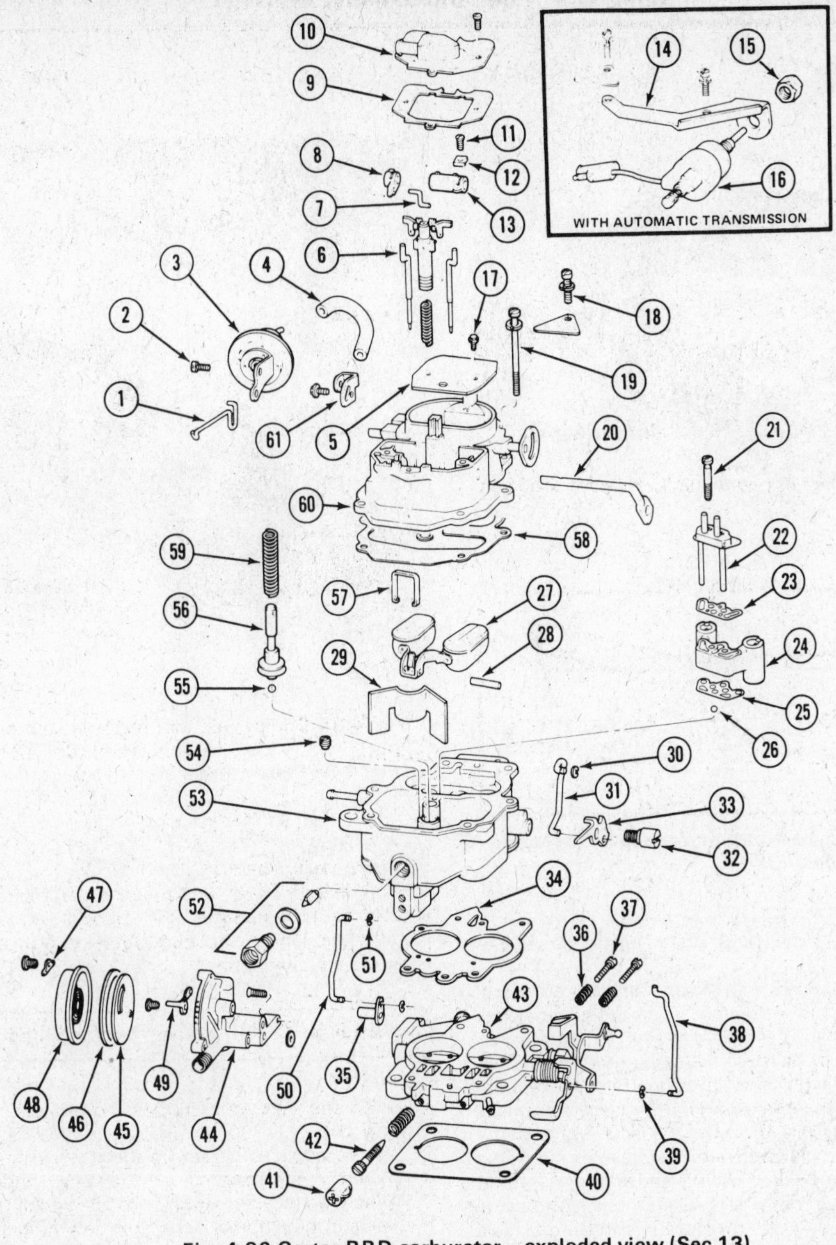

Fig. 4.36 Carter BBD carburetor – exploded view (Sec 13)

1 Diaphragm connector link
2 Screw
3 Choke vacuum diaphragm
4 Hose
5 Valve
6 Metering rod
7 S-link
8 Pump arm
9 Gasket
10 Rollover check valve
11 Screw
12 Lock
13 Rod lifter
14 Bracket
15 Nut
16 Solenoid
17 Screw
18 Air horn retaining screw (short)
19 Air horn retaining screw (long)
20 Pump lever
21 Venturi cluster screw
22 Idle fuel pick-up tube
23 Gasket
24 Venturi cluster
25 Gasket
26 Check ball (small)
27 Float
28 Fulcrum pin
29 Baffle
30 Clip
31 Choke link
32 Screw
33 Fast idle cam
34 Gasket
35 Thermostatic choke shaft
36 Spring
37 Screw
38 Pump link
39 Clip
40 Gasket
41 Limiter cap
42 Screw
43 Throttle body
44 Choke housing
45 Baffle
46 Gasket
47 Retainer
48 Choke coil
49 Lever
50 Choke rod
51 Clip
52 Needle and seat assembly
53 Main body
54 Main metering jet
55 Check ball (large)
56 Accelerator pump plunger
57 Fulcrum pin retainer
58 Gasket
59 Spring
60 Air horn
61 Lever

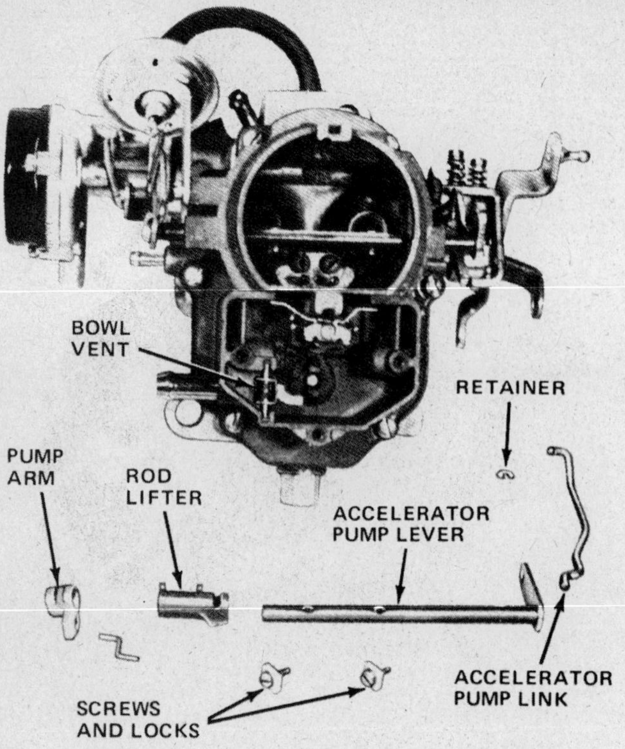

Fig. 4.37 BBD carburetor accelerator pump and lever assembly (Sec 13)

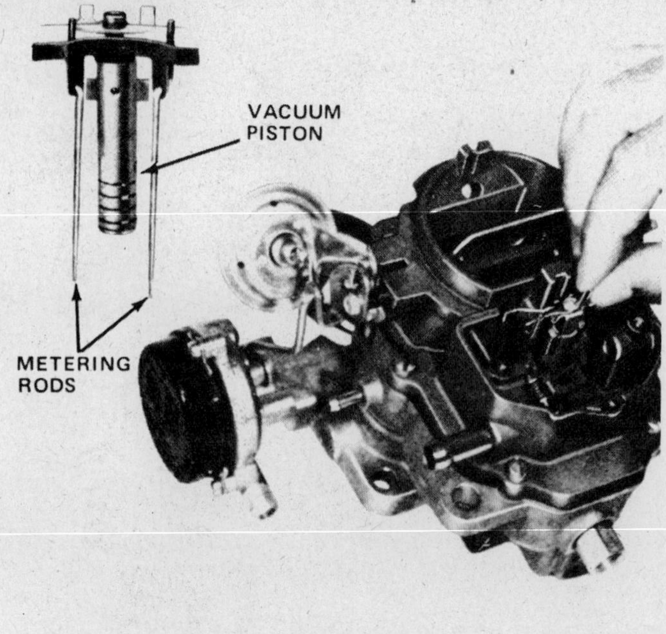

Fig. 4.38 Piston and metering rod assembly removal (BBD carburetor) (Sec 13)

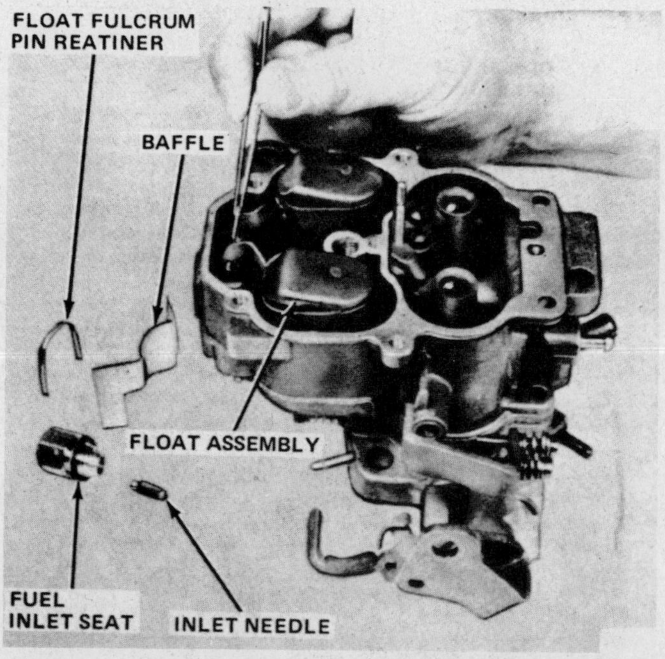

Fig. 4.39 Float assembly components (BBD carburetor) (Sec 13)

20 Don't dismantle the valve plates and shafts unless needed to replace worn parts.
21 Clean and inspect all components, and replace any that are worn.
22 Reassembly is the reverse of disassembly, using the new gaskets and components from the rebuild kit. After installing the accelerator pump discharge and intake check balls, fill the carburetor bowl about half-full with clean gasoline. Insert the pump piston into the cylinder and work it up-and-down to expel any air. Hold the discharge check ball down with a brass rod, raise and lower the accelerator pump piston and make sure no fuel is emitted from the intake or discharge passages. If there is leakage and the passages and ball seats are in good condition, replace the main body. During reassembly, measure the float setting as described below and reset the idle mixture screws to their original positions (Step 18).

Float level adjustment
23 With the fuel inlet valve and floats installed in the carburetor, invert the body so the weight of the floats is on the valve.
24 Place a straightedge across the float bowl and measure the distance from the surface of the bowl edge to the crown of each float at its center. Check this measurement against the Specifications.
25 If adjustment is needed, bend the float lever. Always release the floats from the needle before adjusting to avoid damage to the synthetic rubber tip.

Vacuum piston gap adjustment
26 Check the vacuum piston gap measurement and check it against the Specifications. Adjust as necessary by turning the adjusting screw at the top.

Vacuum piston adjustment
27 With the vacuum piston and metering rod assembly correctly installed, back off the curb idle screw to close the throttles. Note the number of turns required for ease of resetting.
28 Depress the piston completely while applying moderate pressure to the rod lifter tab and tighten the rod lifter screw.
29 Release the piston and rod lifter. Return the curb idle screw to the original position.

Accelerator pump adjustment
30 Back off the curb idle adjusting screw to completely close the throttle plate and open the choke plate so the fast idle cam will allow the throttle plates to seat in the bores.
31 Back off the curb idle screw until it just contacts the stop, then back it off an additional two turns.
32 Measure the distance from the surface of the air horn to the top of the accelerator pump shaft and compare it to the Specifications.
33 To adjust, loosen the pump arm adjusting lock screw and rotate the sleeve to adjust the pump travel. Tighten the lock screw.

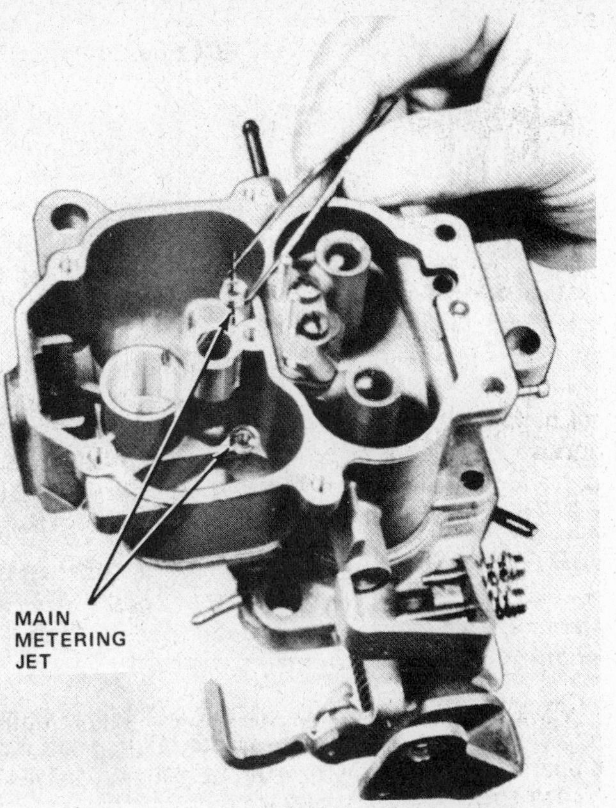

Fig. 4.40 BBD carburetor main metering jets (Sec 13)

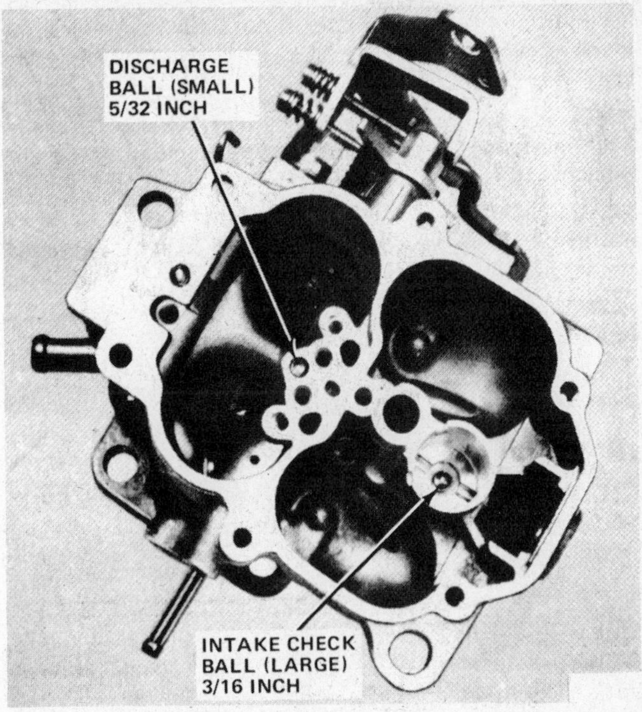

Fig. 4.41 Check ball locations (BBD carburetor) (Sec 13)

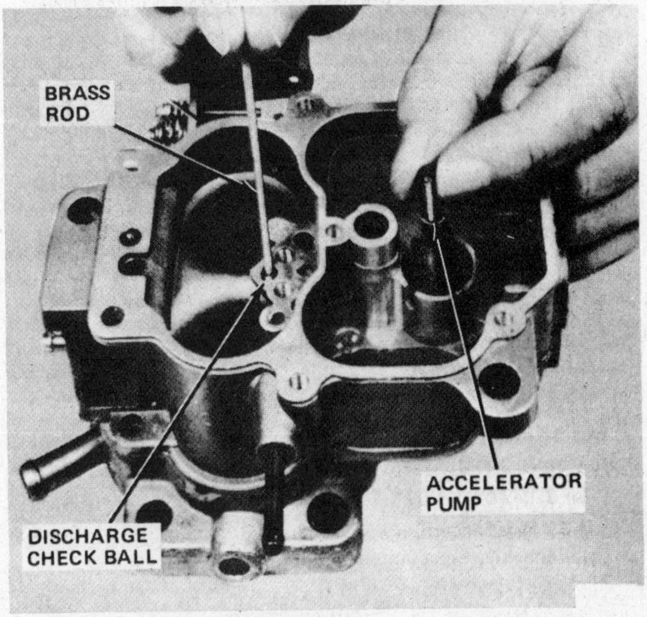

Fig. 4.42 Checking the BBD carburetor accelerator pump system (Sec 13)

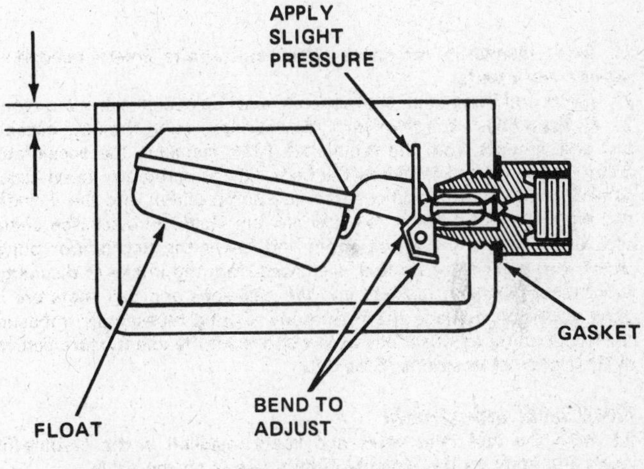

Fig. 4.43 BBD carburetor float level adjustment (Sec 13)

Initial choke valve clearance adjustment

34 Loosen the cover screws and rotate the choke $\frac{1}{4}$-turn in the rich direction. Tighten one screw.

35 Open the throttle plate sufficiently to place the fast idle screw on the high step of the cam.

36 Apply 19 inches of vacuum to the diaphragm to pull the plunger against the stop.

37 Measure the choke plate-to-air horn wall clearance and check it against the Specifications.

38 Bend the diaphragm connector link to adjust.

Fast idle cam position adjustment

39 Perform the operations described in Steps 34 and 35.

40 Measure the choke plate-to-air horn wall clearance with a suitable gauge or drill bit shank. There should be a slight drag when the drill or gauge is removed, if the adjustment is correct.

41 To adjust, bend the fast idle connector rod as necessary.

Choke unloader adjustment

42 With the throttle held in the wide open position, apply light pressure to the choke plate and hold it in place.

43 Measure the choke plate-to-air horn wall clearance with a suitable gauge or drill bit shank.
44 Adjust by bending the unloader tang, making sure that it operates smoothly after adjustment.

Curb idle speed adjustment

45 The curb idle speed must be adjusted under the following conditions:

Transmission in Neutral (manual) or Drive (automatic)
Parking brake securely set
Engine at normal operating temperature
Air cleaner installed
Tachometer properly attached

46 Turn the adjustment screw to attain the specified idle speed.
47 If the carburetor is equipped with a solenoid, turn the nut on the solenoid to adjust the idle rpm, then tighten the locknut.
48 Disconnect the solenoid wire and adjust the carburetor idle screw to obtain a 500 rpm idle speed. Reconnect the solenoid wire.

Mixture adjustment

49 The mixture adjustment preparations are the same as those for curb idle adjustment described in Step 45. Adjust the idle mixture

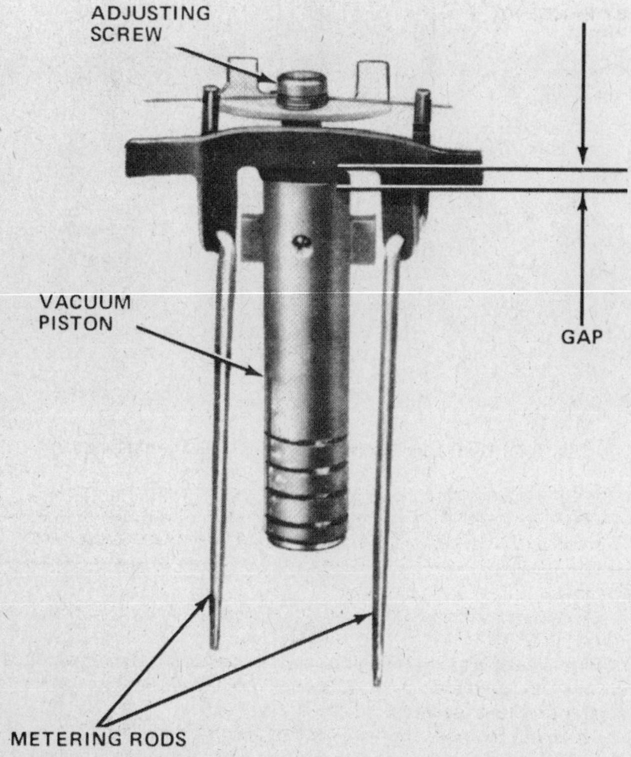

Fig. 4.44 Vacuum piston gap check (BBD carburetor) (Sec 13)

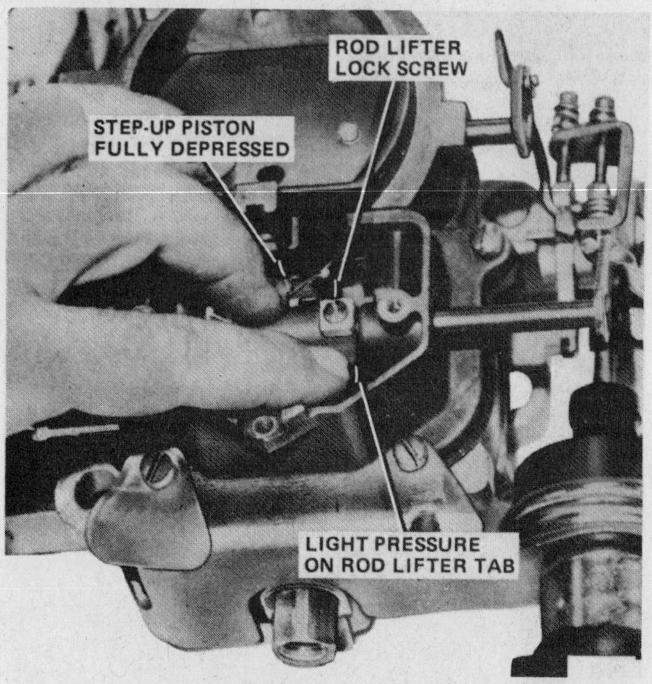

Fig. 4.45 Vacuum piston adjustment (BBD carburetor) (Sec 13)

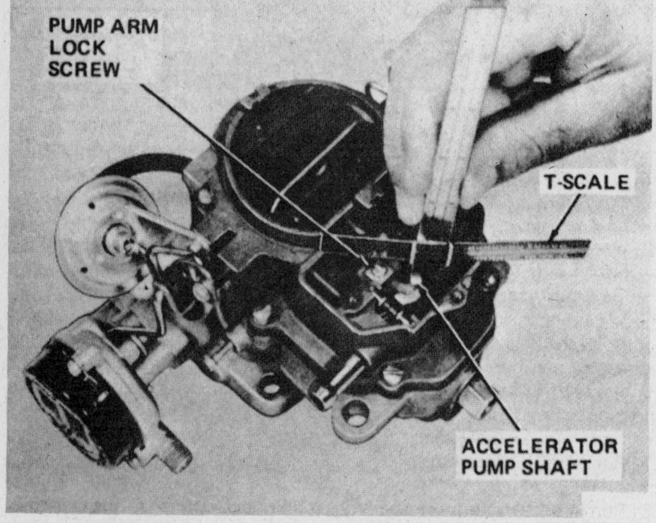

Fig. 4.46 BBD carburetor accelerator pump adjustment (Sec 13)

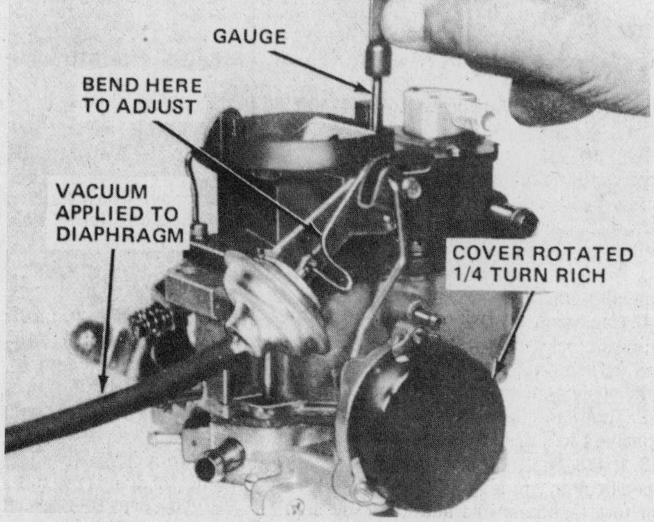

Fig. 4.47 Initial choke valve adjustment (BBD carburetor) (Sec 13)

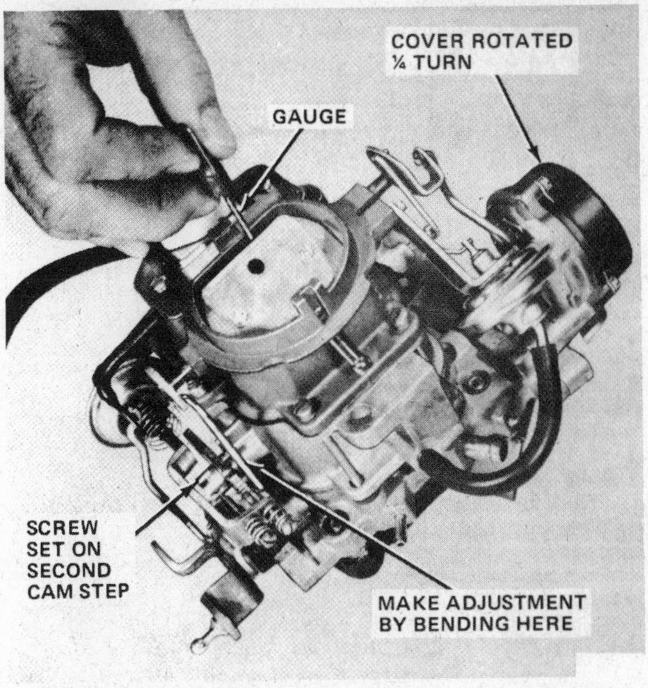

Fig. 4.48 Fast idle cam adjustment (BBD carburetor) (Sec 13)

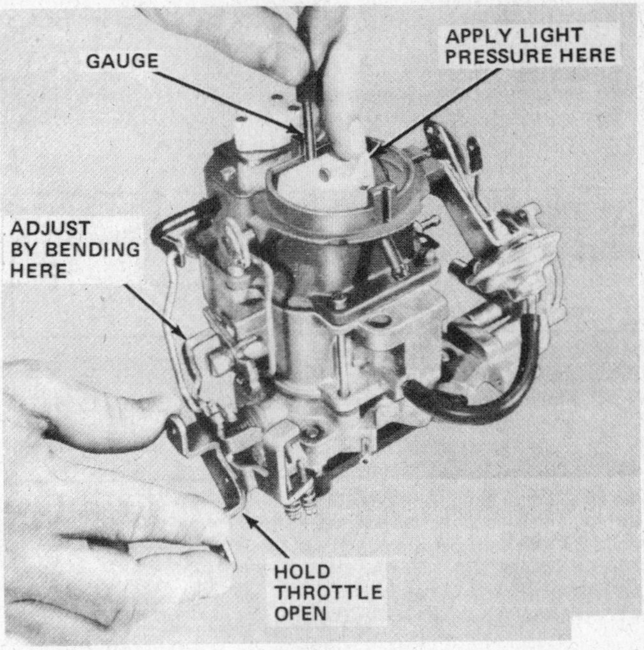

Fig. 4.49 BBD carburetor unloader adjustment (Sec 13)

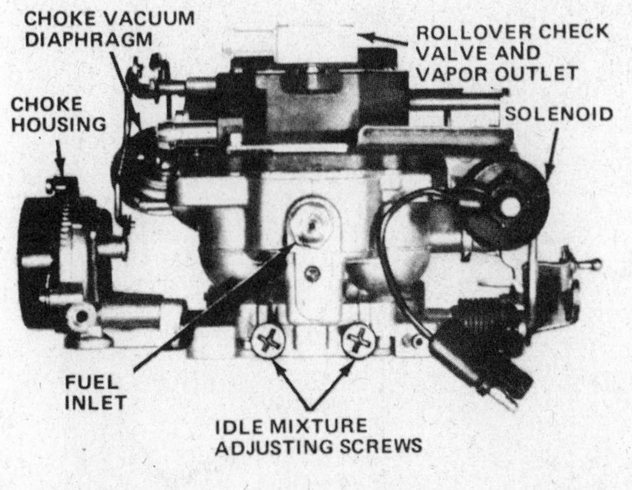

Fig. 4.50 BBD carburetor idle mixture adjusting screw locations (Sec 13)

screws to the full rich stop (counterclockwise), note the position of the screw-head slots and remove the plastic limiter caps. This can be accomplished by using a No. 10 sheet metal screw threaded into the center of the cap.

50 Adjust the idle speed. Use the procedures in Steps 47 and 48 for solenoid-equipped models.

51 Beginning at the full rich position (Step 49), turn the mixture screws clockwise in the lean direction until there is an rpm drop. Turn the screws in the counterclockwise direction until the highest rpm previously achieved is obtained. This is called the lean best idle.

52 Turn the idle mixture screws in small, even increments until the specified idle drop is reached.

53 If the final reading varies more than 30 rpm from the curb idle specification, repeat the idle speed adjustment, followed by the mixture lean best idle and idle drop adjustments (Steps 51 and 52).

54 Install the new idle mixture screw limiter caps with the limiter cap ear against the full rich stop. Be careful not to move the mixture settings.

14 Holley-Weber 5210 carburetor – overhaul and adjustment

Overhaul

1 Disconnect the choke rod from the plastic retainer on the lower end of the lever.

2 Remove the air horn retaining screws, lock washers and identification tag and lift the air horn from the main body. Be careful not to damage the float assembly.

3 Remove the choke rod and dust seal from the air horn.

4 With the air horn upside down, remove the float pin. Remove the float and needle from the air horn and remove the needle from the float.

5 Remove the washer, retainer and seal from the fuel bowl vacuum vent assembly.

6 Remove the power enrichment diaphragm from the air horn.

7 Remove the inlet needle seat and gasket.

8 Turn the air horn right side up and remove the vacuum vent diaphragm housing. Remove the spring and diaphragm.

9 Remove the idle solenoid from the main body.

10 Remove the retaining ring, electric coil and ground ring from the choke housing.

11 Remove the choke lever sleeve and the choke housing.

12 Remove the choke diaphragm cover. Remove the spring and cover. Rotate the choke shaft cam in order to slide the diaphragm shaft out of the housing.

Note: *Do not try to remove the metal choke housing as it may cause damage to the carburetor body.*

13 Remove the pump discharge nozzle retaining screws and remove the nozzle and gaskets.

14 Turn the main body upside down and catch the weight ball and check ball as they drop out.

15 Note the position of the main well air bleed jets and record their respective numbers for assembly reference.

16 Remove the primary air bleed. Turn the main body upside down and catch the primary main well tube. Record the number stamped on the tube for assembly reference.

17 Repeat the procedure for the secondary air bleed and main well tube.

18 Remove the primary metering jet and record the jet number for assembly reference. Repeat the procedure for the secondary main metering jet.

19 Remove the power valve.

4

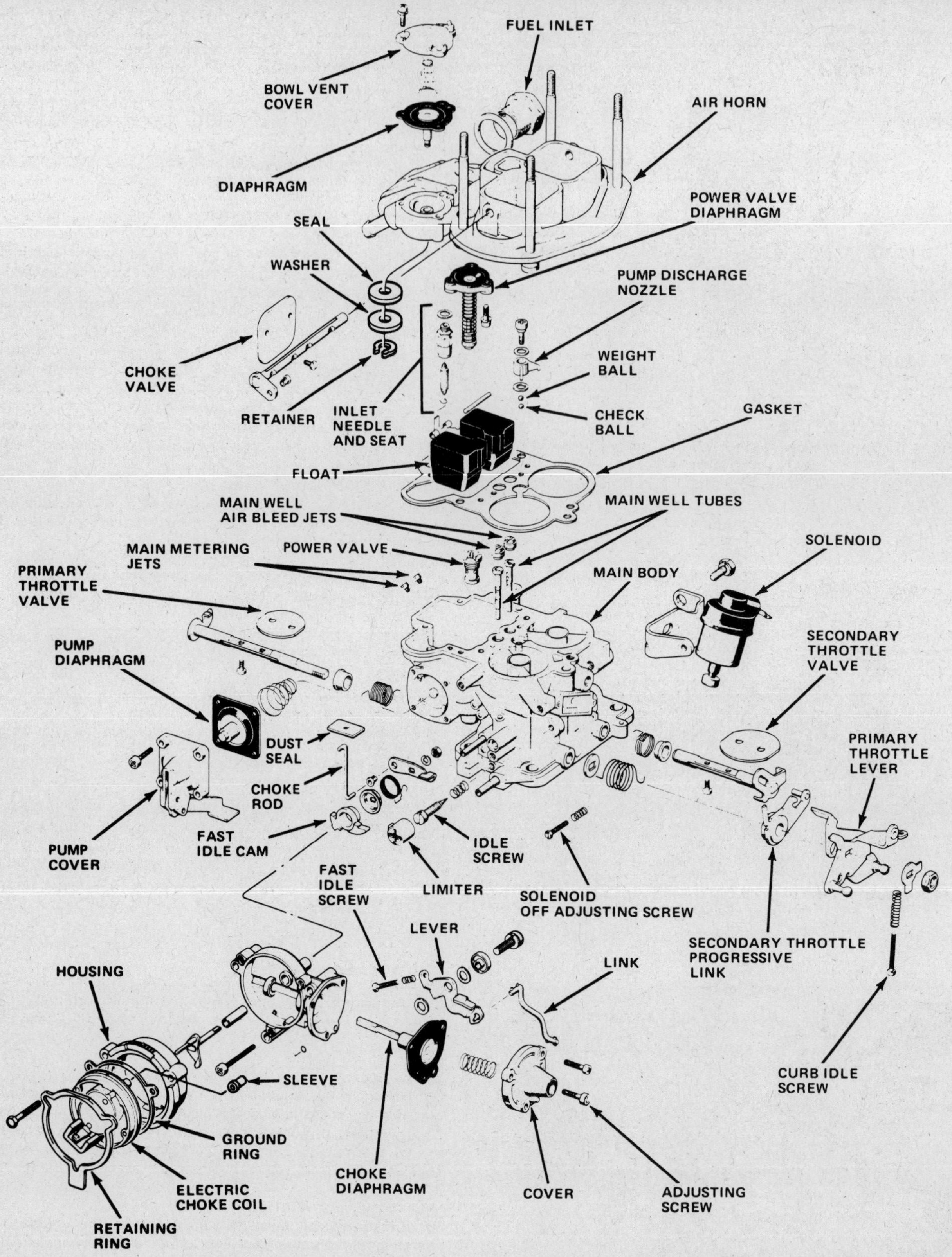

Fig. 4.51 Holley-Weber 5210 carburetor – exploded view (Sec 14)

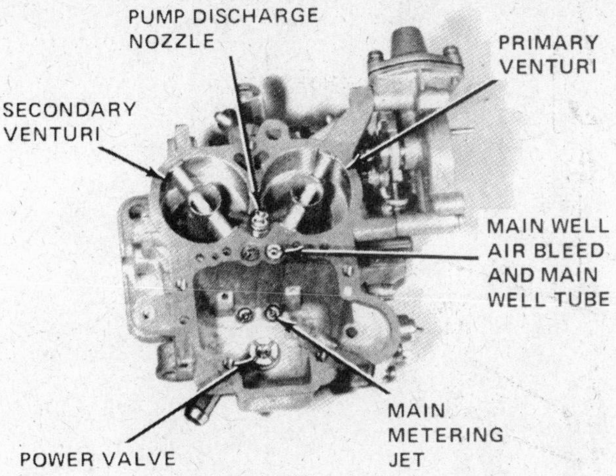

Fig. 4.52 Interior view of the fuel bowl and venturis (540 carburetor) (Sec 14)

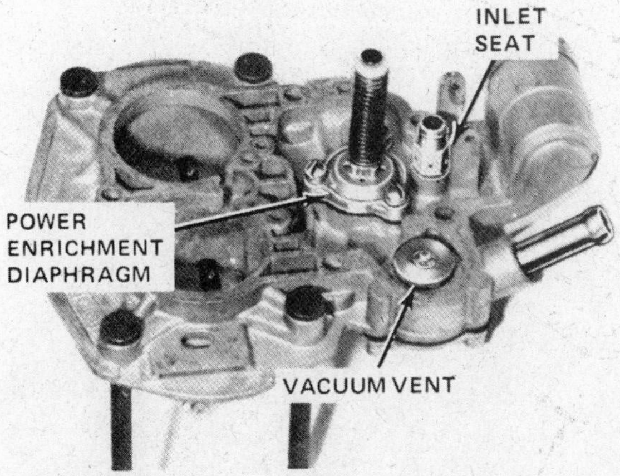

Fig. 4.53 Bottom view of the 5210 carburetor air horn (Sec 14)

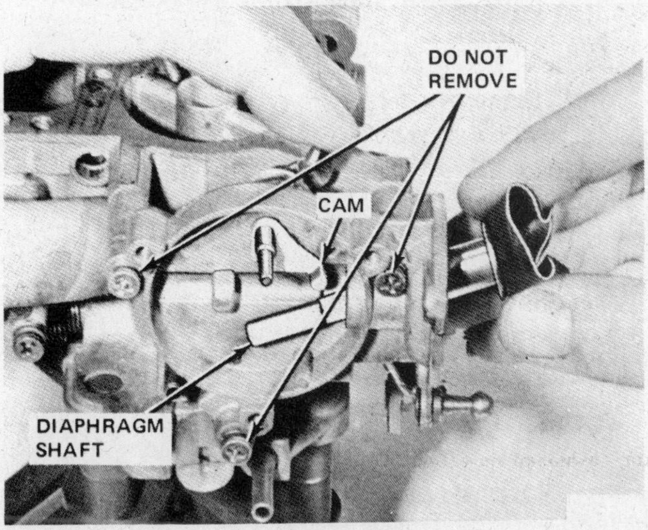

Fig. 4.54 The metal choke housing of the 5210 carburetor is not removable (Sec 14)

20 Remove the accelerator pump cover and remove the pump diaphragm and spring.

21 Before removing the idle limiter cap, count the number of turns needed to lightly seat the screw for assembly reference. Remove the idle mixture screw and spring.

22 Disassembly is now complete and all parts should be thoroughly cleaned with solvent. **Note:** *Do not submerge the main body choke housing in solvent as the diaphragm vacuum passage between the choke housing and main body is sealed with an O-ring. Cleaning solvent could damage this O-ring.*

23 Remove any sediment from the fuel bowl and passages, taking care not to scratch any of the passages. Remove all traces of gaskets with a scraper.

24 Reassembly is basically the reverse of disassembly, but check the holes in the new gaskets to be sure they are properly punched and free of foreign material.

Float level measurement and adjustment

25 Hold the bowl cover in the inverted position and with the float tang resting lightly on the spring loaded fuel inlet needle, carefully measure the clearance between the edge of the float and the bowl cover. See the Specifications for correct dimensions. For this job a ruler and drill is necessary. If this reading is not correct, carefully adjust it by bending the arm between the pivot and the float at the float end.

Automatic choke adjustment

26 Loosen the choke cover screws and rotate the cover in the desired direction. The rich setting is to the right (clockwise) and the lean setting to the left (counterclockwise).

Initial choke plate measurement and adjustment

27 Remove the choke coil retaining screws. Remove the retaining ring and electric coil.

28 Using a screwdriver or suitable tool, push the choke diaphragm shaft against the stop.

29 Position a suitable gauge or drill bit shank (see the Specifications) on the downstream side of the primary choke plate.

30 Take all slack out of the choke linkage.

31 If necessary, adjust the clearance by turning the Allen bolt adjuster on the end of the diaphragm cover.

Fast idle cam adjustment

32 With the air cleaner removed, insert a drill bit of suitable size (see the Specifications) between the lower edge of the choke plate and the air intake wall.

33 Hold the idle screw on the second step of the fast idle cam and measure the clearance between the tang of the choke lever and the arm on the fast idle cam. If the clearance is not correct, bend the choke lever up or down as necessary.

Choke unloader adjustment

34 Insert a suitable gauge or drill bit (see the Specifications) between the lower edge of the choke plate and the air horn wall.

35 If necessary, adjust the clearance by bending the tang on the fast idle lever.

Fast idle speed adjustment

36 Connect a tachometer to the engine and set the fast idle speed with the fast idle adjusting screw against the index mark (located on the second step) of the fast idle cam. The engine must be at normal operating temperature and the EGR and TCS solenoid disconnected. Turn the adjustment screw to obtain the specified setting.

Idle speed adjustment

37 The idle speed must be adjusted with the engine at normal operating temperature, the air cleaner assembly installed and the transmission in Drive (automatic) or Neutral (manual). *Because the automatic transmission must be in Drive during adjustment, make sure the parking brake is firmly set.*

38 With a tachometer connected and the engine at idle, turn the adjustment screw to obtain the specified idle speed. If the carburetor is equipped with a solenoid, turn the hex screw on the solenoid to adjust the idle speed. Disconnect the solenoid wire and then adjust the idle speed screw to obtain an idle of 500 rpm. Reconnect the wire to the solenoid.

4

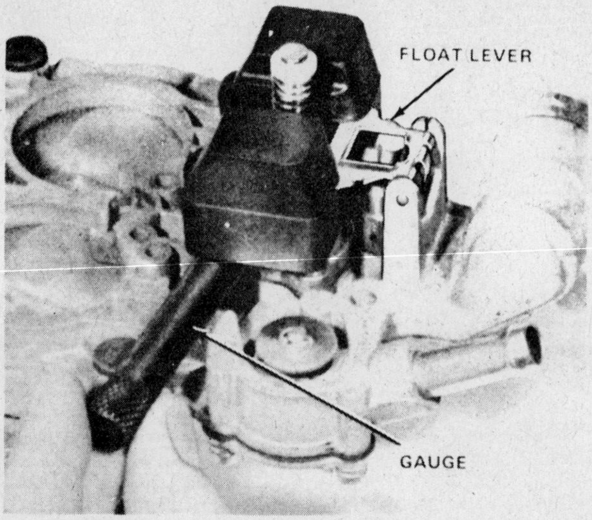

Fig. 4.55 Float level adjustment (5210 carburetor) (Sec 14)

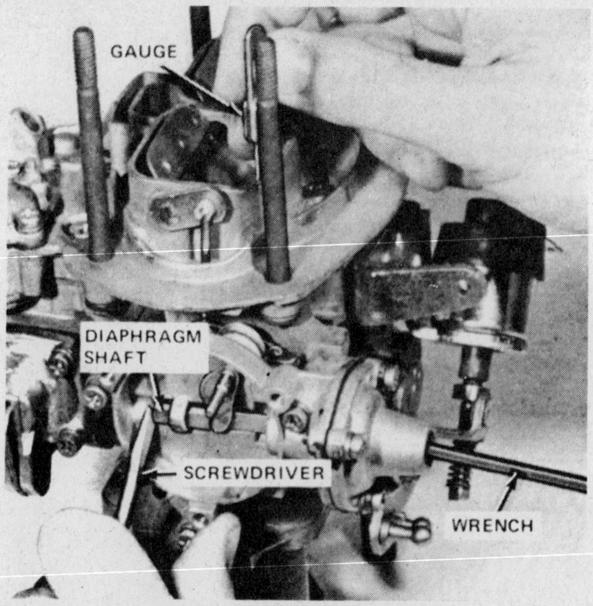

Fig. 4.56 Adjusting the initial choke valve clearance (5210 carburetor) (Sec 14)

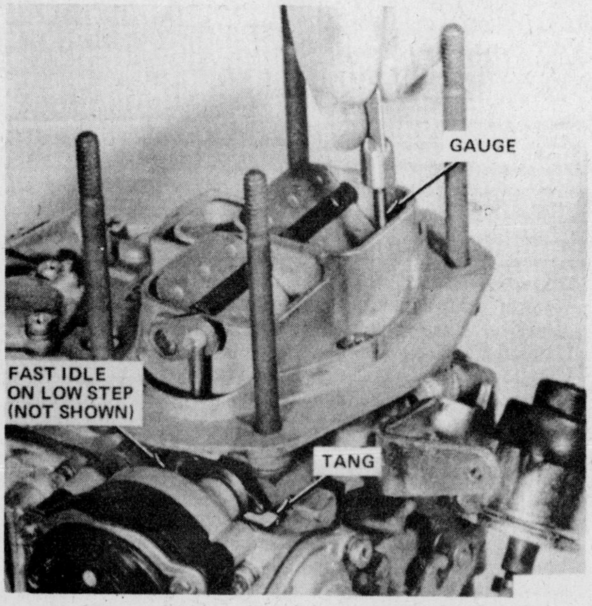

Fig. 4.57 Fast idle cam adjustment (5210 carburetor) (Sec 14)

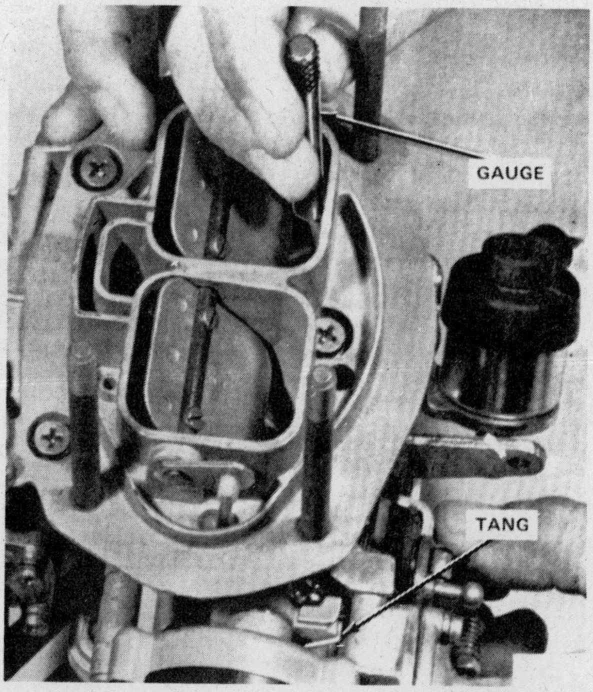

Fig. 4.58 Choke unloader adjustment (5210 carburetor) (Sec 14)

Mixture adjustment

39 The manufacturer recommends that mixture adjustment on these models may be accomplished with special infra-red equipment. Consequently, the vehicle should be taken to a dealer or properly equipped shop for this adjustment.

15 Rochester 2SE and E2SE carburetors – overhaul and adjustment

Overhaul

1 Mount the carburetor on a holding fixture to prevent damage to the throttle valves. If no holding fixture is available, a suitable-size punch securely set in a vise is a good alternative (photo).

2 Remove the gasket from the air horn and the fuel inlet nut and filter assembly.

3 Remove the pump lever attaching screw, disconnect the pump rod from the lever and remove the lever (photo).

4 Disconnect the vacuum break diaphragm hose from the throttle body.

5 Remove the screws that secure the idle speed solenoid/vacuum break diaphragm bracket (if equipped) (photo).

6 Lift off the idle speed solenoid/vacuum break diaphragm assembly and disconnect the air valve rod from the outside vacuum break plunger (if equipped) (photo).

7 Disconnect the vacuum break rod (if equipped) from the inside vacuum break diaphragm plunger.

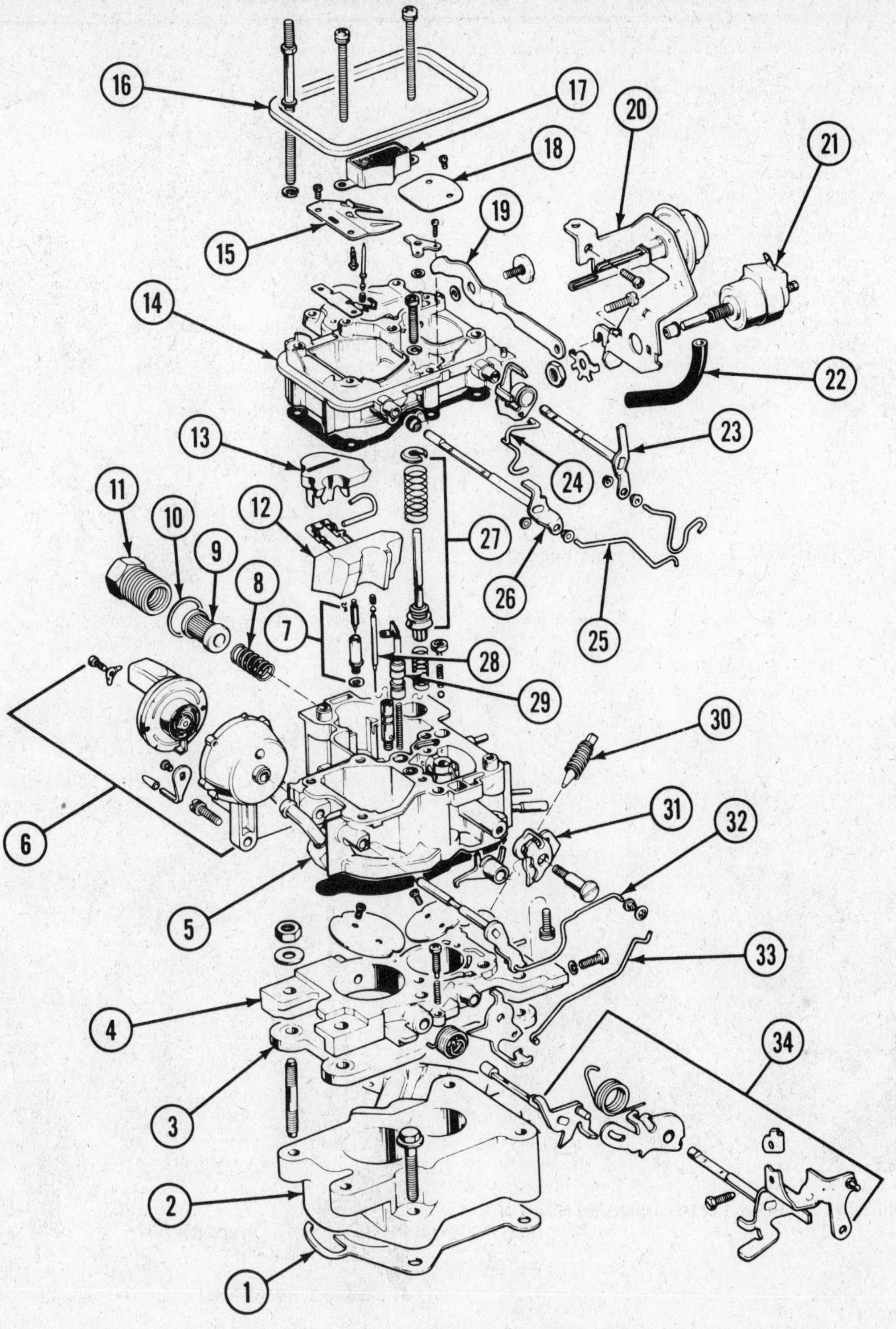

Fig. 4.59 Rochester 2SE carburetor – exploded view (Sec 15)

1 Gasket
2 Intake adapter
3 Insulator
4 Throttle body
5 Main body
6 Electric choke cover and coil
7 Needle seat assembly
8 Spring
9 Fuel filter
10 Gasket
11 Fuel inlet fitting
12 Float assembly
13 Filler block
14 Air horn
15 Air valve
16 Gasket
17 Vent screen
18 Choke plate
19 Pump lever
20 Vacuum break and bracket
21 Idle stop solenoid
22 Vacuum hose
23 Vacuum break lever
24 Choke link
25 Air valve rod
26 Air valve lever
27 Accelerator pump
28 Metering rod
29 Power piston
30 Idle needle and spring
31 Fast idle cam
32 Intermediate choke rod
33 Pump rod
34 Throttle lever assembly

8 Pry off the clip that secures the intermediate choke rod lever and separate the rod from the lever (photo).
9 Remove the screws that secure the vent/screen assembly to the air horn and lift off the assembly.
10 Remove the retaining screws and lift the solenoid from the air horn (photo).
11 Remove the air horn retaining screws. If the carburetor is equipped with a hot idle compensator, it must be removed to gain access to the short air horn screw.
12 Rotate the fast idle cam up, lift off the air horn and disconnect the fast idle cam rod from the fast idle cam (photo).
13 Disengage the fast idle cam rod from the choke lever and save the bushing for later reassembly (photo).
14 If the pump plunger did not come out of the air horn during removal, remove the plunger from the pump well in the float bowl.
15 Compress the pump plunger spring and remove the spring retainer clip and spring from the piston.
16 Remove the air horn gasket from the float bowl.
17 Remove the pump return spring from the pump well.
18 Remove the plastic filler block that covers the float (photo).
19 Pull up on the retaining pin and remove the float valve and float assembly.
20 On E2SE carburetors, remove the float valve seat and gasket and the extended metering jet (photo).
21 On 2SE carburetors, refer to the accompanying illustration for the power piston removal operation.
22 Use needle-nose pliers to pull out the white plastic retainer and then remove the pump discharge spring and check ball (photo).
23 Remove the choke housing from the throttle body (photo).
24 Remove the four retaining screws and separate the throttle body from the float bowl.
25 Carefully file off the heads of the rivets securing the choke cover. Use a hammer and small punch to tap out the remainder of the rivet.
26 Remove the choke coil lever screw and lift out the lever.
27 Remove the intermediate shaft and lever assembly by sliding it out the lever side of the float bowl.

15.1 A punch held in a vise can be used to support the carburetor if a stand is not available

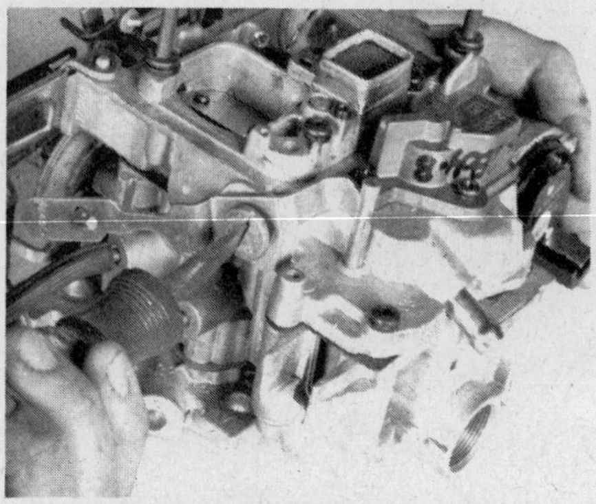

15.3 Removing the pump lever attaching screw

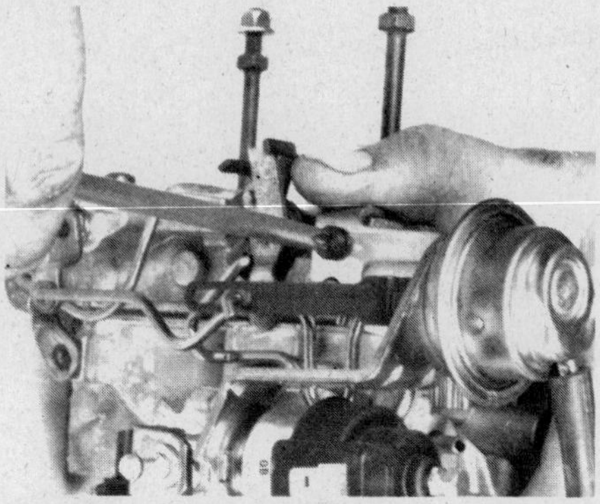

15.5 Removing the idle speed solenoid/vacuum break diaphragm bracket

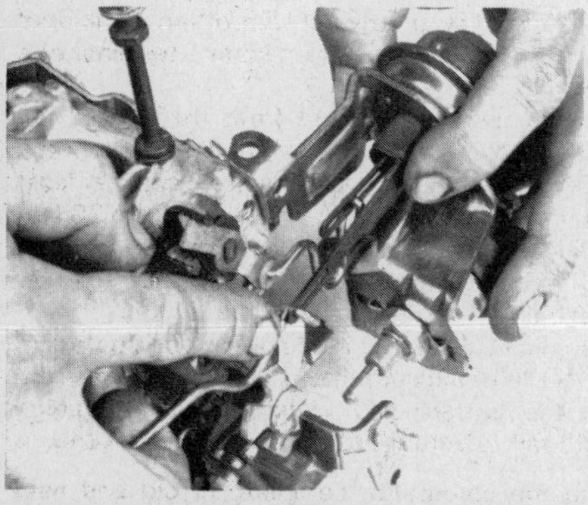

15.6 Lift off the idle speed solenoid vacuum break unit. Disconnect air valve rod from vacuum break plunger

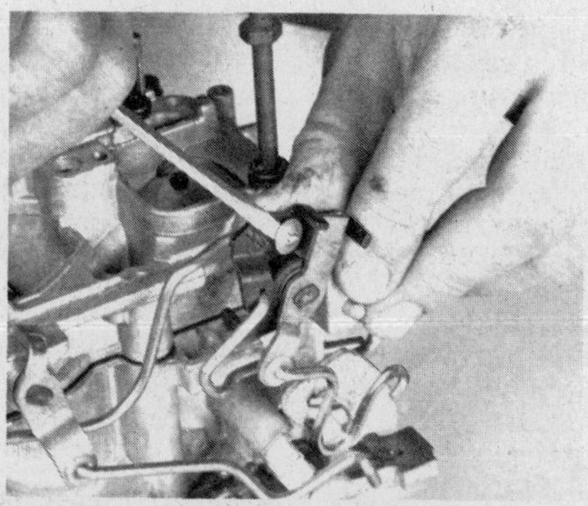

15.8 Pry off the clip securing the intermediate choke rod to the choke lever. Separate the rod from the lever

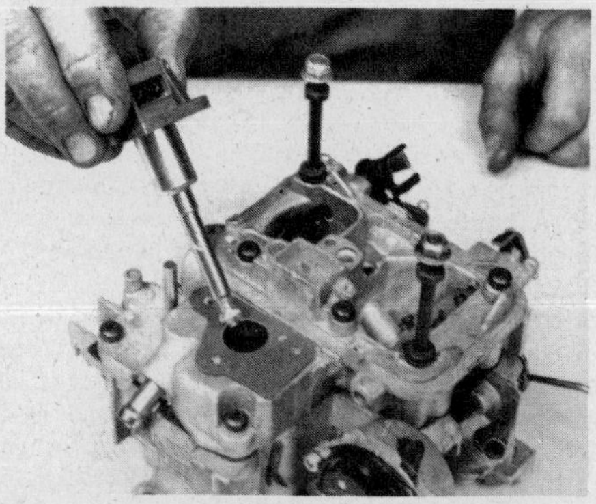

15.10 After removing the retaining screws, use a slight twisting motion while lifting the solenoid out

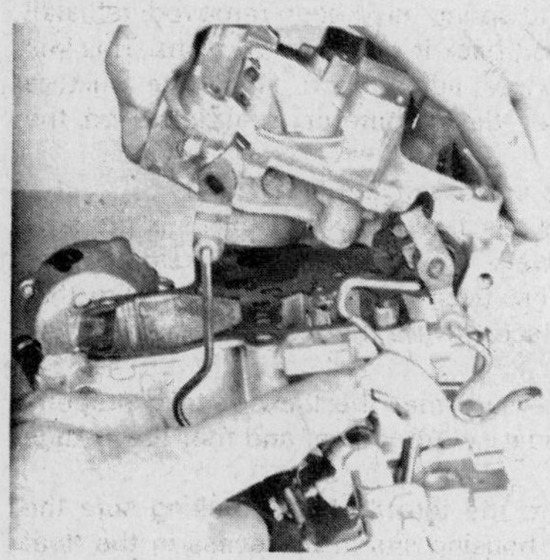

15.12 Removing the air horn

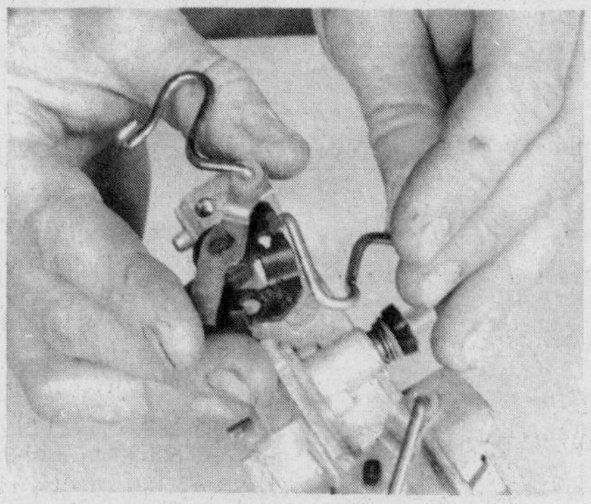

15.13 Removing the fast idle cam from the choke lever

15.18 Lifting out the filler block

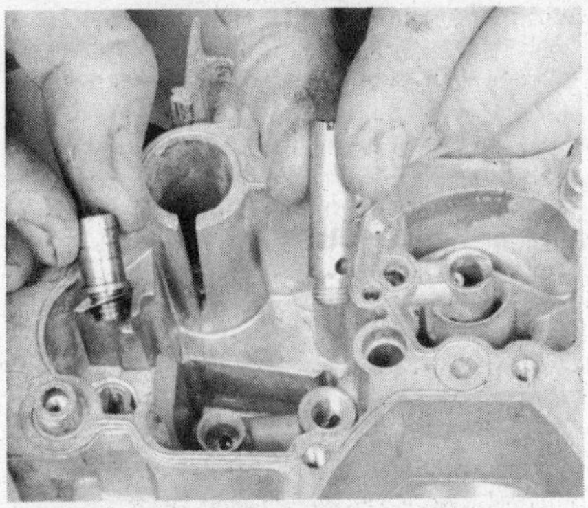

15.20 On E2SE carburetors, remove the float valve seat and gasket and the extended metering jet from the float bowl

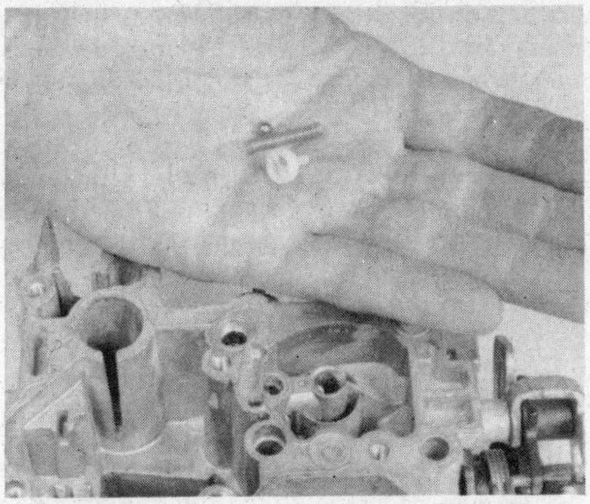

15.22 When removing the discharge spring and check ball, do not pry on the white plastic retainer

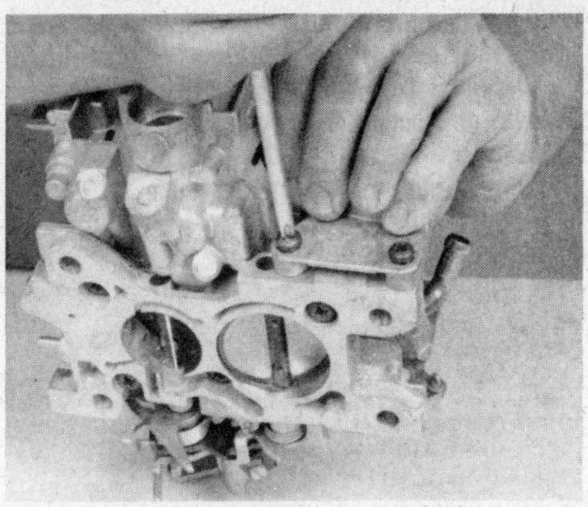

15.23 Removing the choke housing-to-throttle body screws

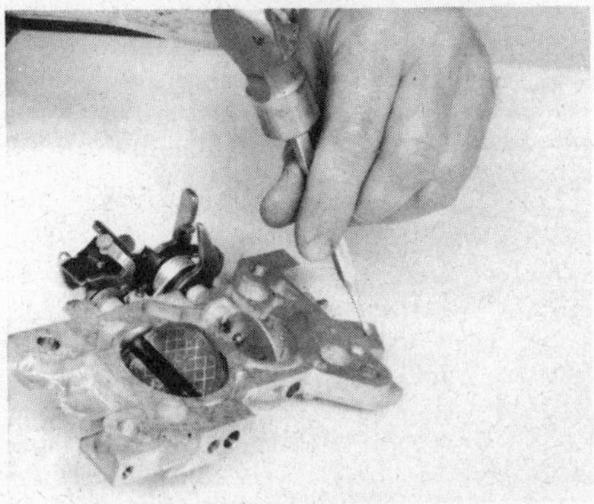

15.28 Use a punch to break out the throttle body casting, then drive out the idle mixture needle cover plug

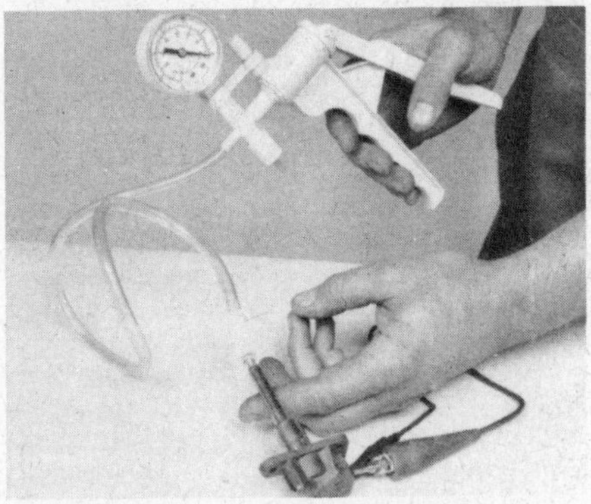

15.41 Testing the mixture control solenoid with a vacuum pump

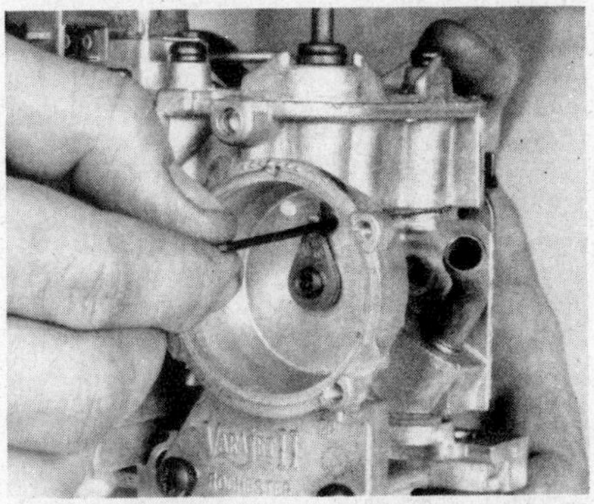

15.49 Installing the thermostatic coil lever with an Allen wrench

28 The plug covering the idle mixture needle should not be removed unless the needle needs replacing or normal cleaning procedures fail to clean the idle mixture passages. If removal is required, use a punch and hammer to drive the plug out (photo).

29 Clean the air horn, float bowl, throttle body and related components with clean solvent and blow them out with compressed air. A can of compressed air such as is available at camera stores can be used if an air compressor is not available. *Do not use a piece of wire for cleaning the jets and passages.*

30 The idle speed solenoid, mixture control solenoid, throttle position sensor, electric choke, pump plunger, diaphragm, plastic filler block and other electrical, rubber and plastic parts should *not* be immersed in carburetor cleaner, as they will harden, swell or distort.

31 Make sure all fuel passages, jets and other metering parts are free of burrs and dirt.

32 Inspect the upper and lower surfaces of the air horn, float bowl and throttle body for damage. Be sure all material has been removed.

33 Inspect all lever holes and plastic bushings for excessive wear and out-of-round conditions and replace if necessary.

34 Inspect the float valve and seat for dirt, deep wear grooves and scoring and replace if necessary.

35 Inspect the float valve pull clip for proper installation and adjust if necessary.

36 Inspect the float, float arms and hinge pin for distortion or binding and correct or replace as necessary.

37 Inspect the rubber cup on the pump plunger for excessive wear or cracking.

38 Check the choke valve and linkage for excessive wear, binding or distortion and correct or replace as necessary.

39 Inspect the choke vacuum diaphragm for leaks and replace if necessary.

40 Check the choke valve for freedom of movement.

41 Check the mixture control solenoid for binding or leaking in the following manner:

a) Connect one end of a jumper wire to either end of the solenoid connector and the other end to the positive terminal of a battery.
b) Connect another jumper wire between the other terminal of the solenoid connector and either the negative terminal of a battery or a ground.
c) Remove the rubber seal and retainer from the end of the solenoid stem and attach a hand vacuum pump to it (photo).
d) With the solenoid fully energized (lean position), apply at least 25 Hg-in of vacuum and time the leak-down rate from 20 Hg-in to 15 Hg-in. The leak-down rate should not exceed five (5) Hg-in in five (5) seconds. If leakage exceeds that amount, replace the solenoid.
e) To check if the solenoid is sticking in the down position, again pump about 25 Hg-in of vacuum into it, then disconnect the jumper lead to the battery and watch the pump gauge reading. It should fall to zero in less than one (1) second.

42 Prior to reassembling the carburetor, compare all old and new gaskets back-to-back to be sure they match perfectly. Check especially that all the necessary holes are present and in the proper position in the new gaskets.

43 If the idle mixture needle and spring have been removed, reinstall by lightly seating the needle, then back it off three (3) turns. This will provide a preliminary idle mixture adjustment. Final idle mixture adjustment must be made after the carburetor is installed on the vehicle.

44 Install a new gasket on the bottom of the float bowl.

45 Mount the throttle body on the float bowl so that it is properly aligned over the locating dowels on the bowl and reinstall the attaching screws, tightening them evenly and securely. Be sure that the steps on the fast idle cam face toward the fast idle screw on the throttle lever when installed.

46 Inspect the linkage to make sure that the lockout tang properly engages in the slot of the secondary lockout lever and that the linkage moves freely without binding.

47 Attach the choke housing to the throttle body, making sure the locating lug on the rear of the housing sits in its recess in the float bowl.

48 Install the intermediate choke shaft and lever assembly into the float bowl by pushing it through from the throttle lever side.

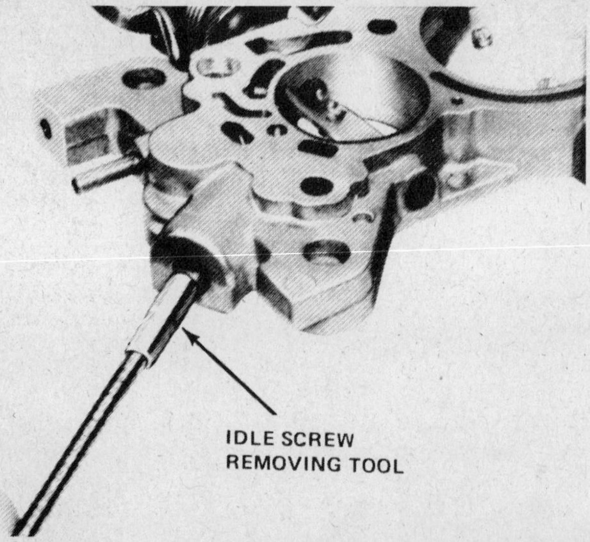

Fig. 4.60 Removing the idle mixture screw (2SE/E2SE carburetor) (Sec 15)

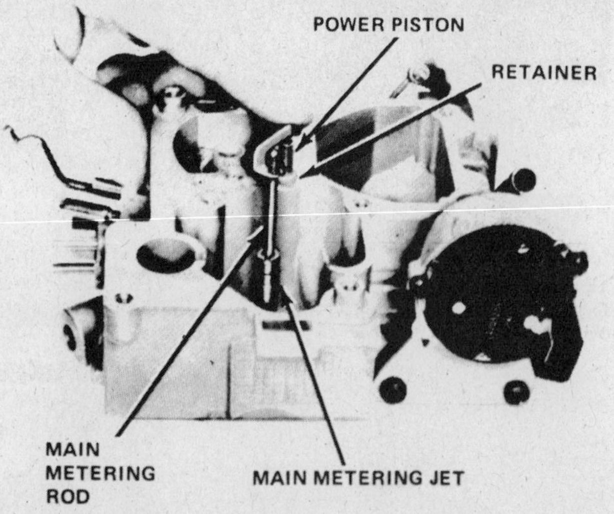

Fig. 4.61 Power piston removal (2SE/E2SE carburetor) (Sec 15)

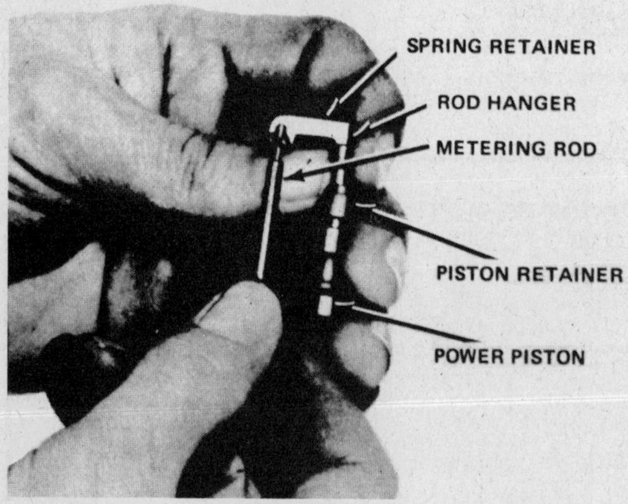

Fig. 4.62 Remove the metering rod from the 2SE carburetor power piston by compressing the spring on the top and aligning the groove with the slot in the holder (Sec 15)

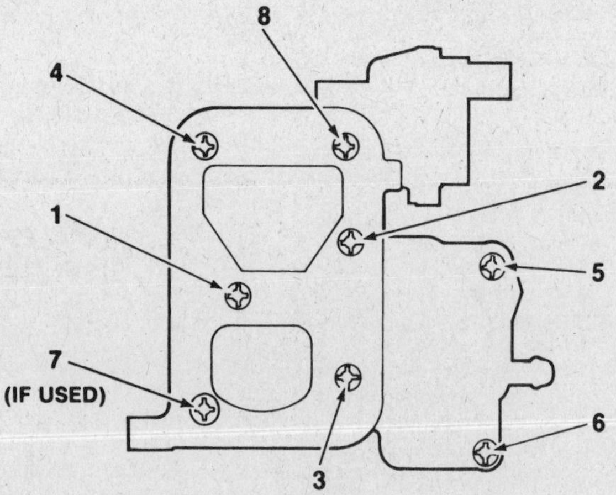

Fig. 4.63 Air horn screw tightening sequence (2SE/E2SE carburetor) (Sec 15)

49 Position the intermediate choke lever in the up position and install the thermostatic coil lever onto the end sticking into the choke housing. The coil lever is properly aligned when the coil pick-up tang is in the 12 o'clock position (photo). Install the attaching screw in the end of the intermediate shaft to secure the coil lever.
50 Three self-tapping screws supplied in the overhaul kit are used in place of the original pop rivets to secure the choke cover and coil assembly to the choke housing. Start the three screws into the housing, checking that they start easily and are properly aligned (photo), then remove them again.
51 Place the fast idle screw on the highest step of the fast idle cam, then install the choke cover on the housing, aligning the notch in the cover with the raised casting projection on the housing cover flange.
52 When installing the cover, be sure the coil pick-up tang engages the inside choke lever.
53 With the choke cover in place, install the three self-tapping screws and tighten them securely.
54 Install the pump discharge check ball and spring in the passage next to the float chamber, then place a new plastic retainer in the hole so that its end engages the spring and tap it lightly into place until the retainer top is flush with the bowl surface.
55 Install the main metering jet in the bottom of the float chamber.
56 Install the float valve seat assembly with its gasket.
57 To make float level adjustments easier, bend the float arm up slightly at the notch shown in the photo before installing.
58 Attach the float valve to the float arm by sliding the lever under the pull clip. The correct installation of the pull clip is to hook the clip over the edge of the float on the float arm facing the float pontoon (photo). Install the float retaining pin in the float arm, then install the float assembly by aligning the valve in its seat and the float retaining pin in its locating channels in the float bowl.

Float level adjustment

59 Adjust the float level in the following manner. While holding the float retaining pin firmly in place, push down on the float arm at its outer end, against the top of the float valve, so the top of the float is the specified distance from the float bowl surface. Bend the float arm as necessary to achieve the proper measurement by pushing down on the pontoon. See the Specifications for the proper float measurement for your vehicle. Visually check the float level following adjustment.

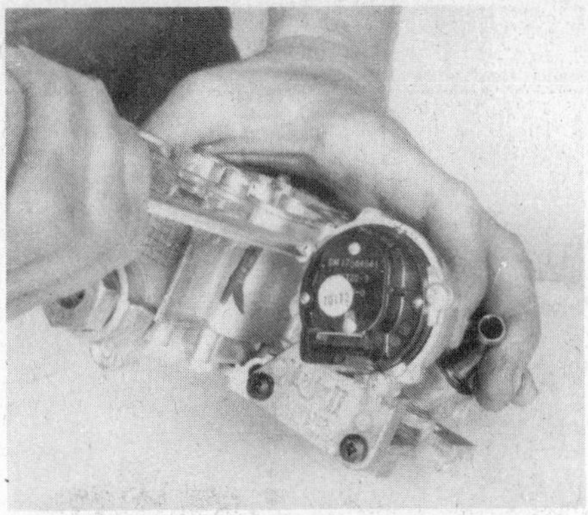

15.50 Reinstalling the choke cover using the self-tapping screws supplied with the overhaul kit

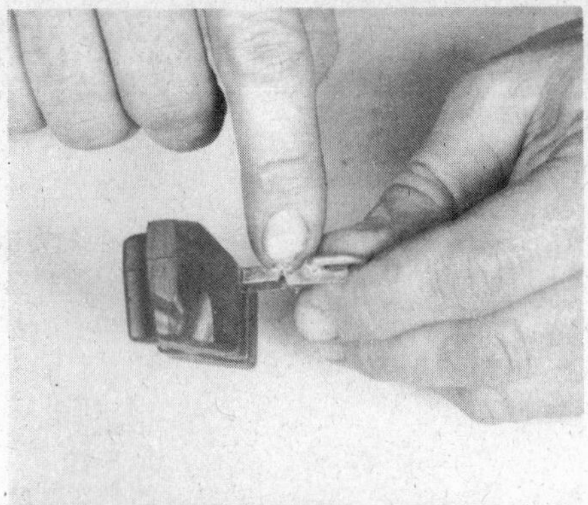

15.57 Prior to installation, bend the float arm slightly at the point indicated

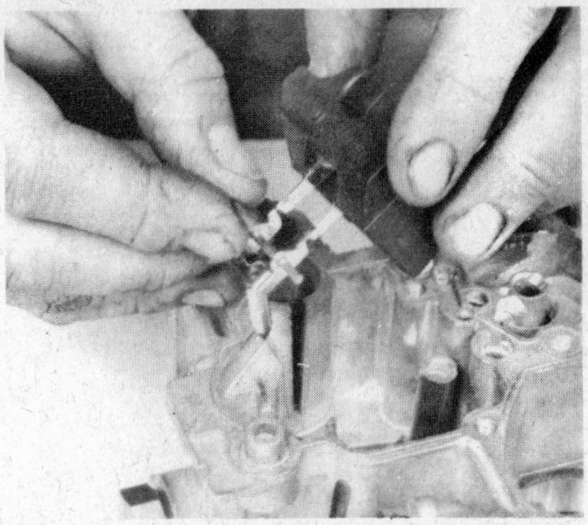

15.58 During installation the float valve should be positioned on the arm as shown

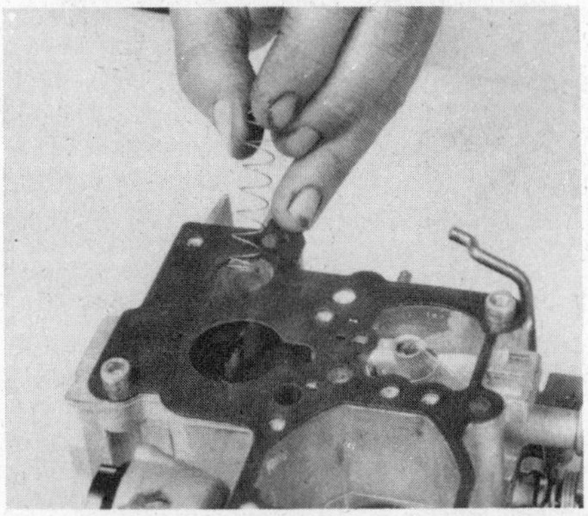

15.64 Installing the pump return spring into the pump well

15.65 Installing the pump plunger into the pump well

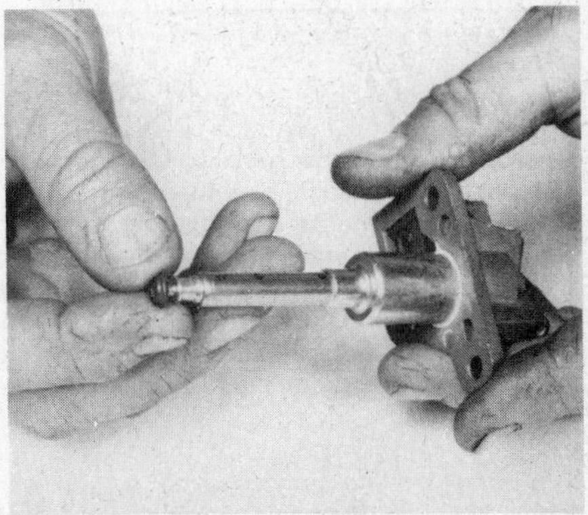

15.73 Fitting a new rubber seal onto the end of the mixture control solenoid

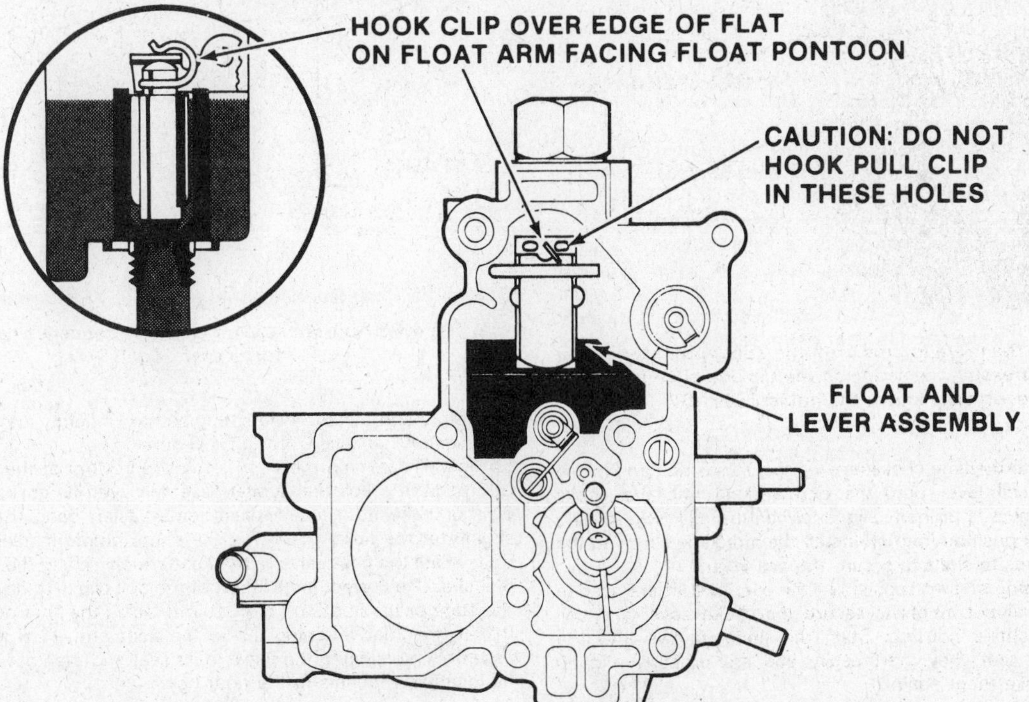
HOOK CLIP OVER EDGE OF FLAT
ON FLOAT ARM FACING FLOAT PONTOON
CAUTION: DO NOT
HOOK PULL CLIP
IN THESE HOLES
FLOAT AND
LEVER ASSEMBLY

Fig. 4.64 Float needle pull clip installation (2SE/E2SE carburetor) (Sec 15)

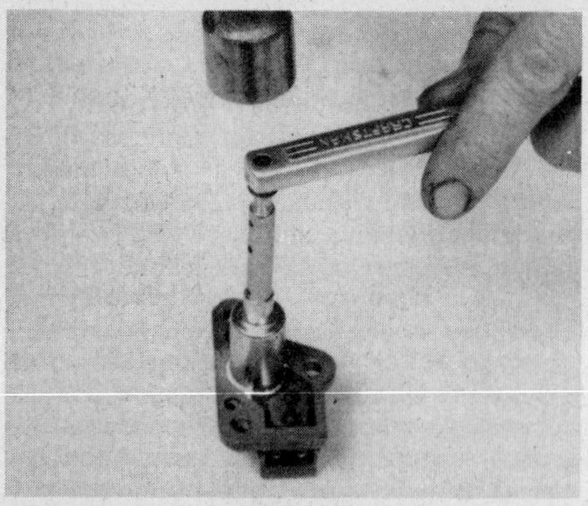

15.74 Tap the seal onto the mixture control stem using a hammer and socket

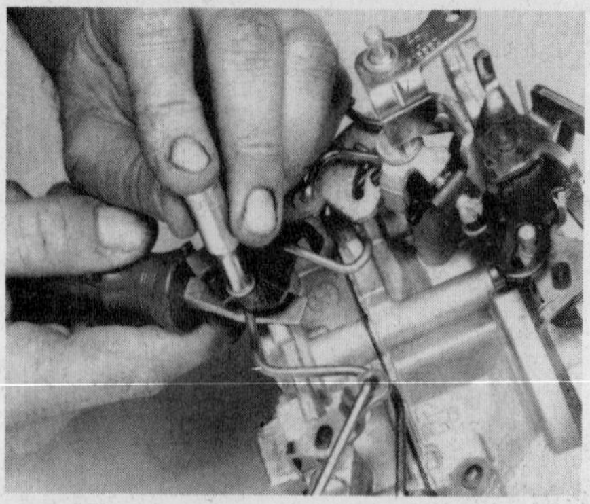

15.77 Install the retaining clip onto the intermediate choke rod to secure the choke lever

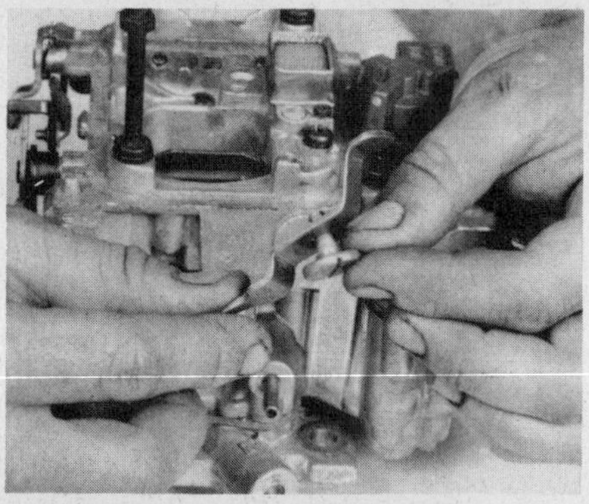

15.79 Inserting the pump rod mounting screw through the pump rod prior to installation

60 On 2SE carbs, install the power piston spring into the piston bore. If the metering rod has been removed from the power piston assembly, reinstall the rod into its holder, making sure the spring is on top of the arm. Then install the assembly in the float bowl. Use care when installing the metering rod into the main metering jet so as not to damage the metering rod tip. Press down firmly on the power piston's plastic retainer until it is firmly seated in its recess and the top is flush with the top of the bowl casting. Light tapping may be required.
61 Install the plastic filler block over the float valve so that it is flush with the float bowl surface.
62 If the carb is equipped with a throttle position sensor, install the TPS return spring in the bottom of the well in the float bowl. Then install the TPS connector assembly by aligning the groove in the electrical connector with the slot in the float bowl. When properly installed, the assembly should sit below the float bowl surface.
63 Install a new air horn gasket on the float bowl.
64 Install the pump return spring in the pump well (photo).
65 Reassemble the pump plunger assembly, lubricate the plunger cap with a thin coat of engine oil, and install the pump plunger in the pump well (photo).
66 If used, remove the old pump plunger seal and retainer and the old TPS plunger seal and retainer in the air horn. Install new seals and retainers in both locations and lightly stake both seal retainers in three places other than the original staking locations.
67 Install the fast idle cam rod into the lower hole of the choke lever.
68 If so equipped, apply a light coating of silicone grease or engine oil on the TPS plunger and push it through its seal in the air horn, so that about one-half of the plunger extends above the seal.
69 Prior to installing the air horn, apply a light coating of silicone grease or engine oil to the pump plunger stem to aid in slipping it through its seal in the air horn.
70 Rotate the fast idle cam to the up position so it can be engaged with the lower end of the fast idle cam rod and, while holding down on the pump plunger assembly, carefully lower the air horn onto the

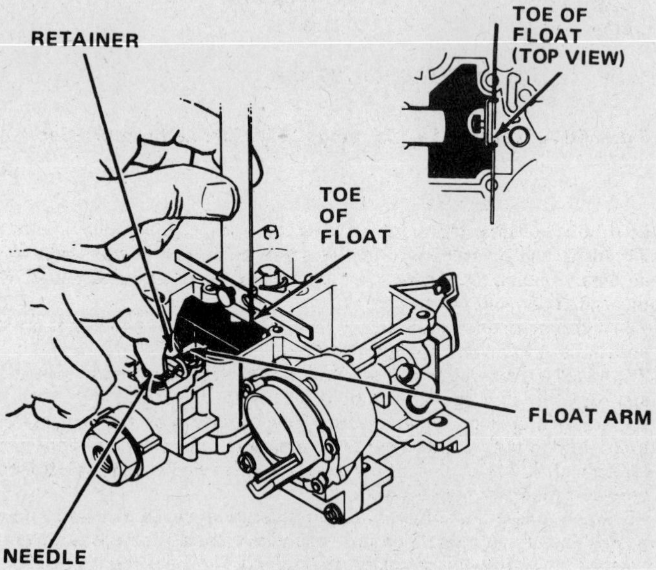

Fig. 4.65 Float level adjustment (2SE/E2SE carburetor) (Sec 15)

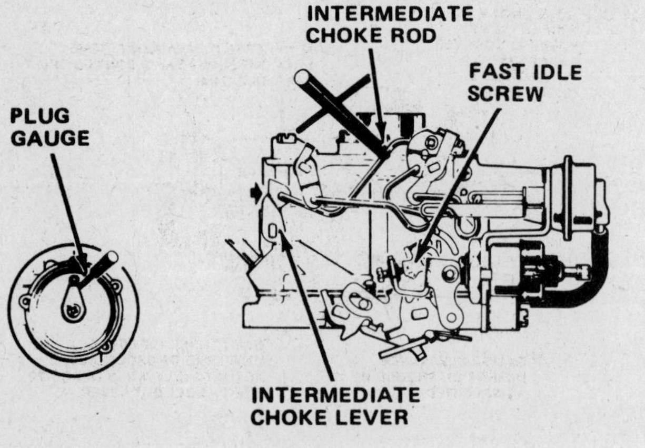

Fig. 4.66 Choke coil lever adjustment (2SE/E2SE carburetor) (Sec 15)

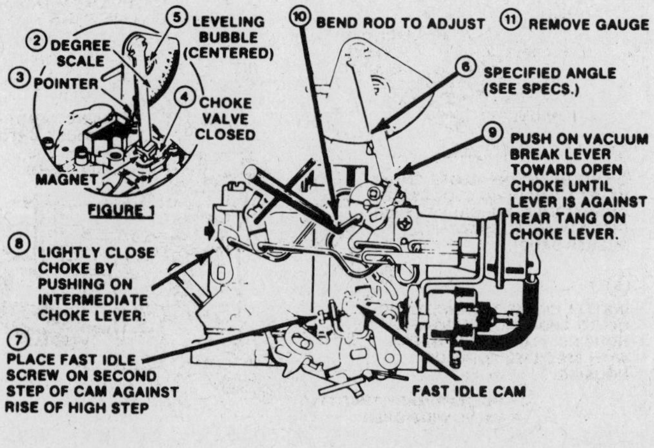

Fig. 4.67 Fast idle cam position (2SE/E2SE carburetor) (Sec 15)

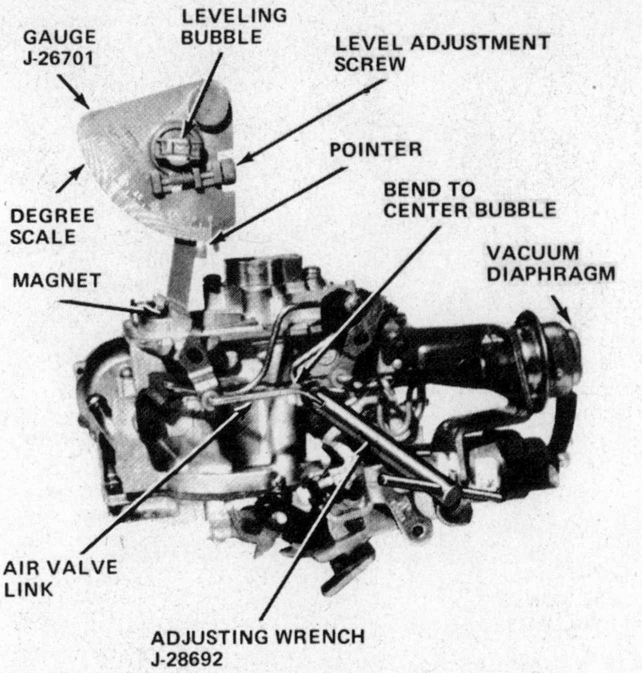

Fig. 4.68 Air valve rod adjustment (2SE/E2SE carburetor) (Sec 15)

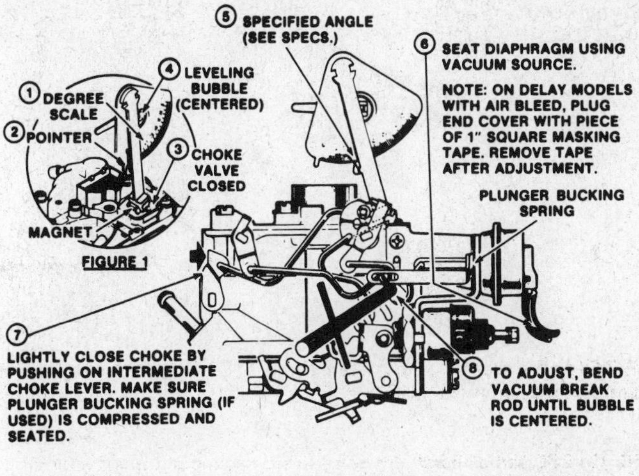

Fig. 4.69 Primary vacuum break adjustment (2SE/E2SE carburetor) (Sec 15)

float bowl, guiding the pump plunger stem through its seal.

71 Install the six air horn attaching screws and lock washers and two air cleaner bolts, tightening them in the proper sequence as shown in the accompanying illustration.

72 If so equipped, install a new seal in the recess of the float bowl and the hot idle compensator valve.

73 Install a new rubber seal on the end of the mixture control solenoid stem until it is up against the boss on the stem (photo).

74 Using a $\frac{3}{16}$-inch socket or other appropriate tool and a hammer (photo) drive the retainer over the mixture control solenoid stem just far enough to retain the rubber seal, while leaving a slight clearance between them for seal expansion.

75 Apply a light coat of engine oil on the rubber seal and, using a new gasket, install the mixture control solenoid in the air horn. Use a slight twisting motion while installing the solenoid to help the rubber seal slip into its recess.

76 Install the vent/screen assembly onto the air horn.

77 Install a plastic bushing in the hole in the choke lever with the small end facing out. Then with the intermediate choke lever at the 12 o'clock position, install the intermediate choke rod in the bushing. Install a new retaining clip on the end of the rod. An effective way of doing this is to use a broad regular screwdriver and a $\frac{3}{16}$-inch socket as shown in the photo. Make sure the clip is not seated tightly against the bushing and that the linkage moves freely.

78 Engage the vacuum break rod with the inside vacuum break diaphragm plunger and the air valve rod with the outside plunger and mount the idle speed solenoid/vacuum break diaphragm assembly.

79 Engage the pump rod with the pump rod lever and mount the pump lever on the air horn with its washer in between the lever and the air horn (photo).

80 Reconnect the vacuum break diaphragm hose to its fitting on the carburetor body.

81 Install the fuel filter so that the hole faces toward the inlet nut.

82 Place a new gasket on the inlet nut and install the nut. Be careful not to overtighten the nut, as this could damage the gasket and cause a fuel leak.

83 Install a new gasket on the top of the air horn.

Idle speed and mixture adjustment

84 Prior to adjusting the idle speed or mixture, the following precautions must be taken and conditions exist:

Parking brake securely set
Engine at normal operating temperature
Transmission in Drive (automatic) or Neutral (manual)
Tachometer connected to the ignition coil or pigtail wire connector

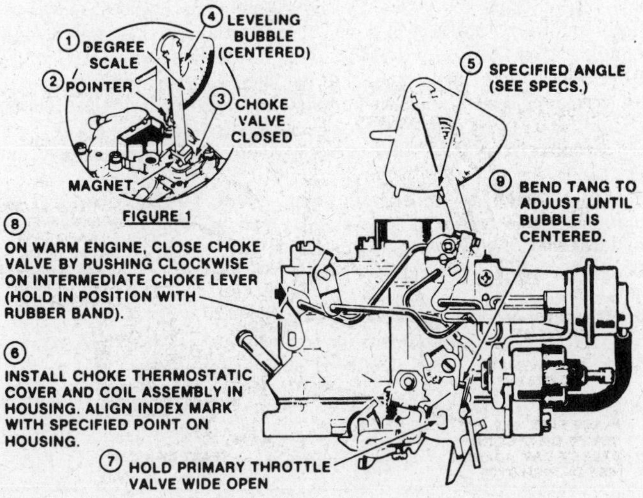

Fig. 4.70 Choke unloader adjustment (2SE/E2SE carburetor) (Sec 15)

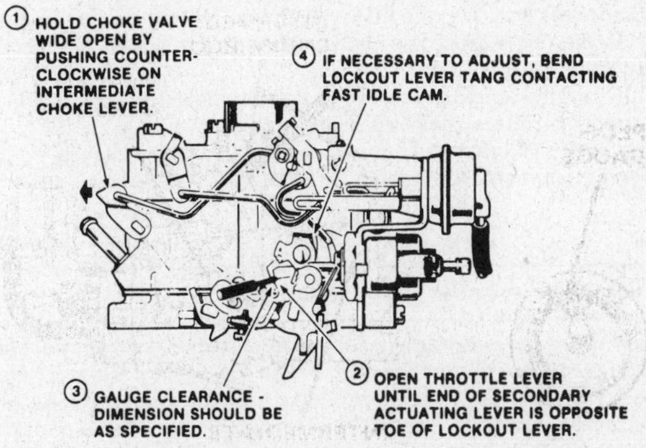

Fig. 4.71 Secondary lockout adjustment (2SE/E2SE carburetor) (Sec 15)

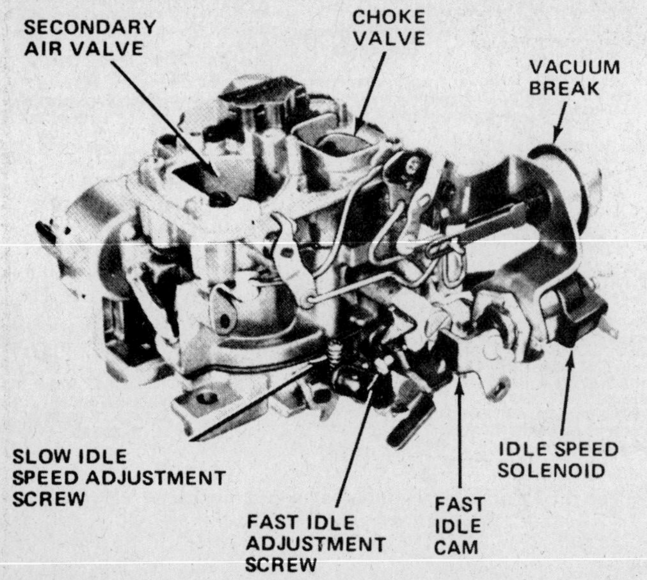

Fig. 4.72 2SE carburetor external component locations (Sec 15)

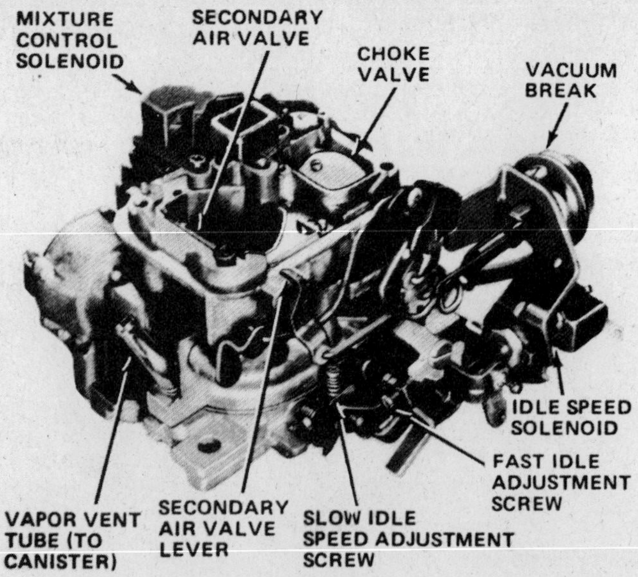

Fig. 4.73 E2SE carburetor adjustment locations (Sec 15)

The air cleaner should be installed and all hoses connected or, if removed, the hoses should be plugged and the choke plate must be open
The air-conditioner compressor wire must be unplugged and the deceleration vacuum hose disconnected and plugged
The ignition timing must be correctly adjusted
The engine must not be operated at idle for more than three (3) minutes

85 Disconnect and plug the distributor vacuum hose and connect a timing light to the engine.
86 Adjust the ignition timing with the engine at or below the specified idle speed.
87 Connect the distributor vacuum hose and remove the timing light.
88 Disconnect the deceleration valve and purge hose from the vapor canister and plug the hoses. Remove the air cleaner if necessary for access.
89 On air-conditioned models, adjust the idle speed screw to achieve the specified idle speed. Turn the air-conditioning switch on, open the throttle momentarily and make sure the solenoid armature is fully extended. Adjust the solenoid idle screw to achieve the specified idle and turn the air-conditioning switch off.
90 On non-air-conditioned models, obtain the specified idle speed by adjusting the solenoid idle screw with the solenoid energized. Disconnect the solenoid wire connector and adjust the idle speed screw to obtain the specified idle speed. Reconnect the solenoid wire.
91 Disconnect and plug the EGR valve hose. With the fast idle speed screw on the top step of the fast idle speed cam, adjust the fast idle speed to the specified rpm.
92 Turn off the engine, remove the tachometer and reinstall any components or hoses removed during this procedure.
93 The fuel mixture adjustment on these models requires special tools and equipment and should be left to your dealer or a qualified shop.

16 Fuel tank – removal and installation

Caution: *Gasoline is extremely flammable and extra precautions must be taken when working on any part of the fuel system. Do not smoke or allow open flames or bare light bulbs near the work area. Also, do not work in a garage if a natural gas type appliance with a pilot light is present.*

1 The fuel tank is located under the rear of the vehicle and is held in place by brackets and bolts.
2 Disconnect the negative battery cable from the battery.
3 Drain or siphon the fuel from the tank so it will be easier to handle.
4 Raise the rear of the vehicle and support it securely.
5 Mark the locations of all hoses attached to the tank, then remove them.
6 Support the tank with a jack, using a board to protect the tank. Remove the retaining bolts and brackets and lower the tank from the vehicle.
7 To install the tank, carefully raise it into position, install the brackets and tighten the bolts securely.
8 Connect the hoses and lower the vehicle.
9 Connect the negative battery cable.

17 Fuel tank – cleaning and repair

1 Drain and remove the fuel tank.
2 Remove the fuel tank gauge unit by removing the retaining screws.
3 Turn the tank over and empty out any remaining fuel.
4 If repair work must be done on the fuel tank that does not involve any heat or flames, the tank can be satisfactorily cleaned by running hot water into it and letting it overflow out the top for at least five (5) minutes. **This method, however, does not remove gasoline vapors.**
5 If repair work involving heat or flame is necessary, have it done by an experienced professional. The following, more thorough procedures should be used to remove all fuel and vapors from the tank.
6 Fill the tank completely with tap water, agitate vigorously and drain.
7 Add a gasoline emulsifying agent to the tank according to the manufacturer's instructions, refill with water, agitate approximately 10 minutes and drain.
8 Once again, flush to overflowing with water for several minutes and drain.
9 The tank is now ready for repair work.
10 Under no circumstances perform repair work involving heat or flame without first carrying out the above procedures.

18 Exhaust system – component replacement

Caution: *Inspection and repair of exhaust system components should be done only after enough time has elapsed after driving the vehicle to allow the system components to cool completely. Also, when working under the vehicle, make sure it is securely supported on jackstands.*

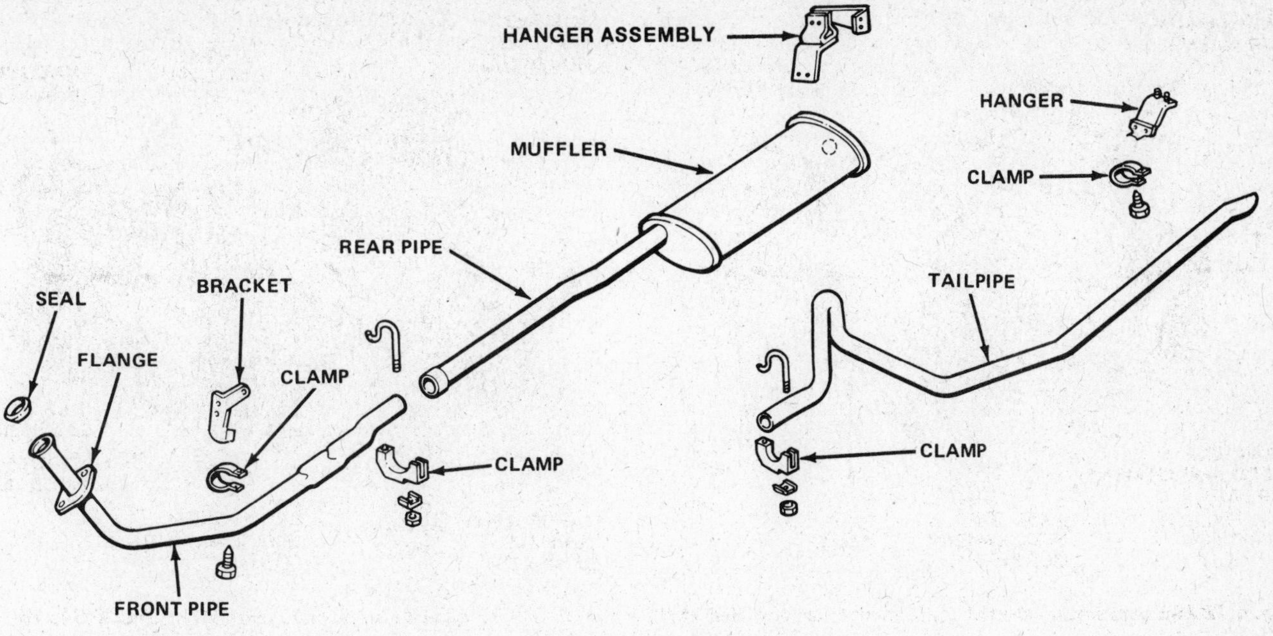

Fig. 4.74 Typical early model exhaust system components (Sec 18)

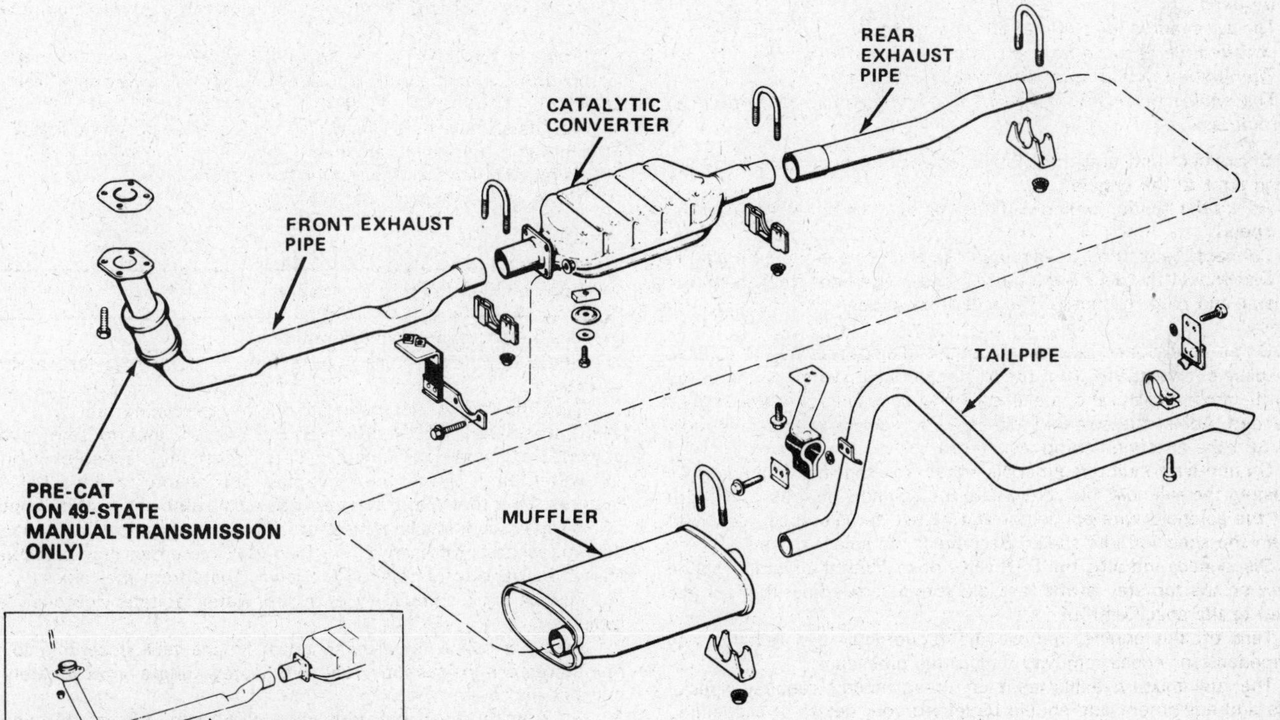

Fig. 4.75 Later model four-cylinder exhaust system and catalytic converter (Sec 18)

1 The exhaust system consists of the exhaust manifold, muffler, catalytic converter (if equipped), tailpipe and connecting pipes, brackets, hangers and clamps. The entire exhaust system is attached to the body or frame with mounting brackets and rubber hangers. If any one of the parts is improperly installed, excessive noise and vibration will be transmitted to the body.

2 Regular inspection of the exhaust system should be made to keep it safe and quiet. Look for any damaged or bent parts, open seams, holes, loose connections, excessive corrosion or other defects. Deteriorated exhaust system components should not be repaired; they should be replaced with new parts. Refer to Chapter 6 for catalytic converter removal and installation procedures.

3 If the components are extremely corroded or rusted together, it may be a good idea to have the work performed by a reputable muffler shop, since welding equipment will probably be required to remove the components.

4 Always work from the back to the front when removing exhaust system components. Penetrating oil applied to mounting bolts and nuts will make them much easier to remove. Always use new gaskets, hangers and clamps and apply anti-seize compound to mounting bolt threads when putting everything back together. Also, when replacing any exhaust system parts, be sure to allow enough clearance from all points on the underbody to avoid overheating the floor pan.

Chapter 5 Engine electrical systems

Contents

Alternator – brush replacement 8
Alternator – removal and installation 7
Battery – emergency jump starting 3
Battery – removal and installation 2
Battery cables – check and replacement 4
Battery check and maintenance See Chapter 1
Charging system – check 5
Contact points and condenser – replacement and adjustment See Chapter 1
Conventional distributor – check 15
Distributor – removal and installation 17
Electronic distributor – check 16
Electronic ignition module – removal and installation 18
Electronic ignition pickup coil – removal and installation 19
Engine drivebelts – check and adjustment See Chapter 1
External voltage regulator – removal and installation 6
General information 1
Ignition coil – removal and installation 14
Ignition system check 13
Ignition timing – check and adjustment See Chapter 1
Integral ignition coil (1980 and 1981 four-cylinder) – removal and installation 15
Spark plug replacement See Chapter 1
Spark plug wires, distributor cap and rotor check and replacement See Chapter 1
Starter motor – brush replacement 11
Starter motor – removal and installation 10
Starter solenoid – removal and installation 12
Starting system – check 9

Specifications

Ignition system type

1980 through 1974 six-cylinder and V8 and 1977 through 1979 four-cylinder	Contact breaker point equipped
1975 through 1983 six-cylinder and V8 and 1980 through 1983 four-cylinder	Electronic

Charging system

Motorcraft alternator output voltage

Temperature (degrees Fahrenheit)	**Acceptable voltage range**
0 to 50	14.8 to 14.1
50 to 100	14.5 to 13.7
100 to 150	14.2 to 13.4
150 to 200	13.8 to 13.1

Ignition system

Coil resistance at 75°F	
Primary coil resistance (six-cylinder and V8)	
1970 through 1974	1.4 to 2.0 ohms
1975 and 1976	1.0 to 2.0 ohms
1977 and 1978	1.25 to 1.4 ohms
1979	1.6 to 1.8 ohms
1980 through 1983	1.13 to 1.23 ohms
Primary coil resistance (four-cylinder)	
1977 through 1979	1.4 to 2.0 ohms
1980 through 1983	Zero or near zero on the low scale
Secondary coil resistance (six-cylinder and V8)	
1970 through 1974	3000 to 20000 ohms
1975	8000 to 12000 ohms
1976 through 1978	9000 to 15000 ohms
1979	8400 to 11700 ohms
1980 through 1983	7700 to 9300 ohms
Secondary coil resistance (four-cylinder)	
1977 through 1979	3000 to 20000 ohms
1980 through 1983	Less than infinity on the high scale

Coil-to-ground resistance (1980 through 1983 four-cylinder)	Infinity
Distributor ignition pickup resistance	
1975 through 1977 six-cylinder and V8	1.6 to 2.4 ohms
1978 through 1983 six-cylinder and V8	400 to 800 ohms
1980 through 1983 four-cylinder	500 to 1500 ohms
Connector-to-ground resistance (1980 through 1983 four-cylinder)	Infinity
Primary voltage (no load)	
1975 through 1977 six-cylinder and V8	6 volts
All others	12 volts

Starting system

Cranking voltage test	
1975 through 1977 six-cylinder and V8	
Switch-on voltage	12 to 13 volts
Cranking voltage	9.6 volts
1978 through 1983 six-cylinder and V8 and 1980 through 1983 four-cylinder cranking voltage	6 volts
Starter motor	
Brush length	0.5 in
Brush wear limit	0.25 in
Brush spring tension	40 oz

Torque specifications

Torque specifications	Ft-lb	Nm
Alternator bracket-to-engine	23 to 30	31 to 41
Alternator pivot bolt	20 to 24	27 to 30
Starter motor-to-bellhousing	15 to 20	21 to 28
Starter solenoid terminal nuts	55 in-lb	6
Distributor clamp bolt	14 to 17	19 to 23

1 General information

The engine electrical system consists of the starting, charging and ignition systems.

The starting system is made up of the battery, the starter solenoid, the starter motor and the attendant wiring. Automatic transmission equipped models feature a Neutral start switch in the system to prevent starting except when in Neutral or Park.

The charging system consists of the alternator, voltage regulator, battery and associated wires and cables. On later models the voltage regulator is an integral part of the alternator.

The ignition system consists of the distributor, coil, spark plugs, battery and assocated wiring. Later models use electronic ignition components to perform some of the mechanical functions of the distributor (such as the spark advance for improved performance and emissions).

2 Battery – removal and installation

1 The battery is located in the engine compartment to the right of the engine. It is held in place by a hold-down frame and wing nuts or bolts and clamps at the base of the battery.

2 Because the battery produces hydrogen gas, keep open flames and lighted cigarettes away from the battery at all times.

3 Avoid spilling any of the electrolyte on the vehicle or yourself. Always keep the battery in an upright position. Any spilled electrolyte should be immediately flushed with large quantities of water. Wear eye protection when working with the battery to prevent eye damage from splashed electrolyte.

4 Always disconnect the negative (–) battery cable first, followed by the positive (+) cable.

5 After the cables are disconnected from the battery, remove the clamp bolts or wing nuts and hold-down frame.

6 Carefully lift the battery from the tray and out of the engine compartment.

7 Prior to installation, make sure the negative cable is properly grounded with a secure connection.

8 Place the battery in position in the tray and apply a thin coat of light grease or petroleum jelly to the posts.

9 Connect the positive cable first, followed by the negative cable.

10 Install the retaining clamps and bolts or hold-down frame, taking care not to over-tighten them (which would distort the battery).

3 Battery – emergency jump starting

Refer to the Booster battery (jump) starting procedure at the front of this manual for this procedure.

4 Battery cables – check and replacement

1 Periodically inspect the full length of each battery cable for damage, cracked insulation and corrosion. Poor battery cable connection can cause starting system failure and decreased engine performance.

2 Check the cable-to-terminal connections at the ends of the cables for breaks, loose strands and corrosion. The presence of white fluffy deposits under the insulation at the cable terminal connection is a sign that the cable is corroded and should be replaced. Check the terminals for distortion, missing bolts or nuts and corrosion.

3 When removing the cables, always disconnect the negative (–) cable from the battery first. If only the positive cable is being replaced, disconnect the negative cable first.

4 Disconnect and remove the cable(s) from the battery and engine/body. Make sure the replacement cable(s) is of the same length and thickness.

5 Clean the threads of the starter or ground cable connection with a wire brush to remove any rust or corrosion. Apply a light coat of petroleum jelly to the threads for ease of installation and to prevent future corrosion. Inspect these connections to ensure that they are secure and will provide good electrical continuity.

6 Attach the cable(s) to the starter or ground and tighten the retaining nut(s) securely.

7 Before connecting the new cable(s) to the battery, make sure they reach their respective terminals without stretching.

8 Connect the positive cable first, followed by the negative cable, tighten the nuts and apply a thin coat of petroleum jelly to the terminal and cable connections.

5 Charging system – check

1 When a problem develops in the charging system, the first check should be for the obvious. Inspect all wires for damage, corrosion and loose connections. Check the drivebelts to make sure they are in good condition and properly tensioned (see Chapter 1 for more information).

2 If the charging system is not working properly (indicated by the warning light staying on, ammeter showing discharge or a battery that is constantly discharged or overcharged), the alternator output should be checked.

Motorcraft alternator

3 Connect a voltmeter to the battery with the voltmeter positive lead on the positive terminal and negative lead on the negative terminal.

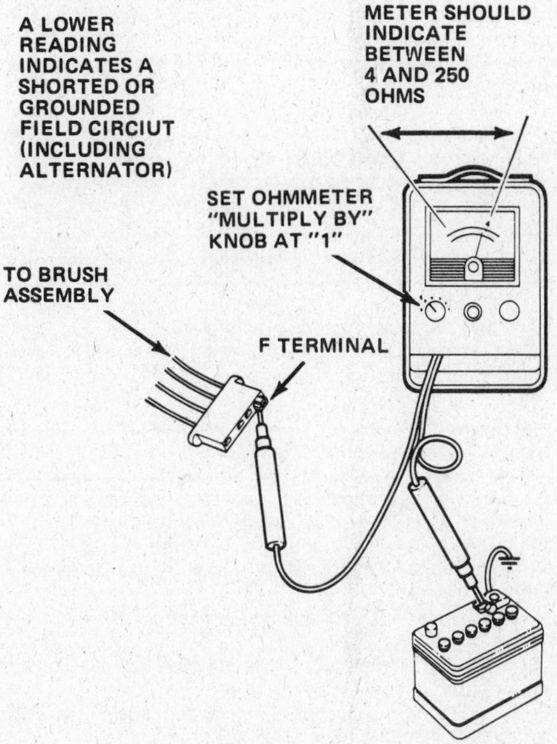
A LOWER READING INDICATES A SHORTED OR GROUNDED FIELD CIRCIUT (INCLUDING ALTERNATOR)
METER SHOULD INDICATE BETWEEN 4 AND 250 OHMS
SET OHMMETER "MULTIPLY BY" KNOB AT "1"
TO BRUSH ASSEMBLY
F TERMINAL

Fig. 5.1 Checking the Motorcraft alternator charging system for an open circuit (Sec 5)

4 Apply a load to the system by turning on the headlights and heater or air conditioner blower motor.

5 Start the engine and slowly increase the speed to approximately 2000 rpm.

6 When the voltage stabilizes, compare the reading to the chart in the Specifications. If the reading is correct, the alternator (and charging system) is operating properly. If the reading is high, the system is overcharging and if it is low, it is undercharging. Proceed with the appropriate checks to verify the conditions and locate the fault.

Undercharging

7 If the system is undercharging, turn off the engine and accessories and note the battery voltage at the terminals.

8 Start the engine, turn on the electrical accessories and slowly increase the engine speed to approximately 2000 rpm.

9 Note the voltage reading and compare it to the one taken in Step 7. If the reading has increased at least 0.5 volt, the charging system

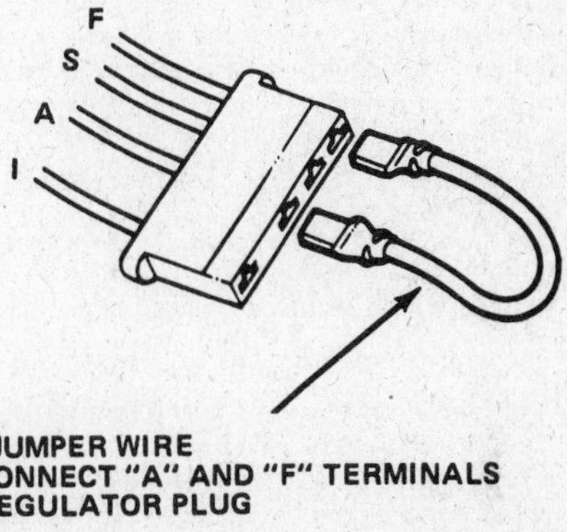
F
S
A
I
USE JUMPER WIRE TO CONNECT "A" AND "F" TERMINALS AT REGULATOR PLUG

Fig. 5.2 Using a jumper wire on the voltage regulator plug (Motorcraft alternator) (Sec 5)

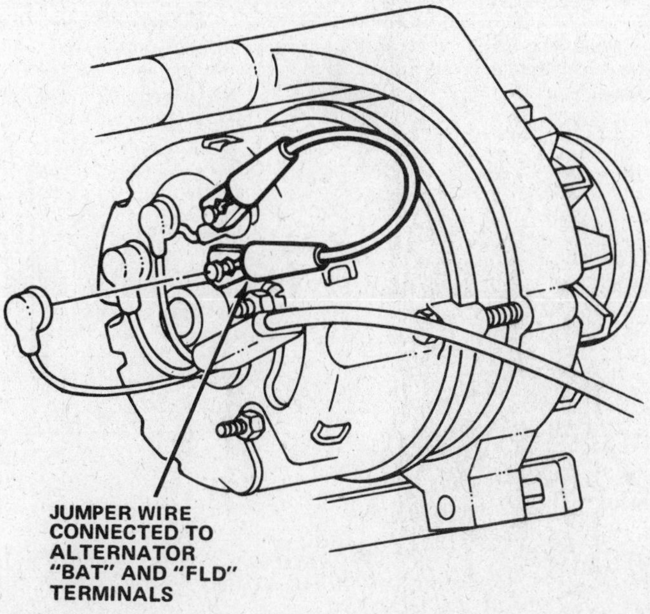
JUMPER WIRE CONNECTED TO ALTERNATOR "BAT" AND "FLD" TERMINALS

Fig. 5.3 Motorcraft alternator jumper wire connections (Sec 5)

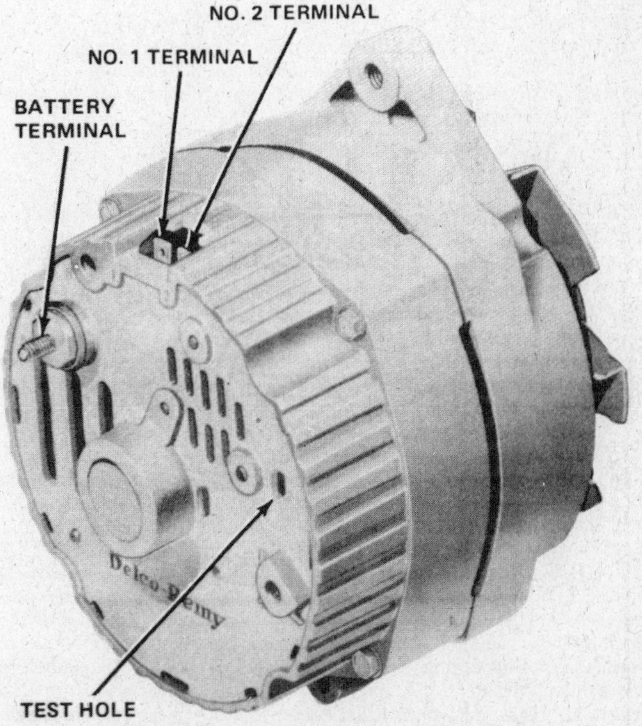
NO. 2 TERMINAL
NO. 1 TERMINAL
BATTERY TERMINAL
TEST HOLE

Fig. 5.4 Typical Delco alternator check connections (Sec 5)

is operating properly. If the increase is less than 0.5 volt, the system is undercharging.

10 If the test indicates undercharging, turn the ignition switch on and check for battery voltage at the voltage regulator S terminal. If there is no voltage, or if it is less than that of the battery, check the yellow wire for an open circuit and for a faulty connection at the regulator or the starter solenoid.

11 If no fault is found, disconnect the voltage regulator wire connector and attach one lead of the ohmmeter to the F terminal and the other to a good ground as shown in the accompanying illustration. The ohmmeter reading should be less than 250 ohms and more than four (4) ohms. If the reading is not as specified, the alternator should be replaced or overhauled.

12 If the reading is as specified, connect the ohmmeter between the I and F terminals of the voltage regulator. No resistance should be indicated. If the reading is approximately ten (10) ohms, the regulator is damaged and should be replaced with a new one.

13 To further check the voltage regulator, connect a jumper wire between the A and F terminals of the plug as shown in the accompanying illustration. Repeat the tests in Steps 7 through 9 and if undercharging is indicated, replace the voltage regulator.

14 If the output is as specified, disconnect the jumper wire, leaving the voltage regulator connector unplugged. Disconnect the wiring harness from the alternator field (FLD) terminal and connect a jumper wire between the battery (BAT) and FLD terminals as shown in the accompanying illustration.

15 Repeat the tests in Steps 7 through 9. If the output is as specified, there is a fault in the wiring harness and it should be replaced. If the output is low, there is a fault in the alternator and it should be replaced or overhauled.

Overcharging

16 Connect a voltmeter positive lead to the battery positive terminal and negative lead to the negative terminal. With all electrical accessories turned off, note the voltmeter reading.

17 Start the engine and slowly increase its speed to approximately 1500 rpm. The voltage should increse no more than two (2) volts over the reading noted in the previous Step. If it does increase more than two volts, the overcharging condition is verified.

18 Disconnect the voltage regulator wiring connector and repeat the test. If the voltage is within the specified range, the regulator is faulty and must be replaced with a new one. If the voltage reading is still high, the alternator wiring harness has a short and should be replaced.

Delco alternator

19 These alternators feature an integral voltage regulator and most testing of the charging system requires special equipment. Simple checks for undercharging and overcharging conditions can be made with a voltmeter.

Undercharging

20 With the ignition switch on, check between the alternator No. 1, No. 2 and battery (BAT) terminals and a good ground with a voltmeter. A zero reading indicates an open circuit between the lead connection and the battery. The vehicle should be taken to a properly equipped shop for further testing because of the special equipment and techniques required.

Overcharging

21 Connect the voltmeter between the No. 2 terminal and a ground. If the reading is zero, the No. 2 circuit is open. If the voltmeter reads the correct voltage and an obvious overcharging condition still exists, there is a fault in the alternator.

Motorola alternator

22 Connect a voltmeter to the battery with the voltmeter positive lead on the positive terminal and the negative lead on the negative terminal.

23 Start the engine and turn the headlights on low beam.

24 Operate the engine at 1000 rpm for approximately two (2) minutes. If the voltage reading remains above 13 volts, the alternator and regulator are operating correctly. If the system is overcharging, the fault is in the regulator or the wiring. Check for improper connections, loose ground wires or a short in the alternator wiring harness before replacing the regulator. If the system is undercharging, perform the following test to determine if the alternator or the regulator is at fault.

25 Disconnect the voltage regulator.

26 Connect an ammeter between the battery positive post and the positive terminal (green wire) of the alternator.

27 No less than 1.5 amps and no more than 3 amps should be indicated on the ammeter.

28 Turn the alternator slowly by hand. If the reading varies, the slip rings must be cleaned. Remove the brush assembly (Section 8) and clean the rings with fine crocus cloth.

29 After verifying the condition of the slip rings and brushes, check the ammeter reading again. If the system is overcharging, there is either a short circuit or the voltage regulator is defective. If the system is still undercharging, perform the next test.

30 With the voltage regulator disconnected, connect a voltmeter to the battery. Connect the positive lead to the positive terminal and the negative lead to the negative terminal.

31 Start the engine and observe the voltage reading while slowly increasing the engine rpm.

32 If 16 volts can be attained, the alternator is not defective. **Caution**: *Do not exceed 16 volts, as damage to the electrical components could result.* If 16 volts cannot be reached, the alternator is defective. Replace the alternator or regulator as necessary.

6 External voltage regulator – removal and installation

1 Unplug the connector, remove the attaching screws and lift the voltage regulator from the engine compartment.

2 To install, place the regulator in position, install the screws and plug in the connector.

7 Alternator – removal and installation

1 Before removing the alternator, make sure the ignition switch is off and the negative cable is disconnected from the battery.

2 Disconnect the electrical leads from the alternator.

3 Loosen the adjusting bolt and pivot bolt nut, then remove the drivebelt from the pulley.

4 Remove the mounting bolts and lift the alternator from the engine compartment.

5 To install, hold the alternator in position, align the holes and install the attaching bolts.

6 Place the drivebelt on the pulley, adjust the tension, and tighten the adjusting and attaching bolts (see Chapter 1).

7 Connect the electrical leads to the alternator.

8 Connect the negative cable to the battery.

8 Alternator – brush replacement

1 Worn or damaged brushes can reduce the alternator output. The brushes generally do not require replacement because of wear until the vehicle has covered considerable mileage (generally over 75 000 miles).

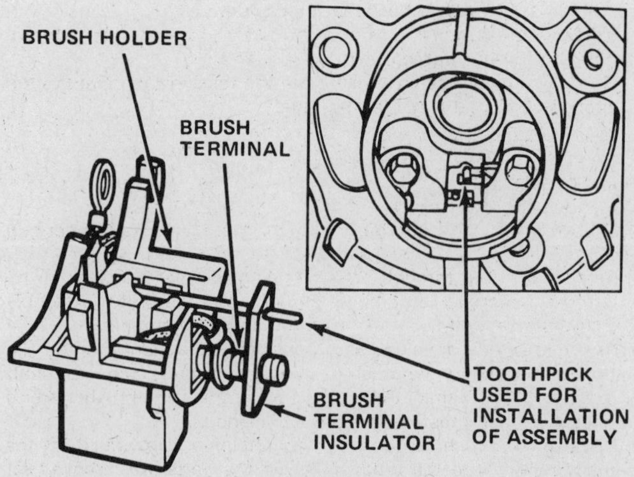

Fig. 5.5 Using a toothpick to retract the brushes on the Motorcraft alternator (Sec 8)

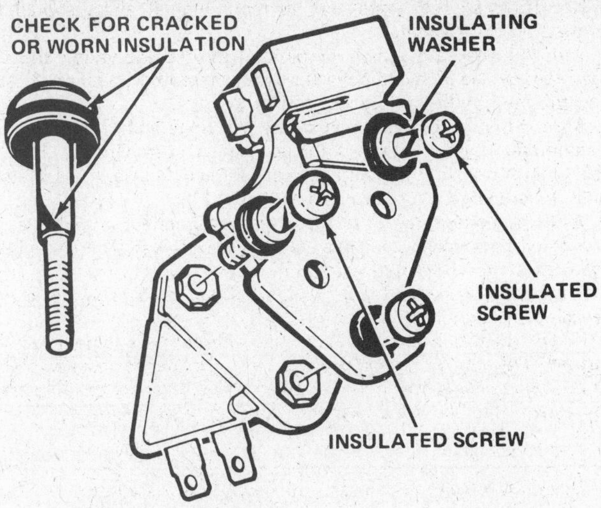

Fig. 5.6 Delco alternator brush holder inspection (Sec 8)

Motorola alternator

2 On these models the brush assembly can be replaced with the alternator in place in the vehicle. *Disconnect the negative (–) cable from the battery before proceeding*

3 Disconnect the field lead from the alternator.

4 Remove the two self-tapping retaining screws and the brush assembly cover.

5 Pull the brush assembly back carefully until it just clears the locating pins, tip it away from the housing and remove it. *Do not pull the assembly straight back as the brushes can break off and fall into the alternator.*

6 Installation is the reverse of removal.

Motorcraft alternator

7 Remove the alternator (Section 7) and scribe a line along the housing to assure correct reassembly. Remove the three housing through-bolts and the nuts and insulators from the rear housing. Make a careful note of the insulator locations.

8 Withdraw the rear housing section from the alternator.

9 Remove the brushes and springs from the brush holder assembly, which is located inside the rear housing.

10 Install the springs and brushes into the holder assembly and retain them by inserting a toothpick through the rear housing as shown in the accompanying illustration. Make sure enough of the toothpick protrudes through the rear of the housing that it can be withdrawn later.

11 Attach the stator to the rear housing, rotor and front housing assembly, making sure the scribed marks line up.

12 Install the three housing through-bolts and the rear end insulators and nuts, but do not tighten them.

13 Carefully remove the toothpick from the rear housing and tighten the through-bolts and rear housing nuts.

14 Install the alternator.

Delco alternator

15 Remove the alternator.

16 Scribe marks on the alternator case for alignment reference during reassembly.

17 Remove the four through-bolts retaining the rear housing.

18 Use a screwdriver to carefully pry between the stator assembly and front housing and separate the alternator components.

19 As the rotor and drive end assemblies are separated from the slip ring housing assembly, the brushes will spring out onto the rotor shaft and can become contaminated with grease. If the same brushes are to be reinstalled, they must be thoroughly cleaned.

20 Remove the brush holder assembly retaining screws and lift the assembly away. Note the order in which the parts are removed for ease of reassembly.

21 If the same brushes and holder assembly are to be reinstalled, inspect the brushes for wear and contamination and the brush springs for damage and corrosion. Check the insulating screws for cracked and worn insulation.

22 Install the springs and brushes in the brush holder. The brushes must slide in and out freely after installation, with no binding.

23 Retain the brushes in the holder by inserting a toothpick into the hole at the bottom of the frame.

24 Install the brush holder with the toothpick protruding through the hole in the alternator end frame.

25 Make sure the rotor shaft bearing surfaces are clean and position the housings with the scribe marks aligned. Install the through-bolts and nuts. Remove the toothpick from the holder assembly.

9 Starting system – check

Note: *In order for the starting system to operate, the battery must be in a fully charged condition and the transmission must be in Neutral or Park. If the battery is not fully charged, or if the Neutral start switch is faulty, recharge the battery or make any necessary repairs before trying to diagnose the starting system.*

1 If the starter does not turn, switch on the headlights and turn the key to Start. If the headlights did not come on, or if they dim or go out when the starter is engaged, the battery (see note above) or cable connections are at fault. If the headlights remain bright, but the starter does not crank the engine, there is an open circuit somewhere in the system (some possible locations are the ignition switch and connections, the starter motor brushes and the solenoid). If the solenoid clicks once when the key is turned to Start, the battery and cable connections should be checked. It should be noted that a jammed starter drive, defective starter motor, engine mechanical problems and extremely low outside temperatures can affect starting system operation, but the previously mentioned possible problems are the most common.

2 The most likely cause of starting system problems (and one that is very easy to fix) is loose, corroded or defective battery cables and cable connections. Inspect the cables and check and clean the connections as described in Section 4 of Chapter 1.

3 Also, check the wiring and connections between the solenoid and the ignition switch. Look for broken wires, burned insulation and loose or dirty connections.

Cranking voltage test (1975 through 1983 six-cylinder and V8)

4 The cranking voltage test will indicate whether the system is developing sufficient voltage to operate properly and requires a 0-to-16 volt voltmeter.

5 Connect the voltmeter positive lead to the coil positive terminal and the negative lead to the coil negative terminal (on 1978 and later models, connect the negative lead to an engine ground). 5

6 Turn the ignition switch to the On position and record the voltage reading (1975 through 1977 models only).

7 Crank the engine over and record the voltage reading.

8 If the voltage readings are lower than specified, check the battery, battery cables, ignition switch and the wiring between the battery and coil for damage, corrosion and loose connections.

Cranking voltage test (1980 through 1983 four-cylinder)

9 The vehicle should be taken to a dealer or properly equipped shop for this test because of the special equipment and techniques required.

Voltage drop test

10 Next, attach the meter leads to the battery positive post and the solenoid or starter switch battery terminal. Turn the ignition switch on and note the voltmeter reading. It should be extremely low (approx. 0.2 volts or less). If not, there is excessive resistance (such as a dirty or loose connection) in that part of the circuit.

11 Repeat the test with the voltmeter leads attached to the negative post and the starter motor housing and the leads attached to the solenoid and starter switch battery and motor terminals. Remember, a high voltage reading means excessive resistance in that part of the circuit. Each wire and connector can be checked in the same way.

12 If the voltage drop tests do not produce conclusive results and if you know the battery is good, then it is very likely that the starter motor is defective. It should be replaced with a new or rebuilt unit

(refer to the appropriate Section in this Chapter for removal, installation and brush replacement procedures).

10 Starter motor – removal and installation

1 Disconnect the negative battery cable from the battery.
2 Disconnect the leads from the solenoid or starter switch, marking them as necessary for reinstallation in their original positions. On some models it will be necessary to raise the front of the vehicle and support it securely on jackstands to gain access to the starter motor from underneath the vehicle.
3 Unscrew and remove the starter motor mounting bolts and withdraw them from the engine bellhousing. On 151 cu in four-cylinder engines, take care to remove any spacer shims along with the starter motor and reinstall them in their original positions.
4 Installation is the reverse of removal.

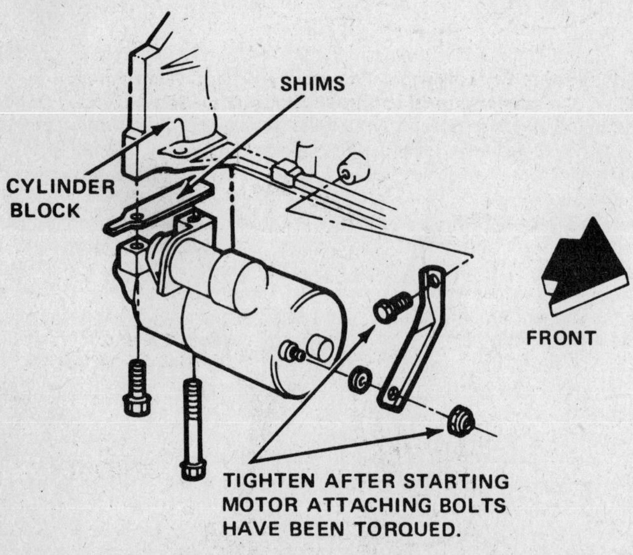

Fig. 5.7 151 cu in four-cylinder engine starter motor and shim installation (Sec 10)

11 Starter motor – brush replacement

1 The starter motor brushes should be replaced after the vehicle has covered considerable mileage (approximately 75 000 miles). Brushes which are worn, damaged or operating with low spring pressure will reduce the starter speed.
2 Remove the starter motor (Section 10)

Prestolite starter motor (in-line six-cylinder and V8)

3 Remove the brush cover band and the starter motor drive yoke cover.
4 Withdraw the brushes from the holders, using a hooked piece of wire to retract the springs. Remove the retaining screws from the leads and lift the brushes from the starter. On some models it will be necessary to remove the through-bolts and disassemble the starter motor for access to the insulated brush leads if the brushes are sufficiently worn to require replacement. Cut off the brush leads as close as possible to the field coil connection.
5 With the brushes removed, check the brush spring tension with a spring scale to make sure it is within the limits specified. Adjust the tension by bending the spring with long-nosed pliers.
6 Solder the insulated brush leads to the field coil, using *rosin* core solder.
7 Pull back the springs with the hooked piece of wire and install the brushes. Connect the electrical lead screws.
8 Reassemble the starter motor and install the brush cover band and drive yoke cover.

Delco 5MT starter motor (151 cu in four-cylinder)

9 Disconnect the field winding connection from the solenoid terminal, remove the starter motor through-bolts, followed by the end frame.
10 Remove the retaining screw and lift out the brush.
11 Inspect the brush holder for distortion and discoloration, indicating overheating which could reduce the tension placed on the brushes. Replace the brush holder with a new one if its condition is suspect.
12 Clean the brush assembly carefully and install the new brush. Check the movement of the brush in the holder to make sure there is no binding and that the brush contacts the commutator evenly and completely.
13 Install the retaining screw and reassemble the starter motor.

12 Starter solenoid – removal and installation

Prestolite starter motor (in-line six-cylinder and V8)

1 The solenoid on these models is mounted separately from the starter motor and is located on the inner fender panel.
2 Disconnect the negative battery cable from the battery.
3 Disconnect the cables and wires from the solenoid.
4 Remove the retaining bolts and lift the solenoid from the engine compartment.
5 Installation is the reverse of removal. Connect the negative battery cable when installation is complete.

Delco 5MT starter motor (151 cu in four-cylinder)

6 Disconnect the negative battery cable from the battery, followed by the solenoid field strap.
7 Remove the solenoid attaching bolts and motor terminal bolt. Grasp the solenoid and twist it to withdraw it from the starter motor.
8 Installation is the reverse of removal. Be sure to reconnect the negative battery cable.

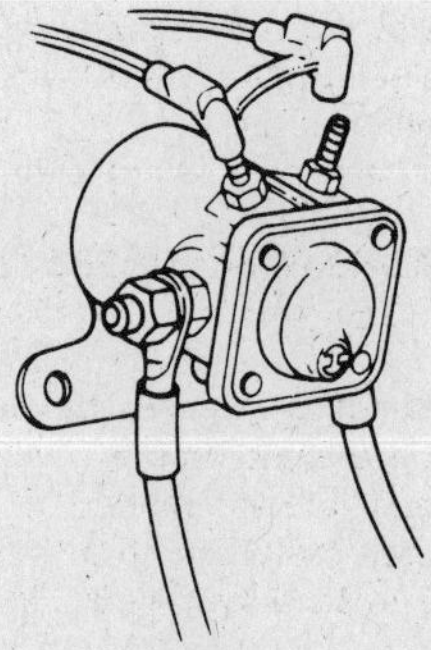

Fig. 5.8 Typical remote mounted in-line six-cylinder and V8 starter solenoid installation (Sec 12)

13 Ignition system check

1 Before beginning the ignition system check, make sure that the battery cable clamps are clean and tight and check the electrolyte level and specific gravity. The battery must be fully charged or the ignition system check will not be conclusive.
2 Check the fuses and fusible links to make sure none of them are blown. Check the ignition system wiring for damaged insulation and loose connections.

Secondary circuit

3 Remove the coil high tension lead from the distributor cap and hold the end about $\frac{1}{4}$-inch from a good engine ground. Have an assistant crank the engine over and check for a bright, blue, well-defined spark between the coil lead and ground. **Caution:** *Do not crank the engine for more than a few seconds when making this check.* If a spark is produced, the ignition system is functioning; if not, proceed to Step 9.

4 Disconnect the wire from one of the spark plugs and remove the plug from the engine. Reattach the wire securely to the plug and hold it against the engine while an assistant operates the starter. Do this with each plug.
5 If all of the spark plugs fired, the ignition system is operating properly. If some of the plugs fired, proceed to Step 6 or 7.
6 *On breaker point-equipped ignitions,* lift the cap from the distributor and gently separate the breaker points with your fingertips to inspect their condition. Points in good condition have a reasonably smooth surface with a dull grey color. If the point contact surfaces are pitted or if they have a black-and-blue appearance, they should be replaced. When replacing points, always replace the condenser, too (see Chapter 1). Wipe the distributor clean and apply a thin film of the proper lubricant to the point cam.
7 *On all models,* wipe the distributor cap both inside and outside with a clean cloth. Gently separate the spark plug cables from the cap, one at a time, and inspect the tower for physical damage and the inside of the tower for evidence of corrosion. Inspect the condition of the tower terminals on the inside of the cap. Look for burned terminals and carbon tracks. Corrosion inside the cap towers can be removed with a small round wire brush. Evidence of other physical defects necessitates cap replacement. Always replace the rotor when replacing the cap on the breaker point-equipped ignition systems. Be sure all connections are secure and tight.
8 Check the condition of the spark plug wires (see Chapter 1). Also check the condition of the spark plugs and set the gaps. Replace the wires or plugs (as a set) if necessary (Chapter 1).
9 Check the condition of the high tension wire between the distributor cap and the ignition coil. Replace it if necessary. Next, check the resistance in the primary and secondary coils.

Ignition coil resistance (all models except 1980 through 1983 four-cylinder)

10 With the engine at normal operating temperature and the ignition switch off, disconnect the positive and negative coil wires.
11 Connect an ohmmeter (set at low scale and calibrated to zero) to the positive and negative terminals of the coil and compare the readings to the primary coil specifications.
12 To check the secondary resistance, first disconnect the coil high tension lead. Connect the ohmmeter leads to the center tower and either the positive or negative terminal.
13 If either of the resistance checks is not within the Specifications, replace the coil with a new one.

Ignition coil resistance (1980 through 1983 four-cylinder engine)

14 With the ignition off, tag and disconnect the wires from the ignition coil.
15 Connect an ohmmeter (set at high resistance scale) between the positive terminal and the grounded frame of the coil. Compare the reading to the coil-to-ground Specifications.
16 Connect the ohmmeter between the positive and negative terminals (using the low resistance scale) to check the primary resistance.
17 To check the secondary resistance, disconnect the coil high tension lead. Connect the ohmmeter leads to the negative terminal and the high voltage terminal, using the high resistance scale.
18 Check all of these readings against the Specifications. Replace the ignition coil with a new one if any of the readings are out of the specified range.

Primary circuit – electronic ignition systems only

Trigger wheel and pickup assembly (1975 through 1977 six-cylinder and V8)

19 With the ignition switch off, disconnect the pickup connector and insert the ohmmeter leads into the distributor side of the pickup connector. Use the low scale setting.
20 Wiggle the wires and note the reading. The reading should remain constant despite the wire movement.
21 If the ohmmeter reading is not within the Specifications, replace the pickup assembly with a new one.

Trigger wheel and pickup assembly (1978 through 1983 six-cylinder and V8)

22 With the engine at normal operating temperature and the ignition off, disconnect the pickup connector leading from the distributor.
23 With the ohmmeter set on the mid-range scale, insert the leads into the B2 and B3 terminals of the connector as shown in the accompanying illustration.
24 If the ohmmeter reading is not within the Specifications, replace the pickup coil assembly with a new one.

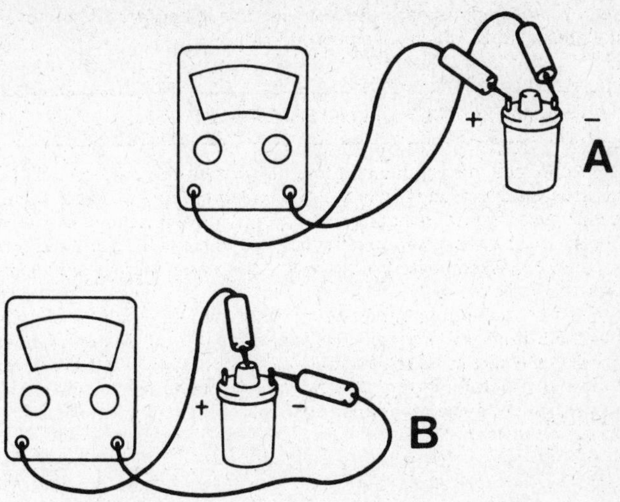
+
–
A
+
–
B

Fig. 5.9 Checking the coil primary (A) and secondary (B) resistance (through 1977 models) (Sec 13)

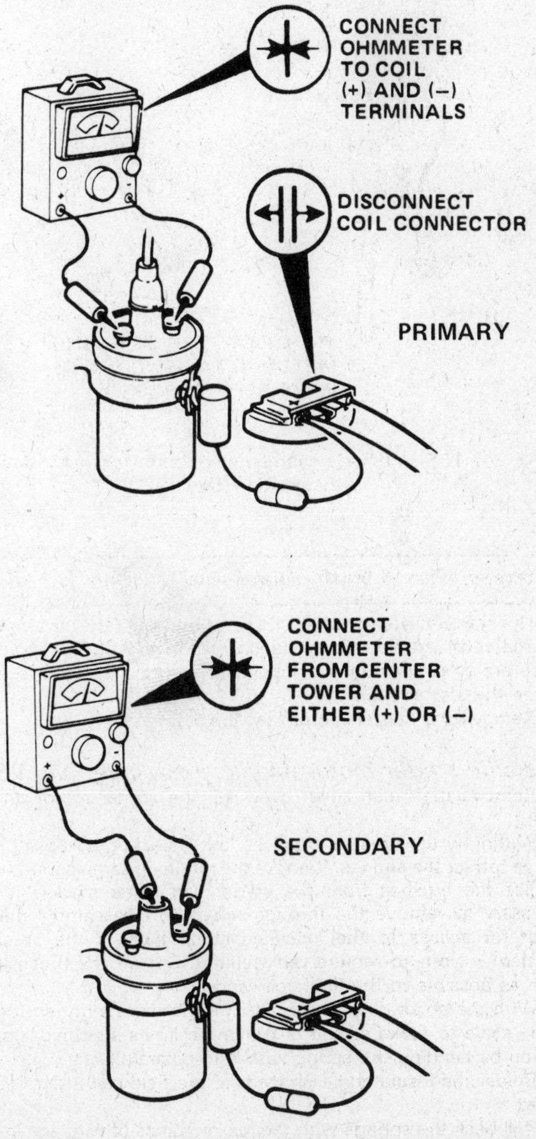
CONNECT
OHMMETER
TO COIL
(+) AND (–)
TERMINALS
DISCONNECT
COIL CONNECTOR
PRIMARY
CONNECT
OHMMETER
FROM CENTER
TOWER AND
EITHER (+) OR (–)
SECONDARY

Fig. 5.10 Checking the primary (top) and secondary (bottom) resistance (1978 through 1983 in-line six-cylinder and V8 models) (Sec 13)

Trigger wheel and pickup assembly (1980 through 1983 four-cylinder)

25 Remove the distributor cap and disconnect the pickup from the module. Connect a vacuum pump or source to the advance control unit and apply 20 inches of vacuum.

26 With the ohmmeter set at mid-range, attach one lead to the connector and the other to a good ground, such as the distributor body, as shown in the accompanying illustration. The ohmmeter reading should not change when vacuum is applied to the advance control unit.

27 Attach both leads to the connector and check the resistance.

28 If either reading is not within the Specifications, replace the pickup with a new one.

Primary circuit – all models

29 Locate the wire lead at the primary terminal on the distributor body. Turn the ignition switch to the On position and measure the voltage at the terminal. Compare the reading to the Specifications.

30 If you measure the specified voltage, proceed to Step 32.

31 If you did not measure the specified voltage, check the internal wire lead (distributor primary terminal-to-breaker points, if equipped) for an open or short circuit. Replace it with a new one if necessary.

32 Disconnect the primary terminal wire lead on the distributor body and turn the ignition switch on. Measure the voltage at the negative terminal of the ignition coil. Compare the reading to the primary voltage specification.

33 If you measured the specified voltage, check the wire between the negative terminal of the coil and the primary terminal of the distributor for an open or short circuit. Repair or replace it with a new one if necessary.

34 If you did not measure the specified voltage, measure the voltage at the positive terminal of the ignition coil. It should be as specified.

35 If you measured the specified voltage at the positive terminal, replace the coil with a new one.

36 If you did not measure the specified voltage, measure the voltage at both ends of the coil external resistor (if so equipped). It should be as specified.

37 If you measure the specified voltage at both ends, check the wiring harness from the resistor to the positive terminal of the coil for a broken wire. Repair or replace as necessary.

38 If you did not measure the specified voltage at either end, check the wiring harness from the battery to the resistor, the connector, the ignition switch and the fuse. Repair or replace components as needed.

39 If you measured the voltage at one end only, disconnect the wire from the resistor terminal where no voltage existed and measure the voltage of the resistor. It should be battery voltage.

40 If you measured the specified voltage, check the wiring harness from the resistor to the ignition coil for a short circuit. Repair or replace it as necessary.

41 If you did not measure the specified voltage, replace the resistor with a new one.

42 Be sure that all of the connections are secure and all mounting hardware is tight.

Centrifugal advance check (breaker point-equipped ignitions)

43 On models eequipped with breaker point ignition systems, check the action of the mechanical advance weights by twisting the rotor in the normal direction of rotation. When released, the rotor should snap back into its released position. Failure of the rotor to snap back indicates defective springs or sticking weights.

Centrifugal advance check (all models)

44 With a timing light installed and the engine running at idle speed, disconnect the vacuum hose from the vacuum advance control unit on the distributor.

45 Observe the timing marks on the front of the engine and slowly accelerate the engine. The timing mark on the crankshaft pulley should appear to move smoothly in a direction away from the stationary mark on the timing tab. When the engine is slowed down, the mark should return to its original position.

46 If the above conditions are not met, the advance mechanism inside the distributor should be checked for broken governor springs and other problems.

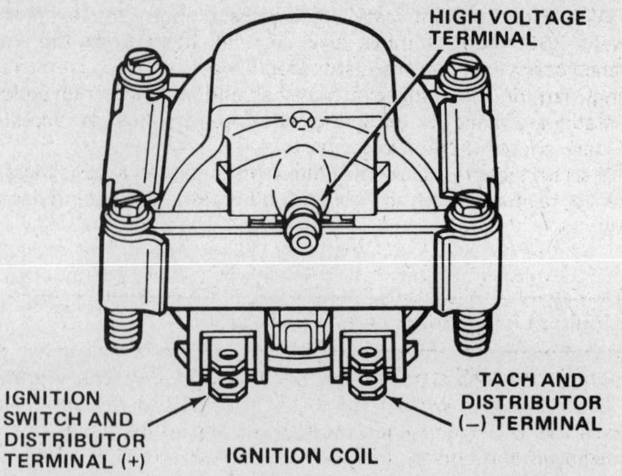

Fig. 5.11 1980 through 1983 four-cylinder engine ignition coil connectors (Sec 13)

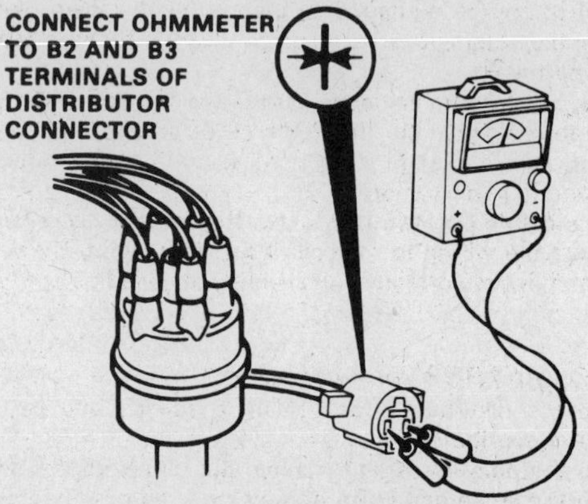

Fig. 5.12 Ohmmeter connections used for later model six-cylinder and V8 electronic ignitions (Sec 13)

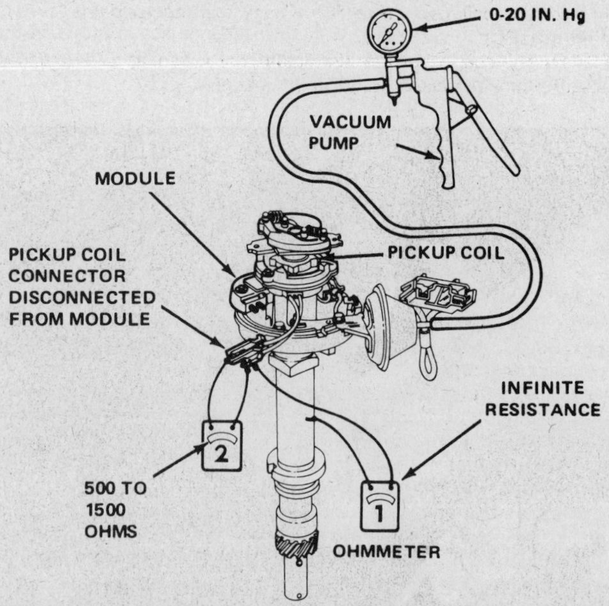

Fig. 5.13 1980 through 1983 four-cylinder distributor pickup circuit test (Sec 13)

1 *Checking pickup-to-ground resistance*
2 *Checking resistance at the connector*

Vacuum advance check (all models)

47 With a timing light installed and the engine running at approximately 2500 rpm, remove the vacuum hose from the vacuum advance control unit on the distributor. When the hose is removed, the timing mark on the crankshaft pulley should appear to move closer to the stationary mark on the timing tab. When the hose is reconnected, the mark should move away again.

48 If reconnecting the vacuum hose produces an abrupt increase in advance, or none at all, the vacuum advance control unit is probably faulty.

14 Ignition coil – removal and installation

Six-cylinder, V8 and 1977 through 1979 four-cylinder

1 Disconnect all wires from the coil. On 1978 through 1983 V8 models this is accomplished by grasping the white plastic connector, squeezing it and pulling it away from the coil. On all models, remove the high tension coil wire by grasping the boot, twisting it one-half turn and pulling it from the coil. It is a good idea to mark all wires and connections with tags so they will be reinstalled in their original positions. This is very important on later model electronic ignition systems, which can be damaged by incorrectly installed wiring.

2 Remove the retaining screws or bolts and lift the coil from the engine compartment.

3 If a new coil is to be installed, great care must be taken to obtain the proper replacement unit. Problems associated with installation of the incorrect coil can range from hard starting to, on later models, damage to the ignition system.

4 Place the coil in position and install the retaining screws or bolts.

5 Reconnect the wiring to the coil. After installation, check all wires to make sure they are correctly and securely installed before turning on the ignition.

1980 through 1983 four-cylinder

6 Remove the distributor cap attaching screws and pull the cap away from the distributor.

7 Remove the plug wires and remove the cap from the distributor.

8 Remove the three coil cover screws and remove the cover.

9 Remove the four coil attaching screws and lift the coil leads from the distributor cap.

10 If a new coil is to be installed, great care must be taken to obtain the proper replacement unit. Problems associated with installation of the incorrect coil can range from hard starting to damage to the ignition system.

11 Place the coil in position and install the retaining screws and coil leads. Be sure the leads are properly installed.

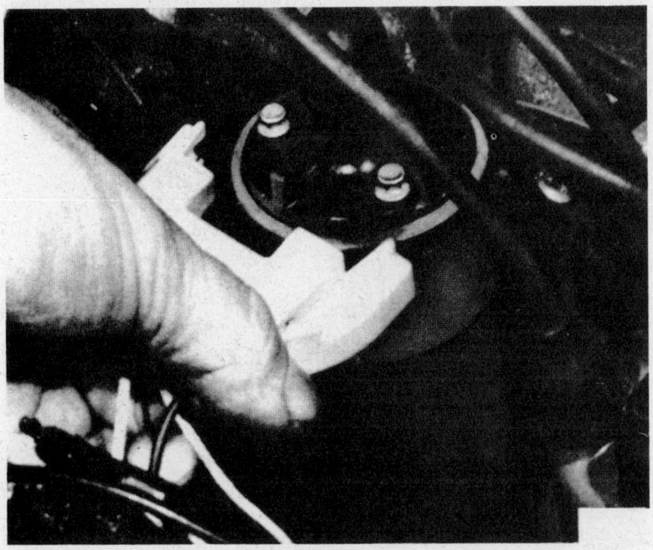

Fig. 5.14 The coil connector on 1978 through 1983 six-cylinder and V8 disconnected by grasping it and pulling it off (Sec 14)

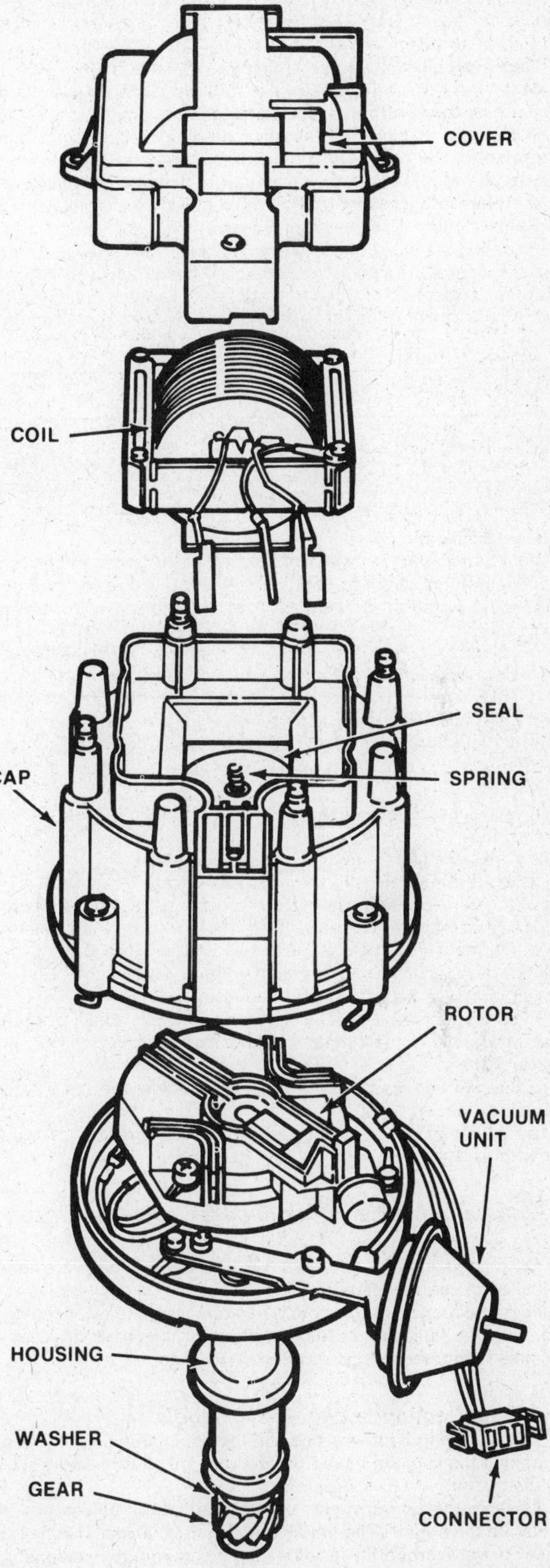

Fig. 5.15 The 1980 and 1981 four-cylinder ignition coil is located on the distributor (Sec 14)

5

12 Reinstall the coil cover.
13 Replace the distributor cap and plug wires, making sure the wires are securely fastened.

15 Conventional distributor – check

1 Remove the distributor cap and rotor.
2 Rotate the engine until the point rubbing block is on one of the high points of the cam. Grasp the distributor shaft firmly and move it back-and-forth while observing the points. If there is enough play in the shaft bushing to allow the points to open, the distributor is badly worn and should be replaced with a new or rebuilt unit.
3 As a further test, connect a dwell meter as described in Chapter 1. Start the engine and observe the dwell meter reading. If the dwell varies more than two or three degrees, as the engine is revved up, the distributor is worn and should be replaced with a new or rebuilt unit.

16 Electronic distributor – check

1 Remove the distributor cap and rotor.
2 Grasp the distributor shaft firmly and move it back-and-forth. If there is perceptible movement, the bushings are worn and the distributor should be replaced with a new or rebuilt unit.

17 Distributor – removal and installation

1 Disconnect the negative battery cable from the battery. Unplug or disconnect all wires from the distributor body and remove the distributor cap.
2 Disconnect the vacuum hose from the vacuum advance control unit on the distributor.
3 Pull the spark plug wires off the spark plugs. Pull only on the rubber boot or damage to the spark plug wire could result. It is a good idea to number each wire using a piece of tape.
4 Remove the spark plugs, then place your thumb over the Number one spark plug hole and turn the crankshaft in a *clockwise* direction until you can feel the compression pressure in the number one cylinder. Continue to slowly turn the crankshaft until the notch in the crankshaft pulley lines up with the O or TDC on the timing mark tab. At this point the number one piston is at TDC on the compression stroke. **Note:** *On in-line six-cylinder engines it is crucial to make sure the number one cylinder is on the compression stroke because the crankshaft pulley mark also aligns with the TDC mark when the number six cylinder is on the exhaust stroke.*

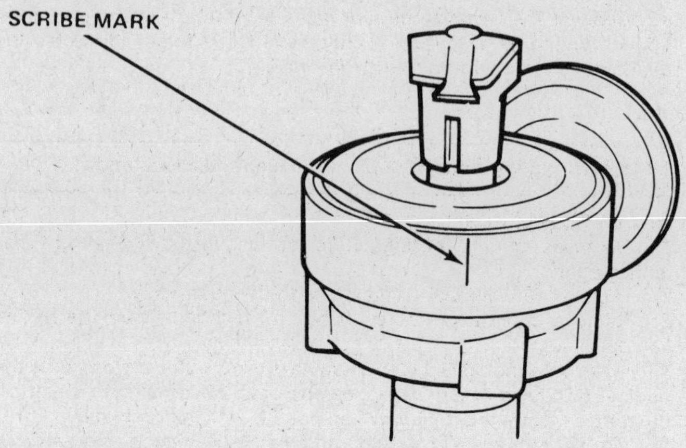

Fig. 5.16 Scribe a mark on the distributor housing opposite the rotor tip before removal (Sec 17)

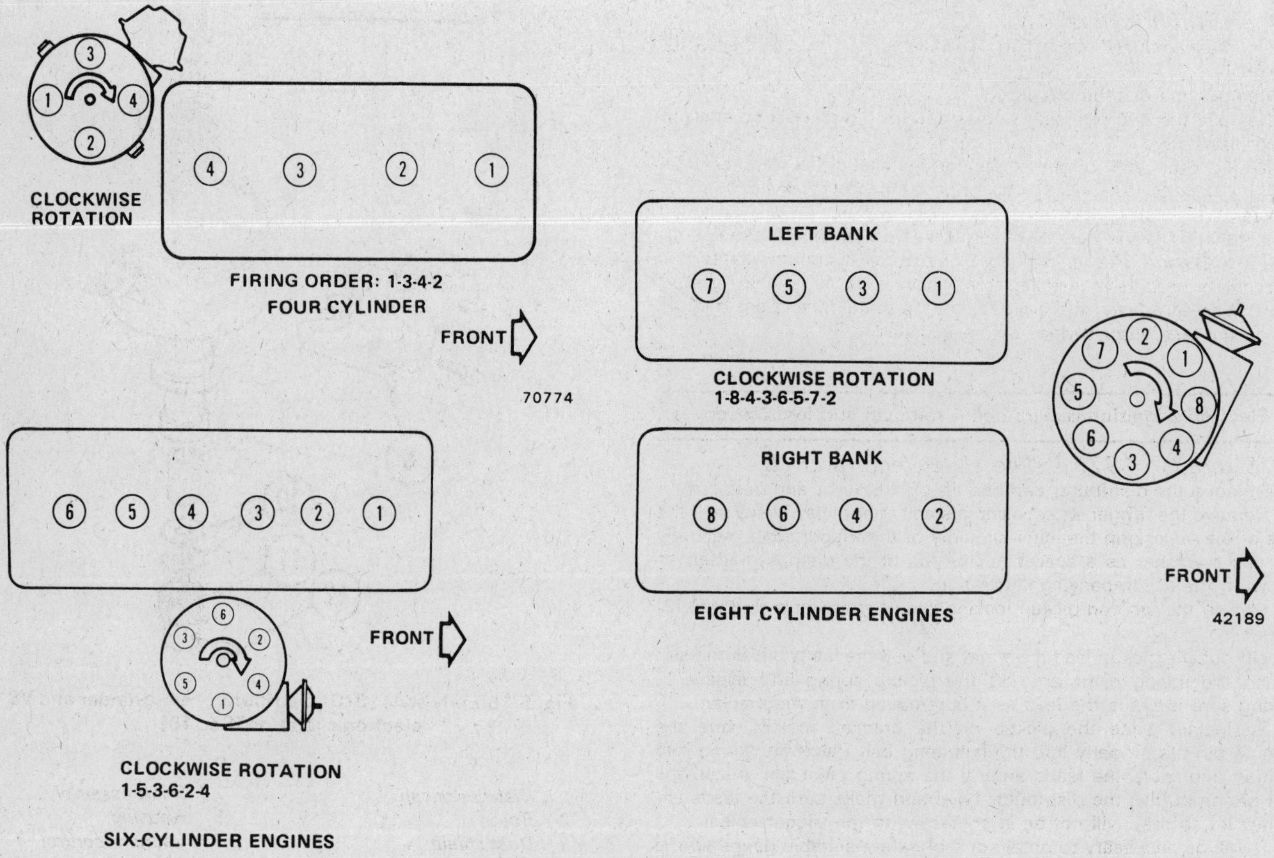

Fig. 5.17 Engine cylinder numbering and firing order (Sec 17)

5 Scribe a line on the distributor housing and make a corresponding mark on the engine. Mark the position of the rotor in relation to the distributor housing and the engine.
6 Remove the bolt and clamp and carefully withdraw the distributor by pulling it straight out of the engine.
7 *Do not allow the engine to be cranked until the distributor has been reinstalled.*
8 To install the distributor, line up the mating marks on the housing and engine. Slide the distributor into place. It may be necessary to move the distributor back-and-forth slightly to engage the gear. After the distributor is securely seated the rotor must be in its original position.
9 Install the bolt and clamp finger tight.
10 Replace the spark plugs and install the plug wires.
11 Install the distributor cap and connect the wires and vacuum hose.
12 Connect the negative battery cable to the battery and check the ignition timing as described in Chapter 1. Don't forget to tighten the distributor hold-down bolt when finished.

18 Electronic ignition module – removal and installation

In-line six-cylinder and V8

1 On these models the module is located on the firewall or inner fender panel.
2 Unplug the electrical connections from the module.
3 Remove the retaining screws and lift the module from the engine compartment.
4 Make sure the replacement module is exactly the same type as the original. Modules of similar appearance can have different electrical properties which could lead to damage of the ignition system.
5 Place the module in position and install the attaching screws.
6 Apply dielectric silicone grease to the cavities and blades of the connectors to assure good electrical contact and plug them securely into the module.

151 cu in four-cylinder

7 On these models the ignition module is part of the distributor assembly.
8 Remove the distributor cap.
9 Remove the two retaining screws and lift the module up and out of the distributor.
10 Noting the color of the wires for installation in their original position, unplug the pickup coil wire connector and remove the module.
11 Installation is the reverse of removal. Do not remove the special dielectric silicone grease from the module or distributor base. If a replacement module is installed it will have a package of the grease with it. Spread a layer of the grease on the metal face of the module and on the distributor surface before installation.

19 Electronic ignition pickup coil – removal and installation

1975 through 1977 in-line six-cylinder and V8

1 Remove the distributor cap and lift off the rotor and dust cap.
2 Remove the trigger wheel using a small gear puller. Make sure the jaws of the puller grip the inner shoulder of the trigger wheel securely and use a washer as a spacer on the top of the distributor shaft as shown in the accompanying illustration.
3 Loosen the ignition pickup locking screw approximately three (3) turns.
4 Lift out the pickup lead grommet and pull the leads out of the slot around the spring pivot pin. Lift the pickup spring and release it, making sure it clears the lead as it is removed from the bracket.
5 To install, place the pickup on the bracket, making sure the locating pin fits properly into the summing bar. Place the spring into position and route the leads around the spring pivot pin. Install the lead grommet into the distributor bowl and make sure the leads are positioned so they will not be in contact with the trigger wheel.
6 It will be necessary to obtain or fabricate a suitable gauge so the pickup can be accurately positioned. Install the gauge and tighten the retaining screw. Position the pickup and remove the gauge. Repeat the operation until the gauge can be removed and replaced without any

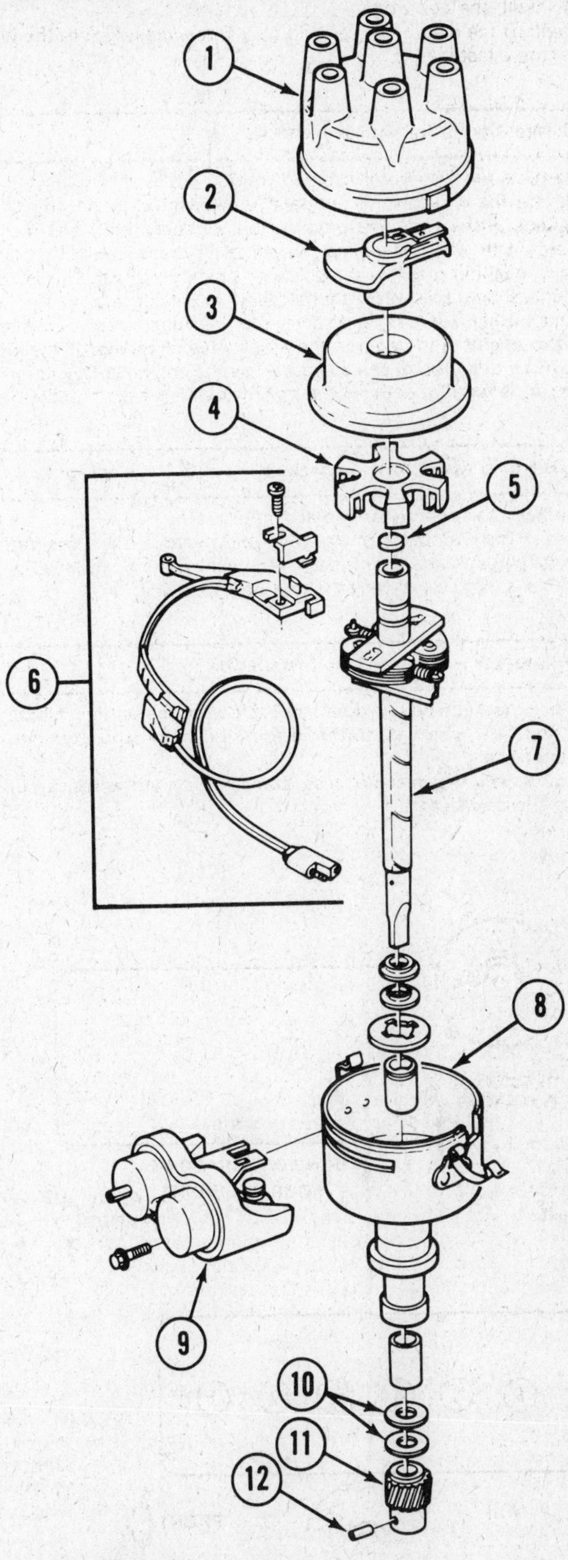

Fig. 5.18 Early style (BID) distributor – six-cylinder and V8 electronic ignition (Sec 19)

1 *Distributor cap*
2 *Rotor*
3 *Dust shield*
4 *Trigger wheel*
5 *Felt wick*
6 *Sensor assembly*
7 *Shaft assembly*
8 *Housing*
9 *Vacuum control*
10 *Shim*
11 *Drive gear*
12 *Pin*

5

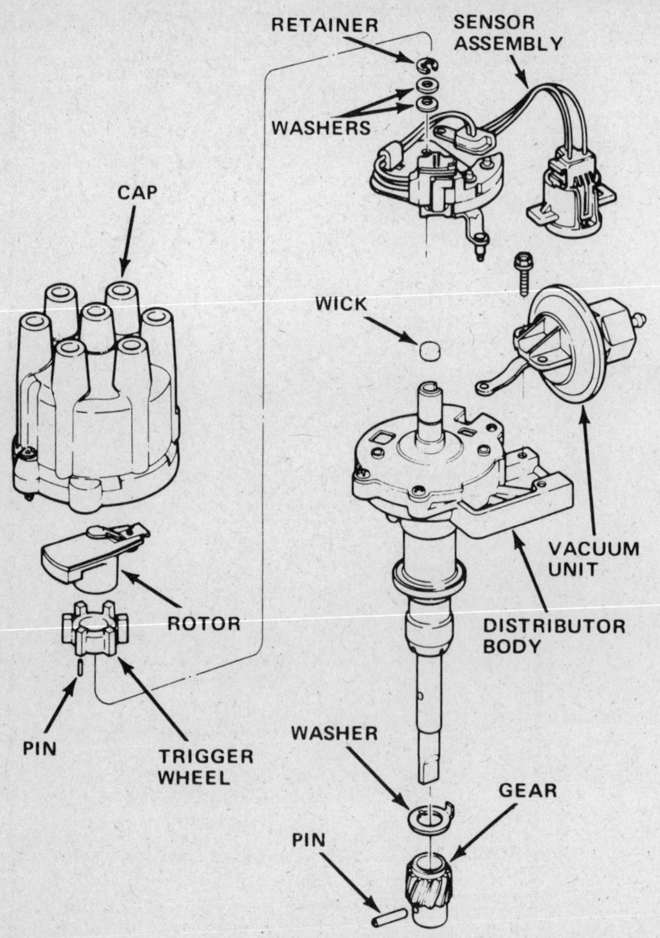

Fig. 5.19 Late style (SSI) distributor – six-cylinder and V8 electronic ignition (Sec 19)

side movement of the pickup.

7 Tighten the retaining screw securely after the pickup has been positioned and remove the gauge.

8 Set the trigger wheel in position and check that the pickup core is positioned in the center of the trigger wheel teeth so the teeth cannot touch it.

9 Use a deep socket to push the trigger wheel into place and tap it into position with a hammer. Bend a 0.050 inch wire (usually included with the new part) and check the trigger wheel-to-pickup base clearance as shown in the accompanying illustration. The trigger wheel should just touch the gauge in the installed position.

10 Add five drops of light engine oil to the felt wick at the top of the yoke and install the dust shield, rotor and cap.

1978 through 1983 in-line six-cylinder and V8

11 Remove the distributor cap and rotor. Remove the trigger wheel. This can be accomplished either by using a small gear puller with a washer used as a spacer on the top of the distributor or by using two screwdrivers to lever the wheel off. Remove the pin from the wheel.

12 On six-cylinder engines, remove the pickup coil retainer and washers from the base plate pivot pin.

13 On V8 engines, remove the snap-ring which retains the pickup to the shaft. Remove the vacuum advance mechanism and move it out of the way.

14 Remove the harness tab ground screw and lift the pickup assembly from the distributor.

15 To install, place the pickup assembly in position. On six-cylinder engines, insert the pickup coil pin into the hole in the vacuum advance mechanism link. On V8 engines, attach the vacuum advance mechanism lever and retainer to the pickup coil pin.

16 On six-cylinder engines, install the washers and retainers onto the pivot pin so the pickup coil is secured to the base plate. On V8 engines, install the snap ring.

17 Place the wiring harness in the distributor housing slot and install the ground screw through the tab.

18 Position the trigger wheel on the distributor shaft with the long portion of the teeth up. After aligning the trigger wheel with the slot in the shaft, insert the retaining pin into the locating groove and tap it into place with a suitable small drift and hammer.

19 Install the rotor and cap.

151 cu in four-cylinder

20 Remove the distributor.

21 Mark the relative location of the distributor gear on the shaft, drive out the roll pin and remove the gear.

22 Remove the distributor shaft, complete with the rotor and advance weights.

23 Remove the snap-ring on the top of the pickup coil, disconnect the wire from the module and remove the pickup coil and plate assembly. *The three screws should not be removed.*

24 Installation is the reverse of removal. Be sure to align the distributor gear with the marks made during removal.

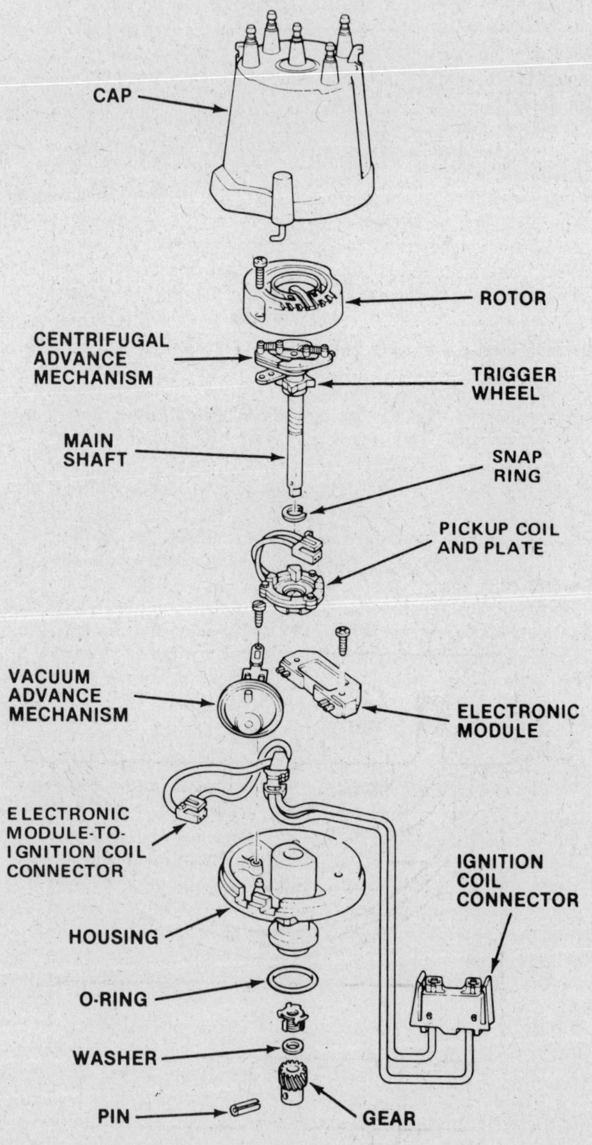

Fig. 5.20 Four-cylinder (HEI) electronic ignition distributor (typical) (Sec 19)

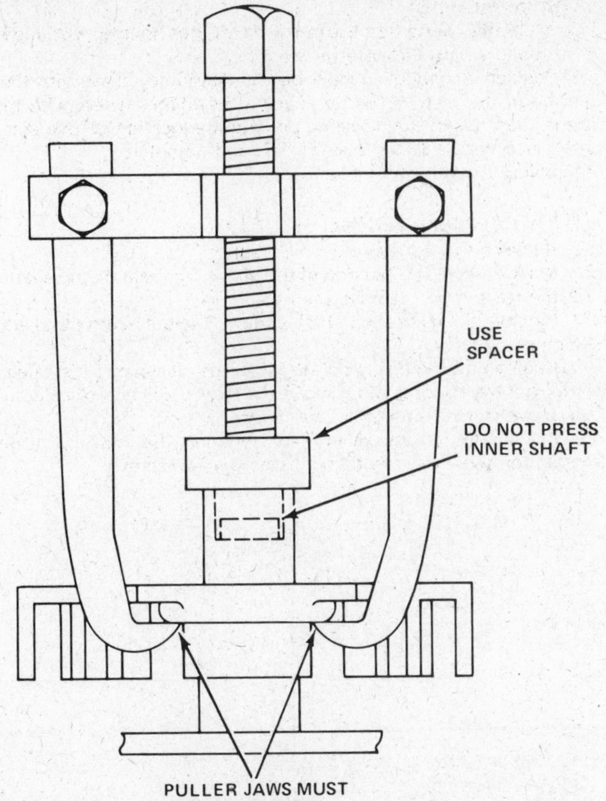

Fig. 5.21 Using a small gear puller to remove the trigger wheel (Sec 19)

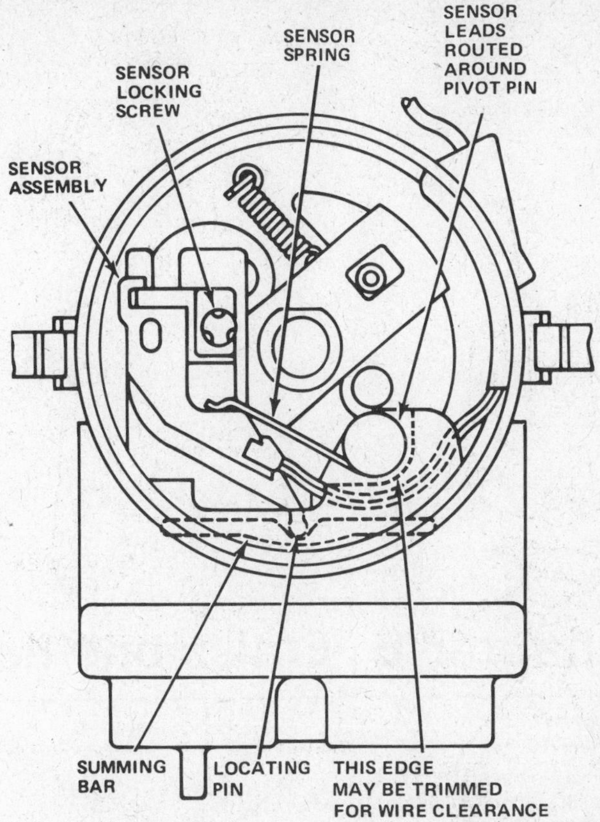

Fig. 5.22 1975 through 1977 ignition pickup coil installation (Sec 19)

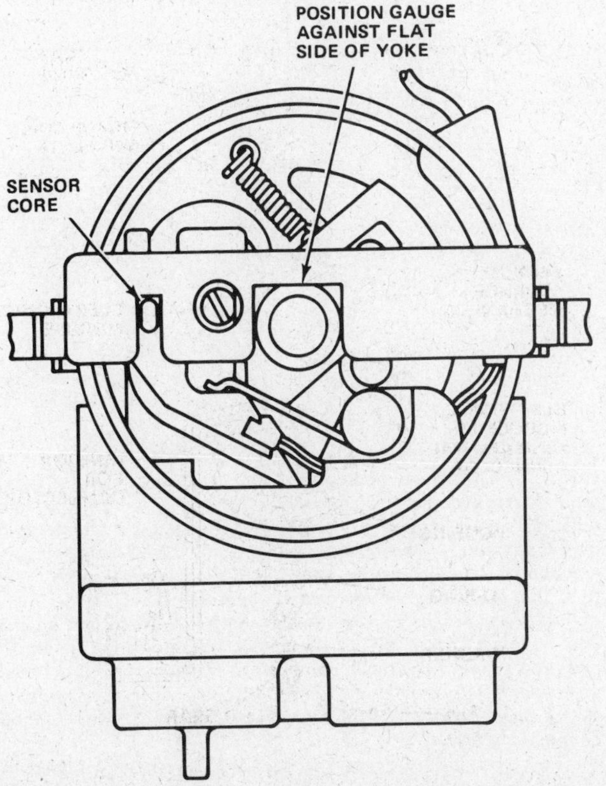

Fig. 5.23 Using a gauge to position the pickup coil (Sec 19)

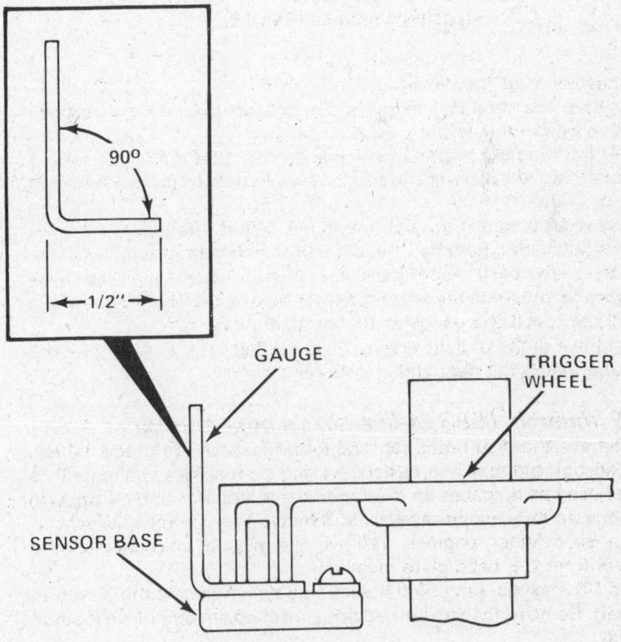

Fig. 5.24 Checking the trigger wheel-to-pickup base clearance (1975 through 1977) (Sec 19)

5

Chapter 6 Emissions control systems

Contents

Air injection system	4
Altitude compensation circuit	9
Catalytic converter	6
Exhaust Gas Recirculation (EGR) system	5
Forced air pre-heat systems	8
Fuel vapor control system	3
General information	1
Positive Crankcase Ventilation (PCV) system	2
Spark control systems	7

Specifications

Torque specifications

	Ft-lb	Nm
Air injection manifold fittings		
Four-cylinder engine	28	38
Six-cylinder engine	20	27
V8 engine	38	52
Air pump adjusting bolt		
Four-cylinder engine	28	38
Six-cylinder and V8 engines	20	27
Air pump pivot bolt		
Four-cylinder engine	28	38
Six-cylinder and V8 engines	20	27
Air injection manifold check valve	25	34

1 General information

To prevent pollution of the atmosphere, a number of emission control systems are required. The combination of systems used depends on the year in which the vehicle was manufactured, the locality to which it was originally delivered and the engine type. The systems and engine combinations include:

Positive Crankcase Ventilation (PCV) system
Fuel vapor control system
Air injection system
Exhaust Gas Recirculation (EGR) system
Catalytic converter
Spark control system
Forced air preheat system
Altitude compensation circuit

The Sections in this Chapter include general descriptions, checking procedures (where possible) and component replacement procedures (where applicable) for each of the systems listed above.

Before assuming that an emission control system is malfunctioning, check the fuel and ignition systems carefully. In some cases, special tools and equipment, as well as specialized training, are required to accurately diagnose the causes of a rough running or difficult to start engine. If checking and servicing become too difficult or if a procedure is beyond the scope of the home mechanic, consult a dealer service department. This does not necessarily mean, however, that the emission control systems are all particularly difficult to maintain and repair. You can quickly and easily perform many checks and do most (if not all) of the regular maintenance at home with common tune-up and hand tools. **Note:** *The most frequent cause of emission system problems is simply a loose or broken vacuum hose or wiring connection. Therefore, always check hose and wiring connections first.*

Pay close attention to any special precautions outlined in this Chapter (particularly those concerning the catalytic converter).

It should be noted that the illustrations of the various systems may not exactly match the system installed on your particular vehicle (due to changes made by the manufacturer during production or from year-to-year).

2 Positive Crankcase Ventilation (PCV) system

General description

1 This system is designed to reduce hydrocarbon emissions (HC) by routing blow-by gases (fuel/air mixture that escapes from the combustion chambers past the piston rings into the crankcase) from the crankcase to the intake manifold and combustion chamber where they are burned during engine operation.
2 The system is very simple and consists of rubber hoses and a PCV valve.

Checking and component replacement

3 Checking, cleaning and replacement of the PCV system components is a routine maintenance procedure. Refer to Chapter 1 for details.

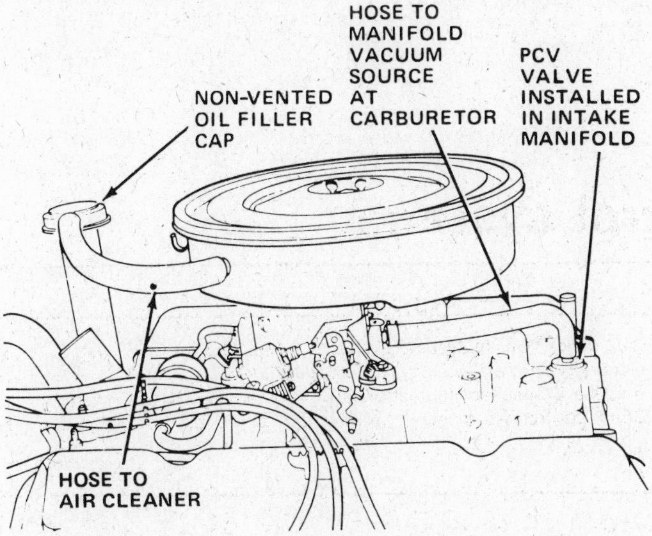

Fig. 6.1 Typical V8 PCV system (similar to the four and six-cylinder systems) (Sec 2)

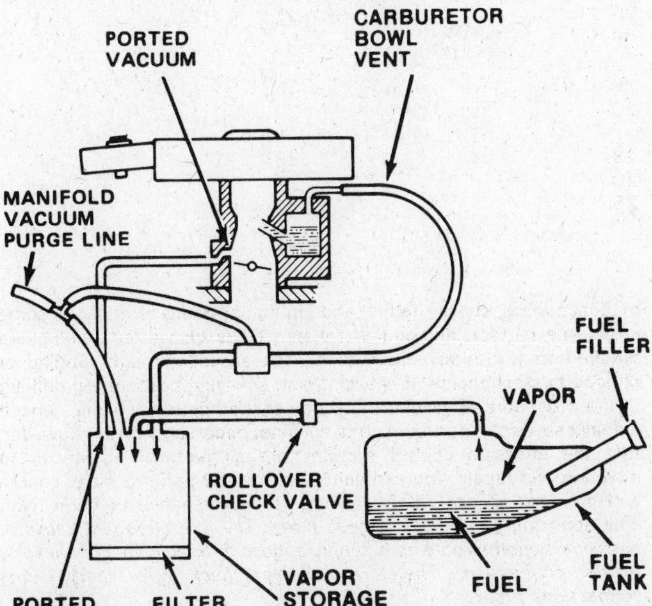

Fig. 6.2 Typical fuel vapor control system (Sec 3)

3 Fuel vapor control system

General description

1 Although the vapor control system is one of the most complex looking, it is in actuality one of the most basic and trouble-free portions of the emissions network. Its function is to reduce hydrocarbon emissions. Basically, it is a closed fuel system which reroutes fuel back to the gas tank and stores fuel vapors instead of venting them to the atmosphere.
2 Due to the fact that it has few moving parts, the vapor control system requires no periodic maintenance except for replacement of the filter in the bottom of the charcoal canister at the recommended intervals.
3 A tip-off that this system is not operating properly is the strong smell of fuel vapors or fuel starvation during acceleration.
4 A pressure/vacuum gasoline filler cap must be used, as a standard cap may render the system ineffective and could possibly collapse the fuel tank. Other components which make up this system include a special gas tank with fill limiters and vent connections, a charcoal canister with integral purge valve and filter which stores vapor from the fuel tank to be burned by the carburetor, a carburetor bowl vent valve and various hoses linking the main components.

Checking

5 As mentioned earlier, this system requires little maintenance. However, if a problem is suspected the system should be inspected.
6 With the engine cold, disconnect the fuel tank line at the charcoal canister. The canister is located inside the engine compartment. Each of the hose connections is labeled.
7 As this hose is disconnected, check for the presence of liquid fuel in the line. Fuel in this vapor hose is an indication that the vent controls or pressure/vacuum relief valve in the gas cap is not functioning properly.
8 Hook up a pressure/suction device to the end of the fuel vapor line. Apply 15 psi pressure to the line and watch for excessive loss of pressure.
9 Check for a fuel vapor smell in the engine compartment and around the gas tank.
10 Remove the fuel filler cap and check for pressure in the gas tank.
11 If there is no pressure in the tank or a fuel odor, inspect all lines for leaks or deterioration.
12 With the fuel filler cap removed, apply pressure again and check for obstructions in the vent line.

Component replacement

13 Chapter 1 contains all information concerning the servicing of the fuel vapor control system, in particular the replacement of the canister filter.

6

4 Air injection system

General description

1 The function of the air injection system is to reduce hydrocarbons (HC), and carbon monoxide (CO) in the exhaust. This is done by pumping fresh air directly into the exhaust manifold ports of each engine cylinder or, in some cases, the catalytic converter. The fresh oxygen-rich air helps complete combustion of the unburned hydrocarbons before they are expelled as exhaust.
2 This system operates at all engine speeds and will bypass air only for a short time during deceleration and at high speeds. In these cases the additional fresh air added to the over-rich fuel/air mixture may cause backfiring or popping through the exhaust.
3 This system as it is used on most AMC engines consists of the air injection pump (with supporting brackets and drivebelt) at the front of the engine, an air diverter valve, the manifold and injection tubes running into each port at the exhaust manifold(s) and a check valve for the aforementioned injection tubes.
4 The in-line diverter valve is located between the air pump and the injection tubes. It momentarily diverts air pump output from the exhaust manifold during rapid engine deceleration. It also functions as a pressure release valve when the pump output pressure simply becomes excessive.

5 The check valve, located on the air injection manifold, prevents the reverse flow of engine exhaust to the air pump, avoiding possible damage to the pump.
6 Some later model vehicles are equipped with a dual air injection system. This system is easily identifiable by a third valve (the air control valve) located in the line between the diverter valve and the check valve. The air control valve operates from a solenoid hooked up to the Computerized Emission Control (CEC) system. The valve directs air pressure either into the exhaust manifolds or into the dual bed catalytic converter to mix with the exhaust gases and reduce HC and CO emissions.

Checking

7 Properly installed and adjusted air injection systems are fairly reliable and seldom cause problems. However, a malfunctioning system can cause engine surge, backfiring and overheated spark plugs. The air pump is the most critical component of this system and the belt at the front of the engine which drives the pump should be your first check. If the belt is cracked or frayed, replace it with a new one. Check the tension of the drivebelt by pressing it with your finger. There should be about $\frac{1}{2}$-inch of play in the belt when pushed half-way between the pulleys.
8 The adjusting or replacement procedures for the drivebelt depend on the mounting of the air pump. On some models, a single belt is used for both the air pump and the alternator. If this is the case, loosen the mounting bolt and the adjusting bolt for the alternator and then push against the alternator to tighten the belt. Hold in this position while the two bolts are tightened. The procedure is basically the same for air pumps which use their own belt, except it will be the air pump which will be loosened.
9 To check for proper air delivery from the pump, follow the hoses from the pump to where they meet the injection tube/manifold assembly on each side of the engine. Loosen the clamps and disconnect the hoses.
10 Start the engine and, with your fingers or a piece of paper, check that air is flowing out of these hoses. Accelerate the engine and observe the air flow, which should increase in relation to engine speed. If this is the case, the pump is working satisfactorily. If air flow was not present, or did not increase, check for crimps in the hoses, proper drivebelt tension, and for a leaking diverter valve which can be heard with the pump operating.
11 To check the diverter valve, sometimes called the 'gulp' valve or anti-backfire valve, make sure all hoses are connected and start the engine. Locate the muffler on the valve, which is a canister unit with holes in it.
12 Being careful not to touch any of the moving engine components, place your hand near the muffler outlet holes and check that little or no air is escaping with the engine at idle speed. Now have an assistant depress the accelerator pedal to accelerate the engine and then quickly let off the pedal. A momentary blast of air should be felt discharging through the diverter valve muffler.
13 If no air discharge was felt, disconnect the smaller vacuum hose at the diverter valve. Place your finger over the end of the hose and again have your assistant depress the accelerator and let it off. As the engine is decelerating, a vacuum should be felt. If vacuum was felt, replace the diverter valve with a new one. If no vacuum was felt, the vacuum hose or engine vacuum source is plugged, requiring a thorough cleaning to eliminate the problem.
14 The check valve is located on the air manifold assembly and its function is to prevent exhaust gases from flowing back into the air pump. To find out if they are functioning properly, disconnect the air supply hose where it attaches to the check valve. Start the engine and, being careful not to touch any moving engine components, place your hand over the outlet of the check valve. The valve can be further checked by turning off the engine, allowing it to cool, and orally blowing through the check valve (toward the air manifold). Then attempt to suck back through it. If the valve is allowing you to suck back towards the air pump, it is bad and should be replaced.
15 Another check for this system is for leaks in the hose connections and/or hoses themselves. Leaks can often be detected by sound or feel with the pump in operation. If a leak is suspected, use a soapy water solution to verify this. Pour or sponge the solution of detergent and water on the hoses and connections. With the pump running, bubbles will form if a leak exists. The air delivery hoses are of a special design to withstand engine temperatures, so if they are replaced make sure the new hoses are of the proper standards.

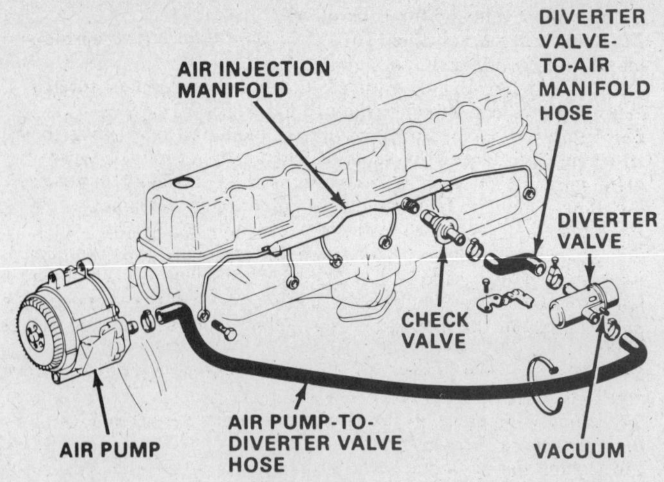

Fig. 6.3 Typical single air injection system (six-cylinder shown) (Sec 4)

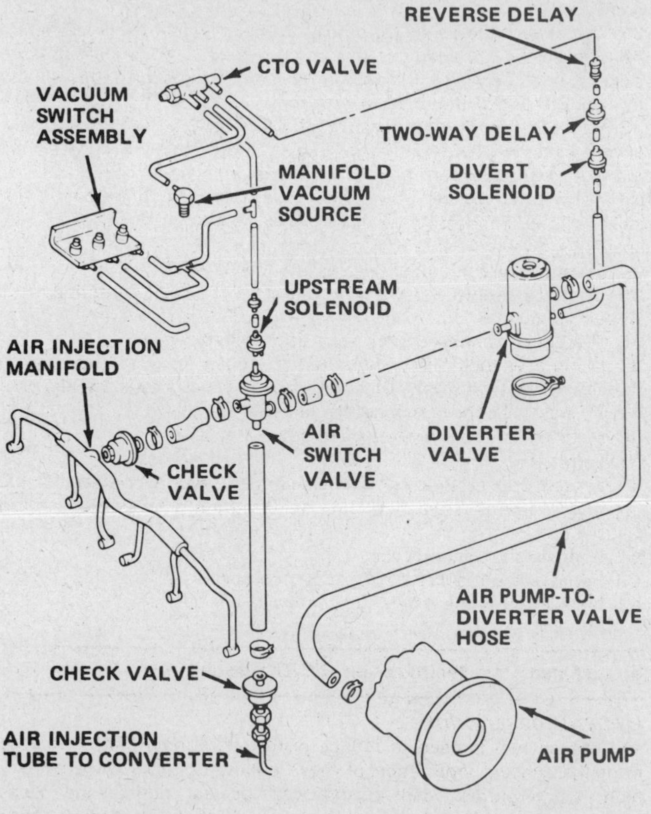

Fig. 6.4 Typical dual air injection system (six-cylinder shown) (Sec 4)

Component replacement

Air pump

16 As mentioned earlier, some air pumps share a common drivebelt with the alternator where others use their own belt. This will affect the removal and installation procedure somewhat.
17 Disconnect the air delivery hoses at the air pump. Note the position of each hose for reassembly.
18 Disconnect the vacuum source hose at the diverter valve.
19 Compress the drivebelt to keep the air pump pulley from turning and remove the bolts and washers securing the pulley to the pump.
20 To get some slack in the belt, loosen the alternator adjusting bolt

and the pivot bolt. Push the alternator in until the belt and air pump pulley can be removed from the pump.
21 Remove the bolts which secure the air pump to its brackets and then lift the pump from the engine compartment.
22 Check the pump for evidence that exhaust gas has entered it, indicating a failure of one or both of the check valves.
23 Attach the air pump to its engine mounting brackets with the attaching bolts loose. The exception to this is on models where the mounting bolts are inaccessible with the pulley installed. In this case, the pump mounting bolts should be tightened at this point.
24 Install the pump pulley with the bolts only hand tight.
25 Place the drivebelt into position on the air pump pulley and adjust the belt by gently prying on the alternator until about $\frac{1}{2}$-inch of play is felt in the belt when pushed with your fingers half-way between the pulleys. Tighten the alternator bolts, keeping the belt tension at this point.
26 Keep the pump pulley from turning by compressing the drivebelt and torque the pulley bolts to specifications.
27 Connect the hoses to the air pump and diverter valve. Make sure the connections are tight.
28 Tighten the mounting bolts for the pump.
29 Check the operation of the air pump as outlined previously.

Air manifold and injection tubes

30 Due to the high temperatures in this area, the connections at the exhaust manifold may be difficult to loosen. Commercial penetrating oil applied to the threads of the injection tubes may help in the removal procedure.
31 Disconnect the air delivery hose at the manifold check valve.
32 Loosen the threaded connectors on the exhaust manifold at each exhaust port. Slide the connectors up on the injection tubes so the threads are out of the exhaust manifold.
33 Pull the injection tube/air manifold assembly from the engine exhaust manifold and out of the engine compartment. To install the manifold, thread each of the injection tube connectors loosely into the exhaust manifold, using an anti-seize compound on the threads. After each of the connectors is sufficiently started, tighten each one securely.
34 Connect the air supply hose to the check valve.
35 Start the engine and check for leaks as previously described.

Check valve

36 Disconnect the air supply hose at the check valve.
37 Using a wrench on the hex fitting, remove the check valve from the air manifold assembly. Be careful not to bend or twist the delicate manifold or injection tubes as this is done.
38 Installation is the reverse of removal.

Diverter valve

39 The diverter valve is not serviceable and must be replaced if it is defective. To remove the diverter valve, disconnect the air hoses at the valve.
40 Remove the vacuum hose.
41 Remove the bracket clamp, if so equipped.
42 Installation is the reverse of removal.

5 Exhaust Gas Recirculation (EGR) system

General description

1 This system is used to reduce oxides of nitrogen (NOx) emitted from the exhaust. Formation of these pollutants takes place at very high temperatures; consequently, it occurs during the peak temperature period of the combustion process. To reduce peak temperatures, and thus the formation of NOx, a small amount of exhaust gas is taken from the exhaust system and recirculated in the combustion cycle.
2 Very little maintenance other than occasionally inspecting the vacuum hoses and the EGR valve is required. Besides the heart of the system – the EGR valve – the only moving part which can wear out is a thermal vacuum switch (TVS) which controls the vacuum signal to the EGR valve at varying engine temperatures.
3 The EGR system does not recirculate gases when the engine is at idle or during deceleration. The system is also regulated by the thermal vacuum switch, which does not allow the system to operate until the engine has reached normal operating temperature.
4 Common engine problems associated with the EGR system are rough idling or stalling when at idle, rough engine performance during light throttle application and stalling during deceleration.

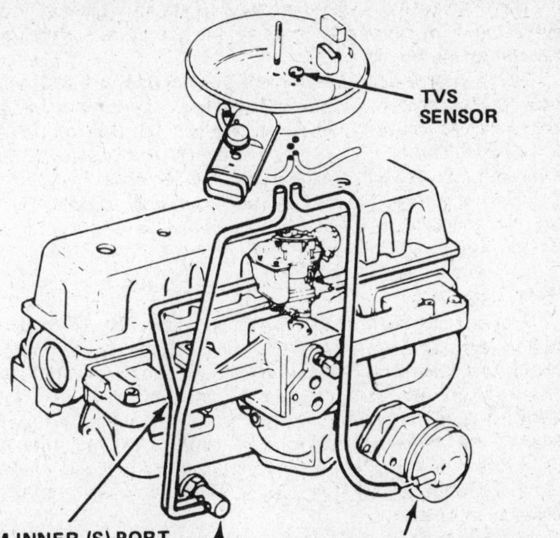

Fig. 6.5 Typical EGR system (six-cylinder shown) (Sec 5)

Checking

EGR valve

5 Refer to Chapter 1 for the procedure to follow when checking the EGR valve.

TVS switch

6 The TVS switch opens as the coolant temperature increases, allowing vacuum to reach the EGR valve. The exact temperature varies from year to year, but is indicative of the normal operating temperature of the particular engine.
7 The best way to test the switch is with a vacuum gauge, checking the vacuum signal with the engine hot.
8 Disconnect the vacuum hose at the EGR valve, connect the vacuum gauge to the disconnected end of the hose and start the engine. Note the reading on the vacuum gauge with the engine at an idle and then have an assistant depress the accelerator slightly and note the reading again. As the accelerator is depressed, the vacuum reading should increase.
9 If the gauge does not respond to the throttle opening, disconnect the hose which leads from the carburetor to the thermal vacuum switch. Repeat the test with the vacuum gauge installed in the vacuum hose end at the switch. If the vacuum gauge responds to accelerator opening, the thermal vacuum switch is defective and should be replaced with a new one.
10 If the gauge still does not respond to an increase in throttle opening, check for a plugged hose or defective carburetor.

Component replacement

EGR valve

11 Remove the air cleaner assembly if necessary to gain adequate working space.
12 Label and disconnect the vacuum hoses.
13 Remove the valve retaining nuts from the manifold.
14 Remove the EGR valve, gaskets and restrictor plate or spacer, if equipped. Be sure to remove all traces of the gasket.
15 Installation is the reverse of removal. Be sure to use a new gasket. If a restrictor plate is used, place it between two replacement gaskets.

TVS switch

16 Remove the air cleaner cover and disconnect the TVS switch from the vacuum hoses.
17 Remove the retaining clips which attach the TVS to the air cleaner and remove the TVS.
18 Installation is the reverse of removal.

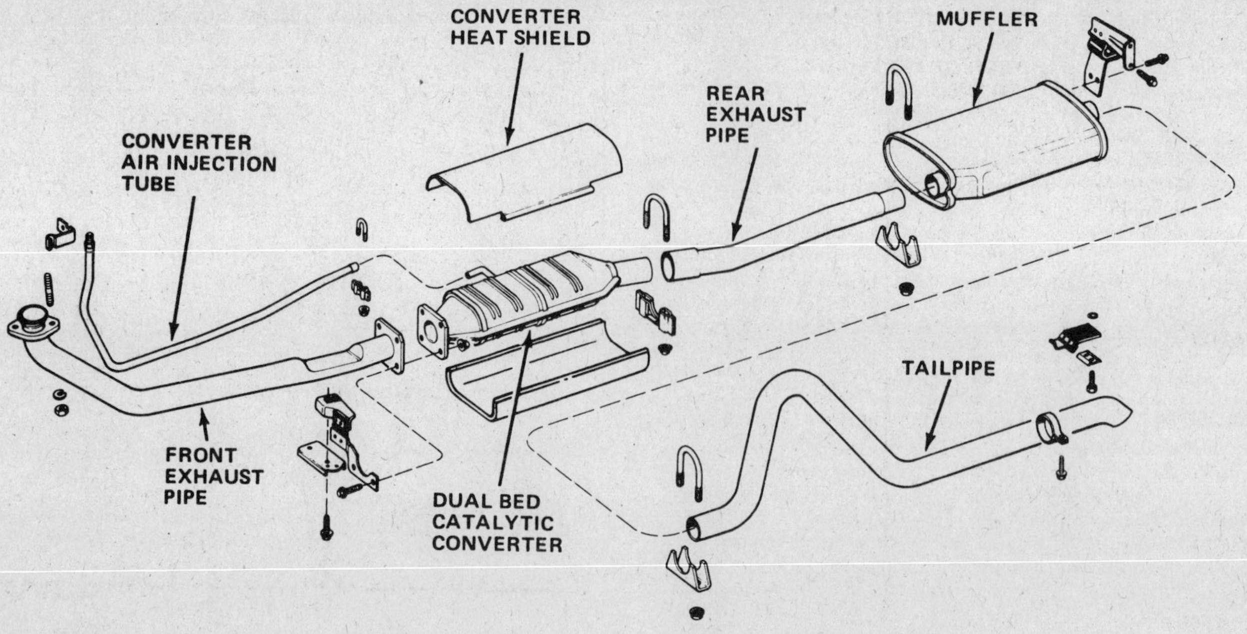

Fig. 6.6 Typical dual-bed, monolythic type catalytic converter (Sec 6)

6 Catalytic converter

General description

1 The catalytic converter is designed to reduce hydrocarbon (HC) and carbon monoxide (CO) pollutants in the exhaust. The converter oxidizes these components and converts them to water and carbon dioxide.
2 The converter is located in the exhaust system and closely resembles a muffler. AMC vehicles are equipped with either a monolithic type or a pelletized type converter.
3 **Note:** *If large amounts of unburned gasoline enter the catalyst, it may overheat and cause a fire. Always observe the following precautions:*

Use only unleaded gasoline
Avoid prolonged idling
Do not prolong engine compression checks
Do not run the engine with a nearly empty fuel tank
Avoid coasting with the ignition turned Off
Do not dispose of a used catalytic converter along with oily or gasoline soaked parts

Checking

4 The catalytic converter requires little if any maintenance and servicing at regular intervals. However, the system should be inspected whenever the vehicle is raised on a lift or if the exhaust system is checked or serviced.
5 Check all connections in the exhaust pipe assembly for looseness or damage. Also check all the clamps for damage, cracks, or missing fasteners. Check the rubber hangers for cracks.
6 The converter itself should be checked for damage or dents (maximum $\frac{3}{4}$-inch deep) which could affect its performance and/or be hazardous to your health. At the same time the converter is inspected, check the metal protector plate under it as well as the heat insulator above it for damage and loose fasteners.

Component replacement

7 Do not attempt to remove the catalytic converter until the complete exhaust system is cool. Raise the vehicle and support it securely on jackstands. Apply some penetrating oil to the clamp bolts and allow it to soak in.
8 Remove the bolts and the rubber hangers, then separate the converter from the exhaust pipes. Remove the old gaskets if they are stuck to the pipes.
9 Installation of the converter is the reverse of removal. Use new exhaust pipe gaskets and tighten the clamp bolts to the specified torque. Replace the rubber hangers with new ones if the originals are deteriorated. Start the engine and check carefully for exhaust leaks.

7 Spark control systems

General description

1 The spark control system is designed to reduce hydrocarbon and oxides of nitrogen (NOx) emissions by advancing the ignition timing only when the engine is cold. On some models, the ignition timing is also advanced when the vehicle is at cruising speed.
2 The system includes a distributor mounted vacuum unit, a coolant temperature override valve (CTO) and a delay valve (or check valve). Also, a transmission solenoid control switch was used on AMC models manufactured from 1972 to 1979.
3 Depending on engine coolant temperature, throttle position and, on some models, the speed of the vehicle, vacuum is applied to the diaphragm in the distributor vacuum unit. The ignition timing is then changed to reduce emissions and improve cold engine driveability.

Checking

Delay valve (pre-1981 models)

4 To test the delay valve used on vehicles manufactured before 1981, you will need a vacuum gauge. Disconnect the vacuum hose from the vacuum advance unit on the distributor.
5 Connect the vacuum gauge to the disconnected hose.
6 Start the engine. The vacuum gauge should indicate manifold vacuum.
7 Stop the engine and observe the gauge. If the vacuum pressure falls off rapidly, the delay valve is defective (a very gradual loss is normal).

Delay valve (1981 through 1983 models)

8 A vacuum gauge will be needed to test the delay valve used on vehicles manufactured from 1981 through 1983.
9 Connect a T-fitting at port 1 of the delay valve (see the accompanying illustration).
10 Connect the vacuum gauge to the T-fitting.
11 Start the engine. Be careful of the moving parts at the front of the engine when carrying out the following checks.
12 Observe the vacuum gauge. When the throttle is suddenly depressed, the vacuum should instantly decrease.
13 Stop the engine. Disconnect the T-fitting from port 1 of the delay

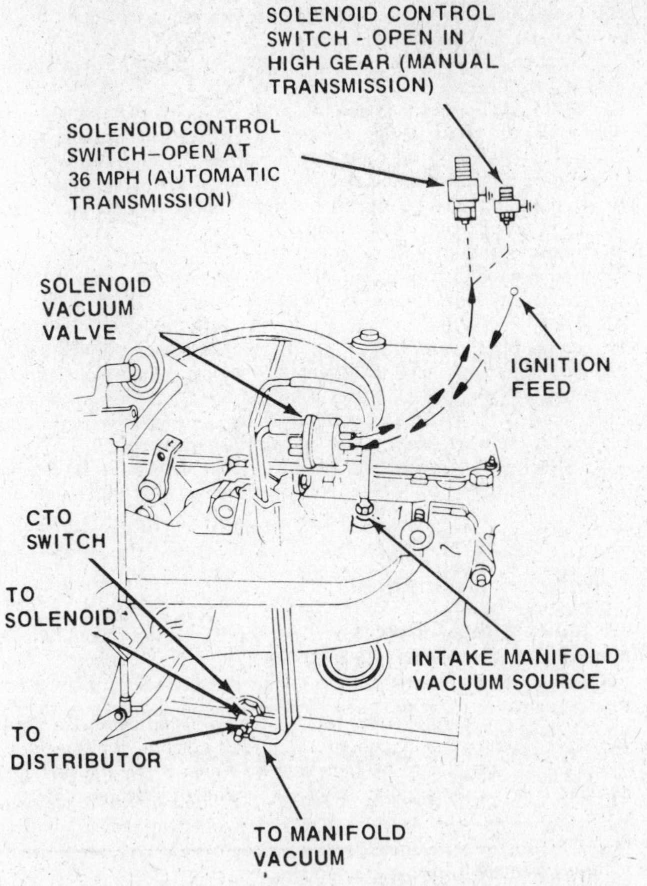

Fig. 6.7 Typical TCS system used from 1972 to 1979 (six-cylinder shown) (Sec 7)

valve and connect it to port 4 on the valve.

14 Start the engine and observe the gauge. When the throttle is suddenly depressed, the vacuum should be maintained.

15 Stop the engine and remove the gauge and T-fitting.

16 Some later model vehicles are equipped with a forward delay valve to maintain the spark advance during sudden throttle closings. An indication of a defective forward delay valve would be a rough running engine during sudden deceleration while the engine is still cold.

CTO valve

17 The CTO valve permits either manifold or carburetor ported vacuum to pass to the distributor vacuum unit, depending on the engine coolant temperature. This improves driveability when the engine is cold. The CTO valve is located on the bottom of the intake manifold on four-cylinder and early V8 engines, and at the left side of the cylinder block on six-cylinder engines. On later V8 models, the CTO valve is located in the thermostat housing.

18 You will need a vacuum gauge to test the CTO valve. To test the switch on engines manufactured from 1972 through 1979, connect the vacuum gauge to the center port (D) of the CTO valve.

19 Start the engine.

20 When the engine is cold, manifold vacuum should be indicated. This would be demonstrated by a vacuum reading on the gauge while the engine is at idle speed.

21 Allow the engine to warm up. Carburetor ported vacuum should be indicated. This would show up as a vacuum reading on the gauge only after the throttle has been depressed to achieve an engine speed of 1000 rpm.

22 Stop the engine and disconnect the vacuum gauge. Be sure to reconnect the vacuum hose to the CTO valve port.

23 Engines manufactured from 1980 through 1983 incorporate a delay valve through which manifold vacuum is routed. To test the CTO valve on these models, first check the manifold vacuum as described earlier in Steps 4 through 6. Be sure the engine is cold.

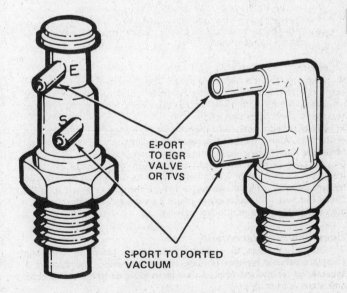

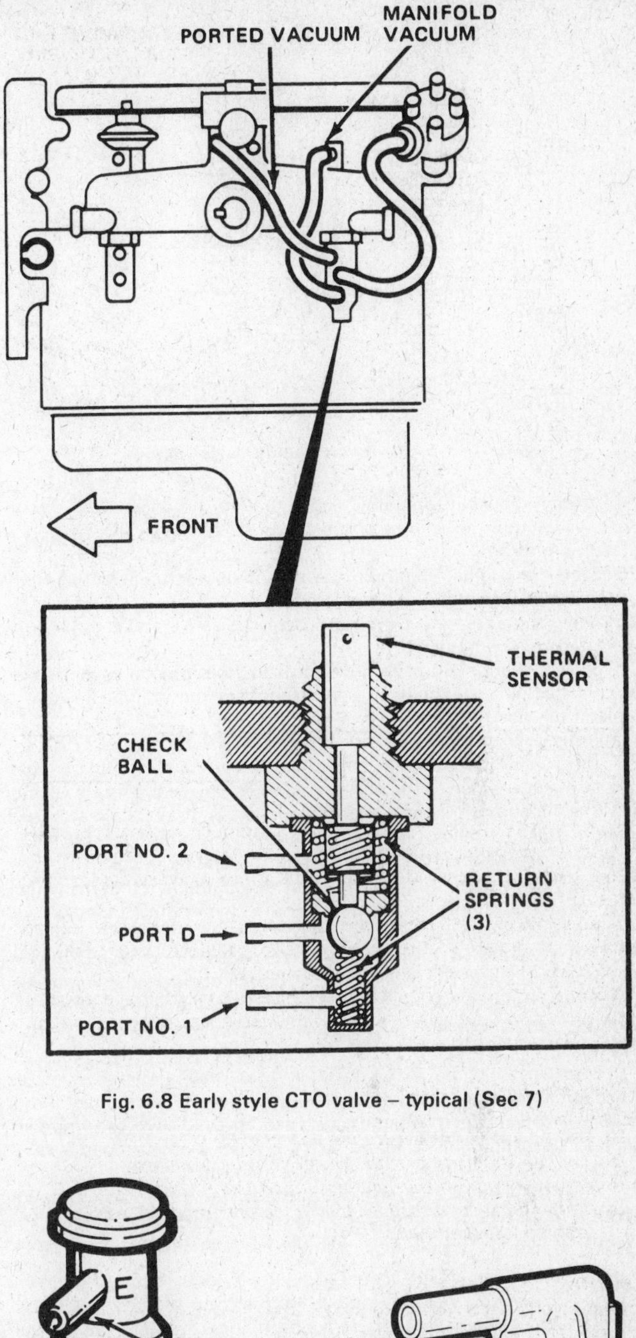

Fig. 6.8 Early style CTO valve – typical (Sec 7)

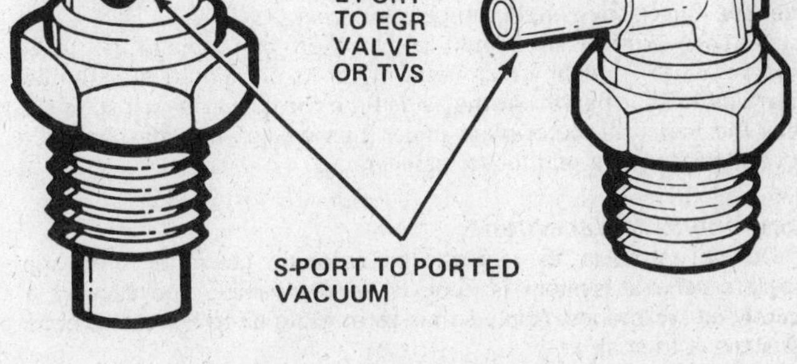

Fig. 6.9 CTO valve typical of later models (Sec 7)

6

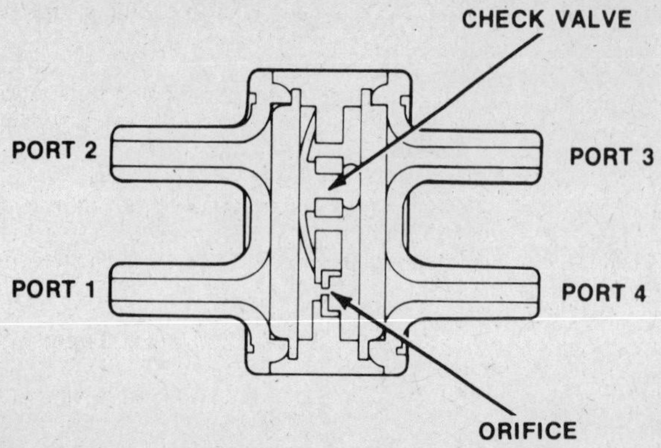

Fig. 6.10 Typical vacuum delay valve (Sec 7)

24 After establishing manifold vacuum, stop the engine and disconnect the vacuum hose from port 4 of the delay valve. Cap the port so that it is airtight.
25 Start the engine. Manifold vacuum should *not* be indicated on the gauge while the engine is cold.
26 Allow the engine to warm up. There should be a vacuum reading indicated on the gauge.
27 Stop the engine and remove the cap from the delay valve port. Reconnect the vacuum hose and disconnect the gauge. Be sure to replace the hose on the CTO valve port.

Transmission controlled spark system (1972 through 1979)

28 The TCS system reduces emissions by lowering the peak combustion temperature during the power stroke. This system permits vacuum spark advance only in high gear (manual transmissions) or at speeds greater than 36 miles per hour (automatic transmissions). The CTO valve will defeat the TCS system when the engine is cold.
29 The TCS system is difficult to check due to the fact that the vehicle must be in operation. This means that the checks must be made with the vehicle travelling at speed.
30 If a problem in this system is suspected, first check that all electrical wires and connections are in good condition and intact. Also inspect the vacuum hoses at the CTO valve and the distributor vacuum advance unit. A blown fuse in the fuse box can also cause problems in this system.
31 To ascertain if the TCS system is in fact malfunctioning, connect a vacuum gauge in the hose between the solenoid and the distributor. A length of vacuum hose must be used to enable you to route the gauge inside the vehicle. Make sure the hose is not crimped and will not be damaged by moving or hot engine parts.
32 Drive the vehicle and have an assistant watch the vacuum gauge. Make a log of vacuum gauge readings and transmission gears. If the system is functioning properly, the following conditions will be met:

a) When the engine is cold, vacuum will show on the gauge until the engine has warmed up to operating temperature.
b) At normal operating temperature there should be vacuum showing on the gauge in high gear (manual transmissions) or beyond speeds of 36 mph (automatic transmissions) only.

33 The system should be tested with the engine cold and also after it has reached normal operating temperature.
34 If a fault is detected during the driving test, check the transmission switch (located on the transmission case) as described in the next Step.
35 With the engine warm and running, have an assistant put the transmission in a low forward gear (make sure the front wheels are blocked, parking brake is on and the assistant has the brake pedal depressed). There should be no vacuum going to the distributor. If there is vacuum going to the distributor, remove the transmission switch connection. Replace the transmission switch if the vacuum stops when the transmission switch connection is removed.
36 To check the solenoid vacuum valve (TCS system), set the parking brake.
37 Place the gearshift lever in the Neutral position if your vehicle is equipped with a manual transmission. If your vehicle is equipped with an automatic transmission, place the gearshift lever in Park.
38 Disconnect the vacuum line at the solenoid vacuum valve.
39 Connect a vacuum gauge to the solenoid vacuum valve where the distributor line was disconnected.
40 Start the engine and run it at 1000 to 1500 rpm. No vacuum should be indicated on the gauge.
41 Maintain engine speed and, being careful of moving engine parts, disconnect the two-wire connector from the solenoid. There should be a reading on the gauge, indicating ported vacuum. Connect and disconnect the wire several times to verify the test. The valve cannot be repaired and must be replaced if defective. Disconnect the vacuum gauge and reconnect the vacuum hose.

Distributor vacuum unit

42 Remove the distributor cap and rotor. Mark the hoses attached to the distributor vacuum unit, then disconnect them.
43 Attach a separate section of hose to one of the ports and apply a vacuum at the hose with your mouth. When a vacuum is applied, the vacuum unit shaft (inside the distributor) should retract and rotate the breaker plate. Repeat the check with the hose attached to the other port. **Note**: *If the diaphragm canister is equipped with two ports, block off one of them with your finger when making the check.*
44 If the breaker plate fails to move, the diaphragm is probably ruptured and the entire vacuum unit must be replaced with a new one.

Component replacement

CTO valve

45 The CTO is threaded into a cooling system passage and its removal requires draining of the cooling system (see Chapter 1). Mark the hoses, to simplify installation, before disconnecting them. Apply thread sealant to the new valve before installing it and be sure to hook up the hoses correctly.

Check valve(s), delay valve(s), solenoid switch and solenoid vacuum valve

46 Replacement of these components is a simple matter of removing the faulty component and installing a new one. Be sure to mark the hoses before disconnecting them to ensure that they are correctly connected to the new component(s).

Distributor vacuum unit

47 Since replacement of this component may require removal and partial disassembly of the distributor, refer to Chapter 5 for additional information.

8 Forced air pre-heat systems

General description

1 While coming under different names, the end result from this system is the same – to improve engine efficiency and reduce hydrocarbon emissions during initial engine warm-up.
2 There are two different methods used to achieve this goal. First, a thermo controlled air cleaner is used to draw warm air from the exhaust manifold directly into the carburetor. Second, some form of exhaust valve is incorporated inside the exhaust pipe to recirculate warm exhaust gases, which are then used to pre-heat the carburetor and choke.
3 It is during the first few miles of driving (depending on outside temperature) that this system has its greatest effect on engine performance and emissions output. Once the engine has reached normal operating temperature, the flapper valves in the exhaust pipe and air cleaner open, allowing for normal engine operation.
4 Because of this cold-engine only function, it is important to periodically check this system to prevent poor engine performance when cold, or overheating of the fuel mixture once the engine has reached operating temperatures. If either the exhaust heat valve or air cleaner valve sticks in the 'no heat' position, the engine will run poorly, stall and waste gas until it has warmed up on its own. A valve sticking in the 'heat' position causes the engine to run as if it is out of tune due to the constant flow of hot air to the carburetor.
5 The components which make up this system include a heat valve inside the exhaust pipe on the right side of the engine (called an exhaust manifold heat valve), and a thermostatic air cleaner consisting of a temperature sensor, thermostat or vacuum diaphragm, air valve door and heat stove.

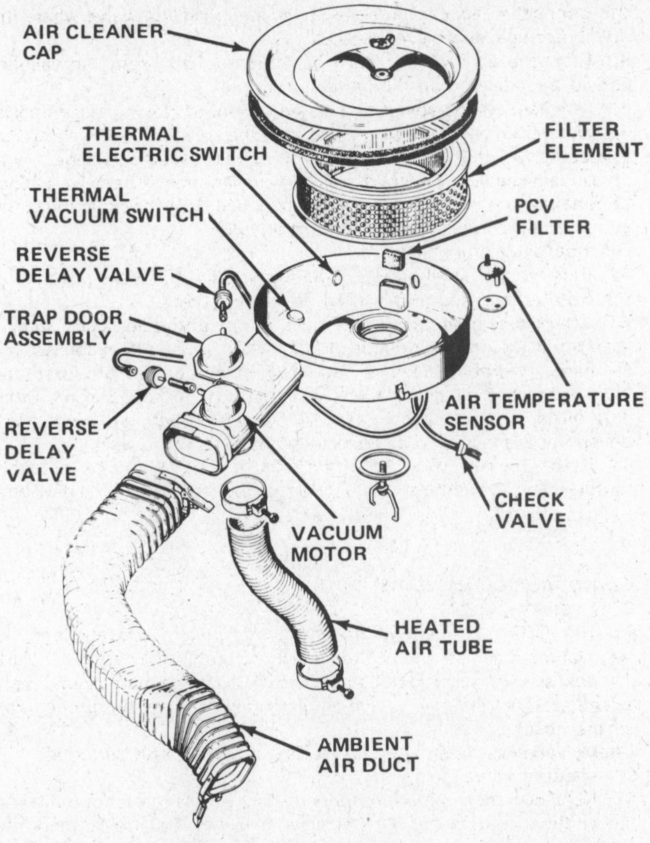

Fig. 6.11 Air cleaner assembly equipped with the TAC system (later six-cylinder model shown) (Sec 8)

Checking

6 Refer to Chapter 1 for procedures used to check the exhaust manifold heat valve and the thermo controlled air cleaner.

Component replacement

Exhaust manifold heat valve (four and six-cylinder)

7 Remove and separate the intake and exhaust manifolds (Chapter 2).
8 Remove the manifold heat valve assembly by cutting the heat valve shaft on both sides of the valve.
9 Lift the valve out of the manifold. Using a punch and hammer, drive out the remaining shaft sections and bushings.
10 Install the replacement bushings using the heat valve shaft as a guide pin.
11 Ream out the replacement bushings with a $\frac{5}{16}$-inch drill bit to remove all burrs.
12 Position the heat valve in the Off (unweighted) position and install the shaft and counterweight assembly.
13 Rotate the counterweight until the spring stop contacts the bottom of the manifold boss.
14 Install the heat valve on the shaft, but do not tighten the retaining screw yet.
15 With the heat valve closed, install the tension spring with the hook end up and pointing away from the manifold. Hook the spring under the support pin.
16 Operate the heat valve several times to allow the shaft to center.
17 Hold the shaft in place and move the valve as far as possible toward the weighted position. Tighten the retaining screw.
18 Check the operation of the valve.
19 Install the intake and exhaust manifolds.

Exhaust manifold heat valve (V8)

20 Disconnect and lower the exhaust pipes.
21 Remove the heat valve assembly from the right side exhaust manifold.
22 Remove all traces of the old exhaust pipe gasket.
23 Install the new heat valve assembly along with a new valve gasket.
24 Install a new exhaust pipe gasket.
25 Align the exhaust pipes and thread the attaching nuts onto the manifold studs. Tighten the nuts alternately until the exhaust flange is evenly seated.

Air valve and trap door vacuum motor

26 Remove the air cleaner assembly from the engine and disconnect the vacuum hose from the motor.
27 Drill out the two spot welds which secure the vacuum motor retaining strap to the snorkel tube.
28 Remove the motor attaching strap.
29 Lift up the motor, cocking it to one side to unhook the motor from the air valve or trap door assembly.
30 Insert the vacuum motor linkage into the air valve or trap door assembly.
31 Using a new rivet, attach the motor and retaining strap to the snorkel. Make sure the rivet does not interfere with the operation of the valve or trap door.
32 Connect the vacuum hose to the motor and install the air cleaner assembly.

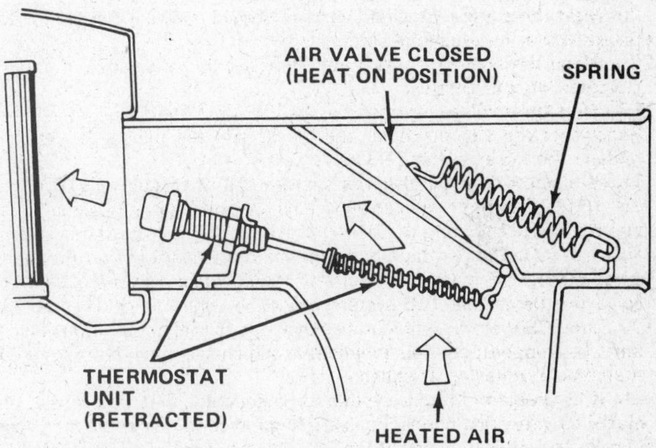

Fig. 6.12 TAC system operation (early six-cylinder model shown) (Sec 8)

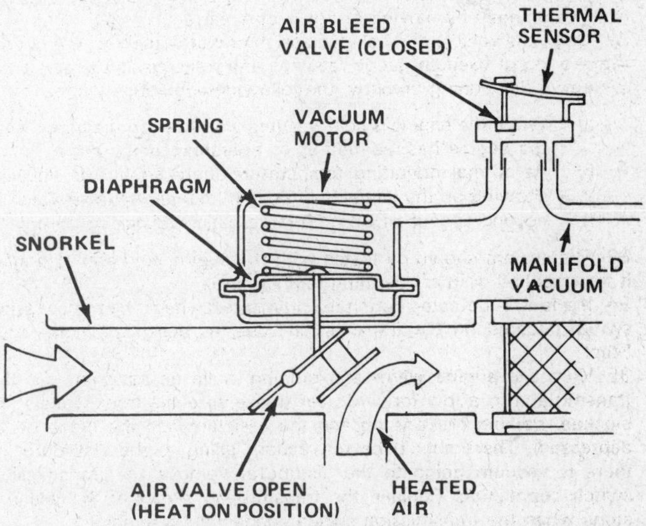

Fig. 6.13 TAC system operation (later four-cylinder model shown) (Sec 8)

6

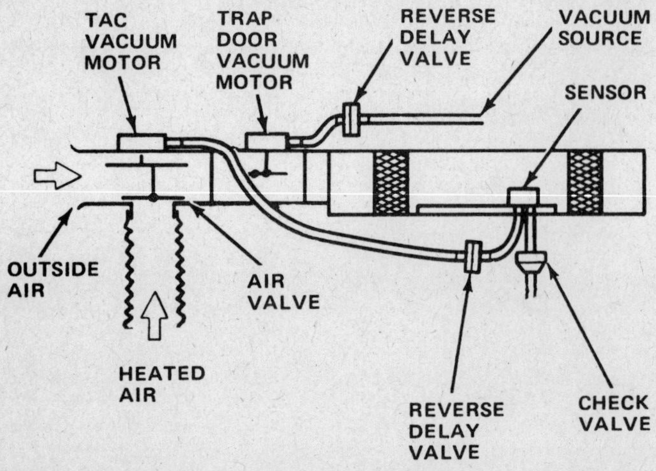

Fig. 6.14 TAC system typical of later six-cylinder models – includes trap door assembly to prevent fuel vapor from escaping after engine is shut off (Sec 8)

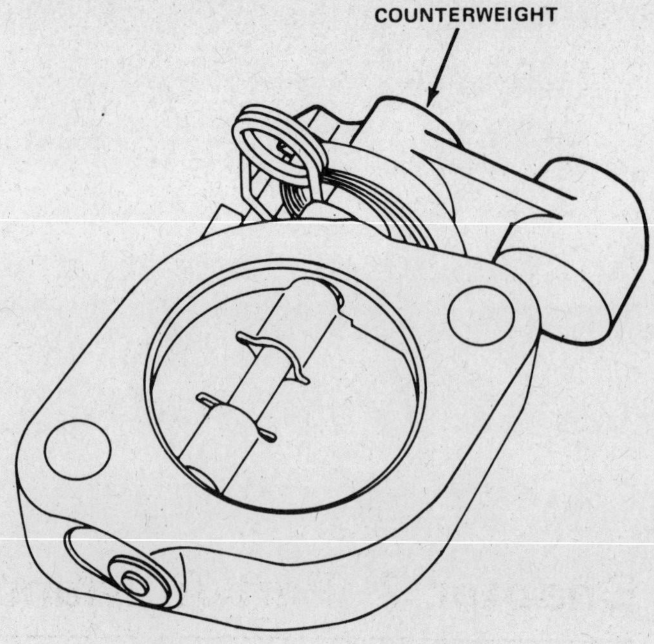

Fig. 6.15 Exhaust manifold heat valve (V8 engine shown) (Sec 8)

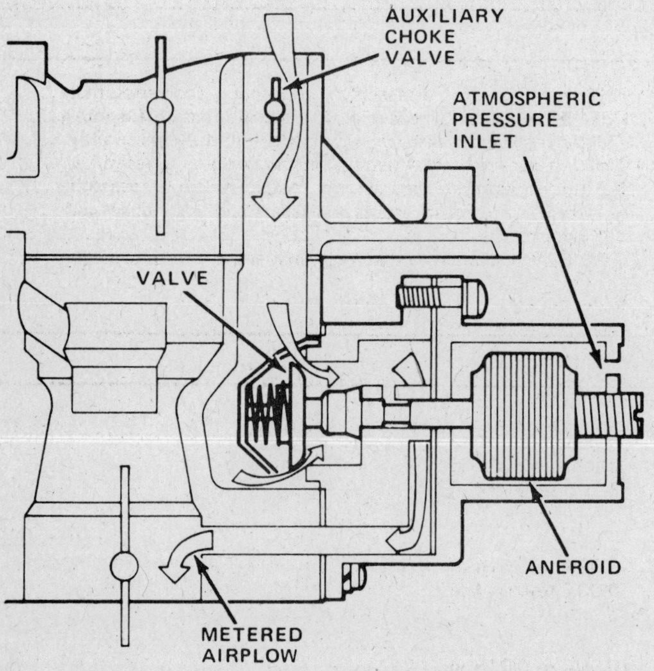

Fig. 6.16 High altitude compensation circuit (model 2150 carburettor shown) (Sec 9)

Thermal switch

33 Remove the air cleaner from the engine and disconnect the vacuum hoses at the sensor.

34 Carefully note the position of the sensor. The new sensor must be installed in exactly the same position.

35 Pry up the tabs on the sensor retaining clip and remove the sensor and clip from the air cleaner.

36 Install the new sensor with a new gasket in the same position as the old one.

37 Press the retaining clip on the sensor. Do not damage the control mechanism in the center of the sensor.

38 Connect the vacuum hoses and attach the air cleaner to the engine.

9 Altitude compensation circuit

General description

1 On some V8 models sold for use above 4000 feet, an altitude compensation circuit is incorporated in the carburetor. This prevents the engine from running rough at high altitudes due to an over-rich fuel/air mixture. The circuit, at high altitudes, supplies the extra air necessary to lean out the mixture. Air flows into an auxiliary chamber and passes into the main venturis via a spring loaded valve. An aneroid diaphragm expands and contracts according to atmospheric pressure in order to open or close the auxiliary air valve.

Checking

2 Any checks to assess the condition of the aneroid diaphragm or air valve will have to be done by your AMC dealer.

Component replacement

3 If the diaphragm is found to be defective, it can be replaced by removing the attaching screws and separating the compensation assembly from the carburetor body.

4 Remove the diaphragm-to-chamber attaching screws and remove the diaphragm and gasket from the chamber.

5 Remove the carburetor body-to-chamber gasket from the carburetor (or chamber). Be sure to scrape off all traces of the old gasket.

6 Installation is the reverse of removal. Use new gaskets on the diaphragm and carburetor-to-chamber mating surface.

Chapter 7 Part A Manual transmission

Contents

Extension housing oil seal – replacement 6
Gearshift lever – removal and installation 4
General information 1
Planning major transmission work 3
Removal and installation 7
Shift linkage adjustment 5
Transmission application and identification 2
Transmission oil level check .... See Chapter 1
150T transmission – disassembly, inspection and reassembly 12
HR1 transmission – disassembly, inspection and reassembly 8
SR4 transmission – disassembly, inspection and reassembly 13
T-4 transmission – disassembly, inspection and reassembly 14
T-5 transmission – disassembly, inspection and reassembly 15
T-10 transmission – disassembly, inspection and reassembly 9
T-14 and T-15 transmissions – disassembly, inspection and reassembly 11
T-96 transmission – disassembly, inspection and reassembly 10

Specifications

HR1 transmission

Second gear end play	0.004 to 0.014 in
3 – 4 synchronizer end play	0.004 to 0.014 in
Countershaft gear end play	0.006 to 0.018 in

SR-4 transmission

Second gear end play	0.004 to 0.014 in
3 – 4 synchronizer end play	0.004 to 0.014 in

150-T transmission

Reverse idler gear end play	0.004 to 0.018 in
Second gear end play	0.004 to 0.014 in
Countershaft gear end play	0.004 to 0.018 in

T-14 transmission

First gear end play	0.003 to 0.012 in
Second gear end play	0.003 to 0.018 in
Countershaft gear end play	0.005 to 0.019 in

T-15 transmission

First gear end play	0.003 to 0.014 in
Second gear end play	0.003 to 0.018 in
Countershaft gear end play	0.005 to 0.018 in

T-10 transmission

Interlock sleeve clearance	0.002 to 0.008 in

T-96 transmission

Second gear end play	0.003 to 0.010 in
Interlock sleeve clearance	0.001 to 0.007 in

Torque specifications

	Ft-lb	Nm
Front bearing cap bolts	13	18
Transmission-to-clutch housing bolts	55	74
Support cushion bolts	22	30
HR1 support cushion bolts	35	47
Reverse lever pivot bolt	20	27
Transmission cover bolts	10	14
U-joint clamp strap bolts	14	19
Filler plug	15	20
TCS switch and backup light switch	15	20
Extension housing bolts	23	31
HR1 extension housing bolts	34	46

1 General information

The AMC vehicles covered in this manual and equipped with manual transmissions are outfitted with three, four and five-speed transmissions. Every transmission, with the exception of the optional overdrive, is covered in this Chapter.

2 Transmission application and identification

1 The T-96 transmission was used on 1971 and 1972 Gremlin and Hornet models equipped with 232-cubic-inch engines.
2 The T-10 transmission was used on 1971 and 1972 Hornet models equipped with 360-cubic-inch engines and all 1973 and 1974 models equipped with four-speed transmissions.
3 The T-14 transmission was used on 1971 and 1972 Gremlin and Hornet models equipped with 258-cubic-inch engines and all 1973 and 1974 models equipped with three-speed transmissions. It was also used on all 1976 model Gremlins.
4 The T-15 transmission was used on 1972 Hornet models with 360-cubic-inch engines.
5 The 150-T transmission was introduced in 1975 and used on all three-speed models in that year. It was also used on all 1976 Hornets and 1977 and 1978 AMC models equipped with three-speed transmissions. Finally, it was used on the 1979 Spirit equipped with the 232-cubic-inch engine.
6 The HR1 four-speed transmission was used only on 1978 and 1979 models equipped with a four-cylinder engine.
7 The SR4 transmission was the only four-speed transmission used in 1977 and 1978 and was standard equipment on 1979 models with six and eight cylinder engines.
8 The T-4, T-5 and SR4 transmissions are used on all models from 1982 on.

3 Planning major transmission work

1 Before beginning transmission disassembly, read through the entire procedure to familiarize yourself with the scope and requirements of the job.
2 One of the biggest problems a beginner will face when dismantling an assembly as complex as a transmission is trying to remember exactly where each part came from. To help alleviate this problem, it may be helpful to draw your own simple diagrams or take instant photos during the disassembly process. Laying each part out in the order in which it was removed and tagging parts may also be useful.
3 Try to anticipate which parts may have to be replaced and have them available before beginning. Regardless of broken or badly worn components, there are certain items which must be replaced as a matter of course when the transmission is reassembled. These include gaskets, snap-rings, oil seals and sometimes bearings. You will also need some multi-purpose grease and an RTV-type gasket sealer to properly reassemble the transmission.
4 Cleanliness is extremely important when working on a precision piece of equipment such as a transmission. The working area should be kept as clean and free of dirt and dust as possible. Also, adequate space should be available to lay out the various parts as they are removed.

4 Gearshift lever – removal and installation

T-10 transmission

1 Insert a 0.015 to 0.020 inch feeler gauge blade alongside the driver's side of the lever between the spring steel barb and the lower part of the gearshift lever.
2 Grasp the bottom of the lever and the blade at the same time and pull up and out of the assembly.
3 To install the lever, simply push it back down into the assembly.

T-96 and T-14 transmission

4 Remove the gearshift lever bezel and rubber boot.
5 Remove the lever retainer bolts and remove the retainer.
6 Remove the shift lever crossover spring while lifting the lever out of the assembly.
7 Remove the shift rod cotter pins and anti-rattle washers. Slide the shift rods forward for removal.
8 Installation is the reverse of removal.

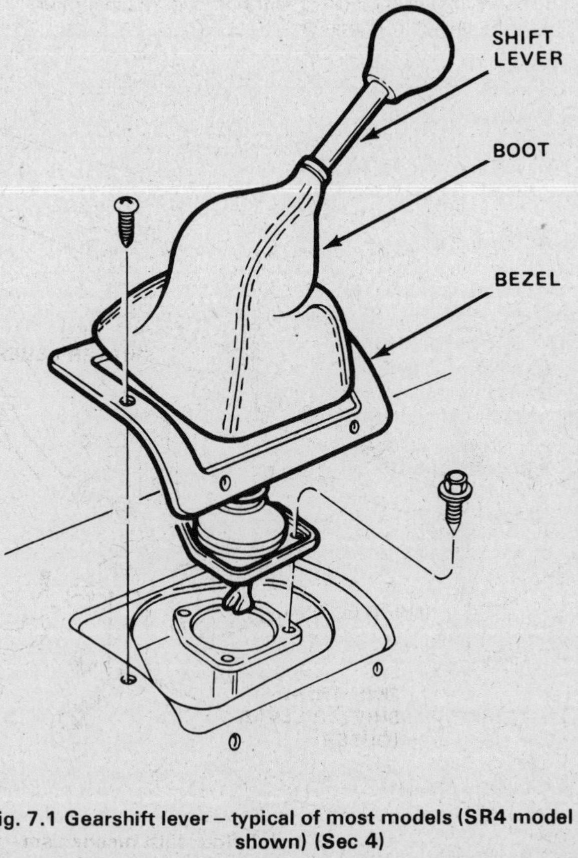

Fig. 7.1 Gearshift lever – typical of most models (SR4 model shown) (Sec 4)

150-T transmission

9 Remove the gearshift level bezel and slide the rubber boot up.
10 Remove the lever retainer bolts, unhook the crossover spring and remove the lever along with the crossover spring.
11 Disconnect the shift rods from the transmission shift levers and slide the rods forward and out of the retainer bushings.
12 Remove the lever retainer mounting bolts and remove the retainer.
13 Installation is the reverse of removal.

SR4, T-4, and T-5 transmissions

14 Shift the transmission into Neutral.
15 Remove the gearshift lever bezel and slide the rubber boot up.
16 Remove the two bolts attaching the lever to the lever mounting flange on the transmission extension housing.
17 Pull the lever straight up and out of the housing.
18 Installation is the reverse of removal. Be sure the gearshift lever fork is seated on the offset lever bushing. Tighten the lever-to-flange bolts to 18 ft-lb (24 Nm).

HR1 transmission

19 Shift the transmission into Neutral.
20 Remove the bezel and slide the inner and outer boots up.
21 Remove the E-clip retainer and slide the lever spring up.
22 Fold the carpet back and straighten the gearshift lever lock tabs. Unthread the plastic locknut from the extension housing.
23 Lift the lever up and out of the housing.
24 Installation is the reverse of removal. Be sure the shift rail insulator is straight and facing down on the shift rail before installing the lever.

5 Shift linkage adjustment

Floor shift

1 Place the levers attached to both shift fork shafts in the Neutral position.
2 Loosen the Second-Third shift lever attaching nut and adjustment bolt.
3 Place the First-Reverse shift rod in the Neutral position.
4 Align the Second-Third shift rod notch with the First-Reverse shift rod notch and tighten the adjustment bolt and attaching nut.
5 Check the gearshift operation.

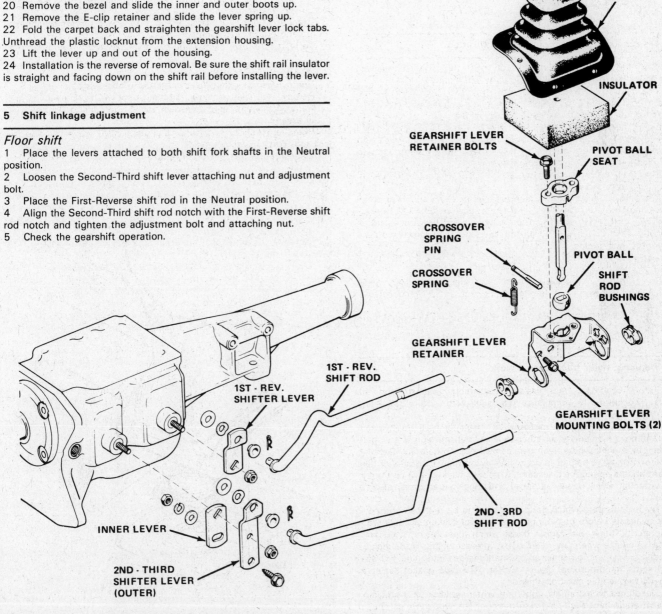

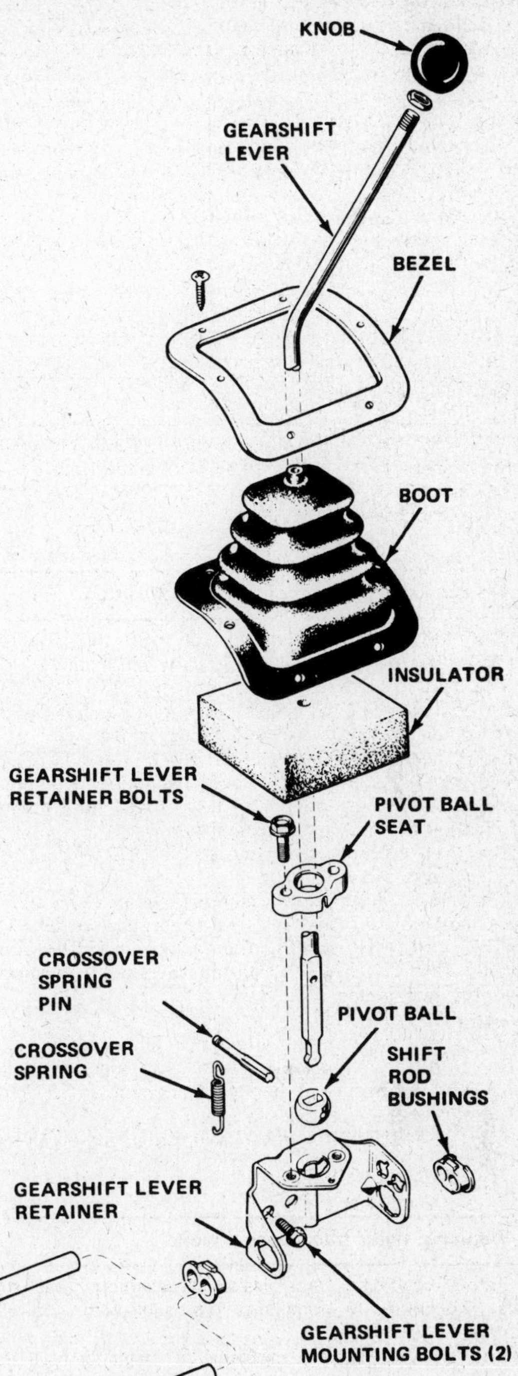

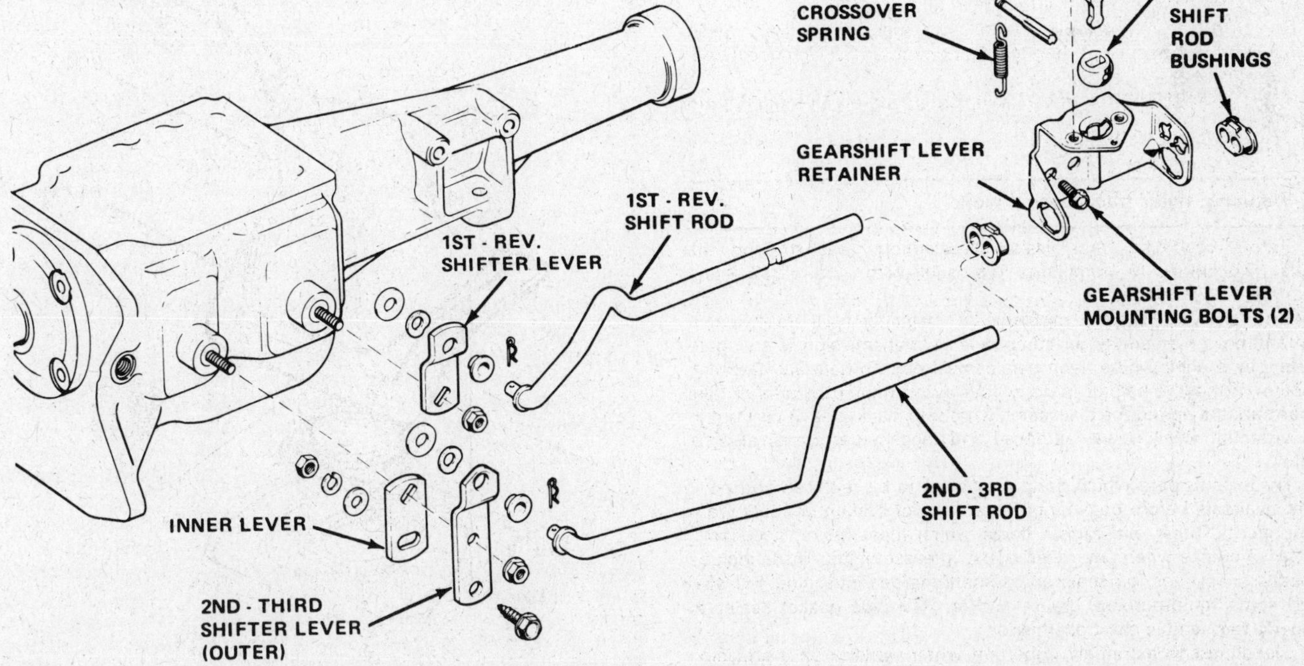

Fig. 7.2 Floor shift mechanism – typical of many models (150T shown) (Sec 5)

Column shift

6 Disconnect the shift rods from the shift levers on the outside of the transmission.
7 Insert a guide pin, $\frac{3}{16}$-inch in diameter, through the steering column shift levers. Position the column shift lever in Reverse and lock the steering column.
8 Place the First-Reverse lever (on the transmission) in Reverse and then adjust the shift rod trunnion so the guide pin slides freely through the outer shift lever on the transmission. Tighten the trunnion locknuts.
9 Unlock the steering column and move the column shift lever to Neutral, making sure that both of the outer shift levers are also in Neutral.
10 Adjust the Second-Third gearshift rod trunnion to provide the guide pin with a sliding fit in the column levers. Tighten the shift rod trunnion locknuts. Remove the guide pin and check gear selection, finally selecting Reverse and checking that the steering column lock operates without binding.

6 Extension housing oil seal – replacement

1 The extension housing oil seal can be replaced without dismantling or removing the transmission.
2 Raise the rear of the vehicle and support it securely on jackstands. Be sure to block the front wheels to keep the vehicle from rolling. If the seal is leaking, transmission lubricant will be built up on the front of the driveshaft.
3 Refer to Chapter 8 and remove the driveshaft.
4 Using a screwdriver or pry bar, carefully pry the oil seal and dust seal out of the rear of the transmission. Do not damage the splines on the transmission output shaft.
5 Using a large section of pipe or a very large deep socket as a drift, install the new oil seal. Drive it into the bore squarely and make sure that it is completely seated.
6 Lubricate the splines of the transmission output shaft and the outside of the driveshaft sleeve yoke with lightweight grease, then install the driveshaft. Be careful not to damage the lip of the new seal.
7 Lower the vehicle, test drive it and check for leaks.

7 Removal and installation

1 Remove the gearshift lever as described in Section 4.
2 Open the hood. Raise the vehicle and support it firmly on jackstands.
3 Mark the driveshaft and rear axle yokes for assembly reference.
4 Remove the rear axle yoke U-bolts and remove the driveshaft.
5 Disconnect the speedometer cable and backup light switch wires. Disconnect the transmission controlled spark wire, if so equipped.
6 On vehicles equipped with an HR1 transmission, disconnect the starter motor cable and remove the starter motor. Remove the clutch throwout lever protective boot and loosen the clutch cable locknut. Back off the cable adjuster nut to create slack in the cable and disengage the cable from the lever. Finally, on HR1 models, remove the inspection cover at the front of the clutch housing.
7 On all models except the HR1 transmission, install a support stand under the clutch housing to support the engine when the transmission and rear crossmember are removed.
8 On vehicles equipped with an HR1 transmission, place a support stand under the front of the engine.
9 Remove the catalytic converter support bracket, if so equipped, from the transmission.
10 On some V8 models, it may be necessary to remove the exhaust pipes to gain adequate clearance for transmission removal.
11 Remove the nuts and bolts attaching the transmission support cushion to the crossmember. Remove the crossmember attaching nuts and remove the crossmember.
12 Support the transmission using a sturdy floor jack, preferably one equipped with wheels or casters.
13 On vehicles equipped with T-10, T-14 and T-96 transmissions, the column shift rods and reverse lock-up rod must be disconnected. On these vehicles, lower the engine until adequate clearance for transmission removal is obtained.
14 On T-10, T-14 and T-96 models, remove two of the transmission-to-clutch housing bolts and install two AMC guide pins no. J-1434 or two pins of a suitable size. Remove the two remaining bolts on these models and carefully remove the transmission.
15 On vehicles equipped with 150-T, SR4, HR1, T-5 and T-4 transmissions, remove the transmission-to-clutch housing attaching bolts and carefully remove the transmission. **Note**: *Be careful not to damage the clutch shaft, pilot bushing and driven plate during transmission removal.*
16 Remove the throwout bearing (if applicable) and remove the pilot bushing lubricating wick, if so equipped. Soak the lubricating wick in engine oil.
17 Installation is the reverse of removal. Be sure to tighten all bolts to the specified torque.

8 HR1 transmission – disassembly, inspection and reassembly

Disassembly

1 Pull the throwout lever straight out of the lever opening in the clutch housing to disengage the lever retaining clip from the pivot ball stud.
2 Remove the throwout lever and bearing as an assembly by sliding them off the bearing cap.
3 Remove the clutch housing-to-transmission bolts and remove the clutch housing.
4 Remove the dynamic absorber and transmission support cushion adapter bracket from the extension housing.
5 Remove the back-up light switch from the extension housing.
6 Insert a $\frac{5}{16}$-inch diameter rod through the access plug hole to remove the interlock plate retaining pin. Remove the interlock pin.
7 Using a $\frac{5}{32}$-inch pin punch, remove the selector arm roll pin.
8 Tap the front end of the shift rail until it displaces the large plug at the back of the extension housing. Remove the shift rail from the back of the extension housing.
9 Remove the selector arm, interlock plate and shift forks from the transmission case. Note the location and position of these components for assembly reference.
10 Remove the bolts attaching the front bearing cap to the transmission case. Remove the bearing cap and bearing cap O-ring.
11 Using a screwdriver, pry out the front bearing cap oil seal. A small, sharp chisel can be used to partially collapse the metal wall of the seal if it is difficult to remove the seal. If this is necessary, be careful not to nick or gouge the seal bore.
12 Remove the front bearing retaining and locating snap-ring from the clutch shaft.
13 Using a bearing removal tool, remove the front bearing from the clutch shaft. AMC bearing remover no. J-8157-01, puller bolts no. J-26827 and puller assembly J-25132 or a suitable bearing removal tool can be used.
14 Remove the extension housing-to-transmission case bolts. Tap the extension housing with a soft-faced hammer to loosen it from the case.
15 Remove the clutch shaft from the transmission case.
16 Remove the extension housing and output shaft geartrain from the back of the transmission case. Do not let the Third-Fourth synchronizer sleeve separate from the hub during shaft removal.
17 Using a screwdriver, pry out the shift rail oil seal from the rear of the transmission case.
18 Remove the pilot roller bearing from the clutch shaft bore or from the output shaft pilot bearing hub.
19 Use AMC slide hammer no. J7004-1 and shaft remover no. J-26856 or a suitable slide hammer and shaft remover to remove the Reverse idler gearshaft. Thread the shaft remover into the idler shaft and thread the slide hammer bolt into the shaft remover.
20 Remove the Reverse idler gear along with the gear spacer from the transmission case. Note the position of the gear spacer for assembly reference.
21 Remove the countershaft during AMC countershaft loading tool no. J-26826 or a suitable length of pipe of the correct diameter.
22 Remove the shift fork from the Reverse lever. Note its position for assembly reference.
23 Remove the Reverse lever retaining clip and remove the Reverse lever and lever spring. Note the spring position for assembly reference.
24 Remove the countershaft gear and the loading tool as an assembly. Remove the loading tool, needle bearings and four bearing retainers. Note that there are two different thicknesses of bearing retainers and two different lengths of needle bearings.
25 Remove the thrust washers from the countershaft gear.

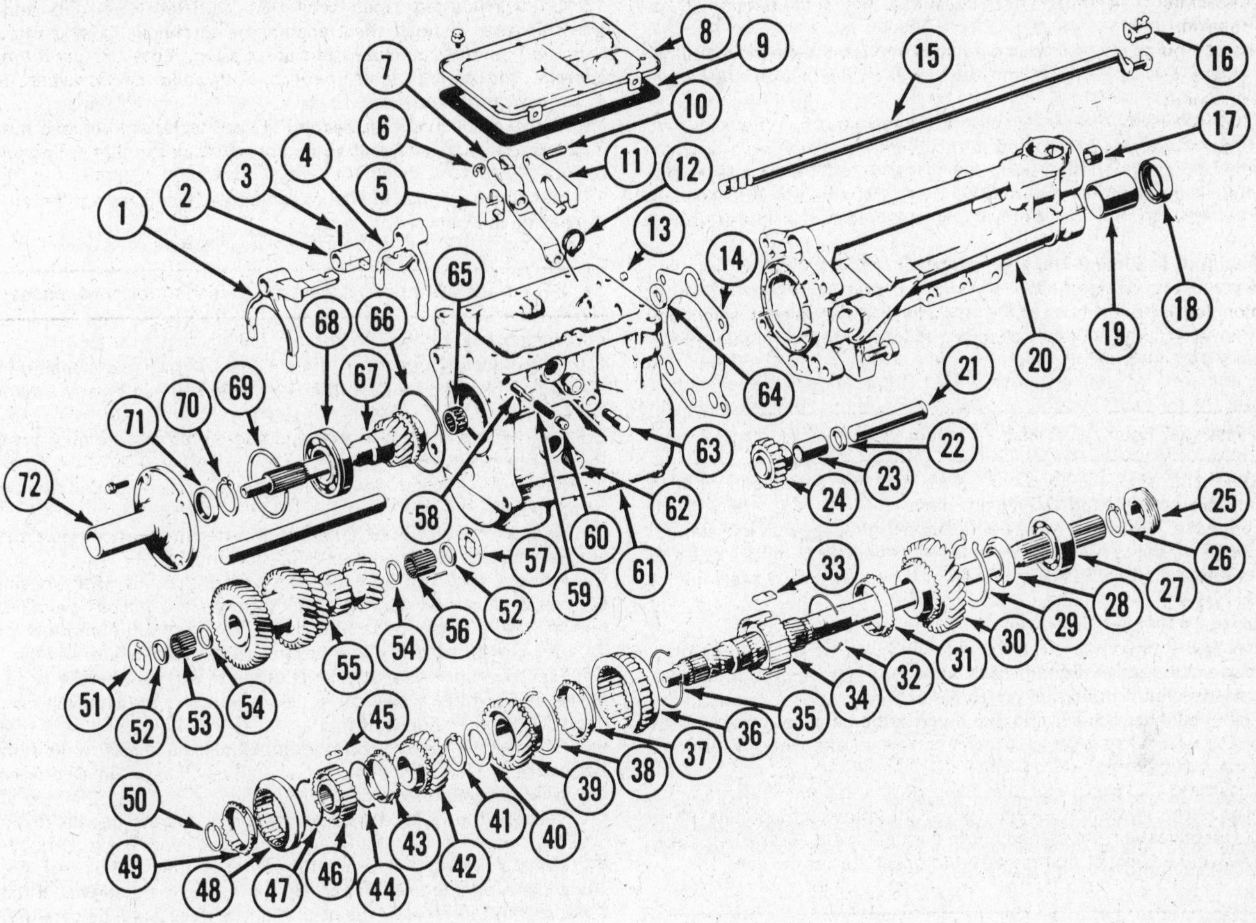

Fig. 7.3 Exploded view of the HR1 transmission components (Sec 8)

1 *Third-fourth shift fork*
2 *Selector arm*
3 *Selector arm roll pin*
4 *First-second shift fork*
5 *Reverse lever shift fork*
6 *Reverse lever spring clip*
7 *Reverse lever*
8 *Top cover*
9 *Top cover gasket*
10 *Interlock plate retaining pin*
11 *Interlock plate*
12 *Reverse lever spring*
13 *Interlock retaining pin access plug*
14 *Extension housing gasket*
15 *Shift rail*
16 *Shift rail insert*
17 *Shift rail bushing (nylon)*
18 *Extension housing seal*
19 *Extension housing bushing (serviced as part of housing)*
20 *Extension housing*
21 *Reverse idler gear shaft*
22 *Reverse idler gear spacer*
23 *Reverse idler gear bushing (serviced as part of gear)*
24 *Reverse idler gear*
25 *Speedometer gear*
26 *Rear bearing snap ring*
27 *Rear bearing*
28 *Oil slinger/spacer*
29 *Output shaft rear snap ring*
30 *First gear*
31 *First gear blocking ring*
32 *First-second synchronizer insert spring*
33 *First-second synchronizer insert (3)*
34 *Output shaft and first-second synchronizer hub assembly (serviced as assembly only)*
35 *First-second synchronizer insert spring*
36 *First-second synchronizer sleeve*
37 *Second gear blocking ring*
38 *Second gear stop ring (installed on gear)*
39 *Second gear*
40 *Second gear spacer*
41 *Second gear snap ring*
42 *Third gear*
43 *Third gear blocking ring*
44 *Third-fourth synchronizer insert spring*
45 *Third-fourth synchronizer insert (3)*
46 *Third-fourth synchronizer hub*
47 *Third-fourth synchronizer insert spring*
48 *Third-fourth synchronizer sleeve*
49 *Fourth gear blocking ring*
50 *Output shaft front snap ring*
51 *Countershaft thrust washer (metal face)*
52 *Countershaft bearing retainer (thick)*
53 *Countershaft front bearings (short - 19 reqd)*
54 *Countershaft bearing retainer (thin)*
55 *Countershaft gear*
56 *Countershaft rear bearings (long – 19 reqd)*
57 *Countershaft thrust washer (metal face)*
58 *Detent plunger*
59 *Detent spring*
60 *Detent plug*
61 *Transmission case*
62 *Fill plug*
63 *Reverse lever pivot (serviced as part of case)*
64 *Shift rail oil seal*
65 *Clutch shaft roller bearing*
66 *Front bearing cap O-ring*
67 *Clutch shaft*
68 *Front bearing*
69 *Front bearing locating snap ring*
70 *Front bearing retaining snap ring*
71 *Front bearing cap oil seal*
72 *Front bearing cap*

26 Remove the Fourth gear blocking ring from the Third-Fourth synchronizer.
27 Remove the rear snap-ring from the output shaft. To do this, compress the ring with needle-nose pliers and slide it toward First gear until it clears the extension housing.
28 Using a soft-faced hammer, tap on the end of the output shaft to loosen the bearing from the extension housing.
29 Remove the front snap-ring from the output shaft.
30 Remove the Third-Fourth synchronizer assembly. Mark the synchronizer sleeve and hub for assembly reference and separate the sleeve from the hub. Remove the synchronizer inserts and insert springs.
31 Remove Third gear and the Third gear blocking ring.
32 Using snap-ring pliers with 45° angle tips, unseat the rear bearing snap-ring and slide it toward the speedometer drivegear.
33 Remove First gear, the first gear spacer, the rear bearing and the speedometer gear as an assembly using a bearing remover such as AMC no. J-8157 and an arbor press. The bearing remover should contact the forward face of First gear. Do not let the First gear blocking ring become caught between the bearing remover and the gear.
34 Remove the First gear blocking ring.
35 Mark the First-Second synchronizer hub and sleeve and remove them. Remove the inserts and the insert springs. The First-Second synchronizer hub is part of the output shaft and is not removable.
36 Remove the extension housing oil seal using AMC tool no. J26829 and slide hammer no. J-7004-1.

Inspection

37 Inspect the disassembled parts after cleaning them with solvent and drying them thoroughly. Needle bearings can be cleaned by wrapping them in a cloth and submerging the cloth and bearings in solvent.

Transmission case and extension housing

38 Check the transmission case and extension housing for cracks and damage, especially at the bearing outer race bosses. Small nicks and burrs can be removed with a fine file.

Mainshaft

39 Check the mainshaft for worn or damaged gear mounting areas and worn or damaged splines. Check the First speed gear for damage and wear.

Main drivegear

40 On the main drivegear assembly, check the front end outer diameter and the inner diameter of the needle bearing contact areas for damage and wear. Check the synchronizer cone surfaces for wear and damage. Check the splines for wear and damage and check the fit of the clutch disc on the shaft. It should move freely on the splines, but must not be excessively loose. Check for worn thrust washers.

Gears

41 Check all gears for worn and damaged teeth. Check the inner diameter and both ends of each gear for wear and damage. Also, check the contact surface of the synchronizer cone for wear and damage.

Blocking rings

42 Check the gear teeth and cone inside diameter for wear and damage.

Synchronizer sleeve and hub

43 With the hub and sleeve assembled, see if the sleeve slides smoothly. Also, check for excessive looseness in the direction of rotation. If either part is defective, both the hub and sleeve must be replaced as an assembly.

Synchronizer inserts and spring

44 Check the synchronizer inserts for wear and damage, especially at the projection. Check the springs for deterioration and cracks.

Reverse idler gear and shaft

45 Inspect the teeth and both sides of the gear for wear and damage. Check the shaft for cracks, evidence of seizure and wear.

Control lever and shift forks

46 Check the upper and lower levers for chatter marks and the stop plate for wear. Inspect the nylon inserts on the shift forks.

Needle and ball bearings

47 Check the needle bearings for roller surface damage such as pitting, cracks and scoring. Assemble the needle bearings and gears on their respective shafts and check to see if they rotate smoothly and quietly. Inspect all ball bearings for wear and damage. See if they rotate smoothly and quietly. If there is any doubt as to the condition of a bearing, replace it.
48 During transmission overhaul, always replace all oil seals and gaskets.

Reassembly

49 Using a soft-faced hammer, install the rear bearing in the extension housing bore. Be sure to seat the bearing completely.
50 Select the thickest possible output shaft rear snap-ring that will fit in the snap-ring groove of the extension housing. The snap-rings are available in varying thicknesses.
51 Remove the snap-ring and rear bearing from the extension housing.
52 Lubricate the output shaft and gear components with transmission lubricant. Lubricate the tapered blocking ring surfaces of all gears with petroleum jelly.
53 Install the synchronizer spring and inserts in the First-Second hub and install the First-Second synchronizer sleeve over the hub and inserts. Position the hub and the sleeve using alignment marks. Also, be sure to position the open ends of each spring so they face away from one another (engage the tang end of each insert spring in the same synchronizer insert).
54 Install the blocking ring on Second gear and install the ring and gear on the output shaft. Be sure to engage the synchronizer inserts in the blocking ring notches.
55 Install the Second gear thrust washer and snap-ring, seating the tabbed end of the snap-ring in the machined groove of the output shaft.
56 Using a feeler gauge, measure Second gear end play. End play should be 0.004 to 0.014-inch (0.1016 and 0.3556 mm). If the end play exceeds this, replace the thrust washer, snap-ring and, if necessary, the gear.
57 Install the blocking ring on First gear and install the ring and gear on the output shaft.
58 Install the oil slinger/spacer on the output shaft. Be sure the oil slinger grooves face First gear.
59 Install the rear snap-ring (see Step 50) over the oil slinger/spacer and against First gear.
60 Install the rear bearing on the output shaft using AMC tool no. J-25678-01 or another suitable tool. Be sure to completely seat the bearing.
61 Install the thickest possible replacement snap-ring in the output shaft groove.
62 Seat the speedometer gear on the output shaft using AMC positioning gauge J-26832 or another suitable tool.
63 Using an arbor press and rear bearing installer no. J-25678-01 or another suitable tool, press the speedometer gear onto the output shaft until the positioning gauge contacts the rear bearing.
64 Install Third gear and the blocking ring on the output shaft.
65 Assemble the Third-Fourth synchronizer components and install the assembly on the output shaft. Install the output shaft front snap-ring.
66 Measure the Third-Fourth synchronizer end play. End play should be 0.004 to 0.014-inch (0.1016 to 0.3556 mm). If the end play exceeds this, replace the snap-ring, synchronizer hub and, if necessary, the synchronizer sleeve.
67 Install the output shaft and geartrain into the extension housing. Tap the front end of the output shaft with a soft-faced hammer to seat the rear bearing in the extension housing.
68 Install the rear snap-ring in the extension housing snap-ring groove.
69 Lubricate all components with transmission lubricant (unless otherwise noted) as they are installed in the case.
70 Insert the countershaft loading tool into the countershaft gear bore.
71 Coat the countershaft needle bearings and bearing retainers with petroleum jelly.

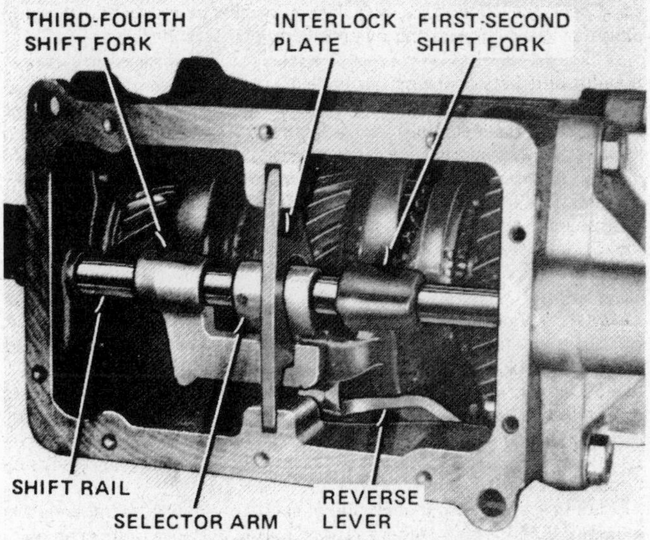

Fig. 7.4 Shift mechanism components (HR1 transmission) (Sec 8)

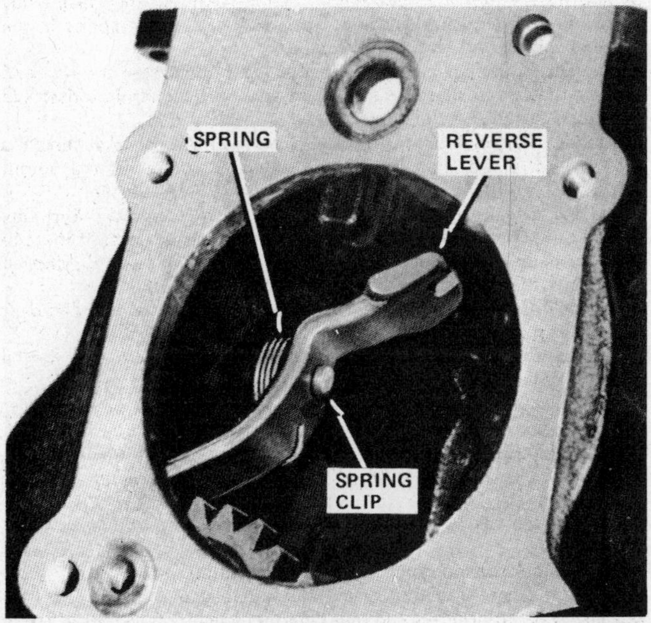

Fig. 7.5 Installed position of Reverse lever (HR1 transmission) (Sec 8)

72 Install a thin bearing retainer in each end of the countershaft gear.
73 Install 19 *long* needle bearings at the *rear* of the countershaft gear.
74 Install 19 *short* needle bearings at the *front* of the countershaft gear.
75 Install a thick bearing retainer in each countershaft bore.
76 Coat the replacement countershaft thrustwashers with petroleum jelly.
77 Position the thrust washer over the bearing bore at the front of the countershaft gear. Push the loading tool toward the front of the gear and through the thrust washer, extending the loading tool just far enough to hold the washer in position.
78 Align the thrust washer tab with the locating notch and install the gear in the case.
79 Align the thrust washer and loading tool with the front countershaft bore in the case. Push the loading tool into the case front bore just enough to hold the thrust washer and countershaft gear in position.
80 Turn the case on end with the rear bearing bore facing up. Align the rear thrust washer tab with the case notch and install the washer between the gear and the case.
81 Align the countershaft gear rear bore, case rear bore and rear thrust washer. Insert the countershaft through the rear bore and into the rear bore of the countershaft gear.
82 Turn the case back to its original position. Be sure the step machined in the rear end of the countershaft is in a horizontal position and that the lower step is facing down.
83 Countershaft end play should be 0.006 to 0.018 inch (0.524 to 0.457 mm). Replace the thrust washers if the end play exceeds the limit.
84 Install the Reverse lever fork in the Reverse lever. Install the Reverse lever and spring on the pivot shaft in the case and install the retaining clip.
85 Position the Reverse idler gear and gear spacer. Install the idler gear shaft from the rear of the case. Be sure the Reverse lever fork is engaged with the idler gear.
86 Install the replacement shift rail oil seal in the counterbore at the rear of the case. Use a suitable size socket to install the seal.
87 Coat the output shaft pilot bearing with petroleum jelly and install it in the clutch shaft bore.
88 Install the blocking ring on the clutch shaft and install the clutch shaft in the transmission case.
89 Place a new gasket on the extension housing.
90 Insert the output shaft into the transmission case and install it on the clutch shaft.
91 Coat the extension housing bolts with non-hardening gasket sealer and, lining up the clutch and output shafts, install the extension housing. Be sure the notch in the countershaft is aligned with the recess in the extension housing. Tighten the housing bolts only finger tight at this time.
92 Install the front bearing using a tool such as AMC bearing installer no. J-5590.
93 Install the bearing retaining and locating snap-rings.
94 Install a new front bearing oil seal using a tool such as AMC tool no. J-26540.
95 Install a new bearing cap O-ring and install the front bearing cap.
96 Install the shift forks in the synchronizer sleeves.
97 Install the interlock plate using a new retaining pin.
98 Lubricate the shift rail with transmission lubricant and install the shift rail. Slide the shift rail through the First-Second shift fork and the interlock plate.
99 Install the selector arm on the shift rail and slide the rail through the Third-Fourth shift fork and into the case front bore.
100 Install the selector arm roll pin in the arm and shift rail. Be sure the pin is flush with the selector arm surface.
101 Install the detent plunger, spring, and plug in the transmission case. Tighten the plug to 9 ft-lb (12 Nm).
102 Tighten the front bearing cap bolts to 9 ft-lb (12.2 Nm) and the extension housing bolts to 34 ft-lbs (46.1 Nm).
103 Install new access plugs in the extension housing shift rail bore and in the transmission case (the interlock plate retaining pin access hole).
104 Install a new extension housing oil seal using a tool such as AMC tool no. J-26830.
105 Pour 2.4 pints (1.13 liters) of transmission lubricant into the case and install a new top cover gasket. Install the top cover and tighten the bolts to 10 ft-lb (14 Nm).
106 Install the dynamic absorber and transmission support cushion adapter bracket on the extension housing.
107 Install the clutch housing, throw-out lever and throw-out bearing. Tighten the clutch housing-to-case bolts to 55 ft-lb (75 Nm).

7A

9 T-10 transmission – disassembly, inspection and reassembly

Disassembly

1 Remove the shift rods from the shift levers. Remove the shift mechanism attaching bolts and remove the shift mechanism.
2 Drain the transmission lubricant and shift the transmission into second gear.

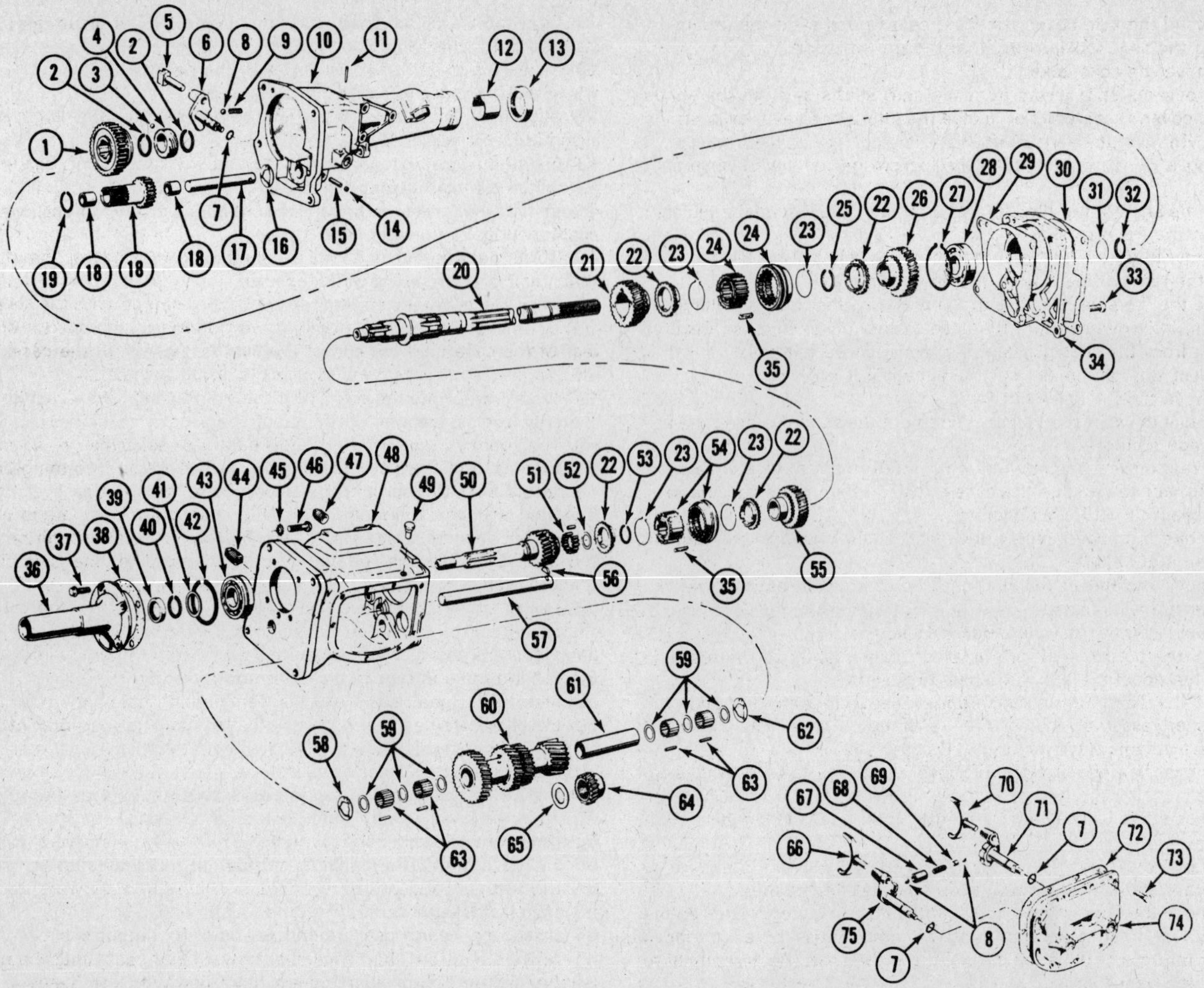

Fig. 7.6 Exploded view of the T-10 transmission components (Sec 9)

1 *Reverse gear*
2 *Speedometer drive gear ring*
3 *Speedometer drive gear ball*
4 *Speedometer drive gear*
5 *Shifter reverse fork*
6 *Shifter fork reverse shaft*
7 *Shifter fork shaft seal*
8 *Speed finder interlock poppet*
9 *Speed finger interlock poppet reverse spring*
10 *Reverse gear housing*
11 *Shifter fork shaft retaining pin*
12 *Reverse gear housing bushing*
13 *Reverse gear housing seal*
14 *Idler gear shaft pin access plug*
15 *Idler gear shaft retaining pin*
16 *Idler gear shaft thrust washer*
17 *Idler gear shaft*
18 *Reverse idler gear and bushings*
19 *Reverse idler rear snap ring*
20 *Spline shaft*
21 *Second gear*
22 *Clutch friction ring set*
23 *Shaft plate retaining spring*
24 *First and second gear clutch assembly*
25 *First and second snap ring*
26 *First gear*
27 *Rear ball bearing lockring*
28 *Rear ball bearing*
29 *Gasket*
30 *Gasket*
31 *Rear ball bearing washer*
32 *Rear ball bearing lockring*
33 *Bolt*
34 *Reverse gear housing adapter*
35 *Clutch shaft plate*
36 *Front bearing cap*
37 *Bolt*
38 *Front bearing cap shim*
39 *Front bearing oil seal*
40 *Front ball bearing snap ring*
41 *Front ball bearing washer*
42 *Front ball bearing lockring*
43 *Front ball bearing*
44 *Drain plug*
45 *Lock washer*
46 *Bolt*
47 *Filler plug*
48 *Case*
49 *Case breather*
50 *Clutch shaft*
51 *Spline shaft pilot bearing roller*
52 *Spline shaft pilot bearing roller spacer*
53 *Third and fourth gear snap ring*
54 *Third and fourth gear clutch assembly*
55 *Third gear*
56 *Key*
57 *Countershaft*
58 *Front countershaft gear thrust washer*
59 *Countershaft gear bearing roller washer*
60 *Countershaft gear*
61 *Countershaft gear roller bearing spacer*
62 *Rear countershaft gear thrust washer (less lip)*
63 *Countershaft gear bearing roller*
64 *Reverse idler gear*
65 *Reverse idler gear thrust washer*
66 *Shifter third and fourth gear fork*
67 *Speed finder interlock sleeve*
68 *Speed finder interlock poppet spring*
69 *Second finder interlock pin*
70 *Shifter first and second gear fork*
71 *Shifter fork first and second gear shaft*
72 *Gasket*
73 *Bolt*
74 *Cover*
75 *Shifter fork third and fourth gear shaft*

3 Remove the side cover attaching screws and slide the assembly, including the shift forks, away from the transmission.
4 Remove the shift forks.
5 Remove the shift levers from the shift shafts and tap the shafts from the cover. Be careful not to lose the interlock sleeve, balls, spring and pin. Remove the shift shaft seals.
6 Using a $\frac{1}{8}$-inch punch, drive the lockpin out of the Reverse shift shaft.
7 Pull the shaft out of the case about $\frac{1}{8}$-inch and disengage the shift fork from the Reverse sliding gear.
8 Remove the Reverse gearcase attaching screws and tap the case toward the rear to free it from the adapter plate.
9 Slide the Reverse gearcase to the rear until the Reverse idler shaft clears the idler gear. Rotate the case to the left to free the Reverse shift fork from the sliding gear collar and remove the case.
10 Inspect the idler gear shaft. Replace it if it is worn.
11 Remove the Reverse shift fork.
12 Remove the shift shaft lever and tap out the shaft. Remove the ball bearing and spring from the case.
13 The rear oil seal can now be removed from the Reverse gearcase. Be careful not to damage the case bushing when removing the seal. Pry the seal out with a screwdriver.
14 Remove the speedometer drivegear, snap-rings and ball bearing from the output shaft.
15 Remove the Reverse sliding gear from the shaft and remove the idler gear from the case.
16 Remove the adapter plate securing bolt.
17 Slide the output shaft and adapter plate slightly to the rear and remove the adapter plate with snap-ring pliers.
18 Shift the Third-Fourth synchronizer sleeve forward and slide the output shaft assembly out of the transmission case. The 16 clutch shaft roller bearings will fall into the case.
19 Remove the Reverse front idler gear and steel thrust washer from the case.
20 Remove the washer and snap-ring from the end of the output shaft.
21 Remove the Third-Fourth synchronizer assembly and Third gear.
22 Remove the center bearing snap-ring and flat washer.
23 Remove the bearing from the shaft by inserting steel plates on the front side of First gear and using an arbor press or a soft-faced hammer to press or drive the bearing from the shaft. Be careful not to damage the gear teeth.
24 Remove First gear.
25 Remove the snap-ring and remove the First-Second synchronizer assembly. Mark the position of the synchronizer hub for assembly reference.
26 Remove Second gear.
27 Use a dummy shaft machined to 0.870 x 7 inches or AMC countershaft loading tool no. J-5589 to drive the countershaft out of the rear of the case.
28 Remove the Woodruff key from the countershaft.
29 Remove the front bearing cap and bearing snap-ring.
30 Tap the clutch shaft assembly to the rear and remove it from the transmission case.
31 Remove the clutch shaft snap-ring.
32 Press the front bearing from the clutch shaft with a suitable bearing puller or AMC puller no. J-6654.

Inspection

33 See Section 8 for information on inspecting the transmission components.

Reassembly

34 Insert the dummy shaft into the countershaft and install the spacer and bearing washer. Coat 20 needle bearings with petroleum jelly and install them around the dummy shaft.
35 Install a bearing washer, 20 more coated needle bearings, and another bearing washer on the shaft.
36 Repeat the procedure on the other end of the countershaft gear and install the bronze thrust washers at each end of the transmission case. Align the washer tabs with the recesses in the case.
37 Place the countershaft gear assembly in the bottom of the case.
38 Press the front bearing onto the clutch shaft using a bearing puller such as AMC no. J-6654-01.
39 Coat the 16 clutch shaft roller bearings with petroleum jelly and install them in the clutch shaft bore.
40 Install the clutch shaft assembly in the case.
41 Install the flat washer in the shaft bore.
42 Align the front bearing with the case bore and tap the clutch shaft assembly into place.
43 Install the front bearing snap-ring and the clutch shaft snap-ring.
44 Install the front bearing cap.
45 Install the front Reverse idler gear with the thrust washer positioned in front of the gear.
46 Raise the countershaft gear assembly to mesh with the clutch shaft gear and install the Woodruff key.
47 Align the countershaft so that the key is lined up with the keyway in the rear face of the transmission case. Tap the countershaft in at the rear of the case until the end of the shaft is flush with the case.
48 Install Third gear on the front of the output shaft.
49 Install the friction ring on Third gear and install the Third-Fourth synchronizer assembly.
50 The front output shaft snap-rings are available in selective thicknesses. Install the thickest snap-ring that will fit into the groove.
51 Install Second gear and the Second gear friction ring.
52 Hold the synchronizer hub so that one synchronizer plate is in the 12 o'clock position. Place either tang on the plate and install the ring in a clockwise direction. Repeat the procedure on the other side of the synchronizer hub.
53 Install the First-Second synchronizer assembly on the output shaft.
54 Install the thickest snap-ring that will fit into the groove adjacent to the First-Second synchronizer assembly.
55 Install First gear and the First gear friction ring.
56 Press the center bearing on with the bearing snap-ring groove facing first gear.
57 Install the flat washer and lock ring.
58 Install the adapter with a new gasket and secure it to the bearing with the snap-ring.
59 Move the First-Second synchronizer assembly forward to the Second gear position to facilitate the output shaft installation.
60 Move the Third-Fourth synchronizer assembly forward to the Fourth gear position.
61 Install the Fourth gear friction ring and the output shaft.
62 Move the output shaft assembly forward and check that the three notches in the Fourth gear friction ring align with the plates in the Third-Fourth synchronizer assembly.
63 Align the adapter dowel with the hole in the transmission case and tap the shaft assembly forward.
64 Install the special self-locking bolt in the adapter plate and secure it to the transmission case.
65 Move the synchronizer sleeves to the Neutral positions.
66 Install the Reverse idler gear through the adapter plate opening and engage the splines with the Reverse front idler gear.
67 Install the Reverse sliding gear on the output shaft.
68 Install a new gasket with non-hardening gasket sealer on the rear face of the adapter.
69 Install the speedometer drivegear snap-ring, gear and ball bearing. Index the gear on the ball bearing, and install the second snap-ring.
70 If the Reverse idler shaft was removed, it can be installed at this time.
71 Install the Reverse shift shaft detent spring and ball. Hold the detent ball down and install the shift shaft.
72 Install the replacement shift shaft seal after coating it with transmission lubricant.
73 Install the Reverse shift lever.
74 Apply a film of grease to the Reverse shift fork and install it in the shift shaft.
75 With the Reverse shift shaft in the rear (Reverse) position, pull the shift shaft out from the case to allow the shift fork to engage the Reverse gear sleeve.
76 Carefully install the Reverse gear housing, guiding the idler gearshaft into the idler gear and aligning the shift fork with the Reverse gear collar.
77 When the shift fork engages, push the Reverse shift shaft back into position.
78 Move the Reverse sliding gear to the rear and complete the installation of the gearcase, aligning it with the counterbore and dowel pin of the adapter.
79 Install the case attaching bolts. Install the identification tag.

80 Install the Reverse shift shaft tapered pin.
81 Install a new rear oil seal with an oil seal installation tool such as AMC no. J-9617.
82 Install the shift forks in the shift shafts.
83 Move the First-Second synchronizer sleeve forward to the Second gear position.
84 Move the First-Second shift lever forward to the Second gear position. Align the shift forks with the synchronizer sleeves and install the shift cover with a new gasket and sealer.
85 The lower right bolt requires non-hardening sealer applied to the threads, as the bolt hole is a through hole.
86 Tighten the bolts to 20 ft-lb and check the transmission shifting operation.

10 T-96 Transmission – disassembly, inspection and reassembly

Disassembly 1 Disconnect the clutch throw-out lever from the throw-out bearing. This is achieved by pulling the lever away from the bearing so the pegs disengage from the bearing groove.
2 Withdraw the throw-out lever and bearing from the bellhousing.
3 Unbolt the bellhousing from the transmission and remove it. Remove the top cover from the transmission.
4 From the front face of the case, remove the front bearing cap.
5 Remove the two bearing snap-rings. The bearing must now be pulled off of the clutch shaft. To do this, a puller must be used which will grip the outer track of the bearing and exert pressure on the front of the clutch shaft in order to prevent damage to the gears (J6654-01 and J2040).
6 With the clutch shaft bearing removed, extract the oil slinger.
7 Unscrew and remove the four bolts which secure the extension housing to the transmission case and withdraw the housing.
8 Replace the extension housing rear oil seal and bushing (if worn), by driving them out with a piece of pipe.
9 Remove the speedometer drive gear snap-rings and remove the gear from the rear end of the mainshaft. Remove the gear locking ball.
10 Move the mainshaft assembly toward the rear about one-half inch, then, by lowering the front end of the clutch shaft and raising its rear end above the countershaft, the clutch shaft can be removed from the front of the transmission.
11 Inspect the condition of the needle roller bearings in the rear end of the clutch shaft. All 21 bearings must be replaced if they are worn or pitted.
12 Remove the Second-Third gear shift fork and then tilt the mainshaft so the synchro unit snap-ring can be removed.
13 Pull the synchro unit, Second gear and First-Reverse gears from the front end of the mainshaft.
14 Remove the First-Reverse gearshift fork.
15 Remove the mainshaft and rear bearing from the rear of the transmission case.
16 Support the mainshaft rear bearing and press the mainshaft from it.

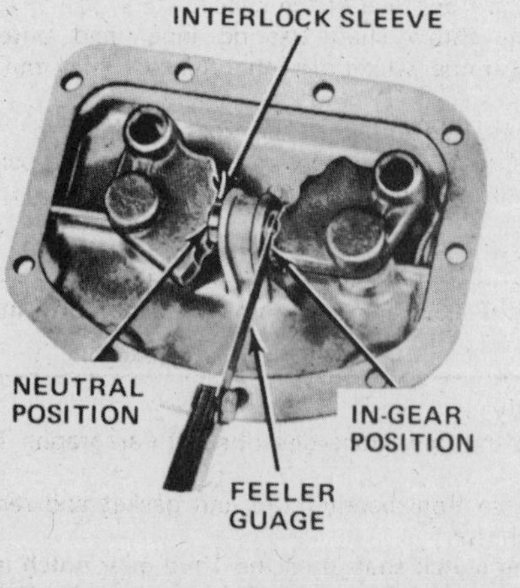

Fig. 7.7 Measuring the interlock sleeve and clearance (Sec 10)

17 Remove the Reverse idler and countershaft lockplate.
18 Using a dummy shaft, the length of the countergear assembly and of slightly smaller diameter than the countershaft, drive out the countershaft. With the dummy shaft retaining the needle bearings in position, lower the countergear assembly to the bottom of the transmission.
19 Remove the Reverse idler gear after driving the shaft out of the rear of the transmission using a brass drift.
20 The countergear assembly can now be lifted from the bottom of the case. Note carefully the position of the two thrust washers.
21 Remove the external gearshift levers and the shift shaft lock pin.
22 Remove the gearshift shafts from the inside of the transmission case taking care to catch the two interlock balls. Finally, remove the sleeve, pin, spring and the O-ring seals from the shift shafts.

Inspection

23 With the transmission completely dismantled, examine all components for wear. If a gear must be replaced then the gear with which it meshes must also be replaced. Replace the synchro unit if noisy shifting was evident before disassembly.
24 At the time of major overhaul, always replace oil seals, O-rings and gaskets with new ones.
25 Clean out the interior of the transmission case and examine it for cracks, particularly around the bolt holes.

Reassembly

26 Begin reassembly by installing new O-ring seals on the shift shafts and installing them, liberally coated with oil, in the case. Install the interlock components and then position the shift mechanism as though a gear was selected. With one end of the interlock sleeve against the shift shaft quadrant, measure the clearance between the opposite end of the sleeve and the quadrant on the other shaft. This clearance should be between 0.001 and 0.007 inch, otherwise change the interlock sleeve for one of alternative length.
27 When adjustment is correct, lock the gearshift shafts with their lock pins and install the shift levers.
28 Using thick grease, stick the needle bearings in both ends of the countergear, again using the dummy shaft to position them. Make sure that the spacer and washers are correctly installed within the countergear.
29 Lower the countergear assembly, complete with dummy shaft, to the bottom of the transmission case.
30 Again using thick grease to retain them, stick the bronze thrust washer to the interior front of the case and the other thrust washers to the interior rear of the case, making sure that the tabs on the washers engage with the notches in the case.
31 Install the Reverse idler gear (chamfered edge of teeth toward the front of the transmission). Drive in the Reverse idler shaft from the rear of the case so the notch on the shaft is toward the rear and faces the countershaft in order to accept the lockplate.
32 Raise the countergear assembly from the bottom of the case and drive in the countershaft from the rear of the case. Make sure that the lockplate notch in the countershaft is correctly aligned to receive the plate and that as the countershaft displaces the dummy shaft, the needle rollers and the thrust washers are not ejected or trapped. Install the lockplate so that it engages securely in the notches of the countershaft and the Reverse idler shaft.
33 Press on a new mainshaft rear bearing and install the inner and outer snap-rings.
34 Install the mainshaft through the opening in the rear of the transmission.
35 Install the shift forks.
36 Install First/Reverse gear, Second gear and the synchro unit. Make sure that the projecting face of the synchro hub is toward the front of the transmission.
37 Attach the snap-ring to the front of the mainshaft. If new components are being installed, use a snap-ring which is the thickest that the groove will accept. Snap-rings are available in various thicknesses.
38 Press the synchro hub against the snap-ring and, using a feeler gauge, check the clearance between Second gear and the shoulder of the mainshaft. The clearance should be between 0.003 and 0.010 inch.
39 Position the 21 needle rollers in the recess at the rear end of the clutch shaft using thick grease.
40 Attach the blocking ring and the clutch shaft to the front end of the

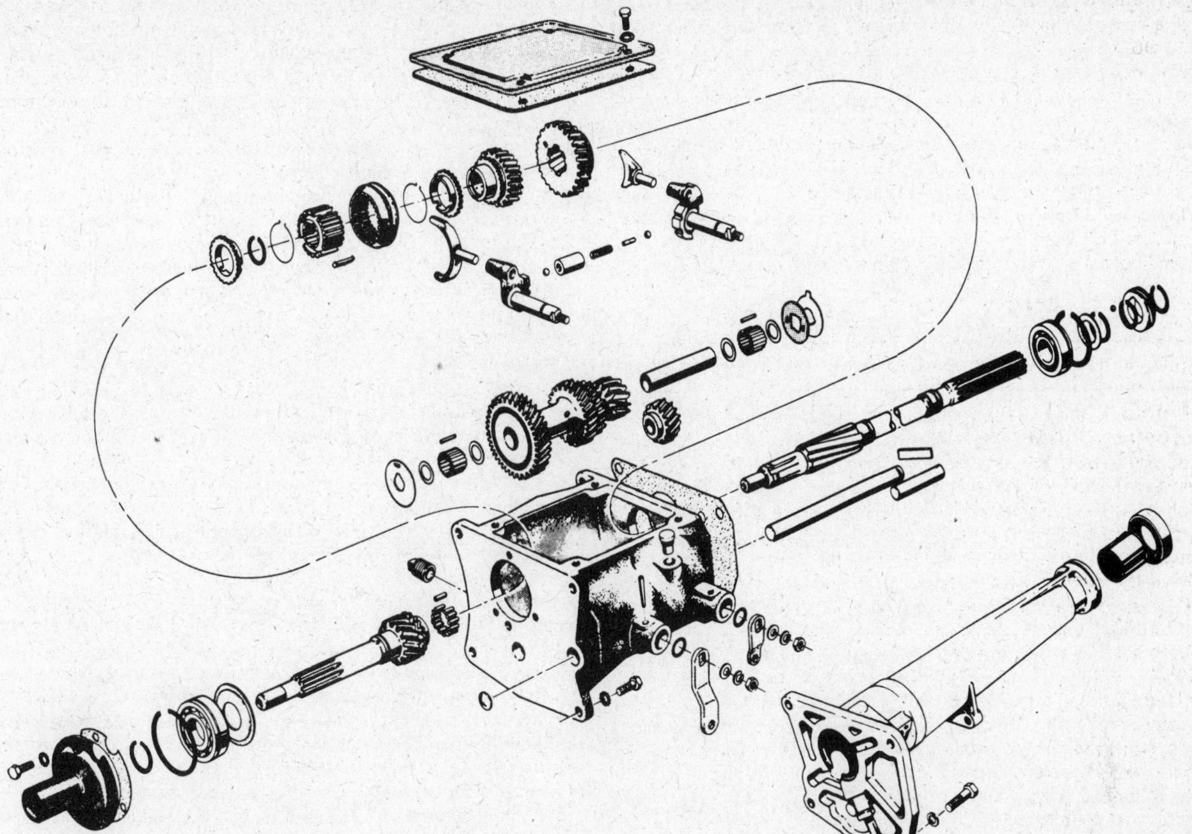

Fig. 7.8 Exploded view of the T-96 transmission components (Sec 10)

mainshaft. To achieve this, move the mainshaft rear bearing into the transmission case recess at the same time aligning the shift forks and gears. It should be noted that the mainshaft bearing outer snap-ring should be the thickest that the groove will accept. Snap-rings are available in various thicknesses.

41 Install the speedometer drivegear snap-ring to the mainshaft, the lock ball, the gear and the second snap-ring.

42 Install the extension housing using a new gasket.

43 Install the oil slinger (concave side facing to the rear) on the front of the clutch shaft.

44 Install the clutch shaft bearing. The bearing can be driven on using a piece of tubing applied to the center race only. Support the rear face of the third gear on the clutch shaft using a suitable plate and clamp anchored to the front face of the case.

45 Install the clutch shaft bearing inner and outer snap-rings, selecting snap-rings which are the thickest that the grooves will accept.

46 Using a new gasket, install the front bearing cap.

47 Check the gearshift mechanism for smooth and positive operation and then install the top cover with a new gasket.

Fig. 7.9 Guiding the end of the output shaft into the clutch shaft bearing (T-96 transmission) (Sec 10)

11 T-14 and T-15 transmissions – disassembly, inspection and reassembly

Disassembly

1 Carry out the operations described in Paragraphs 1 through 4 in Section 10.

2 Remove the front bearing cap and gasket and remove the two snap-rings (photo).

3 Rotate the clutch shaft until the Third gear notch is at its lowest point and withdraw the clutch shaft/bearing assembly (photo).

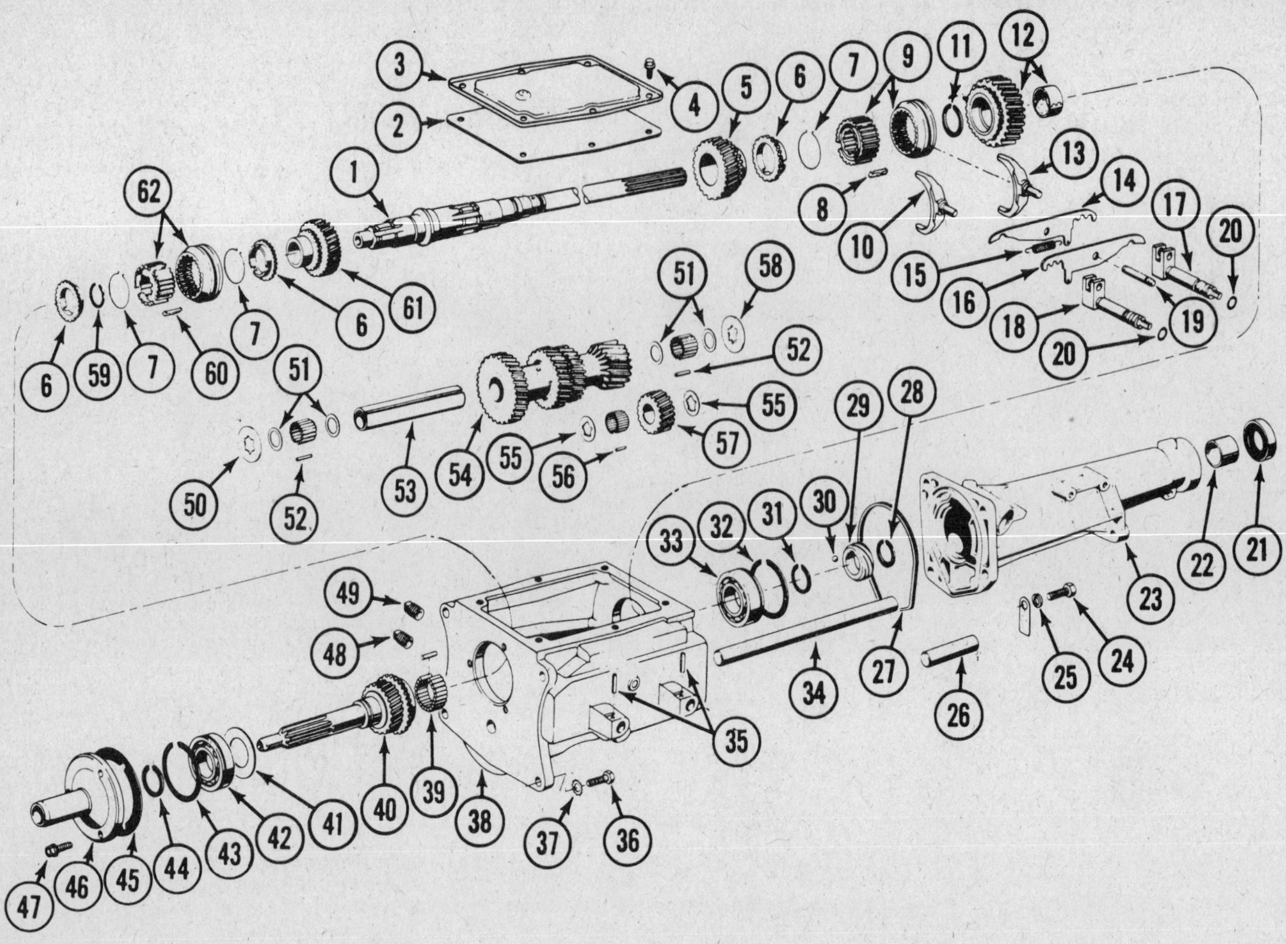

Fig. 7.10 Exploded view of the T-14 transmission components (Sec 11)

1 Main shaft
2 Gasket
3 Case cover
4 Bolt
5 First gear
6 Clutch friction ring set
7 Shaft plate retaining spring
8 Clutch shaft first and reverse shift plate
9 First and reverse clutch assembly
10 Shifter second and high fork
11 Clutch first and reverse gear snap ring
12 Reverse gear
13 Shifter first and reverse R fork
14 Shifter interlock first and reverse lever
15 Interlock poppet spring
16 Shifter interlock second and third lever
17 Shifter fork first and reverse shaft
18 Shifter fork second and third shaft
19 Shifter fork interlock lever pivot pin
20 Shifter fork shaft seal
21 Oil seal
22 Bushing
23 Extension housing
24 Bolt
25 Lock washer
26 Idler gear shaft
27 Gasket
28 Speedometer drive gear ring
29 Speedometer drive gear
30 Speedometer drive gear ball
31 Rear bearing lockring
32 Rear bearing lockring
33 Rear bearing
34 Countershaft
35 Shifter fork retaining pin
36 Bolt
37 Lock washer
38 Case
39 Spline shaft pilot bearing roller
40 Clutch shaft
41 Front bearing washer
42 Front bearing
43 Front bearing lockring
44 Front bearing snap ring
45 Gasket
46 Front bearing cap
47 Bolt
48 Drain plug
49 Filler pipe plug
50 Front countershaft gear thrust washer
51 Countershaft gear bearing roller washer
52 Countershaft gear bearing roller
53 Countershaft gear roller bearing spacer
54 Countershaft gear
55 Reverse idler gear bearing roller washer
56 Reverse idler gear bearing roller
57 Reverse idler gear
58 Rear countershaft thrust
59 Clutch second and third snap ring
60 Clutch shaft second and third shift plate
61 Second and third clutch assembly
62 Second gear

11.2 Removing the front bearing cap

11.3 Removing the clutch shaft (T-14 transmission)

11.7 Removing the mainshaft rear bearing

11.9 Removing the mainshaft assembly

11.12 Shift shaft interlock levers (T-14 transmission)

11.15 The countershaft and reverse idler gear

11.22 Installing second gear and the second-third gear synchronizer blocking ring (T-14 transmission)

11.23A Installing the second-third gear synchronizer assembly on the output shaft (T14-transmission)

11.23B Correct installation of the second-third synchronizer assembly

11.25 Installing the reverse gear on the rear end of the mainshaft

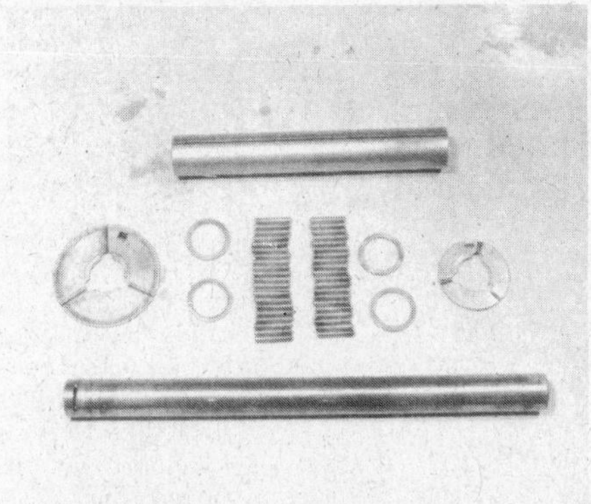

11.26A Countershaft thrust washers and needle bearing components

11.26B Installing the countershaft gear needle bearings

11.35 Installing a shift fork

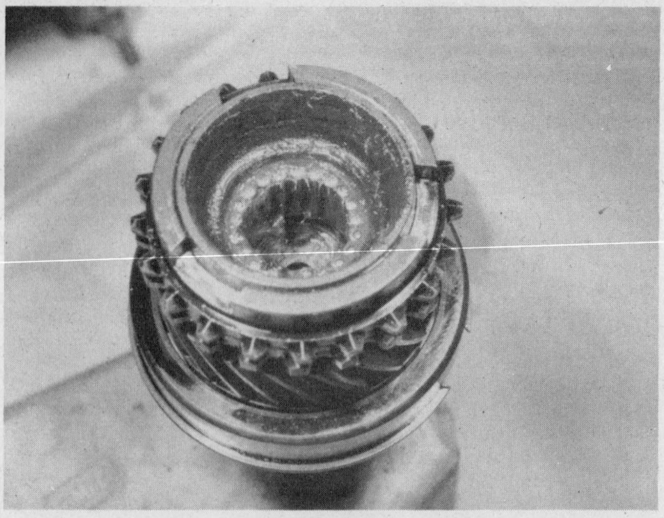

11.39 The pilot needle bearings installed in the clutch shaft

4 Using a press or puller, remove the bearing from the clutch shaft.
5 Unbolt and remove the rear extension housing.
6 Remove the speedometer drivegear snap-ring, the drivegear, the lock ball and the second snap-ring from the rear of the mainshaft.
7 Remove the two mainshaft rear bearing snap-rings and, using a suitable puller, remove the mainshaft rear bearing (photo).
8 Push the mainshaft to one side and then remove both shift forks.
9 Pry the front synchro unit toward the rear of the transmission and then remove the mainshaft assembly by tilting its front end up and out through the top of the case (photo).
10 Remove the TCS switch (emissions control system), if so equipped.
11 Drive out the pins from the shift shafts.
12 Push the shift shafts into the case and remove the shift and detent components (photo).
13 Tap the Reverse idler shaft and the countershaft toward the back of the case to remove tension from the shaft lockplate, which can then be removed.
14 Drive the Reverse idler shaft from the case, taking care to retain the needle roller bearings.
15 Make up a dummy countershaft the same length as the countergear and slightly smaller in diameter so that when it is used to drive out the countershaft, it will retain the needle rollers and thrust washers and enable the complete countergear assembly to be lifted from the transmission (photo).
16 Dismantle the mainshaft by removing the front snap-ring, Second-Third synchro unit and Second gear.
17 Slide Reverse gear off the rear end of the mainshaft, followed by the snap-ring, First-Second synchro unit and First gear.

Inspection

18 Clean all components and examine them for wear and damage. Where noisy gearshifts were evident before disassembly, replace the synchro units as necessary. Always replace gaskets, oil seals and O-rings. Examine the case for cracks, particularly around bolt holes.

Reassembly

19 Begin reassembly by applying oil to the rear end of the mainshaft and installing First gear and First-Second synchro blocking ring.
20 Install the First-Second synchro unit on the mainshaft so that the groove in the synchro sleeve is nearer First gear. Install the shaft snap-ring, which should be the thickest that the groove will accept from the selective thicknesses which are available.
21 Measure the end play (using a feeler gauge) between First gear and the collar on the mainshaft. If the end play exceeds that specified, replace the gear, synchro unit or mainshaft individually or complete as one or all components are worn.
22 Install the Second gear and the Second-Third synchro unit blocking ring on the front of the mainshaft (photo).
23 Install the Second-Third synchro unit so that the end which mates with the blocking ring faces the rear of the mainshaft (photo). If the synchro unit has been dismantled, it must be reassembled as described in the preceding Section (photo).
24 Install the Second gear snap-ring, using the thickest one the groove will accept. Measure the end play (with a feeler gauge) between Second gear and the collar on the mainshaft. This must be between 0.003 and 0.018 inch. If the end play exceeds that specified, replace the gear, synchro unit or mainshaft as individual components or complete as one or more components is worn.
25 Install Reverse gear on the rear of the mainshaft (photo).
26 Using thick grease, stick the needle bearings in both ends of the countergear, again using the dummy shaft to position them. Make sure that the spacer and washers are correctly installed within the countergear (photos).
27 Stick the thrust washers in the case, install the countergear, complete with dummy shaft, and then tap in the countershaft with a soft-faced hammer so displacing the dummy shaft without moving or trapping the needle rollers or thrust washers. Make sure that the notch in the countershaft is at the rear and that it is correctly aligned to receive the lockplate.
28 If the Reverse idler gear needle roller bearings have been displaced, stick them in position using thick grease.

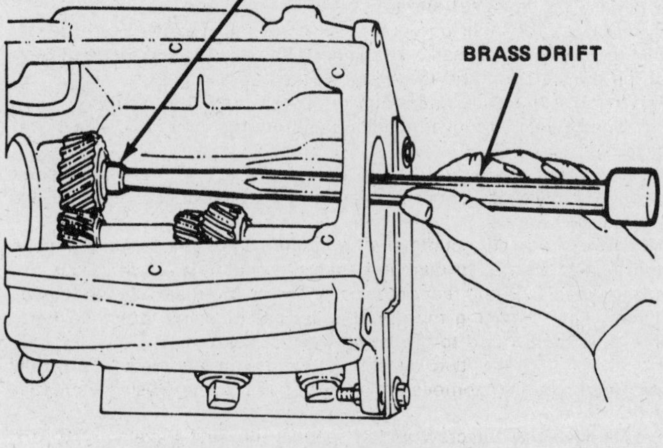

Fig. 7.11 Removing the Reverse idler gearshaft (T-14 transmission) (Sec 11)

29 Install the Reverse idler gear, using thrust washers and idler shaft, making sure that the notch in the shaft is correctly aligned to receive the lockplate.
30 Partially install the shift fork shafts in the case. The First-Reverse shift lever is positioned nearer to the inside of the case and the notches on the tops of both shift levers must be located behind the stud.
31 Align the shift detent assembly with the shift fork shafts and case stud.
32 Push the shift detent assembly and shift fork shafts into position and install new roll pins.
33 Install the TCS switch.
34 Set the Second-Third synchro unit on the Second gear position and then insert the mainshaft assembly into the case.
35 Push the mainshaft assembly to one side so the shift forks can be installed by pulling up the detent levers and locating the forks in the synchro unit grooves (photo).
36 Place a suitable supporting block between the front end of the mainshaft and the inside front face of the case and then install the mainshaft rear bearing using a piece of pipe as a drift applied to the bearing inner. Install the rear bearing snap-rings, making sure that they are the thickest that will fit into the grooves.
37 Install the speedometer drivegear lock ball and drivegear and snap-ring on the mainshaft.
38 Press a new bearing onto the clutch shaft. Apply pressure to the center race only and make sure that the outer snap-ring groove is nearer the front of the shaft.
39 Using thick grease, stick the needle rollers inside the recess at the rear end of the clutch shaft. Place the blocking ring on the front end of the mainshaft and then pass the clutch shaft through the opening in the front of the case and connect it to the mainshaft (photo).
40 Install the clutch shaft bearing snap-rings and a new gasket and bolt on the bearing cap, Make sure that the oil hole in the cap aligns with the one in the case.
41 Install the rear extension housing complete with a new oil seal.
42 Install the external shift levers and check that gear selection is smooth and positive.
43 Use a new gasket and install the top cover. Make sure that the breather vent is clear.

12 150T Transmission – disassembly, inspection and reassembly

Disassembly

1 Remove the clutch throwout lever and bearing and unbolt the clutch bellhousing from the transmission.
2 Remove the top cover and gasket.
3 From the left-hand side of the case, remove the TCS (emissions control) switch.
4 From the left-hand side of the extension housing, remove the backup light switch.
5 Remove the long detent spring from the hole in the case upper flange and then invert the transmission so the detent plunger falls out.
6 Unbolt and remove the extension housing and its gasket.
7 From the rear end of the mainshaft, remove the snap-ring, the speedometer drivegear and lock ball.
8 Remove the inner and outer mainshaft rear bearing snap-rings.
9 Make alignment marks on the front bearing cap and the front face of the transmission and then remove the cap and gasket.
10 Remove the outer snap-ring from the clutch shaft bearing.
11 Unscrew and remove the filler plug from the right-hand side of the case.
12 Drive out the countershaft roll pin, which is now accessible through the filler plug hole. Retrieve the pin later after removal of the internal components.
13 Using a dummy countershaft the same length as the countergear and slightly smaller in diameter than the countershaft, drive out the countershaft from the rear of the case. The countergear, complete with dummy shaft retaining the needle roller bearings and thrust washers, may now be lowered to the bottom of the case.
14 Check that the two synchro units are in the neutral position (centered) and then remove the mainshaft rear bearing using a suitable puller.
15 Remove the setscrew which secures the First-Reverse shift fork and then slide the shift rail from the rear of the case. The First-Reverse fork is located at the rear of the case and it is larger than the Second-Third shift fork. Push the First-Reverse synchro sleeve and gear as far foward as possible and then turn the First-Reverse shift fork up and extract it from the case.
16 Push the Second-Third shift fork to the rear and remove the securing setscrew. Rotate the shift rail through 90° using a pliers so that the detent plug can be cleared. Now tip the case so that the interlock plunger is ejected.
17 Remove the Second-Third shift rail by using a long thin drift inserted through the hole in the rear of the case. As the shift rail is moved, the sealing plug at the front of the rail will be ejected.
18 Remove the bottom detent plug and short detent spring from the case. Turn the Second-Third shift fork up and remove it from the case.
19 Using a suitable puller, remove the clutch shaft, clutch shaft bearing and blocking ring as an assembly.
20 Remove the mainshaft assembly from the case by tilting the end of the shaft down and lifting the front end so that the First-Reverse synchro sleeve and gear pass through the cut-out on the right at the rear end of the case.
21 Lift the countergear assembly (complete with dummy shaft, needle rollers and thrust washers) from the bottom of the case. Retrieve the countershaft roll pin.
22 Remove the two shift fork shafts.
23 Remove the dummy countershaft, noting that there are 25 needle rollers at each end of the countergear.
24 Remove the Reverse idler gear and thrust washers by tapping the shaft until the securing roll pin emerges from the counterbore and the shaft can be gripped and extracted.
25 To dismantle the mainshaft, extract the snap-ring from the front of the shaft and withdraw the Second-Third synchro unit and Second gear. If the synchro unit is to be dismantled, mark the relationship of the hub and sleeve so they can be reassembled in their original positions.
26 Remove the snap-ring and thrust washer from the mainshaft and pull off the First gear and the blocking ring.
27 Remove the snap-ring which retains the First-Reverse synchro hub. Remove the synchro sleeve and gear, springs and three inserts from the hub. The hub must now be pressed from the shaft using a press.
28 To dismantle the clutch shaft, extract the snap-ring and press the shaft out of the bearing using a press.

Inspection

29 Clean all components and examine them for wear and damage. If noisy gearshifts were evident before disassembly, replace the synchro units as necessary. Always replace gaskets, oil seals and O-rings. Examine the case for cracks, particularly around bolt holes.

Reassembly

30 Lubricate all components as they are installed.
31 Begin reassembly by installing the Reverse idler gear and shaft. Use thick grease to retain the thrust washers and make sure that the idler shaft roll pin seats correctly in the counterbore. Check the Reverse idler gear end play by inserting a feeler gauge between the gear and thrust washer. The correct end play is between 0.004 and 0.018 inch and where it is outside the specified tolerance, change the thrust washers.
32 Set up the countergear so the spacer, needle rollers and retaining rings are all held in position with grease and the dummy shaft passes through them. Again using grease, stick the countergear thrust washers to the case interior, making sure that the tangs on the washers locate correctly.
33 Install the countershaft from the rear of the case, inserting it just far enough to hold the rear thrust washer in position. Now install the countergear and push in the countershaft so that it almost (but not completely) displaces the dummy shaft. Now measure the countergear end play with a feeler gauge inserted between the thrust washer and countergear. This should be between 0.004 and 0.018 inch. If the end play is greater than that specified, replace the thrust washers. When the end play has been correctly established, reinsert the dummy shaft and lower the countergear assembly, complete with dummy shaft and needle rollers, to the bottom of the case.
34 With the case standing the correct way up, insert the short lower detent spring in its hole and allow the spring to drop into place at the bottom of the Second-Third shift rail hole. Insert the lower detent plunger and allow this plunger to drop into place on top of the detent spring.
35 Attach the First-Reverse synchro hub to the mainshaft ensuring that the face of the hub which has the slots faces the front of the shaft.

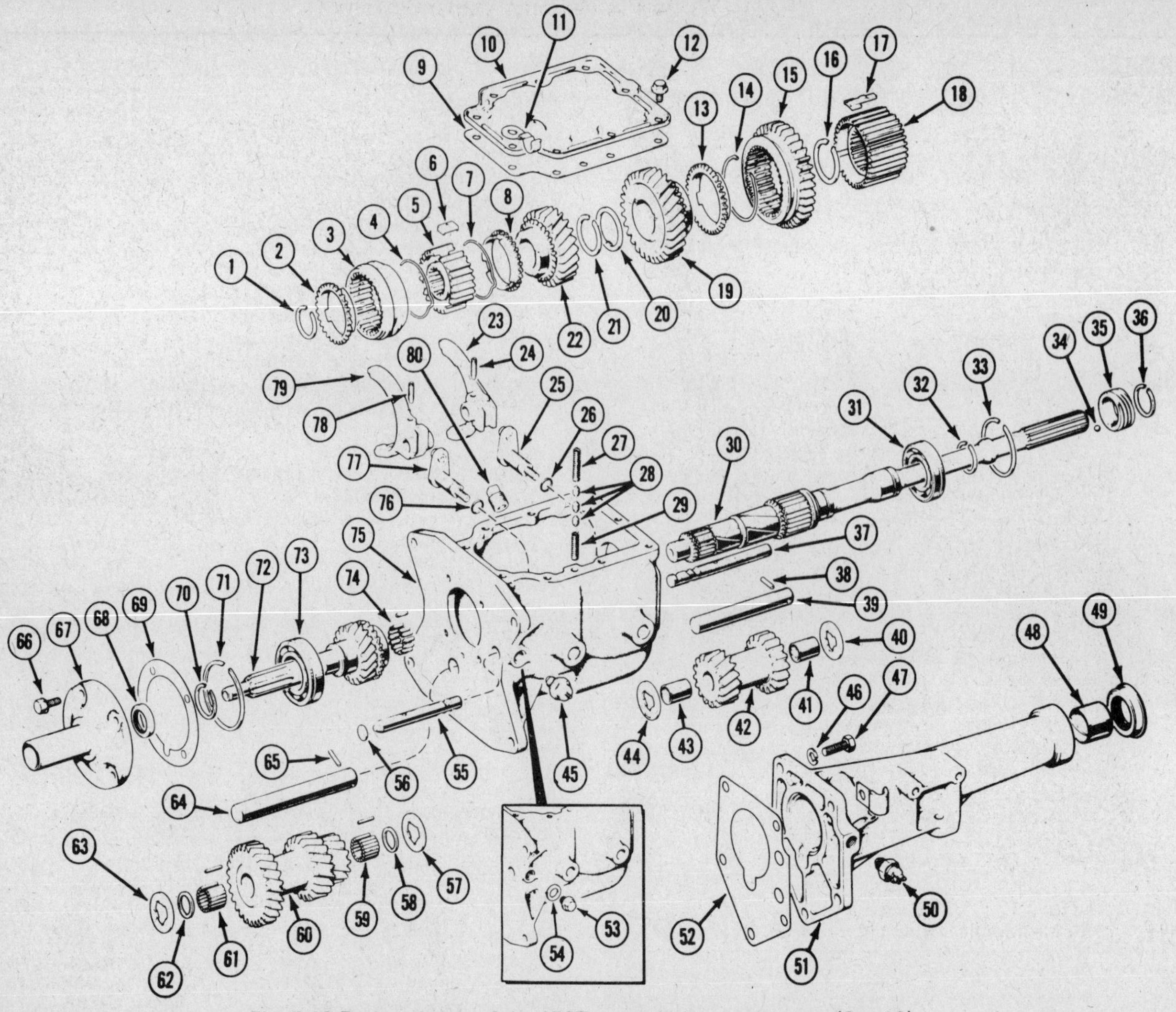

Fig. 7.12 Exploded view of the 150T transmission components (Sec 12)

1 *Ring, retaining (snap) output shaft*
2 *Ring, blocking, second-third synchronizer*
3 *Sleeve, second-third synchronizer*
4 *Spring, insert, second-third synchronizer*
5 *Hub, second-third*
6 *Insert, second-third synchronizer*
7 *Spring, insert, second-third synchronizer*
8 *Ring, blocking, second-third synchronizer*
9 *Gasket, top cover*
10 *Top cover, case*
11 *Clip, TCS switch wire harness*
12 *Bolt, top cover (9)*
13 *Ring, blocking, first-reverse synchronizer*
14 *Spring, insert, first-reverse synchronizer*
15 *Sleeve and gear, first-reverse*
16 *Ring, retaining (snap) first-reverse hub*
17 *Insert, first-reverse synchronizer (3)*
18 *Hub, first-reverse*
19 *Gear, first*
20 *Washer, thrust (tabbed) first gear*
21 *Ring, retaining (snap) first gear*
22 *Gear, second*
23 *Fork, first-reverse shifter*
24 *Setscrew, first-reverse shifter fork*
25 *Shaft, shifter fork*
26 *O-ring, shifter shaft*
27 *Spring, upper detent (long)*
28 *Plugs, gear shift detent and interlock*
29 *Springs, lower detent (short)*
30 *Shaft, output*
31 *Bearings, rear*
32 *Ring, retaining (snap) rear bearing*
33 *Ring, locating (snap) rear bearing*
34 *Lock ball, $\frac{1}{4}$ diameter – speedometer gear*
35 *Gear, speedometer drive*
36 *Ring, retaining (snap) speedometer drive gear*
37 *Shift rail, first–reverse*
38 *Pin, roll, reverse idler gear shaft*
39 *Shaft, reverse idler gear*
40 *Washer, thrust, reverse idler gear*
41 *Bushing, reverse idler gear (included with gear)*
42 *Gear, reverse idler*
43 *Bushing, reverse idler gear (included with gear)*
44 *Washer, thrust, reverse idler gear*
45 *Switch, TCS (Calif. only) or inhibitor (with overdrive)*
46 *Lockwasher, extension housing bolt (5)*
47 *Bolt, extension housing (5)*
48 *Bushing, extension housing (included with housing)*
49 *Seal, oil, extension housing*
50 *Switch, backup light*
51 *Extension housing*
52 *Gasket, extension housing*
53 *Plug (nationwide) without overdrive*
54 *Gasket (nationwide) without overdrive*
55 *Shift rail second-third*
56 *Plug, expansion*
57 *Washer, thrust, countershaft gear*
58 *Retainer, countershaft needle bearing*
59 *Needle bearing, countershaft gear (25)*
60 *Gear, countershaft*
61 *Needle bearing, countershaft gear (25)*
62 *Retainer, countershaft needle bearing*
63 *Washer, thrust, countershaft gear*
64 *Countershaft*
65 *Pin, roll, countershaft*
66 *Bolt, front bearing cap (4)*
67 *Cap, front bearing*
68 *Oil seal, front bearing cap*
69 *Gasket, front bearing cap*
70 *Ring, retaining (snap), front bearing to clutch shaft*
71 *Ring, locating (snap), front bearing*
72 *Shaft, clutch*
73 *Bearing, front*
74 *Bearings, clutch shaft roller*
75 *Case, transmission*
76 *O-ring, shifter shaft*
77 *Shaft, shifter fork*
78 *Setscrew, second-third shifter fork*
79 *Fork, second-third shifter*
80 *Plug, transmission fill*

Fig. 7.13 Removing the output shaft rear bearing (typical)

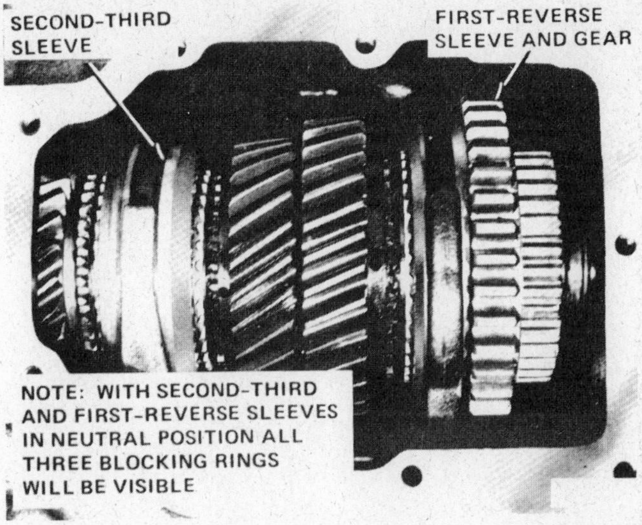

Fig. 7.14 The output shaft geartrain (150T transmission) (Sec 12)

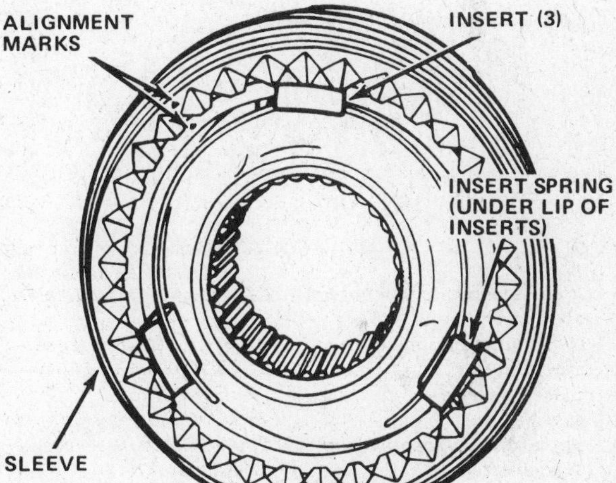

Fig. 7.15 The second-third synchronizer assembly (150T transmission) (Sec 12)

Use a press to bottom the hub on the shaft and then install the snap-ring in the groove which is nearer the rear.

36 Install the First-Reverse synchro sleeve and gear onto the hub with the gear nearest the rear end of the mainshaft. Make sure the hub-to-sleeve alignment marks made before dismantling are correctly mated. Reassemble the inserts and springs.

37 Place the First gear blocking ring on the cone of the gear and attach the gear to the mainshaft. Rotate the gear until the notches in the blocking ring engage with the inserts in the synchro hub, then install the tabbed thrust washer (sharp edge facing out). Also, install the retaining snap-ring on the mainshaft.

38 Install Second gear and the Second-Third synchro unit in a similar manner to that just described for First gear, but note the following points. The ends of both insert springs must cover the same slots in the synchro hub and not be staggered. When the components have been installed on the mainshaft and the snap-ring fitted, check the end play between the snap-ring and the synchro hub using a feeler gauge. The end play should be between 0.004 and 0.014 inch. If the specified tolerance is exceeded, replace the mainshaft thrust washer and all shaft snap-rings.

39 Install the shift fork shafts after they have been equipped with new O-ring seals; the shafts are interchangeable.

40 Install the mainshaft assembly in the case, making sure that the First-Reverse synchro sleeve and gear is in neutral (centered) to pass through the case cut-out.

41 Move the Second-Third synchro sleeve to the rear to Second gear position and then locate the Second-Third shift fork in the groove of the synchro sleeve. Make certain that the setscrew hole in the fork is facing up. The Second-Third fork is the smaller of the two shift forks. Engage the fork with the shift shaft and then pass the Second-Third shift rail through the front of the case and into the shift fork. Note that the tapered end of the rail faces the front of the case.

42 Rotate the shift rail until the detent notches are toward the bottom of the case. Now insert a screwdriver into the detent hole and depress the lower detent plunger, then push the shift rail into the rear support hole. Now move the rail until the detent plunger engages with the forward notch in the rail (Second gear position). Secure the shift fork to the rail with the setscrew.

43 Move the Second-Third synchro unit to the neutral (centered) position and install the interlock plunger in its bore. Move the First-Reverse synchro unit forward to First gear position. Position the First-Reverse shift fork in the synchro sleeve groove and make sure that the setscrew hole in the fork is facing up. Rotate the fork and engage it with the shift fork shaft and then pass the First-Reverse shift rail through the rear of the case into the shift fork.

44 Turn the First-Reverse shift rail until the detent notches face up and then move the rail until the setscrew holes in the fork and rail are aligned. Install the setscrew.

45 Set the First-Reverse synchro sleeve and gear in the neutral (centered) position.

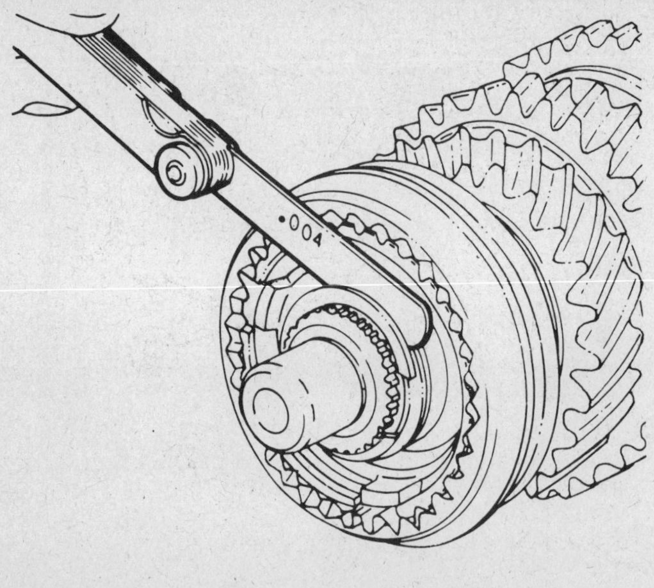

Fig. 7.16 Measuring the second-third gear synchronizer end play (150T transmission) (Sec 12)

46 Press the bearing onto the clutch shaft using the bearing inner race only as a pressure point and having the outer snap-ring groove nearer the front of the shaft. Install the bearing inner and outer snap-rings.
47 Using grease, stick the 15 needle roller bearings into the recess at the rear of the clutch shaft.
48 Locate the Second-Third blocking ring on the cone at the front of the Second gear on the mainshaft.
49 Pass the clutch shaft through the hole in the front face of the case and engage it with the mainshaft, making sure that none of the needler rollers are displaced. Tap the shaft/bearing assembly into place with a soft-faced hammer.
50 Position a new bearing cap gasket on the front face of the case, making sure that the oil return hole is not blocked off.
51 Install the bearing cap, equipped with a new oil seal, and align the marks made before removal to ensure that the oil return holes in the cap and case are opposite each other.
52 Install the mainshaft rear bearing using a piece of pipe as a drift. Make sure that the outer snap-ring groove is nearer the rear of the shaft.
53 Install the speedometer gear lock ball, gear and snap-ring.
54 Drive in the countershaft, displacing the dummy shaft. Make sure that the countershaft roll pin hole is correctly aligned with the holes in the case.
55 Install the extension housing complete with new oil seal and joint gasket. Apply sealant to the securing bolts (**not** the lower drain bolt).
56 Install the plug in the front end of the Second-Third shift rail. Drive it in so that it is about $\frac{1}{16}$-inch below the surface of the case.
57 Insert the upper detent plunger and the long spring.
58 Check the operation of the gearshift is smooth and positive in all positions.
59 Bolt on the top cover using a new gasket.
60 Attach the gearshift levers to the shift fork shafts. Install the back-up light switch and the TCS switch.

13 SR4 transmission – disassembly, inspection and reassembly

Disassembly

1 Using a hammer and punch, remove the large access plug from the extension housing.
2 Remove the flanged nut which attaches the shift rail to the offset lever. Remove the offset lever.
3 Remove the drain bolt (the bottom extension housing attaching bolt) and drain the transmission lubricant.
4 Remove the rest of the extension housing attaching bolts. Remove the housing.
5 Using a screwdriver, pry out the extension housing oil seal.
6 Remove the transmission cover attaching bolts and remove the transmission cover assembly. Note the locations of the two alignment (dowel) bolts for assembly reference. Discard the transmission cover gasket.
7 Remove the C-clip that attaches the Reverse lever to the Reverse lever pivot bolt.
8 Remove the Reverse lever pilot bolt. Remove the Reverse lever and Reverse lever fork as an assembly.
9 Punch or scribe some alignment marks in the front bearing cap and transmission case for assembly reference.
10 Remove the bearing cap and gasket. Discard the gasket.
11 Remove the speedometer gear snap-ring from the rear of the output shaft. Remove the speedometer gear and drive ball.
12 Remove the retaining snap-rings from the front and rear bearings. Remove the locating snap-rings from the front and rear bearings.
13 Using a bearing removal tool, remove the front bearing from the clutch shaft. AMC bearing remover no. J-8157-01, puller bolts no. J-26636, puller assembly J-25152 or a suitable bearing removal tool can be used.
14 Remove the clutch shaft from the transmission case.
15 Using the same bearing removal tool, remove the rear bearing from the output shaft.
16 Remove the output shaft with the geartrain intact. Do not let the First-Second or Third-Fourth synchronizer sleeves separate from the hubs during shaft removal.
17 Push the Reverse idler gear shaft out of the back of the transmission case. Remove the shaft and Reverse idler gear.
18 Remove the countershaft from the back of the transmission case using AMC countershaft tool no. J-26624 or a suitable length of pipe of the proper diameter.
19 Remove the countershaft gear and loading tool as an assembly. Remove the countershaft gear thrust washers and any clutch shaft pilot bushings that fell into the transmission during disassembly. **Note:** *The front countershaft gear thrust washer is plastic. The rear washer is metal.*
20 Remove the countershaft loading tool from the countershaft gear. Remove the needle bearing retainers and needle bearings.
21 Before disassembling the output shaft geartrain, scribe alignment marks on the Third-Fourth synchronizer hub and sleeve for assembly reference.
22 Remove the snap-ring from the front of the output shaft. Remove the Third-Fourth synchronizer assembly.
23 Remove the blocking rings from the Third-Fourth synchronizer assembly. Remove the insert springs and inserts. Separate the synchronizer sleeve from the hub.
24 Remove Third gear from the output shaft.
25 Remove the Second gear retaining snap-ring and thrust washer. Remove Second gear and the blocking ring.
26 Using a pair of side cutters, remove the First gear roll pin from the output shaft.
27 Remove First gear and the First gear blocking ring.
28 Scribe alignment marks on the First-Second synchronizer sleeve and the output shaft for assembly reference.
29 Remove the insert spring and the inserts from the output shaft. **Note:** *The First-Second-Reverse hub is assembled and machined with the output shaft and is not removable.*
30 Remove the detent plug, spring and plunger. Place the selector arm plates and the shift rail in the neutral position (centered).
31 Rotate the shift rail counterclockwise until the selector arm disengages and the selector arm roll pin is accessible.
32 Remove the shift rail until the selector arm contacts the First-Second shift fork.
33 Using a $\frac{3}{16}$-inch pin punch, remove the roll pin and remove the shift rail.
34 Remove the shift forks, selector arm plates, selector arm and interlock plate.
35 Pry out the shift rail oil seal and O-ring with a screwdriver.
36 Using a hammer and punch, remove the shift rail plug.
37 Remove the nylon inserts and selector arm plates from the shift forks. Note their position for assembly reference.

Inspection

38 See Section 8 for information on inspecting the transmission components.

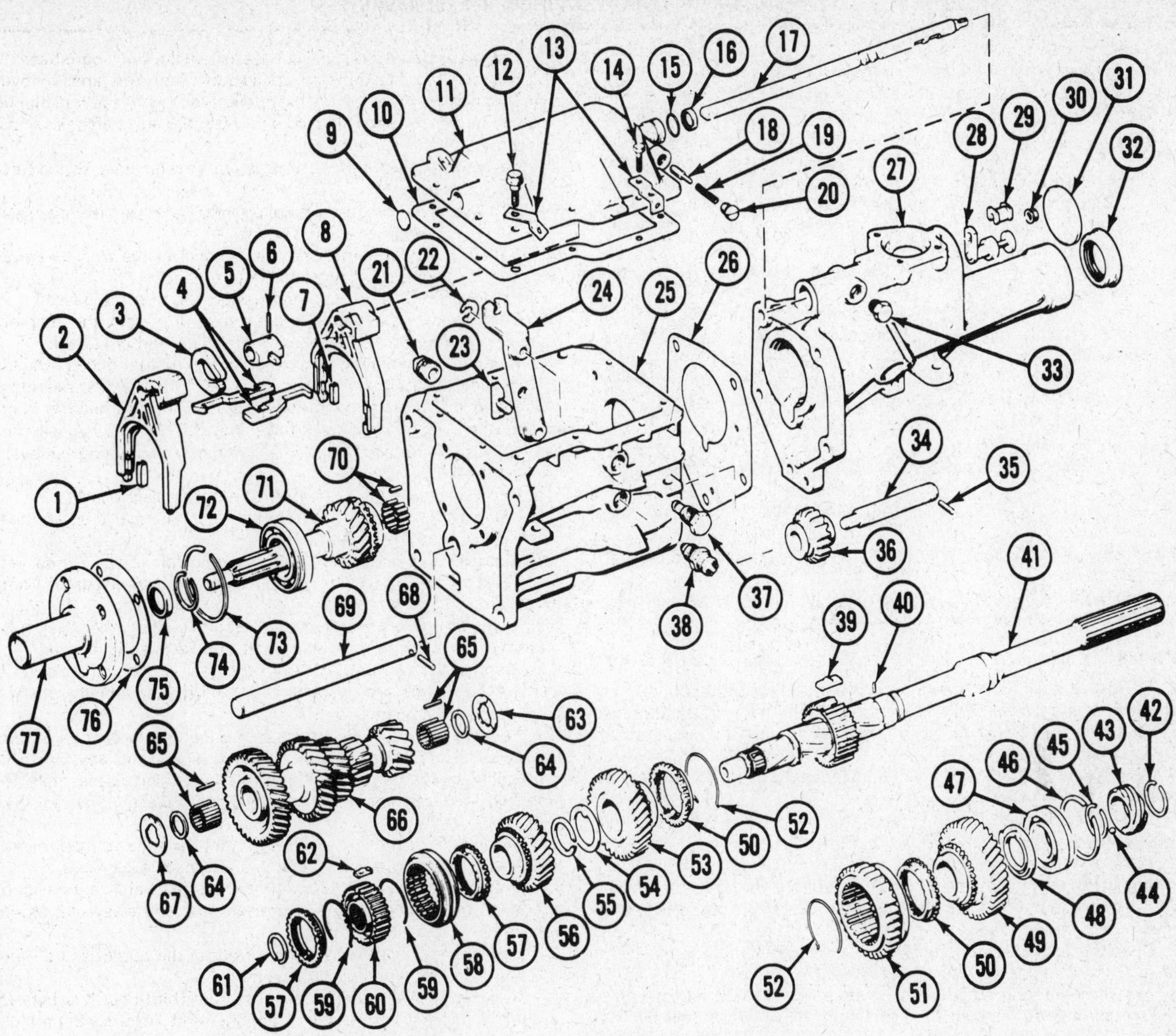

Fig. 7.17 Exploded view of the SR4 transmission components (Sec 13)

1 Third-fourth shift fork insert
2 Third-fourth shift fork
3 Selector interlock plate
4 Selector arm plate (2)
5 Selector arm
6 Selector arm roll pin
7 First-second shift fork insert
8 First-second shift fork
9 Shift rail plug
10 Transmission cover gasket
11 Transmission cover
12 Transmission cover dowel bolt (2)
13 Clip
14 Transmission cover bolt (8)
15 Shift rail O-ring seal
16 Shift rail oil seal
17 Shift rail
18 Detent plunger
19 Detent spring
20 Detent plug
21 Fill plug
22 Reverse lever pivot bolt C-clip
23 Reverse lever fork
24 Reverse lever
25 Transmission case
26 Extension housing gasket
27 Extension housing
28 Offset lever
29 Offset lever insert
30 Offset lever retaining nut
31 Access plug
32 Extension housing oil seal
33 Threaded plug
34 Reverse idler shaft
35 Reverse idler shaft roll pin
36 Reverse idler gear
37 Reverse lever pivot bolt
38 Backup lamp switch
39 First-second synchronizer insert (3)
40 First gear roll pin
41 Output shaft and hub assembly
42 Speedometer gear snap ring
43 Speedometer gear
44 Speedometer gear drive ball
45 Rear bearing retaining snap ring
46 Rear bearing locating snap ring
47 Rear bearing
48 First gear thrust washer
49 First gear
50 First-second synchronizer blocking ring (2)
51 First-reverse sleeve and gear
52 First-second synchronizer insert spring (2)
53 Second gear
54 Second gear thrust washer (tabbed)
55 Second gear snap ring
56 Third gear
57 Third-fourth synchronizer blocking ring (2)
58 Third-fourth synchronizer sleeve
59 Third-fourth synchronizer insert spring (2)
60 Third-fourth synchronizer hub
61 Output shaft snap ring
62 Third-fourth synchronizer insert (3)
63 Countershaft gear rear thrust washer (metal)
64 Countershaft needle bearing retainer (2)
65 Countershaft needle bearing (50)
66 Countershaft gear
67 Countershaft gear front thrust washer (plastic)
68 Countershaft roll pin
69 Countershaft
70 Clutch shaft roller bearings (15)
71 Clutch shaft
72 Front bearing
73 Front bearing locating snap ring
74 Front bearing retaining snap ring
75 Front bearing cap oil seal
76 Front bearing cap gasket
77 Front bearing cap

Reassembly

39 Install the nylon inserts and selector arm plates in the shift forks.
40 Apply sealer to the shift rail plug and install it.
41 Coat the shift rail and rail bores with petroleum jelly and insert the shift rail into the cover until the rail is flush with the inside edge of the cover.
42 Install the First-Second shift fork (the larger of the two forks) in the cover and push the shift rail through the fork.
43 Position the selector arm and the C-shaped interlock plate in the cover. Insert the shift rail through the arm.
44 Position the Third-Fourth shift fork with the selector arm plate under the First-Second plate.
45 Push the shift rail through the transmission cover bore.
46 Rotate the shift rail until the forward arm plate faces away from, but is parallel to, the cover.
47 Align the roll pin holes and install the roll pin. Be sure the pin is flush with the selector arm surface.
48 Install the detent plunger, spring and plug.
49 Install the shift rail O-ring.
50 Install the shift rail oil seal by first placing an oil seal protector tool such as AMC no. J-26628-2 over the threaded end of the shift rail.
51 Lubricate the lip of the oil seal and slide it over the protector and onto the shift rail.
52 Seat the oil seal in the transmission cover using an oil seal installer tool such as AMC no. J-26628-1.
53 Coat the output shaft and gear bores with transmission lubricant.
54 Install the First-Second synchronizer sleeve on the output shaft using the reference marks for alignment.
55 Install three synchronizer inserts and two insert springs in the First-Second synchronizer sleeve. The insert spring tangs engage in the same synchronizer insert, but the open ends of the springs face away from each other.
56 Assemble First gear and the blocking ring and install them on the output shaft. Be sure the synchronizer inserts engage the blocking ring notches.
57 Install the First gear roll pin and then install the Second gear and blocking ring on the output shaft. Be sure to engage the blocking ring notches.
58 Install the Second gear thrust washer and snap-ring. The sharp edge of the washer faces out. Also, be sure to engage the washer tab in the output shaft notch.
59 Using a feeler gauge, measure Second gear end play between the gear and thrust washer. End play should be 0.004 to 0.014 inch (0.1016 to 0.3556 mm). If end play exceeds the limit, replace the thrust washer, snap-ring and, if necessary, the synchronizer hub. **Note:** *If any output shaft gear is replaced, the countershaft gear must also be replaced.*
60 Assemble Third gear and the blocking ring and install them on the output shaft.
61 Install the Third-Fourth synchronizer sleeve on the output shaft using the reference marks for alignment.
62 Install three synchronizer inserts and two insert springs in the Third-Fourth synchronizer sleeve. Install the insert springs as described in Step 55.
63 Install the Third-Fourth synchronizer assembly with the machined groove in the synchronizer hub facing forward and install the snap-ring.
64 Measure the Third-Fourth synchronizer end play. End play should be 0.004 to 0.014 inch (0.1016 to 0.3556 mm). If end play exceeds the limit, replace the snap-ring and inspect the synchronizer hub for excessive wear on the thrust faces.
65 Coat the countershaft gear washers with petroleum jelly and position them in the transmission case. Install the plastic washer in the front of the case.
66 Insert the countershaft loading tool in the countershaft gear, install the 50 needle bearings in the front and rear of the gear and install the needle bearing retainers. Coat the bearings with petroleum jelly during installation.
67 Install the countershaft gear from the rear of the case. Be careful not to displace the thrust washers.
68 Install the Reverse idler gear from the rear of the case. The shift lever groove faces the front of the case.
69 Install the output shaft and geartrain. Be careful not to displace the synchronizer assemblies.
70 Install the Fourth gear blocking ring in the Third-Fourth synchronizer sleeve.

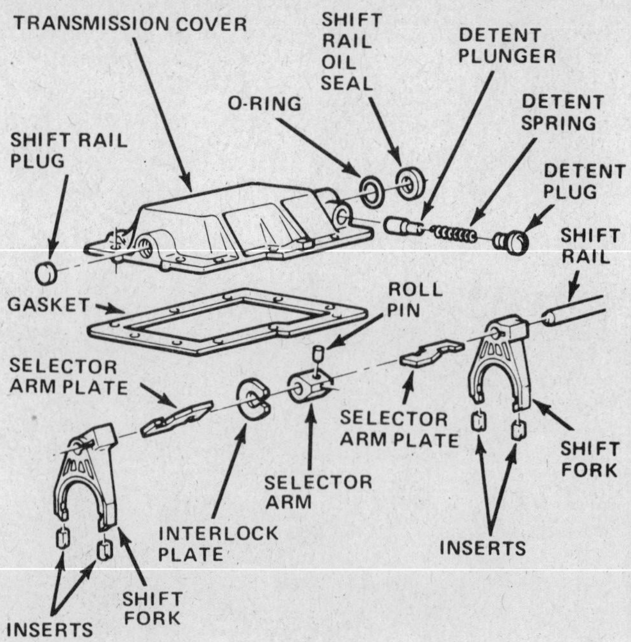

Fig. 7.18 Transmission cover assembly (SR4 transmission) (Sec 13)

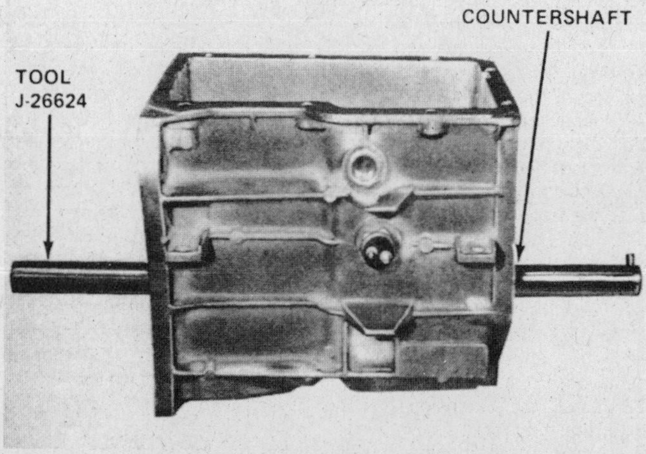

Fig. 7.19 Countershaft removal (typical)

71 Coat the pilot roller bearing bore of the clutch shaft with petroleum jelly and install 15 roller bearings. Install the clutch shaft and engage it with the Third-Fourth synchronizer sleeve and the blocking ring.
72 Using a bearing installation tool such as AMC no. J-22697, install the front bearing. Position the output shaft First gear against the rear of the case, align the bearing and install it completely onto the clutch shaft and into the case. **Note:** *The front bearing does not have an identifying notch in the race. The rear bearing has this notch.*
73 Install the front bearing retaining and locating snap-ring.
74 Using an oil seal installation tool such as AMC no. J-26625, install the front bearing cap oil seal.
75 Install the front bearing cap gasket and front bearing cap. Be sure to align the groove in the cap and the cut-out in the gasket with the oil hole in the case. Coat the bearing cap bolts with non-hardening gasket sealer and install the bolts. Tighten the bolts to 13 ft-lb (17.6 Nm).

Fig. 7.20 Reverse lever and geartrain assembly (SR4 transmission) (Sec 13)

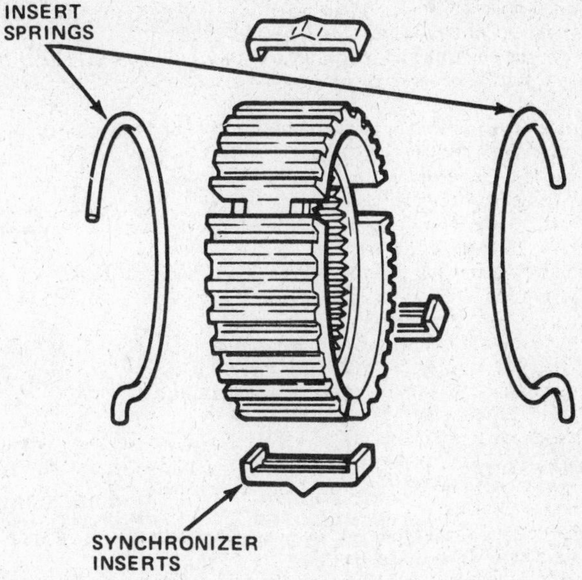

Fig. 7.21 The insert springs and synchronizer hub (typical of later model transmissions)

76 Install the First gear thrust washer on the output shaft, facing the oil groove toward First gear.
77 Install the rear bearing using a bearing installation tool such as AMC no. J-25234.
78 Install the retaining and locating snap-rings on the rear bearing.
79 Install the speedometer gear drive ball, gear and snap-ring.
80 Apply non-hardening gasket sealer to the threads of the Reverse lever pivot bolt. Install the Reverse lever and pivot bolt in the case and install the spring clip. Tighten the pivot bolt to 20 ft-lb (27.1 Nm). Be sure the Reverse lever fork is engaged in the Reverse idler gear.
81 Rotate the clutch shaft and observe the blocking rings. If they tend to stick on the gear cones, gently pry them off the cones with a screwdriver.
82 Place the Reverse lever in the Neutral position and install the cover gasket and cover on the case. Install the cover bolts and tighten each one alternately until a final torque of 10 ft-lb (13.5 Nm) is achieved. Be sure the two dowel bolts are in their proper locations.
83 Install the extension housing gasket and carefully install the extension housing.
84 Apply non-hardening gasket sealer to the extension housing access plug and install the plug.
85 Pour three pints (1.41 liters) of transmission lubricant into the transmission case and install the filler plug. Tighten the plug to 23 ft-lb (31.1 Nm).
86 Using an oil seal installation tool such as AMC no. J-9617, install the extension housing oil seal.
87 Install the rear crossmember on the extension housing (if removed) and tighten the attaching bolts to 22 ft-lb (29.8 Nm).

14 T-4 transmission – disassembly, inspection and reassembly

Disassembly

1 Remove the transmission filler plug and remove the lubricant using a siphon pump.
2 Remove the offset lever roll pin using a pin punch and hammer.
3 Remove the extension housing-to-transmission case bolts. Remove the housing and offset lever as an assembly.
4 Remove the detent ball, spring, and roll pin from the offset lever.
5 Remove the countershaft rear thrust bearing and race.
6 Remove the transmission cover attaching bolts and remove the cover. Note the location of the dowel-type alignment bolts for assembly reference.
7 Remove the Reverse lever C-clip and the Reverse lever pivot bolt. Remove the Reverse lever and Reverse lever fork as an assembly.
8 Punch alignment marks on the front bearing cap and the transmission case and remove the front bearing cap.
9 Remove the front bearing race and end play shims. Pry out the oil seal with a screwdriver.
10 Rotate the clutch shaft until the gear flat faces the countershaft and remove the clutch shaft.
11 Remove the thrust bearing and the roller bearings.
12 Remove the output shaft bearing race by tapping the front of the shaft with a soft-faced hammer.
13 Lift out the shaft assembly.
14 Remove the countershaft rear bearing using a brass drift and an arbor press.
15 Move the countershaft to the rear and lift the shaft out of the case. Remove the countershaft front washer from the case.
16 Remove the countershaft rear bearing spacer.
17 Remove the Reverse idler shaft roll pin and remove the Reverse idler shaft and gear.
18 Remove the countershaft rear bearing using an arbor press.
19 Remove the clutch shaft from the front bearing using a bearing removal tool such as AMC no. J-29721 and J-22912.
20 Remove the extension housing rear seal using a flat drift and a hammer.
21 Remove the back-up light switch from the case.
22 To disassemble the output shaft geartrain, first remove the thrust bearing washer from the front of the output shaft.
23 Remove the Third-Fourth synchronizer blocking ring, sleeve and hub as an assembly after scribing alignment marks on the sleeve and hub.
24 Remove the Third-Fourth synchronizer springs and inserts. Separate the synchronizer hub from the sleeve.
25 Remove Third gear from the shaft.
26 Remove the Second gear snap-ring and thrust washer and remove Second gear.
27 Remove the output shaft bearing using the AMC puller set no. J-29721 and AMC adapters no. 293-39 or a similar bearing puller set.
28 Remove the First gear thrust washer, roll pin (using diagonal pliers), First gear and the blocking ring.
29 Scribe alignment marks on the First-Second gear synchronizer sleeve and the output shaft and remove the insert spring and inserts from the First-Reverse sliding gear. Remove the gear from the output shaft. **Note:** *The First-Second-Reverse hub is part of the output shaft and is not removable.*

7A

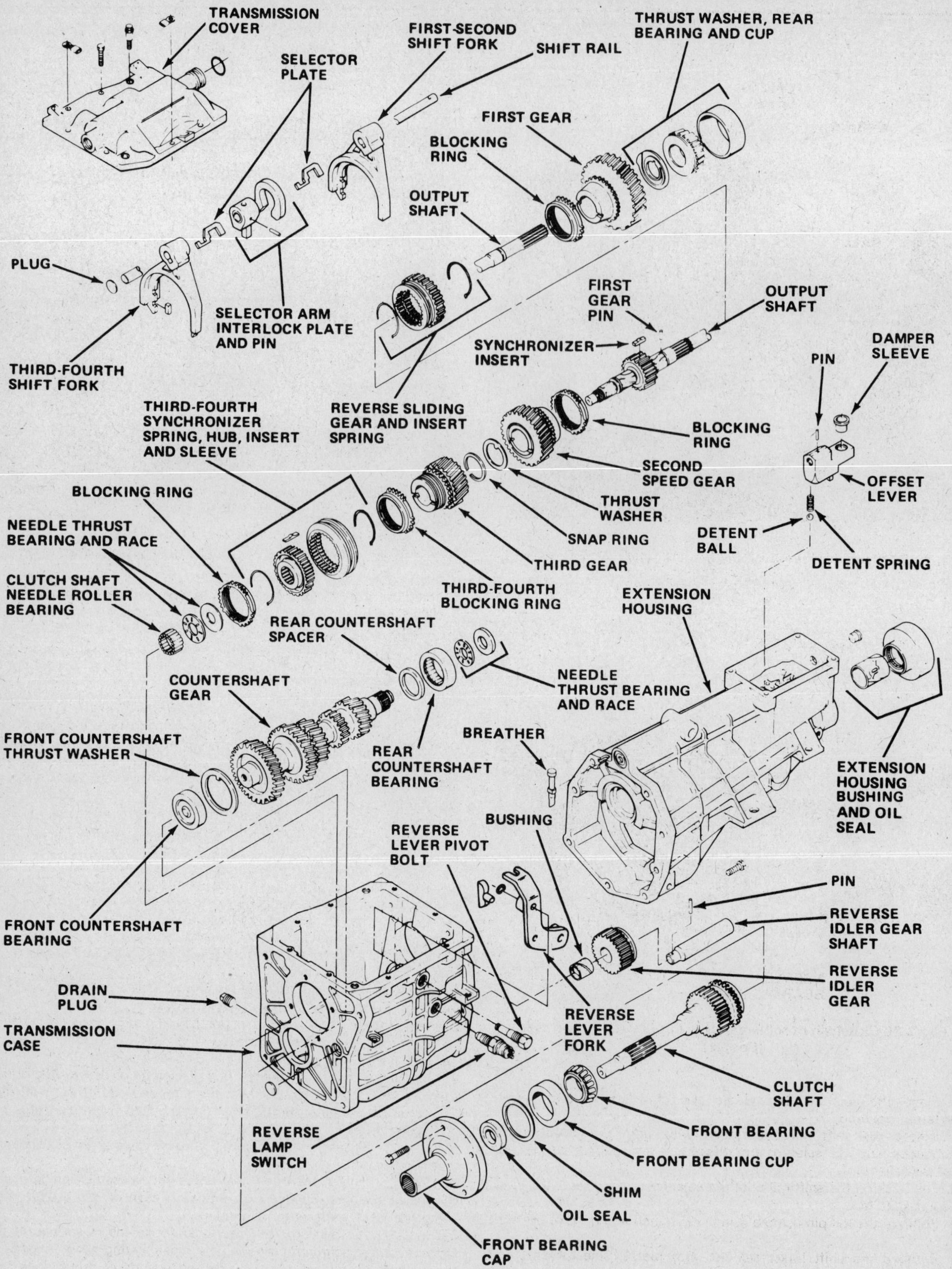

Fig. 7.22 Exploded view of the T-4 transmission components (Sec 14)

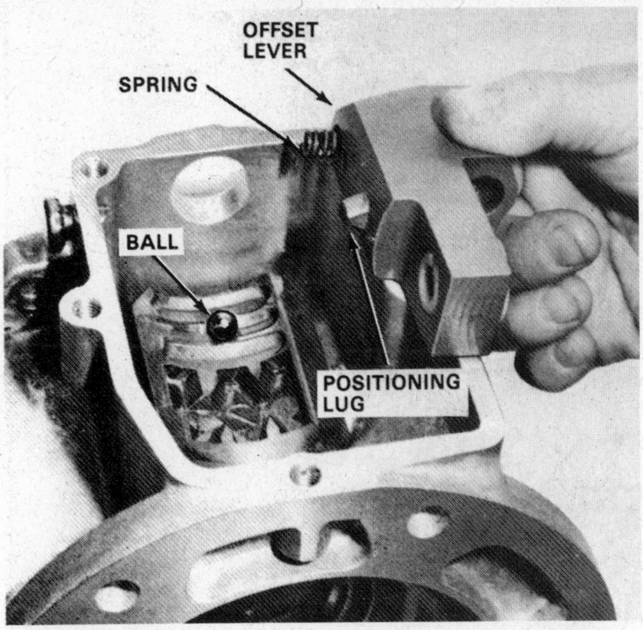

Fig. 7.23 Offset lever removal and installation (T-4 transmission) (Sec 14)

Fig. 7.24 Reverse lever and pivot bolt (T-4 transmission) (Sec 14)

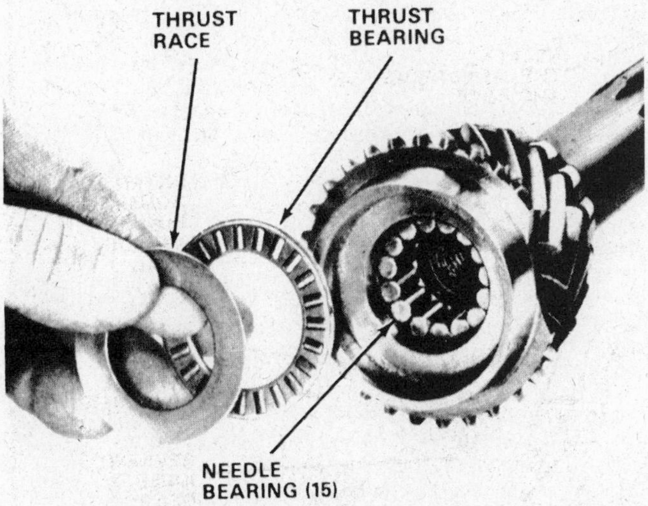

Fig. 7.25 Clutch shaft roller bearing, thrust bearing and race (Sec 14)

30 Place the selector arm plates and shift rail in the Neutral (centered) position.
31 Rotate the shift rail counterclockwise until the selector arm disengages from the selector arm plates and the selector arm roll pin is accessible.
32 Pull back on the shift rail until the selector arm contacts the First-Second shift fork.
33 Remove the roll pin using a $\frac{3}{16}$-inch pin punch and remove the shift rail.
34 Remove the shift forks, selector arm plates, selector arm and interlock plate.
35 Pry out the shift rail oil seal and O-ring using a screwdriver.
36 Remove the shift rail plug using a hammer and punch.
37 Remove the nylon inserts and selector arm plates from the shift forks, noting their position for assembly reference.

Inspection

38 See Section 8 for information on inspecting the transmission components.

Reassembly

39 Install the nylon inserts and selector arm plates in the shift forks.
40 Coat the edges of the shift rail plug with sealer and install the plug.
41 Coat the shift rail and shift rail bores with petroleum jelly and insert the rail in the cover until the end is flush with the inside edge of the cover.
42 Position the First-Second shift fork in the cover and push the shift rail through the fork. **Note**: *The First-Second shift fork is the larger of the two shift forks.*
43 Position the selector arm and interlock plate and insert the shift rail. The widest part of the plate faces away from the cover and the roll pin faces down and toward the rear of the cover.
44 Position the Third-Fourth shift fork with the selector arm plate under the First-Second shift fork selector arm plate.
45 Insert the shift rail through the Third-Fourth shift fork and into the shift rail bore in the cover.
46 Rotate the shift rail until the selector arm plate at the forward end faces away from, but is parallel to, the cover.
47 Align the roll pin holes and install the roll pin. Be sure it is installed flush with the selector arm surface.
48 Install the O-ring in the shift rail oil seal groove.
49 Install the shift rail oil seal by first placing an oil seal protector tool such as AMC no. J-26628-2 over the threaded end of the shift rail.
50 Lubricate the lip of the oil seal and slide it over the protector and onto the shift rail.
51 Seat the oil seal in the transmission cover using an oil seal installer tool such as AMC no. J-26628-1.
52 Coat the output shaft and gear bores with transmission lubricant.
53 Install the First-Second synchronizer sleeve on the output shaft using the reverse marks for alignment.
54 Install three synchronizer inserts and two insert springs in the First-Second synchronizer sleeve. The insert spring tangs engage in the same synchronizer insert but the open ends of the springs face away from each other.
55 Install the blocking ring and Second gear on the output shaft.
56 Install the thrust washer and Second gear snap-ring. Be sure the washer tab is seated in the output shaft notch.

57 Install the blocking ring and First gear on the output shaft and install the First gear roll pin.
58 Install the rear bearing on the output shaft using a bearing installer such as AMC tool no. J-2995 and an arbor press.
59 Install the First gear thrust washer.
60 Install Third gear, the Third and Fourth gear synchronizer hub inserts and the sleeve on the output shaft. The hub offset faces forward.
61 Install the thrust bearing washer on the output shaft.
62 Coat the countershaft front bearing outer cage with Loctite 601 or the equivalent and install the countershaft front bearing flush with the case using an arbor press.
63 Coat the countershaft thrust washer with petroleum jelly. Install the washer with the tab corresponding to the depression in the case.
64 Stand the case on end and install the countershaft in the front bearing bore.
65 Install the countershaft rear bearing spacer.
66 Coat the rear bearing with petroleum jelly and install it with a bearing installer such as AMC tool no. J-29895 and a hammer. The installed bearing should extend 0.125 inch beyond the case surface.
67 Position the Reverse idler gear and install the idler shaft from the rear of the case. Install the roll pin.
68 Install the output shaft.
69 Install the front clutch shaft bearing on the clutch shaft using a bearing installer such as AMC tool no. J-2995 and an arbor press.
70 Coat 15 roller bearings with petroleum jelly and install them in the clutch shaft.
71 Install the thrust bearing and race.
72 Install the Fourth gear blocking ring and rear bearing race.
73 Install the clutch shaft, engaging it in the Third-Fourth synchronizer sleeve and blocking ring.
74 Install the new front bearing cap oil seal with an installation tool such as AMC no. J-26625.
75 Install the new extension housing oil seal with an installation tool such as AMC no. J-29184.
76 Temporarily install the front bearing race in the front bearing cap. Do not install the shims yet.
77 Temporarily install the front bearing cap.
78 Install the Reverse lever, pivot pin and C-clip. Coat the pin threads with sealer. Be sure the Reverse lever fork engages the Reverse idler gear.
79 Coat the countershaft rear bearing race and thrust bearing with petroleum jelly and install it in the extension housing.
80 Temporarily install the extension housing.
81 Turn the transmission case on end and mount a dial indicator on the extension housing with the indicator stylus on the end of the output shaft.
82 Rotate the output shaft and zero the dial indicator.
83 Pull up on the output shaft until the end play is removed. Read the dial indicator and use the dimension to determine the thickness of the bearing preload shim.
84 Select a shim pack measuring 0.001 to 0.005 inch (0.003 to 0.13 mm) thicker than the end play.
85 Set the transmission down on its side and remove the bearing cap and race.
86 Add the necessary shims to the bearing cap and install the clutch shaft bearing race in the cap.
87 Apply some non-hardening gasket sealer to the case mating surface of the front bearing cap. Install the cap using the alignment marks and tighten the attaching bolts to 13 ft-lb (18 Nm).
88 Recheck the end play. There must be no end play.
89 Remove the extension housing.
90 Move the shift forks and synchronizer rings to the Neutral position.
91 Apply non-hardening gasket sealer to the cover mating surfaces of the transmission case. Lower the cover assembly while aligning the shift forks and synchronizer sleeves. Center the cover to engage the Reverse lever and install the two dowel bolts.
92 Install the remaining cover bolts and tighten them to 10 ft-lb (14 Nm). Apply non-hardening gasket sealer to the extension housing mating surface of the transmission case and install the extension housing to a position where the shift rail just enters the shift cover opening.
93 Install the offset lever and spring with the detent ball in the neutral guide plate detent.
94 Install the extension housing bolts and tighten them to 23 ft-lb (31 Nm).
95 Insall the roll pin and the damper sleeve in the offset lever.
96 Coat the back-up light switch with non-hardening gasket sealer and install the switch in the case.

15 T-5 transmission – disassembly, inspection and reassembly

Disassembly

1 Remove the transmission filler plug and remove the lubricant using a siphon pump.
2 Remove the offset lever roll pin using a pin punch and hammer.
3 Remove the extension housing-to-transmission case bolts. Remove the housing and offset lever as an assembly.
4 Remove the detent ball, spring, and roll pin from the offset lever.
5 Remove the plastic funnel, thrust bearing race and thrust bearing from the end of the countershaft or the inside of the extension housing.
6 Remove the transmission cover attaching bolts and remove the cover. Note the location of the dowel-type alignment bolts for assembly reference.
7 Remove the roll pin from the Fifth gear shift fork using a hammer and punch. **Note:** *To prevent damage to the Reverse shift rail, place a wood block under the Fifth gear shift fork during roll pin removal.*
8 Remove the Fifth gear synchronizer snap-ring and shift fork. Remove the Fifth gear synchronizer assembly and remove Fifth gear from the rear of the countershaft.
9 Remove the insert retainer, insert springs and inserts from the Fifth gear synchronizer sleeve. Mark the position of the sleeve and hub for assembly reference.
10 Remove the snap-ring and remove the Fifth speed driven gear from the rear of the output shaft using a puller such as AMC puller assembly no. J-25215.
11 Punch alignment marks on the front bearing cap and the transmission case for assembly reference.
12 Remove the bearing cap attaching bolts and remove the bearing cap.
13 Remove the bearing race and end play shims from the cap. Pry out the bearing cap oil seal with a screwdriver.
14 Rotate the clutch shaft until the gear flat faces the countershaft and remove the clutch shaft from the transmission case. Remove the clutch shaft needle bearings, thrust bearing and race.
15 Remove the output shaft rear bearing race and lift the shaft assembly out of the case.
16 Unhook the overcenter link spring from the rear of the case. A homemade spring removal tool made of welding rod or a similar material would be helpful here.
17 Remove the Reverse lever C-clip.
18 Rotate the Reverse shift rail until it disengages from the Reverse lever and remove the rail from the rear of the case.
19 Remove the Reverse lever pivot pin, disengage the Reverse lever from the idler gear and remove the Reverse lever and fork assembly from the transmission case.
20 Remove the rear countershaft snap-ring and spacer.
21 Using an arbor press and a brass drift inserted through the clutch shaft opening in the front of the case, carefully press the countershaft assembly to the rear to remove the countershaft bearing.
22 Move the countershaft assembly to the rear and lift it out of the transmission case.
23 Remove the countershaft rear bearing spacer.
24 Remove the idler shaft roll pin.
25 Remove the idler shaft and gear from the transmission case.
26 Using an arbor press, remove the countershaft front bearing from the case.
27 Remove the clutch shaft front bearing using a bearing removal tool such as AMC no. J-29721 and J-22912-01.
28 Remove the rear extension housing seal using a flat drift and a hammer.
29 Remove the thrust bearing washer from the output shaft.
30 Remove the Third-Fourth synchronizer assembly and blocking ring. Mark the sleeve and hub for assembly reference.
31 Remove the Third-Fourth synchronizer insert springs and inserts and remove the sleeve from the hub.
32 Remove Third gear from the output shaft.
33 Remove the Second gear snap-ring, tabbed thrust washer and second gear from the shaft.
34 Remove the output shaft rear bearing using a puller such as AMC no. J-29721 and adapters no. 293-39.

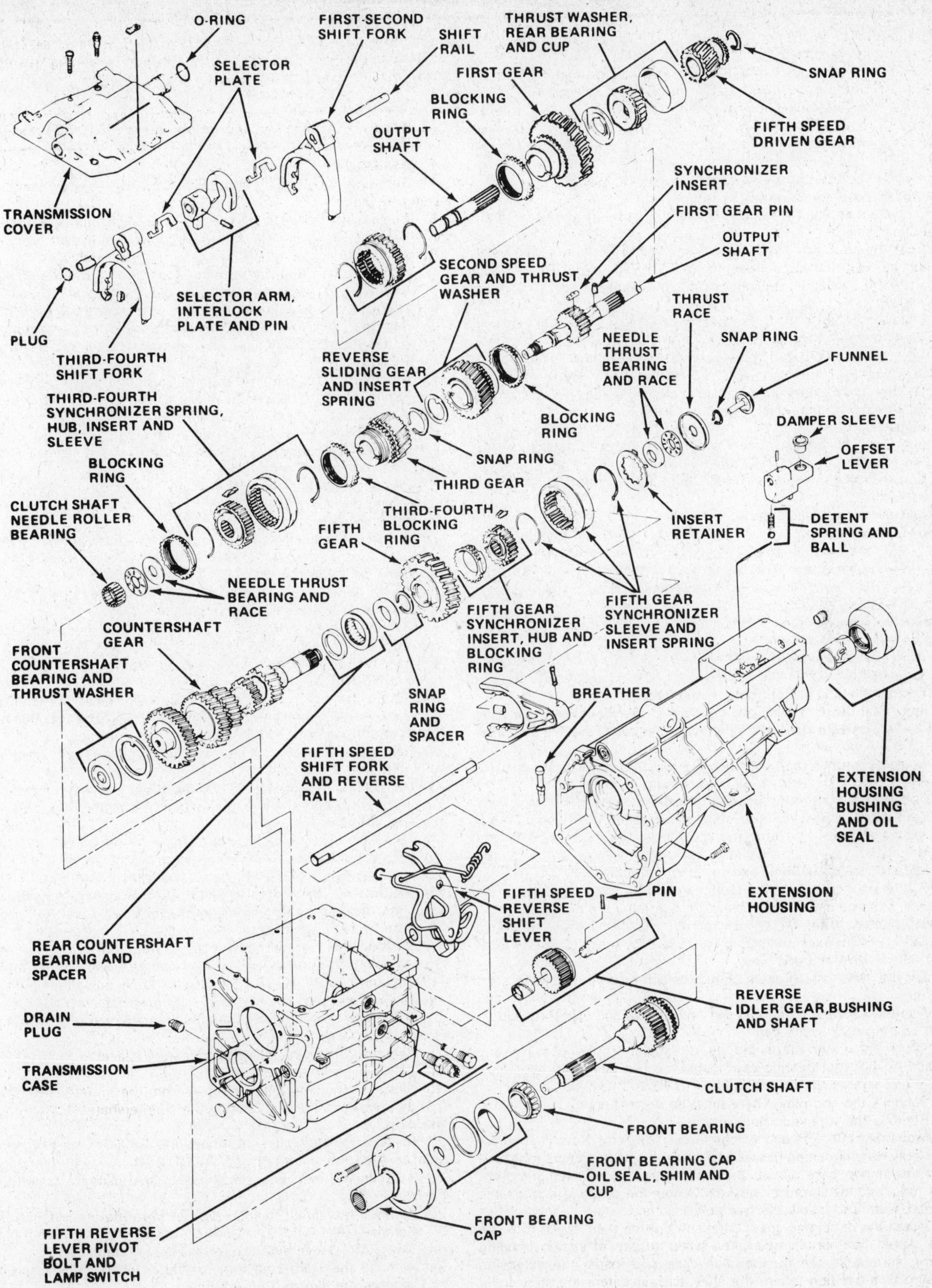

Fig. 7.26 Exploded view of the T-5 transmission components (Sec 15)

7A

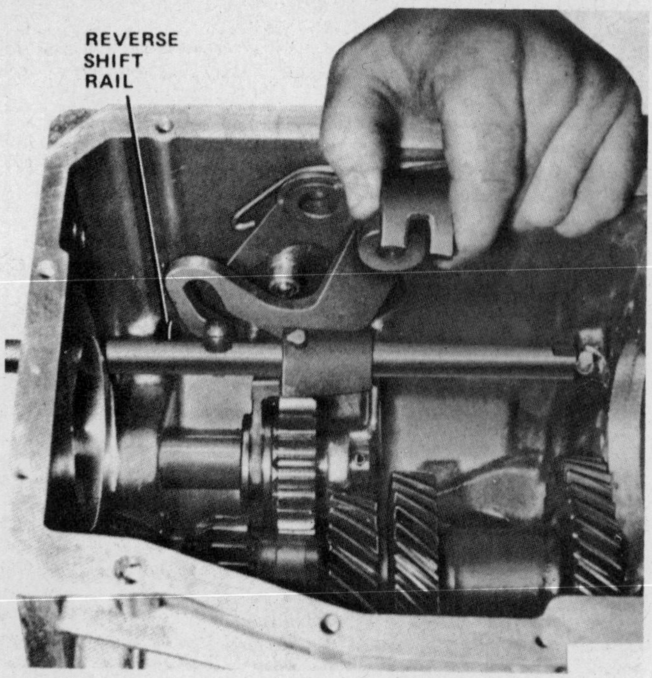

Fig. 7.27 Reverse shift rail removal and installation (T-5 transmission) (Sec 15)

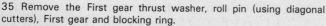

Fig. 7.28 Fifth gearshift fork and synchronizer sleeve (T-5 transmission) (Sec 15)

35 Remove the First gear thrust washer, roll pin (using diagonal cutters), First gear and blocking ring.
36 Scribe alignment marks on the First-Second gear synchronizer sleeve and the output shaft hub for assembly reference.
37 Remove the insert spring and inserts from the First-Reverse sliding gear and remove the gear from the output shaft hub. **Note**: *The First-Second-Reverse hub is part of the output shaft and is not removable.*
38 Place the selector arm plates and shift rail in the Neutral (centered) position.
39 Rotate the shift rail counterclockwise until the selector arm disengages from the selector arm plates and the selector arm roll pin is accessible.
40 Pull back on the shift rail until the selector arm contacts the First-Second shift fork.
41 Remove the roll pin using a $\frac{3}{16}$-inch pin punch and remove the shift rail.
42 Remove the shift forks, selector arm plates, selector arm and interlock plate.
43 Pry out the shift rail oil seal and O-ring using a screwdriver.
44 Remove the shift rail plug using a hammer and punch.
45 Remove the nylon inserts and selector arm plates from the shift forks, noting their position for assembly reference.

Inspection

46 See Section 8 for information on inspecting the transmission components.

Reassembly

47 Install the nylon inserts and selector arm plates in the shift forks.
48 Coat the edges of the shift rail plug with sealer and install the plug.
49 Coat the shift rail and shift rail bores with petroleum jelly and insert the rail into the cover until the end is flush with the inside edge of the cover.
50 Position the First-Second shift fork in the cover and push the shift rail through the fork. **Note**: *The First-Second shift fork is the larger of the two shift forks.*
51 Position the selector arm and interlock plate and insert the shift rail. The widest part of the plate faces away from the cover and the roll pin faces down and toward the rear of the cover.
52 Position the Third-Fourth shift fork with the selector arm plate under the First-Second shift fork selector arm plate.
53 Insert the shift rail through the Third-Fourth shift fork and into the shift rail bore in the cover.
54 Rotate the shift rail until the selector arm plate at the forward end faces away from, but is parallel to, the cover.
55 Align the roll pil holes and install the roll pin. Be sure it is installed flush with the selector arm surface.
56 Install the O-ring in the shift rail oil seal groove.
57 Install the shift rail oil seal by first placing an oil seal protector tool such as AMC no. J-26628-2 over the threaded end of the shift rail.
58 Lubricate the lip of the oil seal and slide it over the protector and onto the shift rail.
59 Seat the oil seal in the transmission cover using an oil seal installer tool such as AMC no. J-26628-1.
60 Coat the output shaft and gear bores with transmission lubricant.
61 Install the First-Second synchronizer sleeve on the output shaft using the reference marks for alignment.
62 Install three synchronizer inserts and two insert springs in the First-Second synchronizer sleeve. The insert spring tangs engage in the same synchronizer insert but the open ends of the springs face away from each other.
63 Install the blocking ring and Second gear on the output shaft.
64 Install the thrust washer and Second gear snap-ring. Be sure the washer tab is seated in the output shaft notch.
65 Install the blocking ring and First gear on the output shaft.
66 Install the First gear roll pin.
67 Install the rear bearing on the output shaft using a bearing installer such as AMC tool no. J-2995 and and arbor press.
68 Install the First gear thrust washer.
69 Install Third gear, the Third and Fourth gear synchronizer hub inserts and the sleeve on the output shaft. The hub offset faces forward.
70 Install the thrust bearing washer on the output shaft.
71 Coat the countershaft front bearing outer cage with Loctite 601 or the equivalent and install the countershaft front bearing flush with the case using an arbor press.
72 Coat the countershaft thrust washer with petroleum jelly. Install the washer with the tab corresponding to the depression in the case.
73 Stand the case on end and install the countershaft in the front bearing bore.
74 Install the countershaft rear bearing spacer.
75 Coat the rear bearing with petroleum jelly and install with a bearing installer such as AMC no. J-29895 and a sleeve tool such as

AMC no. J-33032. The installed bearing should extend 0.125 inch beyond the case surface.
76 Position the Reverse idler gear and install the idler shaft from the rear of the case. Install the roll pin.
77 Install the output shaft.
78 Install the front clutch shaft bearing on the clutch shaft using a bearing installer such as AMC tool no. J-2995 and an arbor press.
79 Coat 15 roller bearings with petroleum jelly and install them in the clutch shaft.
80 Install the thrust bearing and race in the clutch shaft.
81 Install the rear output shaft bearing race cap.
82 Install the Fourth gear blocking ring.
83 Install the clutch shaft, engaging it in the Third-Fourth synchronizer sleeve and blocking ring.
84 Install the front bearing cap oil seal using an oil installation tool such as AMC no. J-26625.
85 Install the front bearing race in the front bearing cap but do not yet install the preload shims.
86 Temporarily install the front bearing cap.
87 Install the Reverse lever, pivot bolt and C-clip. Coat the pivot bolt threads with non-hardening gasket sealer. Be sure the Reverse lever fork engages the idler gear.
88 Install the Fifth speed driven gear and snap-ring.
89 Install Fifth gear on the countershaft.
90 Insert the Reverse rail from the rear of the case and rotate it until it engages in the Fifth speed Reverse lever.
91 Install the Reverse lever overcenter link spring.
92 Using reference marks for alignment, assemble the Fifth gear synchronizer sleeve, insert springs and insert retainer.
93 Install the plastic inserts on each side of the Fifth speed shift fork.
94 Place the Fifth gear synchronizer assembly on the Fifth speed shift fork and slide them onto the countershaft and Reverse rail.
95 Place a wood block under the rail and fork assembly and install the roll pin.
96 Install the thrust race against the Fifth speed synchronizer hub and install the snap-ring.
97 Coat the thrust race and bearing with petroleum jelly and install the bearing against the thrust race.
98 Install the lipped thrust race over the thrust bearing and install the plastic funnel in the end of the countershaft gear.
99 Temporarily install the extension housing.
100 Turn the transmission case on end and mount a dial indicator on the extension housing with the indicator stylus on the end of the output shaft.
101 Rotate the output shaft and zero the dial indicator.
102 Pull up on the output shaft until the end play is removed. Read the dial indicator and use the dimension to determine the thickness of the bearing preload shim.
103 Select a shim pack measuring 0.001 to 0.005 inch (0.003 to 0.13 mm) thicker than the end play.
104 Set the transmission down on its side and remove the bearing cap and race.
105 Add the necessary shims to the bearing cap and install the clutch shaft bearing race in the cap.
106 Apply some non-hardening gasket sealer to the case mating surface of the front bearing cap. Install the cap using the alignment marks and tighten the attaching bolts to 13 ft-lb (18 Nm).
107 Recheck the end play. There must be no end play.
108 Remove the extension housing.
109 Move the shift forks and synchronizer rings to the Neutral position.
110 Apply non-hardening gasket sealer to the cover mating surfaces of the transmission case. Lower the cover assembly while aligning the shift forks and synchronizer sleeves. Center the cover to engage the Reverse lever and install the two dowel bolts.
111 Install the remaining cover bolts and tighten them to 10 ft-lb (14 Nm). Apply non-hardening gasket sealer to the extension housing mating surface of the transmission case and install the extension housing to a position where the shift rail just enters the shift cover opening.
112 Install the offset lever and spring with the detent ball in the neutral guide plate detent.
113 Install the extension housing bolts and tighten them to 23 ft-lb (31 Nm).
114 Install the roll pin and the damper sleeve in the offset lever.
115 Coat the back-up light switch with non-hardening gasket sealer and install the switch in the case.

Chapter 7 Part B Automatic transmission

Contents

Automatic transmission diagnosis 17
Automatic transmission fluid change .... See Chapter 1
General information 16
Fluid level check .... See Chapter 1
Kickdown (front) band – adjustment 21
Neutral safety switch – check and replacement 18
Removal and installation 22
Shift linkage – adjustment 20
Throttle linkage and cable – adjustment 19

Specifications

Kickdown band adjustment

(backed off from 72 in-lb)*	
1971	
M-43 and M-44 transmission	$\frac{3}{4}$ of a turn
M-11B and M44 transmission	$1\frac{1}{4}$ turns
1972	
360 cubic-inch engine	$2\frac{1}{2}$ turns
All other models	2 turns
1973 through 1976	
360 cubic-inch engine with HD 727 transmission	2 turns
Other models with standard and HD 727 transmission	$2\frac{1}{2}$ turns
All other models	2 turns
1977 and 1978	
304 cubic-inch engine with HD 727 transmission	$2\frac{1}{2}$ turns
360 cubic-inch engine with standard HD 727 transmission	$2\frac{1}{2}$ turns
360 cubic-inch engine with HD 727 transmission	2 turns
All other models	2 turns
1979 and 1980 (all models)	2 turns
1981 (all models)	$2\frac{1}{2}$ turns
1982 and 1983	
Four-cylinder engine with 904 transmission	$2\frac{1}{2}$ turns
Six-cylinder engine with 904 transmission	2 turns
Six-cylinder engine with 998 transmission	3 turns

**If an adapter tool such as AMC no. J-24063 is used with the torque wrench, the adjustment should be backed off from a torque valve of 36 in-lb.*

Torque specifications

	Ft-lb*	Nm
Cooler line fitting	160 in-lb	18
Converter housing-to-engine bolts	54	73
Kickdown band adjusting screw locknut	35	47
Shift linkage control lever screw	95 in-lb	11
Neutral safety switch	24	33
Oil pan bolts	150 in-lb	17
Rear cushion-to-crossmember bolt	25	34
Rear support bracket-to-rear cushion bolt	48	65
Rear support bracket-to-transmission bolt	48	65
Speedometer adapter clamp screw	100 in-lb	11
Starter motor-to-converter housing bolt	54	73
Starter motor-to-converter housing hex nut	33	45
Transmission-to-engine bolts	28	38

**Unless otherwise stated*

16 General information

Due to the complexity of the clutches and the hydraulic control system, and because of the special tools and expertise required to perform an automatic transmission overhaul, it should not be undertaken by the home mechanic. Therefore, the procedures in this Chapter are limited to general diagnosis, routine maintenance and adjustment and transmission removal and installation.

If the transmission requires major repair work, it should be left to an AMC dealer service department or a reputable automotive or transmission repair shop specializing in this type of work. You can, however, remove and install the transmission yourself and save the expense, even if the repair work is done by a transmission specialist. **Caution:** *Never tow a disabled vehicle at speeds greater than 30 mph or distances over 50 miles unless the driveshaft is removed. Failure to observe this precaution may result in severe transmission damage caused by a lack of lubrication.*

17 Automatic transmission diagnosis

Automatic transmission malfunctions may be caused by four general conditions: poor engine performance, improper adjustments, hydraulic malfunctions and mechanical malfunctions. Diagnosis of these problems should always begin with a check of the easily repaired items: fluid level and condition, shift linkage adjustment and throttle linkage adjustment. Next, perform a road test to determine if the problem has been corrected or if more diagnosis is necessary. If the problem persists after the preliminary tests and corrections are completed, additional diagnosis should be done by an AMC dealer service department or a reputable automotive or transmission repair shop.

18 Neutral safety switch – check and replacement

1 To test the Neutral safety switch, first block both the front and back of one wheel to keep the vehicle from rolling. Remove the wiring connector from the switch on the transmission housing.
2 Use a circuit tester or an ohmmeter to check for continuity between the center terminal pin and the transmission case. *Continuity should exist only when the transmission is in Park or Neutral.*
3 If the switch is not functioning properly, check the shift linkage adjustment (Section 20) before replacing the switch.
4 If the switch must be replaced, position a drain pan under the transmission, as there will be a slight loss of fluid during switch removal.
5 Move the selector lever to the Park and then to the Neutral position. Inspect the switch operating lever fingers to ensure that they are properly centered in the switch opening in the case.
6 Install the new switch and seal in the transmission case. Tighten the switch to the specified torque.
7 Add transmission fluid as needed and connect the wire connector.
8 The engine should start only with the transmission in the Neutral and Park positions.

19 Throttle linkage and cable – adjustment

Throttle linkage adjustment

1 Remove the air cleaner assembly, then remove the throttle control rod spring at the carburetor.
2 Hook the throttle control rod spring onto the throttle control lever on the transmission case. Stretch the spring forward and attach the other end to maintain forward tension on the throttle control lever.
3 Block the choke open and set the carburetor throttle off the fast idle cam. Also, on carburetors equipped with a throttle operated solenoid valve, turn the ignition lock to the On position and energize the solenoid. Open the throttle halfway to allow the solenoid to lock and return the carburetor to the idle position.
4 Loosen the retaining bolt(s) on the throttle control adjusting link. On V8 models, remove the spring clip and move the nylon washer to the rear of the link.
5 Lengthen or shorten (depending on linkage type) the adjusting link to eliminate all play. Tighten the link retaining bolt(s).

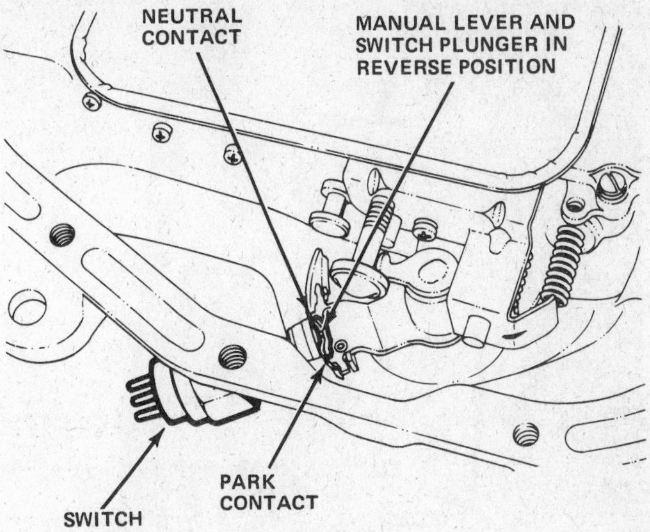

Fig. 7.29 Neutral safety (and back-up light) switch components – typical (Sec 18)

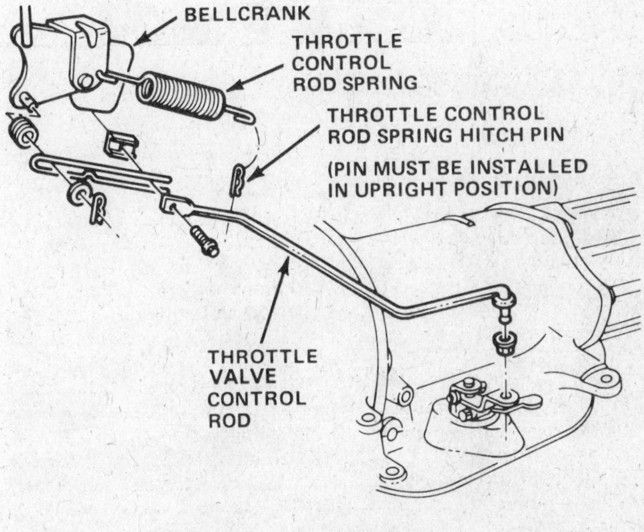

Fig. 7.30 Throttle control rod assembly – typical (Sec 19)

7B

6 On V8 models, install the nylon washer and spring clip.
7 Reinstall the spring on the throttle control rod and install the air cleaner.

Throttle cable adjustment

8 It may be necessary to remove the air cleaner and strut rod bushing heat shield in order to gain access to the throttle control lever. Move the spark plug wires aside if necessary.
9 Use a spare spring to hold the throttle control lever to the rear, against the stop.
10 Block the choke open and set the carburetor throttle off the fast idle cam.
11 On four-cylinder models without air conditioning, turn the ignition key to the On position to energize the throttle stop solenoid.
12 Using a small screwdriver, release the cable adjuster T-clamp.
13 Grasp the cable outer sheath and move the cable and sheath forward to eliminate any cable load on the throttle cable bellcrank.
14 Adjust the cable by moving the cable and sheath to the rear until there is zero lash between the plastic cable end and the bellcrank ball.

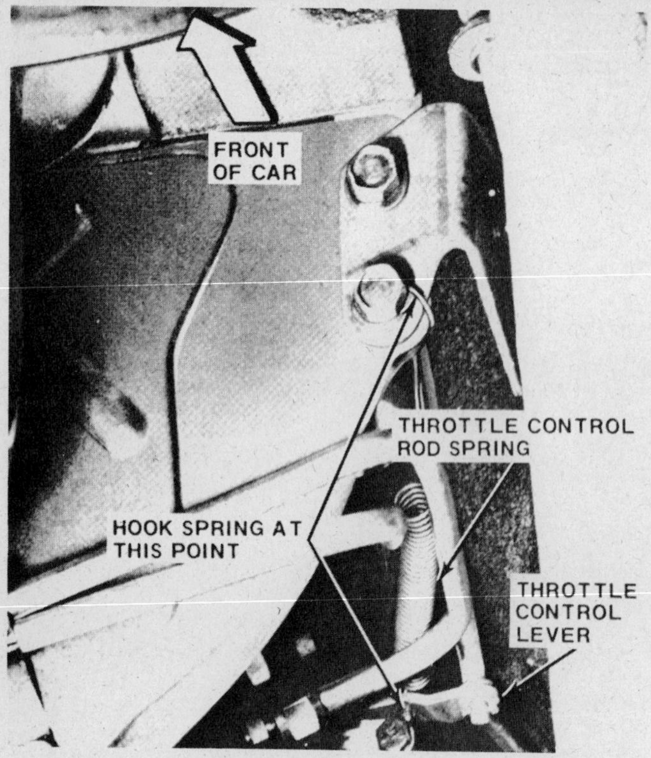

Fig. 7.31 Throttle control lever tension spring – typical of early AMC models (Sec 19)

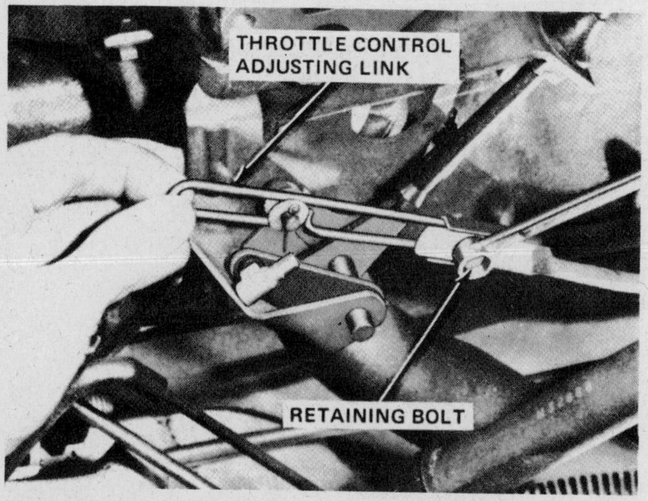

Fig. 7.33 Tightening the adjusting link retaining bolt – typical of four and six-cylinder throttle linkages (Sec 19)

15 When zero lash is achieved, lock the cable by pressing the T-clamp back into place.

16 Turn the ignition off (if applicable) and reinstall any components which were removed. Remove the holding spring from the throttle control lever.

20 Shift linkage – adjustment

1 Raise the vehicle and support it securely on jackstands.

2 Loosen the shift rod trunnion set screw or jam nuts.

3 Remove the lockpin attaching the shift rod to the bellcrank on

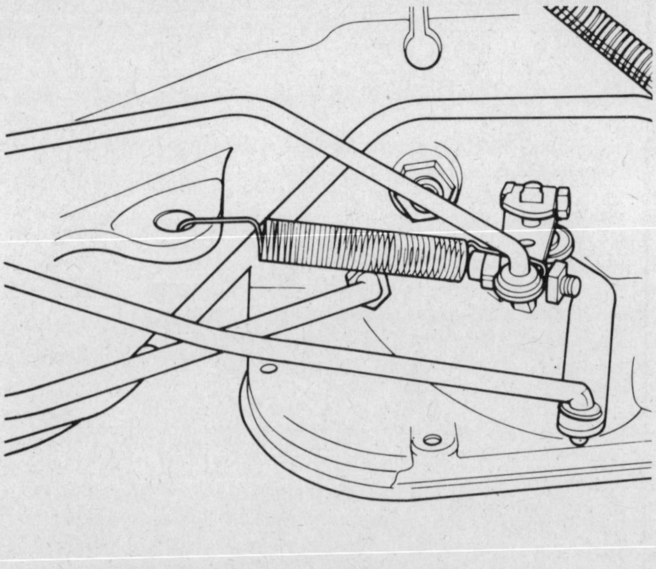

Fig. 7.32 Throttle control lever tension spring – typical of later AMC models (Sec 19)

column shift models. Remove the lockpin attaching the shift rod to the transmission lever on floor shift models.

4 Place the gearshift lever in the Park position and lock the steering column.

5 Move the lever on the transmission to the Park (rear) position. Be sure the lever is moved to the rear as far as possible.

6 Adjust the shift rod trunnion until the lockpin will fit easily into the bellcrank arm without binding. **Note**: *On column shift models, all gearshift linkage lash must be eliminated in order to obtain a proper adjustment. When making the adjustment, eliminate any lash by pulling down on the shift rod and pressing up on the outer bellcrank.*

7 Tighten the trunnion set screw or jam nuts, being careful not to change the adjustment.

8 Check for positive engagement of the park lock by trying to turn the driveshaft. The shaft should not rotate.

9 Move the gearshift lever to the Park and Neutral positions. The engine should start in these positions only. If the engine starts in any other position, the adjustment is incorrect or the Neutral safety switch is defective.

10 Check the steering lock operation, if equipped with tilt steering.

11 Lower the vehicle.

21 Kickdown (front) band – adjustment

1 Raise the vehicle and support it securely on jackstands.

2 On some later models, it may be necessary to remove the driveshaft to gain adequate working clearance.

3 Loosen the adjusting screw locknut and back it off *five* turns.

4 Check to be sure the adjusting screw turns freely in the case.

5 Using a torque wrench, tighten the adjusting screw to the specified torque.

6 Back off the adjusting screw the specified number of turns.

7 Tighten the adjusting screw locknut to the specified torque. Do not allow the adjusting screw to rotate when tightening the locknut.

22 Removal and installation

1 Disconnect the battery cables from the battery. Disconnect the Neutral safety switch wire.

2 Remove the fan shroud.

3 Disconnect the fluid filler tube.

4 Disconnect the selector linkage.

5 Disconnect the speedometer drive cable.

6 Disconnect the vacuum hose and the solenoid electrical lead from the transmission (M series).

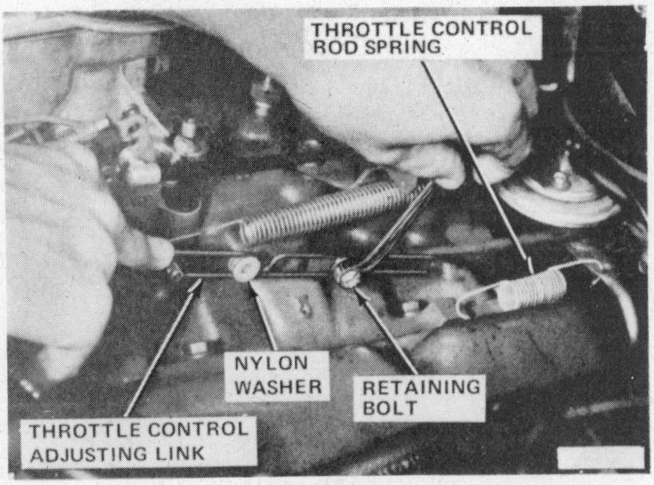

Fig. 7.34 Tightening the adjusting link retaining bolt – typical of V8 throttle linkages (Sec 19)

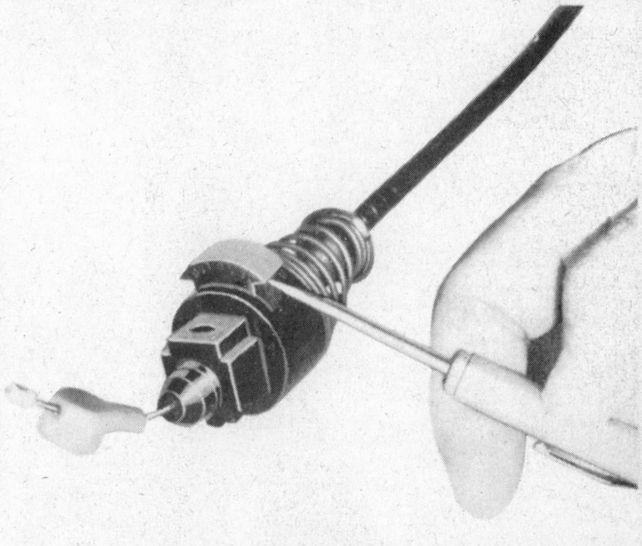

Fig. 7.35 Releasing the throttle cable adjuster T-clamp – typical (Sec 19)

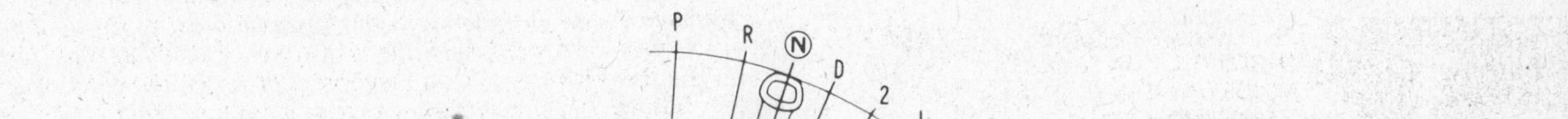

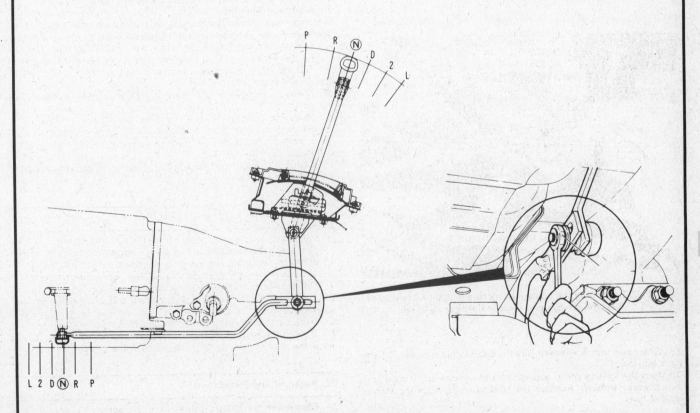

Fig. 7.36 Shift linkage control rod adjustments – typical (Sec 20)

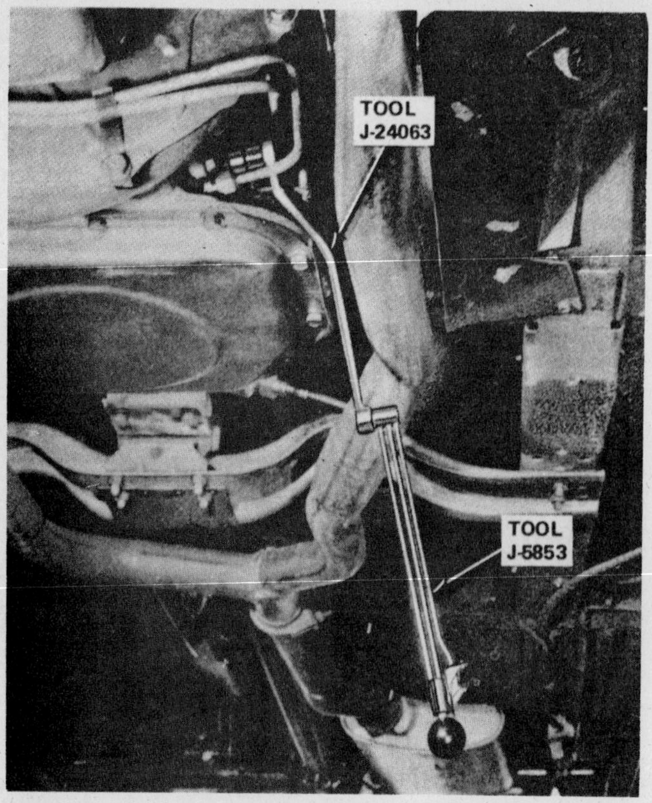

Fig. 7.37 Front band adjustment requires a torque wrench adapter – typical (Sec 21)

7 Raise the vehicle high enough to allow removal of the transmission from beneath the vehicle. Support the vehicle securely on jackstands.
8 Disconnect the exhaust pipe from the manifold and the exhaust pipe support bracket.
9 Remove the inspection cover from the front of the torque converter housing.
10 Remove the starter motor.
11 Remove the driveshaft.
12 Disconnect the fluid cooler lines (model 904).
13 Disconnect the oil line to the TCS switch (model 904).
14 Disconnect the TCS and Neutral switch leads (model 904).
15 Mark the relationship of the driveplate to the torque converter so they can be reassembled in their original positions.
16 Drain the transmission fluid. On model 904 transmissions, the torque converter is equipped with a drain plug, which should also be removed when it is in its lowest position. On M series units, no torque converter drain plug is installed and some loss of fluid must be anticipated as the transmission is withdrawn.
17 Unscrew and remove the bolts which secure the torque converter to the driveplate. The torque converter will have to be turned to bring each of the driveplate bolts into view through the housing opening before each one can be removed. To do this, rotate the crankshaft front pulley bolt with a ratchet handle and socket or box-end wrench.
18 Place a jack under the transmission and remove the rear mount crossmember as a complete assembly.
19 Lower the jack until the torque converter housing will clear the body floorpan as it is withdrawn and then remove the bolts which hold the housing to the engine.
20 Remove the transmission to the rear, supporting its weight and preventing the torque converter from being displaced inside the housing.
21 Installation is the reverse of removal, but make sure that the torque converter tangs engage correctly with the oil pump drive slots and that the marks on the driveplate and torque converter made before removal are in alignment.
22 Finally, refill the transmission and check all the adjustments described in earlier Sections of this Chapter.

Chapter 8 Driveline

Contents

Axle shafts, bearings and oil seals – removal and installation 16
Clutch – removal, inspection and installation 4
Clutch hydraulic system – bleeding 2
Clutch master cylinder – overhaul 8
Clutch master cylinder – removal and installation 7
Clutch pedal – removal and installation 3
Clutch pedal free play check and adjustment ...... See Chapter 1
Clutch release bearing mechanism – disassembly, inspection and reassembly 5
Clutch slave cylinder – overhaul 10
Clutch slave cylinder – removal and installation 9
Differential oil level check ...... See Chapter 1
Differential lubricant change ...... See Chapter 1
Driveshaft – removal and installation 12
General information 1
Pilot bushing – replacement 6
Pinion oil seal – replacement 14
Rear axle assembly – removal and installation 17
Rear axle hub – removal and installation 15
Universal joints – check 11
Universal joints – replacement 13

Specifications

Clutch fluid type

DOT 3 or SAE J-1703 brake fluid

Torque specifications

	Ft-lb	Nm
Clutch cover bolts		
1970 through 1973 all models	40	54
1974 through 1976 six-cylinder	28	38
1974 through 1976 V8	38	52
1977 through 1983 six-cylinder and V8	28	38
1977 through 1983 four-cylinder	23	31
Clutch housing-to-engine dowel bolts		
1970 through 1973 models	45	60
1974 through 1983 models	26	35
Clutch housing-to-starter motor bolts		
V8 and four-cylinder models	45	62
Six-cylinder models	18	24
Clutch housing-to-transmission bolts	55	75
Clutch housing-to-engine bolts		
Four-cylinder engine	50	68
V8 engine	27	37
Six-cylinder engine		
Top mounting bolts	27	37
Bottom mounting bolts	43	58
Clutch housing spacer-to-engine block bolts	12	16
Clutch pedal pivot bolt locknut	50	68
Universal joint clamp strap bolt	14	19
Rear spring U-bolt nuts	50	68
Brake backing plate-to-axle housing bolts	32	43

1 General information

Manual transmission models are equipped with a conventional design clutch utilizing either a mechanical linkage or a hydraulically actuated release mechanism.

Power is transmitted from the transmission to the rear axle by a one-piece driveshaft. Universal joints are located at the front and rear to allow for vertical movement of the rear axle and slight movement of the engine and transmission. A slip-joint is used to allow for fore-and-aft movement of the drivetrain.

The rear axle assembly is conventional in design and consists of a differential carrier, hypoid final drive gears and semi-floating rear axles.

Most rear-end components problems reveal themselves in the form of some sort of noise. The noise may be caused by gears (in the differential carrier assembly) or bearings (in the differential and the outer ends of the rear axle housing).

Gear noise is usually a high-pitched whine, which may be more pronounced at certain speeds or when the vehicle is under load.

Bearing noise is generally a lower-pitched, steady growl. It tends to get louder when accelerating under load. Swerving the vehicle from side-to-side on a flat, level road may help to pinpoint faulty wheel bearings. This practice throws additional side loads on the bearings, which should increase any noise coming from them. A bad bearing could show up in the differential assembly, although bearing failure in this area is much less likely than in the wheel bearings.

Major repair work on the differential (and other rear-end components) requires many special tools and a high degree of expertise, and therefore should not be attempted by the home mechanic. If major repairs become necessary, we recommend that they be performed by an AMC dealer service department or a reputable repair shop.

2 Clutch hydraulic system – bleeding

1 If air gets into the clutch release mechanism hydraulic system, the clutch may not release completely when the pedal is depressed. Air can enter the system whenever any part of it is dismantled or if the fluid level in the clutch master cylinder reservoir runs low. Air can also leak into the system through a hole too small to allow fluid to leak out. In this case, it indicates that a general overhaul of the system is required.

2 To bleed the air out, you will need an assistant to pump the clutch pedal, a supply of new brake fluid of the recommended type, an empty glass or plastic container, a plastic or vinyl tube which will fit over the bleeder nipple and a wrench for the bleeder screw.

3 Check the fluid level at the clutch master cylinder reservoir. Add fluid, if necessary, to bring the level up to the Full mark. Use only the recommended brake fluid and do not mix different types. Never use fluid from a container that has been standing uncapped. You will have to check the fluid level in the reservoir often during the bleeding procedure. If the level drops too far, air will enter the system through the master cylinder.

4 Raise the front of the vehicle and set it securely on jackstands.

5 Remove the bleeder screw cap from the bleeder screw on the slave cylinder.

6 Attach one end of the clear plastic or vinyl tube to the bleeder screw nipple and place the other end in the glass or plastic container, submerged in clean brake fluid.

7 Loosen the bleeder screw slightly, then tighten it to the point where it is snug yet easily loosened.

8 Have the assistant pump the pedal several times and hold it in the fully depressed position.

9 With pressure on the pedal, open the bleeder screw approximately one-half turn. As the fluid is flowing through the tube and into the jar, tighten the bleeder screw. Again, pump the pedal, hold it in the fully depressed position and loosen the bleeder screw momentarily. Do not allow the pedal to be released with the bleeder screw in the open position.

10 Repeat the procedure until no air bubbles are visible in the fluid flowing through the tube. Be sure to check the fluid level in the clutch master cylinder reservoir while performing the bleeding operation.

11 Tighten the bleeder screw completely, remove the plastic or vinyl tube and install the bleeder screw cap.

12 Check the clutch fluid level in the reservoir to make sure it is adequate, then test drive the vehicle and check for proper clutch operation.

3 Clutch pedal – removal and installation

1 Disconnect the negative battery cable and remove the package tray (Chapter 10).

2 Remove the fuse panel attaching screws and move the panel aside.

3 Disconnect the clutch pedal-to-bellcrank rod.

4 Remove and discard the clutch and brake pedal pivot bolt locknut.

5 Remove the clutch pedal and pivot bolt.

6 If a replacement clutch pedal is being installed, measure and record the height of the rubber stop bumper for assembly reference. Install the original stop bumper in the replacement pedal bracket at the same height as the original pedal stop setup.

7 Installation is the reverse of removal. Lubricate the clutch pedal pivot bolt and bushings with chassis lubricant and be sure to use a replacement pivot bolt locknut. Tighten the pivot bolt locknut to the specified torque.

8 See Chapter 1 for the procedure to follow when adjusting the height and free play of the clutch pedal.

4 Clutch – removal, inspection and installation

Removal

1 Remove the transmission (see Chapter 7A).

2 Remove the starter motor and disconnect the clutch linkage, as applicable.

3 Remove the clutch housing-to-engine bolts and remove the clutch housing.

4 Scribe alignment marks on the clutch cover and the flywheel so they can be reassembled in the same position relative to each other.

5 Remove the clutch cover bolts and separate the clutch cover and disc from the flywheel (photo). Loosen the bolts one-half turn at a time, in a diagonal sequence, to avoid distorting the cover.

Inspection

6 Check the metal parts of the clutch disc for cracks and distortion. Check carefully for broken springs. Slip the clutch disc onto the transmission input shaft and check for excessive play, in the direction of rotation, between the splines of the clutch disc hub and the input shaft. Inspect the clutch disc friction lining for cracks, burned spots and oil stains. If oil is present on the clutch components, the engine rear oil seal or the transmission front oil seal, or both, may be defective and require replacement. Minor oil stains may be removed with lacquer thinner or a similar solvent. Look for broken or loose rivets.

7 Inspect the clutch cover assembly for excessive finger wear, loose strap rivets and cracks. Check the pressure plate for scoring, burn marks and ridges.

8 Look for scoring, burn marks and deep ridges on the flywheel. If any of these problems exist, or if the surface is highly polished, remove the flywheel and have it resurfaced and balanced at a reputable automotive machine shop. Check the pilot bushing in the end of the crankshaft. If the transmission input shaft contact surface is worn or damaged, replace the bushing.

9 Disassemble and check the release bearing and clutch release mechanism as described in Section 5.

Installation

10 Hold the clutch disc and clutch cover assembly in place on the flywheel and loosely install the mounting bolts (be sure to line up the marks on the flywheel and clutch cover). The manufacturer's stamped mark on the clutch disc must face away from the flywheel when the clutch is assembled.

11 Install a clutch disc alignment tool through the clutch disc and into the pilot bushing. This tool will center the clutch disc properly (photo).

12 Tighten the clutch attaching bolts to the specified torque (photo). Use a crisscross pattern and tighten the bolts one turn each at a time so the clutch cover assembly is drawn down onto the flywheel evenly.

13 Remove the clutch disc alignment tool.

5 Clutch release bearing mechanism – disassembly, inspection and reassembly

1 On later four-cylinder models equipped with a hydraulic clutch, the release bearing and lever must be removed as an assembly. Remove

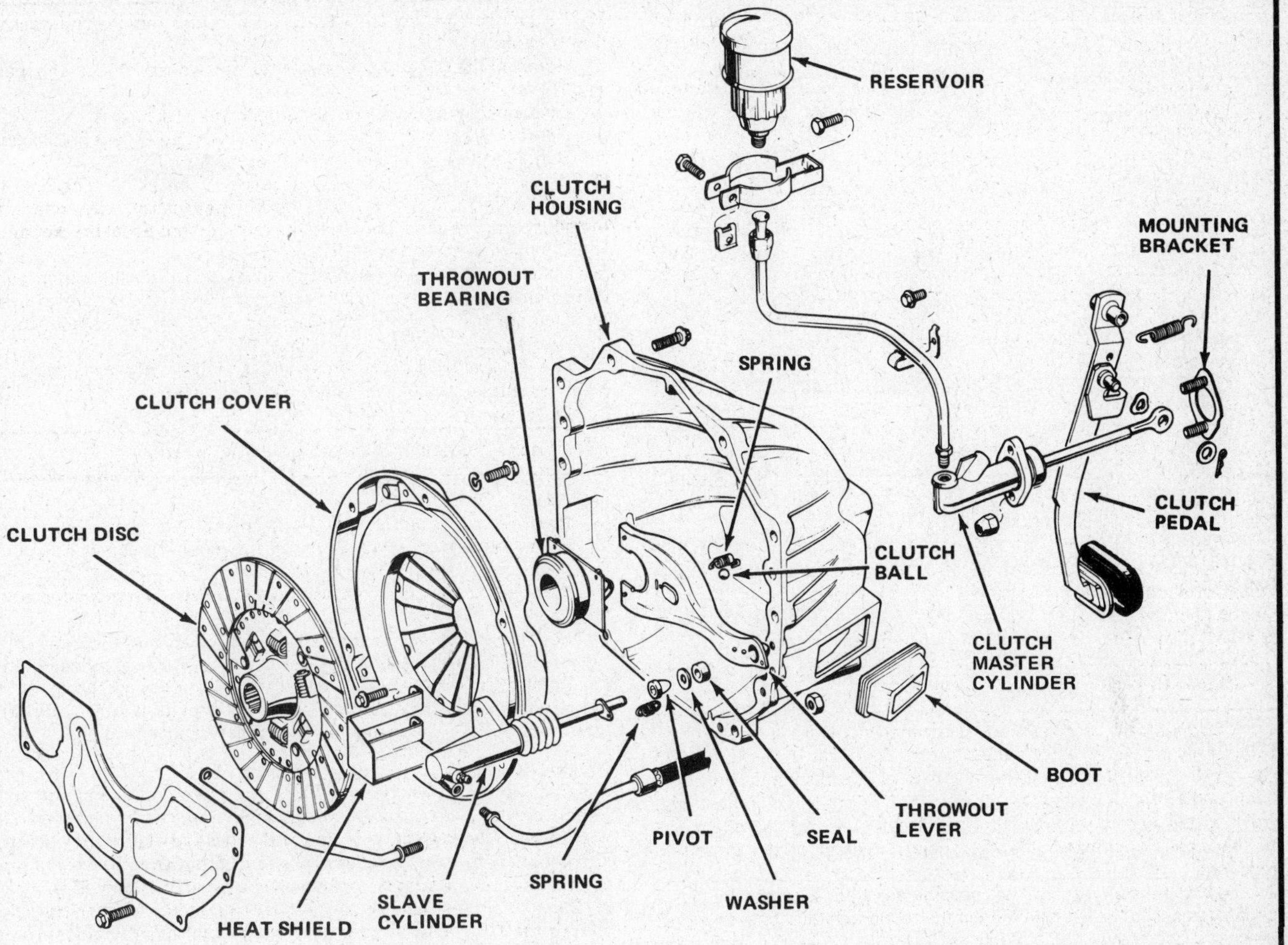

Fig. 8.1 Typical clutch components – exploded view (hydraulic clutch shown) (Sec 4)

4.5 Separating the clutch cover and clutch disc from the flywheel

4.11 If a tool is not available, an old transmission input shaft can be used to center the clutch disc

4.12 Tightening the clutch cover bolts with a torque wrench

the release lever boot from the clutch housing.
2 Disconnect the throwout lever spring and pull the bearing and lever assembly out of the opening in the clutch housing. Remove the bearing from the release lever guide springs.
3 On vehicles equipped with a mechanical clutch linkage, simply disconnect the bearing retaining springs to remove the release bearing. The release lever can then be removed by disconnecting the bellcrank-to-release lever rod and disconnecting the lever springs. Remove the boot with the lever.
4 Check the release bearing for smoothness of operation. It should rotate smoothly and quietly with no excessive play. The prepacked grease will hinder its movement somewhat, but it should spin reasonably freely. Replace the bearing if necessary. *Do not wash the bearing in solvent as it will dissolve the prepacked grease.*
5 Installation is the reverse of removal. On vehicles equipped with mechanical clutch linkages, fill the inner groove of the bearing sleeve with grease before installation.

6 Pilot bushing – replacement

1 Remove the clutch cover and disc (Section 4).
2 On vehicles equipped with a mechanical clutch linkage, remove the pilot bushing lubricating wick and soak it in clean engine oil.
3 Fill the crankshaft pilot bushing bore and the pilot bushing with chassis grease. Insert a round bar of suitable diameter into the bore and tap the bar with a hammer. The hydraulic pressure will force the bushing out.
4 Soak the replacement bushing in clean engine oil before installation.
5 Remove all chassis grease from the bushing bore.
6 Using a pipe or round bar of suitable diameter and a hammer, drive the bushing into the bore until it is seated. Be sure that the installation tool and bushing remain parallel with the crankshaft centerline during installation.
7 Install the pilot bushing lubricating wick, if equipped.

7 Clutch master cylinder – removal and installation

1 Remove the brake master cylinder and power brake unit as an assembly (Chapter 9).
2 Disconnect the hydraulic lines at the clutch master cylinder and disconnect the cylinder pushrod from the clutch pedal.
3 Unbolt the master cylinder from the dash panel and the mounting bracket and remove the cylinder.
4 Installation is the reverse of removal. Bleed the clutch hydraulic system after installing the master cylinder (Section 2). Bleed the brake system after installing the power brake unit and the master cylinder (Chapter 9).

8 Clutch master cylinder – overhaul

1 In order to perform the clutch master cylinder overhaul, you will need a clean place to work, clean rags, a rebuild kit and a container of new, clean brake fluid.
2 Clean the exterior of the clutch master cylinder thoroughly.
3 Remove the rubber dust boot from the cylinder.
4 Remove the pushrod snap-ring and remove the pushrod, seal, washer (if equipped) and retainer washer.
5 To remove the plunger and spring assembly from the cylinder, tap the cylinder on a solid surface until the plunger assembly dislodges from the cylinder.
6 Compress the spring slightly and insert a thin, small blade screwdriver into the rectangular slot in the side of the valve stem retainer (see the accompanying illustration). Pry the tab of the valve stem retainer up and release the retainer, spring and valve stem from the plunger.
7 Remove the spring, valve stem, valve stem and spring retainers and wave washer from the plunger.
8 Remove the seal from the plunger.
9 Remove the seal from the tip of the valve stem, if equipped.
10 Clean all the parts with brake fluid. *Do not use petroleum-based solvents.* Check the bore for score marks and scratches. If it is worn or

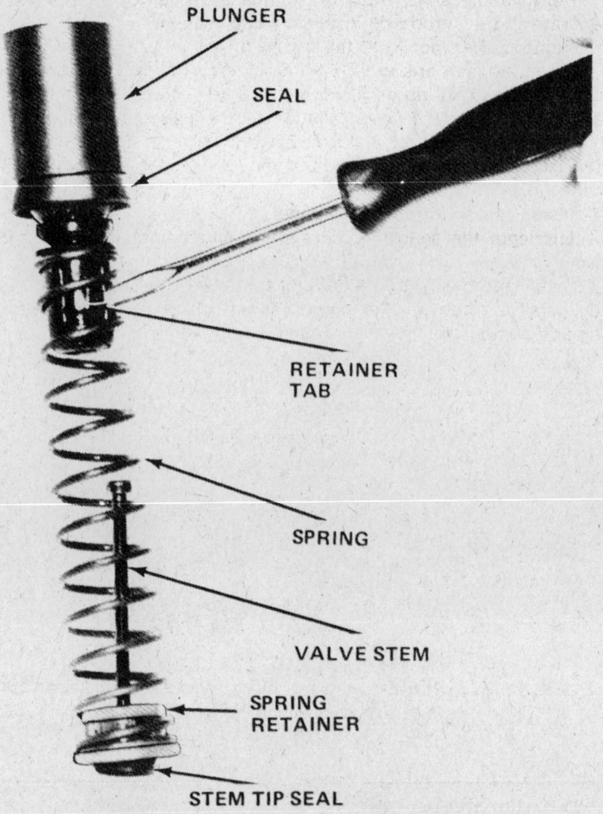

Fig. 8.2 Removing the spring and valve stem from the clutch master cylinder plunger – typical (Sec 8)

damaged, replace the master cylinder with a new or rebuilt unit.
11 To reassemble, first install the new seal on the plunger.
12 Install the new seal on the tip of the valve stem, if equipped.
13 Install the spring, both retainers, the wave washer and valve stem onto the plunger.
14 Lubricate the plunger, plunger seal and clutch cylinder bore with clean brake fluid.
15 Install the plunger and spring assembly in the cylinder bore.
16 Install the pushrod, retainer washer, new pushrod seal and snap-ring in the master cylinder.
17 Slide a new boot over the pushrod and onto the master cylinder. Make sure that the boot is properly seated to form a good seal.

9 Clutch slave cylinder – removal and installation

1 Raise the vehicle and support it securely on jackstands.
2 Disconnect the hydraulic line at the slave cylinder.
3 Disconnect the spring from the cylinder pushrod.
4 Remove the bolts attaching the cylinder and heat shield from the clutch housing and remove the cylinder.
5 Installation is the reverse of removal. Bleed the clutch hydraulic system after installing the slave cylinder (Section 2).

10 Clutch slave cylinder – overhaul

1 In order to perform the clutch slave cylinder overhaul, you will need a clean place to work, clean rags, a rebuild kit and a container of new, clean brake fluid.
2 Clean the exterior of the slave cylinder thoroughly and slide the rubber dust boot off the end of the cylinder.
3 Remove (as a complete assembly) the pushrod, boot, plunger and spring from the cylinder.

4 Remove the spring from the plunger.
5 Remove the seal from the end of the plunger.
6 Remove the snap-ring that retains the pushrod in the plunger. Separate the pushrod and boot from the plunger.
7 Remove the boot from the pushrod.
8 Clean all the parts with brake fluid. *Do not use petroleum-based solvents.* Check the bore for score marks and scratches. If it is worn or damaged, replace the slave cylinder with a new or rebuilt unit.
9 To reassemble, first install the new boot on the pushrod.
10 Install the pushrod in the plunger and install the new pushrod snap-ring.
11 Install the spring on the plunger.
12 Lubricate the seal and the slave cylinder bore with clean brake fluid.
13 Install the pushrod assembly in the slave cylinder.
14 Install the boot on the slave cylinder. Make sure that the boot is properly seated to form a good seal.

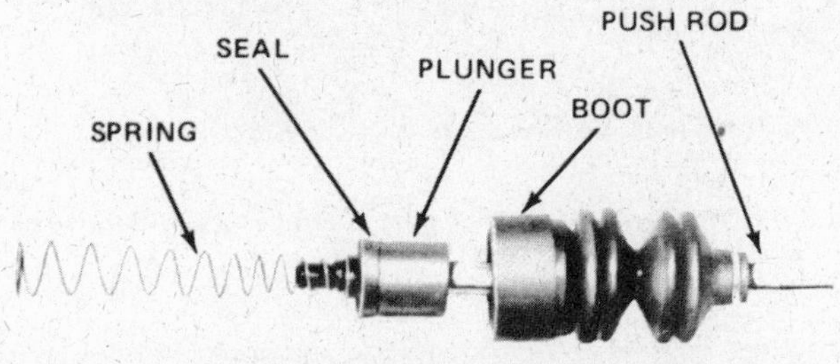

Fig. 8.3 Slave cylinder pushrod, plunger and spring assembly – typical (Sec 10)

11 Universal joints – check

1 Universal joint problems are usually caused by worn or damaged needle bearings. These problems are revealed as vibration in the driveline or clunking noises when the transmission is put in Drive or the clutch is released. In extreme cases they are caused by lack of lubrication. If this happens, you will hear metallic squeaks and, ultimately, grinding and shrieking sounds as the bearings are destroyed.
2 It is easy to check the needle bearings for wear and damage with the driveshaft in place on the vehicle. To check the rear universal joint, turn the driveshaft with one hand and hold the rear axle yoke with the other. Any movement between the two is an indication of wear. The front universal joint can be checked by holding the driveshaft with one hand and the sleeve yoke in the transmission with the other. Any movement here indicates the need for universal joint repair.
3 If they are worn or damaged, the universal joints will have to be disassembled and the bearings replaced with new ones. Read over the procedure carefully before beginning.

12 Driveshaft – removal and installation

1 Raise the rear of the vehicle and set it on jackstands. Block the front tires to keep the vehicle from rolling.
2 Make marks on the driveshaft and the rear axle yoke (where they come together) so the driveshaft can be reinstalled in the same position relative to the rear axle yoke.
3 Remove the bolts and clamp straps that attach the driveshaft to the rear axle yoke.
4 Carefully release the rear of the driveshaft from the differential and slide the driveshaft to the rear, out of the transmission housing (photo). Be very careful not to damage the seal in the end of the transmission housing.
5 Refer to Section 13 for U-joint inspection and repair procedures.
6 Before installing the driveshaft, thoroughly clean the outside surface of the sleeve yoke and apply a coat of multi-purpose grease to it. Also, check the inside of the sleeve yoke to make sure there is no foreign material present.
7 Carefully insert the sleeve yoke into the transmission housing,

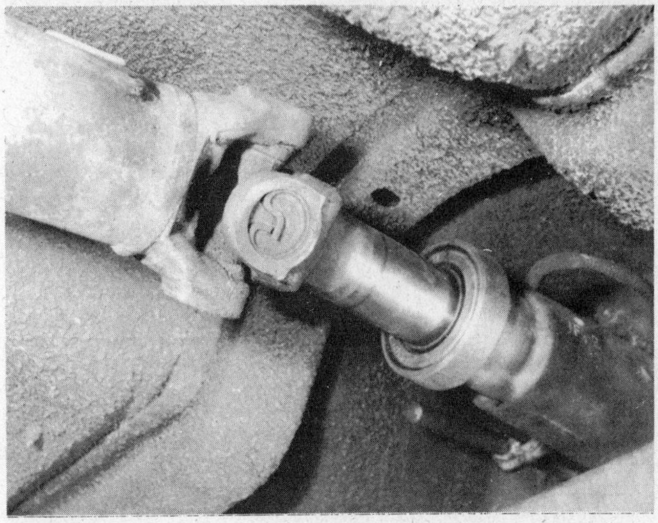

12.4 The front of the driveshaft can be slipped out of the rear of the transmission

lining up the splines inside the sleeve yoke with the splines on the transmission output shaft. Position the driveshaft and install the bolts and clamp straps that attach it to the differential (be sure to line up the marks on the driveshaft and the rear axle yoke). Tighten the bolts to the specified torque.
8 Lower the vehicle to the ground.

13 Universal joints – replacement

1 Mark the driveshaft and the sleeve yoke to ensure reassembly in the correct relationship.
2 Support the universal joint in a vise equipped with soft jaws and remove the snap-rings from the universal joint yokes. It is recommended that eack snap-ring and yoke be marked so the snap-rings can be returned to the same location during reassembly.
3 To remove the bearings from the yokes, you will need two sockets. One should be large enough to fit into the yoke where the snap-rings were installed and the other should have an inside diameter just large enough for the bearings to fit into when they are forced out of the yoke.

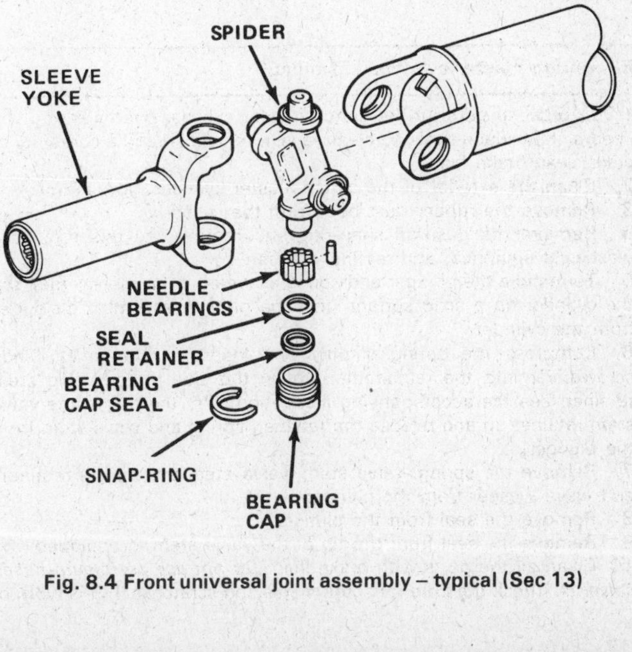

Fig. 8.4 Front universal joint assembly – typical (Sec 13)

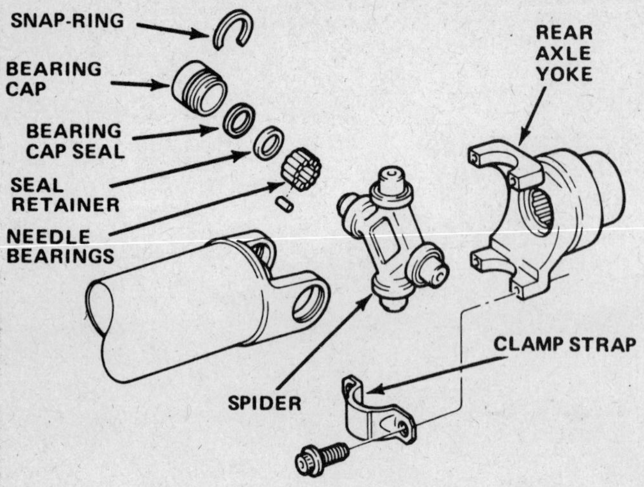

Fig. 8.5 Rear universal joint assembly – typical (Sec 13)

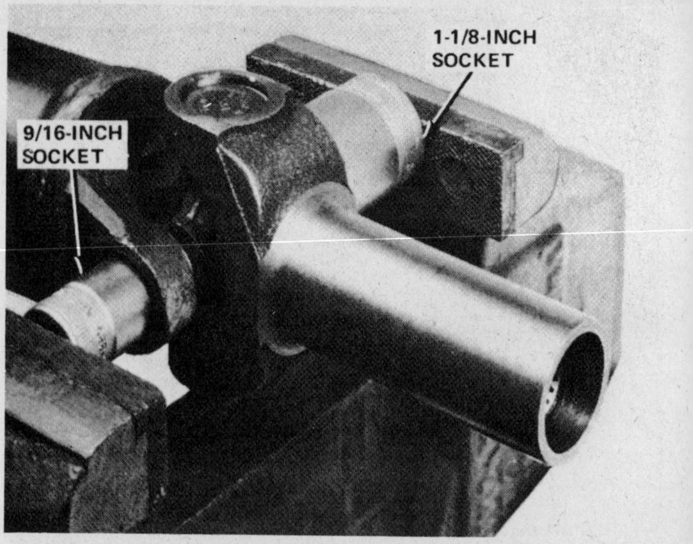

Fig. 8.6 Removing the universal joint bearing caps with a vise and sockets (Sec 13)

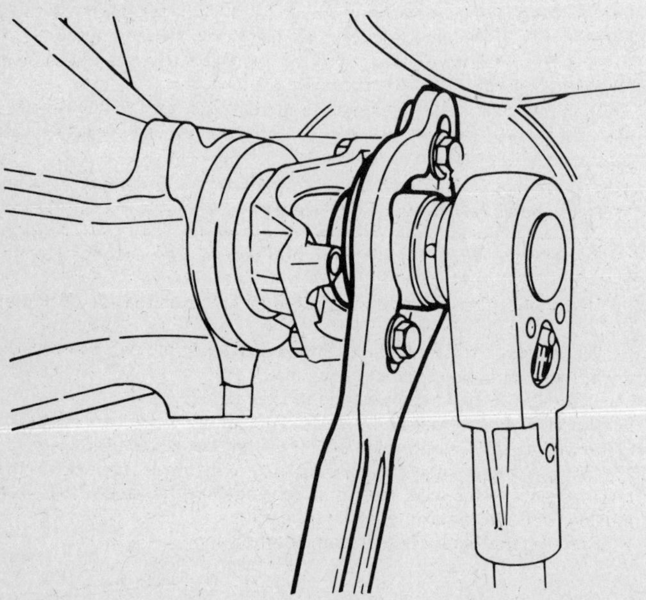

Fig. 8.7 Removing the drive pinion nut (Sec 14)

4 Mount the universal joint in a vise with the large socket on one side of the yoke and the small socket on the other side, pushing against the bearing. Carefully tighten the vise until the bearing is pushed out of the yoke and into the large socket. If it cannot be pushed all the way out, remove the universal joint from the vise and use a pliers to finish removing the bearing.
5 Reverse the sockets and push out the bearing on the other side of the yoke. This time, the small socket will be pushing against the cross-shaped universal joint spider end.
6 Before pressing out the two remaining bearings, mark the spider so it can be installed in the same relative position during reassembly.
7 The remaining universal joints can be disassembled following the same procedure. Be sure to mark all components for each universal joint so that they can be kept together and reassembled in the proper position.
8 Clean the driveshaft yoke and universal joint components with solvent and dry them thoroughly.
9 Inspect the driveshaft for cracks and damage. If possible, check the driveshaft runout with a dial indicator. Replace the driveshaft if defects are noted.
10 Check the spider journals for scoring, needle roller impressions, rust and pitting. Replace them if any of the above conditions exist.
11 Check the sleeve yoke splines for wear and damage.
12 When reassembling the universal joints, replace all needle bearings and seals with new ones.
13 Before reassembly, pack each grease cavity in the spiders with a small amount of grease. Also, apply a thin coat of grease to the new needle bearing rollers and the roller contact areas on the spiders.
14 Apply a thin coat of grease to the seal lips and install the bearings and spider into the yoke using the vise and sockets that were used to remove the old bearings. Work slowly and be very careful not to damage the bearings as they are being pressed into the yokes.
15 Press the bearings in until the snap-ring grooves are completely visible. Install a snap-ring on each side. Tap the yoke with a hammer to move the cups slightly.
16 Make sure that the spider moves freely in the bearings.
17 Assemble the remaining universal joint and install the driveshaft.

14 Pinion oil seal – replacement

1 Severe oil leakage from the differential usually occurs at the pinion oil seal. The oil is usually thrown out in a narrow band on the underside of the floor pan on both sides of the pinion housing. Oil seal leakage can be caused by a blocked differential case vent.
2 Raise the rear of the vehicle and support it securely.
3 Remove the driveshaft as described in Section 12.
4 Remove the rear wheels and brake drums.
5 Using a suitable socket and torque wrench calibrated in in-lb, establish the torque required to turn the drive pinion and record it for use during reassembly.
6 A suitable tool must now be used to hold the rear axle yoke while the self-locking pinion nut is removed. This can easily be made by drilling two holes at the end of a length of flat steel bar and bolting it to the yoke.
7 Unscrew and remove the pinion nut.
8 Mark the relationship of the yoke to the pinion shaft and then withdraw the yoke. If it is tight, use a two or three jaw puller engaged behind the flange. Never attempt to pry behind the deflector or hammer on the end of the pinion shaft.

Fig. 8.8 Removing the rear axle hub with a suitable puller (Sec 15)

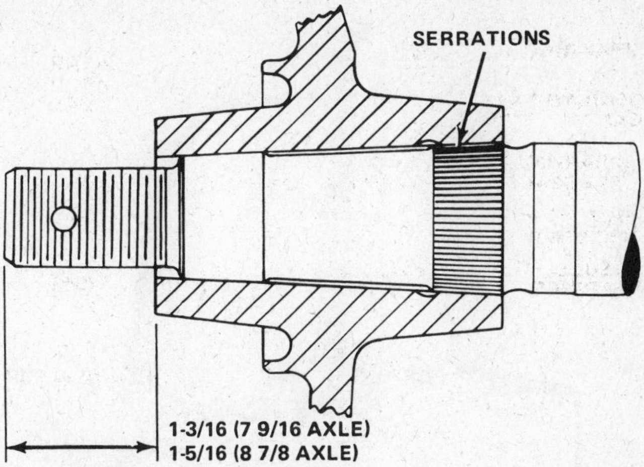

Fig. 8.9 Axle shaft-to-hub face measurement required when installing a replacement hub (Sec 15)

9 Pry out the old oil seal and discard it.
10 Tap the new oil seal into position making sure that it enters the housing squarely and to its full depth.
11 Align the mating marks made before dismantling and install the yoke. If necessary, use a piece of tubing as a spacer and screw on the pinion nut to force the flange completely down on the shaft. Never attempt to hammer the flange home.
12 Install a new pinion nut and tighten it until the pinion end play just disappears, at the same time holding the rear axle yoke in place with the tool.
13 Now measure the torque required to rotate the pinion and tighten the nut a little at a time until the figure compares with that recorded before dismantling. In order to compensate for the drag of the new oil seal, the nut should be further tightened so that the rotational torque of the pinion exceeds that recorded before dismantling by 5 in-lb.
14 Install the driveshaft, brake drums and wheels.
15 Lower the vehicle to the ground. If by any chance the pinion nut is overtightened, the collapsible spacer will be overcompressed. It will be useless to back off the nut to correct the situation. The yoke, pinion front bearing and spacer will have to be removed and a new spacer installed and the tightening operation repeated with greater care.

15 Rear axle hub – removal and installation

1 Remove the hub cap. On vehicles equipped with styled wheels with bolt-on hub caps, raise the vehicle, remove the hub cap retaining bolts and hub cap and reinstall the wheel. Lower the vehicle.
2 Remove and discard the axle shaft nut cotter pin.
3 Remove the axle shaft nut.
4 Raise the vehicle and support it securely on jackstands.
5 Remove the wheels and remove the brake drum retaining screws.
6 Release the parking brake and remove the brake drum. If the drum is difficult to remove, unseat the brake adjuster lever and back off the adjuster screw.
7 With a suitable puller, such as AMC puller tool no. 5-25109-01, remove the axle hub. **Note:** *Do not use a slide hammer, as this type of puller may damage the rear wheel bearings and differential thrust block.*
8 If the original hub is being installed, align the keyway in the hub with the key on the axle shaft.
9 Slide the hub onto the shaft as far as possible and install the nut and thrust washer.
10 Install the brake drum and wheel.
11 Lower the vehicle to the ground and tighten the axle shaft nut to a torque of 250 ft-lb. If the hole for the cotter pin is not in alignment, tighten the nut one more castellation. Install a new cotter pin.
12 If a new hub and drum are being installed, proceed as previously described but use two thrust washers (well greased) under the axle shaft nut. Lower the vehicle to the ground and tighten the nut until the distance between the outer face of the hub and the end of the axle shaft is as shown in the accompanying illustration.
13 Remove the axleshaft nut and remove one of the thrust washers.
14 Install the nut and tighten it to 250 ft-lb. Install a new cotter pin.

16 Axle shafts, bearings and oil seals – removal and installation

1 Remove the wheel, brake drum and rear hub as described in the preceding Section.
2 Disconnect the parking brake cable at the equalizer (see Chapter 9).
3 Disconnect the brake line at the rear wheel cylinder. In order to prevent loss of brake fluid, plug the line.
4 Remove the brake support plate assembly.
5 Remove the oil seal and seat retainer (if equipped) and the axle shims. The shims are only installed on the left-hand side of the vehicle.
6 Using a puller (not a slide hammer) which will correct to the threaded end of the axle shaft and bear against the face of the axle housing, remove the axle shaft and bearing.
7 Remove the inner oil seal from the housing.

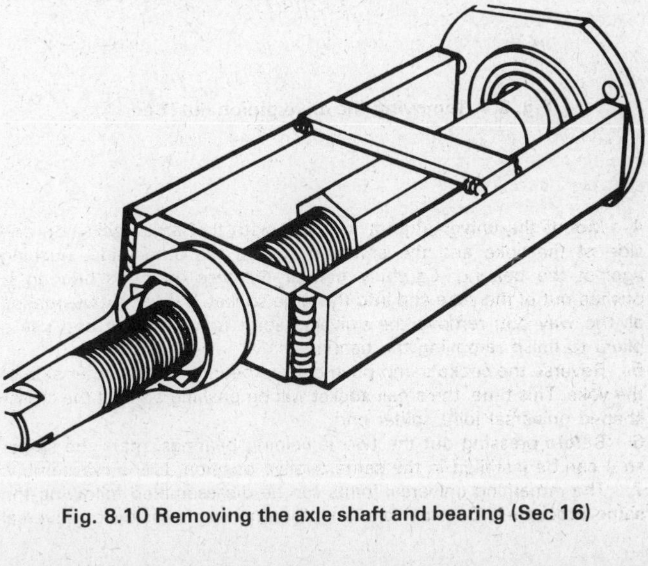

Fig. 8.10 Removing the axle shaft and bearing (Sec 16)

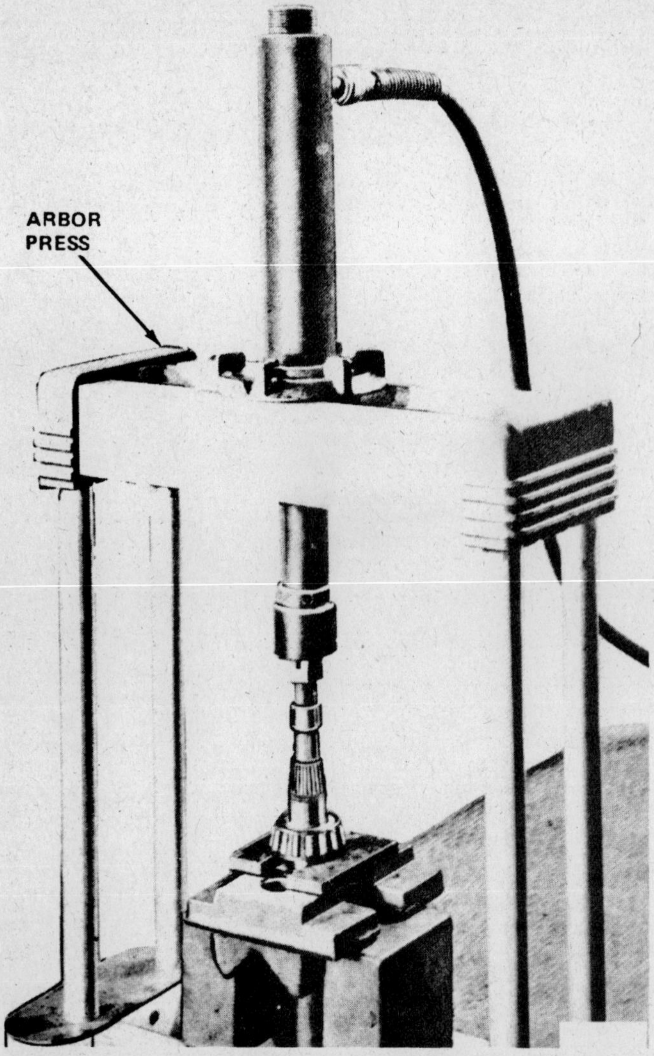

Fig. 8.11 To remove the bearing from the axle shaft, a press is required (Sec 16)

8 Support the bearing center race and press the axle shaft from the bearing using an arbor press.
9 Install the inner seal in the housing using a tubular drift.
10 Press the new bearing onto the axle shaft and liberally apply wheel bearing lubricant to it.
11 Pass the axle shaft into the housing and pick up the splines of the differential gears.
12 Install the bearing outer race, shims, oil seal and brake backing plate, tightening the bolts to the specified torque.
13 Where new components have been installed, check the axle shaft end play. To do this, strike the end of each axle shaft to completely seat the bearing outer races. Use alead or copper hammer for this.
14 Bolt a flat metal bar to the axle shaft and then use a dial indicator or a spacer and feeler gauges to check the end play. If adjustment is required, add or remove shims (which are located only on the left-hand side). Add shims to increase end play or remove them to decrease it.
15 Install the hub and brake drum and reconnect the parking brake and the hydraulic line. Bleed the brakes as described in Chapter 9.
16 Install the wheel and lower the vehicle to the ground.

17 Rear axle assembly – removal and installation

1 Remove the hub cap. On vehicles equipped with styled wheels with bolt-on hub caps, raise the vehicle, remove the hub cap retaining bolts and hub cap and reinstall the wheel. Lower the vehicle.
2 Remove and discard the axle shaft nut cotter pin.
3 Remove the axle shaft nut.
4 Raise the vehicle and support the body securely on jackstands.
5 Remove the rear axle cover and plate and allow the oil to drain out.
6 Remove the wheels, rear hubs and brake drums.
7 Disconnect the parking brake cables at the equalizer.
8 Remove the brake support plates from the axle housing end flanges. Retain the left-hand shims.
9 Remove the axle shafts (Section 16).
10 Remove the driveshaft.
11 Disconnect the rear shock absorber lower mount.
12 Disconnect the hydraulic brake line at the floor pan bracket and plug the line to prevent loss of fluid.
13 Support the axle on a jack placed under the differential unit and then remove the spring U-bolts.
14 Remove the rear axle assembly sideways through the space between the spring and the body.
15 Begin installation by locating the axle on the springs so the spring center bolts align with the axle seat holes. Install the U-bolts and tighten them to the specified torque.
16 Install the driveshaft.
17 Connect the parking brake cables, the hydraulic line and the shock absorbers.
18 Install the axle shafts, brake support plates, hubs and brake drums.
19 Fill the axle with the correct grade and quantity of lubricant.
20 Bleed the brakes and adjust the parking brake (Chapter 9).
21 Install the wheels and lower the vehicle to the ground.

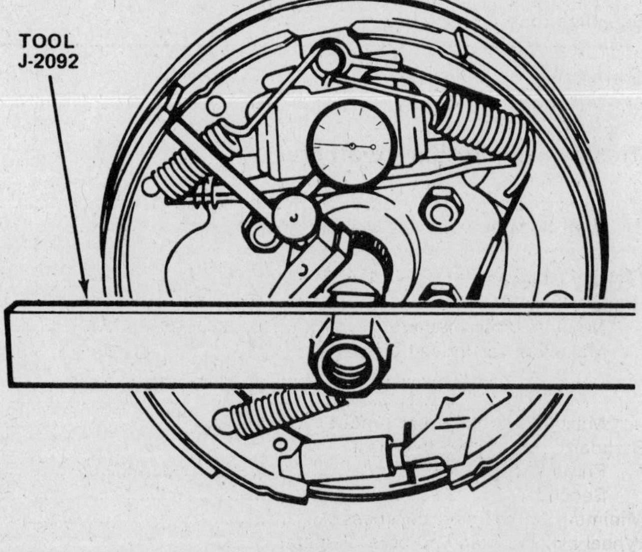

Fig. 8.12 Checking the axle shaft end play with a dial indicator (push-and-pull on the flat bar attached to the axle shaft) (Sec 16)

Chapter 9 Brakes

Contents

Brake disc – inspection, removal and installation 14
Brake drum – removal, inspection and installation ..... See Chapter 1
Brake drums – servicing 11
Brake light switch – removal and installation 2
Brake pedal – removal and installation 3
Brake shoes – adjustment 9
Brake shoes – removal and installation 10
Brake shoes, pads and disc – inspection .... See Chapter 1
Brake system – bleeding procedure 8
Combination valve (disc/drum system) – description and replacement 6
Disc brake caliper – removal, overhaul and installation 13
Disc brake pads – removal and installation 12
General information 1
Hoses and brake lines – inspection and replacement 7
Master cylinder – overhaul 18
Master cylinder – removal and installation 17
Parking brake – description and adjustment 4
Pressure differential valve (drum brake system) – description and replacement 5
Vacuum brake booster – removal and installation 15
Wheel cylinder – removal, overhaul and installation 16

Specifications

General

Brake fluid type	AMC or DOT 3 or SAE J1703

Master cylinder bore diameter

Standard	1.0 in
Front discs	1.0625 in
With booster	1.1250 in

Drum brakes

Brake drums	
Nominal drum diameter	9 in or 10 in, depending on model
Maximum resurfaced diameter	
9 in	9.060 in
10 in	10.060 in
Maximum brake drum runout	0.007 in
Standard brake lining thickness	
Primary	$\frac{3}{16}$ in
Secondary	$\frac{1}{4}$ in
Minimum brake lining thickness	See Chapter 1
Wheel cylinder standard bore diameter	
Rear drums	
1970 through 1976 Gremlin six-cylinder	$\frac{13}{16}$ in
1970 through 1976 Gremlin V8	$\frac{7}{8}$ in
1970 through 1976 Hornet (all models)	$\frac{7}{8}$ in
1977 Gremlin and Hornet (all models)	$\frac{13}{16}$ in
1978 Gremlin six-cylinder and V8	$\frac{13}{16}$ in
1978 Gremlin four-cylinder	0.940 in
1979 Concord (all models)	$\frac{13}{16}$ in
1979 Spirit four-cylinder	0.940 in
1980 through 1982 Eagle (all models)	0.940 in

Front drums	
1970 through 1976 Hornet and Gremlin six-cylinder	1-$\frac{1}{8}$ in
1970 through 1976 Hornet and Gremlin V8	1-$\frac{3}{16}$ in

Disc brakes

Disc thickness	
Standard	
1970 through 1974	1.0 in
1975 and 1976	1.190 in
1977 through 1979	0.870 in
Minimum thickness	
1970 through 1974	0.940 in
1975	1.130 in
Replacement thickness	
1976	1.120 in
1977 through 1979	0.810 in
1980 through 1982	0.815 in
Allowable variation	0.0005 in
Runout limit	
1970 through 1974	0.005 in
1975 through 1982	0.003 in
1981 and 1982 (Eagle only)	0.004 in
Caliper piston diameter	
1970 through 1974	2-$\frac{3}{4}$ in
1975 and 1976	3.10 in
1977 through 1982	2.60 in
Brake pad minimum thickness	See Chapter 1

Torque specifications

	Ft-lb
1970 through 1974 caliper guide pin	35
1975 through 1981 caliper support key retaining screw	15
1982 caliper mounting pin	26
1970 through 1982 caliper anchor plate mounting bolt	80
Master cylinder mounting bolts	30
Wheel cylinder mounting bolts	90

1 General information

The brake system is four wheel hydraulic type with separate circuits for front and rear brakes. The parking brake is foot operated and is connected mechanically to the rear wheels only.

Depending on the year of production and model, either a four wheel drum or a front disc and rear drum system is used. All drum brakes incorporate automatic adjusters, except for certain fleet models and public utility types which have manual adjusters.

A vacuum operated brake booster is optionally available. Depending on the system type, either a pressure differential valve (Section 5) or a combination valve (Section 6) is installed in the engine compartment. Their purpose is to regulate the hydraulic pressures in the two separate brake circuits to prevent the rear wheels from locking before the front wheels during heavy brake applications (disc/drum systems only), and to warn the driver of a pressure differential existing between the two circuits. This function is performed by the movement of a piston (which is normally held in balance), which causes the completion of an electrical circuit and illuminates a warning lamp on the instrument panel. Movement of the piston will be caused by pressure loss in one circuit, due probably to a fluid leak. The brake pedal and brake light switch are non-adjustable.

2 Brake light switch – removal and installation

1 On Spirit and Concord models, remove the package tray, if so equipped.
2 Disconnect the wires at the brake light switch. **Caution:** *The stamped nut and locknut on the brake pedal bolt are not reusable. The brake light switch should not be reinstalled without replacing the stamped nut and locknut with new fasteners.*
3 Remove the stamped nut and the locknut from the brake pedal bolt. Discard the stamped nut and locknut.
4 Remove the brake pedal bolt and spacers.
5 Push the brake light switch bushing out of the master cylinder pushrod bushing and remove the switch.

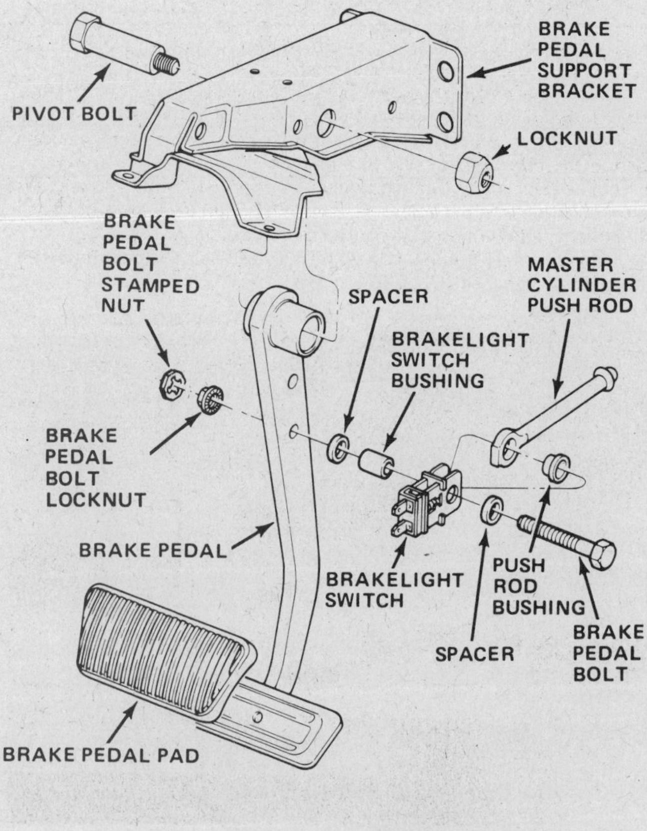

Fig. 9.1 Brake pedal and brake light switch (automatic transmission) – exploded view (Sec 2)

6 Remove the bushing from the master cylinder pushrod eye. Note the position of the bushing for assembly reference.
7 Inspect the brake pedal bolt and all bushings. Replace the bushings if worn, cracked, or galled. Replace the bolt if the threads are torn, galled, or worn or if the non-threaded surface is worn, grooved, or galled.
8 Installation is the reverse of the removal procedure. On vehicles *without* power brakes, be sure to install the brake pedal bolt in the upper mounting hole. On vehicles *with* power brakes, install the bolt in the lower hole.
9 Check switch operation. Press and release the brake pedal several times. Brake lights should illuminate at approximately the first $\frac{1}{2}$ inch (13 mm) of pedal travel and go out when the pedal is released.

3 Brake pedal – removal and installation

1 Before starting work on the brake pedal, disconnect the negative cable from the battery. This allows work to be done around the fuse panel and lead wires without risking fuse blowout due to short circuiting.
2 On Spirit and Concord models, remove the package tray, if so equipped.
3 Remove the fuse panel attaching screws and move the panel aside. **Caution**: *The pivot bolt locknut is not reusable. If the brake pedal is removed, a new locknut must be used upon reassembly.*
4 On vehicles with a manual transmission, disconnect the clutch pushrod at the clutch pedal.
5 Remove the brake pedal bolt and brake light switch as outlined in the previous Section.
6 Remove and discard the pedal pivot bolt locknut and remove the pivot bolt and brake pedal, or clutch and brake pedals.
7 Inspect the brake pedal pivot bushings. Replace the pedal if the bushings are worn, cracked, galled, or cut.
8 Installation is the reverse of the removal procedure.

4 Parking brake – description and adjustment

1 The parking brake is a foot operated unit mounted on a lever and bracket assembly attached to the dash panel.
2 To set the parking brake it is recommended that both the foot brake and parking brake pedals be depressed simultaneously. A hand release lever is pulled to release the brakes (which mechanically operate the rear brakes only, through cables).
3 Adjustment of the parking brake is normally automatic, due to the automatic brake shoe adjusters, but after high mileage, additional adjustment may be required due to cable stretch.
4 Raise the rear of the vehicle and fully release the parking brake.

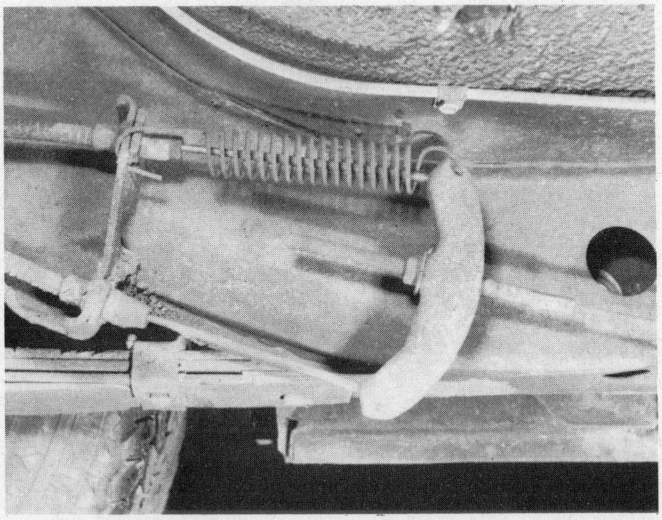

4.5 Parking brake equalizer

5 Release both nuts on the parking brake rod at the equalizer and then turn the nuts until all slack is removed from the cables (photo).
6 Check the rear brakes for drag by turning the wheels.
7 Tighten the equalizer locknuts.

5 Pressure differential valve (drum brake system) – description and replacement

This valve is installed in the hydraulic system of all drum brake layouts. It is located on the engine compartment side of the dash panel, below the heater blower housing. The valve is essentially a cylinder in which a piston is kept in balance when the pressures in the separate front and rear hydraulic circuits are equal.

In the event of a leak or other malfunction in either circuit, the piston is displaced by the loss of pressure and completes an electrical circuit to provide the driver with a visual warning by means of an indicator light.

Whenever the piston is displaced, it will probably have to be centered in its 'in balance' position. To do this, apply slight pressure with the brake pedal while releasing the valve plunger a turn or two.

Replace the valve if any leakage is apparent around the valve assembly. The valve can be removed by disconnecting the brake lines and switch wire at the assembly and removing the attaching bolts. *The brake system must be bled after installation of the replacement valve.*

The pressure differental valve is not repairable and must be replaced as a unit if a malfunction occurs. See Section 8 to follow for special precautions when bleeding the brakes on 1974 and earlier brake systems.

6 Combination valve (disc/drum system) – checking and replacement

This valve has three functions: (a) pressure differential valve similar to that described in Section 5, (b) a pressure regulating valve to prevent the rear brakes from locking before the front ones and (c) a front brake pressure metering valve which allows rear brake circuit pressure to build up while reducing front brake circuit pressure until the rear brake shoe return spring tension has been overcome.

In the event of a leak or other malfunction in either circuit, the piston is displaced by the loss of pressure and completes an electrical circuit to provide the driver with a visual warning by means of an indicator light.

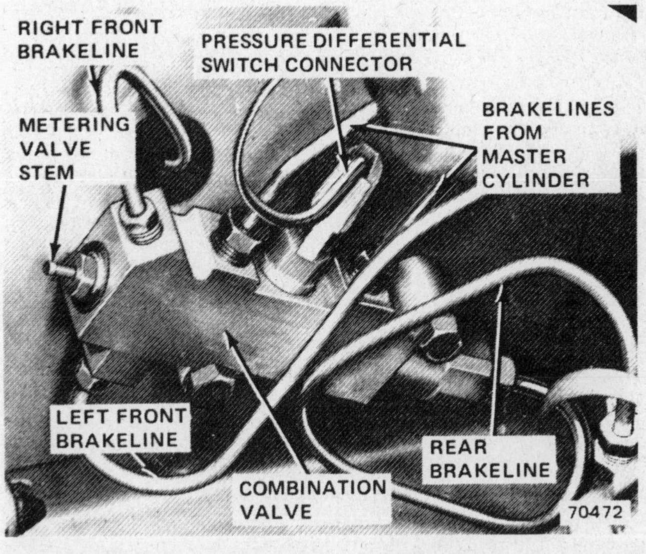

Fig. 9.2 Combination valve assembly (Sec 6)

9

The combination valve is located on the right inner fender panel at the lower rear corner. Whenever the piston in the pressure differential valve is displaced, it has to be recentered. To do this, turn the ignition switch on and press the brake pedal a time or two.

Replace the valve if any leakage is apparent around the valve assembly. The valve can be removed by disconnecting the brake lines and switch wire at the assembly and removing the attaching bolts. *The brake system must be bled after installation of the replacement valve.*

The combination valve is not repairable and must be replaced as a unit if a malfunction occurs.

7 Hoses and brake lines – inspection and replacement

1 Refer to Chapter 1 for a general inspection of the brake hoses and lines.

2 About every six months the flexible hoses which connect the steel brake lines should be inspected for cracks, chafing of the outer cover, leaks, blisters, and other damage. These are important and vulnerable parts of the brake system and inspection should be complete. A light and mirror will be helpful for a thorough check. If a hose exhibits any of the above conditions, replace it with a new one.

3 To undo the locknuts at both ends of the flexible hoses, hold the nut on the flexible hose steady, undo the other union nut and remove the flexible hose and washer.

4 Installation is a reversal of the removal procedure, but carefully check that all the securing brackets are in good condition and that the locknuts are tight.

5 When it becomes necessary to replace steel lines, use only double-walled steel tubing. Never substitute copper tubing, as copper is subject to fatigue cracking and corrosion. The outside diameter of the tubing is used for sizing.

6 Some auto parts stores and brake supply houses carry various lengths of prefabricated brake line. Depending on the type of tubing used, these sections can either be bent by hand into the desired shape or must be bent in a tubing bender.

7 If prefabricated lengths are not available, obtain the recommended steel tubing and steel fitting nuts to match the line to be replaced. Determine the correct length by measuring the old brake line section and cut the new tubing to fit, leaving about $\frac{1}{2}$-inch extra for flaring the ends.

8 Install the fittings onto the cut tubing and flare the ends using a flaring tool.

9 Using a tubing bender, bend the tubing to match the shape of the old brake line.

10 Tube flaring and bending can usually be done by a local auto parts store if the proper equipment mentioned in Paragraphs 8 and 9 is not available.

11 When installing the brake line, leave at least $\frac{3}{4}$-inch clearance between the line and any moving or vibrating parts.

12 If any hoses or lines are replaced, plug the disconnected fittings to keep contaminants out of the brake circuit.

13 Bleed the system according to the bleeding procedure found in this Chapter.

8 Hydraulic brake system – bleeding procedure

1 If the brake system has air in it, oepration of the brake pedal will be spongy and imprecise. Air can enter the brake system whenever any part of the system is dismantled or if the fluid level in the master cylinder reservoir runs low. Air can also leak into the system through a hole too small to allow fluid to leak out. In this case, it indicates that a general overhaul of the brake system is required. **Note**: *Inspect all brake line flexible hoses, rigid tubing and connections. See Chapter 1 for visual inspections before bleeding the system. By doing this, you will save a lot of time and prevent fluid loss.*

2 On drum brake systems manufacture from 1970 through 1974, the pressure differential switch must be disconnected. Disconnect the switch terminal wire. Unscrew and remove the switch terminal, spring and plunger.

3 On disc/drum brake systems manufactured from 1970 through 1977, the metering valve section of the combination valve must be defeated. A special tool is required for this. Use Metering Valve Release Tool J-23774-01 (available from your dealer) to hold the valve stem out at the correct travel with 22 to 35 lbs of pull.

8.9 Bleed tube attached to a caliper bleeder screw

4 To bleed the brakes, you will need an assistant to pump the brake pedal, a supply of new brake fluid, an empty glass jar, a clear plastic or vinyl tube which will fit over the bleeder valve nipple, and a wrench for the bleeder valve.

5 There are five locations at which the brake system is bled: the master cylinder, the front brake wheel cylinder of caliper assemblies and the rear brake wheel cylinders.

6 Check the fluid level at the master cylinder reservoir. Add fluid, if necessary, to bring the level up to the Full mark. Use only the recommended brake fluid, and do not mix different types. Never use fluid from a container that has been standing uncapped. You will have to check the fluid level in the master cylinder reservoir often during the bleeding procedure. If the level drops too far, air will enter the system through the master cylinder.

7 Raise the vehicle and set it securely on jackstands (refer to the *Jacking and towing* procedures at the front of this manual).

8 Remove the bleeder valve cap from the wheel cylinder or caliper assembly that is being bled. If more than one wheel must be bled, start with the one farthest from the master cylinder.

9 Attach one end of the clear plastic or vinyl tube to the bleeder screw and place the other end in the jar submerged in a small amount of clean brake fluid (photo).

10 Loosen the bleeder valve slightly, then tighten it to the point where it is snug yet easily loosened.

11 Have the assistant pump the brake pedal several times and hold it in the fully depressed position.

12 With the pressure on the brake pedal, open the bleeder valve approximately one-half turn. As the brake fluid is flowing through the tube and into the jar, tighten the bleeder valve. Again, pump the brake pedal, hold it in the fully depressed position and loosen the bleeder valve momentarily. Do not allow the brake pedal to be released with the bleeder valve in the open position.

13 Repeat the procedure until no air bubbles are visible in the brake fluid flowing through the tube. Be sure to check the brake fluid level in the master cylinder reservoir while performing the bleeding operation.

14 Fully tighten the bleeder valve, remove the plastic or vinyl tube and install the bleeder valve cap.

15 Follow the same procedure to bleed the other wheel cylinder or caliper assemblies.

16 To bleed the master cylinder, have an assistant pump and hold the brake pedal. Momentarily loosen the brake line fittings, one at a time, where they attach to the master cylinder. Any air in the master cylinder will escape when the fittings are loosened. Brake fluid will damage painted surfaces, so use paper towels or rags to cover and protect the areas around the master cylinder.

17 Reconnect the pressure differential valve wire on 1974 and earlier models.

18 Check the brake fluid level in the master cylinder to make sure it is adequate, then test drive the vehicle and check for proper brake operation.

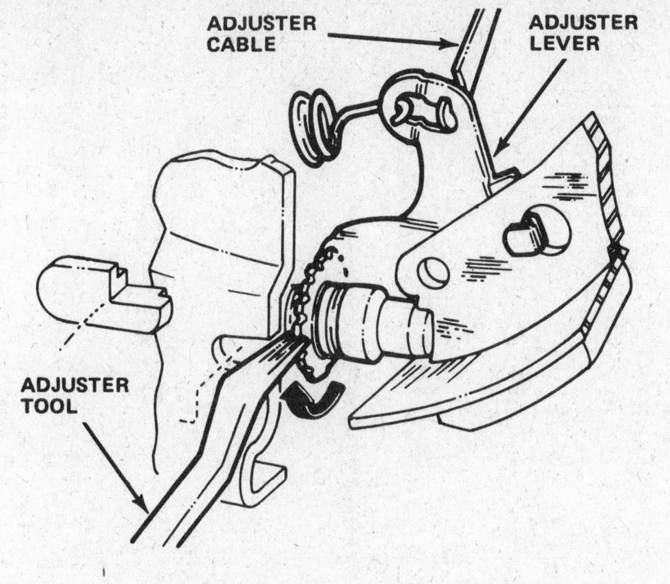

Fig. 9.3 Moving the brake adjuster star wheel to adjust the brake shoes (Sec 9)

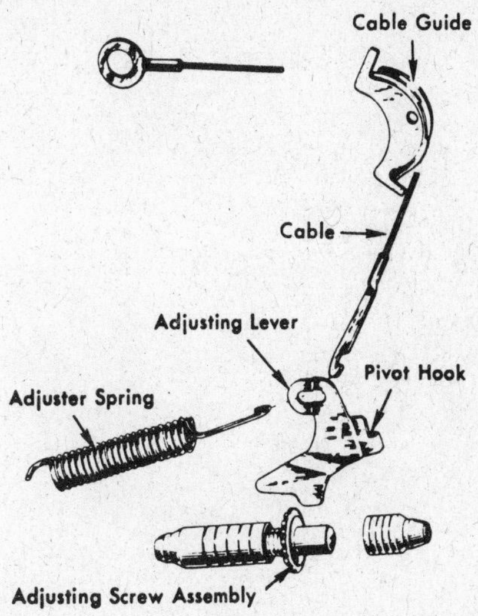

Fig. 9.4 Drum brake automatic adjuster – exploded view (Sec 9)

9.4 Backing plate adjuster slot

9 Brake shoes – adjustment

1 The brake shoe lining-to-drum clearance is automatically adjusted when the brake pedal is depressed during normal vehicle operation. When the brakes are disassembled for servicing, or if the adjuster becomes corroded or gets damaged and fails to function, the shoe clearance can be adjusted manually.

2 When the brakes are being reassembled after servicing, turn the brake adjuster star wheel by hand until the brake drum will just slip over the shoes and into position. The correct clearance will be automatically established as the vehicle is driven.

3 If the automatic adjuster fails to function, the shoe clearance can be temporarily adjusted so that the vehicle can be driven.

4 Remove the rubber plug from the back side of the brake backing plate (photo) and turn the brake adjuster star wheel (with a brake adjusting tool or a screwdriver) in the direction of the arrow (see accompanying illustration). Continue until the wheel is locked against the drum. Mark the star wheel and insert a second screwdriver past the star wheel to force the adjuster lever off the adjuster screw. Back the star wheel off one complete revolution.

5 Replace the rubber plug in the back of the brake backing plate.

6 The brake should be disassembled and the adjuster should be lubricated and checked for proper operation (refer to Section 10).

10 Brake shoes – removal and installation

1 Every 5000 miles, jack up the vehicle, remove each wheel and examine the shoe linings for wear. With riveted type linings, if the friction material has worn down to, or nearly down to, the heads of the rivets, replace the brake shoes as axle sets. With bonded type linings, replace the shoes if the friction material is worn down to within $\frac{1}{16}$-inch of the shoe or rivets.

2 If the linings are in good condition, brush all accumulated dust from the shoes and drum and do not touch the automatic adjuster. Replace the drum.

3 Where the linings must be replaced, replace the complete set of shoes with reconditioned or new ones.

4 To remove the shoes, grip the automatic adjuster lever with a pliers and remove the pivot hook from the hole in the secondary shoe.

5 Detach the shoe return spring (photo).

6 Remove the adjuster cable, cable guide, adjuster lever and spring.

7 Remove the shoe hold down springs by inserting a screwdriver and twisting the springs from their anchor plates (photos).

8 Remove the brake shoes, the adjuster screw assembly and, in the case of the rear brakes, the parking brake strut (photo).

9 Detach the parking brake cable from the lever as the shoe is removed (photo).

10 Place a thick rubber band or a piece of wire around the wheel cylinder pistons to retain them and do not depress the brake pedal while the shoes and drum are removed. 9

11 Clean the backing plate and check for oil leakage. Where evident, this could be due to leaking oil seals or wheel cylinders. Correct the problem before installing the new shoes.

12 Begin reassembly by locating the brake shoes on the backing plate. Make sure that the shoes are positioned correctly with regard to the leading and trailing edges of the linings. Apply a small amount of high melting point grease to the sliding surfaces of the backing plate and to the ends of the shoes where they engage with the adjuster and wheel cylinder slots.

13 Install the hold down springs.

14 Install the primary shoe return spring and then place the adjuster cable eyelet on the anchor pin, position the cable guide and install the secondary return spring.

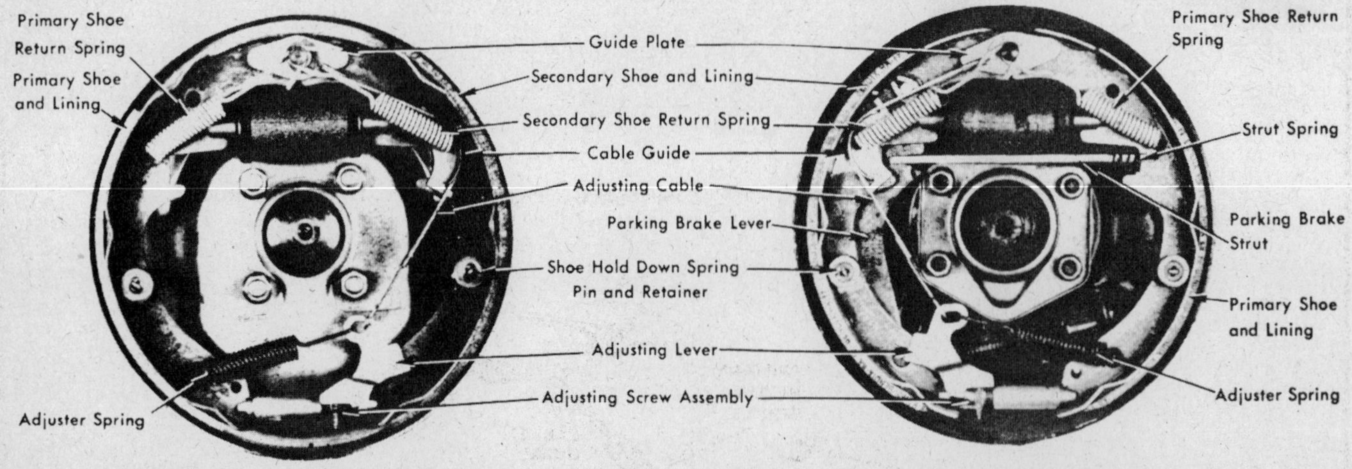

10" Diameter Left Front Brake Assembly — Duo-Servo Type

10" Diameter Right Rear Brake Assembly — Duo-Servo Type

Fig. 9.5 Identification of drum brake components (typical) (Sec 10)

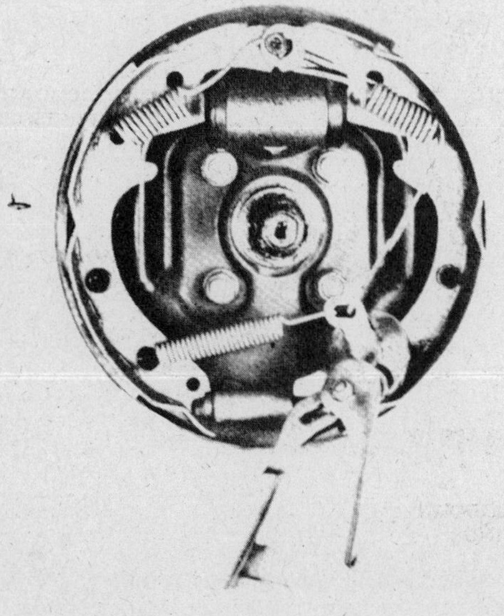

Fig. 9.6 Disconnecting the automatic adjuster lever from the secondary brake shoe (Sec 10)

15 Install the adjuster screw, after making sure that in the case of rear brakes the parking brake strut and the parking brake cable are correctly positioned and attached. Make sure that the adjuster screw is threaded completely into its sleeve (minimum adjustment position) (photo).

16 Place the small hooked end of the adjuster spring in the large hole in the primary shoe and then place the large hooked end of the spring in the adjuster lever.

17 Engage the hooked end of the adjuster cable in the adjuster lever and locate the adjuster cable over its guide.

18 With pliers, position the adjuster lever so the pivot hook engages in the large hole at the bottom of the secondary shoe.

19 Make sure that the shoes are centered on the backing plate and install the brake drum.

20 Remove the plug from the backing plate access slot. Turn the brake adjuster star wheel in the direction of the arrow (see accompanying illustration) until the wheel is locked against the drum. Mark the star wheel and insert a second screwdriver past the star wheel to force the lever off the adjuster screw. Back the star wheel off one complete revolution.

21 Install the plug and the wheel and repeat all operations on the other brakes. **Warning**: *After assembling and adjusting the brakes, check for proper brake operation before driving the vehicle.*

22 After the brakes have been replaced, drive the vehicle in reverse and apply the brake pedal several times. This will center the shoes and actuate the automatic adjuster for final precise adjustment.

11 Brake drums – servicing

1 Refer to Chapter 1 for removal procedures and a visual inspection of the brake drums.

2 If deeply scored, or so worn that the drum has become pocketed to the width of the shoes, then the drums must be replaced with new ones or resurfaced at an automotive machine shop.

3 Measure the inside diameter of the drum and compare it with the Specifications at the front of this Chapter. If your measurements exceed the maximum, then replace the drum with a new one.

4 Also, if the drum is out-of-round, it should be replaced to prevent premature brake shoe wear and wheel wobble during stops.

5 Refer to Chapter 1 for installation of the brake drums.

12 Disc brake pads – removal and installation

1 If the disc pads need to be replaced or if a closer inspection than that outlined in Chapter 1 is required, the calipers must be removed.

2 Raise the front of the vehicle and set it on jackstands. Block the rear tires and set the parking brake to keep the vehicle from rolling. Remove the wheels. It is a good idea to disassemble only one brake at a time so the other brake can be used as a guide if difficulties are encountered during reassembly.

3 Brush away any loose dirt around the caliper.

4 On 1970 through 1974 disc brake models, unscrew the guide pins and positioners which attach the caliper to the adapter (photo). On 1975 through 1982 models, first bottom the caliper piston in the

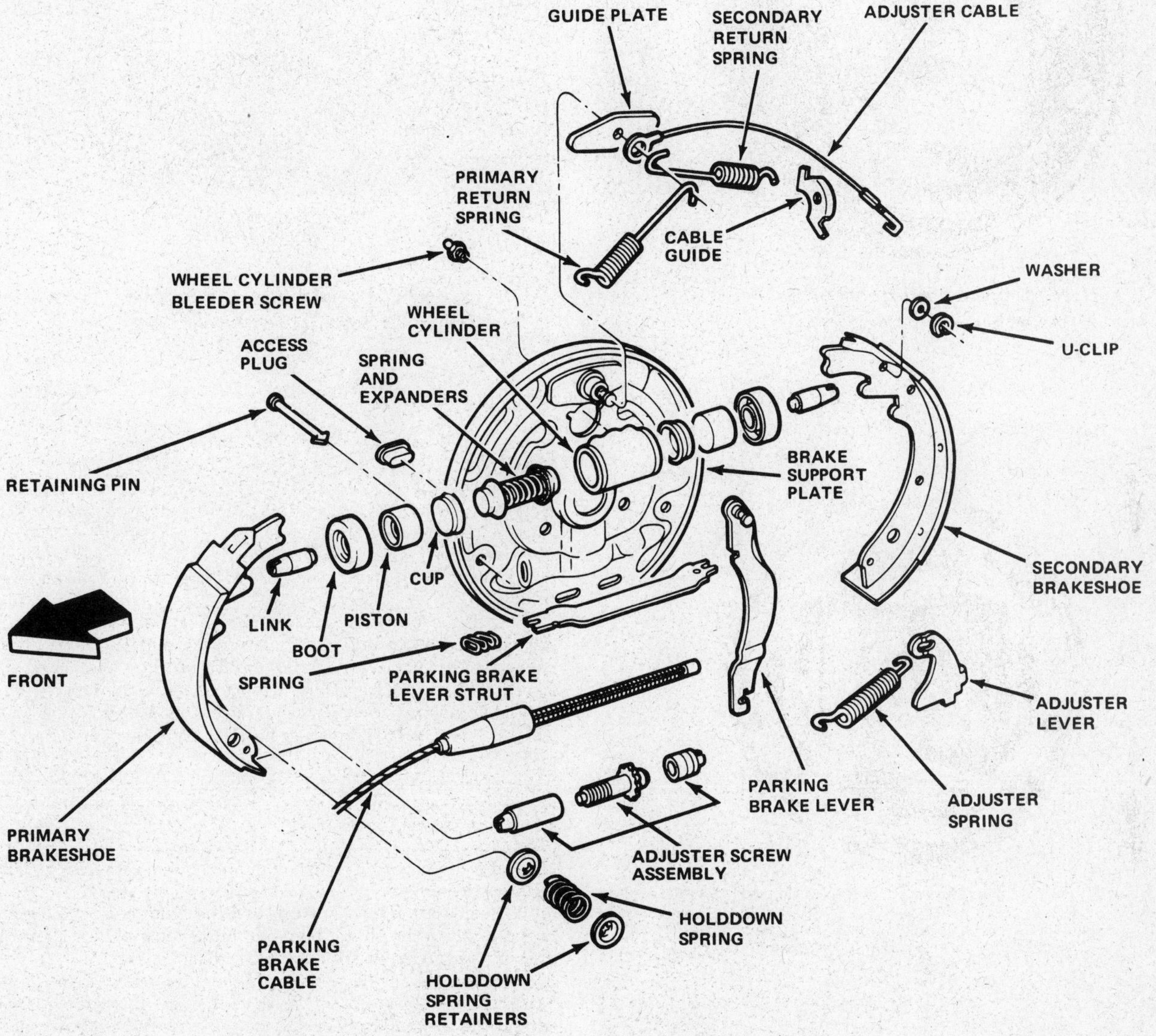
GUIDE PLATE
SECONDARY RETURN SPRING
ADJUSTER CABLE
PRIMARY RETURN SPRING
CABLE GUIDE
WASHER
WHEEL CYLINDER BLEEDER SCREW
U-CLIP
WHEEL CYLINDER
ACCESS PLUG
SPRING AND EXPANDERS
BRAKE SUPPORT PLATE
RETAINING PIN
SECONDARY BRAKESHOE
CUP
LINK
PISTON
BOOT
FRONT
SPRING
PARKING BRAKE LEVER STRUT
ADJUSTER LEVER
PARKING BRAKE LEVER
ADJUSTER SPRING
PRIMARY BRAKESHOE
ADJUSTER SCREW ASSEMBLY
HOLDDOWN SPRING
PARKING BRAKE CABLE
HOLDDOWN SPRING RETAINERS

Fig. 9.7 Drum brake components – exploded view (Sec 10)

10.5 Detaching a shoe return spring

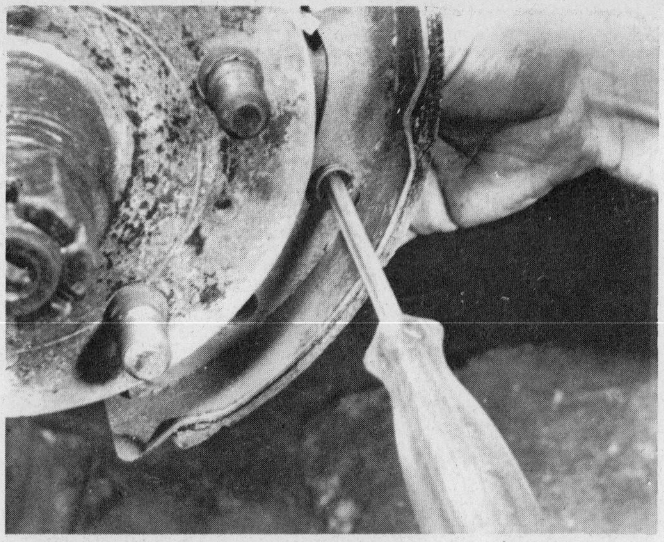

10.7A Unhooking a shoe hold-down spring

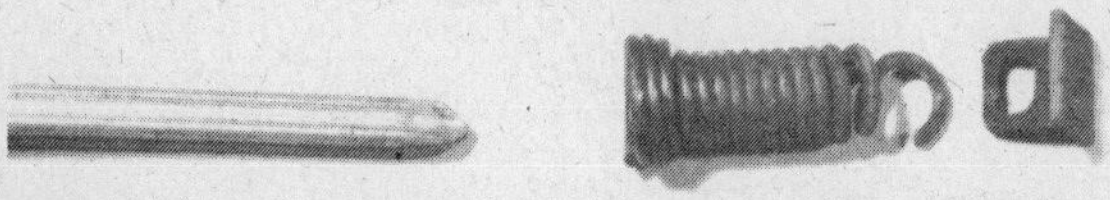

10.7B Shoe hold-down spring and anchor plate

10.8 Removing the parking brake strut (rear brakes)

10.9 Parking brake cable attachment to secondary shoe lever (rear brakes only)

10.15 Installing the automatic adjuster screw

Fig. 9.8 Be sure to lubricate the abutment surface of the caliper and the anchor plate (Sec 12)

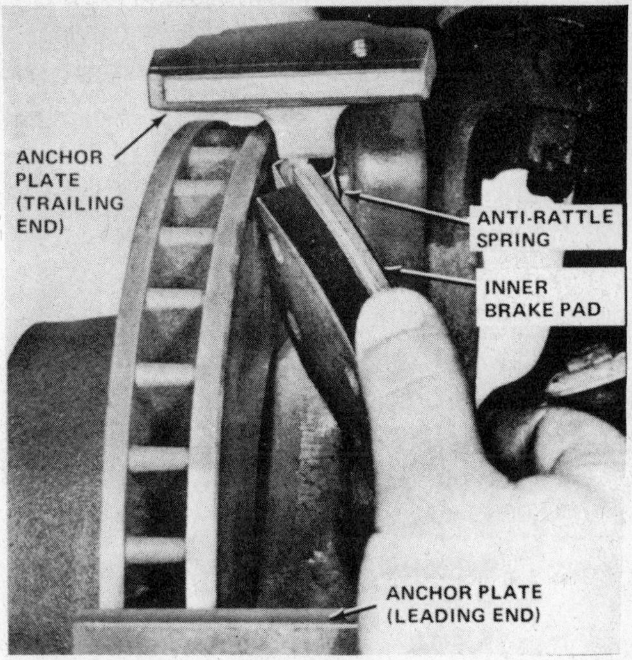

Fig. 9.9 Removal and installation of the inner brake pad (Sec 12)

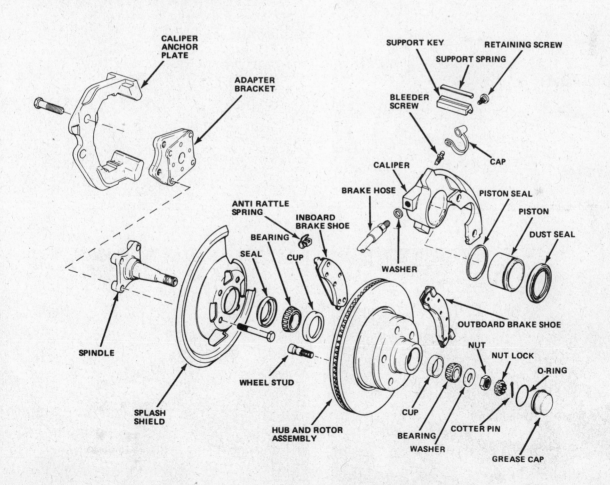

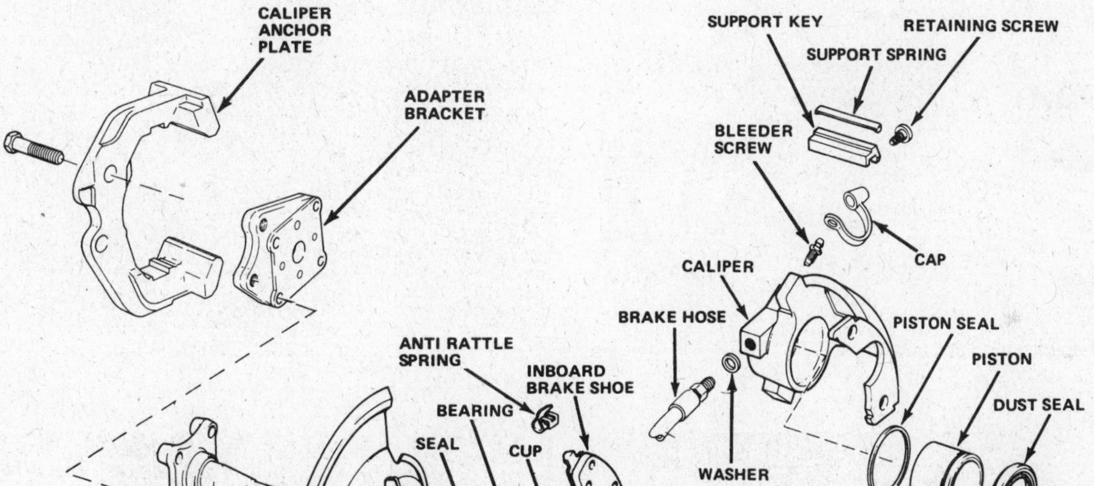

Fig. 9.10 Disc brake components – exploded view (typical) (Sec 12)

piston bore. Insert a screwdriver between the piston and inner disc pad. Pry the piston back into the bore. **Note:** *If the piston cannot be bottomed with a screwdriver, a large C-clamp may be used.*
5 After bottoming the caliper piston, remove the support key retaining screw on 1975 through 1981 models. A $\frac{1}{4}$-inch hex (Allen) wrench will remove the retaining screw.
6 Drive out the caliper support key and support spring with a drift punch and hammer.
7 On 1982 model disc brakes, a new caliper mounting system is used. After bottoming the caliper piston, use a 7 mm hex wrench to remove the mounting pin.
8 Remove the caliper by sliding it from the rotor and then tie it to the suspension with a piece of wire to prevent straining the hydraulic hose.
9 Remove the disc pads by extracting the inner one from the adapter and the outer one from the caliper.
10 The outer rubber bushings should be removed from the caliper and discarded as should the inner flanged bushings and the positioners. New components are supplied with the new disc pads.
11 Before installing the new pads, depress the caliper piston into its bore to accept the thicker linings. This action will cause the fluid in the master cylinder to rise and spill so either draw some from the master cylinder reservoir or release the bleed screw on the caliper as the piston is depressed and eject the displaced fluid.
12 Reassembly is a reversal of disassembly but make sure that the tabs of the positioners are located over the machined surface of the caliper and have their arrows pointing up. Tighten the guide pins to the specified torque.
13 When installation is complete, apply the brake pedal hard several times to bring the pads into contact with the rotor and then check the fluid level in the master cylinder reservoir and top up if necessary.

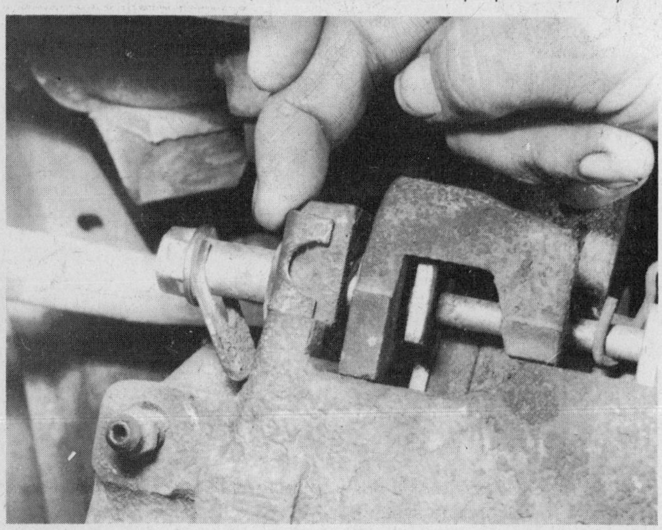

12.4 Removing the caliper guide pin and positioner

13 Disc brake caliper – removal, overhaul and installation

1 If the caliper is leaking fluid around the piston, it should be removed and overhauled to restore braking performance. Before disassembling it, read through this entire procedure and make sure you have the correct rebuild kit. Also, you will need some new, clean brake fluid of the recommended type and some clean rags.
2 **Note:** *Disassembly, overhaul and reassembly of the brake caliper must be done in a spotlessly clean work area to avoid contamination and possible failure of the brake hydraulic system components. If such a work area is not available, have it rebuilt by a dealer service department or a service station.*
3 Before removing the caliper, first disconnect the brake line from the caliper and plug it to keep contaminants out of the brake system and to prevent losing any more brake fluid than is necessary.
4 Remove the caliper as described in Section 12.
5 Clean the exterior of the caliper and drain the hydraulic fluid from it. On 1970 through 1974 disc brake models, remove the inner and outer guide pin.
6 Grip the caliper securely in the jaws of a vise using one of the cylinder body lugs as a pressure area.
7 Apply air pressure to the fluid inlet hole and carefully eject the piston.
8 Remove the dust boot.
9 Extract the piston seal using a wooden or plastic probe to avoid damaging the cylinder bore.
10 Unscrew and remove the bleed screw.
11 Clean all components and examine the piston and cylinder bore for scoring or 'bright' wear areas. Where these are evident, replace the caliper.
12 If the components are in good condition, the caliper can be rebuilt.
13 Dip the new piston seal in clean brake fluid.
14 Install the seat seal using the fingers only to seat it in the groove.
15 Dip the new dust boot in clean brake fluid and install it securely in its groove.
16 Dip the piston in brake fluid and install it in the boot and cylinder. Press the piston in until it is bottomed.
17 Reassemble and install the caliper as described in Section 12, connect the fluid line and bleed the hydraulic system as described in Section 8.

14 Brake disc – inspection, removal and installation

1 Refer to Chapter 1 for a general visual inspection of the brake disc.
2 Measure the disc thickness with a micrometer. If it is less than the Specifications at the front of this Chapter, due to wear or prior refacing, it must be replaced with a new one.
3 If the disc must be refaced, due to scoring or deep grooving, it can be done without removing the disc from the hub.
4 Using a dial indicator gauge, or similar instrument, check the disc runout (warpage). **Note:** *There must not be any excessive looseness in the front wheel bearings when the runout is measured; refer to Chapter 1 for wheel bearing adjustment.* The runout measurement must not exceed the Specifications given in the front of this Chapter. If it does, the disc must be replaced with a new one.
5 Refer to Chapter 1 for removal and installation of the hub/disc assembly.

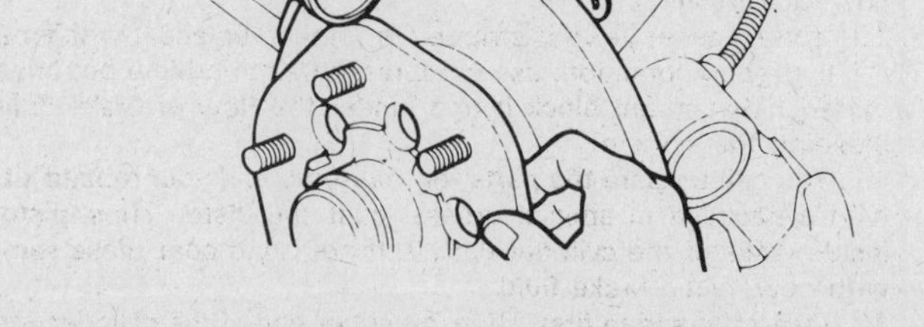

Fig. 9.11 Checking brake disc runout with a dial indicator (Sec 14)

15 Vacuum brake booster – removal and installation

1 Defeat the vacuum in the unit by repeated applications of the brake pedal.
2 Disconnect the vacuum pipe from the check valve on the booster front face.
3 Disconnect the fluid lines from the master cylinder and unbolt the master cylinder from the booster unit.

4 Disconnect the brake operating pushrod from the foot pedal arm.
5 Unbolt and remove the booster unit from the engine compartment rear firewall.
6 *On vehicles with all drum brakes,* a single diaphragm booster unit is used while on vehicles *with front disc brakes,* a tandem diaphragm unit is installed. It is recommended that in the event of a problem in a booster unit that a new or factory reconditioned assembly be installed rather than overhaul the existing unit.
7 Prior to installing a new booster, check the projection of the booster pushrod. For single and tandem diaphragm booster units, the pushrod should project between 1.185 and 1.200 inches above the face of the front housing. If the pushrod is adjustable, hold the pushrod with pliers and turn the nut in or out as necessary to alter its effective length. Where the pushrod is non-adjustable, then the booster has developed an internal fault and must be replaced.

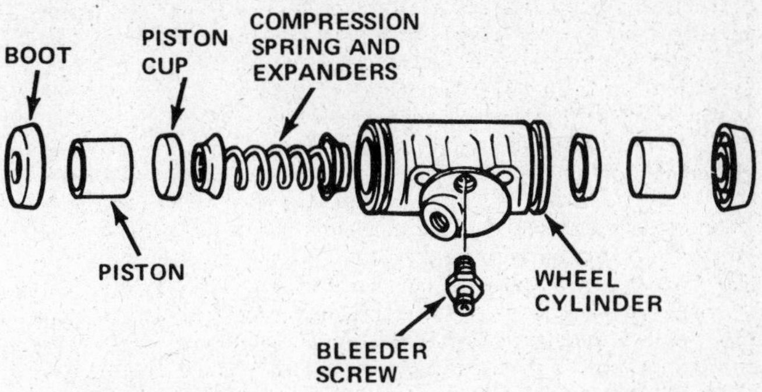

Fig. 9.12 Wheel cylinder components – exploded view (Sec 16)

16 Wheel cylinder – removal, overhaul and installation

1 If the wheel cylinder is leaking fluid around the piston, it should be removed and overhauled to restore braking performance. Before disassembling it, read through this entire procedure and make sure you have the correct rebuild kit. Also, you will need some new, clean brake fluid of the recommended type, and some clean rags. **Note:** *Disassembly, overhaul and reassembly of the wheel cylinder must be done in a spotlessly clean work area to avoid contamination and possible failure of the brake hydraulic system components. If such a work area is not available, have it rebuilt by a dealer service department or a service station.*
2 Refer to Section 10 for the brake shoe removal procedure.
3 Although it is possible to overhaul a wheel cylinder while it is still attached to the backing plate, it is recommended that it be removed. To do this, disconnect the brake line from the cylinder and either plug the line or seal the master cylinder reservoir with a sheet of thin plastic to prevent loss of fluid and to keep contaminants from entering the brake system.
4 Remove the two small bolts, on the back side of the backing plate, which hold the cylinder to the plate. Remove the cylinder.
5 Next, carefully remove the rubber boot with your fingers.
6 You can now remove all the remaining parts within the cylinder housing; both pistons, the cups and the compression spring and expanders. An easy way to remove these parts is by tapping the cylinder on a piece of wood.
7 Examine the mating surfaces of the pistons and the cylinder walls. If there is scoring, evidence of metal-to-metal contact or bright wear areas, replace the complete cylinder assembly with a new one.
8 If the metal components are in good condition, discard the rubber boots and the cylinder cups and replace them with the new parts from the rebuild kit.
9 Thoroughly clean all the parts with new brake fluid. When cleaning the brake cylinder walls, wrap a clean white cloth around the stick and soak it in new brake fluid. Insert the stick, first in one side of the cylinder and then the other, and rotate it several times. Do not use a push-pull movement.
10 If the bleeder valve is stripped or ruined, replace it with a new one. If it's in good condition, use compressed air and blow out any foreign material that might block it and hinder the flow of brake fluid when bleeding the system.
11 You can prepare the parts for reassembly. If your rebuild kit comes with a package of special grease, coat the piston cups, pistons and inside walls of the cylinder with it. If not, then coat these same parts with new, clean brake fluid.
12 Insert the spring first. Then, on either end of the cylinder, insert the piston cups, followed by the pistons. **Note:** *Make sure these parts are inserted correctly.*
13 Coat the inside and outside of the rubber boots with high-temperature brake grease. Install the boots onto the brake cylinder.
14 Refer to Section 10 for the brake shoe installation procedure.

17 Master cylinder – removal and installation

1 Place some old rags underneath the master cylinder to soak up any brake fluid that might spill during the removal. **Note:** *Be careful not to spill any fluid on the painted surfaces of the vehicle; it will damage the paint. If some does spill, wipe it up immediately.*

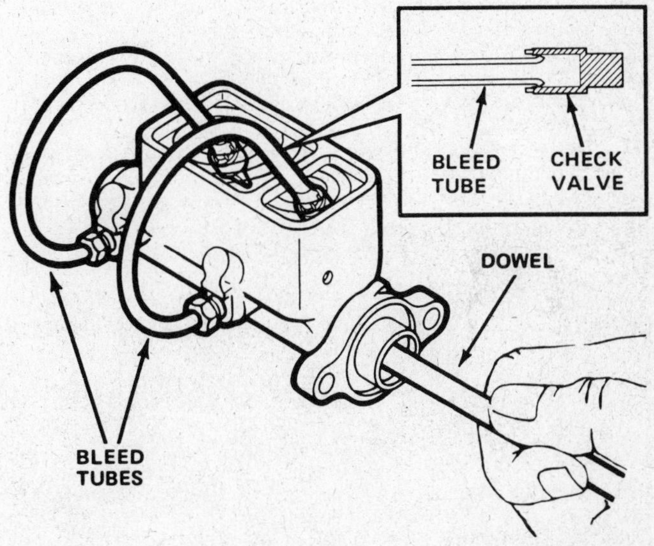

Fig. 9.13 Priming the master cylinder before installation (Sec 17)

2 Disconnect the brake pushrod from the brake pedal (vehicles without power braking system).
3 Disconnect the brake lines from the master cylinder and catch the brake fluid in a suitable container.
4 Unbolt the master cylinder from the engine compartment rear firewall (vehicles without brake booster) or from the front face of the booster (vehicles with power brakes), remove the cover and seal and tip out the fluid.
5 Check for fluid leakage around the flange area at the base of the piston. If there is evidence of leakage, the master cylinder should be overhauled or replaced with a rebuilt unit. Refer to Section 19 for the procedure on master cylinder overhaul.
6 Before the master cylinder is installed, the unit should be bled. Connect two lengths of tubing as shown in the accompanying illustration and actuate the pistons until the unit is primed with clean fluid and all air is bled out. If the master cylinder is not bled before installation, it can be done later as described in Section 9. However, it is recommended, if possible, to prime the unit first.

18 Master cylinder – overhaul

1 If the cylinder is leaking fluid around the piston, it should be removed and overhauled to restore braking performance. Before disassembling it, read through this entire procedure and make sure you have the correct rebuild kit. Also, you will need some new, clean brake

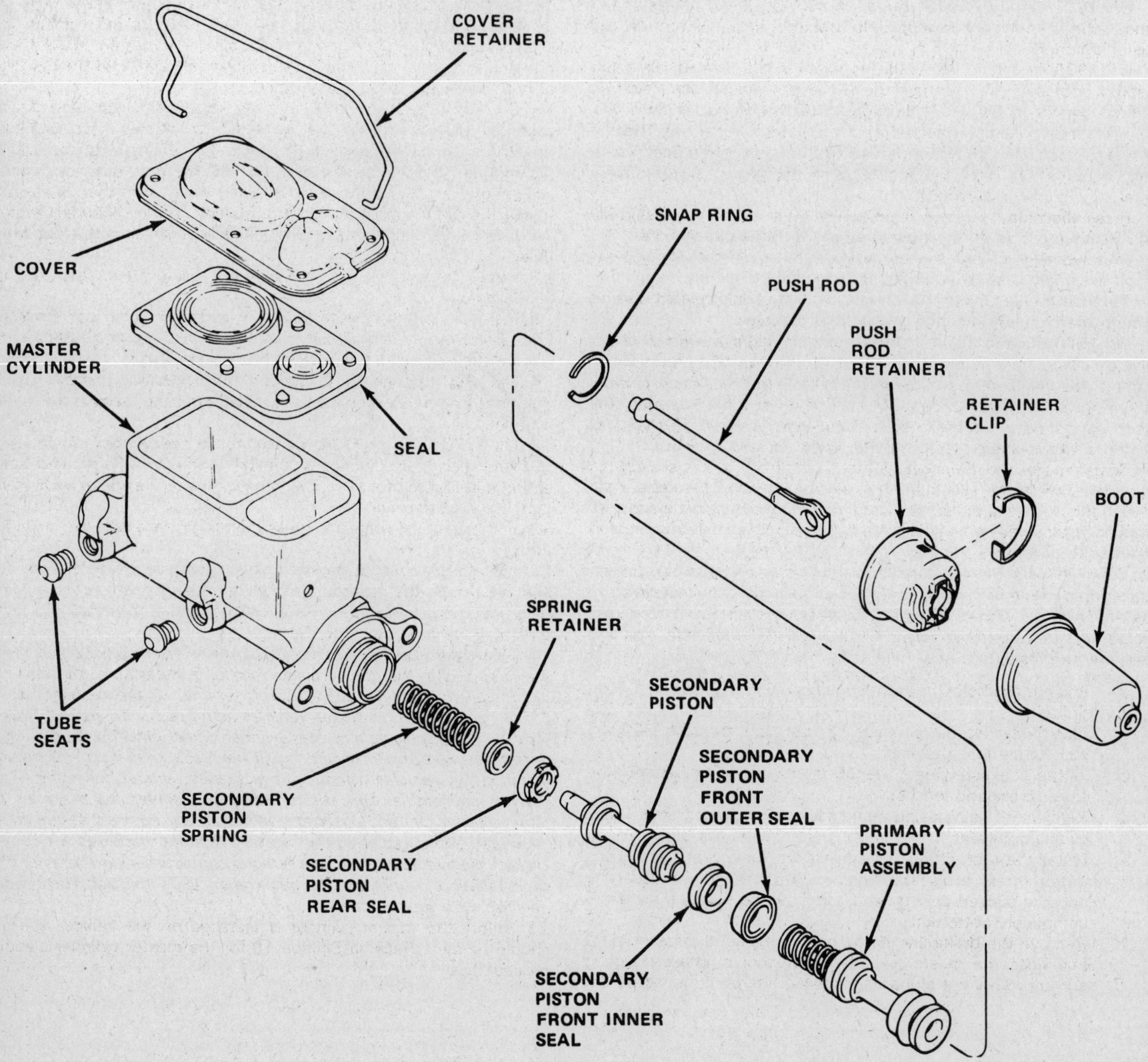

Fig. 9.14 Master cylinder components – exploded view (typical) (Sec 18)

fluid of the recommended type and some clean rags. **Note**: *Disassembly, overhaul and reassembly of the master cylinder must be done in a spotlessly clean work area to avoid contamination and possible failure of the brake hydraulic system components. If such a work area is not available, have it rebuilt by a dealer service department or a service station.*

2 On 1970 through 1976 model master cylinders, unscrew and remove the primary piston stop bolt, located on the bottom on the master cylinder.

3 On 1970 through 1982 vehicles with manual brakes, slide the pushrod boot back and remove the C-shaped retainer clip, retainer, pushrod and boot. On 1970 through 1976 model master cylinders, there might be an exterior snap-ring instead of a retainer clip. There is no retainer, retainer clip or boot on 1970 through 1976 model power brake systems. On 1977 through 1982 model power brake systems, there is no pushrod assembly.

4 Press the primary piston in using the pushrod or other suitable tool. Remove the snap-ring from the groove in the piston bore.

5 Remove and discard the primary piston assembly. A complete piston assembly is supplied with the rebuild kit.

6 Remove the secondary piston assembly by applying air pressure through the compensator port in the front reservoir.

7 On 1970 through 1974 model master cylinders, a residual check valve or valves must be removed. On 1970 through 1974 drum brake systems, the check valves in the front and rear fluid outlet ports must be removed. On 1970 through 1974 front disc brake systems, the check valve for the rear brake system must be removed. This valve is located closer to the piston bore end of the master cylinder.

8 To gain access to the check valves, the outlet port tube seats must be removed with the self tapping screws supplied in the rebuild kit. Thread the self tapping screws into the tube seats and place two screwdriver tips under the screw head. Carefully pry the screw up and remove the tube seat.

9 Clean all metal parts in clean brake fluid or brake cleaning solvent. Use air pressure to remove dirt and cleaning solvent from recesses and internal passages. **Note**: *When you purchase the rebuild kit from your dealer, be sure to get two spare brake line fitting nuts also. You will need them to install the new tube seats,*

- a) Enlarge the holes in the tube seats using a $\frac{13}{64}$ inch (5.1 mm) drill bit.
- b) Place a flat washer on each tube seat and thread a $\frac{1}{4}$-20 x $\frac{3}{4}$ inch screw into the seat.
- c) Tighten the screw until the tube seat is loose and remove the seat, screw and washer.
- d) Remove all chips using compressed air and alcohol or brake cleaning solvent.
- e) Install the tube fitting seats using the spare brake line fitting nuts to press the seats into place. Do not allow the seats to become cocked during installation and be sure the seats are completely bottomed.
- f) Remove the brake line fitting nuts, remove all chips or burrs and rinse the master cylinder in alcohol or brake cleaning solvent. Blow out all passages using filtered compressed air.

10 On 1975 through 1982 model master cylinders, there are no check valves and the tube seats rarely need to be replaced. However, if the seats are cracked, scored, loose, or cocked in the fluid outlet port, they shold be replaced. It might be preferable to buy a rebuilt master cylinder. Read through the entire procedure above before attempting to replace the tube seats on later model master cylinders.

11 Before reassembly, dip each component in clean brake fluid.

12 On 1970 through 1974 models, install the piston washer, rear seal, protector and return spring on the secondary piston. Install the O-ring and front seal on the secondary piston. Be sure that the flat faces of both piston seals face each other.

13 On 1975 through 1982 models, install the rear seal on the secondary piston with the seal lip facing in, towards the piston bore. Install the front inner seal on the secondary piston with the seal lip facing in, towards the cylinder bore. Install the front outer seal on the secondary piston with the seal lip facing away from the piston bore. Install the return spring and spring retainer on the secondary piston.

14 Lubricate the piston bore and piston assemblies with clean brake fluid.

15 Install the secondary piston assembly, spring end first, into the piston bore.

16 Install the primary piston assembly, spring end first, into the piston bore. Press the primary piston in using the pushrod or a suitable tool. Secure the pistons in the bore with the snap-ring.

17 On 1970 through 1976 model master cylinders, place a new O-ring on the primary piston stop and install the piston stop in the master cylinder.

18 On 1970 through 1974 models, place new rubber check valves over the check valve springs and install them in the fluid outlet holes, spring end first. **Note**: *With disc brakes, install the check valve in the rear brake system only.*

19 Install the tube seats and press them into place with the brake line fitting nuts.

20 On vehicles without power brakes, assemble the boot, snap-ring and washer on the pushrod; then install the retainer on the pushrod with the prongs toward the master cylinder end of the rod. The retainer must engage the groove on the rod.

21 Insert the pushrod assembly into the master cylinder and install the snap-ring in the groove of the master cylinder bore. **Caution**: *Do not install the retainer clip, pushrod retainer or the rubber boot on 1970 through 1976 model vehicles equipped with power brakes.* **Note**: *When replacing a master cylinder, the original pushrod must be used. The replacement cylinder will have the snap-ring and retainer installed. On vehicles without power brakes, remove the retainer clip washer and retainer from the replacement cylinder and assemble the boot, retainer clip and pushrod retainer on the pushrod as previously described. When replacing the master cylinder on vehicles with power brakes, remove and discard the retainer clip, washer, and retainer prior to installation. Do not install a pushrod on 1977 through 1982 model vehicles with power brakes.*

22 Before the master cylinder is installed on the vehicle, the unit should be bled. Refer to Section 18 for the master cylinder bleeding procedure.

Chapter 10 Chassis electrical system

Contents

Battery check and maintenance ... See Chapter 1
Bulbs – replacement ... 14
Electrical troubleshooting – general information ... 2
Fuel, coolant temperature and oil pressure gauges – check ... 5
Fuses and fusible links – general information ... 3
General information ... 1
Headlights – adjustment ... 13
Headlights – removal and installation ... 12
Headlight warning buzzer – general information ... 23
Horn and horn relay – general information ... 8
Ignition switch – removal and installation ... 11
Instrument cluster and package tray – removal and installaton ... 9
Neutral safety switch (automatic transmission) – check, adjustment and replacement ... See Chapter 7B
Oil pressure gauge – check ... 7
Oil pressure warning light – check ... 6
Radio – removal and installation ... 19
Radio dial bulbs – replacement ... 18
Rear window defogger – precautions and check ... 17
Seat belt interlock system (1974 and 1975) ... 21
Seat belt warning system (1970 through 1973) ... 20
Seat belt warning system (1976 through 1982) ... 22
Speedometer cable – removal and installation ... 10
Steering column switches – removal and installation ... See Chapter 11
Turn signal and hazard warning lights – check ... 4
Windshield and rear window washers – general information ... 16
Windshield and rear wiper motors – removal and installation ... 15

Specifications

Light bulb application	**Type**
Headlights	
1971 through 1978	6014
1978 Concord only	6052
1979 through 1982	4651 or 4652
Front turn signal and parking lights	
1971 through 1978	1157
1978 Concord only	1157 NA (natural amber)
1979 through 1982	1157 NA
Front side marker lights (all)	194
Rear side marker lights	
1971 through 1977 Hornet	1895
1970 through 1982 (all other models)	194
Stop and taillights (1978 through 1982 Concord)	1157
Rear turn signal lights (1978 through 1982 Concord)	1156
Combination rear signal, stop and taillights (all)	1157
Backup lights (all)	1156
Dome light	
1971 through 1974	562
1975 through 1982	561

1 General information

The AMC vehicles covered in this manual are equipped with a 12-volt, negative-ground electrical system. The system is equipped with fuses and fusible links ("fused" wires) to protect it from damage due to short circuits.

This Chapter covers basic maintenance and repair of the lighting system and interior electrics.

2 Electrical troubleshooting – general information

A typical electrical circuit consists of an electrical component, any switches, relays, motors, etc. related to that component and the wiring and connectors that connect the component to both the battery and the chassis. To aid in locating a problem in any electrical circuit, wiring diagrams for each model are included at the end of this Chapter.

Before tackling any troublesome electrical circuit, first study the appropriate diagrams to get a complete understanding of what makes up that individual circuit. Trouble spots, for instance, can often be narrowed down by noting if other components related to that circuit are operating properly or not. If several components or circuits fail at one time, chances are the problem lies in the fuse or ground connection, as several circuits often are routed through the same fuse and ground connections.

Electrical problems often stem from simple causes, such as loose or corroded connections, a blown fuse or melted fusible link. Prior to any electrical troubleshooting, always visually check the condition of the fuse, wires and connections of the problem circuit.

If testing instruments are going to be utilized, use the diagrams to plan ahead of time where you will make the necessary connections in order to accurately pinpoint the trouble spot.

The basic tools needed for electrical troubleshooting include a circuit tester or voltmeter (a 12-volt bulb with a set of test leads can also be used), a continuity tester (which includes a bulb, battery and set of test leads) and a jumper wire, preferably with a circuit breaker incorporated, which can be used to bypass electrical components.

Voltage checks should be performed if a circuit is not functioning properly. Connect one lead of a circuit tester to either the negative battery terminal or a known good ground. Connect the other lead to a connector in the circuit being tested, preferably nearest to the battery or fuse. If the bulb of the tester goes on, voltage is reaching that point (which means the part of the circuit between that connector and the battery is problem free). Continue checking along the entire circuit in the same fashion. When you reach a point where no voltage is present, the problem lies between there and the last good test point. Most of the time the problem is due to a loose connection. *Keep in mind that some circuits receive voltage only when the ignition key is in the Accessory or Run position.*

A method of finding shorts in a circuit is to remove the fuse and connect a test light or voltmeter in its place to the fuse terminals. There should be no load in the circuit. Move the wiring harness from side-to-side while watching the test light. If the bulb goes on, there is a short to ground somewhere in that area, probably where insulation has rubbed off of a wire. The same test can be performed on other components of the circuit, including the switch.

A ground check should be done to see if a component is grounded properly. Disconnect the battery and connect one lead of a self-powered test light such as a continuity tester to a known good ground. Connect the other lead to the wire or ground connection being tested. If the bulb goes on, the ground is good. If the bulb does not go on, the ground is not good.

A continuity check is performed to see if a circuit, section of circuit or individual component is passing electricity through it properly. Disconnect the battery, and connect one lead of a self-powered test light such as a continuity tester to one end of the circuit being tested and the other lead to the other end of the circuit. If the bulb goes on, there is continuity, which means the circuit is passing electricity through it properly. Switches can be checked in the same way.

Remember that all electrical circuits are composed basically of electricity running from the battery, through the wires, switches, relays, etc. to the electrical component (light bulb, motor, etc.). From there it is run to the vehicle body (ground) where it is passed back to the battery. Any electrical problem is basically an interruption in the flow of electricity to and from the battery.

3 Fuses and fusible links – general information

The electrical circuits of the vehicle are protected by a combination of fuses and fusible links. The fuse box is located on the passenger compartment side of the dash panel, adjacent to the parking brake mechanism. Each of the fuses is designed to protect a specific circuit, as identified on the fuse panel.

If an electrical component has failed, your first check should be the fuse. A fuse which has "blown" can be readily identified by inspecting the metal element inside the housing. If this element is broken the fuse is inoperable and should be replaced with a new one. Fuses are replaced by simply pulling out the old one and pushing in the new one.

It is important that the correct fuse be installed. The different electrical circuits need varying amounts of protection, indicated by the amperage rating on the fuse. A fuse with too low a rating will blow prematurely, while a fuse with too high a rating may not blow soon enough to avoid serious damage to other components or the wiring.

At no time should the fuse be bypassed with metal or foil. Serious damage to the electrical system could result.

If the replacement fuse immediately fails, do not replace it with another until the cause of the problem is isolated and corrected. In most cases this will be a short circuit in the wiring caused by a broken or deteriorated wire.

In addition to fuses, the wiring system incorporates fusible links for overload protection. These links are used in circuits which are not ordinarily fused, due to carrying high amperage loads or because of their location on the chassis. Failure of a fusible link is usually caused by a grounded circuit. The problem must be pinpointed before installing a new link. When replacing a link, disconnect the negative battery cable from the battery and follow the link from the terminal end to the wiring harness. The harness tape must be unwrapped where the link enters the harness and the replacement link soldered to the harness wires. Re-tape any soldered connections.

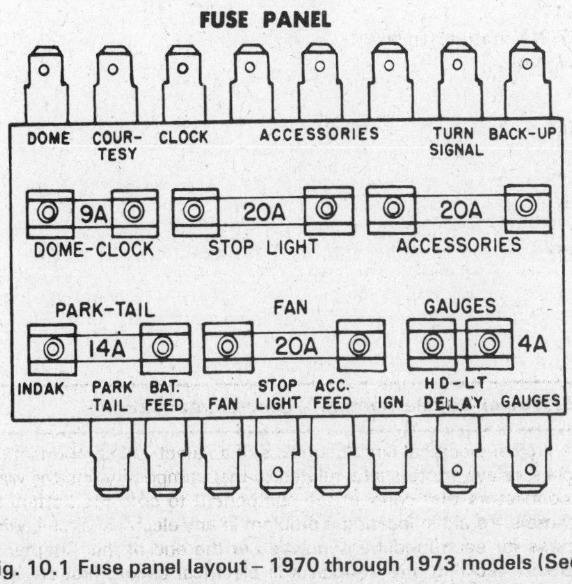

Fig. 10.1 Fuse panel layout – 1970 through 1973 models (Sec 3)

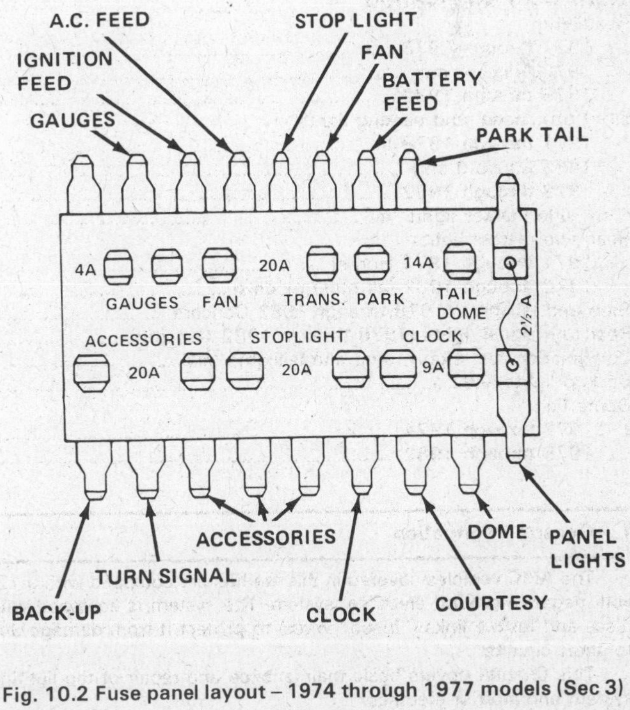

Fig. 10.2 Fuse panel layout – 1974 through 1977 models (Sec 3)

10

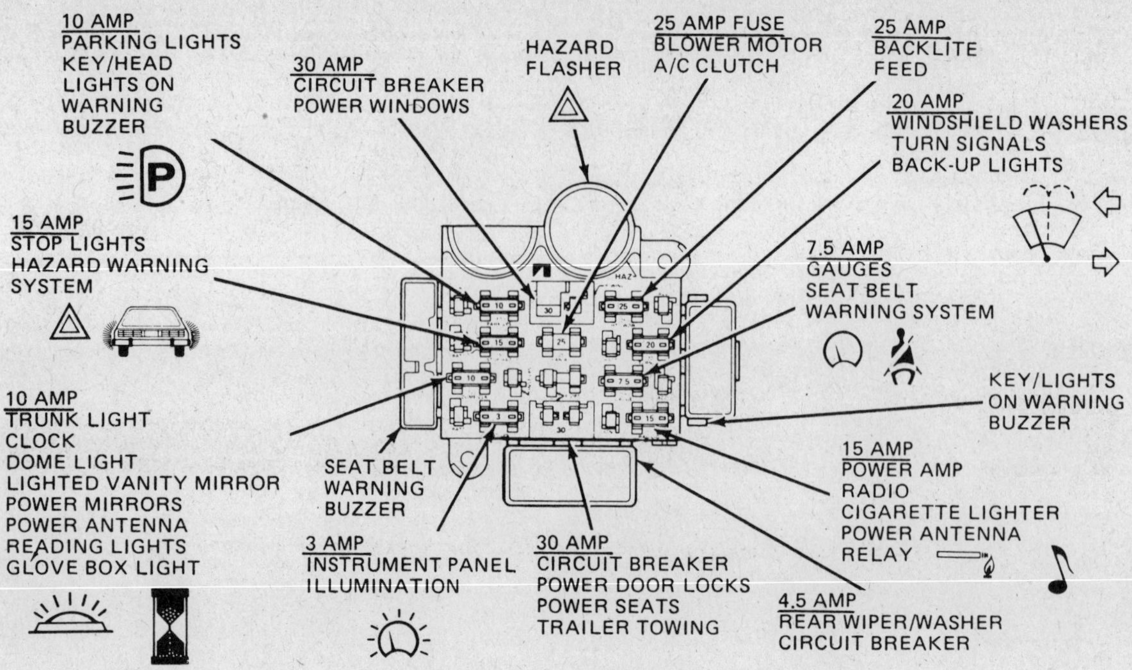

Fig. 10.3 Fuse panel layout – 1978 through 1982 models (Sec 3)

4 Turn signal and hazard warning lights – check

1 If the hazard or turn signal flashers fail to work properly, first check the bulbs, then make sure the nuts which hold the light units to the vehicle are tight and free from corrosion. These complete the circuit and any resistance here could affect the operation of the flasher unit.
2 Check the security of all wiring connectors after reference to the appropriate wiring diagram.
3 If everything seems to be fine, then the hazard warning or flasher indicator units themselves must be faulty (since they cannot be repaired, they must be replaced with new ones).
4 The directional flasher is located either under the fuse panel or in the instrument panel. The hazard warning flasher either attaches to the fuse panel or hangs free from the wiring harness under the steering column.

5 Fuel, coolant temperature and oil pressure gauges – check

1 If the fuel level or coolant temperature gauge pointer is not operating at all, first check the corresponding fuse at the fuse panel. If the fuse is undamaged, proceed to Step 2.
2 If the fuel, coolant temperature or oil pressure gauge pointer is not operating at all, use a circuit tester to test for voltage at the gauge input connection. If no voltage is present, the problem is in the wiring.
3 If voltage is present, check to be sure the gauge ground terminal is connected to a good ground. Next, ground the gauge sender terminal at the back of the gauge to a good ground. If the pointer does not move, replace the gauge. If the pointer moves, the problem is in the sending unit or the sending unit wiring.

6 Oil pressure warning light – check

1 The oil pressure warning light first appeared in 1975 and became standard equipment a year later.
2 If the oil pressure warning light does not operate when the ignition switch is turned on, ground the sending unit wire to the engine. If the indicator lights up, replace the sending unit. If the indicator does not light up, the problem is in the bulb or the wiring. Replace the bulb as a first measure.
3 If the bulb is not defective, find the short circuit in the wiring using a voltmeter or circuit tester.

7 Oil pressure gauge – check

Disconnect the wire from the sending unit located on the engine block. Connect one lead of an ohmmeter to a good ground and the other lead to the sending unit terminal. Reconnect the sending wire. The gauge should read as follows:

1970 through 1975

PSI	Resistance (ohms)
0	73.0 ± 12
5 to 7	44.0 ± 3
77 to 83	10.0 ± 1

1979 through 1982 (optional)

0	240 (approx.)
60	67 (approx.)

8 Horn and horn relay – general information

If the horn is not sounding, use a voltmeter to check the power lead to the horn relay. A zero reading indicates that the fusible link has blown and must be replaced. Trace the cause (probably an open circuit) before installing the new link. If voltage is present, the horn relay is probably faulty.

9 Instrument cluster and package tray – removal and installation

1 Disconnect the negative battery cable from the battery. If your vehicle is equipped with a package tray, follow Steps 2 through 5. If there is no package tray, proceed to Step 6.

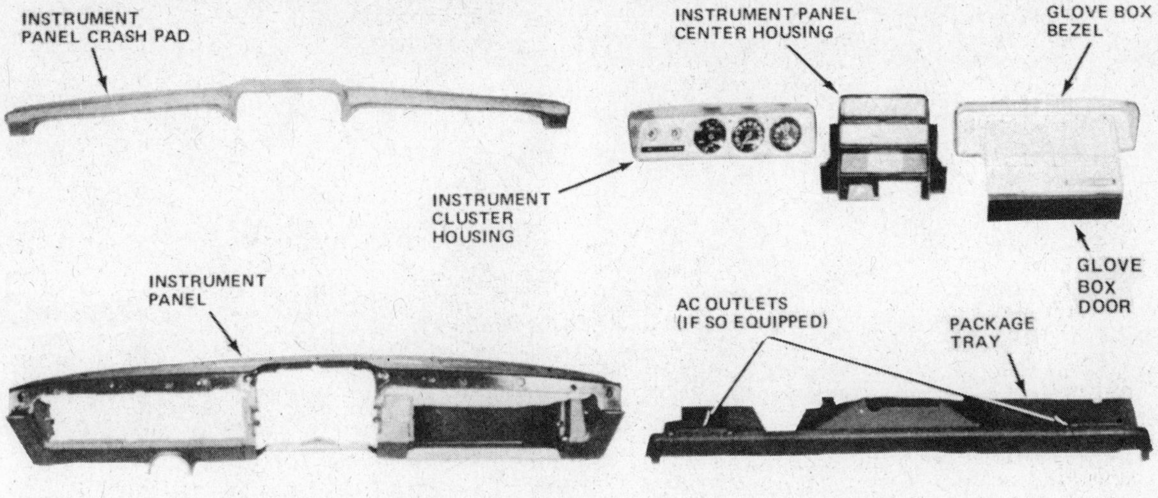

Fig.. 10.4 Instrument cluster and panel – 1970 through 1976 models (Sec 9)

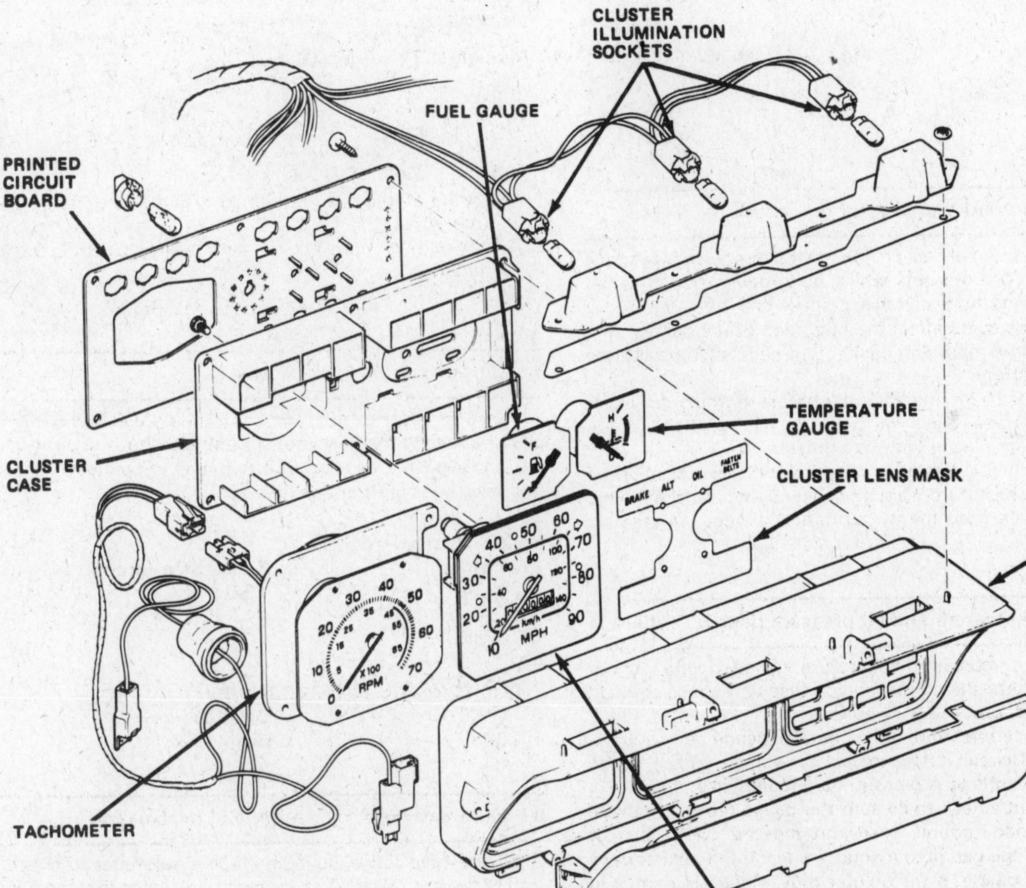

Fig. 10.5 Instrument cluster assembly (1977 through 1982 models) – exploded view (Sec 9)

12.1 Removing the headlight door

12.2 Removing the headlight retaining ring

12.3 Removing the headlight sealed beam unit

14.1 Removing the front turn signal bulb

14.2A Removing the taillight lens

14.2B Rear turn signal, back-up, stop and taillight bulbs

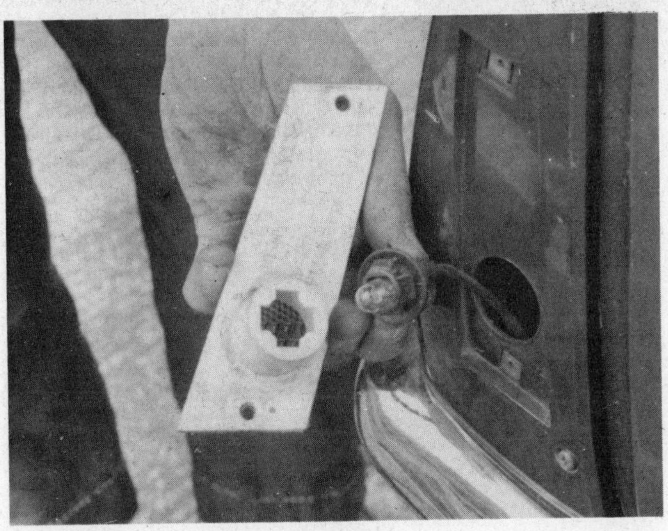

14.3A Removing the front side marker light

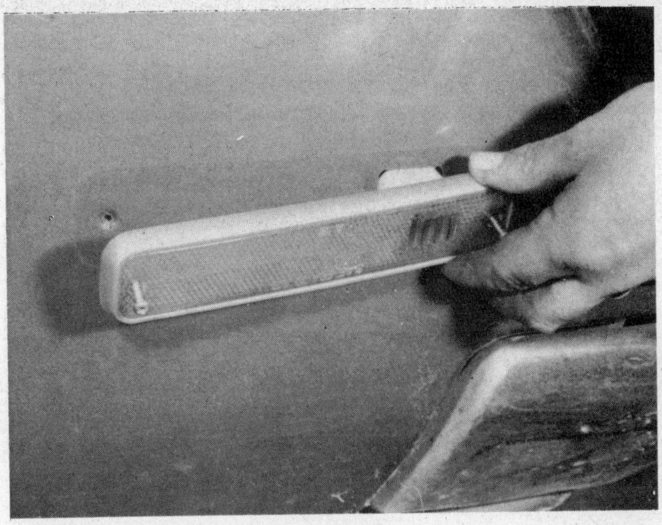

14.3B Removing the rear side marker light

2 Disconnect the wiring harness from the courtesy lights.
3 Remove the screws attaching the package tray to the cowl trim panels.
4 Remove the hood release cable attaching screws, if so equipped.
5 Remove the screws attaching the package tray to the instrument panel and evaporator housing. Remove the package tray.
6 Remove the lower steering column cover, if so equipped.
7 Disconnect the speedometer cable.
8 Remove the gear selector dial actuator cable from the steering column shift shroud, if so equipped (later model automatics only).
9 Remove all the control knobs, switches and retaining nuts.
10 Remove the attaching screws from the instrument cluster bezel.
11 Disengage any tabs and push down on the light housings (if so equipped) in order to clear the instrument panel.
12 Disconnect all switches, wires and lights from the back of the cluster.
13 Installation is the reverse of removal.

10 Speedometer cable – removal and installation

1 Disconnect the speedometer at the transmission end and unhook it from the underbody routing bracket.
2 Remove the package tray, if so equipped (see Section 9).
3 Unscrew the speedometer cable.
4 Remove the cable and grommet from the dash panel.
5 Installation is the reverse of removal.

11 Ignition switch – removal and installation

1 Remove the package tray, if so equipped (see Section 9).
2 Place the key lock in the Off-Lock position and remove the two switch attaching screws.
3 Disconnect the switch from the remote rod.
4 Disconnect the harness connector and remove the switch from the steering column.
5 Installation is the reverse of removal.

12 Headlights – removal and installation

1 Remove the headlight door (photo).
2 Remove the retaining ring (photo).
3 Pull the headlight sealed beam unit out and disconnect the electrical plug (photo).
4 Installation is the reverse of the removal procedure. Be sure that the replacement headlight is the same type and rating as the original.

13 Headlights – adjustment

Due to the legal aspects involved, headlight adjustment should be performed by a qualified mechanic with the appropriate beam-setting equipment.

14 Bulbs – replacement

Front park and turn signal lights

1 Remove the lens attaching screws and detach the lens. Replace the bulb with one of a similar type, noting that it is twin filament with offset pins and can only be installed one way (photo).

Taillight, rear turn signal and backup lights

2 These bulbs are accessible after removal of the lens attaching screws and lens (photos).

Side marker lights

3 Front and rear side marker light bulbs are accessible after removal of the lens. Pull the bulb holder from its securing clip (photos).

License plate light

4 Unscrew and remove the attaching screws from the rear bumper. The bulb is then accessible after removal of the lens.

Interior dome light

5 Pry off the lens with a screwdriver, if necessary, and remove the bulb. Be sure that all bulbs are replaced with ones of similar rating and type.

15 Windshield and rear wiper motors – removal and installation

1 Remove the wiper blades and arms.
2 Disconnect the wiring harness connector at the wiper motor.
3 Remove the securing bolts which hold the wiper motor to the engine compartment firewall. Pull the motor forward to expose the motor crank-to-link stud clip. Pry up the lock tab of the clip and slide the clip from the stud. Remove the motor.
4 To remove the linkage, first unscrew the wiper arm driving pivot shaft nuts. Slide the linkage to the left to disengage the right-hand pivot shaft from its hole and then withdraw the linkage to the right-hand side.
5 Installation is the reverse of the removal procedure, but be sure the motor crank-to-linkage stud clip is securely seated.

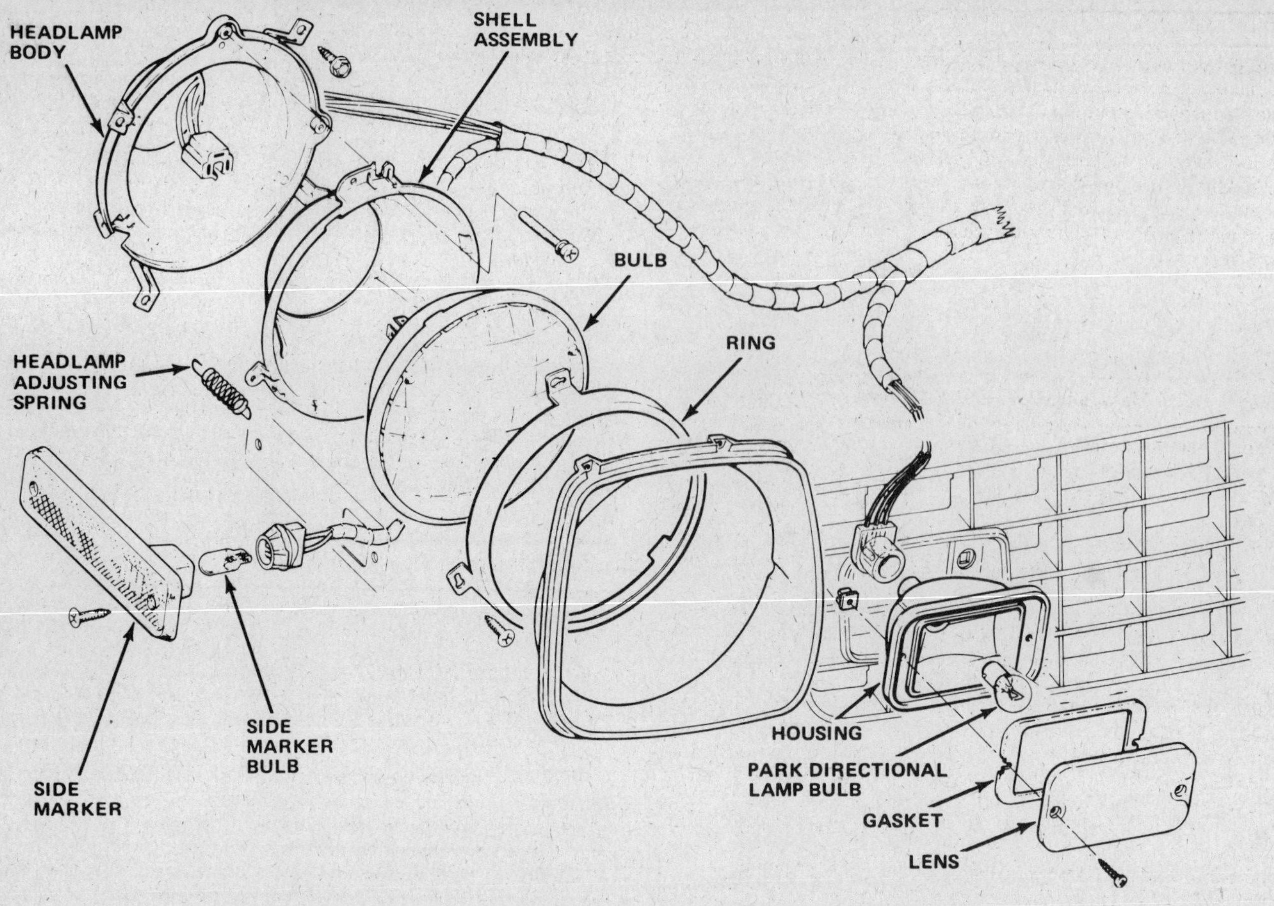

Fig. 10.6 Headlight, parking, directional and side marker lights – Gremlin and Spirit models (Secs 12 and 14)

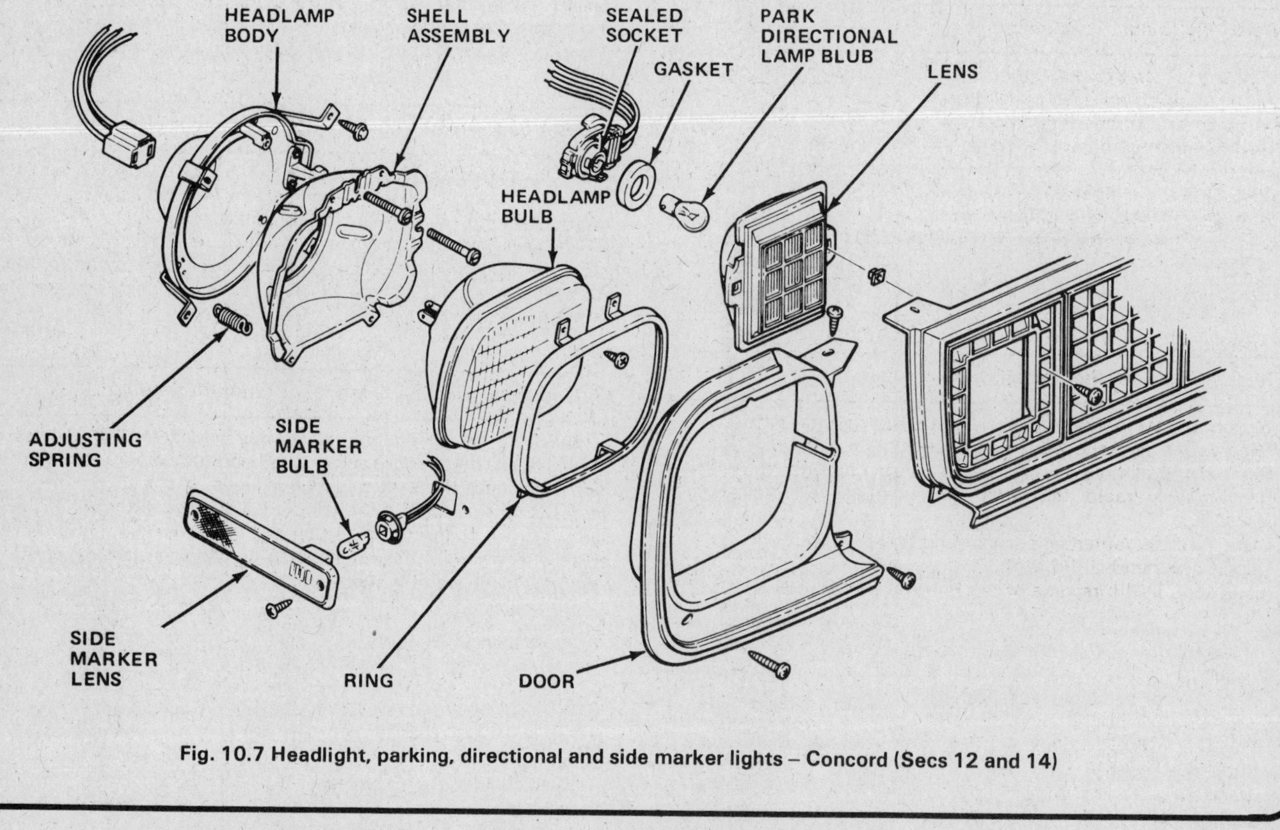

Fig. 10.7 Headlight, parking, directional and side marker lights – Concord (Secs 12 and 14)

16 Windshield and rear window washers – general information

The electric washer pump is located on the washer fluid container. On vehicles equipped with rear window washers, an integral control switch is hooked up to both the front and rear washer pump.

If a washer is not operating properly, first check to be sure the fluid tubes and jets are clear and securely fastened. Check for any loose wiring. If the washer is still not operational, the electric pump must be replaced as a unit.

17 Rear window defogger – precautions and check

1 When cleaning the glass, use a soft dry cloth and wipe the glass carefully in the direction of the wires.
2 Do not use detergents or any glass cleaner which contains abrasives.
3 When testing the wire, do not touch the wire with the tip of the test probe, but fold a piece of aluminium foil over the probe and press the foil against the wire.
4 Connect the positive lead of a 12-volt DC voltmeter to the feed side of the window defogger wiring. Connecting the negative lead to the ground wire at the upper inside corner of the window. A voltage drop of 11 to 13 volts should be indicated.
5 Keep the negative lead connected to the ground. Using the positive lead, carefully contact each grid at the centerline of the window. A voltage drop of half the full amount, approximately 6 volts, indicates a good grid. No voltage drop (0 volts) or a drop of 12 volts indicates a break in the grid.
6 The voltmeter can be moved along the grid to pinpoint the location of the break.
7 You can repair the defogger wire by obtaining a special repair kit from an AMC dealer (or he can repair the grid for you).

18 Radio dial bulbs – replacement

1 Remove the control knobs, nuts and bezel or instrument center housing, depending on dash panel type.
2 Remove the dial cover retainers and the cover.
3 Turn the manual control shaft so that the pointer moves to the extreme left or right.
4 Remove the dial light deflector clips and deflector.
5 Remove the bulb and diffuser. Installation of the new bulb and reassembly is the reverse of the removal procedure.

19 Radio – removal and installation

1 Disconnect the cable from the negative battery terminal.
2 Remove the package tray, if so equipped.
3 Remove the ashtray and bracket, if located beneath the radio.
4 Remove the radio bezel or instrument center housing, as applicable.
5 Disconnect the antenna, speaker and power leads.
6 Unbolt and remove the radio.
7 Installation is the reverse of the removal procedure.

20 Seat belt warning system (1970 through 1973)

1 This system provides both visual and audible warnings when the following conditions exist:

The ignition switch is On
The speed selector control lever (automatic transmission) is in any position other than N or P
Column shift lever (manual transmission) is in any position except Neutral
Floor shift manual transmission parking brake has not been applied

2 Any malfunction of the system should be traced and rectified by checking the circuit fuse, the connecting wiring and switch operation. The passenger seat sensing switch requires a pressure of between 8 and 40 pounds upon the seat cushion to actuate it. The warning buzzer is located under the instrument panel to the left of the instrument cluster. A test light is most suitable for checking the circuit and components of the system.

21 Seat belt interlock system (1974 and 1975)

1 This system prevents the engine from being started unless the following conditions exist:

Driver's door closed and seat belt fastened
Passenger (if carried) door closed and seat belt fastened
Transmission control lever in Neutral or P or N (automatic transmission)

2 Once the engine has been started initially under the correct conditions, it can be restarted again even if the seat belts are unfastened, provided that the ignition is not switched off and the driver's door is not opened and closed.
3 A warning light and buzzer operate as a reminder should the transmission be in gear or a seat belt be left unfastened at an occupied front seat or fastened at an unoccupied front seat.
4 An emergency engine restart relay is located within the engine compartment. The white center button in the relay should be depressed with a pencil or key. As soon as convenient, establish the cause of the system malfunction. Testing of components is not within the scope of the home mechanic but, before seeking professional assistance, check the circuit fuse and wiring connections.

22 Seat belt warning system (1976 through 1982)

1 The seat belt warning light will turn on whenever the ignition is turned on, whether or not the driver has buckled up. The light will automatically go off after four to eight seconds.
2 The seat belt warning buzzer will not sound if the driver buckles up before the ignition is turned on. However, if the driver does not buckle up, the buzzer will sound for four to eight seconds and then automatically go off.

23 Headlight warning buzzer – general information

Available as an option, this device warns the driver that the headlights are on after the engine has been turned off and the driver's door is opened. If the buzzer malfunctions, check to see if the key alarm buzzer functions, if the vehicle is equipped with one. If the key alarm is malfunctioning also, then the buzzer is faulty and must be replaced as a unit. If the key alarm is functioning properly, check the wiring for evidence of a short circuit.

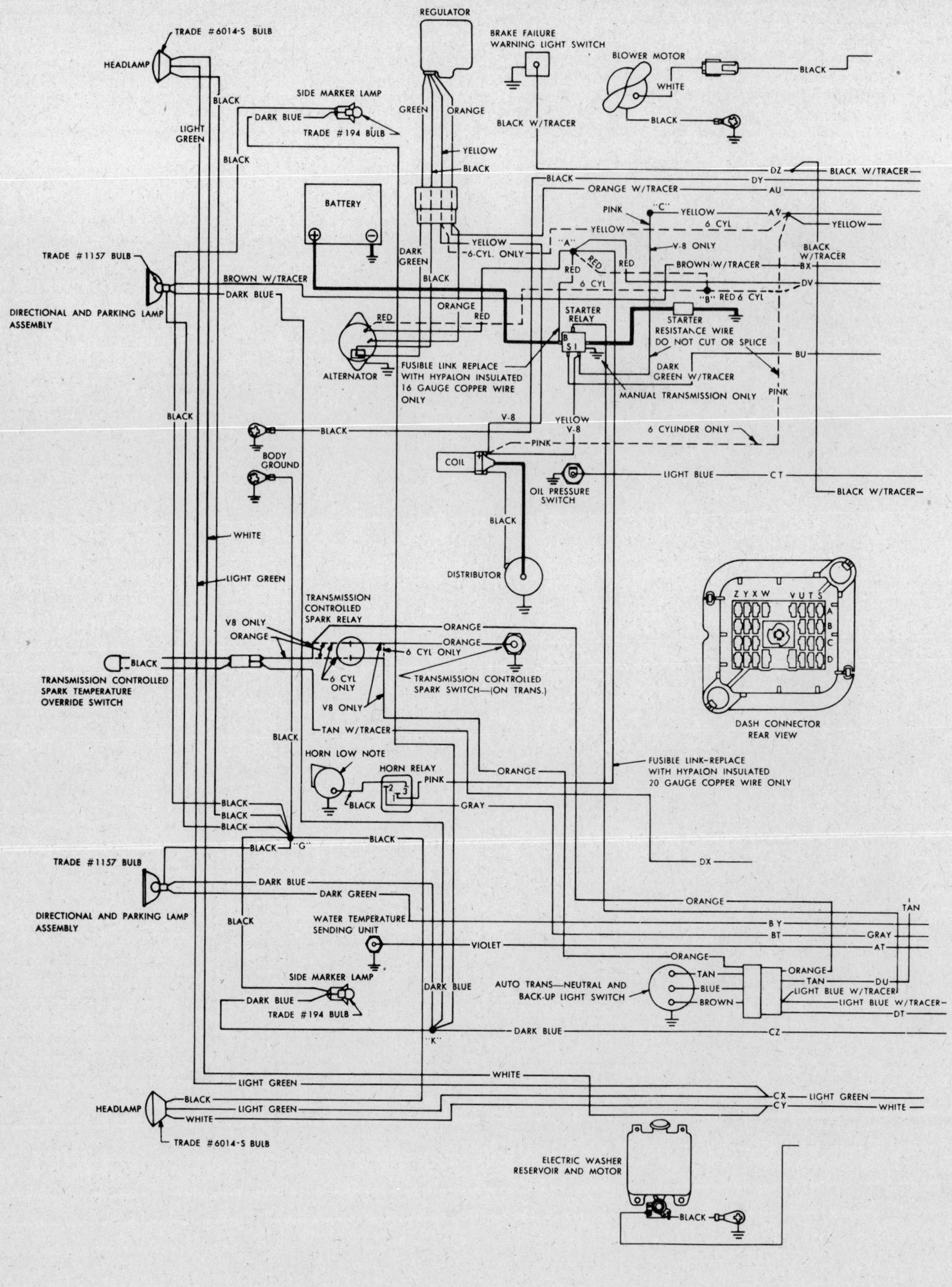

Fig. 10.8 Wiring diagram – 1970 through 1974 models (1 of 3)

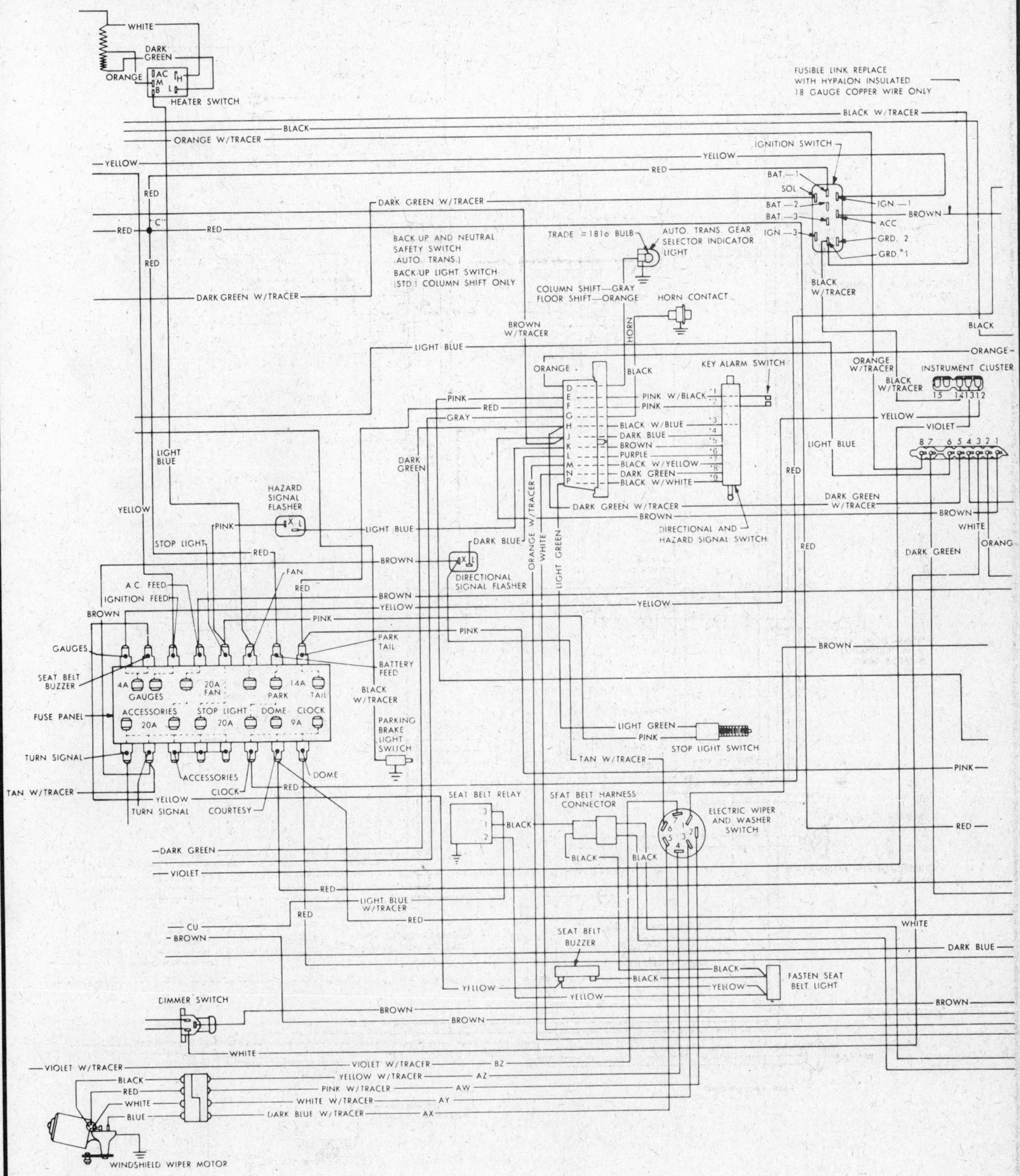

Fig. 10.9 Wiring diagram – 1970 through 1974 models (2 of 3)

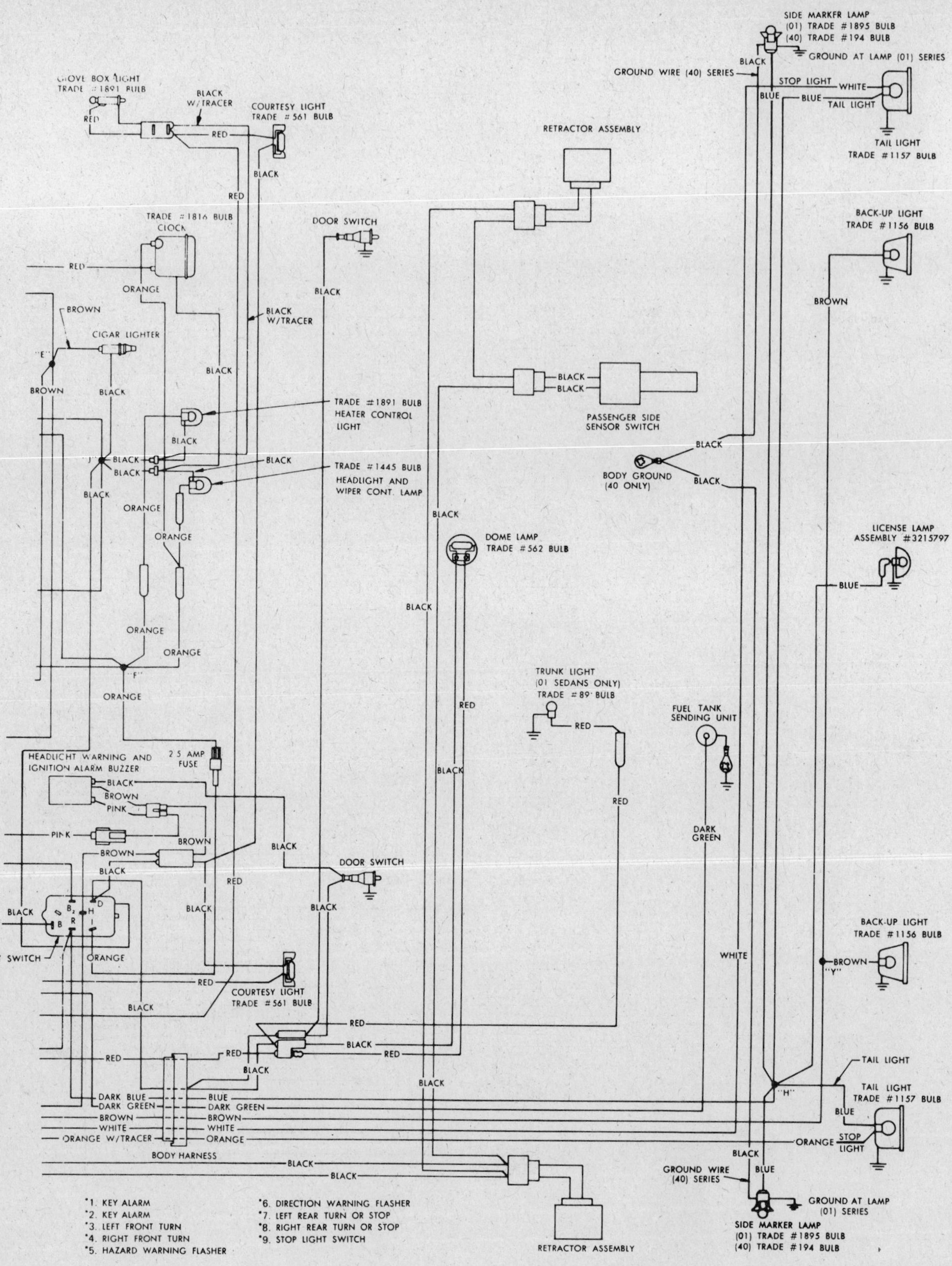

Fig. 10.10 Wiring diagram – 1970 through 1974 models (3 of 3)

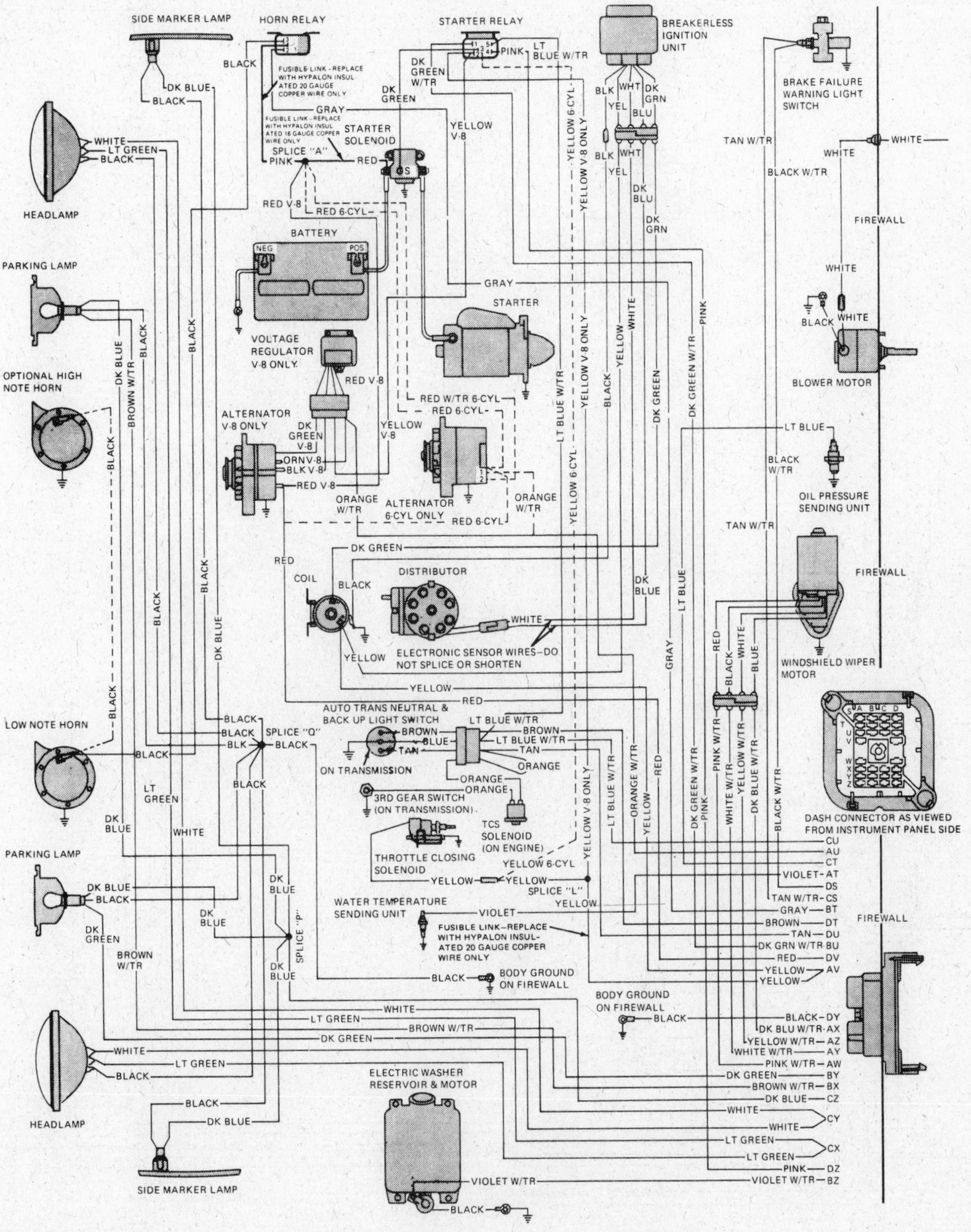

Fig. 10.11 Wiring diagram – 1975 and 1976 models (1 of 3)

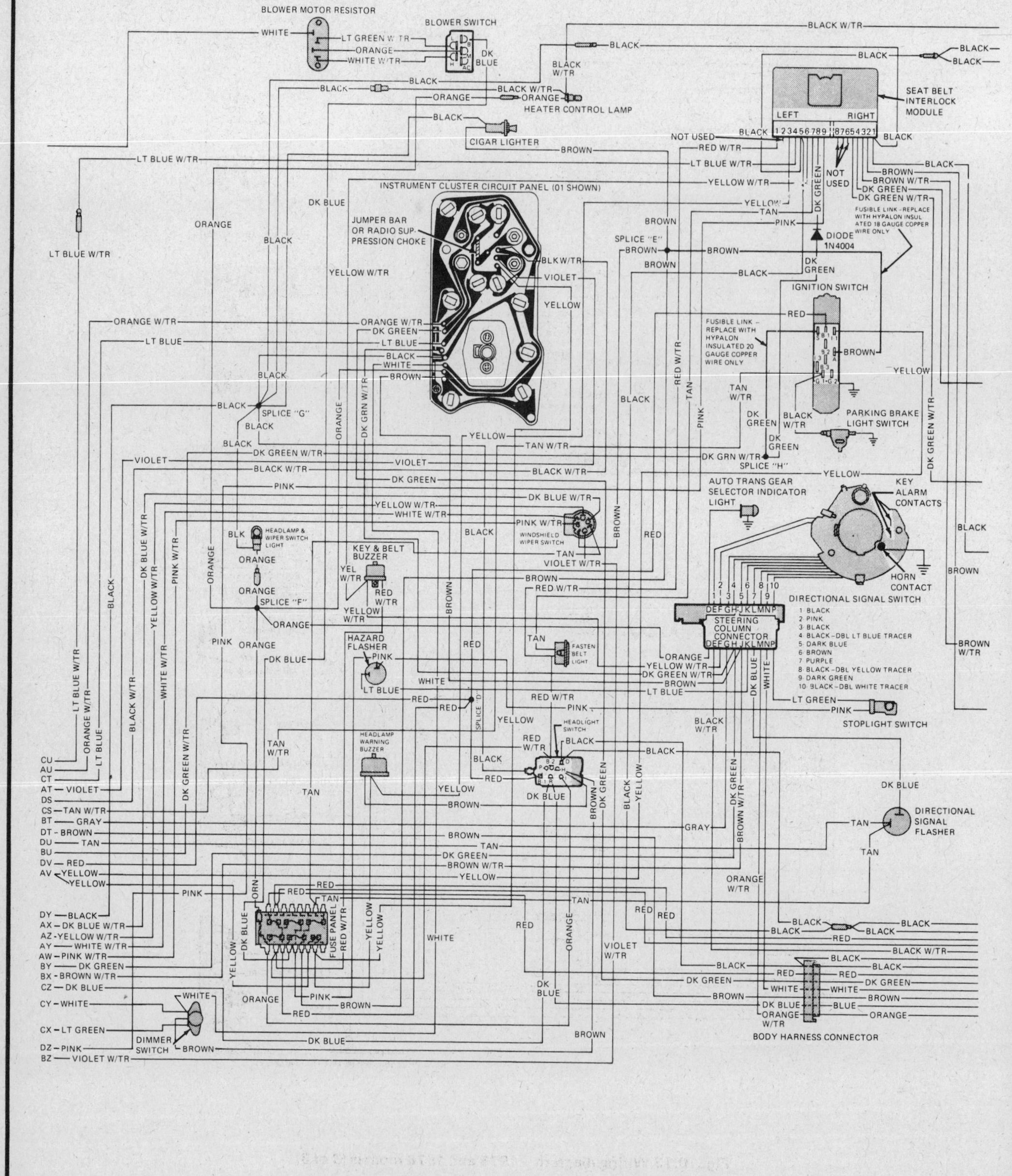

Fig. 10.12 Wiring diagram – 1975 and 1976 models (2 of 3)

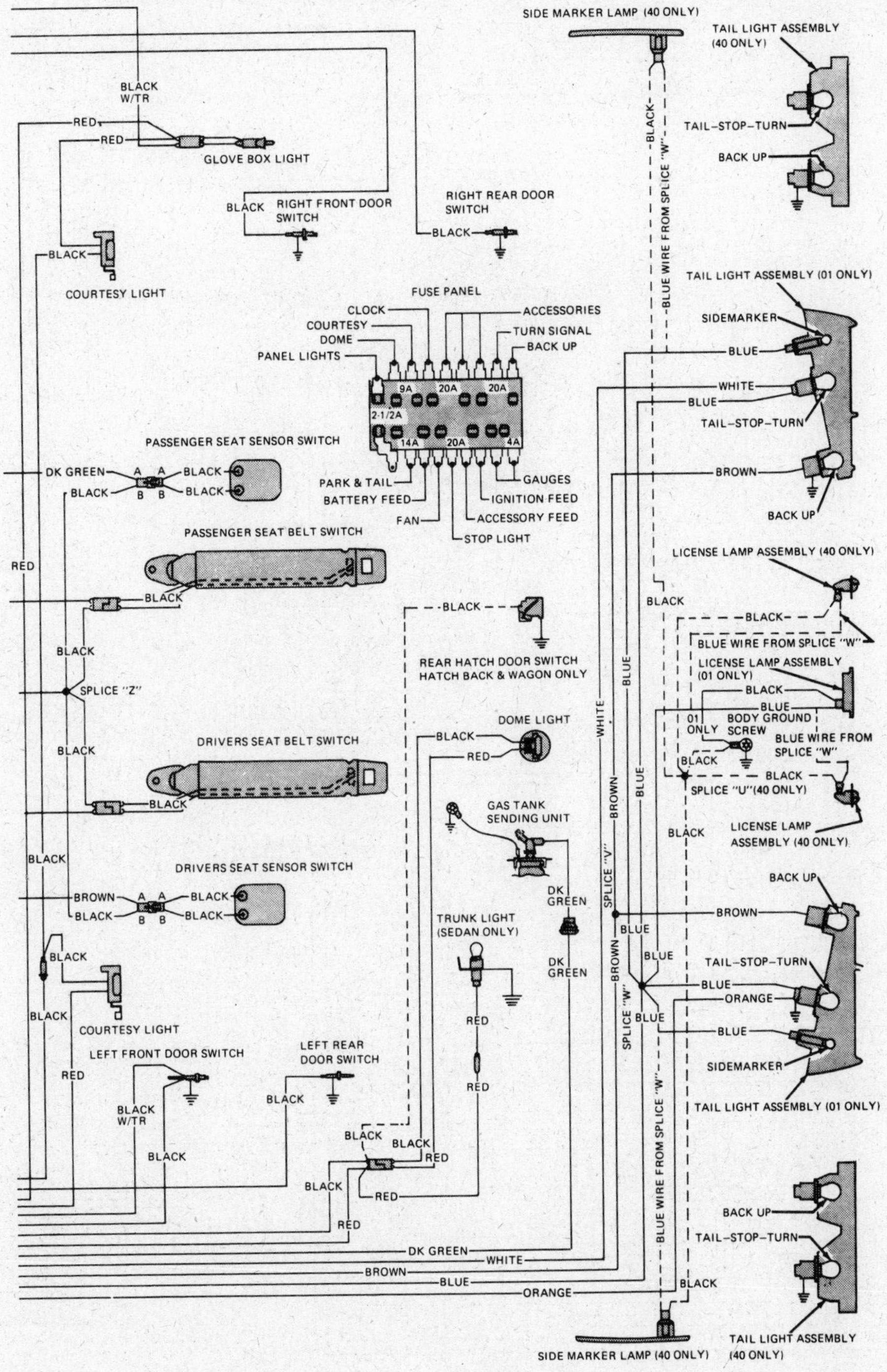

Fig. 10.13 Wiring diagram – 1975 and 1976 models (3 of 3)

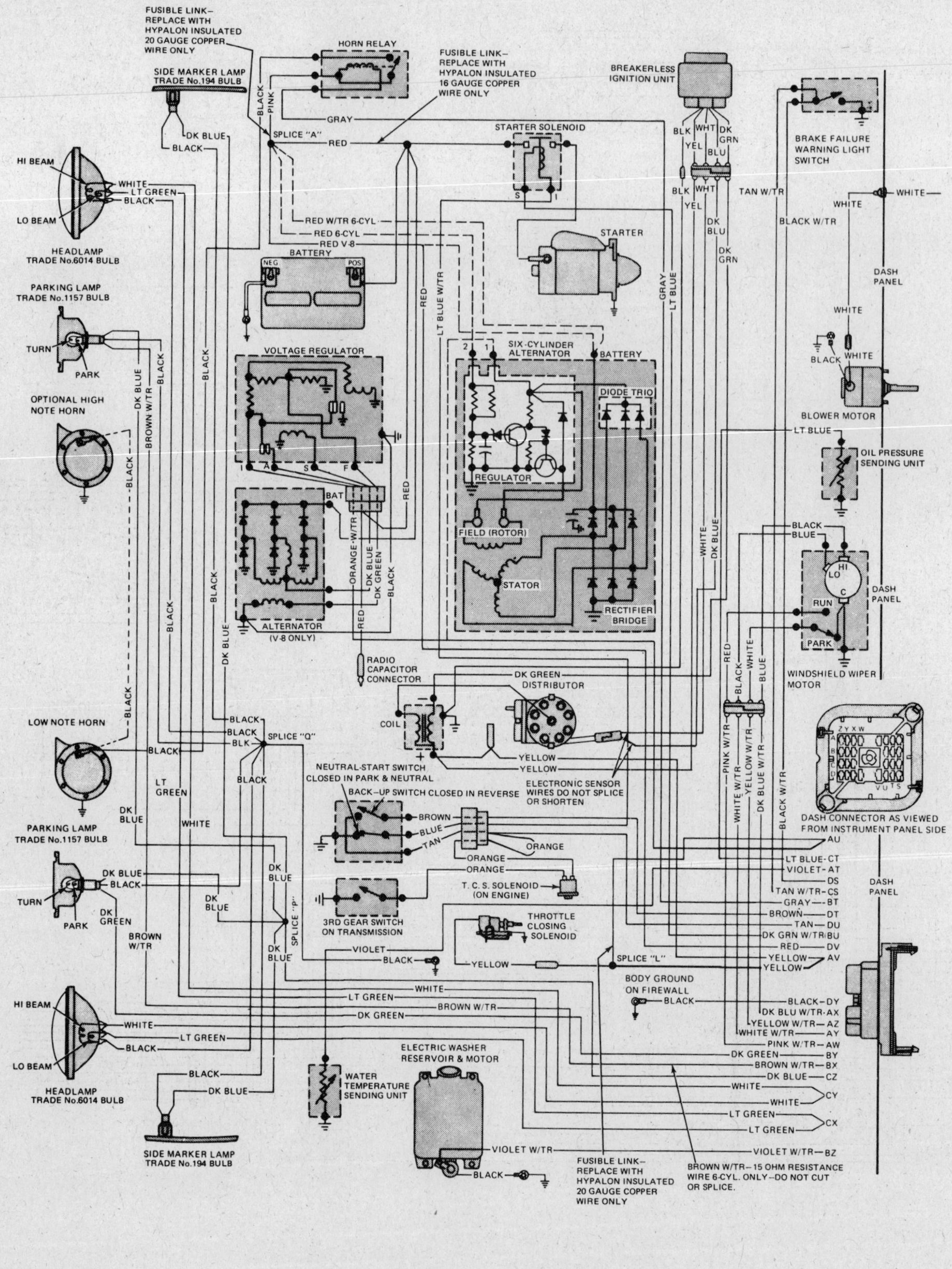
FUSIBLE LINK– REPLACE WITH HYPALON INSULATED 20 GAUGE COPPER WIRE ONLY
HORN RELAY
FUSIBLE LINK– REPLACE WITH HYPALON INSULATED 16 GAUGE COPPER WIRE ONLY
BREAKERLESS IGNITION UNIT
SIDE MARKER LAMP TRADE No.194 BULB
SPLICE "A"
STARTER SOLENOID
BRAKE FAILURE WARNING LIGHT SWITCH
HI BEAM
LO BEAM
HEADLAMP TRADE No.6014 BULB
BATTERY
STARTER
DASH PANEL
PARKING LAMP TRADE No.1157 BULB
TURN
PARK
VOLTAGE REGULATOR
SIX-CYLINDER ALTERNATOR
DIODE TRIO
BLOWER MOTOR
OPTIONAL HIGH NOTE HORN
REGULATOR
OIL PRESSURE SENDING UNIT
FIELD (ROTOR)
STATOR
RECTIFIER BRIDGE
ALTERNATOR (V-8 ONLY)
RADIO CAPACITOR CONNECTOR
WINDSHIELD WIPER MOTOR
DISTRIBUTOR
COIL
LOW NOTE HORN
SPLICE "Q"
NEUTRAL-START SWITCH CLOSED IN PARK & NEUTRAL
BACK-UP SWITCH CLOSED IN REVERSE
ELECTRONIC SENSOR WIRES DO NOT SPLICE OR SHORTEN
DASH CONNECTOR AS VIEWED FROM INSTRUMENT PANEL SIDE
T. C. S. SOLENOID (ON ENGINE)
3RD GEAR SWITCH ON TRANSMISSION
THROTTLE CLOSING SOLENOID
SPLICE "P"
SPLICE "L"
BODY GROUND ON FIREWALL
ELECTRIC WASHER RESERVOIR & MOTOR
WATER TEMPERATURE SENDING UNIT
FUSIBLE LINK– REPLACE WITH HYPALON INSULATED 20 GAUGE COPPER WIRE ONLY
BROWN W/TR– 15 OHM RESISTANCE WIRE 6-CYL. ONLY–DO NOT CUT OR SPLICE.

Fig. 10.14 Wiring diagram – 1977 models (1 of 3)

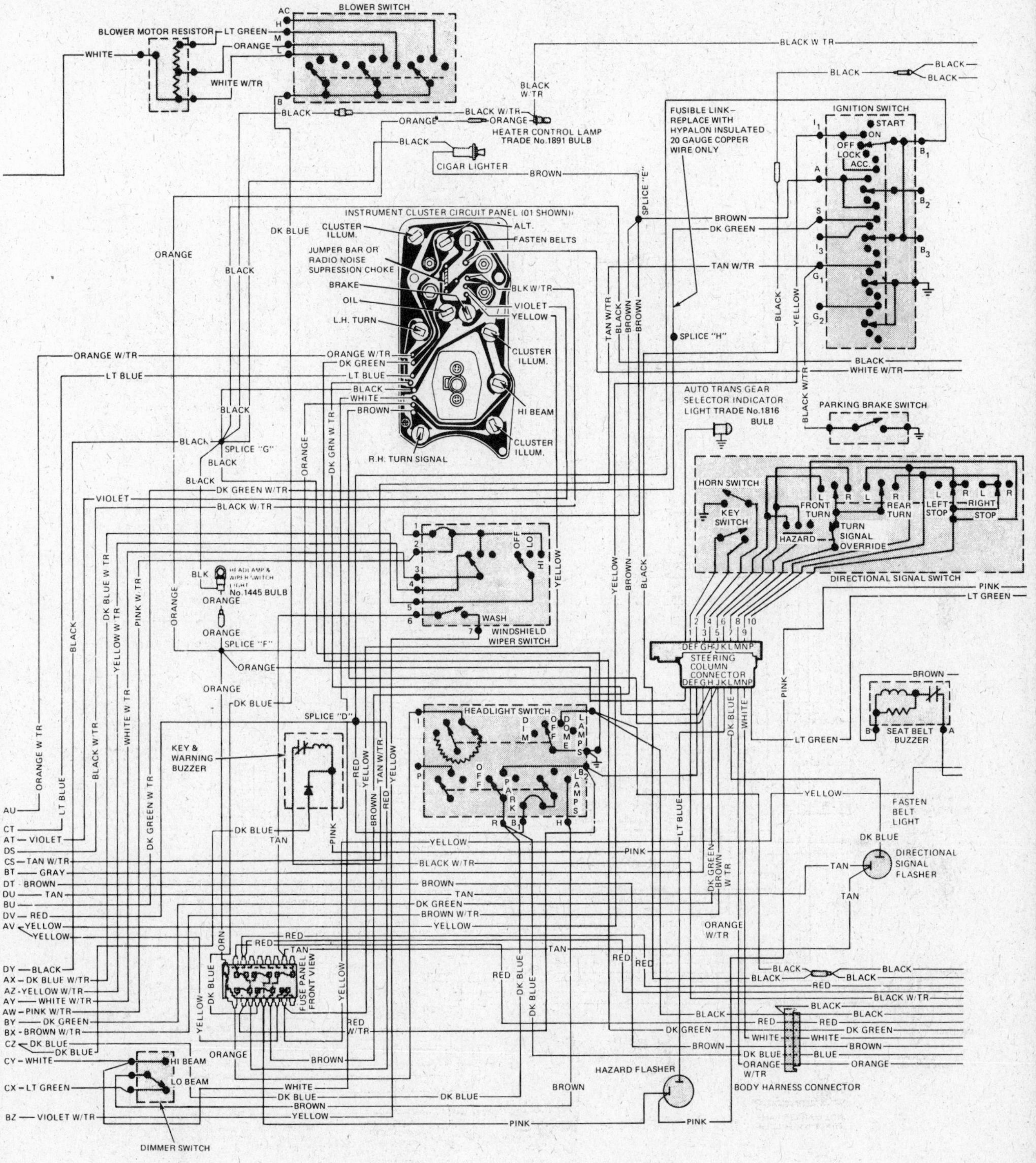

Fig. 10.15 Wiring diagram – 1977 models (2 of 3)

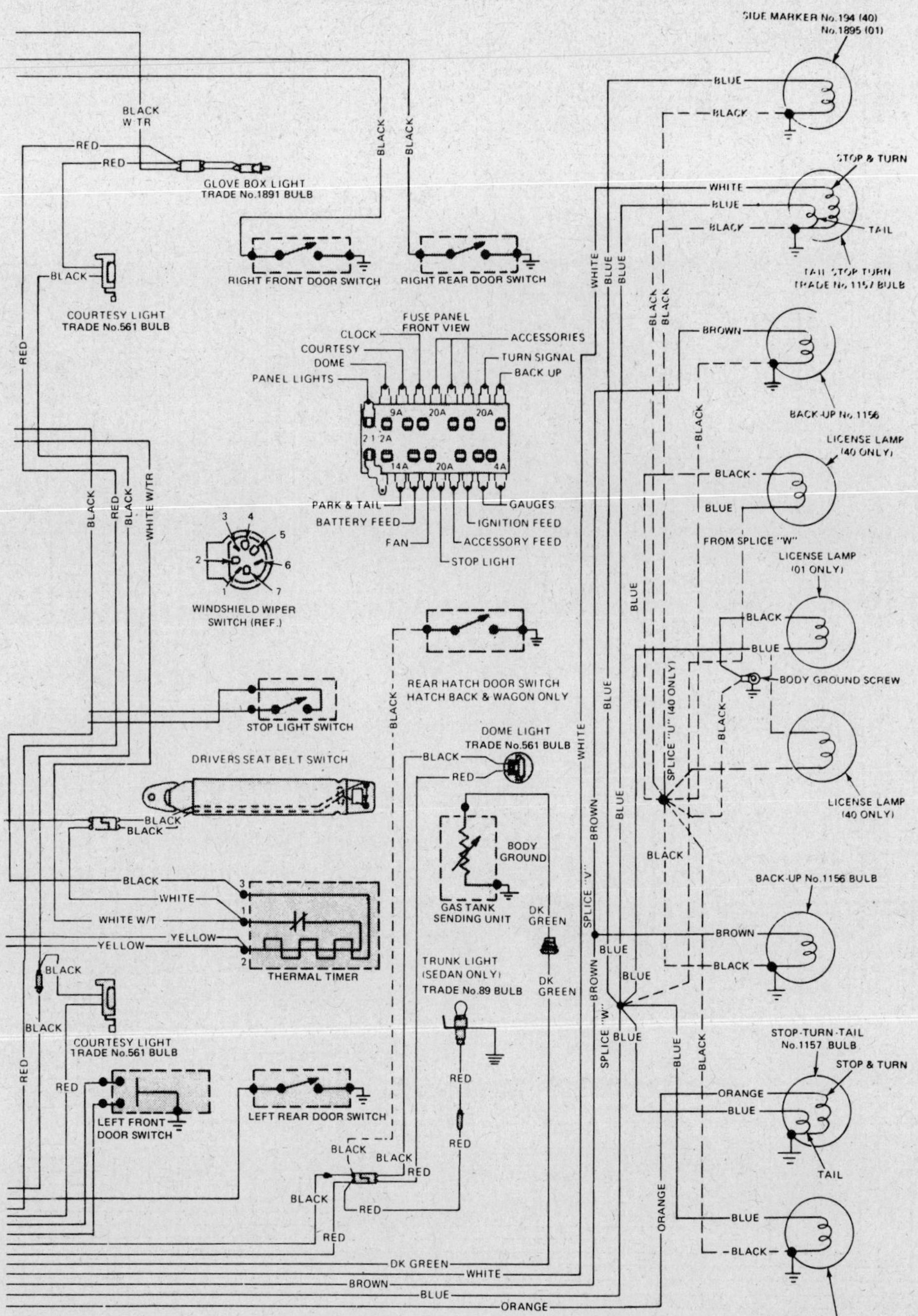

Fig. 10.16 Wiring diagram – 1977 models (3 of 3)

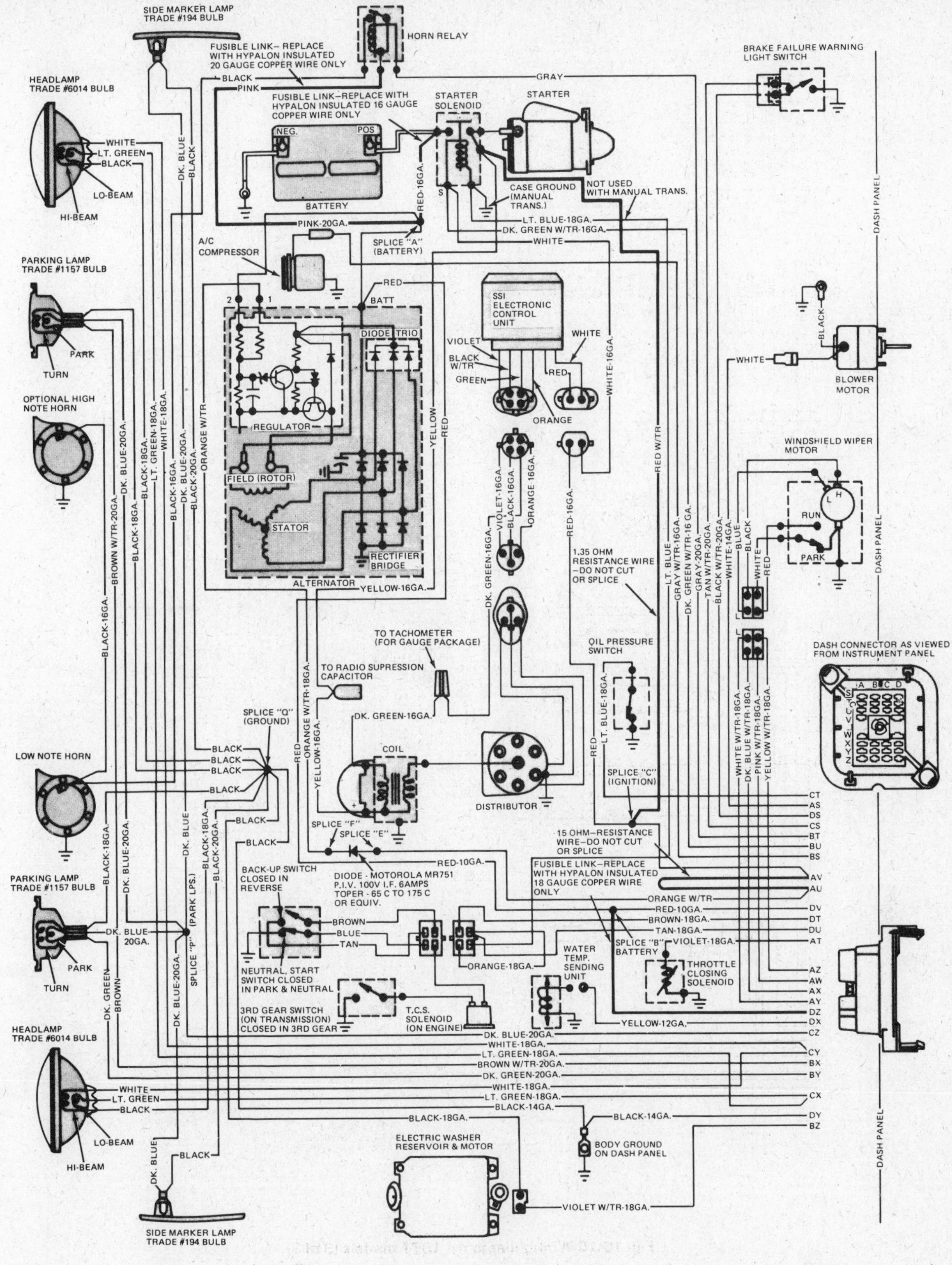
SIDE MARKER LAMP TRADE #194 BULB
HORN RELAY
FUSIBLE LINK– REPLACE WITH HYPALON INSULATED 20 GAUGE COPPER WIRE ONLY
HEADLAMP TRADE #6014 BULB
FUSIBLE LINK–REPLACE WITH HYPALON INSULATED 16 GAUGE COPPER WIRE ONLY
STARTER SOLENOID
STARTER
BRAKE FAILURE WARNING LIGHT SWITCH
BATTERY
CASE GROUND (MANUAL TRANS.)
NOT USED WITH MANUAL TRANS.
LO-BEAM
HI-BEAM
SPLICE "A" (BATTERY)
A/C COMPRESSOR
PARKING LAMP TRADE #1157 BULB
PARK
TURN
SSI ELECTRONIC CONTROL UNIT
DIODE TRIO
REGULATOR
BLOWER MOTOR
OPTIONAL HIGH NOTE HORN
WINDSHIELD WIPER MOTOR
FIELD (ROTOR)
STATOR
RECTIFIER BRIDGE
ALTERNATOR
RUN
1.35 OHM RESISTANCE WIRE –DO NOT CUT OR SPLICE
TO TACHOMETER (FOR GAUGE PACKAGE)
OIL PRESSURE SWITCH
DASH CONNECTOR AS VIEWED FROM INSTRUMENT PANEL
TO RADIO SUPRESSION CAPACITOR
SPLICE "Q" (GROUND)
COIL
LOW NOTE HORN
DISTRIBUTOR
SPLICE "C" (IGNITION)
15 OHM–RESISTANCE WIRE–DO NOT CUT OR SPLICE
SPLICE "F"
SPLICE "E"
DIODE - MOTOROLA MR751 P.I.V. 100V I.F. 6AMPS TOPER - 65 C TO 175 C OR EQUIV.
FUSIBLE LINK–REPLACE WITH HYPALON INSULATED 18 GAUGE COPPER WIRE ONLY
BACK-UP SWITCH CLOSED IN REVERSE
SPLICE "P" (PARK LPS.)
SPLICE "B" BATTERY
NEUTRAL, START SWITCH CLOSED IN PARK & NEUTRAL
WATER TEMP. SENDING UNIT
THROTTLE CLOSING SOLENOID
3RD GEAR SWITCH (ON TRANSMISSION) CLOSED IN 3RD GEAR
T.C.S. SOLENOID (ON ENGINE)
BODY GROUND ON DASH PANEL
ELECTRIC WASHER RESERVOIR & MOTOR
DASH PANEL

Fig. 10.17 Ignition system wiring diagram – 1978 and 1979 six-cylinder models only

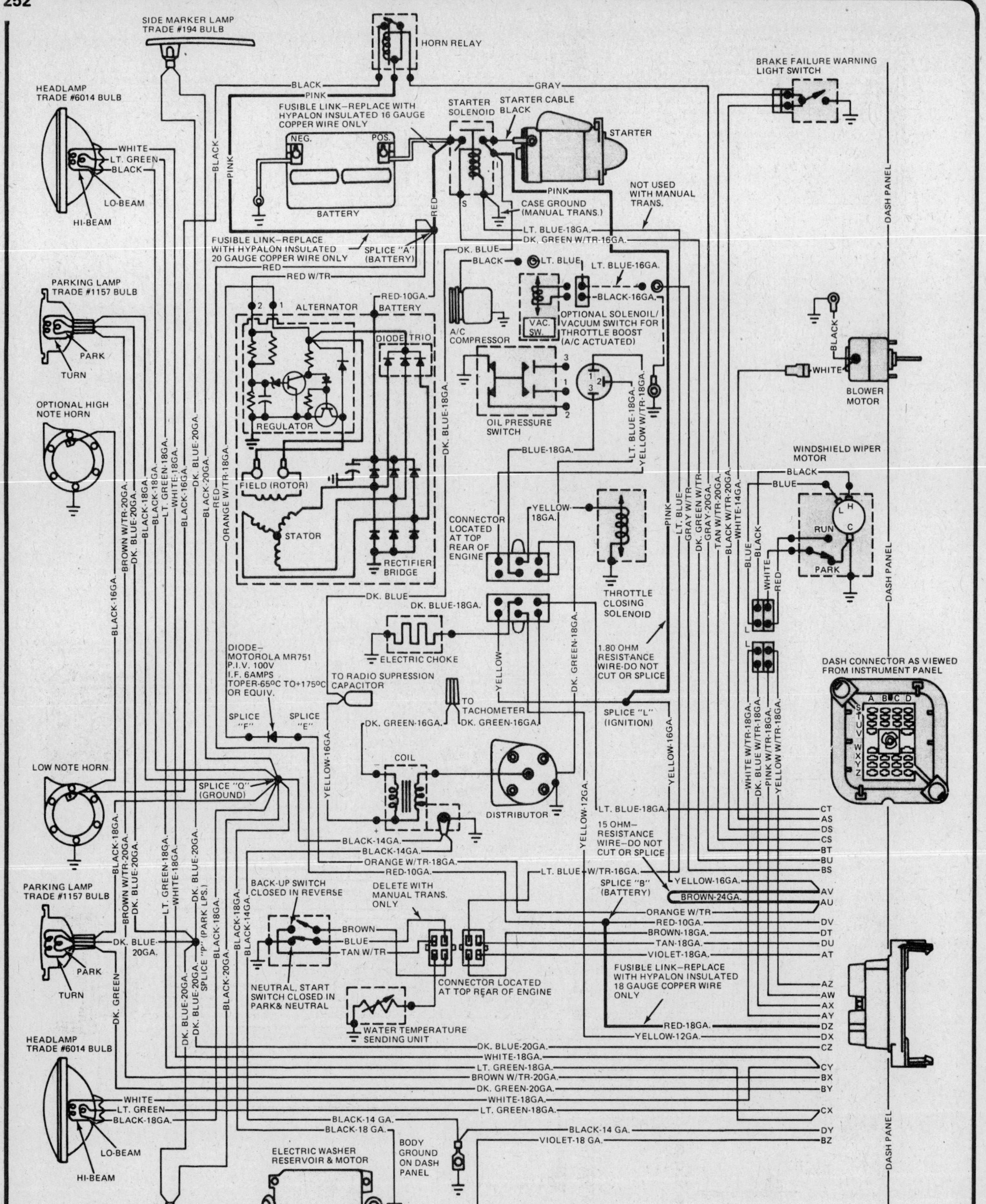
SIDE MARKER LAMP TRADE #194 BULB
HORN RELAY
HEADLAMP TRADE #6014 BULB
WHITE
LT. GREEN
BLACK
LO-BEAM
HI-BEAM
BLACK
PINK
GRAY
FUSIBLE LINK–REPLACE WITH HYPALON INSULATED 16 GAUGE COPPER WIRE ONLY
STARTER SOLENOID
STARTER CABLE BLACK
STARTER
NEG.
POS.
BATTERY
S
PINK
CASE GROUND (MANUAL TRANS.)
NOT USED WITH MANUAL TRANS.
BRAKE FAILURE WARNING LIGHT SWITCH
DASH PANEL
FUSIBLE LINK–REPLACE WITH HYPALON INSULATED 20 GAUGE COPPER WIRE ONLY
SPLICE "A" (BATTERY)
RED
RED W/TR
LT. BLUE-18GA.
DK. GREEN W/TR-16GA.
DK. BLUE
BLACK
LT. BLUE
LT. BLUE-16GA.
BLACK-16GA.
RED-10GA.
BATTERY
ALTERNATOR
DIODE TRIO
REGULATOR
FIELD (ROTOR)
STATOR
RECTIFIER BRIDGE
A/C COMPRESSOR
VAC. SW.
OPTIONAL SOLENOIL/ VACUUM SWITCH FOR THROTTLE BOOST (A/C ACTUATED)
OIL PRESSURE SWITCH
BLUE-18GA.
LT. BLUE-18GA.
YELLOW W/TR-18GA.
BLOWER MOTOR
WINDSHIELD WIPER MOTOR
RUN
PARK
PARKING LAMP TRADE #1157 BULB
PARK
TURN
OPTIONAL HIGH NOTE HORN
YELLOW-18GA.
CONNECTOR LOCATED AT TOP REAR OF ENGINE
THROTTLE CLOSING SOLENOID
DK. BLUE
DK. BLUE-18GA.
ELECTRIC CHOKE
1.80 OHM RESISTANCE WIRE-DO NOT CUT OR SPLICE
DASH CONNECTOR AS VIEWED FROM INSTRUMENT PANEL
DIODE– MOTOROLA MR751 P.I.V. 100V I.F. 6AMPS TOPER-65°C TO+175°C OR EQUIV.
TO RADIO SUPRESSION CAPACITOR
SPLICE "F"
SPLICE "E"
TO TACHOMETER
DK. GREEN-16GA.
SPLICE "L" (IGNITION)
COIL
DISTRIBUTOR
LOW NOTE HORN
SPLICE "Q" (GROUND)
LT. BLUE-18GA.
15 OHM– RESISTANCE WIRE–DO NOT CUT OR SPLICE
BLACK-14GA.
ORANGE W/TR-18GA.
RED-10GA.
LT. BLUE W/TR-16GA.
YELLOW-16GA.
SPLICE "B" (BATTERY)
BROWN-24GA.
ORANGE W/TR
RED-10GA.
BROWN-18GA.
TAN-18GA.
VIOLET-18GA.
BACK-UP SWITCH CLOSED IN REVERSE
DELETE WITH MANUAL TRANS. ONLY
BROWN
BLUE
TAN W/TR
NEUTRAL, START SWITCH CLOSED IN PARK& NEUTRAL
CONNECTOR LOCATED AT TOP REAR OF ENGINE
WATER TEMPERATURE SENDING UNIT
FUSIBLE LINK–REPLACE WITH HYPALON INSULATED 18 GAUGE COPPER WIRE ONLY
RED-18GA.
YELLOW-12GA.
DK. BLUE-20GA.
WHITE-18GA.
LT. GREEN-18GA.
BROWN W/TR-20GA.
DK. GREEN-20GA.
BLACK-14 GA.
BLACK-18 GA.
VIOLET-18 GA.
BODY GROUND ON DASH PANEL
ELECTRIC WASHER RESERVOIR & MOTOR
SPLICE "P" (PARK LPS.)
CT
AS
DS
CS
BT
BU
BS
AV
AU
DV
DT
DU
AT
AZ
AW
AX
AY
DZ
DX
CZ
CY
BX
BY
CX
DY
BZ

Fig. 10.18 Ignition system wiring diagram – 1978 and 1979 four-cylinder models only

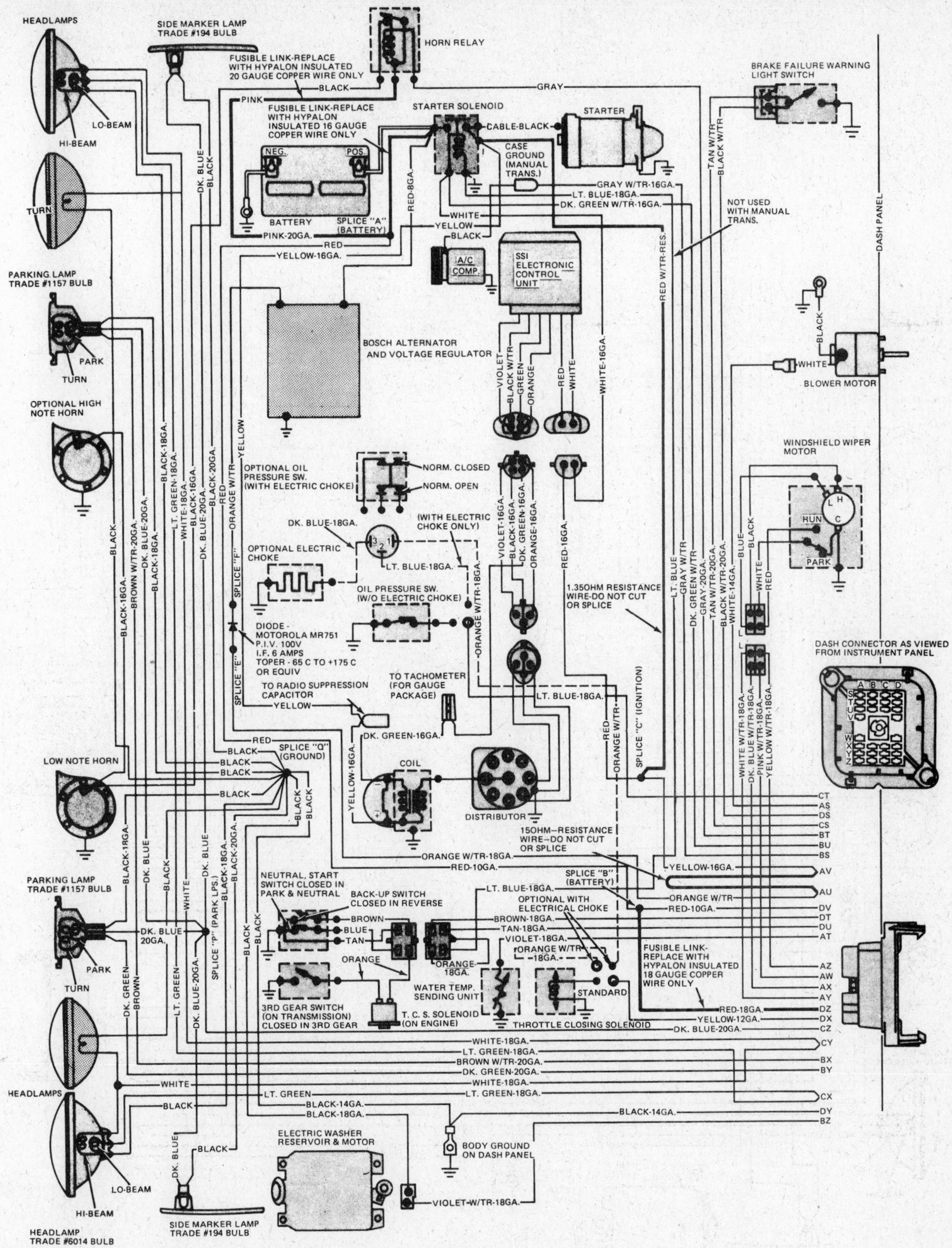
HEADLAMPS
SIDE MARKER LAMP TRADE #194 BULB
HORN RELAY
FUSIBLE LINK-REPLACE WITH HYPALON INSULATED 20 GAUGE COPPER WIRE ONLY
FUSIBLE LINK-REPLACE WITH HYPALON INSULATED 16 GAUGE COPPER WIRE ONLY
STARTER SOLENOID
STARTER
BRAKE FAILURE WARNING LIGHT SWITCH
BATTERY
SPLICE "A" (BATTERY)
CASE GROUND (MANUAL TRANS.)
NOT USED WITH MANUAL TRANS.
SSI ELECTRONIC CONTROL UNIT
A/C COMP.
PARKING LAMP TRADE #1157 BULB
BOSCH ALTERNATOR AND VOLTAGE REGULATOR
BLOWER MOTOR
DASH PANEL
OPTIONAL HIGH NOTE HORN
OPTIONAL OIL PRESSURE SW. (WITH ELECTRIC CHOKE)
NORM. CLOSED
NORM. OPEN
WINDSHIELD WIPER MOTOR
OPTIONAL ELECTRIC CHOKE
(WITH ELECTRIC CHOKE ONLY)
OIL PRESSURE SW. (W/O ELECTRIC CHOKE)
1.35OHM RESISTANCE WIRE-DO NOT CUT OR SPLICE
DIODE - MOTOROLA MR751 P.I.V. 100V I.F. 6 AMPS TOPER - 65 C TO +175 C OR EQUIV
DASH CONNECTOR AS VIEWED FROM INSTRUMENT PANEL
TO RADIO SUPPRESSION CAPACITOR
TO TACHOMETER (FOR GAUGE PACKAGE)
SPLICE "Q" (GROUND)
LOW NOTE HORN
COIL
DISTRIBUTOR
SPLICE "C" (IGNITION)
15OHM-RESISTANCE WIRE-DO NOT CUT OR SPLICE
SPLICE "B" (BATTERY)
NEUTRAL, START SWITCH CLOSED IN PARK & NEUTRAL
BACK-UP SWITCH CLOSED IN REVERSE
OPTIONAL WITH ELECTRICAL CHOKE
SPLICE "P" (PARK LPS.)
3RD GEAR SWITCH (ON TRANSMISSION) CLOSED IN 3RD GEAR
WATER TEMP. SENDING UNIT
T. C. S. SOLENOID (ON ENGINE)
STANDARD
THROTTLE CLOSING SOLENOID
FUSIBLE LINK-REPLACE WITH HYPALON INSULATED 18 GAUGE COPPER WIRE ONLY
ELECTRIC WASHER RESERVOIR & MOTOR
BODY GROUND ON DASH PANEL
HEADLAMP TRADE #6014 BULB
LO-BEAM
HI-BEAM
TURN
PARK

Fig. 10.19 Ignition system wiring diagram – 1978 and 1979 V8 models only

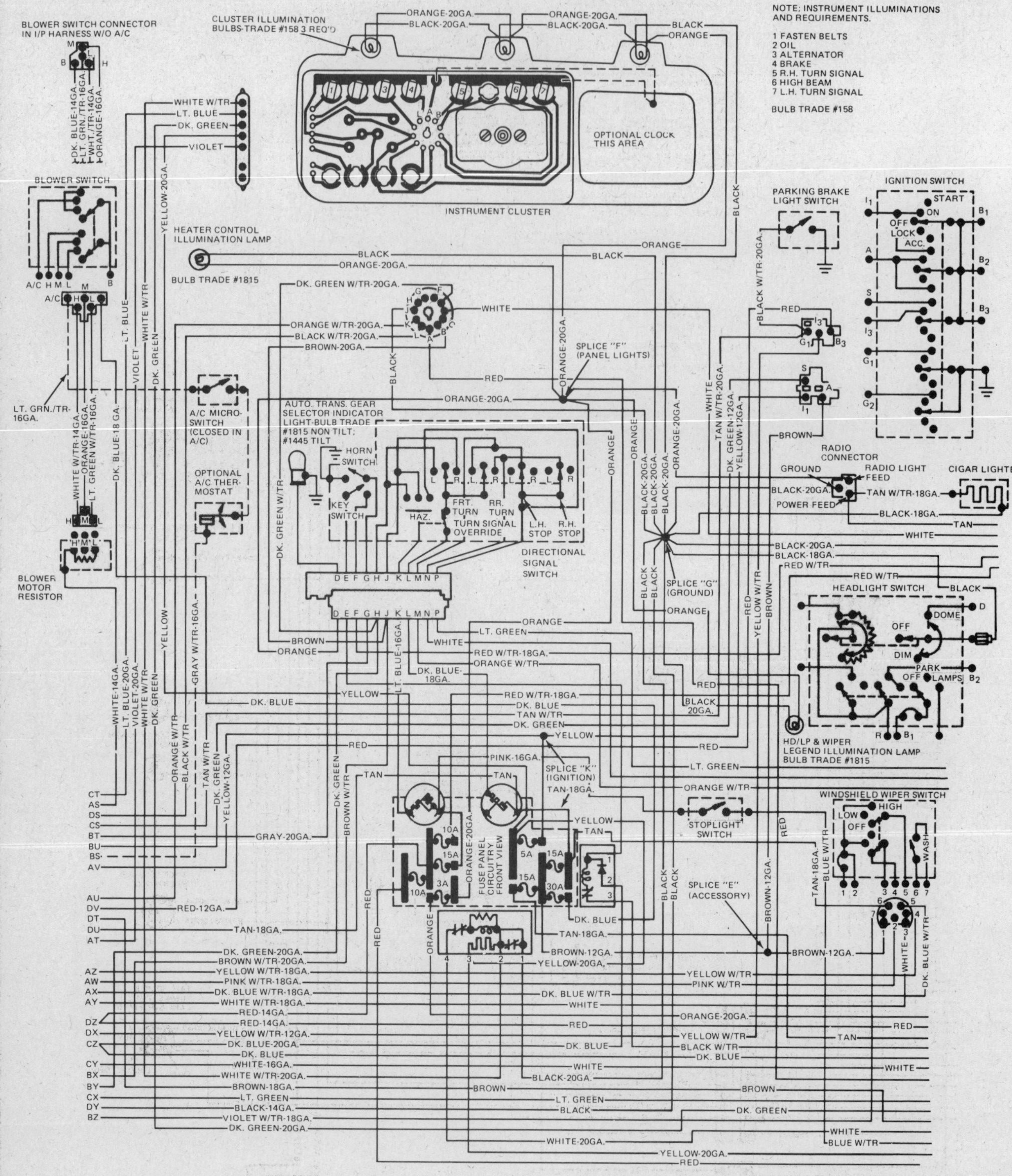

Fig. 10.20 Wiring diagram – 1978 and 1979 (all models) (1 of 2)

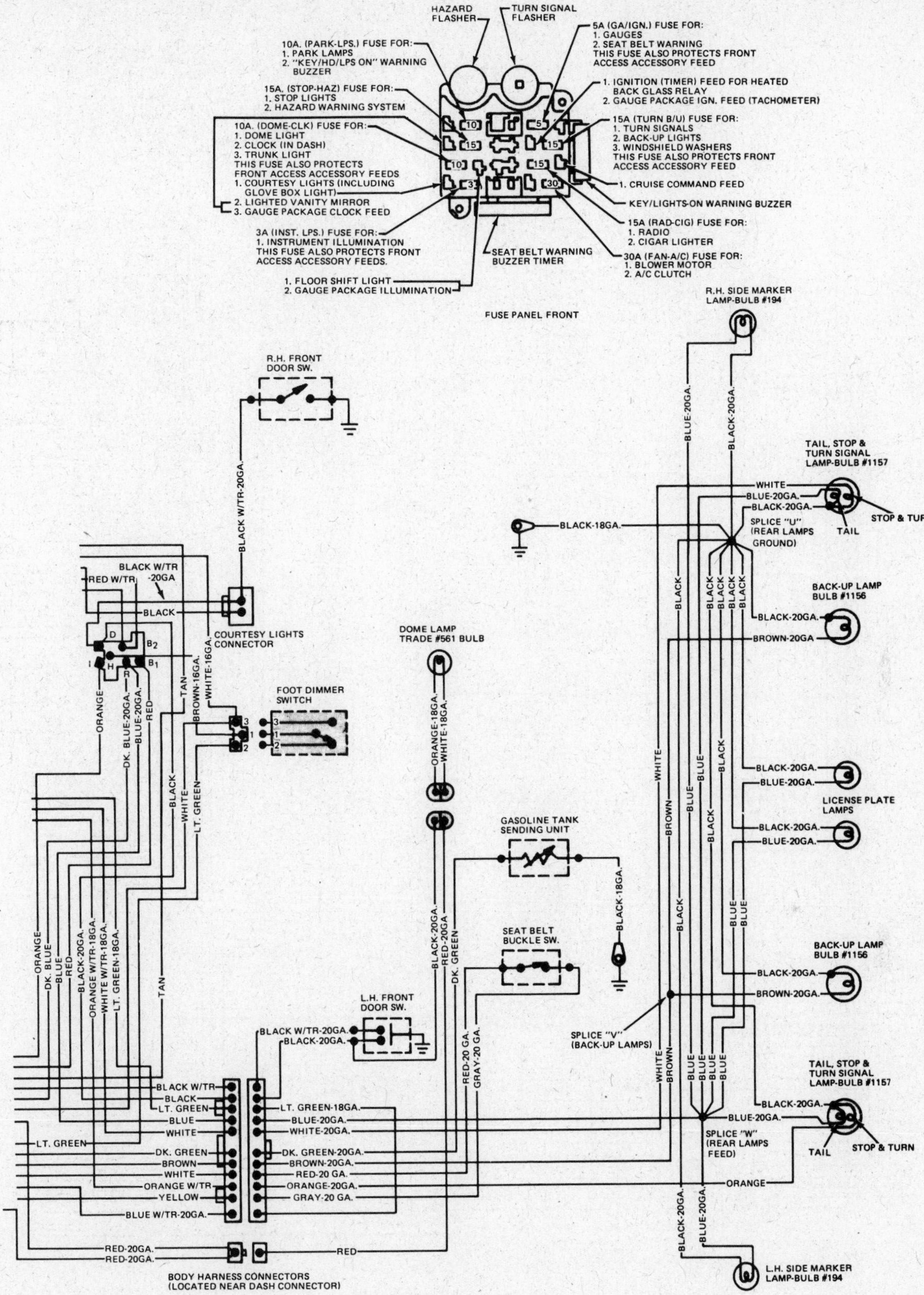

Fig. 10.21 Wiring diagram – 1978 and 1979 (all models) (2 of 2)

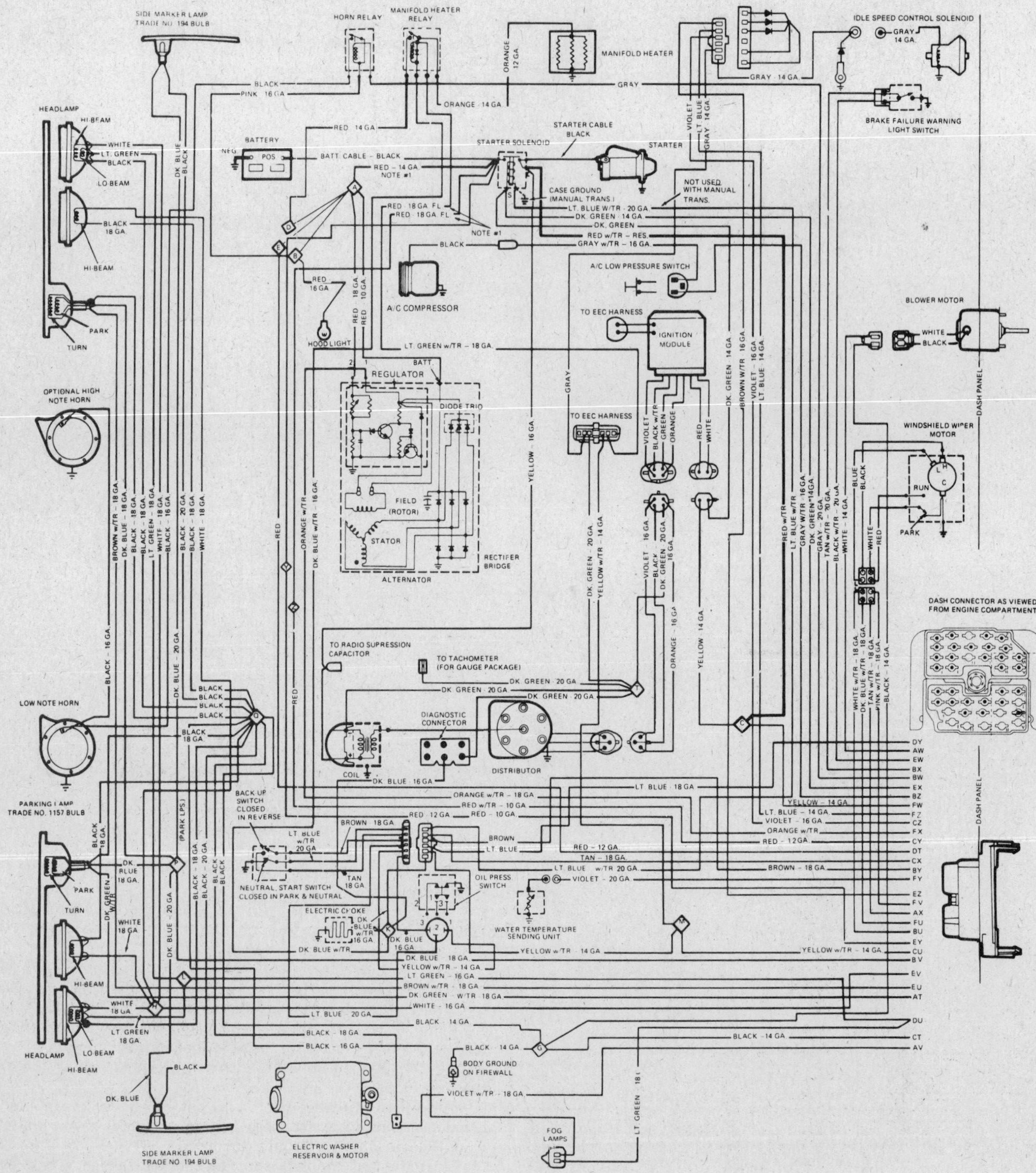

Fig. 10.22 Ignition system wiring diagram – 1980 through 1982 six-cylinder models only

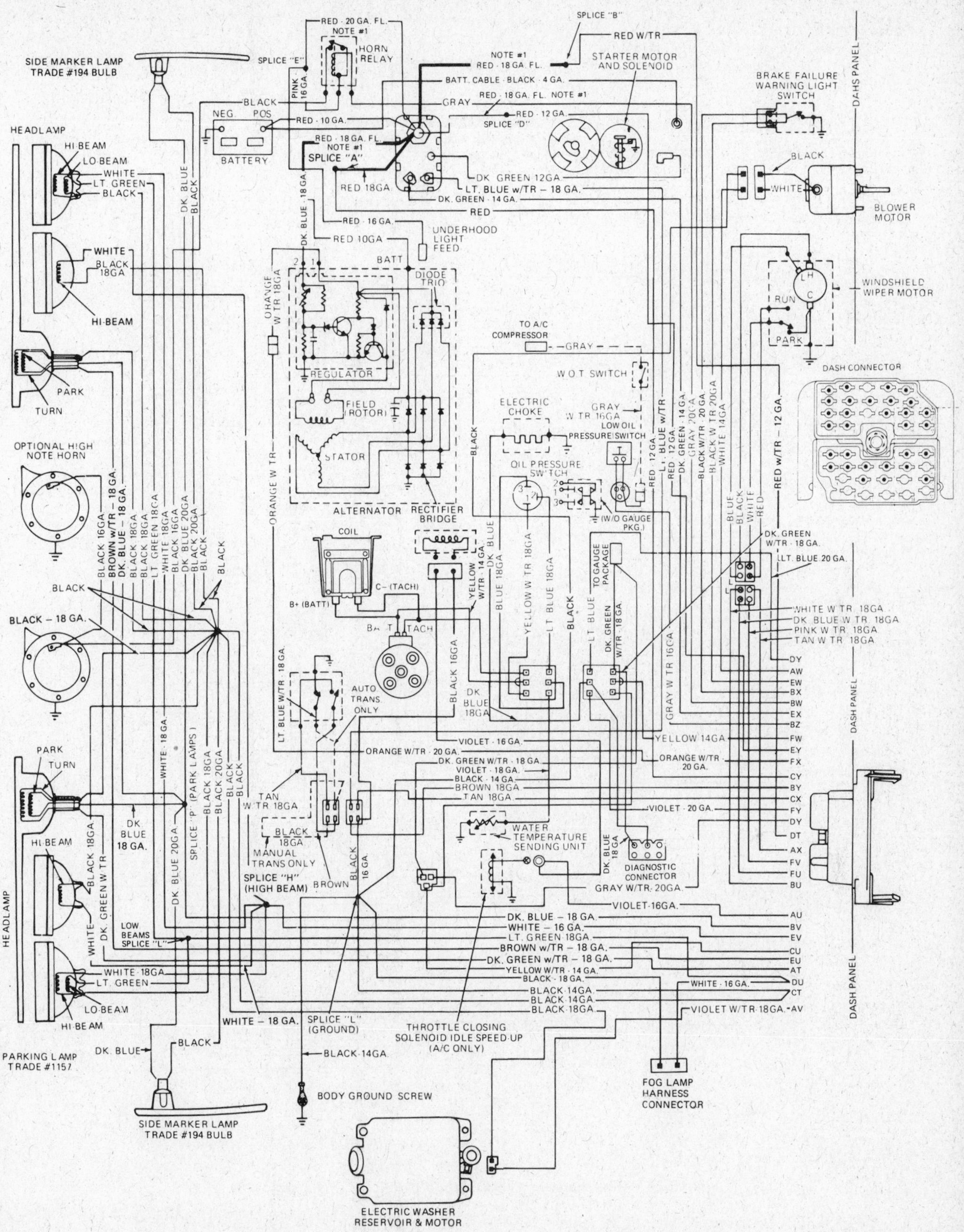

Fig. 10.23 Ignition system wiring diagram – 1980 through 1982 four-cylinder models only

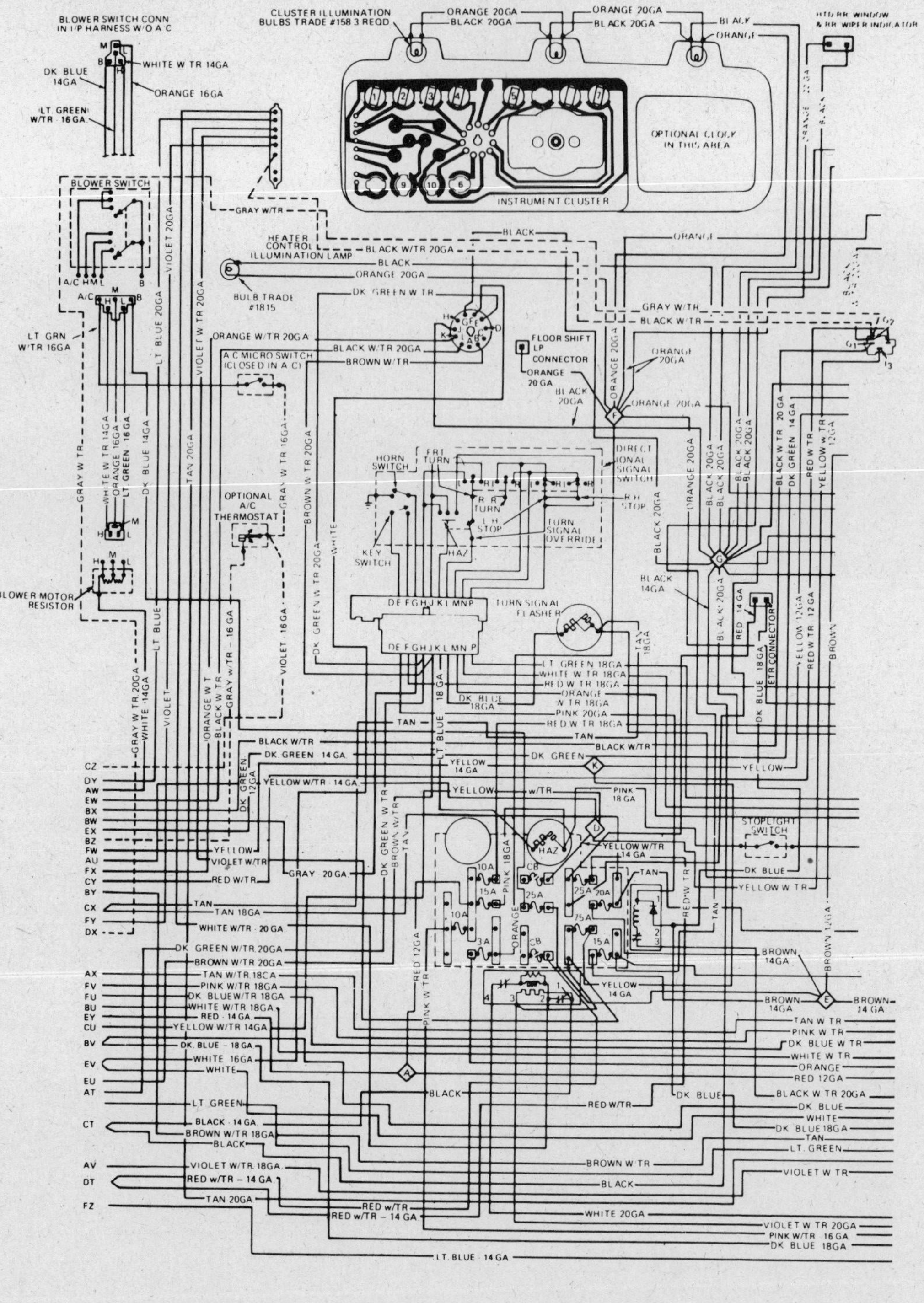

Fig. 10.24 Wiring diagram – 1980 through 1982 (all models) (1 of 3)

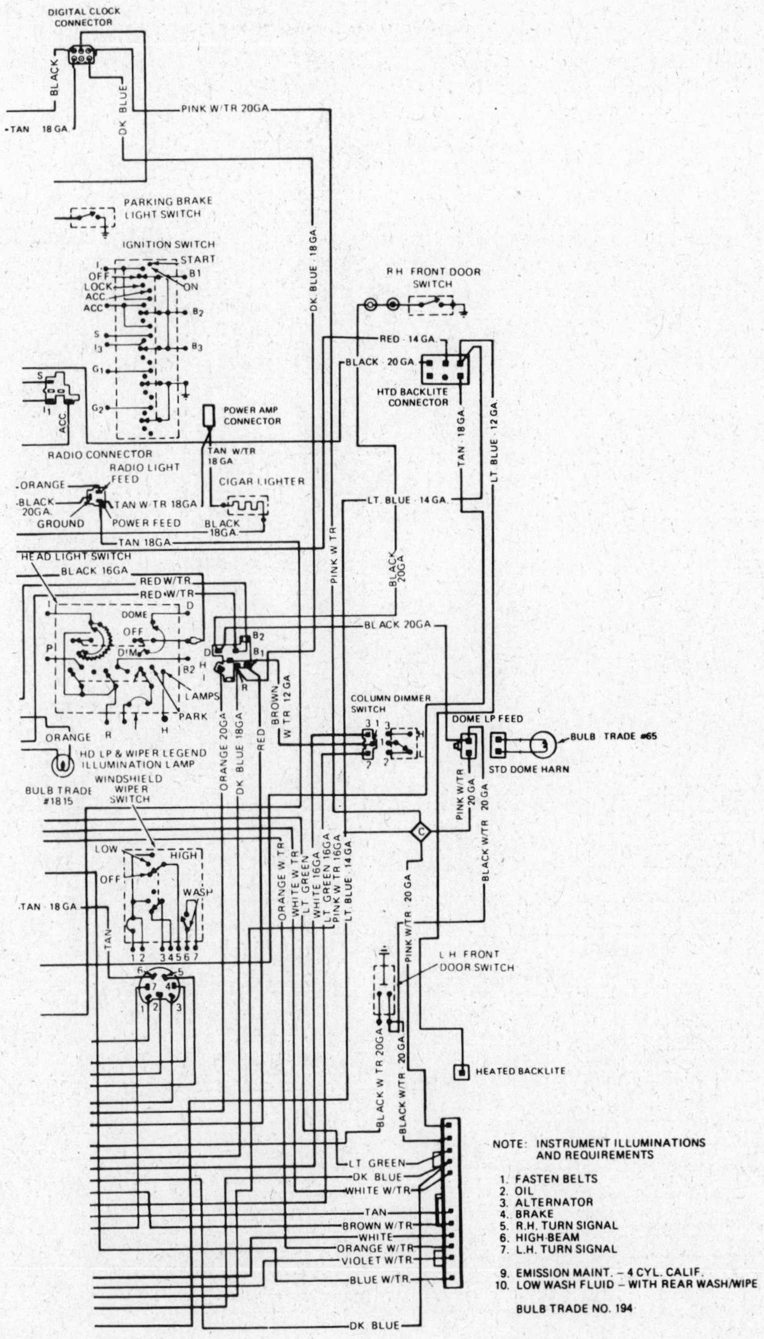

Fig. 10.25 Wiring diagram – 1980 through 1982 (all models) (2 of 3)

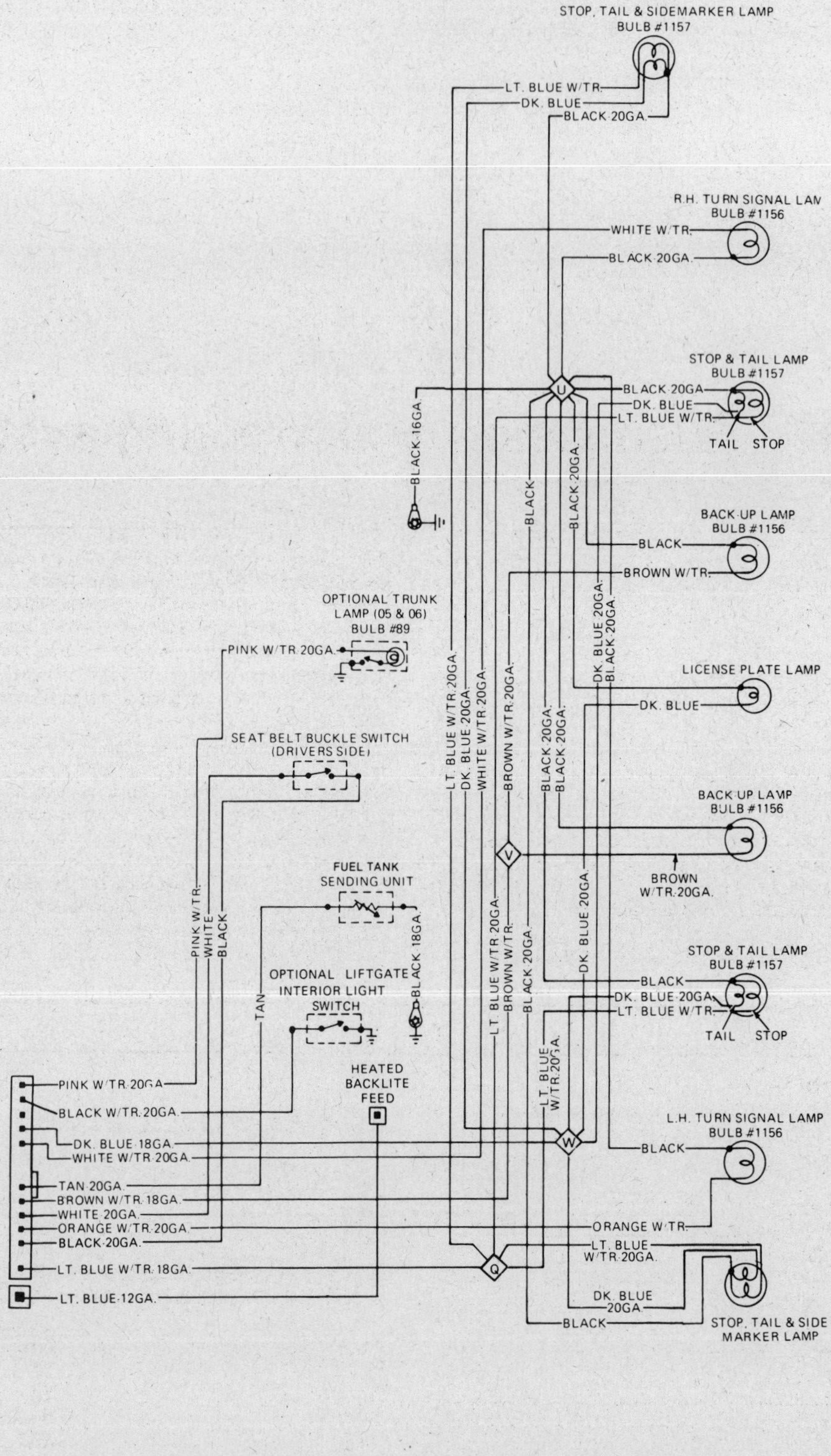

Fig. 10.26 Wiring diagram – 1980 through 1982 (all models) (3 of 3)

Chapter 11 Suspension and steering systems

Contents

Chassis lubrication .... See Chapter 1
Front coil springs – removal and installation 13
Front shock absorbers – removal and installation 4
General information 1
Idler arm – removal and installation 9
Lower control arm – removal and installation 15
Manual steering gear – in-vehicle service and repair 19
Manual steering gear – maintenance and adjustment 18
Manual steering gear – overhaul 21
Manual steering gear – removal and installation 20
Pitman arm – removal and installation 10
Power steering – in-vehicle service and repair 28
Power steering fluid level check .... See Chapter 1
Power steering gear and pump – removal and installation 29
Power steering hydraulic system – bleeding 30
Power steering system – inspection and maintenance 27
Rear shock absorbers – removal and installation 5
Rear spring – disassembly, inspection and reassembly 17
Rear spring – removal and installation 16
Stabilizer bar – removal and installation 6
Steering column – removal and installation 23
Steering column (standard type) – overhaul 24
Steering column (tilt-type with column shift) – overhaul 25
Steering column (tilt-type with floor shift) – overhaul 26
Steering knuckle – removal and installation 11
Steering linkage and balljoints – removal and installation 8
Steering wheel – removal and installation 22
Strut rod – removal and installation 7
Suspension and steering check .... See Chapter 1
Suspension balljoints – removal and installation 12
Tire and tire presure checks .... See Chapter 1
Tire rotation .... See Chapter 1
Upper control arm – removal and installation 14
Wheel alignment – general information 3
Wheel bearing check and service .... See Chapter 1
Wheels – inspection 2

Specifications

Manual steering system

Wormshaft thrust bearing preload	5 to 8 in-lb
Pitman shaft overcenter preload	4 to 10 in-lb (in addition to above)
Total steering gear preload	16 in-lb (max.)

Power steering system

Power steering wormshaft thrust bearing preload	4 to 10 in-lb
Pitman shaft overcenter preload	
New gear (less than 400 miles)	4 to 8 in-lb (in addition to above – 18 in-lb max.)
Used gear (over 400 miles)	4 to 5 in-lb (in addition to above – 14 in-lb max.)

Torque specifications

	Ft-lb	Nm
Idler arm-to-relay rod nut	40	54
Idler arm-to-bracket nut	40	54
Idler arm bracket mounting bolts/nuts	50	68
Pitman arm nut	115	156
Tie-rod adjustable tube clamp bolt	14	19
Tie-rod-to-center link retaining nut	40	54
Tie-rod end retaining nut	35	48
Steering shaft flexible coupling pinch bolt	30	41
Flexible coupling-to-intermediate shaft flange nuts	20	27
Steering gear mounting bolt	65	88
Steering gear side cover bolt	45	61
Power steering hose fittings (at gear)	25	34
Power steering pump mounting bolt	28	38

Balljoint stud nut	75	102
Lower control arm pivot bolt	110	149
Front and rear shock absorber nuts	8	11
Shock absorber mounting bracket bolt	20	27
Spindle-to-anchor plate bolt	55	75
Steering arm bolt	55	75
Strut rod-to-bracket nut	65	88
Strut rod bracket-to-frame sill bolt	75	102
Strut rod-to-lower control arm nut	75	102
Upper control arm inner pivot bolt	65	88
Pitman shaft adjuster locknut	25	34
Power steering pump pulley nut	58	79
Lower spring seat pivot retaining nuts	35	47
Rear spring front eye pivot bolt	110	149
Rear spring shackle pin nuts	30	41
Rear spring hanger mounting stud nuts	45	61
Rear spring U-bolt nuts	50	68
Steering wheel nut	25	34
Intermediate steering shaft-to-column pinch bolts	48	65
Mounting bracket-to-column bolts	20	27

1 General information

The AMC vehicles covered in this book are equipped with an independent front suspension system. This system utilizes upper and lower control arms, coil springs and double-acting shock absorbers. A stabilizer bar is also installed. The rear suspension is composed of semi elliptical leaf springs and double-acting shock absorbers.

The steering linkage consists of a Pitman arm, an idler arm, tie-rods and a relay rod. The steering gear is a worm and nut type with an energy-absorbing, anti-theft steering column. Power steering and an adjustable tilt steering column were installed on some models.

2 Wheels – inspection

1 Wheels can be damaged by an impact with a curb or other solid object. If the wheels are bent, the result is a hazardous condition which must be corrected. Inspect the wheels for obvious signs of damage such as cracks and deformation.

2 Tire and wheel balance is very important to the overall handling, braking and ride performance of the vehicle. Whenever a tire is disassembled for repair or replacement, the tire and wheel assembly should be balanced before being installed on the vehicle.

3 Wheels should be periodically cleaned, especially on the inside, where mud and road salts accumulate and eventually cause rust and, ultimately, wheel failure.

3 Wheel alignment – general information

Note: *Since wheel alignment and testing equipment is generally out of the reach of the home mechanic, this Section is intended only to familarize the reader with the basic terms used and procedures followed during a typical wheel alignment job. In the event that your vehicle needs a wheel alignment check or adjustment, we recommend that the work be done by a reputable front end alignment and repair shop.*

The three basic adjustments made when aligning a vehicle's front end are toe-in, caster and camber.

Toe-in is the amount the front wheels are angled in relationship to the centerline of the vehicle. For example, in a vehicle with zero toe-in, the distance measured between the front edges of the wheels is the same as the distance measured between the rear edges of the wheels. The wheels are running parallel with the centerline of the vehicle. Toe-in is adjusted by lengthening or shortening the tie-rods. Incorrect toe-in will cause tires to wear improperly by making them 'scrub' against the road surface.

Camber and caster are the angles at which the wheel and suspension upright are inclined to the vertical. Camber is the angle of the wheel in the lateral (side-to-side) plane, while caster is the angle of the wheel and upright in the longitudinal (fore-and-aft) plane. Camber angle affects the amount of tire tread which contacts the road and compensates for changes in the suspension geometry when the vehicle is travelling around curves or over an undulating surface. Caster angle affects the self-centering action of the steering, which governs straight-line stability.

4 Front shock absorbers – removal and installation

1 Remove the two lower mounting nuts, washers and grommets.

2 Remove the screws which secure the upper mounting bracket to the fender well.

3 Remove the shock absorber and upper bracket. Remove the brackets from the shock absorber.

4 Installation is the reverse of the removal procedure, but check for correct component installation and tighten the nuts to the specified torque.

5 Rear shock absorbers – removal and installation

1 On most Gremlin models, the upper shock mounting nuts are accessible by removing the cover plate in the rear storage compartment.

2 To gain access on other models, it may be necessary to raise the rear of the vehicle and set it on jackstands. Block the front wheels to keep the vehicle from rolling.

3 Remove the upper mounting nut, retainers and grommets.

4 Remove the lower mounting nut, retainers and grommets, compress the shock absorber by hand and remove it.

5 Installation is the reverse of the removal procedure. Make sure the nuts and washers are installed correctly and be sure the proper end of the shock is facing up. Tighten the nuts to the specified torque.

6 Stabilizer bar – removal and installation

Note: *On some later models, it may be necessary to remove the right front wheel and disconnect the idler arm at the frame in order to gain the necessary clearance for stabilizer bar removal.*

1 Disconnect the strut rods from the ends of the stabilizer bar.

2 Remove the stabilizer bar brackets from the frame.

3 Mark the relative positions of the ends of the bar (left and right) and remove it.

4 Installation is the reverse of the removal procedure but be sure to tighten all nuts to the specified torque.

7 Strut rod – removal and installation

1 Raise the front of the vehicle and support it securely.

2 Remove the adjusting nut and locknut from the mounting bracket end of the rod.

3 Disconnect the rod from the lower control arm and remove it along with the bushings and washers.

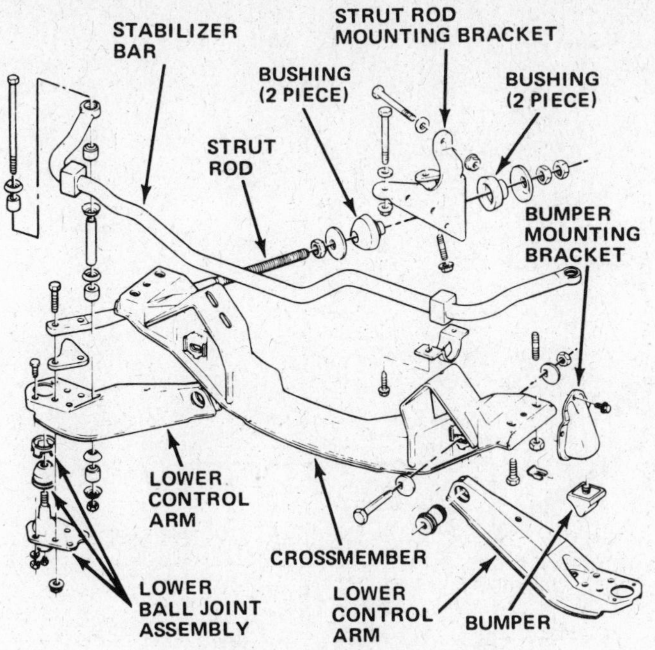

Fig. 11.1 Exploded view of the lower control arm assembly and stabilizer bar components – typical

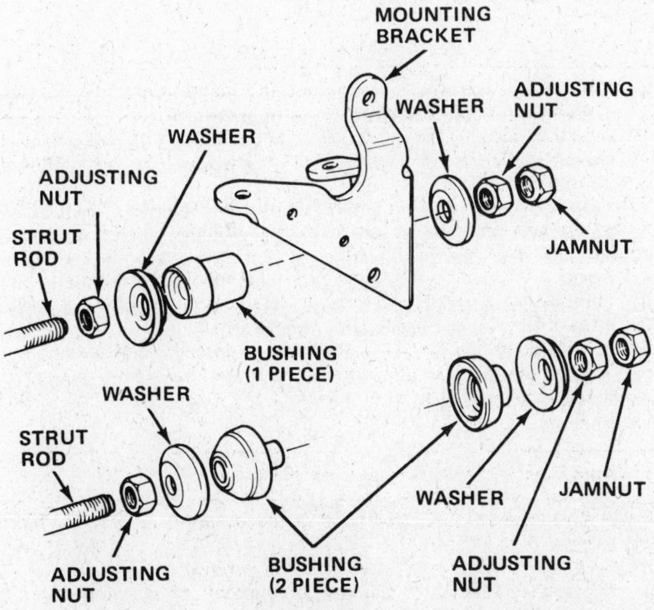

Fig. 11.2 Two different types of strut rod bushings are used – typical

4 The flexible bushings may be one or two-piece types. The one-piece type will probably require a press for removal.
5 Replace the bushings.
6 Installation is the reverse of the removal procedure. Tighten all nuts to the specified torque. After strut rod reinstallation, the vehicle should be taken to a front end alignment shop for inspection of caster angle.

8 Steering linkage and balljoints – removal and installation

1 The balljoints on the two outer tie-rods and those on the relay rod are all connected by a tapered ball stud located in a tapered hole and secured by a self-locking nut or a castle nut and cotter pin.
2 The outer tie-rods are tubular, internally threaded sleeve types and are secured to the tie-rod ends by clamps and bolts (photo).
3 To remove the taper pin, first remove the ball stud nut. On occasion the tapered studs will simply pull out. More often they are wedged in position and a clamp or slotted steel wedges may be driven between the ball unit and the arm to which it is attached. Another method is to place the head of a hammer (or other solid metal object) on one side of the hole in the arm into which the pin is fitted. Then hit it forcefully with a hammer on the opposite side. This has the effect of squeezing the taper out and usually works, provided you can get a good swing at it.
4 Measure the length of exposed thread on each of the tie-rod ends (as a guide to reassembly), release the pinch bolts from the clamps and unscrew the tie-rod end from the tie-rod sleeve.
5 When installing the new tie-rods, screw them into the sleeves approximately the same amount as the original ones.
6 Whenever the steering linkage has been disconnected and a linkage component replaced, the vehicle should be taken to a front end alignment shop for inspection (refer to Section 3).

9 Idler arm – removal and installation

1 Raise the front of the vehicle and set it on jackstands. Block the rear tires and set the parking brake to keep the vehicle fom rolling.
2 Disconnect the idler arm from the relay rod. To do this, remove the cotter pin and loosen the locknut until it is at the end of the stud, covering the last few threads. Pry back the dust cover and slip the jaws of a puller (a gear puller should work fine) between the relay rod end and the idler arm. Tighten the bolt of the puller until it is tight against the stud and tap the head of the puller bolt with a hammer until the connection breaks loose. If it doesn't seem to be working, increase the pressure of the puller by tightening the bolt one-quarter turn and strike the bolt head with the hammer again.
3 Remove the nuts attaching the idler arm support bracket (photo), to the frame rail and lift out the idler arm assembly.
4 Fasten the support bracket to the frame rail and tighten the attaching nuts to the specified torque.
5 Connect the idler arm to the relay rod and tighten the locknut to the specified torque, aligning the cotter pin hole in the stud with one of the slots in the nut. Install a new cotter pin.
6 Lower the vehicle to the ground and test drive it.

10 Pitman arm – removal and installation

1 Raise the front of the vehicle and set it on jackstands. Block the rear tires and set the parking brake to keep the vehicle from rolling.
2 Disconnect the Pitman arm from the relay rod (photo). To do this, remove the cotter pin and loosen the locknut until it is at the end of the stud, covering the last few threads. Pry back the dust cover and slip the jaws of a puller (a gear puller should work fine) between the relay rod end and the Pitman arm. Tighten the bolt of the puller until it is tight against the stud and tap the head of the puller bolt with a hammer until the connection breaks loose. If it doesn't seem to be working, increase the puller pressure by tightening the bolt one-quarter turn and strike the bolt head with the hammer again.
3 At the other end of the Pitman arm, mark the location of the arm on the shaft for assembly reference, then loosen the large nut that attaches the Pitman arm to the steering gear cross-shaft. Back off the nut until it is at the end of the shaft, covering the last few threads.
4 Since this large locknut is installed with a considerable amount of torque, it may be necessary to use a large puller to remove the Pitman arm from the cross-shaft. The gear puller used for the other steering joints may not have enough force to break this connection.
5 With the puller fork, or jaws, behind the Pitman arm and the puller bolt tightened against the end of the cross-shaft, strike the end of the

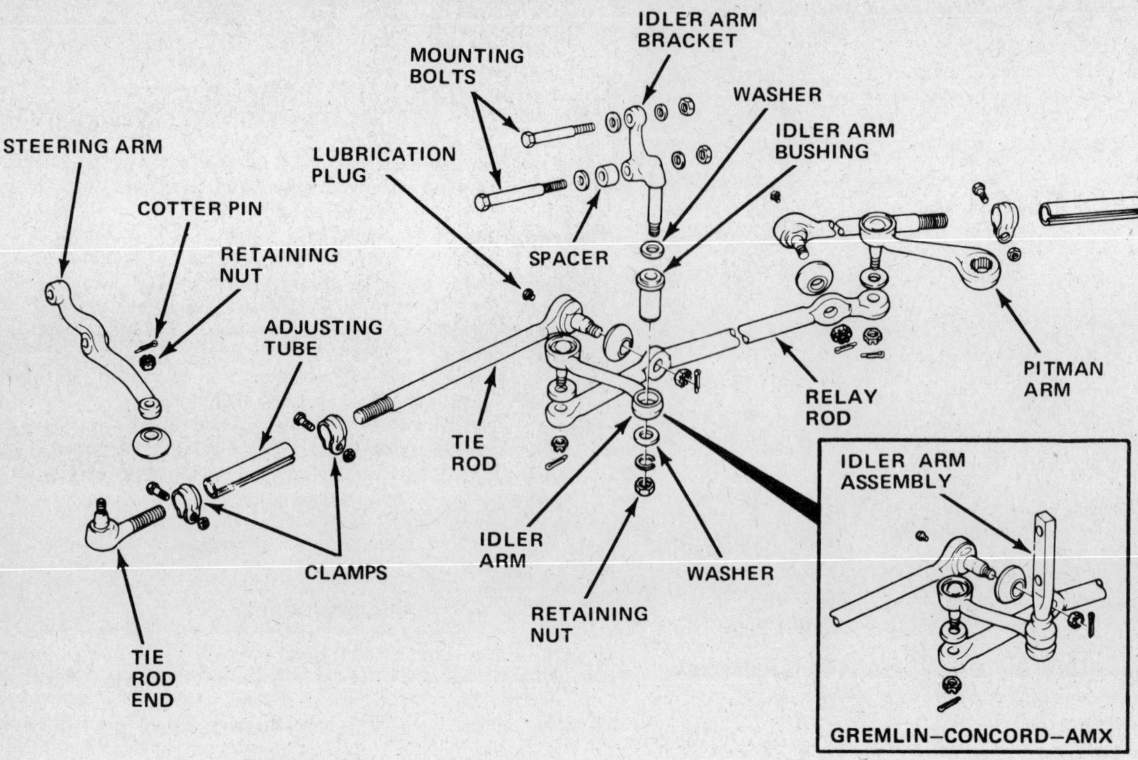

Fig. 11.3 Exploded view of the steering linkage components – typical (Sec 8)

puller bolt with a hammer to break the Pitman arm free from the cross-shaft. It may be necessary to continue tightening and striking the bolt to free the Pitman arm.

6 Remove the Pitman arm from the shaft and check it for deformation, cracks or other damage. If the balljoint at the end of the Pitman arm is loose or shows signs of wear or damage, the Pitman arm/balljoint should be replaced as a unit.

7 Slide the Pitman arm onto the cross-shaft, using the reference marks for alignment. Install the nut and tighten it to the specified torque. Stake the nut to the Pitman shaft threads.

8 Connect the Pitman arm to the relay rod and tighten the locknut to the specified torque, aligning the cotter pin hole in the stud with one of the slots in the the nut. Install a new cotter pin.

9 Lower the vehicle to the ground and test drive it.

11 Steering knuckle – removal and installation

1 Raise the front of the vehicle and support it securely on jackstands.

2 On vehicles equipped with front disc brakes, remove the wheel, tie the caliper out of the way, and remove the caliper anchor plate and adaptor as described in Chapter 9. Remove the hub and rotor assembly.

3 On vehicles equipped with front drum brakes, remove the wheel and brake drum as an assembly by removing the dust cap, cotter key, nut lock and spindle nut. Disconnect the brake line and remove the brake backing plate and shoe assembly as described in Chapter 9.

4 Compress the coil spring with a spring compressor.

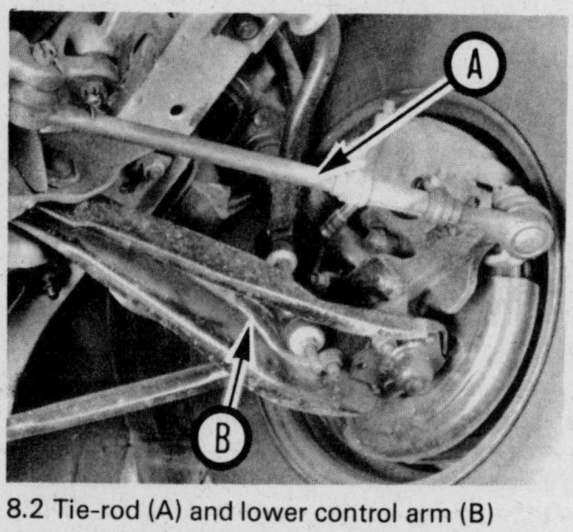

8.2 Tie-rod (A) and lower control arm (B)

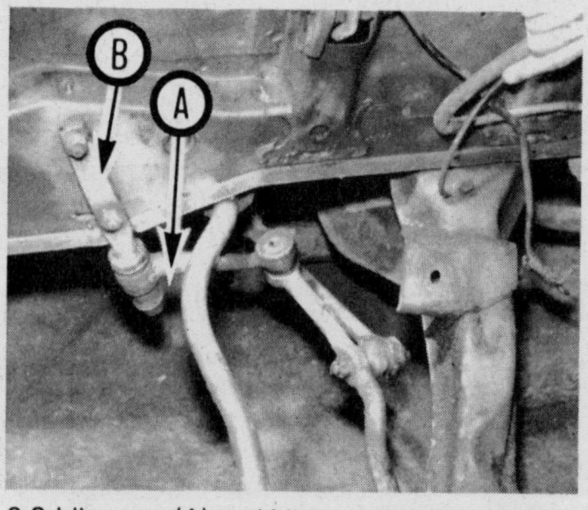

9.3 Idler arm (A) and idler arm bracket (B)

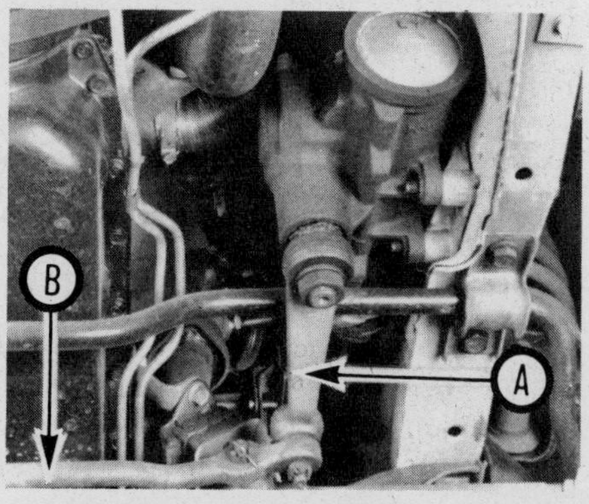

10.2 The Pitman arm (A) and relay rod (B)

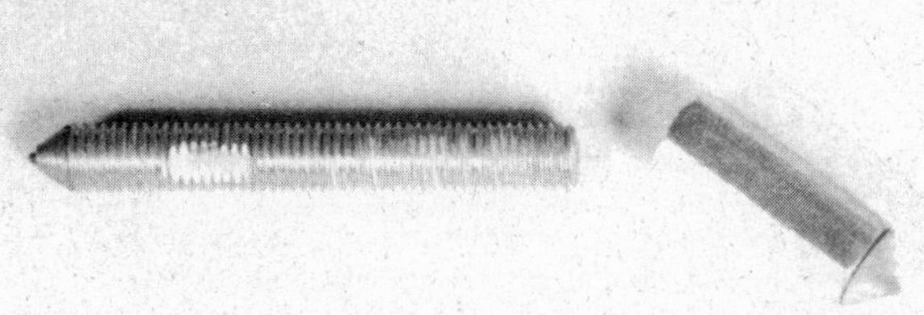

11.9A Homemade suspension balljoint removal tool

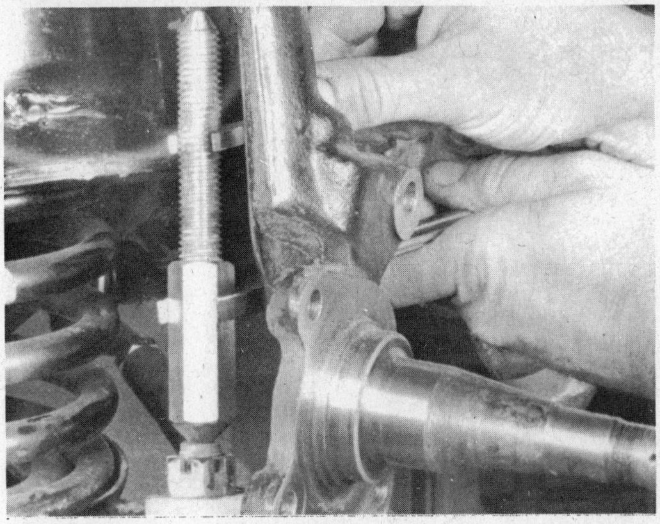

11.9B Forcing the suspension balljoints apart

5 Using a second jack, raise the lower control arm slightly.
6 Remove the steering spindle from the steering knuckle.
7 Remove the steering arm from the steering knuckle.
8 Remove the upper balljoint stud cotter pin. Loosen, but do not remove, the retaining nut.
9 Using factory special tool No. J-9656 or a homemade tool such as the one shown (photo), force the ball studs from the tapered holes in the steering knuckle (photo).
10 Using a soft-faced hammer, rap the knuckle at the top and bottom, where the ball studs are located, until the balljoints are jarred loose.
11 Adjust the frame supporting jacks as necessary in order to completely remove the nuts from the ball studs. Lower the control arm slightly to allow removal of the knuckle.
12 Installation is the reverse of the removal procedure but be sure all nuts are tightened to the specified torque and use new cotter pins.
13 On vehicles equipped with front drum brakes, bleed the hydraulic system as described in Chapter 9.

12 Suspension balljoints – removal and installation

Note: *If the suspension balljoints are removed, but not replaced, new mounting bolts must be purchased before reinstallation. However, it is recommended that the balljoints be replaced whenever they are removed. A steel chisel or grinding tool will be needed to remove the balljoint attaching rivets from the control arm.*

Upper balljoint removal

1 Place a 2 x 4 x 5 inch wood block between the frame side sill and the upper control arm.
2 Raise the front of the vehicle and support it at the frame side sills with jackstands.
3 Remove the wheel for easier access.
4 Remove the balljoint stud cotter pin and retaining nut.
5 Place a support stand under the lower control arm.
6 Using factory special tool No. J-9656 or a homemade tool, force the ball studs from the tapered holes in the steering knuckle (Section 11).
7 Disconnect the upper balljoint stud from the steering knuckle as described in Section 11.
8 Remove the heads from the balljoint attaching rivets using a chisel or grinding tool. Be careful not to damage the control arm.
9 Drive the rivets out of the balljoint and control arm using a hammer and punch.
10 Disengage the balljoint from the control arm.

Lower balljoint removal

11 Follow steps 1 through 3 of this Section. Next, Step 12 of this

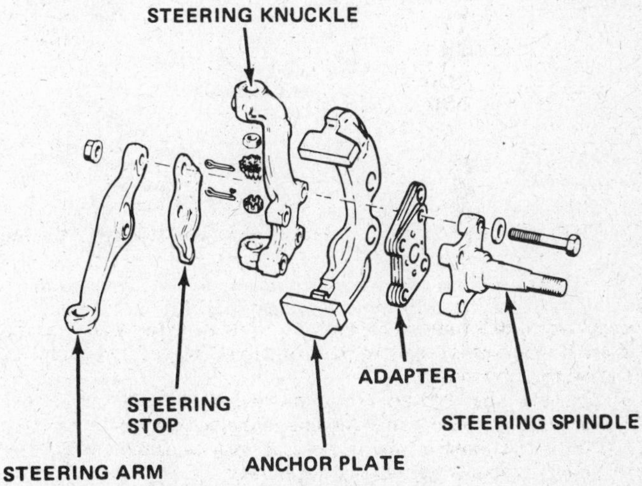

Fig. 11.4 Exploded view of the steering knuckle and related components – typical (Sec 11)

Section may be required in order to gain adequate access to the lower balljoint.
12 On vehicles equipped with front disc brakes, remove the caliper and rotor assembly as described in Chapter 9. On vehicles equipped with front drum brakes, remove the wheel and brake drum as an assembly. Disconnect the brake line and remove the brake support plate and shoe assembly as described in Chapter 9.
13 Disconnect the strut rod at the lower control arm.
14 Disconnect the steering arm from the steering knuckle.
15 Follow Steps 4 through 10 of this Section.

Installation

16 Installation is the reverse of the removal procedure. Balljoint attaching bolts are supplied in the replacement balljoint kit. Use new cotter pins and tighten all nuts to the specified torque.

11

13 Front coil springs – removal and installation

1 Remove the shock absorber.
2 Compress the coil spring, as described in Section 4, with a suitable spring compressor.
3 Remove the nuts from the spring lower seat pivot.

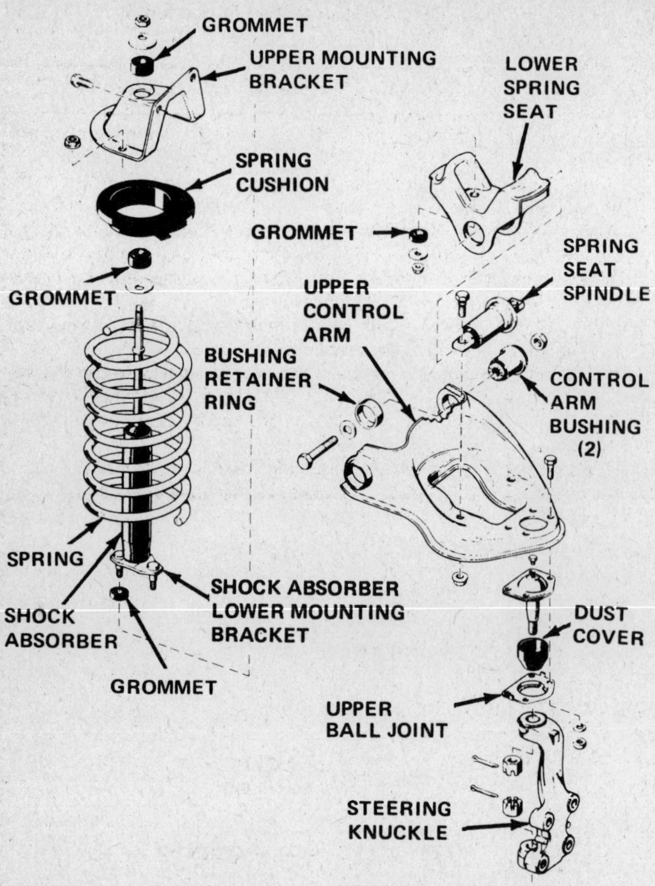

Fig. 11.5 Front suspension spring and upper control arm components – typical (Sec 13)

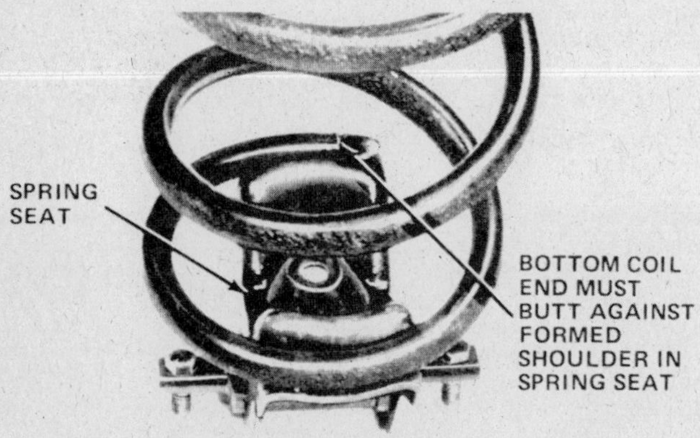

Fig. 11.6 Correct installation of the coil spring (Sec 13)

4 Raise the front of the vehicle under the frame so the suspension control arms fall free of the spring seat.
5 Remove the wheel and take out the spring, still compressed with the compressor in position, and the spring seat.
6 Remove the spring upper cushion.
7 If a new spring is being installed, carefully remove the compressor from the original one and attach it to the new one.
8 Attach the cushion to the top coil of the spring and tape it to hold it in position.
9 Install the spring lower seat and retaining nuts, making sure that the end of the lower coil is towards the engine compartment and up against the shoulder in the spring seat.
10 Install the wheel and raise the upper control arm to provide positive engagement of the spring in its seat. Remove the compressor, tighten the seat pivot nuts to the specified torque and reinstall the shock absorber.
11 Lower the vehicle completely and remove the jack.

14 Upper control arm – removal and installation

1 Remove the shock absorber as described in Section 4.
2 Remove the coil spring as described in Section 13.
3 Raise the front of the vehicle and support it securely under the frame.
4 Remove the wheel.
5 Disconnect the upper balljoint stud from the steering knuckle as described in Section 11. Support the brake assembly in a vertical position to avoid straining the brakeline.
6 Remove the control arm inner pivot bolts and take out the control arm.
7 Replace the balljoint if it is worn (refer to Section 12).
8 If the pivot bushings are worn, you might want to take the control arm to a dealer to have the bushings replaced. Alternatively, you can use factory special tool No. J-23473 or a homemade equivalent to remove the pivot bushings. A long bolt equipped with a nut and two different sizes of washers and tubular spacers can be used for removal and installation.
9 Installation is the reverse of the removal procedure. Tighten all bolts to the specified torque, but do not tighten the inner pivot nuts until the wheels of the vehicle are on the ground.

15 Lower control arm – removal and installation

1 Raise the front of the vehicle and support it securely under the frame.
2 Remove the wheel.
3 Remove the brake assemblies, including the rotor or brake backing plate, depending on the type of front brake system used (refer to Chapter 9).
4 Disconnect the steering arm from the steering knuckle.
5 Disconnect the lower balljoint stud from the steering knuckle as described in Section 11.
6 Unbolt the stabilizer bar from the control arm, if so equipped.
7 Unbolt the strut rod from the control arm.
8 Remove the control arm inner pivot bolt. Remove the control arm from the crossmember.
9 Replace the balljoint if it is worn (refer to Section 12).
10 If the pivot bushings appear to be worn, replace them as described in Section 14.
11 Installation is the reverse of the removal procedure. Tighten all bolts to the specified torque, but do not tighten the inner pivot nuts until the wheels of the vehicle are on the ground.

16 Rear spring – removal and installation

1 Remove the shock absorber as described in Section 5. It is a good idea to remove and replace only one spring at a time so the other spring can be used as a guide if difficulties are encountered during reassembly.
2 Remove the emergency brake cable holder from the bracket on the bottom spring leaf (if equipped).
3 Raise the rear axle housing slightly with a jack and support it on jackstands.
4 Remove the U-bolt nuts, springs clip plates and U-bolts. Remove the clamp bracket and spring isoclamps.
5 Remove the nut from the inside and the bolt from the outside of the front spring eye. If it will not slide out easily, use a soft-faced hammer to tap it out. Once the bolt is removed, disengage the spring from the mounting bracket.
6 Remove the nuts and washers on the inside of the shackle assembly at the rear spring mount. Pull off the shackle plate and

remove the shackle assembly. Remove the rubber bushings from the spring and mount (do not mix them up).

7 Disassemble and inspect the rear spring by referring to Section 17.

8 To install the spring, make sure the rubber bushings are in place, then slip it into position in the front mounting bracket. Install the bolt on the outside and the washer and nut on the inside of the mounting bracket. Tighten the nut to the specified torque.

9 Slip the rubber bushings into the rear spring mount and the eye at the rear of the spring. Install the shackle assembly, the shackle plate and the washers and nuts. The plate fits on the inside of the spring. Tighten the nuts to the specified torque.

10 Hold the spring isoclamp in position (the spring bolt head fits into the center hole in the spring isoclamp), and install the clamp bracket, spring clip plate, U-bolts and nuts. Tighten the U-bolt nuts to the specified torque. Make sure that the same number of threads are visible beyond the nuts on each U-bolt.

11 Lower the vehicle to the ground.

12 Fasten the emergency brake cable holder (if equipped) on the bottom spring leaf.

13 Install the shock absorber as described in Section 5.

17 Rear spring – disassembly, inspection and reassembly

1 Using a screwdriver or pry bar, pry open the spring leaf clamp bands.

2 Mark the front of each spring leaf and remove the clamp bolt that holds the spring leaves together.

3 Remove any rust and loose paint from the spring leaves with a wire brush. Check each spring leaf, clamp, rubber bushing and silencer for wear, cracks and permanent set. Check the bump stop for cracks and distortion. Replace any defective parts.

4 Apply a zinc chromate primer and new paint to each spring leaf. Use new silencers when reassembling.

5 Reassemble the spring leaves in the proper order with the marked ends forward. Line up the center bolt holes and compress the spring leaves together with a C-clamp. Install the center bolt and tighten it securely.

6 Using a large pliers, close the spring leaf clamp bands.

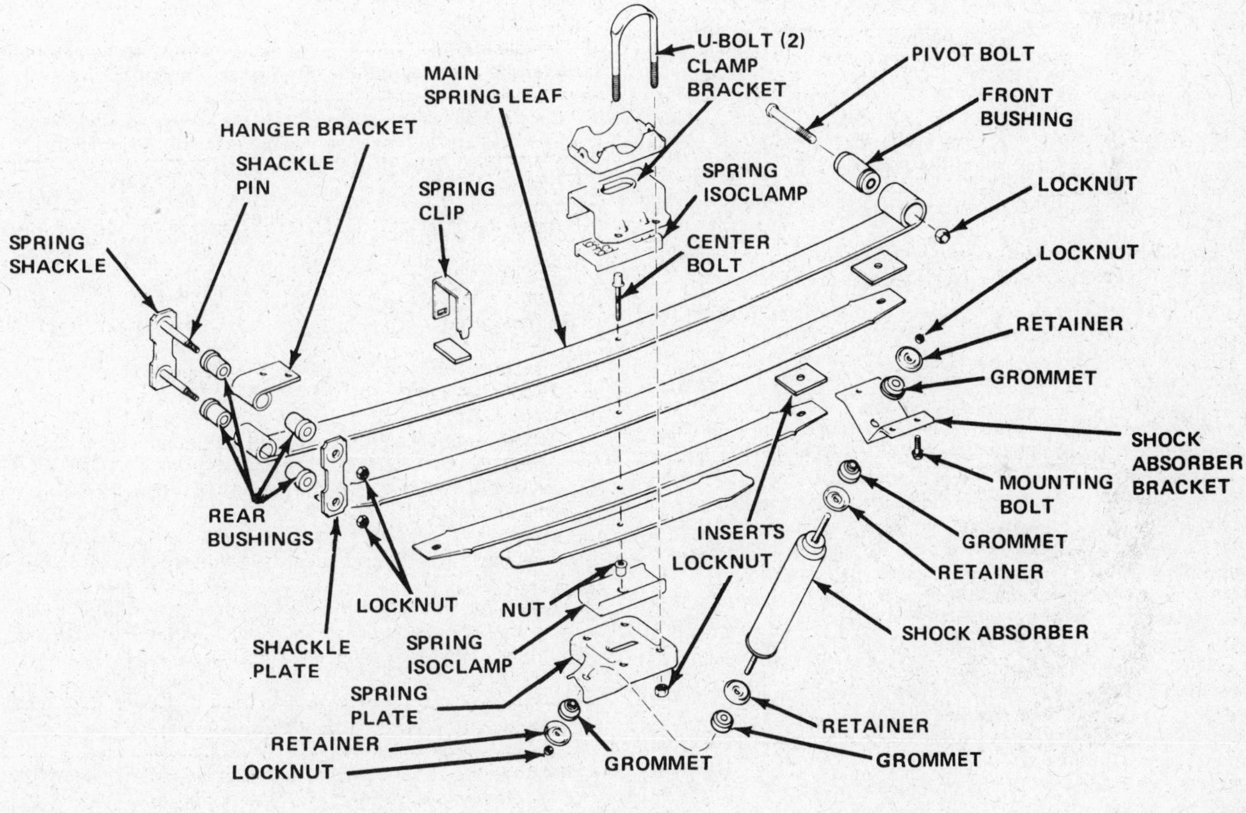

Fig. 11.7 Exploded view of the rear suspension components – typical

18.12 Turning the Pitman shaft adjusting screw

18 Manual steering gear – maintenance and adjustment

1 The steering gear is normally filled with lubricant for life and, unless a severe leak occurs necessitating a complete overhaul, refilling with lubricant will not be required.
2 In order to rectify conditions of lost motion, slackness and vibration which have been found to be directly attributable to the steering gear, carry out the following operations in the sequence described.
3 Disconnect the ground cable from the battery.
4 Remove the nut from the Pitman arm and then mark the relative position of the arm to the Pitman shaft.
5 Using a suitable puller remove the Pitman arm.
6 Loosen the Pitman shaft adjusting screw locknut and back off the screw a few turns.
7 Remove the horn button from the steering wheel.
8 Raise the front of the vehicle and gently turn the steering wheel in one direction until it comes up against the stop. Back off one half turn.
9 Attach a socket to the steering wheel retaining nut and then, either using a torque wrench (in-lb) or a spring balance with a cord wound around the socket, check the worm bearing preload by rotating the steering wheel through a quarter of a turn. The correct preload should be between 5 and 8 in-lb. If not, release the worm bearing adjuster locknut and turn the worm bearing adjuster as necessary. Retighten the locknut to a torque of 25 ft-lb.
10 Now check the overcenter adjustment by gently turning the steering wheel from one stop to the other and counting the exact number of steering wheel turns (mark the wheel rim and a corresponding point on the dashpanel with tape).
11 Turn the steering wheel (from being hard against one stop) half the number of turns counted plus one half turn.
12 Using one of the methods described in paragraph 9, check the torque required to turn the gear through its center of travel. This figure should be a combination of the worm bearing preload (5 to 8 in-lb) plus between 4 and 10 in-lb, but not exceeding a total of 16 in-lb. Adjust, if necessary, by turning the Pitman shaft adjusting screw and then tightening the locknut to 25 ft-lb (photo).
13 Attach the Pitman arm to the shaft making sure that the marks made before removal are in alignment.
14 Tighten the Pitman arm nut to 115 ft-lb and stake the nut.
15 Reconnect the horn button and the battery ground lead.

19 Manual steering gear – in-vehicle service and repair

Pitman shaft grease seal – replacement

1 Remove the Pitman arm, as described in Section 10.
2 Set the steering gear in its center position and then unbolt the side cover and remove the Pitman shaft/side cover assembly from the steering gear housing.
3 Pry the seal out using a screwdriver as a lever.
4 Tap a new seal into position.
5 Separate the side cover from the Pitman shaft.
6 Apply grease to the shaft and install it so that the center tooth of the sector engages with the center groove of the ball nut.
7 Pack the housing with the specified grease to make up for any lost when removing the components.
8 Install the side cover and a new gasket by turning the Pitman shaft adjuster screw counterclockwise to engage the side cover. When the screw bottoms, back it off one-half turn.
9 Install the locknut loosely on the adjuster screw.
10 Install the side cover bolts and tighten them to the specified torque.
11 Carry out the adjustments and install the Pitman arm, as described in Sections 10 and 18.

Side cover and bushing – replacement

12 Wear in the bushing will necessitate replacement of the complete side cover assembly.
13 Remove the Pitman shaft adjusting screw locknut.
14 Remove the side cover retaining bolts.
15 Turn the adjuster screw clockwise to remove the cover.
16 Install the new cover assembly and gasket by turning the adjuster screw counterclockwise.
17 Complete the installation and then check the adjustments described in Section 18.

20 Manual steering gear – removal and installation

1 Set the wheels in approximately the straight-ahead position.
2 Unscrew and remove the flexible coupling flange bolts.
3 Remove the Pitman arm (Section 10).
4 Unscrew and remove the steering gear housing bolts and remove the gear from the engine compartment.
5 The flexible coupling can be removed from the worm shaft after unscrewing the pinch bolt.
6 To install the flexible coupling, make sure that the pointer on the coupling is in alignment with the line (or flat) on the shaft. Tighten the pinch bolt to the specified torque.

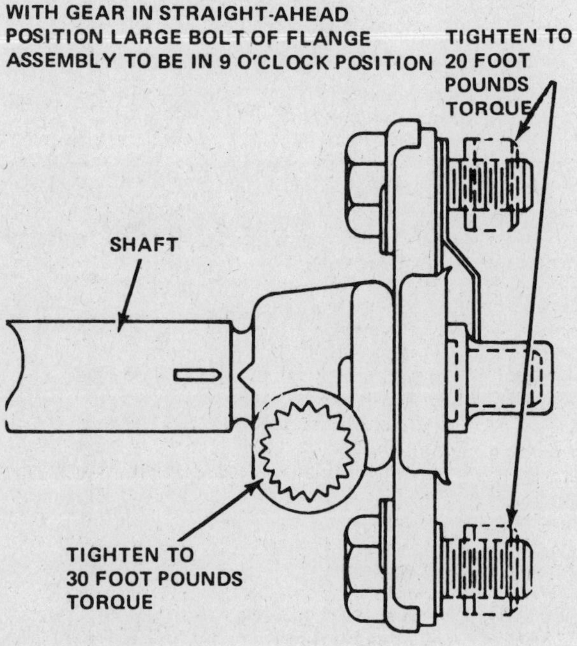

Fig. 11.8 Steering column flexible coupling-to-wormshaft alignment marks – typical (Sec 20)

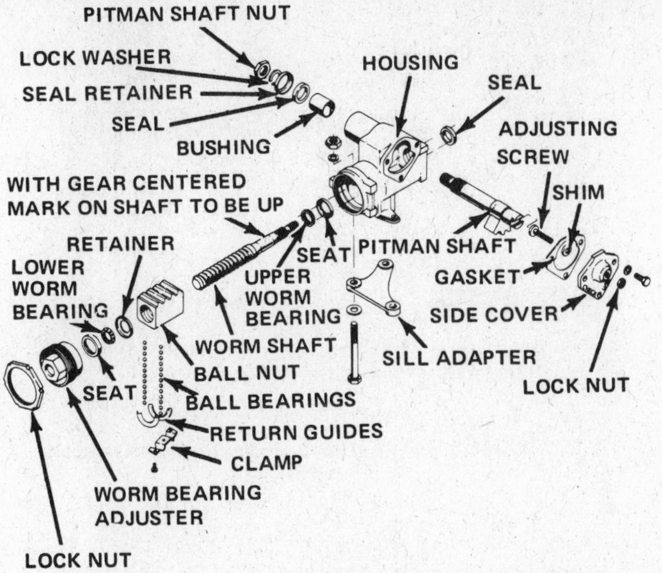

Fig. 11.9 Exploded view of the manual steering gear components – typical (Sec 21)

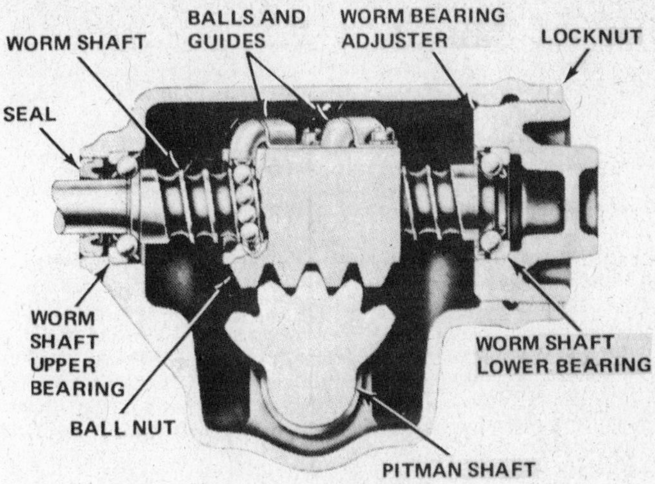

Fig. 11.10 Cross-sectional view of the recirculating ball gear – typical (Sec 21)

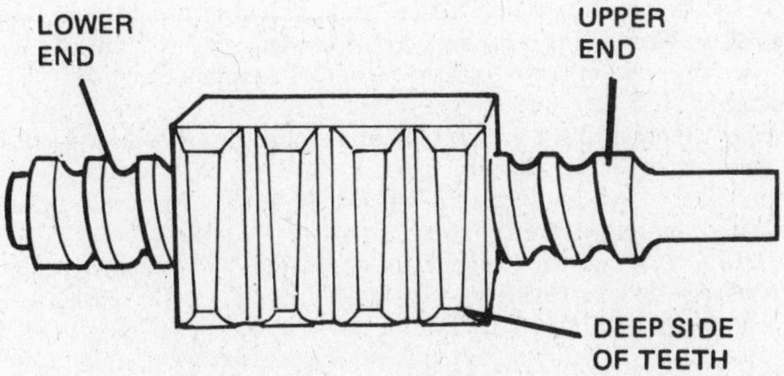

Fig. 11.11 Correct installation of the ball nut on the wormshaft – typical (Sec 21)

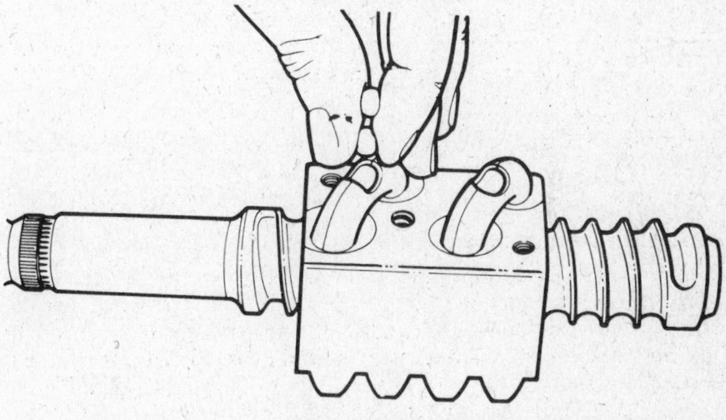

Fig. 11.12 Install the bearings in the ball nut circuits (Sec 21)

7 Align the flexible coupling so the flange securing bolts can be inserted and then install the steering gear housing and bolts. Tighten all bolts to the specified torque.

8 Install and adjust the Pitman arm, as described in Sections 10 and 18.

21 Manual steering gear – overhaul

1 Remove the flexible coupling.

2 Grip the steering housing securely in a vise. **Note**: *Clamp the vise jaws on the gear mounting bosses only.*

3 Rotate the wormshaft until it is centered with the marked (flat) side facing up. If this is not readily apparent, rotate the wormshaft stop-to-stop and count the total number of turns. Turn the wormshaft back one-half of the total number of turns to center the shaft and nut.

4 Remove the three side cover securing screws and adjuster screw locknut.

5 Remove the cover and gasket by turning the adjuster screw in a clockwise direction.

6 Remove the adjuster screw from the slot in the end of the Pitman shaft. Retain the screw shim.

7 Remove the Pitman shaft. If necessary, tap the shaft lightly with a soft-faced hammer to remove it. Be sure not to damage the Pitman shaft seal.

8 Release the worm bearing adjuster locknut using a brass drift and then remove the adjuster and bearing.

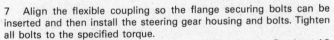

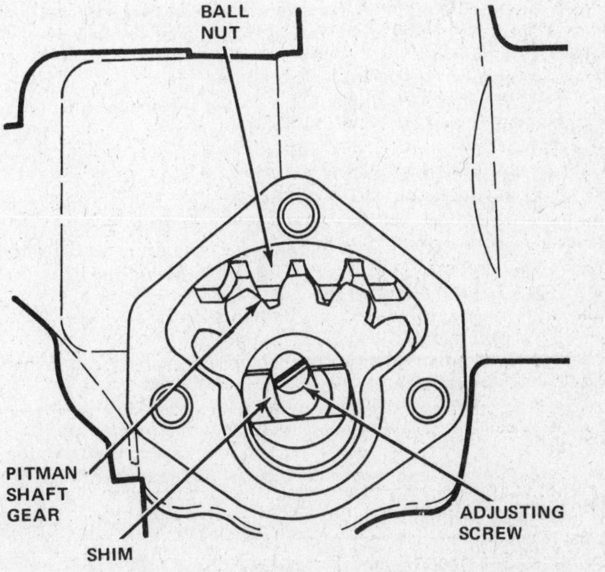

Fig. 11.13 Pitman shaft and ball nut in centered position (Sec 21)

9 Remove the bearing retainer with a screwdriver.
10 Remove the worm/shaft and ball nut/bearing assembly.
11 Remove the ball nut return guide clamp screws and clamp.
12 Remove the guides, turn the ball nut over and extract the balls. Removal of the balls will be facilitated if the wormshaft is rotated slowly from side to side.
13 When all the balls have been extracted, remove the ball nut.
14 Clean all components and the housing with solvent and examine them for wear or damage. Remove and install the shaft bushings and bearing tracks with suitable pullers or a long threaded bolt, nuts, washers and spacers of suitable diameter. Install new seals as a matter of routine at time of major overhaul.
15 Begin reassembly by lubricating the bearings, bushings and seals.
16 Locate the ball nut on the wormshaft so the deeper ends of the grooves are as shown.
17 Divide the balls into equal numbers and insert them initially into the return guides using petroleum jelly to retain them, then insert the remaining balls equally into the ball nut circuits. Do not rotate the shaft during this operation or the balls may enter the crossover passage.
18 Install the return guide clamp and screws.
19 Install the bearing on the wormshaft (above the worm).
20 Center the ball nut on the wormshaft.
21 Slide the steering wormshaft, bearing and ball nut into the steering gear housing, being careful not to damage the housing seal.
22 Locate the bearing in the worm adjuster, install the bearing retainer and the adjuster and locknut (finger-tight at this stage).
23 Install the Pitman shaft adjuster screw and shim the slot in the Pitman shaft. The adjuster screw should turn freely but play should not exceed 0.002 inch, otherwise replace the shim with one of different thickness.
24 Pack the housing with the specified grease. This is best achieved by turning the wormshaft until the ball nut is at one end of its travel. Insert grease and then rotate the shaft so that the ball nut moves to the opposite end of the worm, then insert more grease.
25 Insert the Pitman shaft so that the center tooth of the sector engages with the center groove of the ball nut.
26 Apply more grease and install the side cover and gasket.
27 Carry out the two adjustments described in Section 18 but attaching the torque wrench or cord and spring balance to the splined wormshaft. Do not damage or burr the splines; tape them first to protect them.

22 Steering wheel – removal and installation

1 Set the wheels in the straight-ahead position.
2 Disconnect the cable from the negative battery terminal.
3 Remove the horn button. On steering wheels with center horn buttons, remove the button by simply pulling up and out. On other types, remove the mounting screws at the back of the wheel. Pull the horn wire plastic retainer out of the turn signal cancelling cam and remove the button.
4 Unscrew and remove the steering wheel retaining nut and washer.
5 If the steering wheel does not come off the splined shaft easily, a suitable puller must be used. *Do not attempt to jar it from the shaft or strike the end of the shaft as this will damage the energy absorbing construction of the column.*
6 Attach the wheel to the shaft, making sure that the mating marks are in alignment. Tighten the retaining nut to 20 ft-lb.
7 Reinstall the center horn button by engaging the rubber retaining ring projection with the cup notch using downward pressure.
8 Reconnect the battery cable.

23 Steering column – removal and installation

1 Disconnect the cable from the negative battery terminal.
2 Remove two of the flexible coupling flange connecting bolts.
3 Scratch or paint alignment marks on the upper shaft, lower shaft and wormshaft in order to facilitate reassembly.
4 On 1975 and earlier models, remove the bearing caps and retainer from the upper shaft.
5 Disconnect the column dimmer switch harness, if so equipped.
6 Disconnect the Cruise Command or overdrive harness connectors, if so equipped.

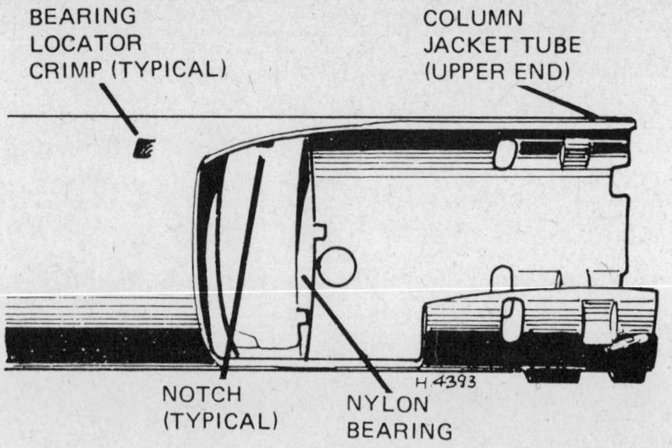

Fig. 11.14 Steering column upper end components – typical (Sec 23)

7 Unhook the shift quadrant pointer cable, if so equipped (column shift models only).
8 With column shift, disconnect the shift linkage.
9 Under the dashboard, depress the locking clip on the column harness connector so the column wiring can be disengaged.
10 Unscrew the column-to-toe board sealing plate.
11 Remove the instrument panel lower crash pad trim plate and column bracket bolts from the instrument panel.
12 Remove the bolts which secure the bracket to the column, taking care not to damage the breakaway capsules.
13 The steering column can now be withdrawn from the vehicle interior.
14 Begin installation by attaching the upper bracket to the column and tightening the bolts to a torque of 15 ft-lb.
15 Install the column and loosely attach it to the instrument panel by the rear mounting bracket studs.
16 Set the shaft marks in alignment and connect the flexible coupling, tightening the bolts to 25 ft-lb.
17 Gently pull the steering column up so the flexible coupling is flat and not distorted. Holding it in this position, tighten the upper bracket nuts to a torque of 10 ft-lb.
18 Install the toe-board sealing plate, connect the electrical leads and reinstall the crash pad.
19 Reconnect the shift linkage on column shift models.
20 Reconnect the battery cable.

24 Steering column (standard type) – overhaul

1 Remove the steering wheel as described in Section 22.
2 If the complete steering column or the lower section assembly is to be overhauled, the steering column must be removed from the vehicle. Upper section overhaul can be carried out with the steering column installed.
3 If necessary, remove the steering column as described in Section 23. If the steering column is to remain installed, follow Steps 1 through 9 of Section 23.

Upper section overhaul

4 Compress the lockplate and unseat the steering shaft snap-ring using factory special compressor tool No. J-23653-A. Steering shafts manufactured after 1978 might have metric threads. Use the appropriate compressor tool.
5 Remove the lockplate compressor tool and remove the steering shaft snap-ring. Discard the snap-ring.
6 Remove the lockplate, canceling cam, upper bearing preload spring and thrust washer.
7 On automobiles without Cruise Command, position the turn signal lever in the right turn position, and remove the lever. Pull straight out to disengage it.
8 On automobiles with Cruise Command, remove the wires from the switch terminal. Fold two of the four wires back along the harness.

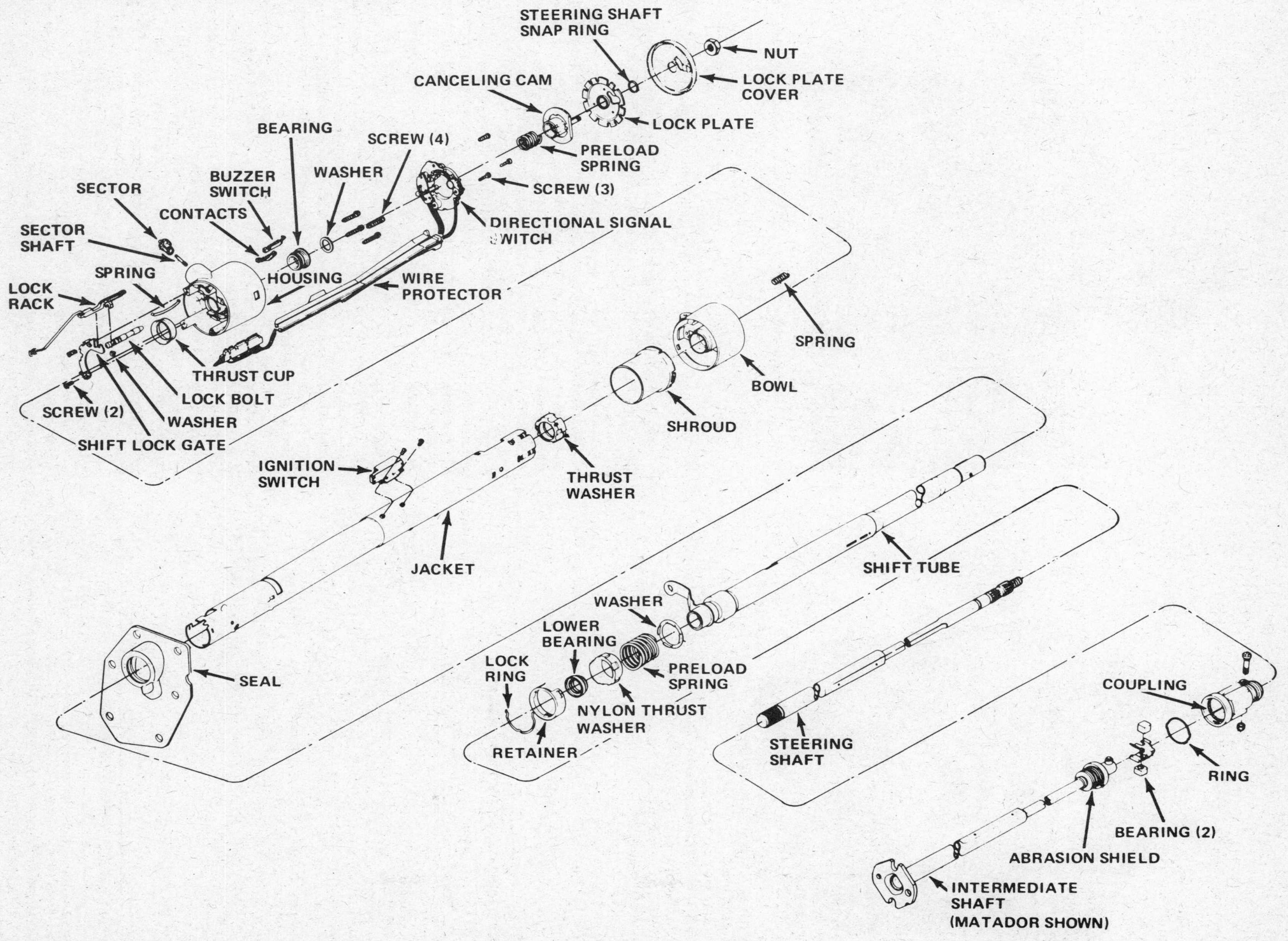

Fig. 11.15 Standard steering column components with column shift automatic transmission – typical (Sec 24)

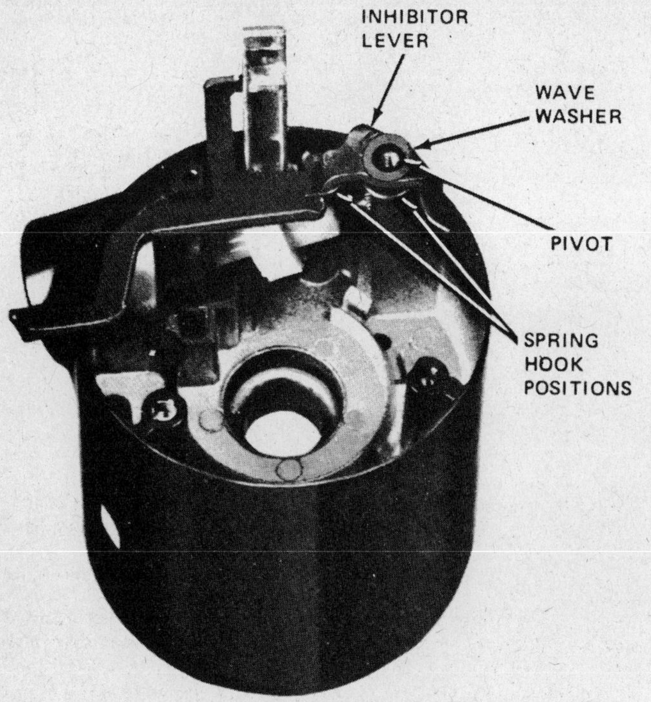

Fig. 11.16 Inhibitor lever assembly on a key release standard column – 1980 and earlier models (Sec 24)

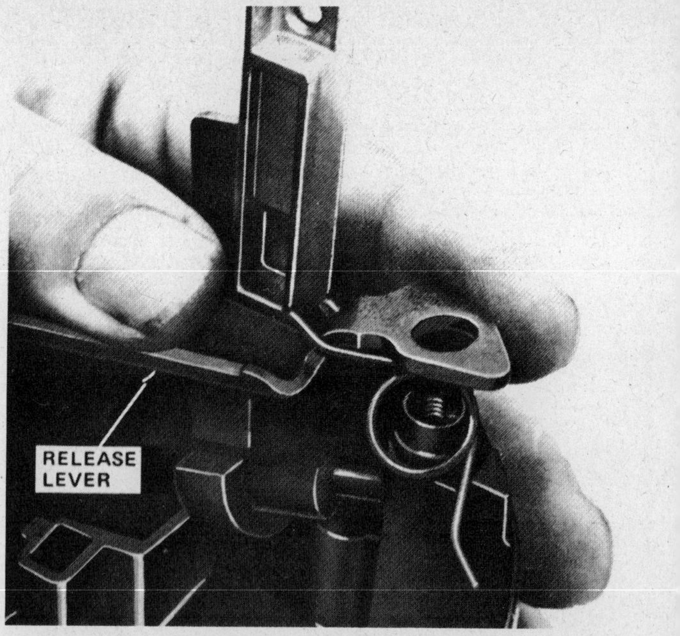

Fig. 11.17 Key release lever and spring installation – typical of standard steering columns (Sec 24)

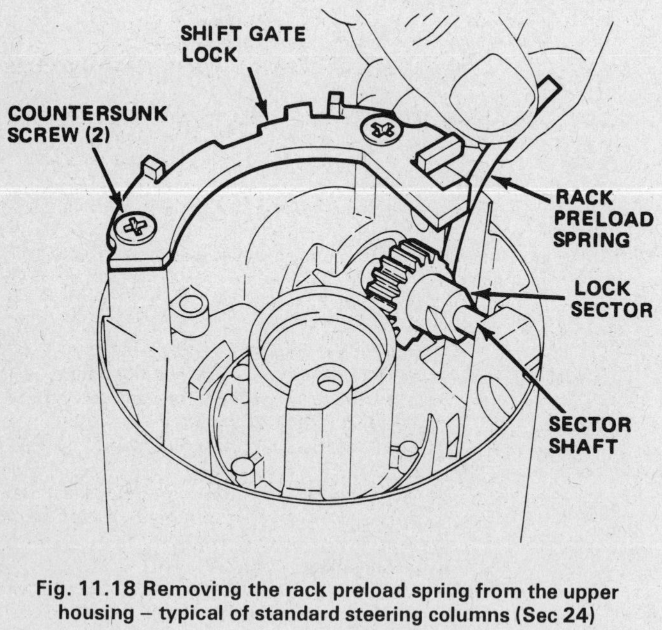

Fig. 11.18 Removing the rack preload spring from the upper housing – typical of standard steering columns (Sec 24)

Tape the wires in place and tape a length of string to the harness to aid the removal.

9 Push in on the hazard warning switch knob and unthread the knob in the counterclockwise direction.

10 On automatic transmission models, place the gearshift lever in the Park position to facilitate removal. Drive the retaining pin out using a small punch and remove the lever. For manual transmission models, place the gearshift lever in the Reverse position and follow the same procedure.

11 Using a stiff wire or paper clip, compress the lock tab that retains the shift quadrant light wire in the connector block and disconnect the wire.

12 On vehicles without Cruise Command, wrap tape around the turn signal switch harness connector to prevent snagging. Remove the turn signal switch attaching screws and remove the switch and harness. Pull the switch straight up and out of the column.

13 On vehicles equipped with Cruise Command, remove the turn signal lever by pulling it straight out. Remove the turn signal and Cruise Command switches as an assembly. Guide the switch harness out of the column using the string previously taped to the harness.

14 Insert the ignition key into the lock cylinder and turn the key to the On position.

15 Remove the key warning buzzer switch and contacts as an assembly using needle nose pliers or a paper clip with a right-angle bend.

16 To remove the lock cylinder on 1981 and 1982 floor shift models, turn the ignition cylinder clockwise two detent positions, past the Off-Lock position. On all other models, place the lock cylinder in the Lock position. Compress the lock cylinder retaining tab with a thin-blade screwdriver and remove the lock cylinder.

17 Remove the ignition switch from the lower end of the steering column. Remove the dimmer switch from the lower end of the column, if so equipped.

18 Remove the upper housing attaching screws and remove the upper housing. The remote rod and shift quadrant light wire, if equipped, will be removed as an assembly along with the upper housing. **Note**: *If you are overhauling a floor shift type of steering column, proceed to Step 26. Steps 19 through 25 are for column-shift models only.*

19 Remove the thrust cup from the upper housing.

20 Note the position of the sector on the shaft for assembly reference and remove the sector using a blunt punch.

21 Remove the shift gate lock from the upper housing. Replace the gate if excessively worn.

22 Remove the shift bowl from the column.

23 Remove the nylon bearing from the upper end of the column jacket tube. **Note**: *If the lower section must also be disassembled, it is easier to remove the nylon bearing after the shift tube has been removed.*

24 Remove the screws attaching the shroud (floor shift) or the shift

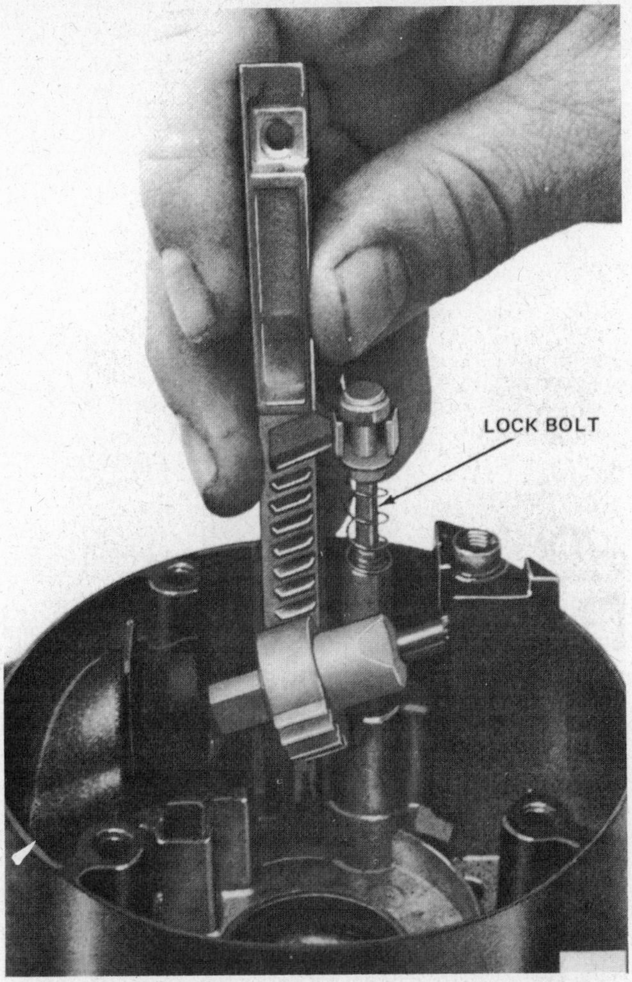

Fig. 11.19 Lock rack and lock bolt removal – typical (Sec 24 through 26)

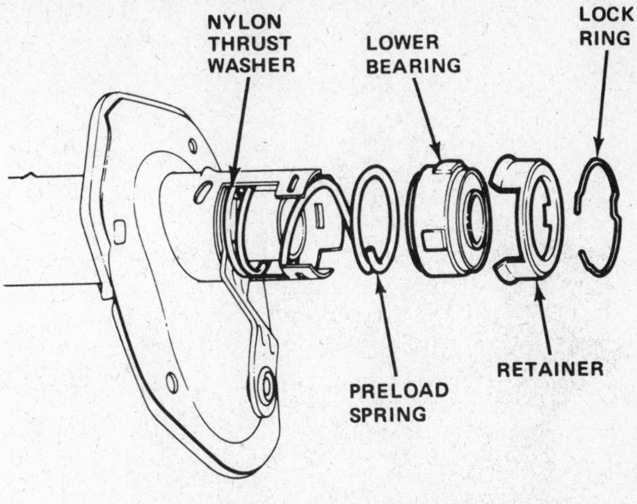

Fig. 11.20 Lower bearing assembly typical of 1974 and later model steering columns – exploded view (Sec 24 through 26)

bowl (column shift) to the column. Remove the shroud or shift bowl.
25 To release the inhibitor lever on key release columns manufactured from 1970 through 1980, first place a rag over the inhibitor lever pivot to prevent the lever spring from flying out.
26 Carefully remove the inhibitor lever (all models).
27 Remove the inhibitor lever spring.
28 Lift the remote lock rod and rack assembly, and lock bolt and spring assembly, out of the housing. If the rack preload spring requires service, remove it at this time.
29 Installation of the upper section assembly is the reverse of the removal procedure.

Lower section overhaul

30 Pull the steering shaft out of the lower end of the column.
31 On vehicles equipped with automatic column shifts, remove the lower bearing retainer ring, lower bearing, preload spring and nylon washer.
32 On vehicles equipped with manual column shifts, remove the back-up light switch. Remove the lower bearing retainer ring and lower bearing.
33 On vehicles equipped with floor mounted shifts, remove the lower bearing retaining ring and lower bearing. The remaining steps pertain only to column shift models.
34 Remove the Low-Reverse shift lever and spacer, if so equipped.
35 Remove the shift tube bearing retaining screws and remove the shift tube.
36 Remove the nylon shift tube bearing if it has not been removed previously.
37 Installation is the reverse of the removal procedure. Apply multi-purpose grease to all friction and bearing surfaces before assembly. Be sure to install the lower bearing with the metal face toward the retainer.
38 On 1970 through 1976 column shift models, insert a 0.005-inch shim between the Low-Reverse shift lever and the lever spacer. Rotate the shift tube bearing assembly clockwise (as viewed from the bottom of the column) until the lever is tight against the shim. Tighten the retaining screws to 10 ft-lb of torque and remove the shim.

25 Steering column (tilt-type with column shift) – overhaul

1 Follow Steps 1 through 17 of Section 24.
2 Rotate the tilt lever counterclockwise and remove it.
3 Remove the cover retaining screws and remove the cover from the column.
4 Remove the lock sector tension spring retaining screw. Unhook the spring from the lock sector shaft and remove the spring.
5 Remove the snap-ring from the lock sector shaft and remove the lock sector, sector shaft and retaining ring.
6 Temporarily install the tilt lever and set the upper column housing in the full tilt up position.
7 Insert a screwdriver in the tilt spring retainer slot and compress the retainer approximately $\frac{3}{16}$-inch. Rotate the retainer $\frac{1}{8}$-turn counter-clockwise and remove the retainer and spring. **Warning**: *The tilt spring is under extreme pressure.*
8 Set the steering housing in the center (non-tilt) position.
9 Remove the two housing pivot pins. You will need factory special tool No. J-21854-1 or a suitable small puller to remove the pins.
10 Lift the tilt lever to disengage the lock shoes.
11 Remove the ball bearing assemblies from the steering housing.
12 Remove the tilt lever.
13 Using a punch, remove the release lever and lock shoe pins. When removing the release lever and lock shoe pins, compress the lock shoe springs to relieve the spring tension on the pins.
14 Remove the lock shoes and lock shoe springs.
15 Disconnect the steering shaft at the lower flange-to-steering gear mount. Loosen the clamp bolt and nut adjacent to the lower column bearing and slide the clamp down to the lower flange coupling. Remove the steering shaft through the upper end of the column. Remove the intermediate clamp.
16 Remove the retainer plate by rotating the shift bowl clockwise, sliding the plate out of the jacket notches, tipping it down toward the shift bowl hub at the 12 o'clock position and removing the plate bottom side first.
17 Remove the wave washer and shift tube spring.
18 Remove the shift bowl from the column.
19 Remove the lower bearing retainer clip.

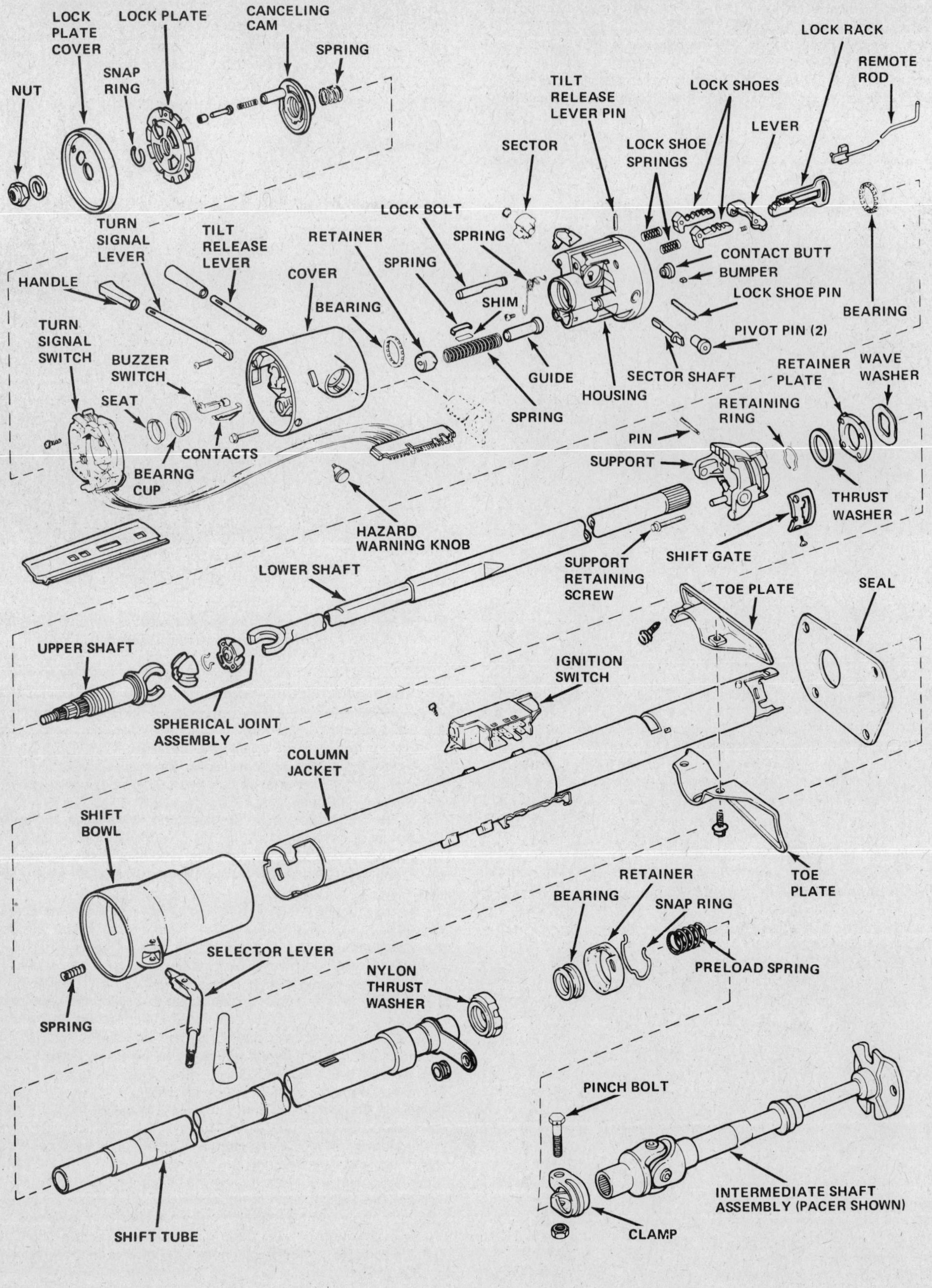

Fig. 11.21 Typical tilt-type steering column components – exploded view (Secs 25 and 26)

20 Remove the lower bearing retainer and remove the lower bearing and bearing adapter assembly.
21 Any further overhaul of the lower section assembly is as described in Section 27.
22 Installation is the reverse of the removal procedure. Apply multi-purpose grease to all friction and bearing surfaces before reassembly.

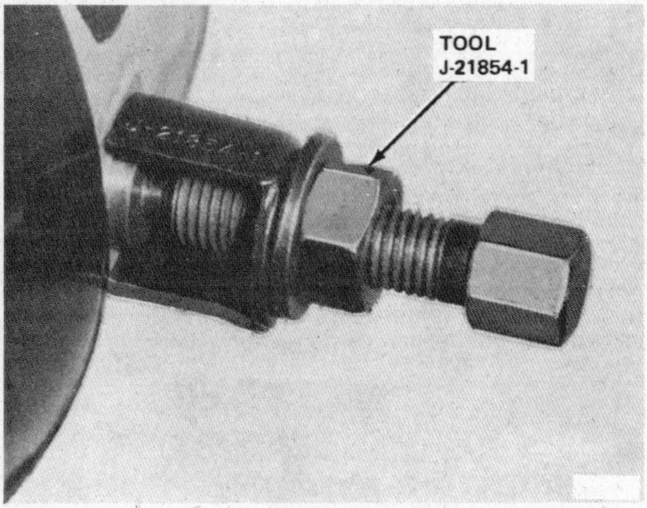

Fig. 11.22 Pivot pin removal on a tilt-type steering column – typical (Secs 25 and 26)

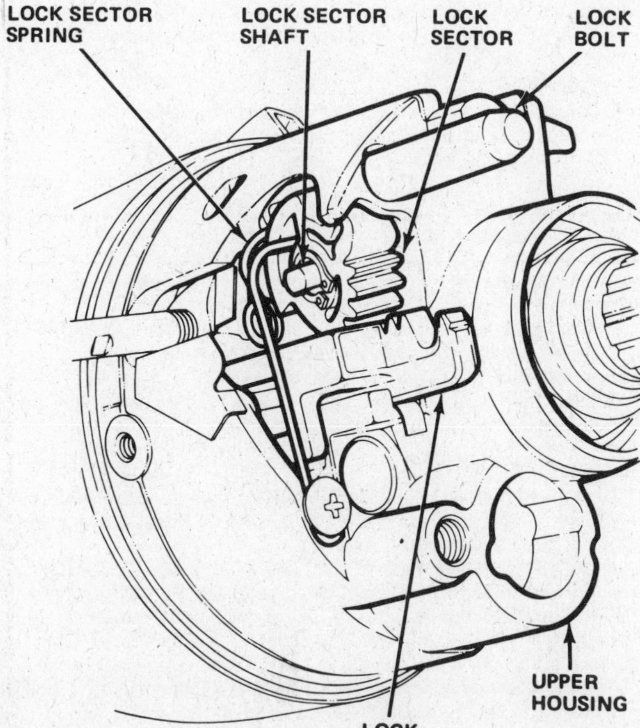

Fig. 11.23 Lock sector assembly on a tilt-type steering column – typical (Secs 25 and 26)

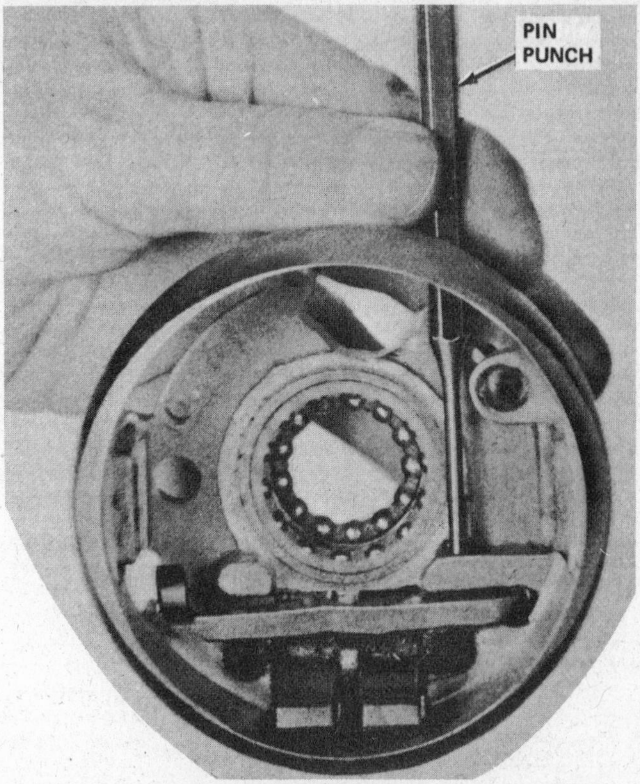

Fig. 11.24 Removing the release lever pin – typical of tilt-type steering columns (Secs 25 and 26)

26 Steering column (tilt-type with floor shift) – overhaul

1 Follow steps 1 through 17 of Section 24.
2 Rotate the tilt lever counterclockwise and remove it.
3 Remove the cover retaining screws and remove the cover from the column.
4 Remove the upper bearing race and bearing seat from the steering shaft.
5 Temporarily reinstall the tilt lever and set the upper column housing in the full tilt up position. **Warning**: *The tilt spring guide is under extreme pressure.*
6 Remove the tilt spring, guide and retainer. Be sure to use the correct size Phillips screwdriver to avoid rounding out the retainer head. To release the retainer spring, press the retainer in and turn it counterclockwise until the retainer tabs align with the housing lugs.
7 Set the steering housing in the center (non-tilt) position.
8 Remove the two housing pivot pins. You will need factory special tool No. J-21854-1 or a suitable small puller to remove the pins.
9 Raise the tilt lever to disengage the lock shoes and remove the housing. Pull the housing up to disengage the shoes. Turn the housing clockwise to separate the lock rack from the remote rod.
10 Remove the tilt lever from the housing.
11 Remove the tilt lever shield from the housing.
12 Remove the lock sector spring retaining screw and remove the spring. Rotate the spring in a clockwise direction to remove it from the screw.
13 Remove the lock sector retaining ring.
14 Remove the lock sector and sector shaft. Tap the shaft through the sector and out of the housing using a hammer and a punch.
15 Remove the lock bolt, lock rack, and lock rack preload spring. Remove the spring shim, if so equipped. Remove the remote rod from the housing.
16 Insert a wedge of some type between the lock shoes and housing to relieve the spring tension on the tilt and lock shoe pins.
17 Using a punch, remove the tilt lever and lockshoe pins from the housing.
18 Remove the lock shoes, springs and wedge.

11

19 Remove the housing upper and lower bearings only if they are worn. If the bearings and races must be replaced, remove them with a hammer and punch.
20 Any further overhaul of the lower section assembly is as described in Sections 24 and 25.
21 Installation is the reverse of the removal procedure. Apply multi-purpose grease to all friction and bearing surfaces before reassembly.

27 Power steering system – inspection and maintenance

1 Check the fluid level and the tension of the steering pump drivebelt as described in Chapter 1.
2 Check the tightness of the hose connections. Check the hoses for leaks and deterioration.
3 A slight hissing noise is normal from the steering gear, especially when turning the steering wheel at very low vehicle speeds, such as during parking or when the steering wheel is at full lock. However, excessive noise can be caused by metal-to-metal contact at the column flexible joint.
4 The flexible coupling should be positioned on the steering gear wormshaft to give $\frac{1}{16}$-inch clearance between the coupling flange and the gearbox. The rubber component of the coupling should be flat and not distorted. Where this cannot be achieved, loosen the column bolts and move the column backward or forward as necessary.

28 Power steering – in vehicle service and repair

Pitman shaft seal – replacement

1 Remove the Pitman arm using a suitable puller, making sure to mark the relative position of the arm to the shaft.
2 Place a drip pan under the steering gear.
3 Remove the seal retaining ring and backup washer.
4 With the engine running, momentarily turn and hold the steering to full left lock. This action will cause pressure to build up and blow out the seals and remaining backup washer.
5 Switch off the engine, clean the shaft and the seal recess.
6 Wrap tape over the Pitman shaft splines to prevent them from damaging the new seal lips. Install the new seals and washers, the correct way around, using a piece of pipe as a drift.
7 Top off the fluid reservoir, start the engine and check for leaks while turning the steering wheel from lock-to-lock.
8 Install the Pitman arm and, after tightening the retaining nut to the specified torque, stake the threads with a center punch.

End cover seal replacement

9 Rotate the end cover retaining ring so that one end of it is over the hole in the side of the housing.
10 Drive the ring from its groove with a punch and remove it.
11 Turn the steering wheel slowly and gently to the left until the rack piston just forces the end cover from the housing. Do not turn the steering wheel any more than necessary or the balls may be ejected from the rack-piston circuit into the rack-piston chamber.
12 Remove and discard the end cover seal and install the new seal, end cover and retaining ring.

Pump shaft seal replacement

Note: *On vehicles equipped with six-cylinder engines, the power steering pump must be removed in order to replace the shaft seal or pump pulley. For six-cylinder models, refer to Section 29, then proceed to the following steps.*
13 Place a drip pan beneath the pump. Remove the pump drivebelt.
14 Remove the pulley attaching nut. Temporarily attach the drivebelt to the steering pump pulley to loosen the nut. Grip the belt very close to the pulley to stop it from rotating and unscrew the nut.
15 Remove the pulley using a suitable puller and pry the Woodruff key from the shaft.
16 Remove the shaft seal by gripping its metal casing with a small puller. Be sure not to scratch or damage the shaft.
17 Tap the new seal into position with a piece of pipe and install the other components, tightening the pulley nut to the specified torque.
18 Adjust the drivebelt tension and top off the reservoir.
19 The repairs described in this Section should be regarded as the limit to which the home mechanic should go in servicing either the gear or pump. After considerable mileage has been covered, it is recommended that any fault in either unit is corrected by exchanging it for a reconditioned or new component. Removal and installation procedures are given in the next Section.

29 Power steering gear and pump – removal and installation

Steering gear removal

1 To remove the power steering gear, set the wheels in the straight-ahead position.
2 Place a drain pan under the steering gear.
3 Disconnect and plug the hoses at the steering gear.
4 Remove the flexible coupling-to-intermediate shaft attaching nuts.
5 Scribe or paint alignment marks on the Pitman arm and Pitman shaft for assembly reference.
6 Remove the Pitman arm as described in Section 10.
7 Remove the steering gear mounting bolts and remove the steering gear.

Pump removal

8 To remove the power steering pump, first place a drain pan under the pump.
9 Remove the ambient air induction flexible hose, if so equipped.
10 Remove the air pump belt adjusting bolt and pivot stud, if so equipped.
11 Remove the air pump drivebelt, if so equipped.
12 If the vehicle is equipped with air conditioning, remove the compressor drivebelt. Remove the drivebelt pulley and pulley bracket as an assembly.
13 Loosen the pump mounting bolts and slide the pump drivebelt off of the pulley.
14 Disconnect the power steering hoses at the pump and plug the ends.
15 It may be necessary to remove the air pump (on vehicles so equipped) to gain adequate clearance for steering pump removal.
16 Remove the pump mounting bolts and remove the pump.

Installation

17 Installation of both units is the reverse of the removal procedure. Tighten all nuts and bolts to the specified torque. Adjust the belts (Chapter 1) and fill and bleed the system (Section 30).

30 Power steering hydraulic system – bleeding

1 This is not a routine operation and will normally only be required when the system has been dismantled and reassembled.
2 Fill the reservoir to the correct level with the recommended fluid.
3 Start the engine and run it for two or three seconds only. Check the reservoir fluid level and top it off if necessary.
4 Repeat the operations described in the preceding paragraph until the fluid level remains constant.
5 Raise the front of the vehicle until the wheels are clear of the ground.
6 Start the engine and increase the speed to about 1500 rpm. Now turn the steering wheel gently from stop-to-stop. Check the reservoir fluid level, adding some if necessary.
7 Lower the vehicle to the ground. With the engine still running, move the vehicle forward sufficiently to obain full right lock followed by full left lock. Recheck the fluid level. If the fluid in the reservoir is extremely foamy, allow the vehicle to stand for a few minutes with the engine switched off and then repeat the operations just described.
8 Air in the power steering system is often indicated by a noisy pump but a low fluid level can also cause this.

Chapter 12 Body

Contents

Body and frame repairs – major damage	7
Body exterior – maintenance	2
Body repair – minor damage	6
Bumpers – removal and installation	18
Door latch assembly – removal and installation	12
Door striker – adjustment	11
Door trim panels – removal and installation	10
Door window glass – removal and installation	13
Door window regulator – removal, installation and adjustment	14
Front fender – removal and installation	19
General information	1
Hinges and locks – maintenance	5
Hood – removal, installation and adjustment	16
Radiator grille – removal and installation	17
Rear liftgate – removal and installation	15
Upholstery and carpets – maintenance	3
Vinyl trim – maintenance	4
Weatherstripping – maintenance and replacement	9
Windshield and rear window glass – replacement	8

Specifications

Torque specifications	Ft-lb
Door hinge bolt	20
Door lock striker	52
Hood hinge-to-hood bolts	23

1 General information

The body and frame are all-steel construction, welded into a single structural unit. With the exception of the bolt-on front fenders, replacement of unrepairable vehicle panels must be carried out by cutting the panel at its welded seams and welding in a new one.

2 Body exterior – maintenance

1 The condition of your vehicle's body is very important as it is on this that the resale value will mainly depend. It is much more difficult to repair a neglected body than to replace mechanical components. The hidden portions of the body, such as the wheel arches, fender wells, frame and engine compartment, are equally important, although obviously not requiring as frequent attention as the paint.

2 Once a year or every 12 000 miles it is a good idea to have the underside of the body steam cleaned. All traces of dirt and oil will have to be removed and the underside can then be inspected carefully for rust, damaged hydraulic brake lines, frayed electrical wiring and similar problems. The front suspension should be greased after completion of this job.

3 At the same time, clean the engine and the engine compartment with a water-soluble de-greaser.

4 The fender wells should be given particular attention, since undercoating can easily come away and stones and dirt thrown up from the wheels can soon cause the paint to chip and flake and allow rust to set in. If rust is found, clean down to the bare metal and apply an anti-rust paint.

5 The body should be washed once a week or when dirty. Thoroughly wet the vehicle to soften the dirt and then wash it down with a soft sponge and water mixed with a mild detergent. If the dirt is not washed off very gently, in time it will wear the paint down.

6 Spots of tar thrown up from the road surfaces should be removed with a cloth soaked in a cleaner made especially for this purpose.

7 Once every six months, or more frequently depending on the weather conditions, give the body and chrome trim a thorough wax job. If a chrome cleaner is used to remove rust from any of the vehicle's plated parts, remember that the cleaner can also remove part of the chrome, so use it sparingly.

These photos illustrate a method of repairing simple dents. They are intended to supplement ***Body repair - minor damage*** **in this Chapter and should not be used as the sole instructions for body repair on these vehicles.**

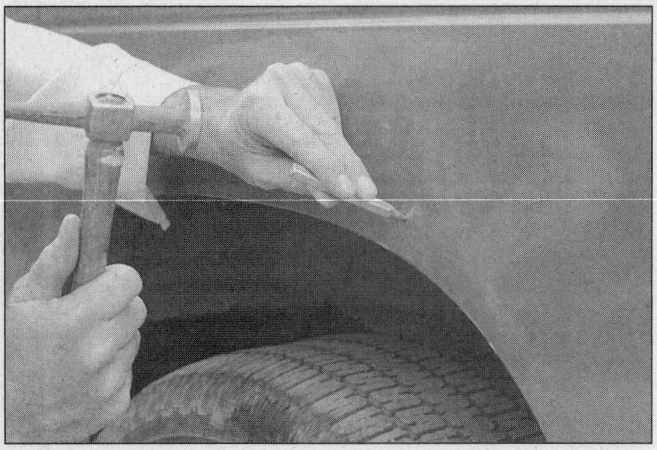

1 If you can't access the backside of the body panel to hammer out the dent, pull it out with a slide-hammer-type dent puller. In the deepest portion of the dent or along the crease line, drill or punch hole(s) at least one inch apart . . .

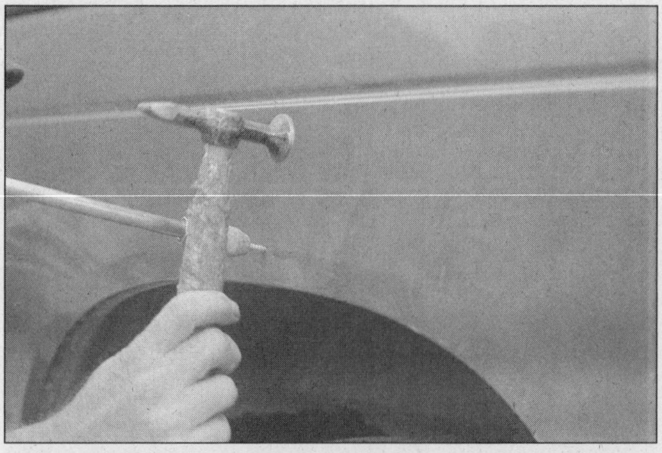

2 . . . then screw the slide-hammer into the hole and operate it. Tap with a hammer near the edge of the dent to help 'pop' the metal back to its original shape. When you're finished, the dent area should be close to its original contour and about 1/8-inch below the surface of the surrounding metal

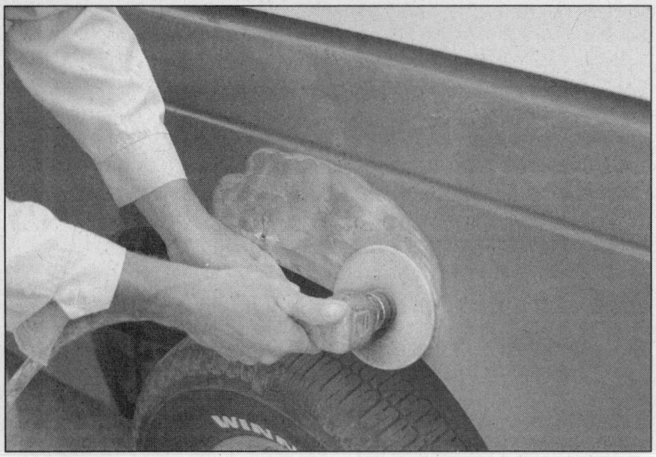

3 Using coarse-grit sandpaper, remove the paint down to the bare metal. Hand sanding works fine, but the disc sander shown here makes the job faster. Use finer (about 320-grit) sandpaper to feather-edge the paint at least one inch around the dent area

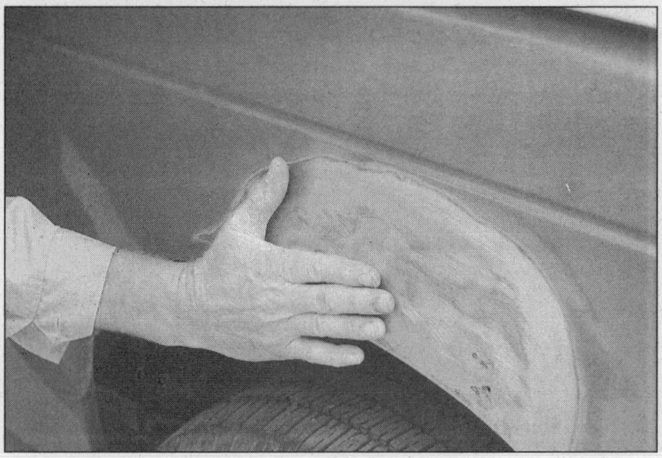

4 When the paint is removed, touch will probably be more helpful than sight for telling if the metal is straight. Hammer down the high spots or raise the low spots as necessary. Clean the repair area with wax/silicone remover

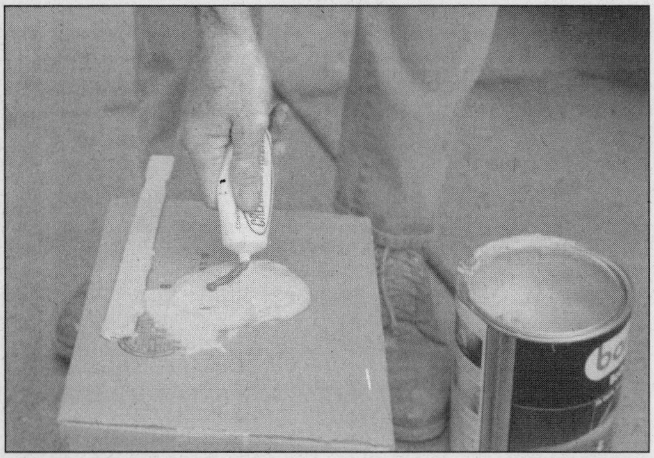

5 Following label instructions, mix up a batch of plastic filler and hardener. The ratio of filler to hardener is critical, and, if you mix it incorrectly, it will either not cure properly or cure too quickly (you won't have time to file and sand it into shape)

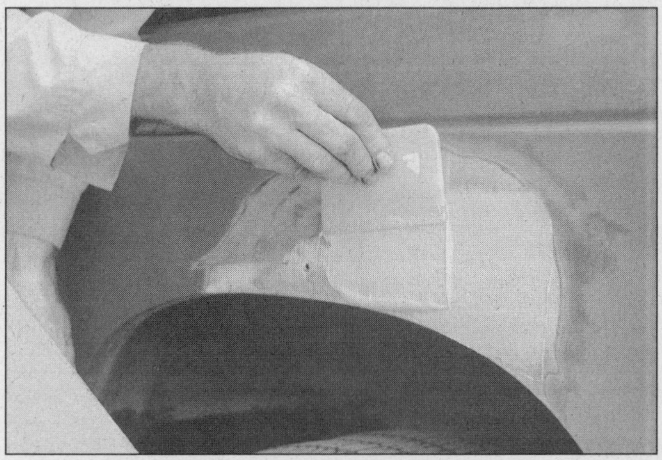

6 Working quickly so the filler doesn't harden, use a plastic applicator to press the body filler firmly into the metal, assuring it bonds completely. Work the filler until it matches the original contour and is slightly above the surrounding metal

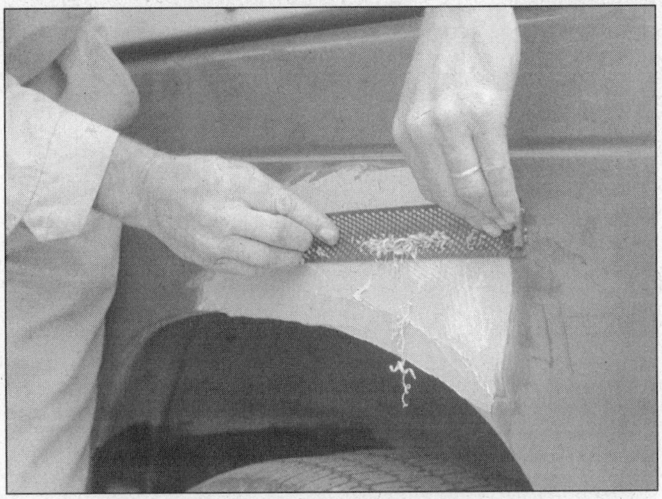

7 Let the filler harden until you can just dent it with your fingernail. Use a body file or Surform tool (shown here) to rough-shape the filler

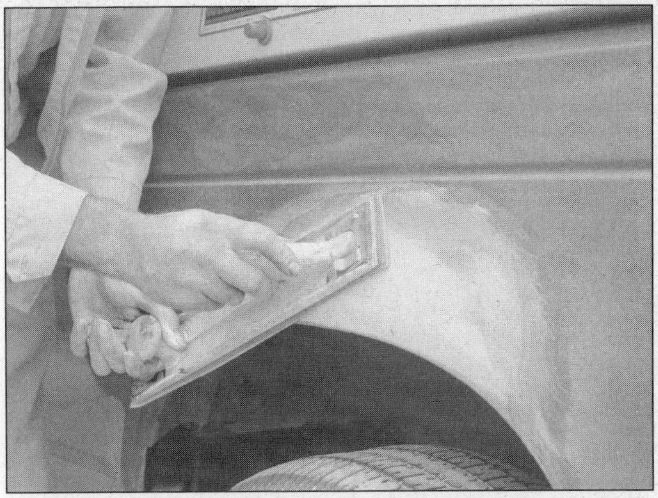

8 Use coarse-grit sandpaper and a sanding board or block to work the filler down until it's smooth and even. Work down to finer grits of sandpaper - always using a board or block - ending up with 360 or 400 grit

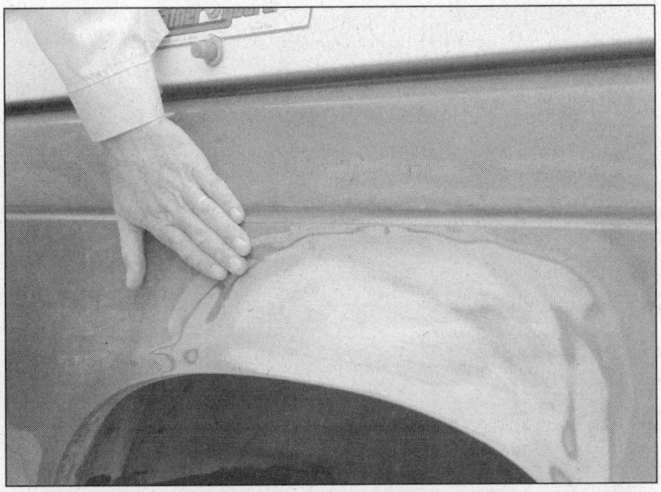

9 You shouldn't be able to feel any ridge at the transition from the filler to the bare metal or from the bare metal to the old paint. As soon as the repair is flat and uniform, remove the dust and mask off the adjacent panels or trim pieces

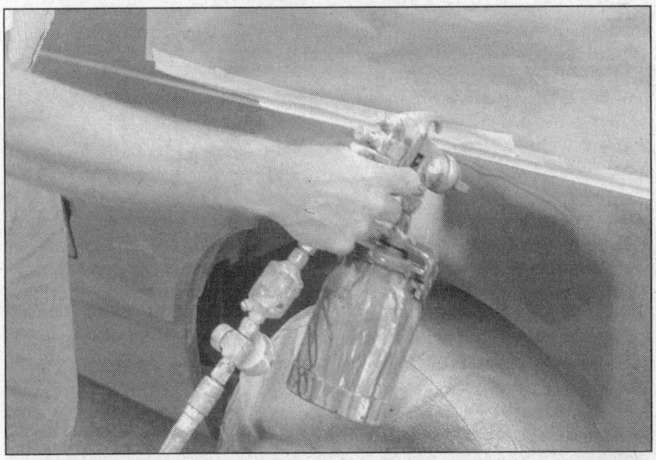

10 Apply several layers of primer to the area. Don't spray the primer on too heavy, so it sags or runs, and make sure each coat is dry before you spray on the next one. A professional-type spray gun is being used here, but aerosol spray primer is available inexpensively from auto parts stores

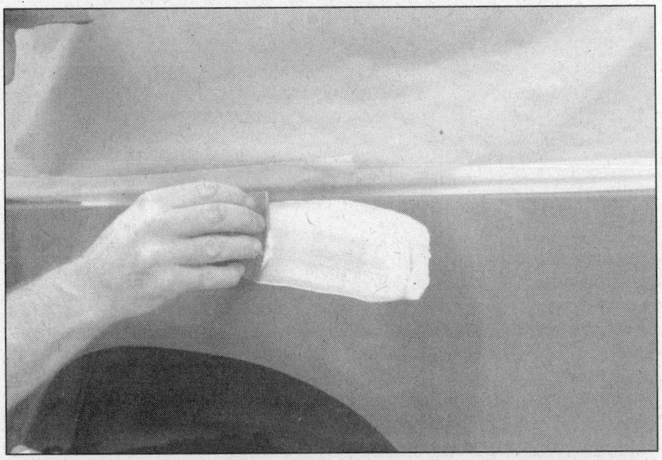

11 The primer will help reveal imperfections or scratches. Fill these with glazing compound. Follow the label instructions and sand it with 360 or 400-grit sandpaper until it's smooth. Repeat the glazing, sanding and respraying until the primer reveals a perfectly smooth surface

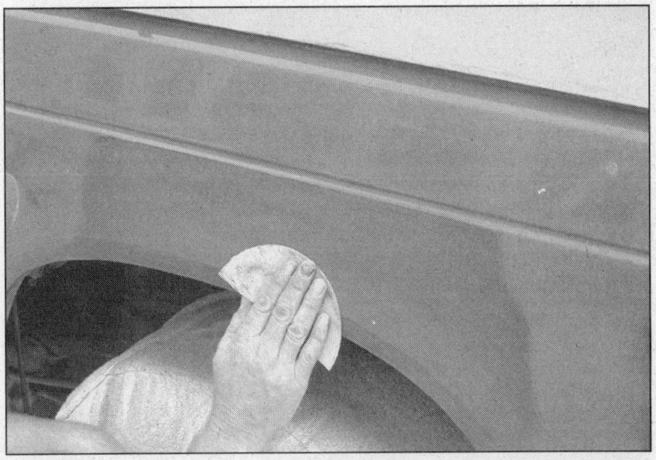

12 Finish sand the primer with very fine sandpaper (400 or 600-grit) to remove the primer overspray. Clean the area with water and allow it to dry. Use a tack rag to remove any dust, then apply the finish coat. Don't attempt to rub out or wax the repair area until the paint has dried completely (at least two weeks)

3 Upholstery and carpets – maintenance

1 Remove the carpets or mats and thoroughly vacuum the interior of the vehicle at least every three months (more frequently if necessary).
2 Beat out the carpets and vacuum them if they are extremely dirty. If the upholstery is soiled, apply an upholstery cleaner with a damp sponge and wipe it off with a clean dry cloth.
3 Consult your local dealer or auto parts store for cleaners made especially for newer automotive upholstery fabrics. Always test the cleaner in an inconspicuous place.

4 Vinyl trim – maintenance

Vinyl trim should not be cleaned with detergents, caustic soaps or petroleum based cleaners. Plain soap and water or a mild vinyl cleaner is best for stains. Test a small area for color fastness. Bubbles under the vinyl can be corrected by piercing them with a pin and then working the air out.

5 Hinges and locks – maintenance

Every 3000 miles or 3 months, the door, hood and trunk hinges and locks should be lubricated with a few drops of oil. The door striker plates should also be given a thin coat of grease to reduce wear and ensure free movement.

6 Body repair – minor damage

Refer to the accompanying color photos which illustrate the following procedures.

Repair of minor scratches

If the scratch is very superficial and does not penetrate to the metal of the body, repair is very simple. Lightly rub the area of the scratch with a fine rubbing compound to remove loose paint from the scratch and to clear the surrounding paint of wax buildup. Rinse the area with clean water.

Apply touch-up paint to the scratch using a small brush. Continue to apply thin layers of paint until the surface of the paint in the scratch is level with the surrounding paint. Allow the new paint at least two weeks to harden, then blend it into the surrounding paint by rubbing with a very fine rubbing compound. Finally, apply a coat of wax to the scratch area.

If the scratch has penetrated the paint and exposed the metal of the body, causing the metal to rust, a different repair technique is required. Remove any loose rust from the bottom of the scratch with a pocket knife, then apply rust inhibiting paint to prevent the formation of rust in the future. Using a rubber or nylon applicator, coat the scratched area with glaze-type filler. If required, this filler can be mixed with thinner to provide a very thin paste which is ideal for filling narrow scratches. Before the glaze filler in the scratch hardens, wrap a piece of smooth cotton cloth around the top of a finger. Dip the cloth in thinner and then quickly wipe it along the surface of the scratch. This will ensure that the surface of the filler is slightly hollowed. The scratch can now be painted over as described earlier in this Section.

Repair of dents

When deep denting of the vehicle's body has taken place, the first task is to pull the dent out until the area nearly attains its original shape. There is little point in trying to restore the original shape completely as the metal in the damaged area will have stretched on impact and cannot be completely restored to its original contours. It is better to bring the level of the dent up to a point which is about $\frac{1}{8}$ inch below the level of the surrounding metal. In cases where the dent is very shallow, it is not worth trying to pull it out at all.

If the underside of the dent is accessible, it can be hammered out gently from behind using a mallet with a wooden or plastic head. While doing this, hold a block of wood firmly against the metal to absorb the hammer blows and prevent large areas of the metal from being stretched out.

If the dent is in a section of the body which has double layers, or some other factor making it inaccessible from behind, a different technique is in order. Drill several small holes through the metal inside the damaged area, particularly in the deeper sections. Screw long self-tapping screws into the holes just enough for them to get a good grip in the metal. Now the dent can be removed by pulling on the protruding heads of the screws with a pair of locking pliers.

The next stage of the repair is the removal of the paint from the damaged area and from an inch or so of the surrounding 'sound' metal. This is easily accomplished by using a wire brush or sanding disc in a drill motor, although it can be done just as effectively by hand with sandpaper. To complete the preparation for filling, score the surface of the bare metal with a screwdriver or the tang of a file (or drill small holes in the affected area). This will provide a really good 'grip' for the filler material. To complete the repair, see the Section on filling and painting.

Repair of rust holes or gashes

Remove all paint from the affected area and from an inch or so of the surrounding 'sound' metal using a sanding disc or wire brush mounted in a drill motor. If these are not available, a few sheets of sandpaper will do the job just as effectively. With the paint removed, you will be able to determine the severity of the corrosion and, therefore, decide whether to replace the whole panel, if possible, or to repair the affected area. New body panels are not as expensive as most people think and it is often quicker and more desirable to install a new panel than to attempt to repair large areas of rust.

Remove all trim pieces from the affected area (except those which will act as a guide to the original shape of the damaged body (ie. headlamp shells, etc.). Then, using metal snips or a hacksaw blade, remove all loose metal and any other metal that is badly affected by rust. Hammer the edges of the hole in to create a slight depression for the filler material.

Wire brush the affected area to remove the powdery rust from the surface of the metal. If the back of the rusted area is accessible, treat it with rust inhibiting paint.

Before filling can be done, it will be necessary to block the hole in some way. This can be accomplished with sheet metal riveted or screwed into place or by stuffing the hole with wire mesh.

Once the hole is blocked off, the affected area can be filled and painted (see the following Section on filling and painting).

Filling and painting

Many types of body fillers are available but generally speaking, body repair kits which contain filler paste and a tube of resin hardener are best for this type of repair work. A wide, flexible plastic or nylon applicator will be necessary for imparting a smooth contoured finish to the surface of the filler material.

Mix up a small amount of filler on a clean piece of wood or cardboard (use the hardener sparingly). Follow the maker's instructions on the package, otherwise the filler will set incorrectly.

Using the applicator, apply the filler paste to the prepared area. Draw the applicator across the surface of the filler to achieve the desired contour and to level the filler surface. As soon as a contour that approximates the correct one is achieved, stop working the paste. If you continue, the paste will begin to stick to the applicator. Continue to add thin layers of filler paste at 20-minute intervals until the level of the filler is just above the surrounding metal.

Once the filler has hardened, excess can be removed using a body file. From then on, progressively finer grades of sandpaper should be used, starting with a 180-grit paper and finishing with 600-grit wet-or-dry paper. Always wrap the sandpaper around a flat rubber or wooden block, otherwise the surface of the filler will not be completely flat. During the sanding of the filler surface, the wet-or-dry paper should be periodically rinsed in water. This will ensure that a very smooth finish is produced in the final stage.

At this point, the repair area should be surrounded by a ring of bare metal, which in turn should be encircled by the finely feathered edge of the good paint. Rinse the repair area with clean water until all of the dust produced by the sanding operation is gone.

Spray the entire area with a light coat of primer. This will reveal any imperfections in the surface of the filler. Repair these imperfections with fresh filler paste or glaze filler and once more smooth the surface with sandpaper. Repeat this spray-and-repair procedure until you are satisfied that the surface of the filler and the feathered edge of the paint are perfect. Rinse the area with clean water and allow it to dry completely.

The repair area is now ready for painting. Paint spraying must be carried out in warm, dry, windless and dustfree atmosphere. These conditions can be created if you have access to a large indoor working area but if you are forced to work in the open, you will have to pick your day very carefully. If you are working indoors, dousing the floor in the work area with water will help to settle the dust which would otherwise be in the air. If the repair area is confined to one body panel, mask off the surrounding panels. This will help to minimize the effects of a slight mismatch in paint color. Trim pieces such as chrome strips, door handles, etc., will also need to be masked off or removed. Use masking tape and several thicknesses of newspaper for the masking operations.

Before spraying, shake the paint can thoroughly, then spray a test area until the technique is mastered. Cover the repair area with a thick coat of primer. The thickness should be built up using several thin layers of primer rather than one thick one. Using 600-grit wet-or-dry sandpaper, rub down the surface of the primer until it is very smooth. While doing this, the work area should be thoroughly rinsed with water, and the wet-or-dry sandpaper periodically rinsed as well. Allow the primer to dry before spraying additional coats.

Spray on the top coat, again building up the thickness by using several thin layers of paint. Begin spraying in the center of the repair area and then, using a circular motion, work out until the whole repair area and about two inches of the surrounding original paint is covered. Remove all masking material 10 to 15 minutes after spraying on the final coat of paint. Allow the new paint at least two weeks to harden, then using a very fine rubbing compound, blend the edges of the paint into the existing paint. Finally, apply a coat of wax.

7 Body and frame repairs – major damage

1 Major damage must be repaired by an auto body/frame repair shop with the necessary welding and hydraulic straightening equipment.
2 If the damage has been serious, it is vital that the frame be checked for correct alignment as the handling of the vehicle will be affected. Other problems, such as excessive tire wear and wear in the transmission and steering may also occur.

8 Windshield and rear window glass – replacement

Because of the special tools, adhesives and techniques required to replace the windshield and rear window glass, it should be done by a dealer service department or reputable auto body shop.

9 Weatherstripping – maintenance and replacement

1 The weatherstripping should be kept clean and free of contaminants such as gasoline and oil. Spray the weatherstripping periodically with silicone lubricant to reduce abrasion and cracking.
2 To remove the weatherstripping from the doors, apply a solvent such as 3M release agent or its equivalent. Work the release agent in between the metal and the rubber strip. Allow two or three minutes for penetration and softening of the adhesive.
3 Lift the weatherstripping from the drain trough before the solvent evaporates and the adhesive resets.
4 If residue remains, remove it with 3M adhesive cleaner or other suitable solvent.
5 Before installation, remove any protective powder from the new weatherstrip with a suitable solvent.
6 Apply a $\frac{1}{8}$-inch bead of weatherstrip adhesive along the inside corners of the drain trough.
7 Position one end of the rubber weatherstrip in the drain trough on either side of the door striker.
8 Install the weatherstripping along the drain trough with a stick or other suitable tool. Do not stretch the rubber.
9 Cut off the excess and bond the ends together with weatherstrip adhesive.

10 Door trim panels – removal and installation

1 Remove the window regulator handle. Remove the nylon washer, if so equipped.
2 Remove any attaching screws from the armrest overlay strip and pull off the overlay strip. If there is no overlay strip, remove the screw hole plugs.
3 Remove the armrest attaching screws and pull off the armrest.
4 On 1970 through 1973 model Gremlins, remove the attaching screws from the medallion plate and door handle bezel. Remove the plate and bezel (photos).
5 Remove the attaching screws from the rear view mirror remote control knob bezel.
6 Carefully slide the mirror knob bezel off of the mirror knob.
7 Remove the attaching screws from the interior door handle bezel and slide the bezel off the handle.
8 On 1979 and later models, remove the power door lock bezel, if so equipped. Remove the lock pushbutton.
9 Remove the screws along the bottom of the trim panel.
10 Carefully pry out the panel-to-door clips with a screwdriver or other suitable tool.
11 On 1979 and later models, remove the panel by pulling out and away from the door while also pulling up on the panel. Earlier model panels should simply slide off after removing the panel-to-door clips.

10.4A Removing the attaching screws from the door handle bezel

10.4B Removing the door handle bezel

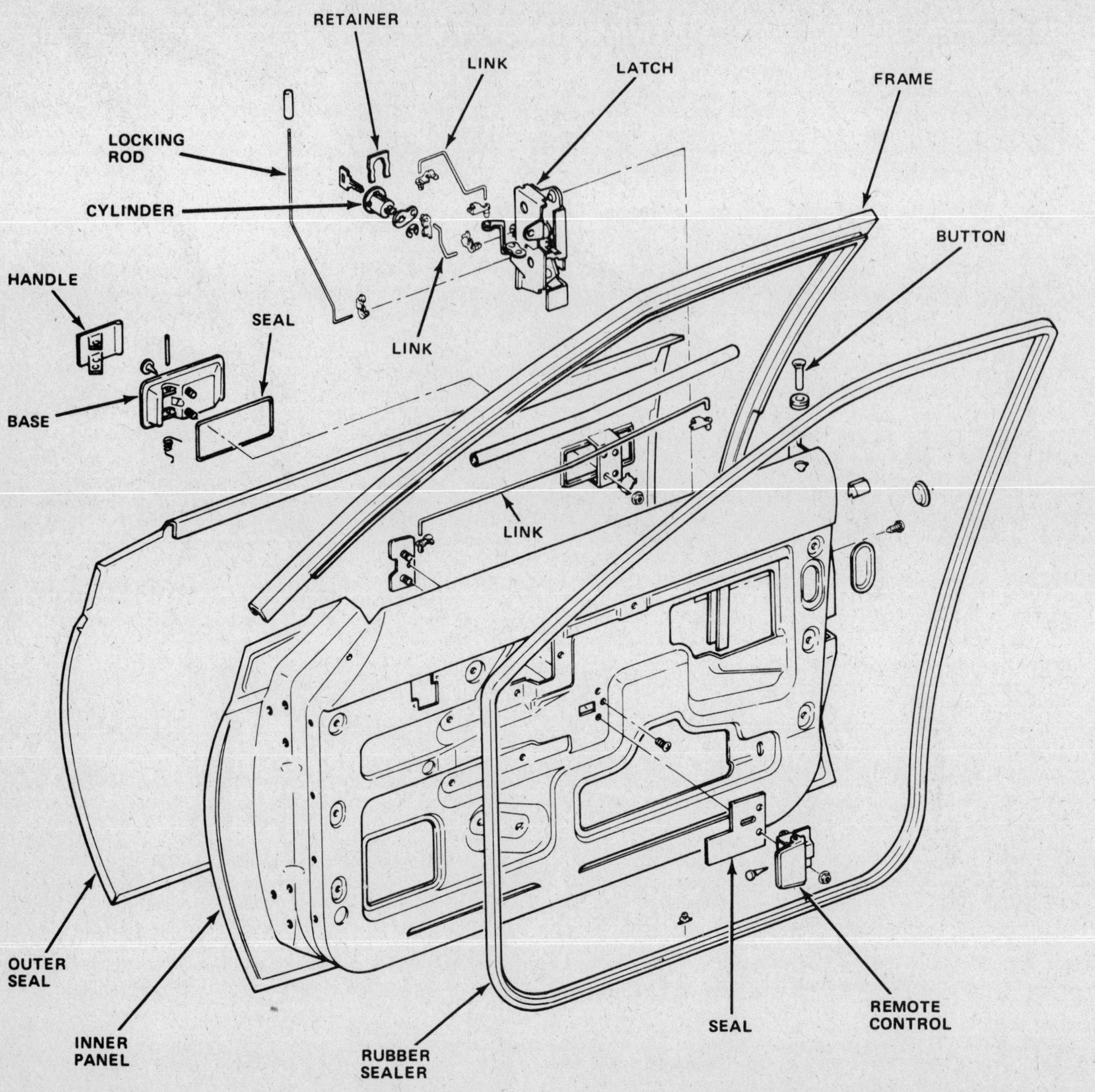

Fig. 12.1 Door components – exploded view (latch and latch linkages represent typical 1978 and later model door assemblies) (Sec 12)

11 Door striker – adjustment

1 If the door does not close smoothly, the door striker should be adjusted.

2 Loosen the mounting screw, adjust the striker and retighten the screws.

3 Repeat the procedure until the door closes properly. **Caution:** *The lock striker should enter the latch smoothly with no up or down movement of the door. The door should open smoothly without dragging on the striker. Double check for proper functioning. It is possible to set the striker in so far that the door is closed tight with only the safety catch engaged.*

12 Door latch assembly – removal and installation

Note: *You will need a TORX bit screwdriver to remove the latch assembly on 1976 and later models.*

1 Remove the door trim panel as described in Section 10.

2 Using a putty knife, carefully remove the water dam paper.

3 Disconnect the remote control rod, locking rods, and outside handle rod.

4 Remove the screws attaching the latch to the door and remove the latch.

5 Installation is the reverse of the removal procedure.

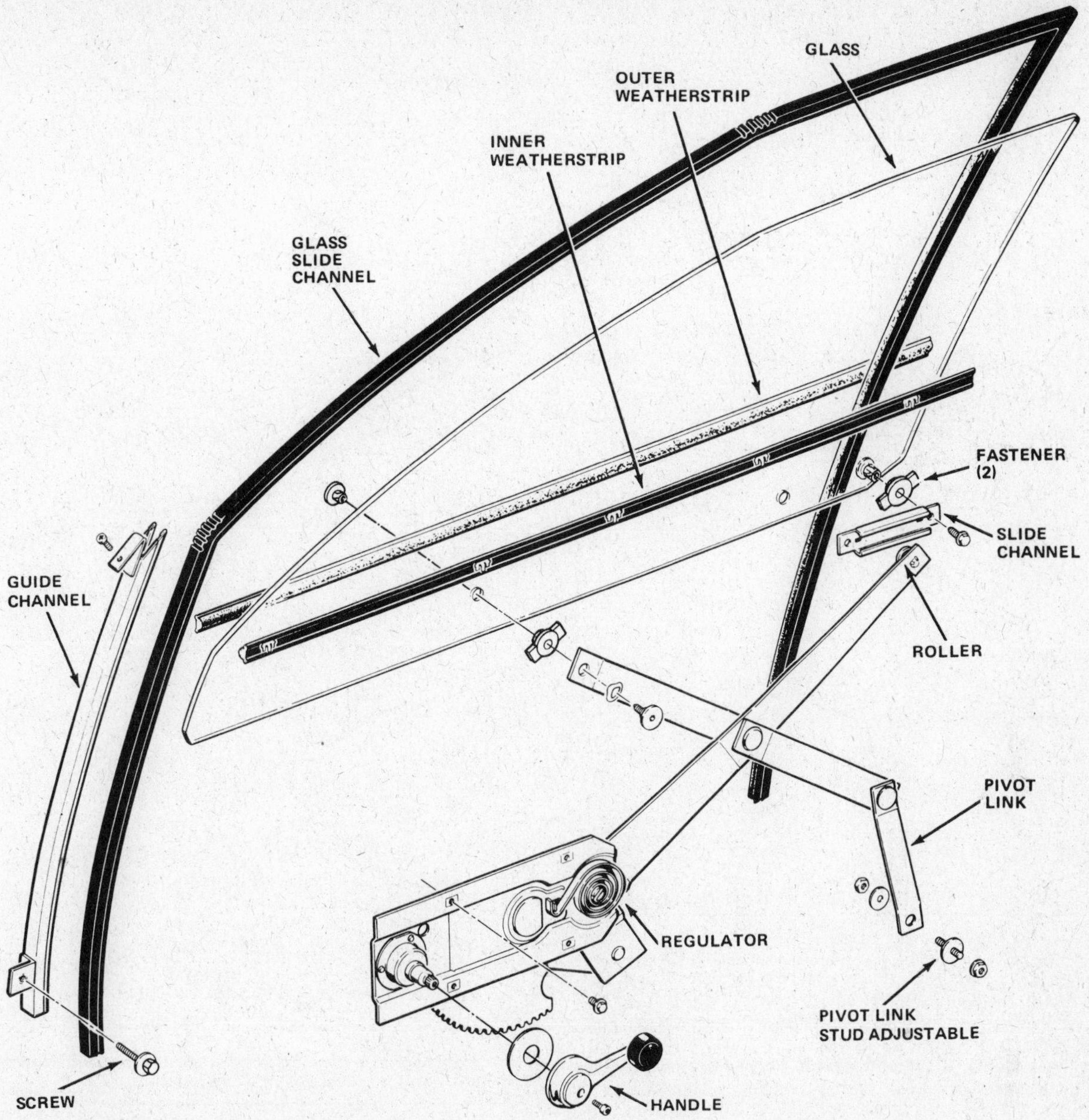

Fig. 12.2 Front door window regulator and window glass – exploded view (typical) (Secs 13 and 14)

13 Door window glass – removal and installation

Front doors – removal

1 Pull the inner glass weatherstrip away from the door panel at the retaining clips. Slightly distort the retaining slots with a screwdriver and remove the weatherstrip.

2 Remove the door trim panel as described in Section 10. Remove the water dam paper using a putty knife.

3 Install the window crank temporarily to raise the glass until the front and rear regulator arm attaching screws are visible through the access holes.

4 Apply masking tape to each side of the glass, over the top of the window frame. This will hold the glass in place while lowering the window regulator.

5 Remove the front regulator arm attaching screw.

6 Remove the two attaching screws from the roller guide channel at the rear of the glass.

7 Carefully roll the regulator to the down-stop.

8 Hold the glass from falling and remove the tape from the glass.

9 Lower the glass carefully while tilting it toward the hinge side of the door to disengage it from the slide channels.

10 Remove the glass by pulling it up and out of the door panel. Keep the glass toward the outside of the window frame.

Rear doors – removal

11 The procedure is slightly different for the Concord and Hornet model rear doors. Follow Steps 1 through 4.

12 Push the glass slightly away from the roller guide plate and pull the tang on the plate out of the hole in the lower window glass bottom channel.

13 Slide the roller guide plate assembly down.

14 Lower the glass to the down-stop.

15 Tilt the glass toward the latch side of the door and disconnect the regulator arm roller from the glass bottom channel.

Installation

16 Installation for the front and rear doors is the reverse of the removal procedure. Straighten the slots on the weatherstrip retaining clips before installing the weatherstrip.

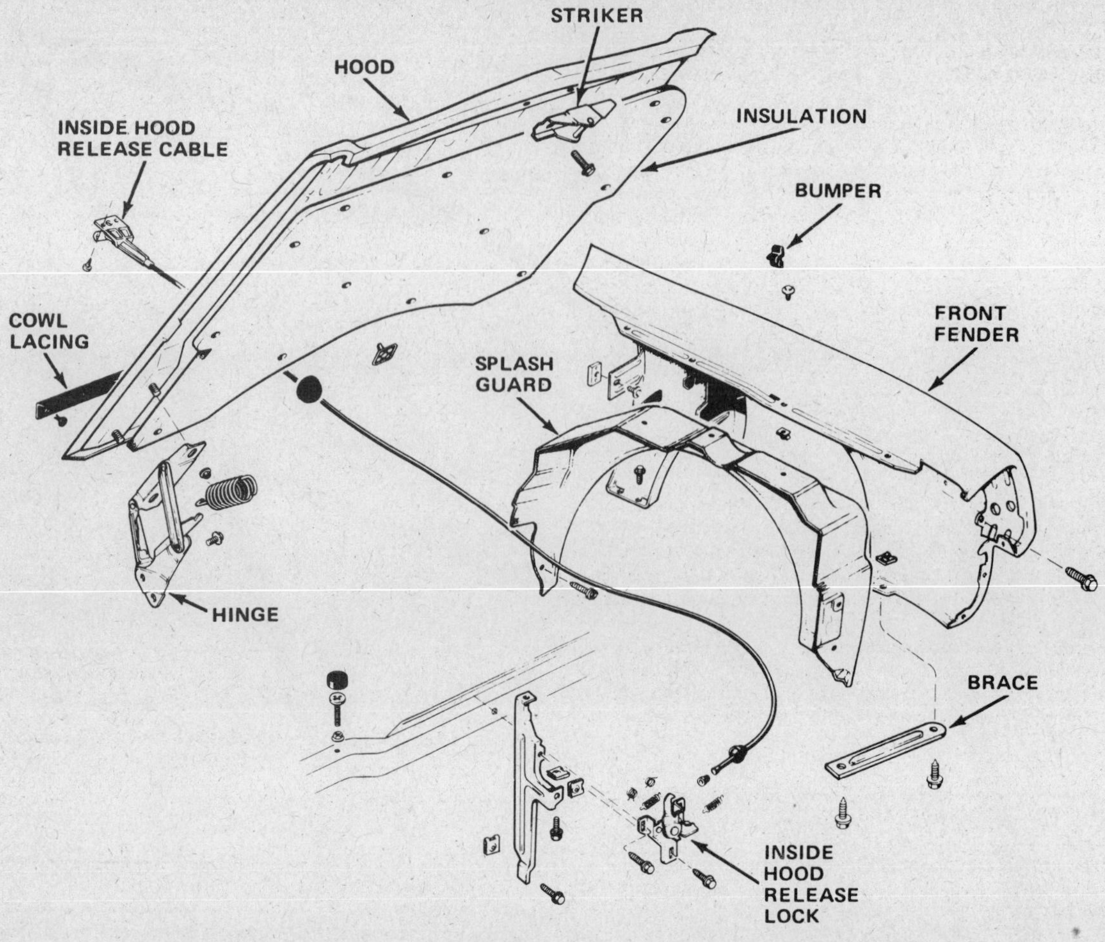

Fig. 12.3 Front fender and hood components – exploded view (typical) (Sec 16)

14 Door window regulator – removal, installation and adjustment

Note: *On 1978 through 1982 model window regulator assemblies, the regulator arm rivets must be drilled out prior to regulator removal. New rivets must be used for reinstallation of the regulator assembly.*

1 Follow steps 2 through 4 of Section 13.

2 Mark the position of the regulator attaching screws before removing the regulator. This will save time during reinstallation.

3 Remove the front regulator arm attaching screw.

4 Remove the forward attaching screw from the roller guide channel.

5 On 1970 through 1977 model door assemblies, remove the four attaching screws from the regulator assembly.

6 On 1978 through 1982 model door assemblies, the regulator attaching rivets must be drilled out. Use a $\frac{1}{4}$-inch drill bit.

7 Remove the attaching screw from the lower regulator arm pivot link.

8 Disengage the roller from the roller guide channel and remove the regulator assembly through the lower access hole.

9 Installation is the reverse of the removal procedure. Use the marked positions to reinstall the regulator assembly. However, if the window glass does not fit properly into the window frame, there are three separate adjustments to correct the problem.

a) Sliding the regulator assembly within its elongated holes will move the entire glass assembly forward or backward without changing the horizontal attitude of the glass.

b) Loosening the locknut on the lower attachment bolt of the glass slide channel facilitates tilt adjustment of the window glass. Turn the slotted screw clockwise to tip the upper edge of the glass out. Turning the screw counterclockwise tips the top of the glass in. Moving the slide channel forward or backward reduces or increases free play between the door frame channels.

c) Loosening the lower regulator arm pivot link facilitates forward and backward tilt. Moving the pivot link up raises the rear portion of the glass. Moving the pivot link down lowers the rear portion of the glass assembly.

15 Rear liftgate – removal and installation

1 Open the liftgate and remove all upper finish moulding.

2 Disconnect the rear wiper wires and remove the grommet, if so equipped.

3 Remove the bolts or retainer clips from the liftgate supports and fold the supports down.

4 Close the liftgate and engage the latch.

5 From inside the vehicle, carefully peel back the headlining (if necessary) and remove the nuts from the hinge studs.

6 Release the latch and remove the liftgate assembly.

7 Installation is the reverse of the removal procedure. Be sure the rubber hinge gaskets are in good condition before reusing them. Check the side gap adjustment before tightening the hinge bolts (the gap should be equal on both sides).

16 Hood – removal, installation and adjustment

Note: *An assistant will be required to help remove the hood.*

1 Prop open the hood and mark with paint (or scribe) the position of the hood hinge brackets. Place protective pads on the vehicle cowling so the hood will not damage the paint if it comes in contact with it. Disconnect the underhood light, if so equipped.

2 Remove the four bolts attaching the hinge brackets to the hood and carefully lift the hood away from the vehicle. Remove the hood

lock assembly. It is held in place by two bolts. Remove the inside release cable, if so equipped.
3 When installing the hood, carefully hold it in place, using the previously scribed marks to align it, and install the four mounting bolts finger tight.
4 Very carefully close the hood and move it, if necessary, until the gaps between the hood and fenders are equal. Raise the hood carefully (so it does not move on the hinge brackets) and tighten the four mounting bolts securely. Lower the hood and recheck the gaps.
5 Next, raise the hood and loosen the jam nuts on the bumper screws at the front of the vehicle.
6 Lower the hood to see if the top of the hood is even with the top of the fenders. If not, raise the hood and screw the bumper screws in or out to move the hood up or down, as necessary. Once the height is correctly adjusted, turn the two bumper screws $\frac{1}{4}$-turn counterclockwise and tighten the jam nuts. Recheck the height one last time.
7 If necessary, the rear height of the hood is adjustable. If the hood is low in relation to the cowl, insert shims between the hinge and the hood at the rear stud. If it is too high at the cowl, insert shims between the hinge and the hood at the front stud.
8 Install the hood lock assembly and tighten the bolts fingertight (so the assembly will move when pushed but is not loose). Close the hood and engage the latch, then pull the hood release handle. Carefully disengage the safety hook, so as not to disturb the position of the hood lock assembly, and raise the hood. Tighten the mounting bolts securely.
9 Close the hood until it latches. It should latch properly when dropped from a height of 12 inches. If excess pressure is required to engage the latch, or if the hood is loose after engaging the latch, adjust the height of the hood lock until the hood latches properly and is not loose.

17 Radiator grille – removal and installation

Note: *On 1975 and 1976 model Gremlins, you will need a special TORX screwdriver (available from your local auto parts store) to remove the headlight doors.*
1 On 1974 through 1976 Gremlins, remove the headlight door and side marker light connectors.
2 On 1970 through 1978 Gremlins and 1978 Concords, disconnect the parking light connectors.
3 Raise the hood and remove the grille attaching screws.
4 On 1975 and 1976 Gremlins, remove the fasteners from the gravel shield.
5 Remove the grille.
6 Installation is the reverse of the removal procedure.

18 Bumpers – removal and installation

1 Non-impact absorbing bumpers installed up until 1973 are removed by simply unbolting the bumper bars from their brackets and, if necessary, the brackets from the frame.
2 From 1973 on, energy absorbing bumpers are used. On the front, a recoverable type bumper strut is used, which utilizes silicone liquid and gas-filled telescopic mounting struts. When removing this type of unit, keep the bumper bar straight (not allowing one end to drop) otherwise the seals in the hydraulic unit may be damaged.
3 On the rear, the bumper is a non-recoverable type. Should these units be damaged due to compression from a rear end collision, they must be replaced.
4 Do not puncture or attempt to dismantle either type of mounting strut.

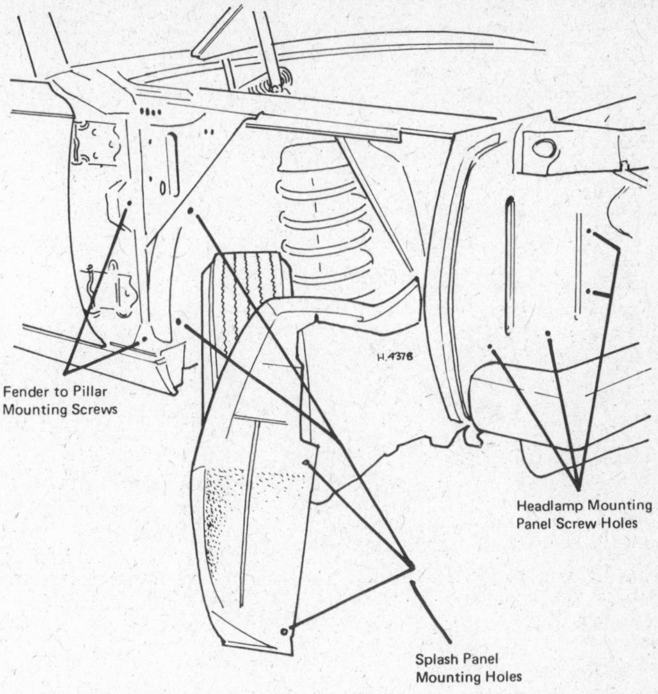

Fig. 12.4 Locations of front fender mounting screws – typical (Sec 19)

19 Front fender – removal and installation

1 Apply several layers of masking tape over the edge of the bumper end to prevent scratching the fender paint.
2 Remove the windshield lower reveal moulding with a suitable tool.
3 Turn the wheels to the side where the fender is to be removed.
4 On 1970 through 1974 model Gremlins and Hornets, open the door and remove the fender-to-cowl top attaching screw.
5 Remove the splash panel mounting screws (usually covered with undercoating) and remove the splash panel. This will expose the screws which attach the fender to the pillar and rocker panel.
6 Remove the fender-to-pillar and fender-to-rocker panel screws.
7 Remove the headlight door and headlight bucket and disconnect the side marker light wires.
8 Disconnect the headlight wiring connector and pull the wiring through the headlight mounting panel.
9 On 1970 through 1974 Gremlins and Hornets, remove the radiator grille as described in Section 17.
10 On all other models, remove the headlight mounting panel-to-radiator support attaching screws. Remove the grille-to-headlight mounting panel plastic fastener.
11 Remove the brace-to-fender skirt screw and the fender-to-lower grille panel screws.
12 Remove the fender-to-wheelhouse screws.
13 Mask the front edge of the door.
14 Tilt the top of the fender out at the front and lift at the rear to remove the fender.
15 Installation is the reverse of the removal procedure.

Conversion factors

Length (distance)						
Inches (in)	X	25.4	= Millimetres (mm)	X	0.0394	= Inches (in)
Feet (ft)	X	0.305	= Metres (m)	X	3.281	= Feet (ft)
Miles	X	1.609	= Kilometres (km)	X	0.621	= Miles
Volume (capacity)						
Cubic inches (cu in; in³)	X	16.387	= Cubic centimetres (cc; cm³)	X	0.061	= Cubic inches (cu in; in³)
Imperial pints (Imp pt)	X	0.568	= Litres (l)	X	1.76	= Imperial pints (Imp pt)
Imperial quarts (Imp qt)	X	1.137	= Litres (l)	X	0.88	= Imperial quarts (Imp qt)
Imperial quarts (Imp qt)	X	1.201	= US quarts (US qt)	X	0.833	= Imperial quarts (Imp qt)
US quarts (US qt)	X	0.946	= Litres (l)	X	1.057	= US quarts (US qt)
Imperial gallons (Imp gal)	X	4.546	= Litres (l)	X	0.22	= Imperial gallons (Imp gal)
Imperial gallons (Imp gal)	X	1.201	= US gallons (US gal)	X	0.833	= Imperial gallons (Imp gal)
US gallons (US gal)	X	3.785	= Litres (l)	X	0.264	= US gallons (US gal)
Mass (weight)						
Ounces (oz)	X	28.35	= Grams (g)	X	0.035	= Ounces (oz)
Pounds (lb)	X	0.454	= Kilograms (kg)	X	2.205	= Pounds (lb)
Force						
Ounces-force (ozf; oz)	X	0.278	= Newtons (N)	X	3.6	= Ounces-force (ozf; oz)
Pounds-force (lbf; lb)	X	4.448	= Newtons (N)	X	0.225	= Pounds-force (lbf; lb)
Newtons (N)	X	0.1	= Kilograms-force (kgf; kg)	X	9.81	= Newtons (N)
Pressure						
Pounds-force per square inch (psi; lbf/in²; lb/in²)	X	0.070	= Kilograms-force per square centimetre (kgf/cm²; kg/cm²)	X	14.223	= Pounds-force per square inch (psi; lbf/in²; lb/in²)
Pounds-force per square inch (psi; lbf/in²; lb/in²)	X	0.068	= Atmospheres (atm)	X	14.696	= Pounds-force per square inch (psi; lbf/in²; lb/in²)
Pounds-force per square inch (psi; lbf/in²; lb/in²)	X	0.069	= Bars	X	14.5	= Pounds-force per square inch (psi; lbf/in²; lb/in²)
Pounds-force per square inch (psi; lbf/in²; lb/in²)	X	6.895	= Kilopascals (kPa)	X	0.145	= Pounds-force per square inch (psi; lbf/in²; lb/in²)
Kilopascals (kPa)	X	0.01	= Kilograms-force per square centimetre (kgf/cm²; kg/cm²)	X	98.1	= Kilopascals (kPa)
Millibar (mbar)	X	100	= Pascals (Pa)	X	0.01	= Millibar (mbar)
Millibar (mbar)	X	0.0145	= Pounds-force per square inch (psi; lbf/in²; lb/in²)	X	68.947	= Millibar (mbar)
Millibar (mbar)	X	0.75	= Millimetres of mercury (mmHg)	X	1.333	= Millibar (mbar)
Millibar (mbar)	X	0.401	= Inches of water (inH$_2$O)	X	2.491	= Millibar (mbar)
Millimetres of mercury (mmHg)	X	0.535	= Inches of water (inH$_2$O)	X	1.868	= Millimetres of mercury (mmHg)
Inches of water (inH$_2$O)	X	0.036	= Pounds-force per square inch (psi; lbf/in²; lb/in²)	X	27.68	= Inches of water (inH$_2$O)
Torque (moment of force)						
Pounds-force inches (lbf in; lb in)	X	1.152	= Kilograms-force centimetre (kgf cm; kg cm)	X	0.868	= Pounds-force inches (lbf in; lb in)
Pounds-force inches (lbf in; lb in)	X	0.113	= Newton metres (Nm)	X	8.85	= Pounds-force inches (lbf in; lb in)
Pounds-force inches (lbf in; lb in)	X	0.083	= Pounds-force feet (lbf ft; lb ft)	X	12	= Pounds-force inches (lbf in; lb in)
Pounds-force feet (lbf ft; lb ft)	X	0.138	= Kilograms-force metres (kgf m; kg m)	X	7.233	= Pounds-force feet (lbf ft; lb ft)
Pounds-force feet (lbf ft; lb ft)	X	1.356	= Newton metres (Nm)	X	0.738	= Pounds-force feet (lbf ft; lb ft)
Newton metres (Nm)	X	0.102	= Kilograms-force metres (kgf m; kg m)	X	9.804	= Newton metres (Nm)
Power						
Horsepower (hp)	X	745.7	= Watts (W)	X	0.0013	= Horsepower (hp)
Velocity (speed)						
Miles per hour (miles/hr; mph)	X	1.609	= Kilometres per hour (km/hr; kph)	X	0.621	= Miles per hour (miles/hr; mph)
Fuel consumption*						
Miles per gallon, Imperial (mpg)	X	0.354	= Kilometres per litre (km/l)	X	2.825	= Miles per gallon, Imperial (mpg)
Miles per gallon, US (mpg)	X	0.425	= Kilometres per litre (km/l)	X	2.352	= Miles per gallon, US (mpg)

Temperature

Degrees Fahrenheit = (°C x 1.8) + 32

Degrees Celsius (Degrees Centigrade; °C) = (°F - 32) x 0.56

**It is common practice to convert from miles per gallon (mpg) to litres/100 kilometres (l/100km), where mpg (Imperial) x l/100 km = 282 and mpg (US) x l/100 km = 235*

Index

A

About this manual – 2
Acknowledgements – 2
Air cleaner, thermo-controlled
check – 44
Air conditioning system
check – 119
compressor
removal and installation – 120
condenser
removal and installation – 120
evaporator
removal and installation – 120
receiver/dryer
removal and installation – 121
servicing – 119
Air filter
replacement – 43
Alternator
brush
replacement – 162
removal and installation – 162
Antifreeze – 116
Automatic transmission – 208 *et seq*
Automatic transmission
diagnosis – 209
fluid change – 55
general information – 209
kickdown (front) band adjustment – 210
neutral safety switch
check and replacement – 209
removal and installation – 210
shift linkage adjustment – 210
specifications – 208
throttle linkage and cable adjustment – 209
torque specifications – 208
troubleshooting – 26
Axle shafts, bearings and oil seals
removal and installation – 219

B

Battery
cables
check and replacement – 160
check and maintenance – 39
emergency jump starting – 160
removal and installation – 160
Bleeding the brakes – 224
Bleeding the clutch – 214
Bleeding the power steering – 276
Body – 277 *et seq*
Body
front fender
removal and installation – 285
general information – 277
maintenance
exterior – 277
hinges and locks – 280
upholstery and carpets – 280
vinyl trim – 280
rear liftgate
removal and installation – 284
repair
major damage – 281
minor damage – 280
torque specifications – 277
weatherstripping
maintenance and replacement – 281
Bodywork repair sequence (color) – 278, 279
Brakes – 221 *et seq*
Brakes
booster
removal and installation – 230
check – 47
combination valve (disc/drum system)
description and replacement – 223
disc
inspection, removal and installation – 230
disc caliper
removal, overhaul and installation – 230
disc pads
removal and installation – 226
drum
servicing – 226
general information – 222
hoses and brake lines
inspection and replacement – 224
light switch
removal and installation – 222
hydraulic system
bleeding procedure – 224
master cylinder
overhaul – 231
removal and installation – 231
parking brake
description and adjustment – 223
pedal
removal and installation – 223
pressure differential valve (drum brakes)
description and replacement – 223
shoes
adjustment – 225
removal and installation – 225
specifications – 30, 221
torque specifications – 222
troubleshooting – 27
wheel cylinder
removal, overhaul and installation – 231
Bulbs, light
replacement – 239
Bumpers
removal and installation – 285

C

Camshaft
installation
6-cylinder engine – 99
V8 engine – 111
removal
6-cylinder engine – 92
V8 engine – 109
Camshaft and bearings
inspection and replacement (6-cylinder engine) – 95
removal and installation (4-cylinder engine) – 81
Capacities – 30
Carburetor
application – 126
choke check – 54

fuel/air mixture adjustment – 55
mounting torque check – 54
overhaul and adjustment
Autolite/Motorcraft – 132
Autolite/Motorcraft 2100 and 2150 – 135
Carter BBD – 140
Holley-Weber 5210 – 145
Rochester 2SE and E2SE – 148
YF – 127
removal and installation – 127
specifications – 122

Charging system
check – 160

Chassis
lubrication – 41

Chemicals, automotive – 18

Clutch
hydraulic system
bleeding – 214
master cylinder
overhaul – 216
removal and installation – 216
pedal
free play check and adjustment – 46
removal and installation – 214
pilot bushing
replacement – 216
release bearing mechanism
disassembly, inspection and reassembly – 214
removal, inspection and installation – 214
slave cylinder
overhaul – 216
removal and installation – 216
specifications – 33, 213
torque specifications – 213
troubleshooting – 25

Coil (ignition) – 167

Compression pressure – 32, 50

Condenser – 52

Contact points and condenser
replacement and adjustment – 52

Conversion factors – 286

Coolant reserve system
testing – 116

Coolant temperature gauge – 236

Cooling, heating and air conditioning systems – 115 *et seq*

Cooling, heating and air conditioning systems
general information – 115
specifications – 115
torque specifications – 115

Cooling system
check – 41
draining, flushing and refilling – 50

Crankshaft
inspection – 64
installation and main bearing oil clearance check
4-cylinder engine – 82
6-cylinder engine – 98
V8 engine – 112
removal
general – 61
4-cylinder engine – 82
V8 engine – 112

Crankshaft pulley hub and front oil seal (4-cylinder engine)
removal and installation – 75

Cylinder compression pressure
check – 50
specifications – 32

Cylinder head
cleaning and inspection – 58
disassembly – 58
installation
4-cylinder engine – 75
6-cylinder engine – 100
V8 engine – 112
reassembly – 60
removal
4-cylinder engine – 75
6-cylinder engine – 92
V8 engine – 107

D

Differential
lubricant
change – 55
pinion oil seal
replacement – 218

Dimensions, general – 10

Distributor
cap and rotor
check and replacement – 50
check
conventional – 168
electronic – 168
removal and installation – 168

Door
latch assembly
removal and installation – 282
striker
adjustment – 282
trim panels
removal and installation – 281
window glass
removal and installation – 283
window regulator
removal, installation and adjustment – 284

Drivebelts – 43

Driveline – 213 *et seq*

Driveline
general information – 214

Driveshaft
removal and installation – 217
troubleshooting – 26

Dwell angle – 54

E

Electrical systems, chassis – 234 *et seq*

Electrical system, chassis
general information – 234
troubleshooting – 234
wiring diagrams – 242 through 260

Electrical systems, engine – 159 *et seq*

Electrical systems, engine
general information – 160
specifications – 159
torque specifications – 160

Emission control systems – 172 *et seq*

Emission control systems
air injection system – 173
altitude compensation circuit – 180
catalytic converter – 176
Exhaust Gas Recirculation (EGR) system – 43, 175
forced air pre-heat systems – 178
fuel vapor control system – 46, 173
general information – 172
Positive Crankcase Ventilation (PCV) system – 43, 46, 173
spark control systems – 176
torque specifications – 172

Engine (four-cylinder) – 69 *et seq*

Engine (four-cylinder)
general information – 71
installation – 83
rejoining to automatic transmission – 83
rejoining to manual transmission – 83
removal – 71
separation from automatic transmission – 71
separation from manual transmission – 71
specifications – 69
torque specifications – 70

Engine (general)
block
cleaning – 62
inspection – 62
disassembly – 57
drivebelts
check and adjustment – 43
idle speed
adjustment – 45
oil and filter
change – 41
overhaul, general – 56
rebuilding alternatives – 57
removal methods and precautions – 57
repair operations possible with engine in vehicle – 56
start-up and break-in after overhaul – 68
troubleshooting – 22
Engine, general overhaul procedures – 56 *et seq*
Engine (six-cylinder) – 84 *et seq*
Engine (six-cylinder)
component designation (oversize and undersize) – 87
components, external
installation – 101
removal – 90
general information – 87
installation (1977 through 1983) – 101
installation with transmission (1970 through 1976) – 101
mount flexible cushions
replacement – 88
oil seals
replacement – 96
removal (1977 through 1983) – 90
removal with transmission (1970 through 1976) – 88
separation from automatic transmission (1970 thru 1976) – 90
separation from manual transmission (1970 thru 1976) – 90
specifications – 84
torque specifications – 86
Engine (V8) – 103 *et seq*
Engine (V8)
component designation (oversize and undersize) – 106
connection to automatic transmission – 114
connection to manual transmission – 114
disassembly and reassembly sequence – 107
general information – 105
installation (1977 through 1983) – 114
installation with transmission (1970 through 1976) – 114
intake manifold
installation – 112
removal – 107
mounts
replacement – 106
oil seal
replacement – 110
removal (1977 through 1983) – 107
removal with transmission (1970 through 1976) – 106
separation from automatic transmission – 107
separation from manual transmission – 107
specifications – 103
torque specifications – 105
Exhaust manifold heat valve
check – 44
Exhaust Gas Recirculation (EGR) system
general information – 175
valve
check – 43
Exhaust system
check – 42
component
replacement – 156
general information – 125

F

Fluids and lubricants
level checks
automatic transmission fluid – 38
brake fluid – 37
differential lubricant – 39
engine coolant – 37
manual transmission lubricant – 38
power steering fluid – 39
windshield washer fluid – 37
Flywheel and rear main oil seal (4-cylinder engine)
removal and installation – 80
Flywheel and starter ring gear (6-cylinder engine)
inspection and servicing – 96
Flywheel/driveplate (6-cylinder engine)
installation – 99
removal – 94
Fuel and exhaust systems – 122 *et seq*
Fuel filter
replacement – 45
Fuel gauge – 236
Fuel lines and hoses
check and replacement – 126
Fuel pump
check – 126
general information – 125
removal and installation – 126
Fuel system
check – 43
general information – 125
specifications – 122
torque specifications – 124
Fuel tank
cleaning and repair – 156
removal and installation – 156
Fuel vapor control system
canister
filter replacement – 46
general information – 173
Fuses and fusible links – 235

G

Gauges
check – 236

H

Hazard warning lights – 236
Headlights
adjustment – 239
removal and installation – 239
warning buzzer – 241
Heater
assembly
removal and installation – 118
control panel
removal and installation – 119
controls
adjustment – 117
Hood
removal, installation and adjustment – 284
Horn and horn relay – 236
Hoses, underhood
check and replacement – 40

I

Idle speed – 32, 45
Ignition switch
removal and installation – 239
Ignition system
check – 164
coil
removal and installation – 167
electronic
distributor – 168
module removal and installation – 169

pick-up coil removal and installation – 169
specifications – 31
timing
check and adjustment – 52
Instrument cluster and package tray
removal and installation – 236

J

Jacking – 19

L

Light bulbs – 239
Lubricants and fluids
general information – 18
recommended – 30
Lubrication system (6-cylinder engine) – **94**

M

Main and connecting rod bearings
inspection – 65
selection
6-cylinder engine – 96
V8 engine – 113
Maintenance, routine – 33, 36
Maintenance techniques – 12
Manifolds
exhaust (4-cylinder engine)
removal and installation – 74
intake (4-cylinder engine)
removal and installation – 74
intake (V8 engine)
installation – 112
removal – 107
Manual transmission – 187 *et seq*
Manual transmission
application and identification – 182
disassembly, inspection and reassembly
HR1 – 184
SR4 – 198
T-4 – 201
T-5 – 204
T-10 – 187
T-14 and T-15 – 191
T-96 – 190
150T – 195
extension housing oil seal
replacement – 184
gearshift lever
removal and installation – 182
general information – 182
planning major work – 182
removal and installation – 184
shift linkage
adjustment – 183
specifications – 187
torque specifications – 182
troubleshooting – 25

O

Oil pan
installation
6-cylinder engine – 99
V8 engine – 112
removal
6-cylinder engine – 92
V8 engine – 107
removal and installation
4-cylinder engine – 78
Oil pressure gauge – 236
Oil pressure warning light – 236
Oil pump (4-cylinder engine)
disassembly, inspection and reassembly – 79
driveshaft
removal and installation – 78
removal and installation – 79
Oil pump (6-cylinder engine)
disassembly, inspection and reassembly – 95
installation – 99
removal – 94
Oil pump (V8 engine)
disassembly, inspection and reassembly – 109
inspection – 111
removal – 109

P

Parts, buying – 10
Piston/connecting rod assembly
inspection – 63
installation and bearing oil clearance check – 66
removal – 60
Piston rings
installation – 65
Positive Crankcase Ventilation (PCV) system
filter
replacement – 43
general information – 173
valve
replacement – 46
Pushrod cover (4-cylinder engine)
removal and installation – 73

R

Radiator
pressure cap rating – 32
removal and installation – 117
servicing – 116
Radiator grille
removal and installation – 285
Radio
dial bulbs
replacement – 241
removal and installation – 241
Rear axle
assembly
removal and installation – 220
axleshafts, bearings and oil seals
removal and installation – 219
hub
removal and installation – 219
Rear axle and differential
troubleshooting – 27
Rear window defogger
precautions and check – 241
Rocker arm cover (4-cylinder engine)
removal and installation – 71
Rocker arms, pushrods and valve springs (4-cylinder engine)
removal and installation (engine in vehicle) – 71
Rocker gear (6-cylinder engine)
inspection and overhaul – 94
installation – 100
removal – 91
Routine maintenance
intervals – 36
introduction – 33

S

Safety first! – 20
Seat belt
interlock system (1974 and 1975) – 241

warning system
1970 through 1973 – 241
1976 through 1982 – 241
Spark plug
conditions (color chart) – 51
replacement – 49
wires
check and replacement – 50
Speedometer cable
removal and installation – 239
Starter motor
brush
replacement – 164
removal and installation – 164
Starter solenoid
removal and installation – 164
Starting system
check – 163
Suspension and steering – 261 *et seq*
Suspension and steering
check – 42
front coil springs
removal and installation – 265
general information – 262
idler arm
removal and installation – 263
lower control arm
removal and installation – 266
manual steering gear
in-vehicle service and repair – 268
maintenance and adjustment – 268
overhaul – 269
removal and installation – 268
Pitman arm
removal and installation – 263
power steering
gear and pump removal and installation – 276
hydraulic system bleeding – 276
inspection and maintenance – 276
in-vehicle service and repair – 276
rear spring
disassembly, inspection and reassembly – 267
removal and installation – 266
shock absorbers, front
removal and installation – 262
shock absorbers, rear
removal and installation – 262
stabilizer bar
removal and installation – 262
steering column
overhaul (standard type) – 270
overhaul (tilt-type with column shift) – 273
overhaul (tilt-type with floor shift) – 275
removal and installation – 270
steering knuckle
removal and installation – 264
steering linkage and balljoints
removal and installation – 263
steering wheel
removal and installation – 270
strut rod
removal and installation – 262
suspension balljoints
removal and installation – 265
torque specifications – 261
troubleshooting – 28
upper control arm
removal and installation – 266

T

Thermostat
removal and installation – 116
Throttle linkage
check and adjustment – 125
Timing chain (V8 engine)
wear checking – 108
Timing chain and sprockets
installation
6-cylinder engine – 99
V8 engine – 111
inspection (6-cylinder engine) – 95
removal (V8 engine) – 108
Timing chain cover (V8 engine)
installation – 111
removal – 108
Timing cover, chain and sprockets (6-cylinder engine)
removal – 92
Timing gear cover (4-cylinder engine)
removal and installation – 76
Timing (ignition) – 52
Tire
check – 40
pressure check – 40
rotation – 44
Tools – 15
Torque specifications, general – 33
Towing – 19
Troubleshooting – 21 *et seq*
Troubleshooting
automatic transmission – 26
brakes – 27
clutch – 25
driveshaft – 26
electrical system – 234
engine and performance – 22
manual transmission – 25
rear axle and differential – 27
suspension and steering – 28
Tune-up and routine maintenance – 30 *et seq*
Tune-up sequence – 33
Turn signal – 236

U

Universal joints
check – 217
replacement – 217

V

Valve lifters, hydraulic (4-cylinder engine)
removal, inspection and installation – 73
Valve lifters, hydraulic (6-cylinder engine)
description and removal – 92
inspection and overhaul – 95
installation – 100
Valves
servicing – 60
Vehicle identification numbers – 11
Voltage regulator, external
removal and installation – 162

W

Water pump
removal and installation – 117
Wheel bearing
check and service – 48
Wheels
alignment – 262
inspection – 262
Windshield and rear window glass
replacement – 281
Windshield and rear window washers – 241
Windshield and rear wiper motors
removal and installation – 239
Wiring diagrams – 242 to 260
Working facilities – 17

Haynes Automotive Manuals

NOTE: New manuals are added to this list on a periodic basis. If you do not see a listing for your vehicle, consult your local Haynes dealer for the latest product information.

ACURA

*1776 **Integra & Legend** all models '86 thru '90

AMC

Jeep CJ - *see JEEP (412)*
694 **Mid-size models,** Concord, Hornet, Gremlin & Spirit '70 thru '83
934 **(Renault) Alliance & Encore** all models '83 thru '87

AUDI

615 **4000** all models '80 thru '87
428 **5000** all models '77 thru '83
1117 **5000** all models '84 thru '88

AUSTIN

Healey Sprite - *see MG Midget Roadster (265)*

BMW

*2020 **3/5 Series** not including diesel or all-wheel drive models '82 thru '92
276 **320i** all 4 cyl models '75 thru '83
632 **528i** & 530i all models '75 thru '80
240 **1500 thru 2002** all models except Turbo '59 thru '77
348 **2500, 2800, 3.0 & Bavaria** all models '69 thru '76

BUICK

Century (front wheel drive) - *see GENERAL MOTORS (829)*
*1627 **Buick, Oldsmobile & Pontiac Full-size (Front wheel drive)** all models '85 thru '95 **Buick** Electra, LeSabre and Park Avenue; **Oldsmobile** Delta 88 Royale, Ninety Eight and Regency; **Pontiac** Bonneville
1551 **Buick Oldsmobile & Pontiac Full-size (Rear wheel drive)** **Buick** Estate '70 thru '90, Electra'70 thru '84, LeSabre '70 thru '85, Limited '74 thru '79 **Oldsmobile** Custom Cruiser '70 thru '90, Delta 88 '70 thru '85,Ninety-eight '70 thru '84 **Pontiac** Bonneville '70 thru '81, Catalina '70 thru '81, Grandville '70 thru '75, Parisienne '83 thru '86
627 **Mid-size Regal & Century** all rear-drive models with V6, V8 and Turbo '74 thru '87
Regal - *see GENERAL MOTORS (1671)*
Skyhawk - *see GENERAL MOTORS (766)*
Skylark '80 thru '85 - *see GENERAL MOTORS (38020)*
Skylark '86 on - *see GENERAL MOTORS (1420)*
Somerset - *see GENERAL MOTORS (1420)*

CADILLAC

*751 **Cadillac Rear Wheel Drive** all gasoline models '70 thru '93
Cimarron - *see GENERAL MOTORS (766)*

CHEVROLET

*1477 **Astro & GMC Safari Mini-vans** '85 thru '93
554 **Camaro V8** all models '70 thru '81
866 **Camaro** all models '82 thru '92
Cavalier - *see GENERAL MOTORS (766)*
Celebrity - *see GENERAL MOTORS (829)*
625 **Chevelle, Malibu & El Camino** all V6 & V8 models '69 thru '87
449 **Chevette & Pontiac T1000** '76 thru '87
550 **Citation** all models '80 thru '85
*1628 **Corsica/Beretta** all models '87 thru '95
274 **Corvette** all V8 models '68 thru '82
*1336 **Corvette** all models '84 thru '91
1762 **Chevrolet Engine Overhaul Manual**
704 **Full-size Sedans** Caprice, Impala, Biscayne, Bel Air & Wagons '69 thru '90
Lumina - *see GENERAL MOTORS (1671)*
Lumina APV - *see GENERAL MOTORS (2035)*
319 **Luv Pick-up** all 2WD & 4WD '72 thru '82
626 **Monte Carlo** all models '70 thru '88
241 **Nova** all V8 models '69 thru '79
*1642 **Nova and Geo Prizm** all front wheel drive models, '85 thru '92
420 **Pick-ups '67 thru '87** - Chevrolet & GMC, all V8 & in-line 6 cyl, 2WD & 4WD '67 thru '87; Suburbans, Blazers & Jimmys '67 thru '91
*1664 **Pick-ups '88 thru '95** - Chevrolet & GMC, all full-size pick-ups, '88 thru '95; Blazer & Jimmy '92 thru '94; Suburban '92 thru '95; Tahoe & Yukon '95
*831 **S-10 & GMC S-15 Pick-ups** all models '82 thru '93
*1727 **Sprint & Geo Metro** '85 thru '94
*345 **Vans - Chevrolet & GMC**, V8 & in-line 6 cylinder models '68 thru '95

CHRYSLER

2114 **Chrysler Engine Overhaul Manual**
*2058 **Full-size Front-Wheel Drive** '88 thru '93
K-Cars - *see DODGE Aries (723)*
Laser - *see DODGE Daytona (1140)*
*1337 **Chrysler & Plymouth Mid-size** front wheel drive '82 thru '93
Rear-wheel Drive - *see Dodge Rear-wheel Drive (2098)*

DATSUN

402 **200SX** all models '77 thru '79
647 **200SX** all models '80 thru '83
228 **B - 210** all models '73 thru '78
525 **210** all models '78 thru '82
206 **240Z, 260Z & 280Z** Coupe '70 thru '78
563 **280ZX** Coupe & 2+2 '79 thru '83
300ZX - *see NISSAN (1137)*
679 **310** all models '78 thru '82
123 **510 & PL521 Pick-up** '68 thru '73
430 **510** all models '78 thru '81
372 **610** all models '72 thru '76
277 **620 Series Pick-up** all models '73 thru '79
720 Series Pick-up - *see NISSAN (771)*
376 **810/Maxima** all gasoline models, '77 thru '84
Pulsar - *see NISSAN (876)*
Sentra - *see NISSAN (982)*
Stanza - *see NISSAN (981)*

DODGE

400 & 600 - *see CHRYSLER Mid-size (1337)*
*723 **Aries & Plymouth Reliant** '81 thru '89
1231 **Caravan & Plymouth Voyager Mini-Vans** all models '84 thru '95
699 **Challenger & Plymouth Saporro** all models '78 thru '83
Challenger '67-'76 - *see DODGE Dart (234)*
236 **Colt** all models '71 thru '77
610 **Colt & Plymouth Champ (front wheel drive)** all models '78 thru '87
*1668 **Dakota Pick-ups** all models '87 thru '93
234 **Dart, Challenger/Plymouth Barracuda & Valiant** 6 cyl models '67 thru '76
*1140 **Daytona & Chrysler Laser** '84 thru '89
*545 **Omni & Plymouth Horizon** '78 thru '90
*912 **Pick-ups** all full-size models '74 thru '91
*556 **Ram 50/D50 Pick-ups & Raider and Plymouth Arrow Pick-ups** '79 thru '93
2098 **Dodge/Plymouth/Chrysler** rear wheel drive '71 thru '89
*1726 **Shadow & Plymouth Sundance** '87 thru '93
*1779 **Spirit & Plymouth Acclaim** '89 thru '95
*349 **Vans - Dodge & Plymouth** V8 & 6 cyl models '71 thru '91

EAGLE

Talon - *see Mitsubishi Eclipse (2097)*

FIAT

094 **124 Sport Coupe & Spider** '68 thru '78
273 **X1/9** all models '74 thru '80

FORD

*1476 **Aerostar Mini-vans** all models '86 thru '94
788 **Bronco and Pick-ups** '73 thru '79
*880 **Bronco and Pick-ups** '80 thru '95
268 **Courier Pick-up** all models '72 thru '82
2105 **Crown Victoria & Mercury Grand Marquis** '88 thru '94
1763 **Ford Engine Overhaul Manual**
789 **Escort/Mercury Lynx** all models '81 thru '90
*2046 **Escort/Mercury Tracer** '91 thru '95
*2021 **Explorer & Mazda Navajo** '91 thru '95
560 **Fairmont & Mercury Zephyr** '78 thru '83
334 **Fiesta** all models '77 thru '80
754 **Ford & Mercury Full-size,** Ford LTD & Mercury Marquis ('75 thru '82); Ford Custom 500,Country Squire, Crown Victoria & Mercury Colony Park ('75 thru '87); Ford LTD Crown Victoria & Mercury Gran Marquis ('83 thru '87)
359 **Granada & Mercury Monarch** all in-line, 6 cyl & V8 models '75 thru '80
773 **Ford & Mercury Mid-size,** Ford Thunderbird & Mercury Cougar ('75 thru '82); Ford LTD & Mercury Marquis ('83 thru '86); Ford Torino,Gran Torino, Elite, Ranchero pick-up, LTD II, Mercury Montego, Comet, XR-7 & Lincoln Versailles ('75 thru '86)
*654 **Mustang & Mercury Capri** all models including Turbo. Mustang, '79 thru '93; Capri, '79 thru '86
357 **Mustang V8** all models '64-1/2 thru '73
231 **Mustang II** 4 cyl, V6 & V8 models '74 thru '78
649 **Pinto & Mercury Bobcat** '75 thru '80
1670 **Probe** all models '89 thru '92
*1026 **Ranger/Bronco II** gasoline models '83 thru '93
*1421 **Taurus & Mercury Sable** '86 thru '94
*1418 **Tempo & Mercury Topaz** all gasoline models '84 thru '94
1338 **Thunderbird/Mercury Cougar** '83 thru '88
*1725 **Thunderbird/Mercury Cougar** '89 and '93
344 **Vans** all V8 Econoline models '69 thru '91
*2119 **Vans** full size '92-'95

GENERAL MOTORS

*829 **Buick Century, Chevrolet Celebrity, Oldsmobile Cutlass Ciera & Pontiac 6000** all models '82 thru '93
*1671 **Buick Regal, Chevrolet Lumina, Oldsmobile Cutlass Supreme & Pontiac Grand Prix** all front wheel drive models '88 thru '95
*766 **Buick Skyhawk, Cadillac Cimarron, Chevrolet Cavalier, Oldsmobile Firenza & Pontiac J-2000 & Sunbird** all models '82 thru '94
38020 **Buick Skylark, Chevrolet Citation, Olds Omega, Pontiac Phoenix** '80 thru '85
1420 **Buick Skylark & Somerset, Oldsmobile Achieva & Calais and Pontiac Grand Am** all models '85 thru '95
*2035 **Chevrolet Lumina APV, Oldsmobile Silhouette & Pontiac Trans Sport** all models '90 thru '94
General Motors Full-size Rear-wheel Drive - *see BUICK (1551)*

GEO

Metro - *see CHEVROLET Sprint (1727)*
Prizm - *see CHEVROLET Nova (1642)*
*2039 **Storm** all models '90 thru '93
Tracker - *see SUZUKI Samurai (1626)*

GMC

Safari - *see CHEVROLET ASTRO (1477)*
Vans & Pick-ups - *see CHEVROLET (420, 831, 345, 1664)*

(Continued on other side)

** Listings shown with an asterisk (*) indicate model coverage as of this printing. These titles will be periodically updated to include later model years - consult your Haynes dealer for more information.*

Haynes North America, Inc., 861 Lawrence Drive, Newbury Park, CA 91320 • (805) 498-6703

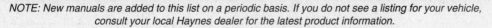

Haynes Automotive Manuals (continued)

NOTE: New manuals are added to this list on a periodic basis. If you do not see a listing for your vehicle, consult your local Haynes dealer for the latest product information.

HONDA
351 **Accord CVCC** all models '76 thru '83
1221 **Accord** all models '84 thru '89
2067 **Accord** all models '90 thru '93
42013 **Accord** all models '94 thru '95
160 **Civic 1200** all models '73 thru '79
633 **Civic 1300 & 1500 CVCC** '80 thru '83
297 **Civic 1500 CVCC** all models '75 thru '79
1227 **Civic** all models '84 thru '91
*2118 **Civic & del Sol** '92 thru '95
*601 **Prelude CVCC** all models '79 thru '89

HYUNDAI
*1552 **Excel** all models '86 thru '94

ISUZU
*1641 **Trooper & Pick-up**, all gasoline models Pick-up, '81 thru '93; Trooper, '84 thru '91

JAGUAR
*242 **XJ6** all 6 cyl models '68 thru '86
*478 **XJ12 & XJS** all 12 cyl models '72 thru '85

JEEP
*1553 **Cherokee, Comanche & Wagoneer Limited** all models '84 thru '93
412 **CJ** all models '49 thru '86
50025 **Grand Cherokee** all models '93 thru '95
*1777 **Wrangler** all models '87 thru '94

LINCOLN
2117 **Rear Wheel Drive** all models '70 thru '95

MAZDA
648 **626** Sedan & Coupe (rear wheel drive) all models '79 thru '82
*1082 **626 & MX-6 (front wheel drive)** all models '83 thru '91
267 **B Series Pick-ups** '72 thru '93
370 **GLC Hatchback (rear wheel drive)** all models '77 thru '83
757 **GLC (front wheel drive)** '81 thru '85
*2047 **MPV** all models '89 thru '94
Navajo-see Ford Explorer (2021)
460 **RX-7** all models '79 thru '85
*1419 **RX-7** all models '86 thru '91

MERCEDES-BENZ
*1643 **190 Series** all four-cylinder gasoline models, '84 thru '88
346 **230, 250 & 280** Sedan, Coupe & Roadster all 6 cyl sohc models '68 thru '72
983 **280 123 Series** gasoline models '77 thru '81
698 **350 & 450** Sedan, Coupe & Roadster all models '71 thru '80
697 **Diesel 123 Series** 200D, 220D, 240D, 240TD, 300D, 300CD, 300TD, 4- & 5-cyl incl. Turbo '76 thru '85

MERCURY
See FORD Listing

MG
111 **MGB** Roadster & GT Coupe all models '62 thru '80
265 **MG Midget & Austin Healey Sprite Roadster** '58 thru '80

MITSUBISHI
*1669 **Cordia, Tredia, Galant, Precis & Mirage** '83 thru '93
*2097 **Eclipse, Eagle Talon & Plymouth Laser** '90 thru '94
*2022 **Pick-up & Montero** '83 thru '95

NISSAN
1137 **300ZX** all models including Turbo '84 thru '89
*1341 **Maxima** all models '85 thru '91
*771 **Pick-ups/Pathfinder** gas models '80 thru '95
876 **Pulsar** all models '83 thru '86
*982 **Sentra** all models '82 thru '94
*981 **Stanza** all models '82 thru '90

OLDSMOBILE
Bravada - *see CHEVROLET S-10 (831)*
Calais - *see GENERAL MOTORS (1420)*
Custom Cruiser - *see BUICK Full-size RWD (1551)*
*658 **Cutlass** all standard gasoline V6 & V8 models '74 thru '88
Cutlass Ciera - *see GENERAL MOTORS (829)*
Cutlass Supreme - *see GM (1671)*
Delta 88 - *see BUICK Full-size RWD (1551)*
Delta 88 Brougham - *see BUICK Full-size FWD (1551), RWD (1627)*
Delta 88 Royale - *see BUICK Full-size RWD (1551)*
Firenza - *see GENERAL MOTORS (766)*
Ninety-eight Regency - *see BUICK Full-size RWD (1551), FWD (1627)*
Ninety-eight Regency Brougham - *see BUICK Full-size RWD (1551)*
Omega - *see GENERAL MOTORS (38020)*
Silhouette - *see GENERAL MOTORS (2035)*

PEUGEOT
663 **504** all diesel models '74 thru '83

PLYMOUTH
Laser - *see MITSUBISHI Eclipse (2097)*
For other PLYMOUTH titles, see DODGE listing.

PONTIAC
T1000 - *see CHEVROLET Chevette (449)*
J-2000 - *see GENERAL MOTORS (766)*
6000 - *see GENERAL MOTORS (829)*
Bonneville - *see Buick Full-size FWD (1627), RWD (1551)*
Bonneville Brougham - *see Buick (1551)*
Catalina - *see Buick Full-size (1551)*
1232 **Fiero** all models '84 thru '88
555 **Firebird** V8 models except Turbo '70 thru '81
867 **Firebird** all models '82 thru '92
Full-size Front Wheel Drive - *see BUICK Oldsmobile, Pontiac Full-size FWD (1627)*
Full-size Rear Wheel Drive - *see BUICK Oldsmobile, Pontiac Full-size RWD (1551)*
Grand Am - *see GENERAL MOTORS (1420)*
Grand Prix - *see GENERAL MOTORS (1671)*
Grandville - *see BUICK Full-size (1551)*
Parisienne - *see BUICK Full-size (1551)*
Phoenix - *see GENERAL MOTORS (38020)*
Sunbird - *see GENERAL MOTORS (766)*
Trans Sport - *see GENERAL MOTORS (2035)*

PORSCHE
*264 **911** all Coupe & Targa models except Turbo & Carrera 4 '65 thru '89
239 **914** all 4 cyl models '69 thru '76
397 **924** all models including Turbo '76 thru '82
*1027 **944** all models including Turbo '83 thru '89

RENAULT
141 **5 Le Car** all models '76 thru '83
Alliance & Encore - *see AMC (934)*

SAAB
247 **99** all models including Turbo '69 thru '80
*980 **900** all models including Turbo '79 thru '88

SATURN
2083 **Saturn** all models '91 thru '94

SUBARU
237 **1100, 1300, 1400 & 1600** '71 thru '79
*681 **1600 & 1800** 2WD & 4WD '80 thru '89

SUZUKI
*1626 **Samurai/Sidekick and Geo Tracker** all models '86 thru '95

TOYOTA
1023 **Camry** all models '83 thru '91
92006 **Camry** all models '92 thru '95
935 **Celica Rear Wheel Drive** '71 thru '85
*2038 **Celica Front Wheel Drive** '86 thru '92
1139 **Celica Supra** all models '79 thru '92
361 **Corolla** all models '75 thru '79
961 **Corolla** all rear wheel drive models '80 thru '87
*1025 **Corolla** all front wheel drive models '84 thru '92
636 **Corolla Tercel** all models '80 thru '82
360 **Corona** all models '74 thru '82
532 **Cressida** all models '78 thru '82
313 **Land Cruiser** all models '68 thru '82
*1339 **MR2** all models '85 thru '87
304 **Pick-up** all models '69 thru '78
*656 **Pick-up** all models '79 thru '95
*2048 **Previa** all models '91 thru '93
2106 **Tercel** all models '87 thru '94

TRIUMPH
113 **Spitfire** all models '62 thru '81
322 **TR7** all models '75 thru '81

VW
159 **Beetle & Karmann Ghia** all models '54 thru '79
238 **Dasher** all gasoline models '74 thru '81
*884 **Rabbit, Jetta, Scirocco, & Pick-up** gas models '74 thru '91 & Convertible '80 thru '92
451 **Rabbit, Jetta & Pick-up** all diesel models '77 thru '84
082 **Transporter 1600** all models '68 thru '79
226 **Transporter 1700, 1800 & 2000** all models '72 thru '79
084 **Type 3 1500 & 1600** all models '63 thru '73
1029 **Vanagon** all air-cooled models '80 thru '83

VOLVO
203 **120, 130 Series & 1800 Sports** '61 thru '73
129 **140 Series** all models '66 thru '74
*270 **240 Series** all models '76 thru '93
400 **260 Series** all models '75 thru '82
*1550 **740 & 760 Series** all models '82 thru '88

TECHBOOK MANUALS
2108 **Automotive Computer Codes**
1667 **Automotive Emissions Control Manual**
482 **Fuel Injection Manual, 1978 thru 1985**
2111 **Fuel Injection Manual, 1986 thru 1994**
2069 **Holley Carburetor Manual**
2068 **Rochester Carburetor Manual**
10240 **Weber/Zenith/Stromberg/SU Carburetors**
1762 **Chevrolet Engine Overhaul Manual**
2114 **Chrysler Engine Overhaul Manual**
1763 **Ford Engine Overhaul Manual**
1736 **GM and Ford Diesel Engine Repair Manual**
1666 **Small Engine Repair Manual**
10355 **Ford Automatic Transmission Overhaul**
10360 **GM Automatic Transmission Overhaul**
1479 **Automotive Body Repair & Painting**
2112 **Automotive Brake Manual**
2113 **Automotive Detaiing Manual**
1654 **Automotive Eelectrical Manual**
1480 **Automotive Heating & Air Conditioning**
2109 **Automotive Reference Manual & Illustrated Dictionary**
2107 **Automotive Tools Manual**
10440 **Used Car Buying Guide**
2110 **Welding Manual**

SPANISH MANUALS
98905 **Códigos Automotrices de la Computadora**
98915 **Inyección de Combustible 1986 al 1994**
99040 **Chevrolet & GMC Camionetas** '67 al '87 Incluye Suburban, Blazer & Jimmy '67 al '91
99041 **Chevrolet & GMC Camionetas** '88 al '95 Incluye Suburban '92 al '95, Blazer & Jimmy '92 al '94, Tahoe y Yukon '95
99075 **Ford Camionetas y Bronco** '80 al '94
99125 **Toyota Camionetas y 4-Runner** '79 al '95

** Listings shown with an asterisk (*) indicate model coverage as of this printing. These titles will be periodically updated to include later model years - consult your Haynes dealer for more information.*

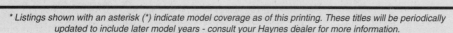

Over 100 Haynes motorcycle manuals also available

Haynes North America, Inc., 861 Lawrence Drive, Newbury Park, CA 91320 • (805) 498-6703